PERSONALITY: THEORY, ASSESSMENT, AND RESEARCH

THIRD EDITION

THIRD EDITION

PERSONALITY: THEORY, ASSESSMENT, AND RESEARCH

Lawrence A. Pervin

Livingston College
Rutgers, The State University

JOHN WILEY & SONS, New York • Chichester • Brisbane • Toronto • Singapore

This book was designed by Judith Fletcher Getman. Photo Research was handled by Stella Kupferberg. Janet Sessa supervised production.

Library of Congress Cataloging in Publication Data:
Pervin, Lawrence A
   Personality: theory, assessment, and research.
   Includes index.
   1. Personality.   I. Title.
BF698.P375 1980   155.2   79-19636

Printed in the United States of America

10 9 8 7 6 5 4 3

TO BOBBIE, DAVID, AND LEVI

PREFACE

The revision of a textbook provides the author with an opportunity to update material and to respond to student feedback concerning earlier presentations. This edition reflects efforts in both directions. In relation to the former, there has been an effort to make sure that the chapters reflect current developments in the field of personality. In particular, a separate chapter has been devoted to social learning theory (Chapter 11), which increasingly influences the thinking and research of many psychologists. In relation to the latter, the entire manuscript has been edited to clarify ambiguities and to remove needlessly technical discussions. At the same time, the effort has been to retain a comprehensive and scholarly approach toward the material.

In my efforts along these lines I have been assisted by many. Students in my classes have been a constant source of stimulation and useful feedback. In terms of outside review, the comments of Professor Rhoda Lindner of California State University-Long Beach have been of invaluable assistance. I would also like to express my appreciation for the helpful reviews of the following professors: Vincent Adesso, University of Wisconsin-Milwaukee; Albert Bandura, Stanford University, Lawrence Gaines, University of Massachusetts Boston; Brendan Maher, Harvard University; Martha T. Mednick, Howard University; and James Uleman, New York University, Research Center for Human Relations. In terms of editorial work, I am indebted to the efforts of Mrs. Alice Greenwald, who assisted in making the text more readable while remaining faithful to the ideas presented. Mr. Jack Burton and Mr. Ron Nelson at Wiley have provided me with useful feedback and constant support during the difficult revision process. Finally, my family, to whom the book is dedicated, has remained a bastion of support and understanding during this as well as the earlier revision of the text.

Princeton, N.J.
July 4, 1979

CONTENTS

1   **PERSONALITY THEORY**   **3**

Defining Personality   4

Personality Theory As An Answer to the Questions
of What, How, and Why   8

Structure   9

Process   10

Growth and Development   11

Psychopathology and Behavior Change   14

Summary   14

Important Issues in Personality Theory   14

Philosophical View of the Person   15

Internal and External Determinants of Behavior   16

The Unity of Behavior and the Concept of the Self   16

Varying States of Awareness and the Concept of the Unconscious   18

The Influences of the Past, Present, and Future on Behavior   18

Summary   19

Theory and Theoretical Issues   19

Evaluation of Theories   21

Theory and the History of Scientific Progress   22

Theory and the Study of Personality   24

Major Concepts and Summary   25

2   **A PSYCHODYNAMIC THEORY:**
FREUD'S PSYCHOANALYTIC THEORY OF PERSONALITY   **27**

Sigmund Freud (1856-1939): A View of the Theorist   29

Freud's View of the Person and Society   34

Freud's View of Science, Theory, and Research Methods   36

Psychoanalysis: A Theory of Personality   38
  Structure   38
  Process   46
  Growth and Development   50
Major Concepts and Summary   65

3   **A PSYCHODYNAMIC THEORY: APPLICATIONS AND**
             EVALUATION OF FREUD'S THEORY   69
Clinical Applications   70
  Psychopathology   70
  Behavior Change   73
A Case Example—Little Hans   78
Related Points of View and Recent Developments   83
  Two Early Challenges to Freud   84
  The Cultural and Interpersonal Emphasis   89
  Recent Developments within Traditional Psychoanalytic Theory   93
Critical Evaluation   95
  Major Contributions   95
  Limitations of the Theory   97
  Summary Evaluation   102
Major Concepts and Summary   102

4   **A PHENOMENOLOGICAL THEORY: CARL ROGERS'**
             PERSON-CENTRED THEORY OF PERSONALITY   107
Carl R. Rogers (1902-   ): A View of the Theorist   109
Rogers' View of the Person   113
Rogers' View of Science, Theory, and Research Methods   114
The Personality Theory of Carl Rogers   117
  Structure   117
  Process   121
  Growth and Development   129
Major Concepts and Summary   135

5   **A PHENOMENOLOGICAL THEORY: APPLICATIONS AND**
             EVALUATION OF ROGERS' THEORY   139
Clinical Applications   140
  Psychopathology   140
  Change   143
A Case Example—Mrs. Oak   151
Related Points of View and Recent Developments   155
  The Human Potential Movement   155
  Rogers' Shift in Emphasis: From Individuals to Groups and Society   159

Critical Evaluation   160
  Phenomenology   161
  The Concept of Self   163
  Conflict, Anxiety, and Defense   165
  Growth and Development   166
  Psychopathology and Change   167
  Summary Evaluation   168
Major Concepts and Summary   170

6   A COGNITIVE THEORY OF PERSONALITY: GEORGE A. KELLY AND HIS PERSONAL CONSTRUCTION THEORY OF PERSONALITY   175
George A. Kelly (1905-1966): A View of the Theorist   177
Kelly's View of the Person   179
Kelly's View of Science, Theory, and Research Methods   181
The Personality Theory of George Kelly   184
  Structure   184
  Process   194
Growth and Development   197
Major Concepts and Summary   198

7   A COGNITIVE THEORY OF PERSONALITY: APPLICATIONS AND EVALUATION OF KELLY'S THEORY   203
Clinical Applications   204
  Psychopathology   204
  Change   209
A Case Example—Ronald Barrett   213
Related Points of View and Recent Developments   216
Critical Evaluation   219
  Kelly and Freud   222
  Kelly and Rogers   223
  Kelly, Freud, and Rogers   225
Major Concepts and Summary   226

8   TRAIT APPROACHES TO PERSONALITY: ALLPORT, EYSENCK, AND CATTELL   231
The Trait Theory of Gordon W. Allport (1897-1967)   234
The Trait-Type, Factor-Analytic Theory of Hans J. Eysenck (1916-   )   237
The Trait, Factor-Analytic Approach of Raymond B. Cattell (1905-   )   242
  Cattell's View of the Person   245
  Cattell's View of Science, Theory, and Research Methods   245
Cattell's Theory of Personality   247
  Structure   248

Process   253
Growth and Development   257
Clinical Applications of Cattell's Theory   259
Psychopathology   259
Change   262
A Case Example   263
Critical Evaluation of Cattell's Theory   265
How Many Factors?   265
Are the Same Factors Identified in Different Studies?   265
Are There Certain Questionable Assumptions in the Factor-Analytic Procedure?   266
How Sure Can We Be that the Factors Identified Have the Same Meaning?   267
Scope of the Effort and Evaluation   269
Trait Theory and Situationist Criticism   270
Major Concepts and Summary   272

9   BEHAVIORAL APPROACHES TO PERSONALITY: UNDERPINNINGS OF LEARNING THEORY AND SKINNER'S OPERANT CONDITIONING   277
The Behavioral View of the Person   280
Behavioral View of Science, Theory, and Research Methods   282
Early Influential Figures in Behavioral Theory—Pavlov and Watson   283
Pavlov's Theory of Classical Conditioning   283
Watson's Behaviorism   286
Skinner's Theory of Operant Conditioning   289
A View of the Theorist   289
Skinner's Theory of Personality   293
Structure   293
Process—Operant Conditioning   293
Growth and Development   296
Clinical Applications of Skinner's Theory   297
Psychopathology   297
Change   300
A Case Example—Joey   304
Critical Evaluation of Skinner's Theory   307
Major Concepts and Summary   308

10   BEHAVIORAL APPROACHES TO PERSONALITY: STIMULUS-RESPONSE (S-R) THEORY AND OVERALL EVALUATION   311
Stimulus-Response Theory   312
A View of the Theorists   313
The S-R Theory of Personality   318

Structure   318
Process   319
Growth and Development   320
Clinical Applications of S-R Theory   322
   Psychopathology   322
   Change   325
   Case Example—A Behavioral Interpretation of Little Hans   333
Recent Developments in Behavioral Approaches to Personality   334
   Statement of Ideology, Utopian Planning, and Social Engineering   335
   Interest in Self-Control and Self-Reinforcement   336
   Increased Range of Application of Behavior Therapy Techniques   337
   Interest in Processes at Work in Behavior Therapy   339
   Interest in a Broader Range of Variables   340
Critical Evaluation of Behavioral Approach to Personality   340
   Oversimplification   341
   Neglect of Important Areas   342
   Learning Theory Interpretations of Behavior Change   343
   The Effectiveness of Behavior Therapy   345
   Moral and Ethical Issues   348
   Summary Evaluation   349
Major Concepts and Summary   350

11   **SOCIAL LEARNING THEORY:**
                BANDURA AND MISCHEL   353
                A View of the Theorists   355
                   Albert Bandura (1925-   )   355
                   Walter Mischel (1931-   )   357
                View of the Person   360
                View of Science, Theory, and Research Methods   362
                Social Learning Theory of Personality   362
                   Process   363
                   Structure   370
                   Growth and Development   371
                Clinical Applications   378
                   Psychopathology   378
                   Change   380
                A Case Example   387
                Critical Evaluation   388
                   Strengths of the Theory   388
                   Limitations of the Theory   391
                Major Concepts and Summary   393

12   **ASSESSMENT:**
        PROJECTIVE AND SUBJECTIVE TESTS   399
        Goals of Tests, Measures, and Assessment Techniques   401
            Reliability   401
            Validity   402
        Classification of Tests   404
            Projective Techniques   406
            Subjective Techniques   419
        Major Concepts and Summary   429

13   **ASSESSMENT: PSYCHOMETRIC TESTS AND**
        BEHAVIORAL OBSERVATIONS   433
        Classification of Tests   434
            Psychometric Techniques   434
            *Objective Techniques: Standardized Performance Tests and Behavioral
            Assessment*   443
        Clinical versus Statistical Prediction   450
            The Statistical Approach   452
            The Clinical Approach   452
            The Evidence and Controversy   453
            Strengths and Limitations of the Two Approaches   455
        A Summary Overview of the Assessment Field   456
        Major Concepts and Summary   460

14   **THEORY AND ASSESSMENT IN THE**
        STUDY OF THE INDIVIDUAL: THE CASE OF JIM HERSH   463
        The Case of Jim Hersh   464
            Rorschach and TAT: Psychoanalytic Theory   465
            Semantic Differential: Phenomenological Theory   470
            Rep Test: Personal Construct Theory   472
            Sixteen Personality Factor Inventory: Trait, Factor-Analytic Theory   474
        Jim Hersh: Five Years Later   479
            Life Experiences Since Graduation—As Told By Jim Hersh   479
            *Brief Personality Description and Changes Since Graduation—
            As Told by Jim Hersh*   481
            *Behavioral Assessment: Reinforcement Survey Schedule and Fear Survey
            Schedule*   482
        Personality Theory and Assessment Data: The Case of Jim Hersh   483

15   **PERSONALITY RESEARCH**   489
        Two Disciplines of Scientific Psychology   491
            Experimental Approach   493

Correlational Approach 498

Summary 499

Tactics of Research and the Concepts of Stress, Helplessness, and Control 500

Naturalistic Observation 501

Laboratory Research 504

Correlational Research and The Use of Personality Questionnaires: Locus of Control 509

Action Research and Clinical Analogues 515

Overlapping Research Efforts and Conclusions Concerning Stress, Control, and Helplessness 520

The Science and Social Psychology of Research 521

Demand Characteristics 522

Experimenter Expectancy Effects 522

Additional Pitfalls in Human Research 524

Research and Public Policy 525

Summary 525

Major Concepts and Summary 526

16   AN OVERVIEW OF PERSONALITY THEORY, ASSESSMENT, AND RESEARCH 531

A Return to Some Issues that Divide Personality Theorists 332

Philosophical View of the Person 532

Internal and External Causes of Behavior 533

The Unity of Behavior and the Concept of the Self 534

Varying States of Awareness and the Concept of the Unconscious 536

Influences of the Past, Present, and Future on Behavior 537

Personality Theory As An Answer to the Questions of What, How, and Why 538

Personality Structure 539

Process 541

Growth and Development 542

Psychopathology 544

Change 545

Relationships Among Theory, Assessment, and Research 547

A Final Summing Up 549

GLOSSARY 551

BIBLIOGRAPHY 561

PHOTO CREDITS 587

INDEX 589

PERSONALITY: THEORY, ASSESSMENT, AND RESEARCH

THIRD EDITION

DEFINING PERSONALITY

PERSONALITY THEORY AS AN ANSWER TO THE QUESTIONS OF WHAT, HOW, AND WHY

Structure

Process

Growth and Development

Psychopathology and Behavior Change

Summary

IMPORTANT ISSUES IN PERSONALITY THEORY

Philosophical View of the Person

Internal and External Determinants of Behavior

The Unity of Behavior and the Concept of the Self

Varying States of Awareness and the Concept of the Unconscious

The Influence of the Past, Present, and Future on Behavior

Summary

THEORY AND THEORETICAL ISSUES

Evaluation of Theories

Theory and the History of Scientific Progress

Theory and the Study of Personality

MAJOR CONCEPTS AND SUMMARY

1 PERSONALITY THEORY

Chapter Focus:

How can we define personality? How can we organize what is known about personality functioning in order to explain certain behavior and point out future directions for research? What do we want a theory of personality to do? How do we know when we have a good theory? Does it matter whether we use one theory or another? These are some of the questions we address in this chapter. We shall discuss what a theory is, what a theory of personality should include, and how to tell how good a theory is. Theories are based on facts but also are influenced by the personalities of the psychologists who develop them. We therefore approach theories from a human as well as a scientific viewpoint. Finally, we shall discuss how competition among theories leads to scientific progress.

Every person is in certain respects
a. like all other people.
b. like some other people.
c. like no other person.
   adapted from KLUCKHOHN *and* MURRAY, 1953, p. 53

Probably no field of psychology has been more perplexing to its students with respect to
theory than that of personality.

SEARS, 1950, p. 115

This book is about personality. It explores ways of approaching psychological functioning, insights into the varied determinants of personality, and increased knowledge of how personality can be studied. In sum, it is an exploration into a greater understanding of why people behave as they do and how we may proceed toward a clearer understanding of behavior.

DEFINING PERSONALITY

Every person and event is unique, if only because everything takes place in time and space and no two things can occur at the same time in the same place. However, there is enough similarity among many people and the events of their lives to consider what they have in common. It is these patterns of human behavior that the psychologist attempts to understand.

personality   In psychology, the field of **personality** is concerned not only with the total individual but also with individual differences. While recognizing that all people are similar in some ways, those interested in personality are particularly concerned with the ways people differ from one another. Why do some achieve and others not? Why do some perceive things one way and others in a different way? Why do talents vary? Why do some people become mentally ill while others do not under similar conditions?

Personality theorists attempt to understand behavior by examining the complex relationships among the different aspects of an individual's functioning, including such aspects as learning, perception, and motivation. Personality research is not the study of perception but rather of how individuals differ in their perceptions and how these differences relate to their total functioning. The study of personality focuses not only on a particular psychological process but also on the relationships of different processes. Understanding how these processes act together to form an integrated whole often involves more than an understanding of each of them separately. People function as organized wholes, and it is in the light of such organization that we must understand them.

There are few aspects of human functioning that do not reflect and express an individual's personality. How, then, are we to define personality? To the general public it may represent a value judgment—if you like someone, it is because he or she has a "good" personality. To the scientist and student of personality, the term *personality* is used to define a field of study. A definition of personality reflects the kinds of problems to be studied and reflects the methods to be used in studying these problems. At present, however, there is no generally agreed-upon single definition of personality.

Some personality psychologists study the biochemical and physiological aspects of how individuals function and use methods appropriate to these areas of investigation. Other personality psychologists look at individuals and observe their overt behavior. Still other psychologists define personality in terms of characteristics, such as unconscious processes, which must be inferred from their behavior and cannot be observed directly. An illustration of this would be the study of what is called "repression." No one can observe directly that an event was forgotten because it is painful to recall. However, one can infer that such a process is taking place, and making this inference helps psychologists explain why some things are remembered and others forgotten. Finally, some psychologists define personality strictly in terms of the ways in which individuals interact with other individuals or in terms of the roles individuals ascribe to themselves and use to function in society. Thus, these and other possible definitions of personality range from processes internal to the organism to overt behavior in an interpersonal context.

It is clear that various definitions of personality are possible and have been used. Each leads to a concentration on different kinds of behavior and to the use of different methods of study. These definitions may be more concrete or more abstract. They may describe what goes on inside individuals, or how individuals interact with each other. They may describe what is directly observable or what must be inferred. They may also define what is unique to particular individuals or what is characteristic of most, or all, individuals.

In considering definitions of personality it is important to keep two issues in mind. First, a definition does and should reflect the kinds of behavior the psychologist will pay attention to and the kinds of methods that will be used to study this behavior. Second, there is no one right or wrong definition of personality. This will remain true until psychologists arrive at a shared understanding of basic aspects of personality functioning. Until then, definitions of personality are not necessarily true or false but are useful to psychologists in assessing personality, in research, and in communicating their findings to others. They are also useful to psychology as a science insofar as they lead to an increase in our ability to understand, predict, and influence behavior.

Some philosophers and psychologists have pointed out that the human organism expresses itself in three ways: biologically, in relationship to others, and in relationship to oneself. It is likely that someday our definition and understanding of personality will integrate the different views of human functioning, so that the definition will reflect our understanding of the relationships among the three. Until such integration takes place, definitions and accompanying research and assessment will focus on more limited aspects of behavior.

For the present, the following is suggested as a working definition of personality: *Personality represents those characteristics of the person or of people generally that account for consistent patterns of response to situations.* A number of points can be made in this context. First, personality concepts must be defined in terms that permit psychologists to agree on ways to observe and measure behavior. To study personality systematically we must be able to agree on what we are looking at and how we are to measure it. Second, personality is characterized by regularities in one individual's functioning as well as by regularities that are similar from person to person. While we are each unique in some ways, in other ways we are like some other people and in some ways we are like all other people. Personality is a concept that expresses such regularities within a person and similarities between people. Personality represents the attributes of individuals that distinguish them from other individuals and make them unique as well as the attributes of functioning that are common to all humans. Third, personality includes both the more stable, unchanging aspects of the person's functioning—sometimes called *structure*—and the more fluid, changing aspects—sometimes called *process.* Just as the system of the physical organism consists of parts of the body and various processes relating these parts to one another, so the psychological organism consists of stable parts and fluid processes that relate these parts to one another. In this sense, the personality is a system. Finally, remember that our working definition of personality indicates that people do not operate in a vacuum, but rather that they respond to and express themselves in relation to situations and circumstances.

Our working definition is based on certain assumptions about the nature of human personality:

1 *The human organism has characteristics distinct from those of other species that are particularly important for the study of personality.* Compared to members of other species, we are less dependent on biological influences and more dependent on psychosocial factors. We

are less dependent than members of other species on primary sources of motivation such as hunger and thirst. Our considerable ability for conceptual thinking and language means that we can communicate and transmit learned patterns of behavior (culture) to a degree unique among the species. This ability also means that we have a lengthened perspective of past and future, and therefore we need not be bound by immediately present stimuli. Further, it means that we can reflect upon ourselves—we can consider ourselves as objects, so to speak. We can both experience and reflect upon our experience; we can be ourselves and think about being ourselves. Finally, and very important for understanding personality—the human organism has a slower rate of maturation than members of other species.

2 *Human behavior is complex.* An understanding of personality must include an appreciation of the complexity of human behavior. Often there are many reasons for any individual's behavior, which may vary from person to person, although the observable behavior may be the same. The same events may be understood differently by different individuals, and the same behavior may have many different roots in different individuals. Complexity also exists because behavior arises not only from personalities but also in relation to situations and circumstances.

3 *Behavior is not always what it appears to be.* There is no fixed relationship between a certain behavior and its causes; there may be different causes for the same behavior shown by two individuals at one time or by the same individual at different times. To understand the significance or meaning of an act for the individual, we must know something about that individual and about the situation in which the act occurred.

4 *We are not always aware of or in control of the factors determining our behavior.* This follows from the concept of the unconscious, although it is not necessary to accept all aspects of the Freudian view of the unconscious to agree with it. This simply suggests that at times people cannot explain why they act in ways contrary to their own expressed wishes. Whether these acts are significant or minor, frequent or infrequent, they occur and remain to be accounted for in some way.

These qualities of human functioning greatly complicate our efforts to measure, interpret, and predict behavior. They suggest that often we capture only glimpses of a person. Although they make the study of personality frustrating, frequent surprises and occasional insights into patterns of behavior also make it exciting.

The scientific exploration of personality, then, attempts to understand how people are alike while recognizing that individuals are unique in some ways. It attempts to discover, understand, and explain regularities in human behavior. Further, it develops theories to help order phenomena and to suggest strategies for further research. There are many theories of personality. They range from those believed by the general public and used by them in their daily living to those developed through the use of sophisticated mathematical techniques and computer technology. Each theory tends to look at a different behavior or to study the same behavior in different ways. It should hardly be surprising that there are so many different theories of personality and that the field, as Sears notes, is so perplexing to students of human behavior.

PERSONALITY THEORY AS AN
ANSWER TO THE QUESTIONS OF WHAT, HOW, AND WHY

Although personality theorists may study one or another aspect of psychological functioning, a complete theory of personality must suggest answers to such questions as: How can people be consistent in their behavior and at the same time show variation over time and place? How does personality develop? How can we account for psychopathology, abnormal behavior due to psychological causes? A theory should be descriptive and explanatory when suggesting answers to these questions. It should tell what is there and suggest reasons for what is observed.

If we study individuals intensively, we want to know what they are like, how they became that way, and why they behave as they do. For an individual or for a group we want a theory to answer the questions of *what, how,* and *why.* The "what" refers to the characteristics of the person and how they are organized in relation to one another. Is the person honest, persistent, and high in need for achievement? The "how" refers to the determinants of a person's current personality. To what extent and in what ways did genetic and environmental forces interact to produce this result? The "why" refers to the reasons for the individual's behavior. Answers refer to the motivational aspects of the individual—why he or she moves at all, and why in a specific direction. If an individual seeks to make a lot of money, why was this particular path chosen? If a child does well in school, is it to please parents, to use talents, to bolster self-esteem, or to show up friends? Is a mother overprotective because she happens to be affectionate, because she seeks to give her children what she missed as a child, or because she seeks to avoid any expression of the resentment and hostility she feels for the child? Is a person depressed as a result of humiliation, because of the loss of a loved one, or because of feelings of guilt? A theory should help us understand to what extent depression is characteristic of a person, how this personality characteristic is developed, why depression is experienced in specific circumstances, and why the person behaves in a certain manner when depressed. If two people tend to be depressed, why does one go out and buy things while another withdraws into a shell?

Structure

structure

Theories can be compared in terms of the concepts they use to answer the what, how, and why of personality. **Structural concepts** refer to the more stable and enduring aspects of personality. They represent the building blocks of personality theory. In this sense they are comparable to parts of the body or to concepts such as atoms and molecules in physics. Such structural concepts as *response, habit, trait,* and *type* have been popular in efforts to conceptualize what people are like. The concept of trait refers to the consistency of individual response to a variety of situations and approximates the kind of concept the layman uses to describe people. Examples of traits are rigidity, honesty, and emotionality. The concept of type refers to the clustering of many different traits. Compared to the trait concept, that of type implies a greater degree of regularity and generality to behavior. Although people can have one or another degree of many traits, they are generally described as being a specific type. For example, individuals have been described as being introverts or extroverts—and in terms of whether they move toward, away from, or against others (Horney, 1945).

It is possible to use conceptual units other than trait or type to describe personality structure. Theories of personality differ in the kinds of units or structural concepts they use. They also differ in the way they conceptualize the organization of these units. Some theories involve a *complex* structural system, one in which many component parts are linked to one another in a variety of ways. Other theories involve a *simple* structural system, in which a few component parts have few connections to one another. The human brain is a far more complex structure than the brain of a fish because it has more parts, which can be distinguished from one another, and more linkages or interconnections among these parts. Theories of personality also differ in the extent to which they view the structural units as organized in a hierarchy; that is, in the extent to which some structural units are seen as higher in order and therefore as controlling the functioning of other units. The human nervous system is more complex than that of other species, not only because it has more different parts and more linkages among them but also because some parts, like the brain, regulate the functioning of other parts in the system. An analogy can be found in business structures. Some business organizations are more complex than others. Complex business organizations have many units, with many linkages among the units, and a ranking of people who have responsibility for making decisions. Simple business organizations have few units, few linkages among the units, and few levels in the chain of command—General Motors as opposed to the mom-and-pop store. Similarly, personality theories differ in the numbers and kinds of structural units they emphasize and in the extent to which they emphasize complexity or organization within the system.

Process

process

As with structure, theories can be compared in terms of the *motivational concepts* they use to account for behavior. These concepts refer to the **process** aspects of human behavior.

Again think of the human body. It can be considered both in terms of the organization of its parts and in terms of the processes that relate the parts to one another. Similarly, a business organization consists of units and processes through which the units function in relation to one another and to the outside world. Organizational processes could, for example, be described in terms of how much conflict exists among the parts and how that conflict is handled.

Some theories view personality processes as resulting from efforts of the individual to reduce tension. Other theories emphasize the efforts of the organism toward growth and self-fulfillment. According to the former view, physiological needs within the organism create tensions that the individual seeks to reduce by satisfying needs. Hunger or thirst creates tension that can be relieved by eating or drinking. According to the latter view, individuals seek to grow and realize their inner potentials even at the cost of increased tension.

The most widely accepted model for earlier theories of motivation was, in fact, that of tension reduction. The organism was viewed as seeking a state of rest, quiet, or balance—often called *homeostasis* or *equilibrium*. Pleasure was to be derived from satisfying needs or reducing tension. Recently, research on animals and humans has suggested that organisms often seek tension. Monkeys, for example, will work to solve puzzles independent of any reward—in fact, rewards may interfere with their performance (Harlow, 1953). They will also work to be able to explore a novel environment (Butler, 1953), and the exploratory and play behavior of members of many species is well known. Observations such as these led White (1959) to formulate a process in human functioning he called **competence motivation**

competence motivation. According to this view, a significant process in personality functioning is the motivation toward dealing competently or effectively with the environment. Individuals appear to take pleasure in increasing tension or excitement and in trying out new behaviors. As individuals mature, more of their behavior appears to be involved with developing skills merely for the sake of mastery or for dealing effectively with the environment, and less of their behavior appears to be exclusively in the service of reducing tension.

The concept of competence motivation has served to emphasize behaviors neglected by earlier theorists, but we need not choose between the tension-reduction and the competence-motivation models of personality dynamics. As one leading motivational theorist (Maslow, 1954) suggests, it is likely that at times the individual is stimulated by physiological needs and seeks to reduce tension, at other times is stimulated by self-fulfilling tendencies, and at yet other times is stimulated by social needs for praise and respect. Such an integrated view is possible, but theorists have tended to use one or another model to account for the more momentary aspects of human behavior.

Growth and Development

growth and development

Growth and **development** are related to the concepts of structure and process in personality theory. An interpretation of growth and development must account for changes in structure from infancy to maturity, and for the corresponding developments in process. A theory of growth must describe the process through which development occurs and must outline the reasons for various patterns of growth. Significant among the *environmental determinants of personality* are experiences individuals have as a result of membership in a particular culture that has its own institutionalized and sanctioned patterns of learned behaviors, rituals, and beliefs. The institutionalization of some behavior patterns means that most members of a culture will have certain personality characteristics in common. Even in a complex society like ours, one in which the number and rigidity of institutionalized patterns of behavior are minimal, the importance of cultural forces in shaping personality functioning is considerable. These forces influence our needs and means of satisfying them, our relationships to authority, our self-concepts, the major forms of anxiety and conflict we experience, and the ways we deal with them. They affect what we think is funny and sad, how we cope with life and death, what we view as healthy and sick. In the words of C. Kluckhohn (1949), "Culture regulates our lives at every turn. From the moment we are born until we die there is, whether we are conscious of it or not, constant pressure upon us to follow certain types of behavior that other men have created for us" (p. 327).

Although certain patterns of behavior develop as a result of membership in a culture, others are developed as a result of membership in some stratified section or class of the population. Few aspects of an individual's personality can be understood without reference to the group to which that person belongs. One's social class group—whether lower class or upper class, working class or professional—is of particular importance. Social class factors help determine the status of individuals, the roles they perform, the duties they are bound by, and the privileges they enjoy. These factors influence how they see themselves and how they perceive members of other social classes, how they earn and spend money. Like cultural factors, social class factors influence the ways individuals define situations and how they respond to them. There is evidence that social class factors are related in a population to the prevalence of mental illness and to the types of mental disorders found. In a study of social class and mental illness, Hollingshead and Redlich (1958) found that while each type of mental disorder occurs in all social classes, proportions in the various classes differ. For example, upper-class patients tended to be neurotic and lower-class patients to be psychotic. Within the neurotic and psychotic categories, members of different classes tended to behave differently.

Beyond the similarities determined by environmental factors such as membership in the same culture or social class, environmental factors lead to considerable variation in the personality functioning of members of a single culture or class. Of particular significance among these is the influence of the family on personality. Although membership in a culture and a social class leads to the use of certain institutionalized child-rearing practices and to conformity with certain patterns of behavior, signigicant differences among families—and the peculiar, individualistic relationships within families—are crucial to personality development. Parents may be warm and loving or hostile and rejecting, overprotective and possessive or aware of their children's need for freedom and autonomy. Each pattern of parental behavior affects the personality development of the child (Becker, 1964).

Some theories of personality attach particular importance to early social interaction between infant and mother. The interpersonal relations theory of Sullivan (1953), for example, suggests that a significant component of personality is the *self-system* (a person's perceptions of the self), which develops out of relationships with significant figures in the environment. During infancy the developing self-system is influenced by the amount of anxiety the mother communicates, often in a subtle way, to the child. In later years, the self-system is influenced by reflected appraisals—how the individual perceives others as perceiving and responding to him or her. Of particular significance here is whether the person sees the self as good or bad as a result of perceptions of the evaluative judgments made by others.

Parents influence their children's behavior in at least three important ways:

1 Through their own behavior they present situations that elicit certain behavior in children (for example, frustration leads to aggression)
2 They serve as role models for identification
3 They selectively reward behaviors

Along with environmental factors, genetic factors play a major role in determining personality, particularly in relation to what is unique in the individual. Although many psychologists historically have argued the relative importance of environmental and genetic factors in shaping personality as a whole, recent theorists have recognized that the importance of these factors may vary from one personality characteristic to another. Genetic factors are generally more important in such characteristics as intelligence and temperament, less important in regard to values, ideals, and beliefs (Vandenberg, 1962). Theorists have also begun to explore possible interactions between genetic and environmental factors. Thus, for example, the concept of *reaction range* (Gottesman, 1963) suggests that while heredity fixes a number of possible behavioral outcomes, environment ultimately determines the behavior.

In summary, personality is determined by many interacting factors, including genetic, cultural, social class, and familial forces. Heredity sets limits on the range of development of characteristics; within this range, characteristics are determined by environmental forces. Heredity provides us talents that a culture may or may not reward and cultivate. It is possible to see the interaction of these many genetic and environmental forces in any significant aspect of personality. One example, from abnormal psychology, is schizophrenia. The study of schizophrenia suggests a *genetic factor*—the greater the genetic similarity between two people the higher the probability that if one is schizophrenic the other is also (Gottesman & Shields, 1966; Kallmann, 1946); a *cultural factor*—a clear relationship between cultural background and overt symptoms (Opler & Singer, 1956; Parsons, 1961); a *social class* factor—(Hollingshead & Redlich, 1958); and a *familial factor*—some evidence that schizophrenics tend to have dominant mothers and passive fathers, and have been brought up in a family characterized by confusing messages or communications between members of the family (Bateson, Jackson, & Weakland, 1956; Frank, 1965). Theories of personality differ in the importance attributed to questions of growth and development, in the relative weight given to genetic and environmental factors, and in interpretations of the mechanisms through which personality development occurs. Ultimately, however, it is the task of any personality theory to account for the development of structures and patterns of behaving. A theory of personality should explain what is developed, how it is developed, any why it is developed.

Psychopathology and Behavior Change

In attempting to account for these varied aspects of human behavior, a complete theory of personality must include analyses of the nature of psychopathology in general and the development of various kinds of psychopathology in particular. Further, such a theory should suggest means or psychotherapies by which such forms of behavior can be modified. What is important is that there be an adequate conceptualization of behavioral change, and that part of this be relevant to an understanding of the process through which the change from psychopathology to health can be helped to take place.

Summary

This section has explored five areas a complete theory of personality must take into account and in relation to which theories of personality can be compared: structure, process, development, psychopathology, and change. These areas represent conceptual abstractions: A person is not structure or process, and what appears structure at one moment may appear process at another. Someone may be said to have a strong conscience (structure) that makes him or her feel guilty (process). Such conceptual abstractions, convenient devices for understanding and explaining human behavior, are found in biology as well as psychology. Similarly, development and change are neither independent of structure or process nor independent of one another. They represent an effort to find pattern and regularity in human behavior, ways in which individuals are similar and ways in which they are unique. The concepts developed by a theory represent efforts toward accounting for the organization of personality characteristics, the conditions under which personality develops, and the processes that characterize personality functioning—what we have labeled the what, how, and why of personality.

IMPORTANT ISSUES IN PERSONALITY THEORY

A theory of personality must conceptualize the varied areas of functioning that have been described. A number of theories have attempted this difficult task. Throughout the relatively brief history of personality theory, a number of issues have confronted theorists repeatedly. The ways in which they treat these issues do much to define the major characteristics of each theoretical position. Thus, in reviewing various personality theories we need to keep certain issues in mind, to see how much attention each theorist gives to these issues and how that theorist resolves each issue.

Philosophical View of the Person

A philosophical view concerning the fundamental nature of the human organism tends to underlie current personality theories. One theory emphasizes the instinctual aspect of humans, another the social; one theory stresses free will, another determinism; one theory discusses simple and mechanistic relationships, another complex and dynamic ones; one theory views the person as an organism that reasons, chooses, and decides (rational view), another views the person as an organism that is driven, compelled, irrational (animal view). A third theory views the person as automatically responding to outside stimuli (machine view), while a fourth views the person as processing information like a computer (computer view).

Philosophical assumptions concerning human nature are important because they focus on specific problems and lead to particular forms of research. Proponents of different points of view have had different life experiences and have been influenced by different historical traditions. Thus, beyond scientific evidence and fact, theories of personality are influenced by personal factors, by the spirit of the time (Zeitgeist) and by philosophical assumptions characteristic of members of a given culture (Pervin, 1978). Although based on observed data, theories selectively emphasize certain kinds of data and go beyond what is known, and therefore can be influenced by personal and cultural factors. In developing a personality theory, individuals are influenced by important events in their own lifetimes. To some extent, in developing psychological theories we talk about ourselves. This in itself is not a problem. Only when personal experiences become more important than other kinds of experience do personal determinants of a theory become a problem.

Along with these personal determinants are the influences on the theorist of the prevailing mood or spirit within the field at the time—the **Zeitgeist**. There are phases in psychology during which one topic of research is emphasized and one point of view stressed. For example, for some time personality theory emphasized the importance of drives or needs that appeared to have some physiological basis. More recent theory has tended to emphasize cognitive factors—how individuals come to organize and conceptualize their environment. Reflecting the *Zeitgeist*, both types of theory emphasize certain kinds of empirical observations and suggest that research follow a defined path.

Zeitgeist

Internal and External Determinants of Behavior

One critical issue that tends to express an underlying philosophical view concerns the relationship between internal and external behavior determinants. All theories of personality recognize that factors inside the organism, and events in the surrounding environment, are important in determining behavior. However, the theories differ in the level of importance given to internal and external determinants and in their interpretation of the relationship between the two (Pervin & Lewis, 1978). Consider, for example, the difference between Freud's theory that we are controlled by unknown, internal forces and Skinner's suggestion that "a person does not act upon the world, the world acts upon him" (1971, p. 211). Whereas the Freudian views the organism as active and responsible for behavior, the Skinnerian views it as a passive victim of controlling events in the environment. The Freudian view suggests that we focus our attention on what is going on *inside* the person; the Skinnerian view suggests that such efforts are foolhardy and that we would be wise to concentrate on environmental variables.

Although the Freudian and Skinnerian views may represent extremes that most psychologists avoid, most psychologists nevertheless weight their theories in the direction of internal or external factors. Periodically there is a shift in emphasis from internal to external factors or vice versa, with an occasional call for investigation of the relationship between the two. For example, in the 1940s one psychologist spoke out against the prevalent tendency to overestimate the unity of internal, and underestimate the importance of external factors in personality (Ichheiser, 1943); in the 1970s another psychologist was asking "Where is the person in personality research?" (Carlson, 1971). Most recently debate concerning the role of internal and external forces in governing behavior has been highlighted in the *person-situation controversy*. In 1968, the social learning theorist Walter Mischel wrote a book, *Personality and Assessment*, that criticized traditional personality theories for their emphasis on stable and enduring internal structures, which leads to the perception of people's behavior as fairly unchanging over time and across situations. Instead of emphasizing broad personality characteristics that function independent of external factors, Mischel suggested that changes in environmental or external conditions modify how people behave. Such changes result in relatively situation-specific behavior: each environmental situation acts independently to affect individual behavior.

Since the publication of Mischel's book and its development of this issue, considerable attention has been given to the internal-external (or person-situation) controversy. First there was debate about whether persons or situations control behavior, then about whether persons or situations are more important, and, finally, acceptance of the view that both are important and interact with one another (Endler & Magnusson, 1976; Magnusson & Endler, 1977). Almost all researchers today suggest an emphasis on person-situation interaction, even though fundamental disagreements remain. Even when persons, situations, and interactions are all accepted as important, there are theoretical differences about *what* in the person interacts *how* and with *what* in the situation. Thus, the internal-external debate remains lively and is an issue to be kept in mind in considering various theoretical points of view.

The Unity of Behavior and the Concept of the Self

Most psychologists agree that human behavior results not only from the operation of specific parts but also from the relationships among these parts. To a certain extent this is true for a mechanical system such as an automobile; it is even more true for a living system such as the human body. Rather than being made up of isolated responses, human behavior generally expresses *pattern, organization* and *integration.* Like a smooth-running car, the parts are operating in harmony with one another. They all seem to function together toward their common goal, instead of each part functioning independently toward different goals that may be in conflict with one another. Indeed, when behavior appears disorganized and disintegrated, we suspect that something is drastically wrong with the person. How, then, are we to formulate this pattern and organization? What is it that **self** gives an integrative quality to behavior? The concept of the **self** has often been used in this regard, but while many personality theorists give major attention to this concept, others choose to disregard it entirely.

Traditionally the concept of the self has been emphasized for three reasons. First, our awareness of ourselves represents an important aspect of our phenomenological or subjective experience. Second, considerable research suggests that how we feel about ourselves influences our behavior in many situations. Third, the concept of the self is used to express the organized, integrated aspects of human personality functioning. In asking whether the concept of the self is necessary, the noted theorist Gordon Allport suggested that many psychologists have tried in vain to account for the integration, organization, and unity of the human person by not making use of the concept of the self. For example, many behavioral psychologists have found it difficult to discuss the person as a whole because they deny the importance of internal factors. Other psychologists, after struggling with a fragmented conceptualization of personality, have returned to the concept of self as a way of representing the coherence, unity, and goal-directedness of human behavior (Allport, 1955).

The concept of the self has been used in a variety of ways, although some theorists have rejected it entirely because they fear it suggests control of our behavior by a strange inner being. But without a concept of self, the theorist is left with the task of developing an alternative concept or set of principles to express the integrated, systematic aspects of human functioning. On the other hand, reliance on the concept of the self leaves the theorist with the task of defining self in a way that does not make it impossible to study systematically. Thus, the various ways to account for the organized aspects of personality, and the utility of the concept of the self in this regard, remain major issues of concern for personality psychologists.

Varying States of Awareness and the Concept of the Unconscious

A fourth issue of continuing concern to most personality theorists is how to conceptualize the role of varying states of consciousness in individual functioning. Most psychologists grant that the potential for different states of consciousness exists. The effects of drugs, along with interest in Eastern religion and techniques of meditation, have served to heighten the concern of personality theorists with the whole range of altered states of consciousness. Most theorists also accept the view that we are not always attentive to or aware of factors that influence our behavior, but many are uncomfortable with Freud's theory of the unconscious. They feel that it is used to account for too much, and that it does not lend itself to empirical investigation. But how are we to account for such diverse phenomena as slips of the tongue, dreams, occasional inability to give a "rational" explanation for our behavior, and our ability under special circumstances to remember events of the past that appeared to have been forgotten? Are these related or separate phenomena? Must they be understood in terms of the working of an unconscious, or are alternative explanations possible? As we shall see, the issue here is important not only in relation to personality theory but also in relation to personality measurement. To what extent can we rely on people to give accurate reports concerning themselves? Must we use tests that will bypass the defenses and get to the unconscious? In relation to the concept of the self, are people aware of all their feelings about and perceptions of themselves? Or are some of these feelings and perceptions unconscious? If we cannot recognize some important feelings about and perceptions of ourselves, what are the implications of this fact on attempts at measurement of the self concept?

The Influences of the Past, Present and Future on Behavior

A final issue that may be noted here is the importance of the past, present, and future in governing behavior. Theorists would undoubtedly agree that behavior can be influenced only by factors operating in the present. In this sense, only the present is important in understanding behavior. But the present can be influenced by experiences of the remote past or of the recent past. Similarly, what one is thinking about in the present can be influenced by thoughts about the immediate future or about the distant future. People vary in the extent to which they worry about the past and the future. And personality theorists differ in their concern with and conceptualization of the past and the future as determinants of behavior in the present. At one extreme lies psychoanalytic theory, which attaches importance to early learning experiences. At the other extreme lies cognitive theory, which emphasizes the individual's plans for the future. However, the issue is not whether events that happened in the past can have lasting effects or whether anticipations about the future can have effects in the present (theorists undoubtedly would agree that both are possible and occur), but how to conceptualize the role of past experiences and future anticipations and connect their influence to what is occurring in the present.

Summary

In attempting to account for the *what, why,* and *how* of human functioning, personality theorists are confronted with many issues. Five issues of particular importance have been mentioned here: the philosophical view of the person, the relation between internal (person) and external (situation) influences in determining behavior, the concept of the self and how to account for the organized aspects of personality functioning, the role of varying states of awareness and the concept of the unconscious, and the role of the past, present, and future in governing behavior. Of course, many other issues concern personality theorists and account for differences among them, but the purpose here has been to point to the main ones. The importance of these and other issues will become increasingly clear as we consider the positions of the various theorists in the chapters that follow.

THEORY AND THEORETICAL ISSUES

theory

A theory of personality suggests ways of bringing together and systematizing a wide variety of findings. It also may suggest which directions in research are the most critical or potentially the most useful. Stated most simply, theories help to pull together what we know and to suggest how we may discover what is as yet unknown. Stated more systematically, a **theory** consists of a set of assumptions and concepts that tie together various empirical findings and suggest new relationships among them that should obtain under certain defined conditions. Viewed in this light, theories involve systematic orderings of ideas and planned approaches to research.

This description could lead to the assumption that the place of theory in psychology is well accepted and that there is consensus about its desirability. However, just as there is disagreement about the view of the person implied in a theory, so there is disagreement concerning the positive contributions of theory and the proper time for its development in psychology. There are those who emphasize that theories sharpen research objectives, make research more organized, and help the psychologist avoid wasting time on meaningless or irrelevant variables. "My argument is that it is only with the rubble of bad theories that we should be able to build better ones, and without theory of some kind, somewhere, psychological observation and description would at best be chaotic and meaningless" (Hebb, 1951, p. 39).

In contrast, there are those who argue that theories inhibit the search for new variables in a variety of areas. Here theory is seen as masking the discovery of new ideas. Accidental discoveries are used to illustrate how science can progress without—indeed, in spite of—theory. Whereas the former view emphasizes the contributions of theory to the development of new lines of research and new techniques, the latter view emphasizes how much of theory-related research takes a wrong path and eventually is discarded (Skinner, 1950).

Those who choose to use theories suggest that facts acquire significance only in the light of theory and that theory makes research cumulative. Those who choose to operate without theory suggest that we should pay attention to gathering facts and develop theories only after we have a considerable body of knowledge upon which to base them. Although some theorists feel that concepts such as drive and need add to understanding, others do not. "In the final analysis of behavior, is it not simpler to say a man drinks because he has been deprived of water for six hours rather than to say because he is thirsty? Such statements as 'thirsty' are perfectly acceptable in common parlance but cannot be allowed in scientific analysis" (Lundin, 1961, p. 40).

Theory is not something that can be taken lightly. It can be useful or destructive, guiding or misleading, revealing or blinding. Yet is it possible to function without theory? B. F. Skinner, a leading learning theorist, believes that it is and argues for caution in the use of theory. On the other hand, others argue that with all the possible variables and phenomena to be studied, only some are chosen, and that the selectivity involved in choice must assume some theory. If selection is not made on the basis of conscious theory, it is made on the basis of unconscious forces (Miller, 1951). To the extent that this may be the case, it seems reasonable to argue in favor of conscious, well-formulated theories.

Yet, of course, all men . . . are theorists. They differ not in whether they use theory, but in the degree to which they are aware of the theory they use. The choice before the man in the street and the research worker alike is not whether to theorize but whether to articulate his theory, to make it explicit, to get it out in the open where he can examine it.

(GAGE, 1963, P. 94)

Evaluation of Theories

What criteria can be used systematically to evaluate theories of personality? The criteria for such an analysis follow from the functions of theory—the organization of existing information and the selection of fruitful areas for investigation. The corresponding criteria for evaluation of theories of personality are *comprehensiveness, parsimony* or *simplicity,* and *research relevance* (Hall & Lindzey, 1957). The first two relate to the organizing function of theory, the third to its guiding function.

A good theory is comprehensive in that it encompasses and accounts for a wide variety of data. Such a theory is directed to each of the realms of behavior discussed previously. It is important to ask how many different kinds of phenomena the theory can account for. However, we must not be merely quantitative. No theory can account for everything, so one must also ask whether the phenomena accounted for by one theory are as important or central to human behavior as the phenomena encompassed by another theory. What constitutes a phenomenon that is critical to our understanding of behavior may often be ambiguous. However, it is important to recognize that comprehensiveness includes both the number and the significance of the facts accounted for by the theory.

Along with being comprehensive, a theory should be simple and parsimonious. It should account for varied phenomena in an economical, internally consistent way. A theory that makes use of a different concept for every aspect of behavior or of concepts that contradict one another is a poor theory. These goals of simplicity and comprehensiveness in turn raise the question of the appropriate level of organization and abstraction of a personality theory. As theories become more comprehensive and more parsimonious, they tend to become more abstract. It is important that, in becoming abstract, theories remain relevant both to groups of people and to specific individuals.

As Hall and Lindzey (1978) point out, a theory is not true or false but useful or not useful. A good theory has research relevance in that it leads to many new hypotheses, which can then be confirmed empirically. It has what Hall and Lindzey call empirical translation: it specifies variables and concepts in such a way that there is agreement about their meaning and about their potential for measurement. Empirical translation means that the concepts in a theory are clear, explicit, and lead to the expansion of knowledge; they must have predictive power. In other words, a theory must contain testable hypotheses about relationships among phenomena. A theory that is not open to the "negative test," one that potentially cannot be shown to be inaccurate, is a poor theory. This would lead to argument and debate, but not to scientific progress. Whatever the life of a theory, if it has led to new insights and new research techniques it has made a valuable contribution to science. "Theories of psychology are seldom disproved; they just fade away. Of course, all present theories of personality are doomed to pass into history. They should be tolerated only in proportion to their heuristic value to research" (Jensen, 1958, p. 295).

These criteria of comprehensiveness, parsimony, and research relevance provide the basis for a comparative evaluation of theories of personality. In comparing theories, however, we should have two questions in mind: Do they address themselves to the same phenomena? Are they at the same stage of development? Two theories that deal with different kinds of behavior may each be evaluated in relation to these three criteria. Nevertheless, we need not choose between the two theories. Each can be allowed to lead to new insights, with the hope that at some point both can be integrated into a single more comprehensive theory. Finally, a new and immature theory may be unable to account for many phenomena but may lead to a few important observations and show promise of becoming more comprehensive with time. Such a theory may be unable to explain phenomena considered to be understood by another established theory but may represent a breakthrough in significant areas formerly left untouched.

Theory and the History of Scientific Progress

We have discussed ways to evaluate theories and the importance of evaluating a theory in relation both to the phenomena it attempts to explain and to its stage of development. A look at the history of developments in most fields of science will help us understand some of the relevant issues. According to Kuhn (1970), there have been three distinct **stages of scientific development**: an early developmental stage, a stage of normal science, and a period of scientific revolution. The *early developmental stage* of scientific activity is characterized by continual competition between a number of distinct schools or views of nature. Each school believes it functions according to the dictates of scientific method and observation. Indeed, what differentiates these competing views is not the degree of commitment to scientific method but rather their differing ways of viewing the world and of practicing science within it. Since at this stage of development there is no common body of data and belief, each school builds the field anew from its own foundation and chooses its own supporting observations and experiments. Fact gathering during this time has a random

stages of scientific development

paradigm

quality. One rarely observes a systematic accumulation of knowledge. Essentially, during the early development stage, the field is without a commonly accepted model, or **paradigm**, that defines the field of observations and the methods to be used in research.

The *stage of normal science* begins with the acceptance of such a paradigm or model and is based on clear scientific achievement. During this stage there is acceptance of and commitment to a model that defines which problems are legitimate areas of inquiry and points out the appropriate methods for research. A more rigid definition of the field occurs, research is more focused, observations more restricted, and knowledge more cumulative. Each new bit of knowledge serves as a building block for the next. The scientists during this period are somewhat tradition-bound and are committed to the accepted model. Instead of many competing schools in the field, there tend to be relatively few, and frequently only one.

Since no paradigm or theory can ever explain all facts, ultimately there are some observations during the period of normal science that do not fit the accepted models. These observations or *anomalies* create a crisis in which tradition is shattered and, after a period of turmoil, a new paradigm is accepted. Copernicus, Newton, and Einstein were each associated with a stage of scientific revolution. In each case, a time-honored theory was rejected in favor of a new theory. In each case also, the new theory was incompatible with the old one and offered explanations of critical observations that could not be explained within the earlier paradigm. However, typically, acceptance of the new paradigm occurs after a period of intense competition among competing views and a period of wide-open research. This period thus shares some characteristics with the early developmental phase—competition among alternative views, wide-open research, debate over fundamental issues, occasional recourse to philosophy, and additions to knowledge that are noncumulative. What differentiates this state from the early development stage is that it follows a period of articulation of a paradigm and is a response to specific observations that have presented problems for that paradigm. Although the new paradigm may not be very well articulated and may be limited in scope, it is accepted because it offers solution to critical issues in the field. Rather than representing a competing paradigm or point of view, it replaces an old one and involves a reevaluation of prior fact. Once accepted, the new paradigm is associated with a new period of normal science until new observations arise and the stage is set for a further scientific revolution. The successive transition from one paradigm to another via revolution is the usual developmental pattern of a mature science.

The field of personality today is filled with issues that divide scientists along sharply defined lines and that lead to alternative, competing schools of thought. It is important to recognize that such theoretical differences exist and that they may not be readily resolved by debate or soon resolved by experimental proof. Kuhn suggests that the social sciences are still in the early developmental stage and have not yet arrived at their first universally received paradigm. If this is the case, we should not be surprised to find competing views that make a common claim to science and emphasize different observations and modes of research. Unfortunately, there may be nothing in the laws of science that allows us to choose among these views. And, though they compete with one another, each may result in significant contributions to knowledge in the field.

Theory and the Study of Personality

What then is the role of theory in the study of personality? The entire plan of this book suggests that theory is important to our goals of understanding and explaining human behavior. It can be said that the current state of personality theory is at a low ebb and that what is available is hardly worth considering. It is true that we have not had a good personality theory in some time; perhaps we have never had a good one. But it is on the basis of our past failures that we will have to build future successes. As a minimum, at least we now know some directions of investigation that are *not* worthy of our efforts. As Kuhn notes, history suggests that the road to a firm research consensus is extraordinarily difficult.

We can be critical of personality theory, as many rightfully have been, and we can even turn away from theory and devote ourselves to detailed research problems, as many psychologists are doing. But, in the final analysis, theory *is* necessary, and a good theory of personality will be developed. The choice is not between "theories or no theories", but rather in the degree to which a theory is so tightly constructed that it narrows the potential for "play in research" and the degree to which a theory is abstract. A theory can be abstract or concrete, complex or simple. It can lead to rigorous research or haphazard research, to the investigation of many problems or the investigation of a few. Freedom to explore and theories of lesser abstraction and complexity are most useful during the early stages of the development of a science. Focused, rigorous, and complex theories are more useful when observation and data are well advanced.

Theory, then, is both inevitable and useful in the study of personality. At this point, our concerns are how explicit we make theories, how good they are, and how well we use them. Theories imply views of humans but we must also appreciate that ". . . in truth, man is at once both biological animal and social product, both master and servant of fate, both rational and irrational, both driver and driven. His behavior can be fully explained only by placing each aspect in its proper perspective. Of all the dynamic physical systems constituting the universe, man is the most complex" (Krech & Crutchfield, 1958, p. 272). Ideally, a theory of personality should involve laws that help us understand how each person is different as well as how all people are the same. In the pursuit of such laws, we must develop theories that will permit coherent organization of what is known, *and* leave room for us to move on to insights into the unknown.

MAJOR CONCEPTS AND SUMMARY

personality	self
structure	theory
process	comprehensiveness, parsimony-simplicity, research relevance
tension-reduction model	
competence motivation	stages of scientific development
Zeitgeist	paradigm
person-situation controversy	

A theory consists of a set of assumptions and concepts that tie together empirical findings and suggests new relationships that should hold true under certain defined conditions. Theories define areas of observation and methods of research. In doing so, they focus attention but may also restrict observation. Theories of personality are expected to answer questions concerning the structure of the organism (what), the processes of personality functioning (why), and the growth and development of these structures and processes (how). In evaluating theories we are interested in the criteria of comprehensiveness, parsimony, and research relevance.

Although it is tempting to believe that science is completely objective and free of personal bias, there is evidence that personal values and arbitrariness affect theories of personality and strategies for research: "An apparently arbitrary element, compounded of personal and historical accident, is always a formative ingredient of the beliefs espoused by a given scientific community in a given time" (Kuhn, 1970, p. 4). Such arbitrariness may be particularly evident during the early developmental stage of a science and may help us understand the conflicting positions that arise in relation to significant issues. Finally, an awareness of the history of scientific progress in other disciplines can help us understand the presence of competing theories of personality today and the potential contributions each may make to future advances.

SIGMUND FREUD (1856-1939): A VIEW OF THE THEORIST

FREUD'S VIEW OF THE PERSON AND SOCIETY

FREUD'S VIEW OF SCIENCE, THEORY, AND RESEARCH METHODS

PSYCHOANALYSIS: A THEORY OF PERSONALITY

Structure
• Levels of Consciousness
• Id, Ego, and Superego

Process
• Life and Death Instincts
• Anxiety and the Mechanisms of Defense

Growth and Development
• The Development of Thinking Processes
• The Development of the Instincts
• Research on Growth and Development

MAJOR CONCEPTS AND SUMMARY

2 A PSYCHODYNAMIC THEORY: FREUD'S PSYCHOANALYTIC THEORY OF PERSONALITY

Chapter Focus:

In this chapter we shall consider psychoanalytic theory as illustrative of a psychodynamic, clinical approach to personality. The psychodynamic emphasis will be clear in the interpretation of behavior as a result of the interplay among motives, drives, needs, and conflicts. The clinical qualities will be apparent in the emphasis on the individual, in the attention given to individual differences, and in attempts to assess and understand the total individual. Research consists mainly of clinical investigation.

It seems like an empty wrangle over words to argue whether mental life is to be regarded as co-extensive with consciousness or whether it may be said to stretch beyond this limit, and yet I can assure you that the acceptance of unconscious mental processes represents a decisive step towards a new orientation in the world and in science.

FREUD, 1924. P. 26

The first personality theory to be considered is that of psychoanalysis. The psychoanalytic theory of Freud is reviewed because of its prominence in the culture of our society, its place in the history of psychology, and its importance as a model of a psychodynamic theory of personality. Psychoanalysis has reflected changing values in our society and has itself played a role in the changing of these values. As noted by Norman O. Brown: "It is a shattering experience for anyone seriously committed to the Western tradition of morality and rationality to take a steadfast, unflinching look at what Freud has to say. It is humiliating to be compelled to admit the grossly seamy side of so many grand ideals . . . To experience Freud is to partake a second time of the forbidden fruit" (1959, p. xi). Freud astutely observed that there had been three hurts to human self-love and self-image—the discovery by Copernicus that the earth was not the center of the universe, the discovery by Darwin that we do not exist independent of other members of the animal kingdom, and the discovery by Freud of the degree to which we are "influenced" by unknown, unconscious, and at times uncontrollable forces.

Psychoanalytic theory was derived from intensive work with individuals and, in turn, was applied to individuals. Although it involves assumptions relevant to all people, psychoanalytic theory has particular relevance to the study of individual differences as well as the total functioning of individuals. Furthermore, psychoanalysis exemplifies a psychodynamic theory in that it gives a prominent role to the complex interplay among forces in human behavior. In psychoanalytic theory behavior is a result of struggles and compromises among motives, drives, needs, and conflicts. Behavior can express a motive directly or in a subtle, disguised way. The same behavior can satisfy different motives in different people, or a variety of motives in one person. For example, eating can satisfy a hunger need but it also can symbolically satisfy a need for love; or being a psychoanalyst can satisfy a need to help others, a wish to discover new aspects of psychological functioning, a wish to satisfy one's curiosity about the private lives of others, or some combination of these as well as other motives. Being a doctor can satisfy a need to help others as well as serve as a way of overcoming anxieties about illness and bodily harm. Thus, any behavior or goal can satisfy a variety of motives at the same time. It is this quality of behavior that forms a major aspect of a psychodynamic theory of personality. "Only when we have begun to understand the subtle interweaving of themes, the 'overdetermination' of any single act, belief, or fantasy, and the multiple functions that every dream, wish, action, and philosophy serves, do we begin to understand something of the individual" (Keniston, 1965, p. 49). Finally, behavior occurs at different levels of awareness, with individuals more or less aware of the forces behind their various behaviors. "The deeper we probe in our study of mental processes, the more we become aware of the richness and complexity of their content. Many simple formulas which seemed to us at first to meet the case turned out later to be inadequate. We are incessantly altering and improving them" (Freud, 1933, p. 121).

In this chapter we shall be analyzing and assessing a theory that is significant in its emphasis on individual differences, the entire personality, behavior as the result of an interplay among forces, personality as involving hierarchical organization, and phenomena as "simple" as the slip of the tongue and as "complex" as the development of culture. To increase the breadth and depth of our perspective, we shall turn our attention first to the life of the individual primarily responsible for psychoanalytic theory, and then to the view of the person and science implicit in his theory. Along with its usefulness for putting psychoanalytic theory into personal and historical perspective, a reading of the biography of Freud (Jones, 1953, 1955, 1957) gives one a sense of the genius and courage of the man responsible for the theory.

SIGMUND FREUD (1856-1939): A VIEW OF THE THEORIST

Sigmund Freud was born in Austria in 1856. He was the first child of his parents; although his father, 20 years older than his mother, had two sons by a previous marriage. His birth was followed by the birth and early death of one sibling and the birth of six more siblings. He is described as having been his mother's favorite and later was to say that "a man who has been the indisputable favorite of his mother keeps for life the feeling of a conqueror, that confidence of success that often induces real success" (Freud, 1900, p. 26). As a boy, he had dreams of becoming a great general or minister of state, but, being Jewish, he was concerned about anti-Semitism in these fields. This led him to consider medicine as a profession. As a medical student (1873-1881), he came under the influence of the noted physiologist Ernst Brucke. Brucke viewed humans in terms of a dynamic physiological system in which they are controlled by the physical principles of the conservation of energy. This view of physiological functioning was the foundation for Freud's dynamic view of psychological functioning.

After obtaining his medical degree, Freud did research and practiced in the field of neurology. Some of his early research involved a comparison of adult and fetal brains. He concluded that the earliest structures persist and are never buried, a view that was paralleled later by his views concerning the development of personality. Professionally, the years after medical school were filled first with theory and research, but then, for financial reasons, there was a turn toward practice. Personally, Freud experienced periodic depressions and attacks of anxiety, occasionally using cocaine to calm the agitation and dispel the depression. During these years he married and had three daughters and three sons. Throughout the later years of the nineteenth century, Freud was concerned about money. He also was subjected to incapacitating spells of migraine. In 1886 he spent a year with the French psychiatrist Jean Charcot, who was having some success in treating neurotic patients with hypnosis. While not satisfied with the effects of hypnosis, Freud was stimulated and excited by the thinking of Charcot and, essentially, changed during this time from a neurologist to a psychopathologist. Jones, the biographer of Freud, comments on Freud's development at this time. "All this work would have established Freud as a first class neurologist, a hard worker, a close thinker, but—with the exception perhaps of the book on aphasia—there was little to foretell the existence of genius" (1953, p. 220).

In 1879, the year following his father's death, Freud began his self-analysis. He continued to be bothered by periods of depression and, while intellectual pursuits helped to distract him from his pain, he looked for answers in his unconscious; "My recovery can only come through work in the unconscious; I cannot manage with conscious efforts alone." For the rest of his life he continued self-analysis, devoting the last half hour of the working day to it. In the 1890's, he tried a variety of therapeutic techniques with his patients. First he used hypnotic suggestion as practiced by Charcot. Then he tried a concentration technique in which he pressed his hand upon the patient's head and urged the recall of memories. During these years he also collaborated with the Viennese physician Joseph Breuer,

catharsis

learning from him the technique of **catharsis** (a release and freeing of emotion through talking about one's problems) and collaborating with him on a book *Studies in Hysteria*. At this point, already in his forties, Freud had developed little, if any, of what was later to become known as psychoanalysis. Furthermore, his judgments of himself and of his work parallel the comment made by his biographer Jones. "I have restricted capacities or talents. None at all for the natural sciences; nothing for mathematics; nothing for anything quantitative. But what I have, of a very restricted nature, is probably very intense."

SIGMUND FREUD

free-association

The momentum in Freud's work and thinking most clearly dates back to his self-analysis and to the beginnings, in 1896, of his use of the **free-association** method with his patients. This method of allowing all thoughts to come forth without inhibition or falsification of any kind resulted, in 1900, in what many still consider to be Freud's most significant work, *The Interpretation of Dreams.* In this book, Freud began to develop his theory of the mind and, although only 600 copies were sold in the first eight years after publication, he began to develop a following. In 1902, a Psychoanalytic Society was formed, and was joined by a number of people who went on to become outstanding psychoanalysts—Alfred Adler, Paul Federn, Otto Rank, and Sandor Ferenczi. Freud's writing and development of theory progressed, but with increased public attention, there was increased public abuse. In 1904, Freud wrote on the *Psychopathology of Everyday Life,* and in 1905 he published *Three Essays On The Theory Of Sexuality.* The latter presented Freud's views on infantile sexuality and its relation to perversions and neuroses. This resulted in ridicule of Freud, who was seen as an evil and wicked man with an obscene mind. Medical institutions were boycotted for tolerating Freud's view; an early follower, Ernest Jones, was forced to resign his neurological appointment for inquiring into the sexual life of his patients.

Freud's ideas at this time were still primitive compared to the elaborate theoretical network he was to develop, but he had already recognized the importance of the unconscious and of infantile sexuality, and made them the groundwork for future developments. In 1909 Freud was invited by G. Stanley Hall to give a series of lectures at Clark University in Worcester, Massachusetts. During this period, Freud was developing his theories of development and infantile fantasies, his theory of the principles of mental functioning, and his views concerning the psychoanalytic process. He had by now achieved sufficient fame and acceptance to have a waiting list of patients.

But Freud had problems, too. By 1919 he had lost all of his savings in the war. In 1920, a daugher, age 26, died. Perhaps of greatest significance was his fear for the lives of two sons who were in the war. It is out of such a historical context that Freud in 1920, at age 64, developed his theory of the death instinct—a wish to die, which is in opposition to the life instinct, or wish for survival. At this time he also developed his theory of group behavior, involving the common identification of members of a group with the leader.

Just as the war appeared to influence his thinking, so apparently did the growth of anti-Semitism during the 1930's. In 1932, for example, the Nazis in Berlin made a bonfire of his books. Shortly thereafter, Freud published his book on *Moses and Monotheism,* in which he suggested that Moses was an Egyptian noble who joined the Jews and gave them a religion. Freud attributed anti-Semitism to resentment against the strict moral code of the Jews and, in this book, appeared to say that it was not a Jew but an Egyptian who bears the onus. In this book Freud also presented some of his views concerning Christianity.

Freud died on September 26, 1939, at the age of 83. Almost to the very end, he was doing analysis daily and continuing his writing. The last 20 years of his life represent a remarkable period of personal courage and productivity. Earlier, it had taken a great deal of courage to go on with his work in spite of considerable attack from the public and his medical colleagues. During this later period, it took considerable courage to go on in spite of the loss of many of his disciples, and in spite of the brutatily of the Nazis. During these later years, Freud continued to work despite extreme physical discomfort and pain, including 33 operations for cancer of the jaw. While not a wealthy man, he turned down lucrative offers which he felt would jeopardize the proper stature of his work. In 1920, he refused an offer from Cosmopolitan magazine to write on topics such as *The Husband's Place in the Home*, saying to the magazine: "Had I taken into account the considerations that influence your edition from the beginning of my career, I am sure I should not have become known at all, either in America or Europe." In 1924 he turned down an offer of $100,000 by Samuel Goldwyn to collaborate in making films of famous love stories.

Most of what we now recognize as the major elements in Freud's theory were developed during these last 20 years. It was during these later years that Freud developed his final ideas concerning civilization, neuroses, psychoses, and perhaps most significant of all, his theory of anxiety and the mechanisms of defense. As a man he was glorified by some as being compassionate, courageous, and a genius. Others take note of his many battles and breaks with colleagues, of his eagerness to defend the "quasi-political" and "quasi-religious" character of the psychoanalytic movement, and see in him a rigid authoritarian, intolerant of the opinions of others, and eager to "be the Moses who showed the human race the promised land" (Fromm, 1959). Whatever the interpretation of Freud's personality, most, if not all, would agree that he had a passionate thirst for truth and pursued his studies with tremendous courage and integrity. Finally, most students of Freud, and psychoanalysis, would agree that factors in Freud's personal life and related historical factors (for example, the Victorian era, World War I, and anti-Semitism) played a part in the final formulation of his theory and in the development of the psychoanalytic movement.

FREUD'S VIEW OF THE PERSON AND SOCIETY

Notwithstanding Freud's statements to the contrary, it can be argued that implicit in psychoanalysis is a view of the person, a view of society, perhaps even a total *Weltanschauung* or philosophy of life. While Freud struggled to develop a theory based on science rather than philosophy, a theory free of biases from his personal life and the historical period of which he was a part, psychoanalytic theory reflects the themes that were current in the lay and scientific communities of late nineteenth-early twentieth century Europe. Freud's theory was based on observations, but these were primarily observations of middle and upper class patients of a Victorian era, and observations by investigators trained to view phenomena in preconceived ways.

What is at the heart of the psychoanalytic view of the person is that the human is an energy system. There is the sense of a system in which energy flows, gets sidetracked, or becomes dammed-up. In all, there is a limited amount of energy, and if it gets used in one way, there is that much less energy to be used in another way. The energy that is used for cultural purposes, is withdrawn from the energy available for sexual purposes, and vice versa. If the energy is blocked from one channel of expression, it finds another, generally along the path of least resistance. Human behavior may take many forms, but basically all behavior is reducible to common forms of energy. The goal of all behavior is **pleasure**, that is, the reduction of tension or the release of energy.

pleasure

Why the assumption of an energy model concerning human behavior? Whatever its scientific merits, the assumption is traceable to the excitement physical scientists were then experiencing in the field of energy dynamics. According to the nineteenth century physicist Helmholtz's principle of the conservation of energy, matter and energy can be transformed but not destroyed. Not only physicists but members of other disciplines were studying intensively the laws of energy changes in a system. As was already noted, while in medical school Freud came under the influence of the physiologist Brucke. Brucke viewed humans as moved by forces according to the principle of the conservation of energy, a view apparently translated by Freud into the psychological realm of behavior. As Hall (1954) notes, the age of energy and dynamics provided scientists with a new conception of humans, "the view that man is an energy system and that he obeys the same physical laws which regulate the soap bubble and the movement of the planets" (pp. 12-13).

Beyond the view of the person as being an energy system, there is the view that humans, like other animals, are driven by sexual and aggressive instincts or drives. Freud's view of the importance of aggression in human behavior was based on observation, but his interpretation of these observations had the definite quality of a philosophical view. For example in *Civilization and Its Discontents* (1930), Freud commented as follows. "The bit of truth behind all this—one so eagerly denied—is that men are not gentle, friendly creatures wishing for love, who simply defend themselves if they are attacked, but that a powerful measure of desire for aggression has to be reckoned as a part of their instinctual endowment" (p. 85). Freud goes on to comment that the instinct of aggression lies "at the bottom of all the relations of affection and love between human beings—possibly with the single exception of that of a mother to her male child" (p. 89). We have already noted that Freud published his theory of aggression and the death instinct in 1920, after the extended and bloody period of World War I.

Along with the aggressive drive, Freud placed great emphasis on the sexual drive, and on the conflict between expression of these drives and society. The emphasis on sexual inhibition in particular, and the inhibition of the expression of instincts in general, appears to relate to the Victorian period of which Freud and his patients were a part. For Freud, the person in pursuit of pleasure was in conflict with society and civilization. People

pleasure principle

function according to the **pleasure principle**, seeking "unbridled gratification" of all desires. Yet, such a mode of operation runs counter to the demands of society and the external world. The energy that would otherwise be released in the pursuit of pleasure and gratification must now be restricted, inhibited, and channeled to conform to the aims of society. "It is impossible to ignore the extent to which civilization is built up on renunciation of instinctual gratifications . . . This 'cultural privation' dominates the whole field of social relations between human beings; we know already that it is the cause of the antagonism against which all civilization has to fight . . . What he (man) employs for cultural purposes he withdraws to a great extent from women and his sexual life" (Freud, 1930, p. 63, p. 73). Freud believed that scientific activities, artistic endeavors, in fact the whole range of cultural productivity, are expressions of sexual and aggressive energy that was prevented from expression in a more direct way.

While such accomplishments represent one outgrowth of the conflict between the instinctual energies of the individual and society's restrictions on the possibilities for gratification, another outgrowth of this conflict is misery and neurosis. In fact, according to Freud, the price of progress in civilization is misery, the forfeiting of happiness, and a heightened sense of guilt. It is even worth the possibility of giving up civilization and returning to primitive conditions!

We can see, then, that beyond the formal conceptualization of a theory of personality, there is implicit in psychoanalysis a view of the person. According to this view humans, like other animals, are driven by instincts or drives and operate in the pursuit of pleasure. People operate as an energy system, building, storing, and releasing, in one form or another, what is basically the same energy. There are no mystical phenomena, no chance behaviors, since all behaviors are determined in the same sense that the behavior of molecules is determined. Not only is all behavior determined, but much of our behavior is determined by forces outside of awareness. "It (psychoanalysis) has furthermore taught us that our intellect is a feeble and dependent thing, a plaything and tool of our impulses and emotions; that all of us are forced to behave cleverly or stupidly according as our attitudes and inner resistances ordain" (Freud, quoted by Jones, 1955, p. 368). In the end, psychoanalysis sides with the instincts and seeks a reduction in the extent to which the instincts are frustrated. In sum, the person is an energy system, driven by sexual and aggressive drives and operating in the pursuit of pleasure (tension reduction), functioning in a regular, lawful way, but often unaware of the forces determining behavior, and basically in conflict with society's restrictions on the expressions of the instincts. While the formal aspects of psychoanalytic theory went through many changes and revisions, the underlying philosophy remained implicit in each phase of Freud's development of the theory.

FREUD'S VIEW OF SCIENCE, THEORY, AND RESEARCH METHODS

It is important to note that in spite of the attention we have given to the philosophical view of the person implicit in psychoanalytic theory, Freud himself disclaimed any relationship between psychoanalysis and philosophy. Freud found the philosopher's thinking too far removed from the rigors of science and viewed psychoanalysis as a branch of psychology and a part of science.

We know that Freud was trained in the techniques of medical research, and that he was aware of issues concerning the definition of concepts and the formulation of a theory. He appreciated the beauty of science, and had a sense of the back-and-forth process between theory and research. Freud felt that the scientific task is the formulation of hypotheses which lead to observations that bring order and clarity into phenomena. He felt a need for sharp definition of concepts, but he also accepted the possibility that vague conceptions and speculative theory might be necessary during the early stages of an empirical science. Thus, Freud could insist on the importance of the instincts while calling them "mythical beings, superb in their indefiniteness." Freud argued for the utility of concepts that appear to organize empirical observations, even if it is not always possible to demonstrate the truthfulness of the concepts.

The true beginning of scientific activity consists rather in describing phenomena and then in proceeding to group, classify, and correlate them. Even at the stage of description it is not possible to avoid applying certain abstract ideas to the material at hand . . . They (the concepts) must at first necessarily possess some measure of uncertainty; there can be no question of any clear delimitation of their content . . . It is only after more searching investigation of the field in question that we are able to formulate with increased clarity the scientific concepts underlying it, and progressively so to modify these concepts so that they become widely applicable and at the same time consistent logically.

FREUD, 1915, PP. 60-61

Although he developed an elaborate theory of personality, Freud's major contribution was in the nature of the observations he made. He was aware that theories could and would change, and he saw these observations as the ultimate contribution of psychoanalysis to the science of psychology, as they related particularly to the functioning of the unconscious. It is important to note that Freud's observations were based on the analysis of patients and, by and large, he had little use for mechanical efforts to verify psychoanalytic principles in the laboratory. When Rosenzweig (1941) wrote to Freud to tell him of his experimental studies of one psychoanalytic concept, Freud wrote back that psychoanalytic concepts were based on a wealth of reliable observations and thus were not in need of independent experimental verification. He was satisfied using the intensive clinical study of the individual case as his major research method.

In analyzing their patients, analysts work as scientists. They have expectations, but they allow the data to come forth. They record many pieces of data which do not appear to fit together and formulate principles to order and organize the data. These principles are then checked against the further observations that are made in the course of the analysis. Observations of one patient are checked against those of another patient, and observations by one analyst are checked against those by another analyst. On a broader scale, observations from work with patients are then checked against cultural documents such as folk tales, rituals, and taboos, and against observations from psychological tests administered to large groups of subjects.

It is debatable whether this approach is merely superficially related to the scientific method or is indeed a close approximation of it. It is clear that this research method allows for the accumulation of considerable data about an individual. There is probably no other position in psychology that even approximates the wealth of material gathered about a single person by the psychoanalyst. On the other hand, as Freud himself pointed out, analysts are unlike other scientists in that they do not use experiments as a significant part of their research. This gap, between the types of observations made by analysts and those made during controlled experiments, has narrowed as experimentally oriented psychologists have become interested in psychoanalysis. While Freud viewed psychoanalysis as a part of the science of psychology, most of the early research was conducted by medical professionals in a therapeutic setting. It is only within the last 20 to 30 years that psychologists have tried to apply the traditional scientific techniques of the discipline to the concepts of psychoanalysis.

PSYCHOANALYSIS: A THEORY OF PERSONALITY

Psychoanalysis is three things — a theory of personality, a method of therapy, and a technique for research. It is important to keep these different aspects in mind, since comments and criticisms appropriate to one may not be relevant to the other. For example, criticism of psychoanalysis as a therapy does not reflect on psychoanalysis as a theory, unless the theory is being tested in the course of therapy. The improvement of a patient in therapy is not critical to the theory, unless the theory makes specific predictions concerning the progress of the patient. Since therapy is such a complex process, and the nature of environmental events outside of therapy can never be predicted, the theory is rarely used to make predictions concerning the outcome of therapy. While keeping these aspects separate, however, we must also seek to see the links between them. We must seek to understand the relationships among theory, assessment and research, to understand how structural units get translated into processes that account for growth and development, psychopathology and behavioral change — all phases of human behavior. At the heart of the psychoanalytic theory we shall find an emphasis on the following concepts: psychological determinism, the unconscious, behavior as goal-directed and expressive of an interplay among forces (dynamics), and behavior as an outgrowth of events that occurred in the past of the individual (genetic approach).

Structure

What are the structural units used by psychoanalytic theory to account for human behavior? Included here are Freud's concepts of the unconscious, the preconscious, and the conscious, as descriptive qualities of mental life. In the early development of the theory the concept of levels of consciousness served as a focal point in psychoanalytic thinking. In fact, Freud claimed that "Psychoanalysis aims at and achieves nothing more than the discovery of the unconscious in mental life" (p. 397).

Levels of Consciousness

conscious

preconscious
unconscious

According to the psychoanalytic theory, psychic life can be described in terms of the degree to which we are aware of phenomena: the **conscious** relates to phenomena we are aware of at any given moment, the **preconscious** to phenomena we are able to be aware of if we attend to them, and the **unconscious** to phenomena that we are unaware of, and *cannot* become aware of except under special circumstances.

Although Freud was not the first to pay attention to the importance of the unconscious, he was the first to explore in detail the qualities of unconscious life and attribute major importance to them in our daily lives. Through the analysis of dreams, slips of the tongue, neuroses, psychoses, works of art, and rituals, Freud attempted to understand the properties of the unconscious and to delineate its importance in behavior. What he found was a quality of psychic life in which nothing was impossible. The unconscious is alogical (opposites can stand for the same thing), disregarding of time (events of different periods may coexist), and disregarding of space (size and distance relationships are neglected, so that large things fit into small things and distant places are brought together). One is reminded of William James' reference to the world of the newly born infant as a "big blooming buzzing confusion."

Within the unconscious, there is a fluidity and plasticity to phenomena that is rarely observed during our rational, waking life. It is in the dream, and in the psychic productions of psychotics, that the workings of the unconscious become most apparent. Here we are exposed to the world of symbols, where many ideas may be telescoped into a single word, where a part of any object may stand for many things. It is through the process of symbolization that a penis can be represented by a snake or nose, a woman by a church, chapel, or boat, and an engulfing mother by an octopus. It is through this process that we are allowed to think of writing as a sexual act — the pen is the male organ, the paper the woman who receives, the ink the semen which flows out in the quick up and down movements of the pen (Groddeck, 1923). Groddeck, who, in *The Book of the It*, gives many fascinating examples of the workings of the unconscious, offers the following as an example of the functioning of the unconscious in his own life.

I cannot recall her (my nurse) appearance, I know nothing more than her name, Bertha, the shining one. But I have a clear recollection of the day she went away. As a parting present she gave me a copper three-pfennig piece. A Dreier . . . Since that day I have been pursued by the number three. Words like trinity, triangle, triple alliance, convey something disreputable to me, and not merely the words but the ideas attached to them, yes, and the whole complex of ideas built up around them by the capricious brain of a child. For this reason, the Holy Ghost, as the Third Person of the Trinity, was already suspect to me in early childhood; trigonometry was a plague in my school days . . . Yes, three is a sort of fatal number for me.

GRODDECK, 1923, P. 9

The unconscious is never observed directly. What evidence then is there that supports the concept of the unconscious? Freud realized the importance of the unconscious after observing hypnotic phenomena. It is well known that while under the effects of hypnosis people can recall things that previously they could not. Furthermore, they will perform things under posthypnotic suggestion without consciously "knowing" that they are behaving in accordance with that suggestion; that is, in the latter case they will fully believe that what they are doing is voluntary and independent of any suggestion by another person.

Psychologists have used perceptual processes to investigate the indirect effects of unconscious forces. An early experiment in this area was performed by McGinnies (1949). Subjects were shown stimuli with a tachistoscope, an apparatus that allows the experimenter to show stimuli to subjects at very fast speeds, so that they cannot be perceived, or at slow speeds. McGinnies presented two types of words to college subjects: neutral words such as apple, dance, child, and emotionally toned words such as rape, whore, penis. McGinnies showed the subjects the words, in random order, first at very fast speeds, and then at progressively slower speeds. He recorded the point at which the subjects were able to identify each of the words and their sweat gland activity (a measure of tension) in response to each word.

McGinnies found that subjects took longer to recognize the emotionally toned words than the neutral words. Also, prior to recognizing both, the subjects showed greater sweat gland activity to the emotional words than to the neutral words. Therefore, there were signs of emotional response to the emotionally toned words prior to their being verbally identified and evidence of a reluctance to perceive these words consciously. McGinnies interpreted these data as proof that an individual can perceive a stimulus before it is brought into conscious awareness. He interpreted the delay between involuntary response to the stimulus and conscious **perceptual defense** identification of the stimulus as evidence of **perceptual defense**, a process by which the individual defends against the anxiety that accompanies actual recognition of a threatening stimulus.

The work by McGinnies was criticized on a number of grounds, including the fact that he did not consider the possibility that subjects identified the emotionally toned words earlier in the process but were reluctant to verbalize them to the experimenter. The research stimulated a host of studies on what has been called "perceptual defense," "perception without awareness," "subliminal perception," and "subception." Various investigators have studied different aspects of the process and some interpret the phenomenon differently, many preferring to avoid relating their findings to the concept of the unconscious. What seems to be clear, however, is that subjects can respond to stimuli and be unable to report conscious recognition of the stimuli (Lazarus and McCleary, 1951; Erdelyi, 1974). Furthermore, there is evidence that the content of a person's imagery can be influenced by stimuli that are not part of conscious awareness and experience (see Box 2.1).

BOX 2.1 **The Concept of the Unconscious**

QUESTION   Does a weak or never consciously perceived stimulus have an effect on people's thinking? Can it be demonstrated that actually reportable perceptions are only a part of a larger group of responses and associations activated by a stimulus?

HYPOTHESIS   An unreported, concealed figure will influence subsequent imagery.

SUBJECTS   310 male and female undergraduates.

METHOD   As the experimental stimulus, use a picture containing two forms, a perceptually dominant tree and a perceptually recessive duck shaped by branches of the tree. As the control stimulus, use a picture containing only a tree, with the branches of the tree so modified as to eliminate the outline of the duck. Instruct the subjects that a picture will flash on the screen (tachistoscopically) three times. For some subjects, use a tachistoscopic exposure of 1 second, for others an exposure of 1/100th second. After the picture goes off, subjects are to sit back, relax, close their eyes, and wait for an image of a nature scene to come to their mind. After obtaining a visual image of the nature scene, each subject is to draw it on a piece of paper and label the various parts. The drawings are then coded and rated by judges for "duck-related" content. Earlier testing suggested that responses such as "duck," "water," "birds," "feather," "animals," "whiteness," "nest," "food," and "humans" could be considered as duck-related content. Experimental subjects see only the picture with the perceptually recessive duck, control subjects only the picture with the duck outline eliminated.

RESULTS   Analyze the data in two ways. First, compare the number of experimental subjects and control subjects who had duck-related images. Second, compare the frequency of duck-related images of the two groups.

BOX 2.1 **The Concept** *continued*
         of the
         Unconscious

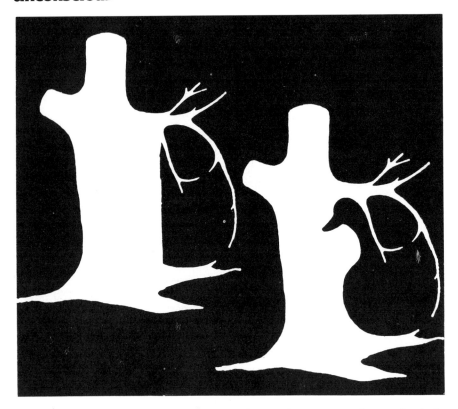

FIGURE 2.1 The figure used as the experimental stimulus (right) contains a perceptually recessive duck, which is eliminated from the control stimulus (left).

1 A greater proportion of experimental than control subjects had duck-related images in their drawings (67 percent of the experimental subjects and 50 percent of the control subjects).

2 The average frequency of duck-related images was greater in the experimental than the control group (only in the 1-second exposure situation).

3 No subject in either group spontaneously reported seeing the duck during the experiment proper. During repeated exposure of the experimental stimulus to both experimental and control groups, including a 30-second exposure with the clue: "There is a duck somewhere in the

picture-find it," well over half the subjects in both groups failed to recognize the duck.

CONCLUSION   Stimuli that are not consciously perceived by subjects may influence their imagery and stream of conscious thought; that is, people may be unaware of the stimuli to which they are responding.

SOURCE   M. Eagle, D. L. Wolitzky, and G. S. Klein, Imagery: Effect of a concealed figure in a stimulus. *Science*, February 18, 1966, 837-839

It is hard to overestimate the importance of the concept of the unconscious to psychoanalytic theory, the moral dilemmas over responsibility that have occurred as a result of it, and the difficulties it has presented to scientists interested in rigorous, controlled investigation. It is important to recognize that acceptance of this concept represents more than just acceptance of the principle that there are aspects of our functioning of which we are not fully aware. Far more than this, the psychoanalytic concept of the unconscious suggests that a significant portion of our behavior, perhaps the major one, is determined by unconscious forces, and that much of our psychic energy is devoted either to finding acceptable expression of unconscious ideas or to keeping them unconscious. The concept of the unconscious is deeply embedded in the rest of psychoanalytic theory. Although many new concepts were added as the theory developed, the concept of the unconscious has always remained as part of the framework for the entire theory.

Id, Ego And Superego

In 1923 Freud developed a more formal structural model for psychoanalysis, defined by the concepts of id, ego, and superego, which refer to different aspects of people's functioning. According to the theory, the **id** represents the biological substratum of humans, the source of all drive energy. The energy for a person's functioning originally resides in the life and death, or sexual and aggressive instincts, which are part of the id. In its functioning, the id seeks the release of excitation, tension, and energy. It operates according to the **pleasure principle** — the pursuit of pleasure and the avoidance of pain. In operating this way the id seeks immediate, total release. It has qualities of a spoiled child: it wants what it wants when it wants it. The id cannot tolerate frustration and is free of inhibitions. It shows no regard for reality and can seek satisfaction through action or through imagining that it has gotten what it wants—the fantasy of gratification is as good as the actual gratification. It is without reason, logic, val-

id

pleasure principle

ues, morals, or ethics. In sum, the id is demanding, impulsive, blind, irrational, asocial, selfish and, finally, pleasure loving.

superego

In marked contrast to the id is the **superego** which represents the moral branch of our functioning, containing the ideals we strive for and the punishments (guilt) we expect when we have gone against our ethical code. This structure functions to control behavior in accordance with the rules of society, offering rewards (pride, self-love) for "good" behavior and punishments (guilt, feelings of inferiority, accidents) for "bad" behavior. The superego may function on a very primitive level, being relatively incapable of reality testing, that is, incapable of modifying its action depending on circumstances. In such cases, the person is unable to distinguish between thought and action, feeling guilty for thinking something even if it did not lead to action. Furthermore, the individual is bound by black-white, all-none judgements and by the pursuit of perfection. Excessive use of words such as good, bad, judgement, and trial are often expressive of a strict superego. But the superego can also be understanding and flexible. For example, people may be able to forgive themselves or someone else if it is clear that something was an accident or done under circumstances of severe stress. In the course of development, children learn to make such important distinctions and see things not only in all or none, right or wrong, black or white terms.

ego

The third structure conceptualized in the theory is that of the **ego**. Whereas the id seeks pleasure and the superego seeks perfection, the ego seeks reality. The function of the ego is to express and satisfy the desires of the id in accordance with reality and the demands of the superego. Whereas the id operates according to the pleasure principle, the ego oper-

reality principle

ates according to the **reality principle** — gratification of the instincts is delayed until an optimum time when the most pleasure can be obtained with the least pain or negative consequences. According to the reality principle, the energy of the id may be blocked, diverted, or released gradually, all in accordance with the demands of reality and the conscience. Such an operation is not in contradiction to the pleasure principle but, rather, represents a temporary suspension of it. It functions, in George Bernard Shaw's words, so as, "to be able to choose the line of greatest advantage instead of yielding in the direction of least resistance." The ego is able to separate wish from fantasy, can tolerate tension and compromise, and changes over time. Accordingly, it expresses the development of perceptual and cognitive skills, the ability to perceive more and think in more complex terms. For example, the person can begin to think in terms of the future and what is best in the long run. All of these qualities are in contrast with the unrealistic, unchanging, demanding qualities of the id.

In comparison with his investigations into the unconscious and the workings of the id, Freud did relatively little work on the functioning of the ego. He pictured the ego as a weak structure, a poor creature that owed service to three harsh masters — the id, reality, and the superego. The "poor" ego has a hard time serving these masters and must reconcile the claims and demands of each. Of particular significance is the relation of the ego to the tyranny of the id.

One might compare the relation of the ego to the id with that between a rider and his horse. The horse provides the locomotive energy, and the rider has the prerogative of determining the goal and of guiding the movements of his powerful mount towards it. But all too often in the relations between the ego and the id we find a picture of the less ideal situation in which the rider is obliged to guide his horse in the direction in which it itself wants to go.

FREUD, 1933, P. 108

In sum, Freud's ego is logical, rational, tolerant of tension, the "executive" of personality, but it is a poor rider on the swift horse of the id and is subject to control by three masters.

Just before his death Freud began to give more attention to the importance of the ego in personality. This attention was then developed by his daughter, Anna Freud, and a number of analysts whose work has been categorized under the heading of ego psychology. Whereas in the earlier view the ego was viewed as existing without energy of its own and obliged to guide the id where it wanted to go, the later view emphasized the importance of the ego in conflict resolution as well as in adaptation. This view left room for the possibility that the individual may experience pleasure through the conflict-free functioning of the ego, and not only through the release of the energies of the id. According to ego psychology, the ego has a source of energy of its own and takes pleasure in mastery of the environment. This concept is related to White's (1959) concept of competence motivation. In its description of personality, this view gave increased importance to the ways in which individuals actively engage their environment and to their modes of thinking and perceiving. While these modes still could be considered as functioning in the service of the id and serving to reduce conflict, they were now viewed as having adaptive functions and importance independent of these other functions. The importance for research of such a change in view will become apparent as we discuss the dynamics (processes) of functioning in the next section.

It is important to understand the status of the concepts used by the theory. The concepts of conscious, unconscious, id, ego, superego are at a high level of abstraction and are not always defined with great precision. For example, the unconscious is at times taken to mean a structure, at times refers to forces pushing toward expression in consciousness and behavior, and at times refers to descriptive properties of psychic phenomena. Furthermore, there is some lack of clarity because the meaning of some concepts changed as the theory developed, but the exact nature of the change in meaning was never spelled out (Madison, 1961). Finally, it should be clear that these are conceptualizations of phenomena. While the language is picturesque and concrete, we must avoid regarding concepts as real things. There is no energy plant inside us with a little person controlling its power. We do not "have" an id, ego, superego but, according to the theory, there are qualities of human behavior which are usefully conceptualized in these structural terms. The structures achieve greater definition in relation to the processes implied in them and it is to these processes that we now turn.

Process

Life and Death Instincts

We have discussed Freud's view of the person as an energy system obeying the same laws as other energy systems. Energy may be altered and transformed but essentially it is all the same energy. Within such an overall framework, the processes (dynamics) involved in psychoanalytic theory relate to the ways in which energy develops and is expressed, blocked, or transformed in some way. According to the theory, the source of all psychic energy lies in states of excitation within the body which seek expression and tension reduction. These states are called **instincts**, or **drives**, and represent constant, inescapable forces. In the earlier view, there were ego instincts, relating to tendencies toward self-preservation, and sexual instincts, relating to tendencies toward preservation of the race. In the later view, there was the **life instinct**, including both of the earlier ego and sexual instincts, and the **death instinct**, involving an aim on the part of the organism to die or return to an inorganic state. The energy of the life instinct was called **libido**. No name has come to be commonly associated with the energy of the death instinct. In fact, the death instinct remains one of the most controversial and least accepted parts of the theory, with most analysts instead referring to the **aggressive instinct**. Both sexual and aggressive instincts are viewed as being part of the id.

In psychoanalytic theory, the instincts are characterized as aiming toward the immediate reduction of tension, toward satisfaction and pleasure. They are gratified by means of external stimuli or objects. In contrast to lower animals, the objects for humans that are capable of gratifying an instinct are many and varied. This provides for uniqueness in personality. Furthermore, in humans the instincts can be delayed and modified before they are released.

In the dynamics of functioning, what can happen to one's instincts? They can, at least temporarily, be blocked from expression or expressed

instincts
drives

life instinct
death instinct

libido

aggressive instinct

without modification. More likely is some change in the quality or direction of the instinct. For example, there may be partial (aim-inhibited) satisfaction of the instincts, in which case there is partial rather than full expression of the instinct. Affection may be a partial, aim-inhibited expression of the sexual instinct, and sarcasm an expression of the aggressive instinct. It is also possible for the object of gratification of the instinct to be changed or *displaced* from the original object to another object. Thus, the love of one's mother may be displaced to the love of one's wife, and the anger at the boss may be displaced to the wife, kids, or dog. Each instinct may be transformed or modified, and the instincts can combine with one another. Football, for example, can gratify both sexual and aggressive instincts; in surgery there can be the fusion of love and destruction. It should already be clear how psychoanalytic theory is able to account for so much behavior on the basis of only two instincts. It is the fluid, mobile, changing qualities of the instincts and their many alternative kinds of gratification that allows for such variability in behavior. In essence, the same instinct can be gratified in a number of ways, and the same behavior can have different causes in different people or multiple gratifications for any one individual.

Virtually every process in psychoanalytic theory can be described in terms of the expenditure of energy in an object (cathexis) or in terms of a force inhibiting the expenditure of energy, that is, inhibiting gratification of an instinct (anticathexis). Because it involves an expenditure of energy, people who direct much of their efforts toward inhibition end up feeling tired and bored. The interplay between the expression of instincts and their inhibition, between cathexis and anticathexis, forms the foundation of the dynamic aspects of psychoanalytic theory. The key to this is the concept of **anxiety**. In psychoanalytic theory, anxiety is a painful, emotional experience, representing a threat or danger to the organism. In a state of "free-floating" anxiety, individuals are unable to relate their state of tension to an external object, in contrast to a state of fear, where the source of tension is known. Freud had two theories of anxiety. In the first theory, anxiety was viewed as a result of undischarged sexual impulses — dammed-up libido. In the later theory, anxiety represented a painful emotion which acted as a signal of impending danger to the ego. Here, anxiety, an ego function, alerts the ego to danger so that it can act.

anxiety

The psychoanalytic theory of anxiety states that at some point the organism experiences a trauma, an incident of considerable harm or injury. Anxiety represents a repetition of the earlier traumatic experience, but in miniature form. Anxiety in the present, then, is related to an earlier danger. It is because the earlier trauma is not recalled that anxiety has its free-floating quality. The sources of anxiety may reside in the id, in the superego, or in reality. Where the id is the source of anxiety, the individual feels threatened with being overwhelmed by impulses. Where the superego is the source of anxiety, the individual experiences guilt and self-condemnation. It is as if the id says "I want it," the superego says "How terrible," and the ego says "I'm afraid." Basically, anxiety develops out of a conflict between the push of the id instincts for expression and the ego's appraisal of external dangers, or between these id instincts and the threat of punishment by the superego.

Anxiety and the Mechanisms of Defense

defense mechanisms

projection

Anxiety is such a painful state that we are incapable of tolerating it for very long. How is it that we are able to deal with such a state? Why are we not anxious more of the time? The answer is that individuals develop **defense mechanisms** against anxiety. Unconsciously, we develop ways to distort reality and exclude feelings from awareness so that we do not feel anxious. What are some of the ways in which this can be done? One of the most primitive defense mechanisms is **projection**. In projection, what is internal and unacceptable is projected out and seen as external. Rather than recognize hostility in oneself, the individual sees others as being hostile. There is in this process a fluidity of boundaries, or a breakdown in the differentiation between what is self and what is other.

In a relevant experimental study, Sears (1936) investigated the degree to which subjects possessed traits such as stinginess, obstinacy, disorderliness, and bashfulness, whether the subjects had insight into their possession of the traits, and the degree to which they attributed the traits to others. He found that subjects who lacked insight into their possession of a trait tended to attribute a greater amount of the trait to others than did subjects who possessed an equal amount of the trait but had insight into this. Furthermore, subjects who lacked insight into their own possession of unacceptable traits gave more extreme ratings on the trait to others and considered the traits to be more unacceptable than did subjects who had insight. Later efforts to study projection experimentally, however, have met with far less success (Holmes, 1978).

denial

A second defense mechanism is that of **denial**. Here there may be either denial of reality, as in the girl who denies she lacks a penis or in the boy who in fantasy denies the lack of power, or denial of impulse, as when an irate person protests "I do not feel angry." The saying "Thou doth protest too much" gives specific reference to this defense. Denial of reality is commonly seen where people attempt to avoid recognizing the extent of a threat. The expression "Oh no!" upon hearing of the death of a close friend represents the reflex action of denial. Children have been known to deny the death of a loved animal and long afterwards to behave as if it were still alive. Denial of reality is also seen when people say, or assume,

"It can't happen to me" in spite of clear evidence of impending doom. This defense was seen in Jews who were victims of the Nazis. Steiner (1966), in his book on the Nazi concentration camp Treblinka, describes how the population acted as if death did not exist, in spite of clear evidence to the contrary all around them. He notes that the extermination of a whole people was so unimaginable that the people could not accept it. They preferred to accept lies rather than to bear the terrible trauma of the truth.

isolation

Another way to deal with anxiety and threat is to isolate events in memory or to isolate emotion from the content of a memory or impulse. In **isolation**, the impulse, thought, or act is not denied access to consciousness, but it is denied the normal accompanying emotion. For example, a woman may experience the thought or fantasy of strangling her child without any associated feelings of anger. The result of using the mechanism of isolation is *intellectualization*, an emphasis on thought over emotion and feeling, and the development of logic-tight compartments. In such cases, the feelings that do exist may be split, as in the case where a male separates women into two categories, one with whom there is love but no sex and the other with whom there is sex but no love (Madonna-prostitute complex).

undoing

People who use the mechanism of isolation also often use the mechanism of **undoing**. Here, the individual magically undoes one act or wish with another act. "It is a kind of negative magic in which the individual's second act abrogates or nullifies the first, in such a manner that it is as though neither had taken place, whereas in reality both have done so" (Freud, 1936, p. 33). This mechanism is seen in compulsive acts in which the person has an unresistable impulse to perform some act (for example, the person undoes a suicide or homicide fantasy by compulsively turning off the gas jets at home), in religious rituals, and in children's sayings such as "Don't step on the crack or you will break your mother's back."

reaction-formation

In **reaction-formation**, the individual defends against expression of an unacceptable impulse by only recognizing and expressing its opposite. This defense is evident in socially desirable behavior that is rigid, exaggerated, and inappropriate. The person who uses reaction-formation can not admit to other feelings, as in overprotective mothers who cannot allow any conscious hostility toward their children. Reaction-formation is most clearly observable when the defense breaks down, as when the good, model boy shoots his parents, or when the man who "wouldn't hurt a fly" goes on a killing rampage. Of similar interest here are the occasional reports of judges who go on to commit crimes.

rationalization

A mechanism often familiar to students is that of **rationalization**. Here an action is perceived, but the underlying motive is not. Behavior is reinterpreted so that it appears reasonable and acceptable. What is of particular interest about rationalization is that with this defense the individual can express the dangerous impulse, seemingly without it being frowned on by the superego. Some of the greatest atrocities of humankind have been committed in the name of the Christian God of love. The leaders of the Inquisition tortured persons who were without a "proper" attitude toward Christ. It is through the defense mechanism of rationalization that we can be hostile while expressing God's will, that we can be immoral in the pursuit of morality.

repression

Finally, we come to the major, primary defense mechanism, **repression**. In repression, a thought, idea, or wish is dismissed from consciousness. It is as if we say, "What we don't know or remember can't hurt us." Repression is viewed as playing a part in all of the other defense mechanisms and, like these other defenses, requires a constant expenditure of energy to keep that which is dangerous outside of consciousness. There has been more experimental research on repression than on any other defense mechanism and perhaps more than on any other single concept in psychoanalytic theory (MacKinnon and Durkes, 1962). An early study in this area was that by Rosenzweig (1941), in which he found that when they were personally involved with the experiment a group of Harvard undergraduates recalled a larger proportion of tasks that they had been able to complete than tasks they had been unable to complete. When the students did not feel threatened, they remembered more of the uncompleted tasks.

sublimation

Before ending this discussion of the defenses, it is important to note one further device that is used to express an impulse free of anxiety. This mechanism, of considerable social importance, is that of **sublimation**. In sublimation, the original object of gratification is replaced by a higher cultural goal, one further removed from direct expression of the instinct. Whereas the other defense mechanisms meet the instincts head on and, by and large, prevent discharge, in sublimation the instinct is turned into a new and useful channel. In contrast to the other defense mechanisms, here the ego does not have to maintain a constant energy output to prevent discharge. Freud interpreted DaVinci's Madonna as a sublimation of his longing for his mother. Becoming a surgeon, butcher, or boxer can represent sublimations, to a greater or lesser degree, of aggressive impulses. Being a psychiatrist can represent a sublimation of "peeping tom" tendencies. In all, as noted, Freud felt that the essence of civilization is contained in a person's ability to sublimate sexual and aggressive energies.

Growth and Development

The psychoanalytic theory of development takes into consideration the development of structures, of thinking processes, of the instincts, and in relation to all of these, the development of character (personality). There are two major aspects to the theory of development. The first is that the individual progresses through stages of development that are rooted in the biological processes of the organism. The second, the genetic approach, emphasizes the importance of early events for all later behavior. An extreme psychoanalytic position would go so far as to say that the most significant aspects of later personality have been formed by the end of the first five years of life.

The Development of Thinking Processes

primary process
secondary process

The psychoanalytic theory of the development of thinking processes focuses on the change from **primary process** thinking to **secondary process** thinking. The primary process is the language of the unconscious, in which reality and fantasy are indistinguishable. The secondary process is the language of consciousness, of learning, thinking, remembering, and reality testing. Parallel to this is the development of the ego and, later, that of the superego. With the development of the ego, the individual becomes more differentiated, as a self, from the rest of the world. There is a decrease in self-preoccupation, an increase in motor ability, an increase in the use of language, and a greater ability to anticipate events and to delay gratification. The development of a healthy superego is reflected in an integrated, conflict-free set of values, an ability to accept blows to the self-esteem (to accept limitations without withdrawal into fantasy), and a sense of pride in accomplishment.

The Development of the Instincts

erogenous zones

The most significant part of the psychoanalytic theory of development concerns the development of the instincts. The source of the instincts is in states of bodily tension, which tend to focus on certain regions of the body, called **erogenous zones**. According to the theory, there is a biologically determined development of, and change in, the major erogenous zones of the body. Although many erogenous zones may be active at any one time, the major source of excitation and energy tends to focus on a particular zone, with the location of that zone changing during the early developmental years. The first erogenous zone is the mouth, the second the anus, and the third the genitals. The mental and emotional growth of the child are dependent on the social interactions, anxieties, and gratifications that occur in relation to these zones.

oral stage

Stages of development   The first major area of excitation, sensitivity, and energy is the mouth. It is this locus of excitation that leads to the name **oral stage**. Early oral gratification occurs in feeding, thumbsucking, and other mouth movements characteristic of infants. In adult life, traces of orality are seen in chewing gum, eating, smoking, and kissing. In the early part of the oral stage the child is passive and receptive. In the late oral stage, with the development of teeth, there can be a fusion of sexual and aggressive pleasures. In children, such a fusion of instinctual gratification is seen in the eating of animal crackers. Other evidence of such a fusion can be seen in cannibalism and in the religious communion ceremony. Five modes of functioning are possible during the oral stage, and these serve as models for dealing with later situations. These modes are taking in and swallowing, holding on, biting, spitting out, and closed mouth. In later life, we see traces of orality in various spheres. For example, academic pursuits can have oral associations within the unconscious — one is given "food for thought," asked to "incorporate" material in reading, and "regurgitate" what has been learned on exams.

anal stage

In the second stage of development, the **anal stage** (ages two and three), there is excitation in the anus and in the movement of feces through the anal passageway. The expulsion of the feces is believed to bring relief from tension and pleasure in the stimulation of the mucous membranes in that region. The pleasure related to this erogenous zone involves the organism in three types of conflict. First, there is the instinctual conflict between elimination and retention. Second, there is the conflict between the instinctual pleasure in release and the ego attempts at control. And, third, there is the conflict between the wish for instinctual pleasure in evacuation and the demands of the external world for delay. This third conflict, which provides the basis for the structural conflict between id and ego, represents the first crucial conflict between the individual and society. Here the environment requires the child to violate the pleasure principle or be punished. External displeasure causes internal displeasure. The child may retaliate against such demands by intentional soiling (diarrhea), come to associate having bowel movements with losing something important which leads to depression, or come to associate having bowel movements with giving a prize or gift to others which may be associated with feelings of power and control.

phallic stage

In the **phallic stage** (ages four and five), excitation and tension come to focus in the genitals. The biological differentiation between the sexes leads to psychological differentiation. The male child develops erections, and the new excitations in this area lead to increased interest in the genitals and the realization that the female lacks the penis. This leads to the

castration anxiety

fear that he may lose his penis — **castration anxiety**. The father becomes a rival for the affections of the mother, suggestion to which is given in the song "I Want a Girl Just Like The Girl That Married Dear Old Dad." The boy's hostility toward the father is projected onto the father with the consequent fear of retaliation. This leads to what is known as the Oedipus complex. According to the Oedipus complex, every boy is fated to kill his father in fantasy and marry his mother. The complex can be heightened by actual seductiveness on the part of the mother. Castration anxiety can be heightened by actual threats from the father to cut off the penis. These threats occur in a surprising number of cases!

The resolution of the complex occurs because of frustrations and disappointments by the mother, because of fear of the father, and because of the possibility of partial gain through identification with the father. For the male child, the Oedipus complex is resolved through keeping the mother as a love object but gaining her through identifying with the father. In identifying with the father, the child assumes many of the same values and morals. It is in this sense that the superego has been called the heir to the resolution of the Oedipus complex.

The developmental processes during this stage are somewhat different for the female. She realizes the lack of a penis and blames the mother, the original love object. Developing **penis envy**, the female child chooses the father as the love object and imagines that the lost organ will be restored by having a child by the father. Whereas the Oedipus complex is abandoned in the boy because of castration anxiety, in the female it is started because of penis envy. As with the male, conflict during this period is in some cases accentuated by seductiveness on the part of the father toward the female child. And, as with the male, the female child resolves the conflict by keeping the father as a love object but gaining him through identification with the mother. Because the female child develops less fear than does the male child (the little girl considers her penis to be already gone), and because the boy must give up an object (mother) that is more salient than the object (father) for the girl, the female child does not resolve the Oedipal issues to the same degree as does the male child. Thus, the female develops a weaker and less harsh superego, which accounts for their being kinder and softer than men.*

The development of an **identification** with the parent of the same sex is a critical issue during the phallic stage and, more generally, is a critical concept in developmental psychology. In identification. Individuals take upon themselves qualities of another person and integrate them into their functioning. Freud distinguished among four types of identification. In *narcissistic* (self-love) *identification*, individuals identify with qualities in those who are similar to themselves. This process leads to group membership. In *goal-oriented identification*, the individual identifies with a successful person. For example, the boy may identify with and assume the values of his father. In *object-loss identification*, the individual attempts to

penis envy

identification

Psychoanalytic theory has been criticized by feminists on a variety of grounds. Perhaps more than any other concept, the concept of penis envy is seen as expressing a chauvinistic, hostile view toward women. This issue will be addressed in Chapter Three in the Critical Evaluation section.

recover a lost object (person) through identification with it. The boy who loses a father early in life may develop an exaggerated identification with the father, or with an idealized image of him. Finally, there is *identification with the aggressor*, in which the individual identifies with a figure in authority so as to avoid punishment. This type of identification also occurs in the development of the superego and is a powerful force in socialization. It is also seen in situations of extreme threat, as in the experiences of prisoners in the Nazi concentration camps. For example, according to accounts of life in the concentration camps, some of the prisoners started to wear whatever pieces of Nazi clothing they could get and, when put in a position of authority, treated the other prisoners in a cruel, inhumane way. Sarnoff (1951) has done some research which suggests that anti-Semitism among Jews can be accounted for in terms of identification with the aggressor.

pregenital

The oral, anal, and phallic stages of development are **pregenital** in the sense that they occur prior to the reproductive potential of the genitals. Sexual pleasure during these stages is of an infantile kind, but it is sexual because it involves the stimulation of erogenous zones, tension reduction, and pleasure. Although Freud gave relatively little attention to developmental factors after the resolution of the Oedipus complex, he did recognize their existence. After the phallic stage, the child enters **latency**, during which there is a lessening of the sexual urge and no new libidinal developments. The meaning of the latency stage has never been clear in psychoanalytic theory. An assumption of a decrease in sexual urges and interest during the ages of six through 13 might have fit observations of Victorian children, but it does not fit observations of children in other cultures. A more plausible assumption, and one more difficult to test, is that there are no new developments during this stage in terms of the ways in which children gratify their instincts.

latency

General lack of interest in the latency stage stems, in part, from the importance attributed to the two events that surround it. Before the latency stage there is the Oedipal period, and after the latency stage there is puberty. The onset of puberty, with the reawakening of the sexual urges and Oedipal feelings, marks the beginning of the **genital stage**. The significance of this period for individuals and for their functioning in society is demonstrated in the initiation rites of many primitive cultures and in the Jewish Bar Mitzvah. Dependency feelings and Oedipal strivings which were not fully resolved during the pregenital stages of development now come back to rear their ugly heads. The turmoil of adolescence is partly attributable to these factors. During this stage, as in the phallic stage, the highest excitation is located in the genitals, but in contrast to the phallic stage, where the aim was forepleasure and autoeroticism, here the aim is pleasure through intercourse. It is here that the psychoanalytic concept of

genital stage

ERIK H. ERIKSON

sexual pleasure most coincides with the commonly accepted meaning of the term. However, in the psychoanalytic view, this sexual pleasure of the genital stage represents nothing more than a later development of the sexual instinct that has been present since birth.

Erikson's psychosocial stages of development   It is probably clear that in the psychoanalytic theory of development, major attention is given to the first five years and to the development of the instincts. Ego psychologists have tried, within this framework, to give greater attention to other developments during the early years and to significant developments which take place during the latency and genital stages. Erik Erikson (1950), for example, one of the leading ego psychoanalysts, describes development in psychosocial terms rather than merely in sexual terms. Thus, the first stage is significant not just because of the localization of pleasure in the mouth, but because in the feeding situation a relationship of trust or mistrust is developed between the infant and the mother. Similarly, the anal stage is significant not only for the change in the nature of the major erogenous zone, but also because toilet-training is a significant social situation in which the child may develop a sense of autonomy or succumb to shame and self-doubt. In the phallic stage the child must struggle with the issue of taking pleasure in, as opposed to feeling guilty about, being assertive, competitive, and successful.

For Erikson, the latency and genital stages are periods when the individual develops a sense of industry and success, or a sense of inferiority, and perhaps most important of all, a sense of identity or a sense of role diffusion. For Erikson, the crucial task of adolescence is the establishment of a sense of ego identity, an accrued confidence that the way one views oneself has a continuity with one's past and is matched by the perceptions of others. In contrast to people who develop a sense of identity, people with role diffusion experience the feeling of not really knowing who they are, of not know whether what they think they are matches what others think of them, of not knowing how they have developed in this way or where they are heading in the future. During late adolescense and the college years, this struggle with a sense of identity may lead to joining a variety of groups and of considerable anguish about the choice of a career. If these issues are not resolved during this time, the individual is, in later life, filled with a sense of despair — life is too short and it is too late to start all over again.

Personality types   As noted, Freud thought that the first five years of life were critical in the development of the individual. During these years, it is possible for a number of failures to occur in the development of the instincts. Such failures in the development are called **fixation**s. If individuals receive too little gratification during a stage of development, so that they are afraid to go to the next stage, or if they receive too much gratification, so that there is no motivation to move on, a fixation will occur. If a fixation occurs, the individual will try to obtain the same type of satisfaction that was appropriate for an earlier stage of development during later stages. For example, the individual partially fixated at the oral stage, may continue to seek oral gratification in eating, smoking, or drinking. A developmental phenomenon related to that of fixation is **regression**. In regression, the individual seeks to return to an earlier mode of satisfaction, an earlier point

fixation

regression

of fixation. Regression will often occur under conditions of stress, so that people may only overeat, smoke, or drink during periods of frustration and anxiety. It is interesting to note in this regard that while research has not demonstrated a relationship between frustration at the oral stage and smoking, a relationship has been found between such frustration and difficulty in giving up smoking (McArthur, Waldron, and Dickinson, 1958).

The concepts of the stages of development, fixation, and regression are of tremendous importance to the psychoanalytic theory of development. One of its most fascinating aspects is the way in which personality characteristics are developed in early life and maintained thereafter. For each of the early stages of development there is a corresponding character type that is developed because of partial fixations at that stage. The characteristics of the **oral personality**, for example, relate to processes going on during the oral stage of development which the individual maintains in later life. Oral personalities are narcissistic in that they are only interested in themselves and do not have a clear recognition of others as separate entities. Other people are seen only in terms of what they can give (feed). Oral personalities are always asking for something, either in terms of a modest, pleading request or an aggressive demand. Either way there is a persistent "sucking" quality to these people. Not being put off by facts or by reason, they "cling like leeches" on others for gratification of their needs.

The oral character may at times appear to be generous. On further inspection, however, the generosity is clearly not genuine; that is, it is based on what they want to give and not on what others want; it is forced so that the other must accept. In giving, they identify with the pleasure of receiving. Furthermore, the underlying feeling is that giving deserves a gift in return. In their work, oral characters seek security, often playing a passive, dependent role. Their pleasures are in taking things into themselves. Most of all, they fear loss, that there will not be enough to go around, and that someone will cheat them or devour them. They are like the rats of Hunt (1941) who, after an early period of food deprivation, followed by a period of consistent feeding, hoarded food to a tremendous degree when a situation of frustration and deprivation was presented to them in later life. In a study of the oral character in children, Blum and Miller (1952) found a relationship between orality (nonpurposive mouth movements) and personality traits such as extreme interest in food (consumption of ice cream and eagerness at lunchtime), social isolation, the need for approval, concern over giving and receiving, and poor tolerance of boredom. In sum, the oral character is demanding, impatient, envious, covetous, jealous, tending toward rage and depression (feeling hollow, empty) when frustrated, and generally pessimistic.

oral personality

anal personality

The **anal personality** stems from the anal stage of development. In contrast to gratification associated with the mouth and oral activity, which can be expressed in adulthood in a relatively unrepressed form, the gratifications of anal impulses must undergo considerable transformation. The general theme here is that the traits of the anal character are related to processes going on at the anal stage of development which have not been completely relinquished. The processes of significance are the bodily processes (accumulation and release of fecal material) and interpersonal relations (the struggle of wills over toilet training). Tying the two together, the anal person sees excretion as symbolic of enormous power. That such a view persists is shown in many everyday expressions such as the reference to the toilet as "the throne." The change from the oral to the anal character is one from "give me" to "do what I tell you," or from "I have to give you" to "I must obey you." The anal character is known by a triad of traits, called the *anal triad*. The triad is: orderliness and cleanliness, parsimony and stinginess, and obstinacy. The emphasis on cleanliness is expressed in the saying "Cleanliness is next to godliness." The anal-compulsive personality has a need to keep everything *clean* and *in order*, representing a reaction formation against an interest in things that are disorderly and unclean. The second trait of the triad, *parsimony-stinginess*, relates to the anal-compulsive's interest in holding on to things, an interest dating back to a wish to retain the powerful and important feces. Such people may even be parsimonious in their use of toilet paper. The third trait in the triad, *obstinacy*, relates to anal character's infantile defiance against parting with their stools, particularly on command by others.

Anal personalities are filled with contradictions and ambivalence. Generally, they are persevering, though at times they will put things off to the last minute. This relates to the conflict between doing things when they are supposed to, as opposed to waiting and experiencing the pleasure in delay. They are generally orderly, but in most cases there is also some trace of messiness. Thus, it is said that every compulsive housewife has a mess closet. The person who keeps an extremely neat desk generally has at least one drawer for all the waste. Often the anal character is submissive and obedient, but then there is an occassional outburst of defiance and vengeance.

Anal characters take pleasure in delay, in the building up of tension, and then pleasure in letting go. This can be seen in their eating habits where they will save the best food for last, then feeling that it is "good to the last drop." Because of their excessive concern with things that are dirty and their tendency to link their impulses with dirtiness, anal characters compulsively and rigidly strive for control over their impulses. They have a harsh conscience which makes them do the right thing at the right time. The vocabulary of such people is filled with words such as should, should not, ought, trial and judgement. The emphasis on order can lead to conservatism and an opposition to innovations; and emphasis on power can lead to a wish to possess what others lack, an underestimation of the contributions of others, and a wish to impose one's own system on everything.

The relationships of the anal character to people and to work are suggested in the above. A central issue in interpersonal relationships is who controls whom, whether to submit or rebel. Anal characters are sensitive to external encroachments on their actual or supposed field of power. They will hold fast to their own way of doing things, expecting compliance from others. They will refuse a request or demand from others, particularly those in authority, but they will do the same things of their own free choice. The self-will and control must be perceived. Thus an anal husband may oppose expenditures of his wife, and then give, "of his own free will," in fact, more than his wife had asked for. Where they are forced to yield to the demands of another person, they will try to maintain a semblance of making a personal decision. Thus, such people may pay even the smallest amount of money by check, as if in fantasy they create their own money for every purchase.

In sum, the anal character possesses traits in adulthood that relate to pleasures dating back to the anal stage and to ways of relating interpersonally which were learned in the toilet-training situation. There is a pleasure in possessions and in having a mass of material stored up, just as earlier there was pleasure in the retention of the feces. Thus, there may be an avoidance of spending money on things that are "passing through", such as concerts and trips, and, instead, an emphasis on storing permanent things, such as records and books. There is a pleasure in storing, pleasure in evacuating, anxiety over waste, and anxiety over the loss of control of one's own impulses or domination by others. The issues are whether to hold on or to let go and whether to submit or to rebel.

phallic character

Just as the oral and anal character types reflect partial fixations at the first two stages of development, so the **phallic character** represents the result of a partial fixation at the stage of the Oedipus complex. Fixation here has different implications for men and women and particular attention has been given to the results of partial fixation for males. Whereas success for the oral person means "I get," and success for the anal person means "I control," success for the phallic male means "I am a man." The phallic male must deny all possible suggestions that he has been castrated. For him success means that he is "big" in the eyes of others. He must at all times assert his masculinity and potency, an attitude reflected in the Rough Riders of Theodore Roosevelt and in the saying "Speak softly but carry a big stick." The excessive, exhibitionistic quality to the behavior of these people is expressive of the underlying anxiety and the efforts to defend against this anxiety. The female counterpart of the male phallic character is known as an hysterical personality. As a defense against Oedipal wishes, the little girl identifies to an excessive extent with her mother and femininity. She uses seductive and flirtatious behavior to maintain the interest of her father but denies their sexual intent. The pattern of behavior then is carried over into adulthood, where she may attract men with flirtatious behavior but deny sexual intent and generally appear to be somewhat naive. Hysterical women idealize life, their partners, and romantic love, often finding themselves surprised by life's uglier moments.

Whereas the phallic person generally strives to be successful, conflicts dating back to the Oedipal period may lead to feelings of guilt over success. For such a person, success means winning out over the father or mother, a breaking of an incest taboo. As with many of the derivatives of earlier fixations, the same conflict can express itself in opposite ways. The male phallic personality type may seek success on the job, many sexual conquests, and many children, all as evidence of potency, or he may be impotent in his work and sexual life because of guilt over competitive strivings with the father. While the behavior found in these two cases may appear to be opposite to one another, they tend to reflect the same issue or conflict in their dynamics. Furthermore, both sets of behaviors reflect an earlier fixation in that they are overdriven, rigid, and unresponsive to reality. Whether giving or taking, submitting or controlling, being successful or being impotent, the oral, anal, and phallic characters are unable to deal with certain types of frustrations, and rigidly adhere to modes of obtaining pleasure that were more appropriate at earlier stages of development.

Research on Growth and Development

The genetic approach to personality evident in psychoanalytic theory emphasizes the importance of events in early life for later personality development. There is a great deal of evidence that this is the case. We have already noted Hunt's research on early frustration and later hoarding behavior in mice. Of related interest is the finding that differences in adult emotionality in rats are related to infantile trauma (Lindzey, Lykken, and Winston, 1960). Harlow (1958) has demonstrated the importance of early experience for later behavior in primates. He separated 60 monkeys from their mothers 6 to 12 hours after birth and suckled them on bottles. One group was fed by a wire-mesh laboratory mother, made warm by radiant heat. A second group was fed by a similar "mother" which also had cloth on it. Harlow found that the contact comfort of the cloth mother was of overwhelming importance in the development of emotional responses in the monkeys, even more important than lactation. The suggestion, in contrast to what might have been expected from psychoanalytic theory, was that the primary function of nursing as an affectional variable was that of ensuring frequent and intimate body contact of the infant with the mother. Beyond this, however, and in support of the genetic approach of psychoanalysis, Harlow found that the monkeys deprived of a real mother as infants became helpless, hopeless, and heartless mothers, almost devoid of maternal feelings. In some further research in support of the genetic approach, Harlow (1962) found that the opportunity for normal infant interaction with other infants is critical for the development of normal sexual relations and later social adjustment.

On the human level, some research by Kagan and Moss (1962) gives support to the importance of events during the early years for later personality development, though it also goes beyond such a generalization to specify some of the relevant variables. These investigators obtained personality data on children between the ages of three and ten and related these observations to their personalities in early adulthood. They concluded that the results offered strong support for the notion that aspects of adult personality begin to develop during childhood. However, they also emphasized that the degree of consistency between behavior in childhood and that in adulthood was dependent on its relationship to traditional sex-role standards. Childhood behavior that is reinforced by cultural standards as appropriate for that sex will tend to be maintained into adulthood. Childhood behavior that is in conflict with such cultural standards will find expression in "theoretically consistent substitute behaviors that are socially more acceptable than the original response" (Kagan and Moss, 1962, p. 269). For example, for males there was a strong relationship between heterosexual and achievement behaviors at ages six through ten and in adulthood, whereas for dependence there was little such relationship. For females, dependence in childhood was related to dependence in adulthood, but heterosexual interests and anger arousal were not. In sum, the degree of continuity or discontinuity of overt patterns of behavior between childhood and adulthood is influenced by the culture's definition of sex-appropriate responses.

It is important to recognize that while studies such as these support the general orientation of the psychoanalytic approach toward growth and development, they say little about the stages of instinctual development and the relevance of these stages for later personality. Is there any evidence of a direct link between events during the stages of instinctual development and later character? One line of evidence comes from anthropological investigation. Cohen (1953), for example, studied 22 societies in terms of early oral socialization practices (for example, gratification, demand feeding versus frustration of the hunger drive) and economic cooperation in adult life. Economic cooperation was defined in terms of an effort to share rather than hoard wealth and economic products such as food. The result was a perfect positive relationship between demand feeding and economic cooperation, while seven societies showed frustration of the hunger drive and economic competition.

A classic in the area of testing personality theory in a cross-cultural setting is the work of Whiting and Child (1953) on child training and personality. Most of the hypotheses investigated in this research were drawn from psychoanalytic theory. Seventy-five societies were studied with regard to child-training practices (for example, weaning, toilet-training, and sex training) and customs relating to illness. The basic hypothesis investigated was that there would be a relationship between socialization anxiety (severe discipline) for a system of behavior, cultural beliefs about the causes of illness, and cultural techniques for treating illness. Socialization anxiety, stemming from factors such as severe and frequent punishment, was viewed as leading to fixation at a stage of development and then to the use of oral, anal, or sexual explanations for illness. Oral explanations for illness would include illness due to ingestion (eating, drinking, food, or poison) or to verbal spells and incantations performed by others; anal explanations would include illness due to defecation, the use of ritual or magic by others, or failure to perform a ritual; sexual explanations would include illness due to sexual behavior, sexual erections, or menstrual blood. A strong relationship was found between oral socialization anxiety and oral therapeutic practices (swallowing) for illness. A similar, though less striking, relationship was found between anal socialization anxiety and anal explanations for illness, and between anal socialization satisfaction and the performance of magical rituals for the treatment of illness. A relationship in support of the hypothesis was found in each of the areas in which socialization anxiety was related to explanations for illness. There was clear confirmation of the hypothesis that a high degree of frustration of behaviors characteristic of a stage of development leads to a continuing fixation of interest in that behavior.

We have, then, some experimental work with animals and some anthropological findings in support of the psychoanalytic theory of growth and development. It is also possible to point to work with individuals from a single culture for support for the theory. One such study (Goldman-Eisler, 1953) obtained ratings on scales measuring character traits and found two distinct clusters of ratings (see Box 2.2). The first cluster of ratings, called oral optimism, had the characteristics of optimism, extraversion, nurturance, sociability, and ambition. The second cluster of ratings, called oral pessimism, had the characteristics of pessimism, passivity, aloofness, withdrawal, and oral aggression. When two groups of subjects were distinguished on the basis of scores on these scales, *oral optimists* and *oral pessimists*, a significant relationship was found between age of weaning and personality. Early weaning was found to be related to oral pessimism and later weaning to be related to oral optimism. Thus, the study offered support to the theory in terms of finding clusters of traits suggested to exist by the theory and in finding a relationship between these personality traits and experiences during an earlier stage of development.

BOX 2.2 **Early Experiences and Later Personality Development: Psychoanalytic Theory of Character Formation**

HYPOTHESIS   On the basis of the psychoanalytic theory of character, we should expect orally satisfied character traits and orally dissatisfied character traits to be opposite. These oral characteristics should be related to differential conditions associated with the oral stage, namely, frustration (early weaning) or gratification (later weaning) during the oral stage.

SUBJECTS   For the research on character traits, use 115 adults (47 men and 68 women) as subjects. For the research on early determinants, use 100 adults as the subject population.

METHOD   (A) Administer 19 rating scales designed to measure many character traits. Most of these scales represent modifications of those developed by H. A. Murray to measure the needs of individuals. Subjects complete their self-ratings anonymously. Analyze the responses to see which kinds of traits tend to go together. (B) After finding two opposite patterns of personality characteristics which appear to be related to psychoanalytic oral character types, determine the age of weaning of "oral optimists" and "oral pessimists." The first part of the research involves determining whether traits which fit psychoanalytic interpretations of character types do in fact go together. The second part of the research involves determining whether subjects who score differently on traits associated with a character type have different childhood experiences. Age of weaning is determined by information obtained from mothers of subjects. Earling weaning is defined as weaning that takes place before the infant is five months, late weaning after the infant is five months of age.

RESULTS

1 Two distinct sets of personality characteristics were found with traits such as pessimism, passivity, aloofness, and oral aggression (verbal) in one set, and traits such as optimism, nurturance, and sociability in the other set. This corresponds, in a striking way, with the psychoanalytic description of the orally gratified type (oral optimist) and the orally frustrated type (oral pessimist).

2 There was a significant difference in personality characteristics.

BOX 2.2   **Early Experiences and Later** *continued*
Personality Development:
Psychoanalytic Theory
of Character Formation

between subjects who were weaned early and those who were weaned late. Those who experience early frustration in breastfeeding tend in their adult character makeup to be oral pessimists, whereas those who enjoy a long period of breastfeeding show a marked tendency to develop oral optimistic character traits.

CONCLUSION   There is evidence that the traits claimed by psychoanalysts to be associated with one another are in fact so associated. This evidence supports the concept of character types. While a variety of factors would appear to be involved in the development of character types, the results indicate that the length of breastfeeding is a significant factor in the etiology of oral pessimism and probably depression.

SOURCE   Frieda Goldman-Eisler. Breastfeeding and character formation. In C. Kluckhohn, H. A. Murray, and D. M. Schneider (Eds.) Personality in nature, society, and culture. New York: Knopf 1953, pp. 146-184.

Despite this evidence concerning the relationship between early experiences and adult personality, the assumptions made by the theory must continue to be treated as assumptions, rather than as facts, and as sources of hypotheses. The relative importance of early experiences for later personality remains an issue of controversy in the field. Kagan, whose earlier research supported the psychoanalytic view, now suggests that less emphasis be given to stages of development and critical periods for growth and development. Instead, he suggests that development consists of more gradual changes and the human organism is remarkably resilient in responding to the effects of early difficulties; that is, early environments that are not beneficial to growth do not necessarily produce difficulties that cannot be reversed (Kagan, 1976). A recent review of the evidence concerning the importance of early years supports Freud's emphasis on these years, particularly in terms of their importance for the development of what Erikson calls basic trust. However, the evidence is less clear concerning other predicted relationships between early experience and later personality development. Finally, as suggested by Kagan, the evidence suggests that while the early years may be important, the later years and different experiences can reshape much of what has been formed earlier (Hunt, 1979).

MAJOR CONCEPTS AND SUMMARY

energy system	erogenous zones
conscious, preconscious, unconscious	oral, anal, phallic stages of developments
id, ego, superego	Oedipus complex
pleasure principle	castration anxiety
reality principle	identification
life and death instincts	fixation
sexual and aggressive instincts	regression
anxiety	oral, anal, and phallic personality types
mechanisms of defense	

Before turning to the clinical applications of psychoanalytic theory and a final evaluation, let us take stock of the essentials of the theory of personality. The chapter began with a discussion of some of the events in Freud's life that played a role in the development of his theory and that influenced his approach toward science. Illustrative of such events were his concerns about death and destruction during World War I, the prevailing concerns in physics and medicine with energy models, and the inhibitions concerning sexuality found in Victorian society broadly and in Freud's patients in particular. In attempting both to help his patients and to develop a lasting theory of personality, Freud developed concepts which often appeared to have explanatory value but proved to be difficult to investigate systematically in nonclinical settings. Freud was impressed with the role of *unconscious forces* in the functioning of his patients. In listening to dreams and slips of the tongue, and in trying to understand the symptoms patients brought to treatment, Freud was struck by the importance of *repressed memories and wishes* in the associations of his patients. Similarly, he was impressed with the conflicts faced by his patients between what they wished and what society or their own conscience would permit. Thus, the development of Freud's concept of *id* to represent the basic sexual and aggressive urges, the concept of the *superego* to represent the conscience or internalization of parental and societal prohibitions, and the *ego* or efforts to find gratification and pleasure in accordance with the demands of reality.

Freud attached particular importance to the role of anxiety in the functioning of his patients. Often they came in with feelings of free-floating anxiety. At the same time, he was impressed with the various devices used to ward off anxiety. Thus, the development of the theory of anxiety and the mechanisms of defense.

The wishes and fears expressed by Freud's patients appeared to relate to experiences they had during their early years. Here Freud was led to his theory of growth and development and to the concepts of *fixation* and *regression*. Experiences during the early years of life were seen as centering around various *erogenous zones*. Changes in the region of special sensitivity as well as in the region of special social contact were expressed in the concepts of the *oral, anal*, and *phallic stages of development*. The person's character or basic personality structure was seen as pretty well established by age five, after the struggles associated with the *Oedipus complex*. The theory of development provides links to many diverse aspects of psychoanalytic theory, including a link to the theory of psychopathology to which we now turn.

CLINICAL APPLICATIONS

Psychopathology

Behavior Change

A CASE EXAMPLE – LITTLE HANS

RELATED POINTS OF VIEW AND RECENT DEVELOPMENTS

Two Early Challenges to Freud
• Alfred Adler
• Carl G. Jung

The Cultural and Interpersonal Emphasis
• Karen Horney
• Harry Stack Sullivan

Recent Developments Within Traditional Psychoanalytic Theory

CRITICAL EVALUATION

Major Contributions

Limitations of the Theory

Summary Evaluation

MAJOR CONCEPTS AND SUMMARY

3 A PSYCHODYNAMIC THEORY: APPLICATIONS AND EVALUATION OF FREUD'S THEORY

Chapter Focus:

In this chapter, we shall continue with our consideration of psycho-analytic theory as illustrative of a psychodynamic, clinical approach to personality. Attention will be given to Freud's attempts to understand and explain the symptoms presented by his patients and his efforts to develop a systematic method of treatment. After considering developments in psychoanalytic theory since Freud, we will turn to a final critical evaluation and summary.

For this next proposition, which we put forward as one of the discoveries of psychoanalysis, consists in the assertion that impulses, which can only be described as sexual in both the narrower and wider sense, play a peculiarly large part, never before sufficiently appreciated, in the causation of nervous and mental disorders. Nay, more, that these sexual impulses have contributed invaluably to the highest cultural, artistic, and social achievements of the human mind.

FREUD, 1924, PP. 26-27

CLINICAL APPLICATIONS

The psychoanalytic theory of psychopathology incorporates the principles concerning structure, process, and growth and development that we have discussed already. Basic to the development of all psychopathology is the way in which the individual strives to obtain gratification of the instincts while avoiding pain. We have noted already the emphasis in psychoanalytic theory on personality development during the first five years of life. We also have noted that frustration may lead to a fixation at any one of the early stages and that later trauma can lead to regression to an earlier mode of functioning. Fixation and regression represent failures in learning or growth and development. This is what psychopathology is about. Psychoanalysis, as a method of therapy, attempts to undo fixations and regressions so that growth and development can be resumed. This is basically what the clinical parts of psychoanalytic theory are concerned with, the details of which are elaborated upon in the following sections.

Psychopathology

Frequently it is difficult for people to appreciate psychoanalytic theory without first appreciating the nature of the often strange and puzzling behaviors that were brought to Freud's attention. Freud spent most of his professional time working with patients with neurotic disorders. In fact, the most critical elements in his theory are based on the observations that came from working with these patients. He tested his theory through observations of these and other patients as well as evaluation of the outcome of his treatment. In the course of his work he decided that the processes of psychological functioning found in his patients were not peculiar to those with neurotic disturbances but could be found, to one degree or another, and in one form or another, in all people. Thus, while originally based on observations with patients, his theory is a general theory of personality functioning rather than only a theory of abnormal behavior.

According to Freud, all psychopathology relates to an effort to gratify instincts that have been fixated at an earlier stage of development. Thus, in psychopathology the individual still seeks sexual and aggressive gratification in infantile forms. However, because of its association with past trauma, expression of this wish may signal danger to the ego and lead to the experience of anxiety. As a result, there is a conflict situation in which the same behaviors are associated both with pleasure and pain. For example, the person may seek to be dependent on others' pleasures but fear that if this is done he or she will be vulnerable to frustration and loss (pain). Another example would be of a wish to indulge in sexual behavior which is blocked by feelings of guilt and fear of punishment or injury. A third example is the conflict between a wish to retaliate against powerful others, representing the parents, and a fear that these figures will themselves retaliate with force and destruction. In each case there is a conflict between a wish and anxiety. In such a situation the result often is that the individual "can't say no," can't be assertive, or otherwise feels blocked and unhappy.

As noted above, a critical part of the conflict is anxiety. To reduce the painful experience of anxiety, defense mechanisms, as outlined in Chapter Two, are brought into play. Thus, for example, the person may deny his or her aggressive feelings or project them onto others. In either case the person no longer has to be afraid of the aggressive feelings. In sum, in psychopathology there is a conflict between a drive or wish (instinct) and the ego's sense (anxiety) that danger will ensue if the wish is expressed (discharged). To guard against this, and ward off anxiety, defense mechanisms are used. In structural terms, a neurosis is a result of conflict between the id and the ego. In process terms, an instinct striving for discharge triggers anxiety, leading to a defense mechanism.

symptom

In many cases the conflict between the id and ego, between instinct and defense, leads to the development of a **symptom**. A symptom, such as a tic, psychological paralysis, or compulsion, represents a disguised expression of a repressed impulse. The meaning of the symptom, the nature of the dangerous instinct, and the nature of the defense all remain unconscious. For example, a mother may be painfully obsessed with the fear that something will happen to her child. Underlying the obsession may be rage at her child and anxiety about the harm she may do to the child. The symptom of the obsession expresses both the mother's feelings that she may harm or injure the child and her defense against it in terms of excessive preoccupation with the child's welfare. To take another example, in a hand-washing compulsion, in which the person feels compelled to wash his or her hands continuously, the symptom may express both the wish to be dirty or do "dirty" things and the defense against the wish in terms of excessive cleanliness. In both of these cases the person is unaware of the wish or the defense and is troubled only by the symptom. Many people do not suffer from such specific problems or symptoms but analysts suggest that all psychological problems can still be understood in these terms.

TABLE 3-1 Psychoanalytic Theory of Psychopathology	ILLUSTRATIVE CONFLICTS		BEHAVIOR CONSEQUENCES OF DEFENSE MECHANISMS
	Wish	*Anxiety*	*Defense*
	I would like to have sex with that person.	Such feelings are bad and will be punished.	Denial of all sexual behavior; obsessive preoccupation with the sexual behavior of others.
	I would like to strike out at all those people who make me feel inferior.	If I am hostile they will retaliate and really hurt me.	Denial of wish or fear: "I never feel angry" or "I'm never afraid of anyone or anything."
	I would like to get close to people and have them feed me or take care of me.	If I do they will smother me or leave me.	Excessive independence and avoidance of getting close to people or fluctuations between approaching people and moving away from them; excessive need to take care of others.

While Freud believed that all pathology centers around the Oedipus complex, frustration and trauma also can lead to regression to an earlier stage of development. The form taken in a neurosis or psychosis (severe thought disturbance) is dependent on the stage to which one regresses. The psychoses represent expressions of a regression back to the oral stage or to an early part of the anal stage (Abraham, 1924). In these forms of pathology the individual is troubled by the wish to gratify primitive instincts. Wishes to devour, or to destroy may threaten the individual. Unconscious impulses and wishes occasionally break into consciousness and there is a return to primitive, primary process thinking. The defenses related to these earlier stages of development are projection and denial, both of which involve considerable distortion of reality. For example, the use of projection ("I do not hate others; others hate me.") leads to paranoid suspicions of the intent of others and delusions of persecution. The neuroses represent expressions of regression back to the anal stage or to the Oedipal stage of development. Since the regression is not as far back in development, the disturbances in functioning are not as severe in the neuroses as they are in psychoses. In each case of abnormal behavior there is an unconscious conflict between a wish and a fear that dates back to an earlier period in childhood. In this sense, as adults there continue to be child-like parts of us that under some conditions, such as those of stress, may become more active and troublesome.

To summarize the psychoanalytic theory of psychopathology, there is an arrest in the development of the person that is associated with conflicts between wishes and fears. The wishes and fears that were part of a specific time period in childhood are now carried over into adolescence and adulthood. The person attempts to handle anxiety that is a painful part of this conflict by using defense mechanisms. However, if the conflict becomes too great the use of defense mechanisms can lead to neurotic symptoms or psychotic withdrawal from reality. In structural terms, neuroses reflect a conflict between id instincts and ego defense mechanisms, both of which are unconscious. In process terms, neuroses reflect the ways in which the individual attempts to use defense mechanisms to avoid anxiety and guilt (from the superego), while still allowing for some instinct gratification. Symptoms express the unconscious conflict between wish or drive and anxiety. In developmental terms, neuroses express fixations at or regressions to gratifications and modes of functioning characteristic of an earlier stage of development. The oral, anal, and phallic stages of development each have associated with them different kinds of wishes and different mechanisms of defense. Thus it is that the symptom and general form of abnormal behavior expressed by the person are tied to the stage of development at which fixation originally occurred and to the stage to which the person has regressed under stress.

Behavior Change

How does behavior change come about? Once having established a behavioral pattern, a way of thinking about and responding to situations, through what process does a change in personality take place? The psychoanalytic theory of growth suggests that there is a normal course of human personality development, one that occurs because of optimum degrees of frustration. Where there has been too little or too much frustration at a particular stage of growth, personality does not proceed normally and a fixation takes place. When this occurs, the individual repeats patterns of behavior regardless of other changes in situations. Given the development of such a neurotic pattern, how is it possible to break the cycle and to move forward? A change in significant parts of the individual's functioning can be regressive or progressive; that is, toward simpler, more rigid, and more child-like ways of functioning or toward more complex, flexible, and adult ways of functioning. Psychoanalytic theory accounts for regressive change in terms of a defensive response to anxiety or trauma. The theory of progressive change is contained in the method of psychotherapy called psychoanalysis.

In his early efforts to effect behavioral change, Freud used a method called cathartic hypnosis. The view then held was that relief from neurotic symptoms would come about through the discharge of blocked emotions. Freud did not like using hypnosis, since not all patients could be hypnotized, the results were often transient, and he did not feel that he was learning much about mental functioning. The second development in

free association

dreams

technique was that of waking suggestion. Here Freud put his hand on the patient's head and assured him that he could recall and face repressed past emotional experiences. With the increased interest in the interpretation of dreams, Freud focused on the **free association** method as basic to psychoanalysis. In free association the patient is asked to report to the analyst every thought that comes to mind, to delay reporting nothing, to withhold nothing, to bar nothing from coming to consciousness. **Dreams** are the "royal road" to the unconscious. Through the free association method the analyst and patient are able to go beyond the manifest (obvious) content of the dream to the latent content, to the hidden meaning which expresses the unconscious wish. Dreams, like symptoms, are disguises and partial wish-fulfillments. In the dream, the person can satisfy a hostile or sexual wish in a disguised, and thereby safe, way. For example, rather than dreaming of oneself killing someone, one may dream of a battle in which a particular figure is killed. In such a case the wish may remain at least somewhat obvious, but in other cases the wish may be much more disguised. Free association allows for the uncovering of the disguise. With the relaxation of conscious control the impulses, wishes, memories, and fantasies of the unconscious break through into consciousness. It is important to realize, however, that the free association process, the stream of consciousness, is not in fact free; it is determined, as is all behavior, by the forces within the individual that are striving for expression. It is also important to recognize that ordinarily one cannot easily or immediately understand the meaning of a dream — it requires a process of uncovering or discovery.

At first, Freud thought that making the unconscious conscious was sufficient to affect change and cure. This was in keeping with the early emphasis on repressed memories as the basis for pathology. As Hendrick (1934) noted, Freud then realized that more than the recovery of memories was involved. Rather, emotional insight into the wishes and conflicts that had remained hidden was necessary.

> He (Freud) would succeed in learning the unconscious wish. He would inform the patient of it; the patient would agree and comprehend; this would effect the patient's intellectual appraisal of his problems, but not the emotional tensions themselves. Thus, early in his work, Freud learned a lesson which many who putter with his techniques have not yet assimilated; that intellectual insight cannot control the forces of the unconscious, that repression is not simply the difference between knowing and not knowing, that cure depends on far more than making conscious.
>
> HENDRICK, 1934, PP. 191-192

What more than "making conscious" does progressive change depend on? The process of therapeutic change in psychoanalysis involves coming to grips with emotions and wishes that previously have been unconscious and struggling with these painful experiences within a relatively safe and benign environment. If psychopathology involves fixation at an early stage of development, then in psychoanalysis individuals become free to resume their normal psychological development. "Analytic therapy may indeed be correctly defined as a technical procedure which awakens conflicts inadequately solved during natural adolescence, and by reducing the need for repression it provides a second chance for a better solution" (Hendrick, 1934, p. 214). If psychopathology involves the damming up of the instincts and the expenditure of energy for defensive purposes, then psychoanalysis involves a redistribution of energy so that more energy is available for mature, guiltless, less rigid, and more gratifying activities. If psychopathology involves conflict and defense mechanisms, then psychoanalysis involves the reduction of conflict and the freeing of the patient from the limitations of the defensive processes. If psychopathology involves an individual dominated by the unconscious and the tyranny of the id, then psychoanalysis involves making conscious what was unconscious and putting under control of the ego what was formerly under the domination of the id or superego.

Our plan of cure is based upon these views. The ego has been weakened by the internal conflict; we must come to its aid. The position is like a civil war which can only be decided by the help of an ally from without. The analytical physician and the weakened ego of the patient, basing themselves upon the real external world, are to combine against the enemies, the instinctual demands of the id, and the moral demands of the superego. We form a pact with each other. The patient's sick ego promises us the most candor, promises, that is, to put at our disposal all of the material which his self-perception provides; we, on the other hand, assure him of the strictest discretion and put at his service our experience in interpreting material that has been influenced by the unconscious. Our knowledge shall compensate for his ignorance and shall give his ego once more mastery over the lost provinces of his mental life. This pact constitutes the analytic situation.

FREUD, 1940, PP. 62-63

In sum, then, psychoanalysis relates to structural, process, and developmental changes. Basically, psychoanalysis is viewed as a learning process in which the individual resumes and completes the growth process that was interrupted when the neurosis began. The principle involved is the reexposure of the patient, under more favorable circumstances, to the emotional situations that could not be handled in the past. The vehicle for such reexposure is the transference relationship and the development of a transference neurosis. The term **transference** refers to the development, on the part of the patient, of attitudes toward the analyst which have as their basis attitudes held by the patient toward earlier parental figures. In the sense that transference relates to distortions of reality based on past

transference

experiences, transference occurs in everyone's daily life and in all forms of psychotherapy. In expressing transference attitudes toward the analyst, patients duplicate in therapy their interactions with people in their outer lives and their past interactions with significant figures. For example, if patients feel that the analyst's taking notes may lead to exploitation by the analyst, they are expressing attitudes they hold towards both people they meet in their daily existence and earlier figures in their lives. In free associating, oral characters may be concerned about whether they are "feeding" the analyst and whether the analyst gives them enough in return; anal characters may be concerned about who is controlling the sessions; phallic characters may be concerned about who will win in competitive struggles. Such attitudes, often part of the unconscious daily existence of the patient, come to light in the course of the analysis.

FREUD'S CONSULTING ROOM

While transference is a part of all relationships and of all forms of therapy, psychoanalysis is distinctive in its use of it as a dynamic force in behavior change. Many of the formal qualities of the analytic situation are structured to enhance the development of transference. The patient lying on the couch supports the development of a dependent relationship. The scheduling of frequent meetings (up to five or six times a week) strengthens the emotional importance of the analytic relationship to the patient's daily existence. Finally, the fact that patients become so tied to their analysts, while knowing so little about them as people, means that their responses are almost completely determined by their neurotic conflicts. The analyst remains a mirror or blank screen on which the individual projects wishes and anxieties.

Thus the technical devices of analysis which best serve for therapy also produce the best experimental situation yet devised for studying the more complex features of human nature . . . Psychoanalysis is the test tube of human experience. For one hour a day, for a limited period, a sample of human thoughts and feelings is examined under controlled conditions. A daily specimen of typical emotional reactions is taken. The endlessly involved complications of everyday life are reduced by the four walls of the treatment room; the multitude of people serving as emotional stimuli and instinctual objects are replaced by a single individual, the analyst.

HENDRICK, 1934, PP. 196-197

The encouragement of transference, or providing the cirumstances that allow it to develop, leads to the development of the transference neurosis. It is here that patients play out, full-blown, their old conflicts. Patients now invest the major aspects of their relationship with the analyst with the wishes and anxieties of the past. The goal is no longer to get well, but to gain from the analyst what they had to do without in childhood. Rather than seeking a way out of competitive relationships, they may only seek to castrate the analyst; rather than seek to become less dependent on others, they may seek to have the analyst gratify all of their dependency needs. The fact that these attitudes have developed within the context of the analysis allows patients and their analysts to look at and understand the instinctual and defensive components of the original infantile conflict. The fact that the patient invests considerable emotion in the situation allows for the increased understanding to be emotionally meaningful. Change occurs when insight has been gained, when patients realize, on both an intellectual and emotional level, the nature of conflicts and feel free, in terms of their new perceptions of themselves and the world, to gratify their instincts in a mature, conflict-free way.

Whereas guilt and anxiety prevented growth in the past, the analytic situation offers the individual the opportunity to deal anew with the old conflicts. Why should the response be any different at this time? Basically, change occurs in analysis because of the three therapeutic factors. First, in analysis the conflict is less intense than it was in the original situation. Second, the analyst assumes an attitude which is different from that of the parents. Finally, patients in analysis are older and more mature, that is they are able to use parts of their ego that have developed to deal with the parts of their functioning that have not. These three factors, creating as they do the opportunity for relearning, provide the basis for what Alexander and French (1946) call the "corrective emotional experience". It should be clear that developments such as these in no way suggest that psychoanalysis is an intellectual experience as opposed to an emotional experience, that insight and understanding are given by the analyst rather than gained by the patient, or that there is a denial of moral responsibility and a sanctioning of sin. Rather, psychoanalytic theory suggests that through insight into old conflicts, through an understanding of the needs for infantile gratifications and a recognition of the potential for mature gratification, through an understanding of old anxieties and a recognition of their lack of relevance to current realities, patients may progress toward maximum instinctual gratification within the limits set by reality and their own moral convictions.

A CASE EXAMPLE — LITTLE HANS

Although many psychiatrists and psychologists have spent considerable time treating patients, Freud is one of the very few who have reported cases in detail. Most of Freud's cases come from early in his career. The famed Dora case, in which Freud analysed the unconscious conflicts behind a number of symptoms, was presented in 1905. The case of an obsessive neurotic, involving fears that something might happen to people, and an obsessive preoccupation with rats, was published in 1909. While these and other case presentations are useful in understanding many aspects of psychoanalytic theory, it is important to remember that they occurred prior to Freud's development of his theory of the sexual and aggressive instincts, prior to the development of the structural model, and prior to the development of the theory of anxiety and defense mechanisms.

The case of Little Hans, published in 1909, involves the analysis of a phobia in a five-year-old boy. It involves the treatment of the boy by his father and does not represent Freud's direct participation in the therapeutic process. The boy was bothered by a hysterical fear that a horse would bite him. Therefore, he refused to leave the house. The boy's father kept detailed notes on his treatment and frequently discussed his progress with Freud. Although the "patient" was not treated by Freud, the case of Little Hans is important because it illustrates the theory of infantile sexuality, the functioning of the Oedipus complex and castration anxiety, the dynamics of symptom formation, and the process of behavior change.

Our account of events in the life of Little Hans begins at age three. At this point he had a lively interest in his penis, which he called his "widdler." What was striking about Hans during this period was his pleasure in touching his own penis and his preoccupation with penises or "widdlers" in others. For example, he wanted to know if his mother had a widdler and was fascinated with the process by which cows are milked. The interest in touching his penis, however, led to threats by his mother. "If you do that, I shall send you to Dr. A. to cut off your widdler. And then what will you widdle with?" Thus, there was a direct castration threat on the part of a parent, in this case the mother. Freud pinpointed this as the beginning of Hans' castration complex.

Hans' interest in widdlers extended to noting the size of the lion's widdler at the zoo and analyzing the differences between animate and inanimate objects — dogs and horses have widdlers, tables and chairs do not. Hans was curious about many things, but Freud related his general thirst for knowledge to sexual curiosity. Hans continued to be interested in whether his mother had a widdler. "I thought you (mother) were so big you'd have a widdler like a horse." When he was three-and-a-half, a sister was born, who also became a focus for his widdler concerns. "But her widdler's still quite small. When she grows up it'll get bigger all right." According to Freud, Hans could not admit what he really saw, namely, that there was no widdler there. To do so would mean that he must face his own castration anxieties. These anxieties occurred at a time when he was experiencing pleasure in the organ, as witnessed in his comments to his mother while she dried and powdered him after his bath.

> HANS Why don't you put your finger there.
>
> MOTHER Because that'd be piggish.
>
> HANS What's that? Piggish? Why?
>
> HANS (laughing) But it's great fun.

Thus Hans, now more than four years old, was preoccupied with his penis, experienced pleasure in it and concern about the loss of it, and began some seduction of his mother. It was at this point that his nervous disorders became apparent. The father, attributing the difficulties to sexual overexcitation due to his mother's tenderness, wrote Freud that Hans was "afraid that a horse will bite him in the street" and this fear seemed somehow to be connected with his having been frightened by seeing a large penis. As you remember, he had noticed at a very early age what large penises horses have, and at that time he inferred that, as his mother was so large, she must "have a widdler like a horse." Hans was afraid of going into the street and was depressed in the evenings. He had bad dreams and was frequently taken into his mother's bed. While walking in the street with his nurse, he became terribly frightened and sought to return home to be with his mother. The fear that horses would bite him became a fear that the horse would come into his room. He had developed a full-blown phobia, an irrational dread or fear of an object (horse). What more can we learn about this phobia? How are we to account for its development? As Freud notes, we must do more than simply call this a small boy's foolish fears.

The father attempted to deal with his son's fear of horses by offering him an interpretation. Hans was told that the fear of horses was nonsense, that the truth was that he (Hans) was fond of mother and the fear of horses had to do with an interest in their widdlers. Upon Freud's suggestion, the father explained to Hans that women do not have widdlers. Apparently there was a period of some relief in Hans, but he continued to be bothered by an obsessive wish to look at horses, though he was then frightened by them. At this point, he had his tonsils taken out and his phobia worsened. He was afraid that a white horse would bite him. He continued to be interested in widdlers in females. At the zoo, he was afraid of all the large animals and was entertained by the smaller ones. Among the birds, he was afraid of the pelican. In spite of his father's truthful explanation, Hans sought to reassure himself. "And everyone has a widdler. And my widdler will get bigger as I get bigger, because it does grow on me." According to Freud, Hans had been making comparisions among the sizes of widdlers and was dissatisfied with his own. Big animals reminded him of this defect and were disagreeable to him. The father's explanations heightened his castration anxiety, as expressed in the words "it does grow on me", as if it could be cut off. Thus, for this reason he resisted the information, and thus it had no therapeutic results. "Could it be that living beings really did exist which did not possess widdlers? If so, it would no longer be so incredible that they could take his own widdler away, and, as it were, make him into a woman."

Around this time, Hans reported the following dream. "In the night there was a big giraffe in the room and a crumpled one; and the big one called out because I took the crumpled one away from it. Then it stopped calling out; and then I sat down on top of the crumpled one." The father's interpretation was that he, the father, was the big giraffe, with the big penis and the mother was the crumpled giraffe, missing the genital organ. The dream was a reproduction of a morning scene in which the mother took Hans into bed with her. The father warned her against this ("The big one called out because I'd taken the crumpled one away from it") but the mother continued to encourage it. The mother encouraged and reinforced the Oedipal wishes. Hans stayed with her and, in the wish-fulfillment of the dream, he took possession of her ("Then the big giraffe stopped calling out; and then I sat down on top of the crumpled one")

Freud's strategy in understanding Hans' phobia was to suspend judgment and to give his impartial attention to everything there was to observe. He learned that prior to the development of the phobia, Hans had been alone with his mother at a summer place. There, two significant events occurred. First, he heard the father of one of his friends tell her that a white horse there bites and that she was not to hold her finger to it. Second, while playing as if they were horses, a friend who rivaled Hans for the affection of the little girls fell down, hit his foot, and bled. In an interview with Hans, Freud learned that Hans was bothered by the blinders on horses and the black around their mouths. The phobia became extended to include a fear that horses dragging a heavy van would fall down and kick their feet. It was then discovered that the exciting cause of his phobia, the event that capitalized on a psychological readiness for the formation of a phobia, was the perception of a horse falling down. While walking outside with his mother one day, Hans had seen a horse pulling a van fall down and begin to kick his feet.

The central feature in this case of little Hans was the phobia about the horse. What is fascinating in this regard is how often associations concerning a horse came up in relation to father, mother, and Hans himself. We have already noticed Hans' interest in his mother's widdler in relation to that of a horse. To his father, he said at one point: "Daddy, don't trot away from me." Can father, who wore a mustache and eyeglasses, be the horse that Hans was afraid of, the horse that would come into his room at night and would bite him? Or, could Hans himself be the horse? Hans was known to play horse in his room, to trot about, fall down, kick about with his feet, and neigh. He repeatedly ran up to his father and bit him, just as he feared the horse would do to him. Hans was overfed. Could this relate to his concerns about large, fat horses? Finally, Hans was known to have called himself a young horse and to have a tendency to stamp his feet on the ground when angry, similar to what the horse did when it fell down. To return to the mother, could the heavily laden carts symbolize the pregnant mother and the horse falling down the birth or delivery of a child? Are such associations coincidental or can they play a significant role in our understanding of the phobia?

According to Freud, the major cause of Hans' phobia was his Oedipus conflict. Hans felt considerable affection for his mother, more than he could handle during the phallic stage of his development. While he had deep affection for the father he also considered him a rival for his mother's affections. When he and mother stayed at the summer cottage and father was away, he was able to get into bed with mother and keep her for himself. This heightened his attraction for his mother and his hostility toward his father. For Freud, "Hans was really a little Oedipus who wanted to have his father 'out of the way', to get rid of him, so that he might be alone with his handsome mother and sleep with her. This wish had originated during his summer holidays, when the alternating presence and absence of his father had drawn Hans' attention to the condition upon which depended the intimacy with his mother which he longed for." The fall and injury to his friend and rival during one of those holidays was significant in symbolizing the defeat for Hans of his rival.

When he returned home from the summer holidays. Hans' resentment toward his father increased. He tried to suppress the resentment with exaggerated affection. He arrived at an ingenious solution to the Oedipal conflict. He and his mother would be parents to children and the father could be the granddaddy. Thus, as Freud notes, "the little Oedipus had found a happier solution than that prescribed by destiny. Instead of putting his father out of the way, he had granted him the same happiness that he desired himself: he made him a grandfather and let him too marry his own mother." But such a fantasy could not be a satisfactory solution and Hans was left with considerable hostility for his father. The exciting cause of the phobia was the horse falling down. At that moment, Hans perceived a wish that his father might in the same way fall down and die. The hostility towards his father was projected onto the father and was symbolized in the horse that would bite him. He feared the father, symbolized in his fear of the horse, because he himself nourished jealous and hostile wishes against him. He feared the horse would bite him because of his wish that his father should fall down, and fears that the horse would come into his room occurred at night when he was most tempted by Oedipal fantasies. In his own play as a horse and in his biting of his father, he expressed an identification with his father. The phobia expressed the wish and the anxiety, and in a secondary way, accomplished the objective of leaving Hans home to be with his mother.

In sum, both his fear that a horse would bite him and his fear that horses would fall down represented the father who was going to punish Hans for the evil wishes he was harboring against him. Hans was able to get over the phobia and, according to a later report by Freud, he appeared to be functioning well. What factors allowed for the change? First, there was the sexual enlightenment by the father. While Hans was reluctant to accept this and it at first heightened his castration anxiety, it did serve as a useful piece of reality to hold onto. Second, the analysis provided by his father and by Freud was useful in making conscious for Hans what had formerly been unconscious. Finally, the father's interest and permissive attitude toward Hans' expression of his feelings allowed for a resolution of the Oedipus conflict in favor of an identification with the father, diminishing both the wish to rival the father and the castration anxiety, and thereby decreasing the potential for symptom development.

The case of little Hans has many problems with it as a piece of scientific investigation. The interviewing was done by the father in an unsystematic way. The father himself was a close adherent of Freud's and therefore was possibly biased somewhat in his observations and interpretations. Freud himself was dependent on second-hand reports. He was aware of the limitations of the data, but he was also impressed with them. Whereas before his theory had been based on the childhood memories of adult patients, with Little Hans there was the beginning of observations of the sexual life of children. It is hard to draw conclusions about the theory in terms of this case. The presentation does not contain all of Freud's observations on Hans. Furthermore, it is but a single case, and it is taken from an early point (1909) in Freud's work. On the other hand, we do get an appreciation of both the wealth of information available to the analyst and, moreover, the problems inherent in evaluating and interpreting such data. We must necessarily get a feeling for Freud's ability to observe and describe phenomena and his efforts to come to terms with the complexity of human behavior. In this one case alone we have descriptions of phenomena relevant to the following: infantile sexuality, fantasies of children, functioning of the unconscious, the process of conflict development and conflict resolution, the process of symptom formation, symbolization, and the dream process. In reading such a case we cannot fail to be impressed by Freud's courageous efforts to discover the secrets of human functioning and by his willingness to pursue the job that needed to be done, in spite of limitations in his observations and in full recognition of the complexity of the phenomena he was trying to understand.

RELATED POINTS OF VIEW AND RECENT DEVELOPMENTS

One interesting aspect of the history of psychoanalytic theory has been the development of schools or groups with different, often antagonistic, points of view. Freud changed many aspects of psychoanalytic theory during the course of his professional career. However, he and his followers clashed on many issues. To a certain extent there was what has been described as a religious or political quality (Fromm, 1959) to psychoanalysis, with the traditional followers being considered among the faithful and those who deviated from the fundamental principles being cast outside the movement. This pattern started during Freud's lifetime and continued afterwards. A theorist such as Erikson is still highly regarded by most traditional psychoanalysts whereas the theorists to be considered below often are not. Frequently it is hard to determine the basis for the response to one or another theorist. However, as a general rule, a theorist must retain a commitment to the following concepts to be considered a part of Freudian psychoanalysis: the sexual and aggresive instincts, the unconscious, and the stages of development. As we shall see, the theories considered below questioned one or another of these concepts and thereby approached understanding humans somewhat differently.

Two Early Challenges to Freud: Alfred Adler and Carl G. Jung

Among the many early analysts who broke with Freud and developed their own schools of thought were Alfred Adler and Carl Jung. Both were early and important followers of Freud, Adler having been president of the Vienna Psychoanalytic Society and Jung president of the International Psychoanalytic Society. Both split with Freud over what they felt was an excessive emphasis on the sexual instincts. The split with Jung was particularly painful for Freud since Jung was to be his "crown prince" and chosen successor. Other individuals also split with Freud and developed their own schools of thought. However, Adler and Jung were among the earliest and remain among the best known.

Alfred Adler (1870-1937)

For approximately a decade, Alfred Adler (1870-1937) was an active member of the Vienna psychoanalytic group. However, in 1911, when he presented his views to the other members of this group, the response was so hostile that he left it to form his own school of *Individual Psychology.* What ideas could have been considered so unacceptable to psychoanalysts? We cannot consider all of Adler's theory, but we can consider some of his early and later views to get a feeling for the important differences between them and psychoanalysis.

Perhaps most significant of all in Adler's split from Freud was his greater emphasis on social urges and conscious thoughts than on instinctual sexual urges and unconscious processes. Early in his career Adler became interested in organ inferiorities and how people compensate for them. A person with a weak organ may attempt to compensate for this weakness by special efforts to strengthen that organ or by efforts to develop other organs. For example, someone who stutters as a child may attempt to become a great speaker, or someone with a defect in vision may attempt to develop special listening sensitivities. Whereas initially Adler was interested in bodily organ weaknesses, gradually he became interested in psychological *feelings of inferiority* and *compensatory strivings* to mask or reduce these painful feelings. Thus, whereas Freudians might see Theodore Roosevelt's emphasis on toughness and carrying a "big stick" as

ALFRED ADLER

a defense against castration anxiety, Adlerians might see him as expressing compensatory strivings against feelings of inferiority associated with boyhood weaknesses. Whereas Freudians might see an extremely aggressive woman as expressing penis envy, Adlerians might see her as expressing a masculine protest or rejection of the stereotyped feminine role of weakness and inferiority. According to Adler, how a person attempts to cope with such feelings becomes a part of his or her *style of life* — a distinctive aspect of his or her personality functioning.

These concepts already suggest a much more social rather than biological emphasis. This social emphasis increasingly became an important part of Adler's thinking. At first Adler spoke of a *will to power* as an expression of the organism's efforts to cope with feelings of helplessness dating from infancy. This emphasis gradually shifted to an emphasis on *striving for superiority*. In its neurotic form this striving could be expressed in wishes for power and control over others; in its healthier form it expressed a "great upward drive" toward unity and perfection. In the healthy person the striving for superiority is expressed in social feeling and cooperation as well as in assertiveness and competition. From the beginning there is in people a social interest, that is an innate interest in relating to people and an innate potential for cooperation.

Adler's theory also is noteworthy for its emphasis on how people respond to feelings about the self, how people respond to goals which direct their behavior toward the future, and how the order of birth among siblings can influence their psychological development. In relation to the latter, many psychologists have noted the tendency for only sons or first-born sons to achieve more than later sons in a family. For example, twenty-one of the first twenty-three American astronauts were first-born or only sons. While many of Adler's ideas have found their way into the general public's thinking and are related to views later expressed by other theorists, the school of Individual Psychology itself has not had a major impact on personality theory and research.

Carl G. Jung (1875-1961)

Jung split with Freud in 1914, a few years after Adler, and developed his own school of thought, *Analytical Psychology*. Like Adler, he was distressed with what he felt was an excessive emphasis on sexuality. Instead, Jung viewed the libido as a generalized life energy. While sexuality is a part of this basic energy, the libido also includes other strivings for pleasure and creativity.

Jung accepted Freud's emphasis on the unconscious but added to it the concept of the *collective unconscious*. According to Jung, people have stored within their collective unconscious the cumulative experiences of past generations. The collective unconscious, as opposed to the personal unconscious, is shared by all humans as a result of their common ancestry. It is a part of our animal heritage, our link with millions of years of past experience: "This psychic life is the mind of our ancient ancestors, the way in which they thought and felt, the way in which they conceived of life

CARL G. JUNG

and the world, of gods and human beings. The existence of these historical layers is presumably the source of the belief in reincarnation and in memories of past lives" (Jung, 1939, p. 24).

An important part of the collective unconscious are universal images or symbols, known as *archetypes*. Archetypes, such as the Mother archetype, are seen in fairytales, dreams, myths, and in some psychotic thoughts. Jung was struck with similar images that keep appearing, in slightly different forms, in far-distant cultures. For example, the Mother archetype might be expressed in a variety of positive or negative forms: as life-giver, as all-giving and nurturant, as the witch or threatening punisher ("Don't fool with

Mother Nature"), and as the seductive female. Archetypes may be represented in our images of persons, demons, animals, natural forces, or objects. The evidence in all cases for their being a part of our collective unconscious is their universality among members of different cultures from past and current time periods.

Another important aspect of Jung's theory was his emphasis on how people struggle with opposing forces within them. For example, there is the struggle between the face or mask we present to others (*persona*) and the private or personal self. If people emphasize the persona too much there may be a loss of sense of self and a doubting about who they are. On the other hand, the persona, as expressed in social roles and customs, is a necessary part of living in society. Similarly, there is the struggle between the masculine and feminine parts of ourselves. Every male has a feminine part (*anima*) and every female has a masculine part (*animus*) to their personality. If a man rejects his feminine part he may emphasize mastery and strength to an excessive degree, appearing cold and insensitive to the feelings of others. If a woman rejects her masculine part she may be excessively absorbed in "motherhood" and unable to accomplish herself in other ways. Psychologists currently interested in stereotyped sex roles would probably applaud Jung's emphasis on these dual aspects in everyone's personality, although they might question his characterizing some as specifically masculine and others as feminine.

Another contrast in Jung's theory is that between *introversion* and *extroversion*. Everyone relates to the world primarily in one of two directions, though the other direction always remains a part of the person. In the case of introversion, the person's basic orientation is inner, toward the self. The introverted type is hesitant, reflective, and cautious. In the case of extroversion the person's basic orientation is outward, toward the outside world. The extroverted type is socially engaging, active, and venturesome. For each person there is the task of finding unity in the *self*. For Jung an important task of life is to be found in bringing into harmony or integrating the above and other opposing forces. The integration of the many opposing aspects of our personality into the self is a lifelong struggle: "Personality as a complete realization of the fullness of our being is an unattainable ideal. But unattainability is no counter argument against an ideal, for ideals are only signposts, never goals" (Jung, 1939, p. 287). The struggle described here can become a particularly important aspect of life once people have passed the age of forty and defined themselves to the outside world in a variety of ways.

As with Adler, we have been able to consider only some of the highlights of Jung's theory. Jung is considered by many to be one of the great creative thinkers of the century and his theory has influenced the thinking of people in many fields outside of psychology. While periodically there are signs of the development of a strong interest in Jung inside of psychology, his views have yet to have a significant impact on the field.

The Cultural and Interpersonal
Emphasis: Karen Horney & Harry Stack Sullivan

With the later shift in psychodynamic thinking from Europe to the United States, one finds theorists emphasizing social rather than biological forces in behavior. Collectively, these theorists are called neo-Freudians, recognizing both their theoretical debt to Freud and their development of new theoretical positions. Some of these theorists, such as Karen Horney, emigrated to the United States prior to the Second World War. Other theorists, notably Harry Stack Sullivan, were born and trained in this country.

Karen Horney (1885-1952)

Karen Horney was trained as a traditional analyst in Germany and came to the United States in 1932. Shortly thereafter she split with traditional psychoanalytic thought and developed her own theoretical orientation and psychoanalytic training program. In contrast to Adler and Jung, she felt that her views built on the tremendous contributions of Freud rather than replaced them. Perhaps the major difference between her and Freud centers on the question of universal biological influences as opposed to cultural influences: "When we realize the great import of cultural conditions on neuroses, the biological and physiological conditions, which are considered by Freud to be their root, recede into the background" (1937, p. viii). She was led to this emphasis by three major considerations. First, Freud's statements concerning women made Horney think about cultural influences: "Their influence on our ideas of what constitutes masculinity or femininity was obvious, and it became just as obvious to me that Freud had arrived at certain conclusions because he failed to take them into account" (1945, p. 11). Second, she was associated with another psychoanalyst, Erich Fromm, who increased her awareness of the importance of social and cultural influences. Finally, Horney's observations of differences in personality structure between patients seen in Europe and the United States confirmed the importance of cultural influences. Beyond this, these observations led her to conclude that interpersonal relationships were at the core of all healthy and disturbed personality functioning.

Horney's emphasis in neurotic functioning is on how individuals attempt to cope with *basic anxiety* — the feeling a child has of being isolated and helpless in a potentially hostile world. According to her theory of neurosis, in the neurotic person there is conflict among three ways of responding to this basic anxiety. These three patterns, or *neurotic trends*, are known as moving toward, moving against, and moving away. All three

KAREN HORNEY

are characterized by rigidity and the lack of fulfillment of individual potential, the essence of any neurosis. In *moving toward* the person attempts to deal with anxiety by an excessive interest in being accepted, needed, and approved of. Such a person accepts a dependent role in relation to others and, except for the unlimited desire for affection, becomes unselfish, undemanding, and self-sacrificing. In *moving against*, the person assumes that everyone is hostile and that life is a struggle against all. All functioning is directed toward denying a need for others and toward appearing tough. In *moving away*, the third component of the conflict, the person shrinks away from others into neurotic detachment. Such people often look at themselves and others with emotional detachment, a way of not getting emotionally involved with others. While each neurotic person shows one or another trend as a special aspect of their personality, the problem is really that there is conflict among the three trends in the effort to deal with basic anxiety.

Before leaving Horney, her views concerning women should be considered. These views date back to her early work within traditional psychoanalytic thought and are reflected in a series of papers in *Feminine Psychology* (1973). As has been noted, from the start Horney had trouble accepting Freud's views of women. She felt that the concept of penis envy might be the result of a male bias in psychoanalysts that treat neurotic women in a particular social context: "Unfortunately, little or nothing is known of psychically healthy women, or of women under different cultural conditions" (1973, p. 216). She suggested that women are not biologically disposed toward masochistic attitudes of being weak, dependent, submissive, and self-sacrificing. Instead, these attitudes indicated the powerful influence of social forces.

In sum, both in her views of women and in her general theoretical orientation Horney rejected Freud's biological emphasis in favor of a social, interpersonal one. Partly as a result of this difference she held a much more optimistic view concerning the person's capacity for change and self-fulfillment.

Harry Stack Sullivan (1892-1949)

Of the theorists considered in this section, Sullivan is the only one born and trained in the United States, the only one who never had direct contact with Freud, and the one who most emphasized the role of social, interpersonal forces in human development. In fact, his theory has been known as the *Interpersonal Theory of Psychiatry* (1953) and his followers consider themselves part of the Sullivan school of interpersonal relations.

Sullivan placed great importance on the early relationship between the infant and the mother in the development of anxiety and in the development of a sense of self. Anxiety may be communicated by the mother in her earliest interaction with the infant. Thus, from the start, anxiety is interpersonal in character. The *self*, a critical concept in Sullivan's thinking, similarly is social in origin. The self develops out of feelings experienced while in contact with others and from *reflected appraisals* or perceptions on the part of the child as to how it is valued or appraised by others. Important parts of the self, particularly in relation to the experience of anxiety as opposed to security, are the *good-me* associated with pleasurable experiences, the *bad-me* associated with pain and threats to security, and the *not-me* or part of the self that is rejected because it is associated with intolerable anxiety.

Sullivan's emphasis on social influences is seen throughout his views on the development of the person. These views are somewhat similar to

HARRY STACK SULLIVAN

Erikson's in their emphasis on interpersonal influences and in their emphasis on important stages beyond the Oedipus complex. Particularly noteworthy here is Sullivan's emphasis on the *juvenile era and preadolescence.* During the juvenile stage, roughly the grammar school years, the child's experiences with friends and teachers begin to rival the influence of parents. Social acceptance becomes important and the child's "reputation" with others becomes an important source of self-esteem or anxiety. During preadolescence a relationship to a close friend of the same sex, or chum, becomes particularly important. This relationship of close friendship, of love, forms the basis for the development of a love relationship with a person of the opposite sex during adolescence. Today, many child psychologists suggest that early relationships with peers may equal in importance the early relationships with the mother (Lewis, M., 1975).

As with the other theorists in this section, we have been able to consider only a few of the major concepts of Sullivan's interpersonal theory. Sullivan's work is noteworthy in its social emphasis, in its emphasis on the development of the self, and in the outstanding contributions that he made to the treatment of schizophrenic patients.

Recent Developments within Traditional Psychoanalytic Theory

Turning to developments within traditional psychoanalytic theory, we can consider progress associated with clinical investigations and progress associated with systematic research efforts. From its inception with Freud and continuing on to date, developments within psychoanalytic theory generally have been based on clinical investigation, that is analysis of individual cases. One important development has been the extension of psychoanalytic investigation to age groups and forms of psychopathology rarely treated by Freud and his followers. As noted, Little Hans was treated by his father. Most psychoanalytic material on childhood and adolescence was based on memories reported by adult parents. The situation changed considerably with the efforts of individuals such as Anna Freud and Melanie Klein who used psychoanalytic concepts in the treatment of children, so that now a major part of the psychotherapy conducted with children and adolescents in Great Britain and the United States is based on psychoanalytic theory. Modifications are made in the treatment procedure according to the age group being treated (for example, with children play therapy is used as a substitute for dream analysis as a route to the unconscious), but the essential theoretical concepts remain the same.

In addition to the expansion of their clinical efforts to treatment of children, psychoanalysts increasingly have been concerned with different types of patient problems than those faced, in the main, by Freud. In the words of one analyst, today's patients come from a different social and cultural context than did Freud's patients and bring with them different problems. Rather than presenting themselves with "typical neuroses" they seek help with depressions, with feelings of emptiness, and with lives "lacking zest and joy" (Wolf, 1977). Such changes in the major problems coming to the attention of analysts have led to new theoretical advances, not from a dissatisfaction with Freudian theory per se but from the need to understand and solve different clinical problems.

Clinical concern with problems of self-definition and excessive vulnerability to blows to one's sense of self-esteem have led psychologists to become increasingly interested in how, during the earliest years, a person develops a sense of self (Kohut, 1977). Thus, many recent theoretical efforts, while not rejecting Freud's views concerning the roles of sex and aggression, have become more concerned with how the person attempts to protect the integrity of the sense of self from threats that arise from within the person and from the surrounding interpersonal environment. To a certain extent, this recent focus on the self represents an extension of the earlier emphasis by other analysts on ego functioning (for example, Hartmann, Kris, Lowenstein, Rapaport, Schafer). However, there is a difference. The earlier emphasis in psychoanalytic ego psychology focused on the undefensive, conflict-free aspects of ego functioning. Such functioning is expressed in artistic, creative productions as opposed disturbed neurotic or psychotic functioning. In contrast, more recently there has been concern with disturbance in the development of ego functioning and the sense of self, and with the implications of such disturbances for the development of psychopathology.

One of the problems with such clinical analyses of the self has been that they are difficult to translate into concepts and procedures that can be used in systematic, empirical investigations. Indeed, some analysts feel that such observations from "depth psychology" are part of a theoretical framework different than personality psychology in general (Kohut, 1971). Other analysts and psychologists, however, have attempted to study psychoanalytic phenomena and principles in the laboratory. Recent reviews of the experimental testing of Freudian concepts come to a variety of conclusions, ranging from the conclusion that many concepts have been certified and generally the theory has fared well (Fisher & Cleveland, 1977; Kline, 1972) to the conclusion that there is no evidence at all for psychoanalytic theory (Eysenck & Wilson, 1973).

One problem in the experimental testing of psychoanalytic concepts has been the difficulty in producing the phenomena of interest in the laboratory. Perhaps some advances are being made. For example, one group of psychologists is attempting to present conflict-related material to subjects at a level just below conscious recognition or through hypnotic suggestion. The effort here is to stimulate unconscious wishes and then observe the effects, on various aspects of psychological functioning (Silverman, 1976). Such observations are of particular significance in relation to the Freudian theory of psychopathology. Along with these efforts are those of other psychologists who are attempting to translate Freud's clinical observations into concepts that are free of metaphor and more open to systematic observation (Klein, 1976: Schafer, 1976; 1978). Instead of concepts such as drive, libido, instinct, and force there would be greater emphasis on behavior, including all private psychological activity that can be made public (dreams, fantasies, fears, etc.).

In sum, recent developments have taken two somewhat divergent trends. On the one hand, there is a concern with new kinds of clinical phenomena without greater concern for the potential for systematic, empirical investigation. On the other hand, there are the efforts of psychologists who are trying to produce in the laboratory the phenomena emphasized by Freud and who are trying to translate Freudian concepts into a language that can better stand the test of scientific criticism. The clinical and laboratory investigators discussed here share a commitment to the basic principles of Freudian psychoanalytic theory.

A CRITICAL EVALUATION

In evaluating psychoanalysis as a theory of personality, we need to keep in mind three points. First, we need to be clear about whether we are considering an early or a later view in the development of the theory. Although the thrust of psychoanalysis, in terms of its emphasis on unconscious forces and on the importance of early events, has remained consistent throughout, major developments in the theory did take place between the publication of *The Interpretation of Dreams* in 1900 and Freud's death in 1939. In considering Freud's view of anxiety, for example, we must be clear that the first theory viewed anxiety as the result of repression and dammed up libido, whereas the second theory viewed anxiety as a signal of impending danger to the ego which leads to repression. Second, in evaluating psychoanalysis we need to be clear about whether we are considering a part of the theory or the theory as a whole. Where consideration is given to a part of the theory, is that part basic to the entire structure or is the rest independent of it? For example, the latency period as a stage of development is not critical to the theory, but the genetic approach is; the theory of dreams as preservers of sleep is not critical to the theory, but the importance of the unconscious is. Finally, in considering psychoanalysis as a theory, we must keep it distinct from psychoanalysis as a method of therapy. The issue of therapeutic success with pychoanalysis has not been dealt with here because it is not critical to an understanding of the theory or an evaluation of it. If psychoanalytic theory did in fact lead to specific predictions concerning therapy, predictions which could be tested in a systematic way, then the results of therapy would be related to the validity of the theory. However, predictions of this nature are rarely made and, therefore, psychoanalysis as a theory of personality must be evaluated on grounds other than those of therapeutic effectiveness.

Major Contributions

How good a theory of personality is psychoanalysis? Clearly, Freud made major contributions to psychology and greatly influenced the developmental approach. Psychoanalysis has led to the use of new techniques, such as those of free association and dream interpretation, and has been a significant force in the development and use of special tests in the assessment of personality. There are two outstanding contributions. First, psychoanalysis made a major contribution to the discovery and investigation of phenomena. Whether ultimately these observations remain part of psychoanalytic theory or are integrated into another theory, the importance of the discovery of these phenomena remains. As we go beyond some of the superficialities of human behavior, we are impressed with the observations made by Freud. These become particularly apparent in clinical work with patients. It is striking for the therapist to observe the paranoid patient's fear that the therapist is out to make a homosexual attack upon him. It is striking to observe the chemist with obsessive-compulsive qualities describe how he first became interested in chemistry because of the "smells, stinks, and explosions" he could make. It is striking to observe the patient fantasy in the transference that the therapist is dependent on the patient's money for his groceries. And it is striking to observe how learning blocks in students may be related to fears that the teacher or other students will "castrate" them, to fears that being intelligent will mean that they are sissies, or to unconscious fears that intellectual curiosity will give rise to their sexual curiosity, just as the word "to know", in the Bible, means knowing someone sexually. Whether we choose to interpret these phenomena as characteristic of all human functioning, as Freud did, or merely as idiosyncratic to neurotics, we are forced to take account of these observations as data concerning human behavior. The importance of Freud's emphasis on certain essentials in human functioning was well expressed by the eminent anthropologist Clyde Kluckhohn.

When I began serious field work among the Navaho and Pueblo Indians, my position on psychoanalysis was a mixed one. I had been analyzed and was thoroughly convinced that Freudian psychology was the only dynamic depth psychology of much importance . . . On the other hand, I tended to believe that psychoanalysis was strongly culture-bound . . . But the facts uncovered in my own field work and that of my collaborators have forced me to the conclusion that Freud and other psychoanalysts have depicted with astonishing correctness many central themes in motivational life which are universal. The styles of expression of these themes and much of the manifest content are culturally determined, but the underlying psychologic drama transcends cultural difference.

This should not be too surprising—except to an anthropologist over-indoctrinated with the theory of culture relativism—for many of the inescapable givens of human life are also universal.

KLUCKHOHN and MORGAN, 1951, P. 120

The first major contribution by Freud, then, was the richness of his observations and the attention he paid to all details of human behavior. The
second was the attention he gave to the complexity of human behavior
at the same time that he developed an extremely encompassing theory.
Psychoanalytic theory emphasizes that seemingly similar behavior can
have very different antecedents and that very similar motives can lead to
quite different behavior. Generosity can express genuine affection or an
effort to deal with feelings of hostility, and the lawyer and the criminal
whom he defends or prosecutes may, in some cases, be closer to one another psychologically than most of us care to realize. Out of this recognition of complexity comes a theory which accounts for almost all aspects of
human behavior. No other theory of personality comes close to psychoanalytic theory in accounting for such a broad range of behavior. Few
others give comparable attention to the functioning of the individual as a
whole.

Many, perhaps most, of our theories of personality deal not with personality as a whole, but
rather with some selected aspect or process. Freudian theory kept the whole personality
more in view . . . Freud produced this general theory not out of a combination of existing
elements, but largely by new creative insights. His theory therefore has a scope, a unity, and a
coherence which is unmatched in psychology.

INKELES, 1963, P. 333

Limitations of the Theory

In making these contributions, Freud stands as a genius and an investigator
of tremendous courage. What then of the limitations of psychoanalysis as
a theory? Comments have been made already in relation to parts of the
theory but what about the theory as a whole? Two major criticisms are
worthy of note. The first involves the psychoanalytic view of the person,
while the second involves the scientific status of psychoanalysis as a theory. In essence, these two criticisms suggest that serious questions can be
raised about the energy model used by psychoanalysis to account for behavior and the ways in which its concepts are defined.

   We already have observed that Freud was influenced by the discoveries
of Helmholtz concerning the conservation of matter and the views of
Brücke concerning the person as an energy system. Basic to the psychoanalytic model is the view that all behavior can be understood in terms of
exchanges and transformations of energy, with the goal of the organism
being tension-reduction. The pleasure principle, the principle fundamental to all behavioral functioning, states that the organism seeks pleasure in
the form of tension reduction. Yet, there is considerable evidence which
suggests that the organism does not always seek tension reduction, in fact,

it often seeks stimulation. Sensory deprivation studies indicate that the organism cannot maintain a prolonged state of rest, free from stimulation and sensory bombardment by the external world. Animals appear to find stimulation of some parts of the brain pleasurable (Olds, 1958) and will work to be able to explore novel environments (Butler, 1954). White (1959), in his review of the relevant literature, notes that there are many behaviors which do not seem to fit the models of physiological drive and tension reduction. These range from the "curiosity of the cat" to the play of children. These behaviors do not appear to be related to any physiological drive, they do not appear to satisfy the organism in the sense that food satisfies a hungry organism, and they do not appear to reduce tension. There is, then, evidence that a tension reduction model alone is inadequate to account for all aspects of human functioning.

Another problem with Freud's energy model is that it tends to shade differences and make too many things equivalent. There is a simplistic quality to the theory which suggests that everything is a result of the sexual and aggressive instincts. For example, a man's love for a woman is viewed by Freud as an aim-inhibited instinct, as a repetition of the incestuous feelings for the mother. For Freud, the sucking of the infant at the breast of the mother is the model for every love relation. Such a view, however, fails to give adequate attention to differences between a child's love and that of an adult, between the love for a mate and the love for a friend, between the love for a person and the love for one's work. It does seem likely that all of these loves have something in common, that in any one individual they share at least some earlier roots and at least some common principles of functioning. On the other hand, to consider all of them partial gratifications of the same instinct hardly seems to do justice to the considerable differences among them.

Thus, the principles concerning the transformations of energy appear to contain both assets and limitations. They provide an appreciation of the possible relationships and similarities among phenomena that might otherwise appear to be isolated and distinct. On the other hand, they tend to reduce too many phenomena to the same thing and thereby to neglect the importance of major differences among them.

In many ways it is this noting of similarities and shadings of differences that gives appeal to the clinician and creates difficulties for the experimenter. In many ways it is the looseness and ambiguity of its concepts that allows psychoanalytic theory to account for so much human behavior. But these factors raise questions concerning the status of psychoanalysis as a scientific theory. The terms of psychoanalysis are ambiguous. There are many metaphors and analogies which can, but need not, be taken literally. Examples would be latency, death instinct, Oedipus complex, and castration anxiety. Does castration anxiety refer to the fear of loss of the penis, or does it refer to the child's fear of injury to his body at a time that his body-image is of increased importance to his self-esteem? The language of the theory is so vague that investigators often are hard-pressed to agree on precise meanings of the terms. How are we to define libido? Furthermore, the same word, such as repression, was used for different concepts at different times, often without a clear definition of the nature of the change of the concept.

Even where the constructs are well defined, ofen they are *too removed from observable and measurable behavior* to be of much empirical use. Concepts such as id, ego, and superego have considerable descriptive power, but it is often hard to translate them into relevant behavioral observations. Robert Sears, who for some time has worked on problems in child development, in general, and the process of identification, in particular, commented on this problem as follows. "We became acutely aware of the difference between the purely descriptive statement of a psychodynamic process and a testable theory of behavioral development. Psychoanalytic theory contained suggestions for the latter, but it did not specify the conditions under which greater or lesser degrees of any particular behavioral product of identification would occur" (Sears, Rau, and Alpert, 1965, p. 241). Here Sears is emphasizing the difference between a descriptive statement involving the use of a concept, and an explicit statement as to how the concept translates itself into quantitative relationships among phenomena. Within psychoanalytic theory, the relationships among phenomena are not always made explicit, and quantitative estimates of relationships are never made.

What we have, then, is a theory that is at times confusing and often difficult to test. This problem is complicated further by the way in which psychoanalysts can account for almost any outcome, even opposite outcomes. If one behavior appears, it is an expression of the instinct; if the opposite appears, it is an expression of a defense; if another form of behavior appears, it is compromise between the instinct and the defense. For example, take Freud's comment on the interpretation of a slip of the tongue. "When a person who commits a slip gives an explanation which fits your views then you declare him to be the final authority on the subject. He says so himself! But if what he says does not suit your book, then you suddenly assert that what he says does not count, one need not believe it. Certainly that is so" (Freud, 1920, p. 46). It does not seem unlikely that such developments take place; that is, that depending on minor shifts in forces, major differences in overt behavior can appear. The problem with the theory is not that it leaves room for such complexity, but that it fails to state which behavior will occur, given a specific set of circumstances. In not providing such statements, psychoanalytic theory does not leave itself open to disproof or the negative test.

Other criticisms are relevant to psychoanalytic theory and the way in which it is defended. Psychoanalysts use observations influenced by the theory to support the theory, without giving adequate consideration to the factors relevant to the social psychology of the experimenter. Committed observers may bias the responses of their subjects and bias their own perceptions of the data. It is also true that analysts often respond to criticism of the theory by suggesting that the critics are being defensive in not recognizing phenomena such as infantile sexuality, that they do not understand the theory, or that one must be psychoanalyzed before one can criticize the theory. To the extent that some psychoanalysts advance such arguments in a routine way, they perpetuate some of the early developments of psychoanalysis as a religious movement, rather than as a scientific theory.

In noting these criticisms of the status of psychoanalysis as a scientific theory, it is important to recognize that Freud was aware of most of these objections. He was not a naive scientist. His position, rather, was that the beginning of scientific activity consists of the description of phenomena, and that at the early stages some imprecision is inevitable. Also, Freud was acutely aware of the difficulties in making use of psychoanalytic insights for predictive purposes. He noted that the analyst was on safe ground in tracing the development of behavior from its final stage backwards, but that if he proceeded in the reverse way, an inevitable sequence of events no longer seemed to be apparent. His conclusion was that psychoanalysis does a better job at analysis than at synthesis, at explaining than at predicting. Freud did not believe that a science consists of nothing but conclusively proved propositions but, rather, insisted that the scientist be content with approximations to certainty.

In carrying on his work with that scientific credo, Freud encountered a number of limitations. For the most part, his direct analytic observations were limited to upper and middle class patients who presented symptoms relevant to the issues dominant in the culture at the time. In seems likely, therefore, that he exaggerated the importance of Victorian issues such as sex, morality, and guilt relative to other human concerns. Because of his training and the scientific spirit of his time. Freud appears to have relied, to an excessive degree, on a physiological energy model to account for psychological phenomena. Finally, it is unfortunate that, at the time of the development of his theory, Freud did not have the benefit of a discipline in psychology which supported his efforts to develop a scientific theory. Unfortunately, Freud was excessively dependent on a medical, therapeutic environment when he was committed to developing a system with broader relevance.

It is interesting to note that Freud's aim was to be both scientific and humanistic, "to bring concepts and order to human concerns and human concerns into the scientific community" (Havens, 1973, p. 2). We have already noted the arguments raised by scientific critics. Psychoanalysis also has been criticized by humanists as being overly intellectual, excessively abstract, and simplistic. Proponents of the existential point of view in psychology and psychiatry have been particularly critical of psychoanalysis along these lines. As has often been the case in the past, some of the harshest and most cogent criticism comes from individuals who themselves are analysts. Thus R.D. Laing (1967), a British analyst, has been critical of the extent to which psychoanalytic concepts may hide and distort human experience and critical of the tendency to label the patient "sick" as opposed to looking at "sickness" in the patient's family or in the broader society. And Thomas Szasz, also an analyst, has argued against the "myth of mental illness" created by the model of abnormal behavior associated with psychoanalysis. Szasz (1961) notes that Freud served a tremendous humanitarian function in demonstrating that mentally "sick" people do not always "will" their pathological behavior and therefore should not be subject to moral outrage. At the same time, Szasz argues that the view of such people as "sick" has led to negative value judgments about them. Furthermore, it has led to serious curtailment of their rights and civil liberties. The criticism of Szasz is not so much against psychoanalytic theory itself as against the medical model of psychopathology that has come to be associated with it and the current social context of that model.

Another aspect of psychoanalytic theory related to the current social context is the criticism it has received from feminists. This has been both because of Freud's views concerning women and because of the influence of these views on female patients and the broader society (Williams, 1976). While Freud often is misinterpreted, he did see certain traits such as receptivity, dependence on others, sensitivity, vanity, and submissiveness as part of the feminine orientation. These characteristics were seen as part of women because of biological influences and because of psychological reactions to their awareness of the lack of a penis—Freud's concept of penis envy. The concept of penis envy symbolizes for many women a "biology is destiny" view on the part of Freud and an inadequate appreciation of cultural factors. Among others, the analyst Karen Horney questioned many of Freud's views concerning women and feminine sexuality, and, as noted earlier, proposed instead a view of feminine development that emphasized cultural influences. It is an interesting aspect of psychoanalysis that while it has come under attack by feminists, perhaps more than any other theory it has almost always had major female figures within its ranks (for example, Anna Freud, Helene Deutsch, Greta Bibring, Margaret Mahler, Clara Thompson, Frieda Fromm-Reichman).

Summary Evaluation

How, then, are we to summarize our evaluation of Freud and psychoanalytic theory? As an observer of human behavior, and as a person with a creative imagination, Freud was indeed a genius with few, if any, equals. The theory he developed certainly has the virtue of being comprehensive. There is no other personality theory that approximates psychoanalysis in the range of behavior considered and interpretations offered. Given such scope, the theory is economical. The structural and process concepts used by the theory are relatively few in number. Furthermore, the theory has suggested many areas for investigation and has led to a considerable amount of research. While relevant to the theory, however, much of this research does not offer an explicit test of a theory-derived hypothesis, and little of it has been used to extend and develop the theory. The major problem with psychoanalytic theory is the way in which the concepts are formulated; that is, ambiguity in the concepts and in the suggested relationships among concepts has made it very difficult to test the theory. The phenomena observed by Freud will have to be incorporated into any further theory of personality. The question for psychoanalytic theory is whether it can be developed to provide for specific tests, or whether it will be replaced in the future by another theory that is equally comprehensive and economical but more open to systematic empirical investigation.

MAJOR CONCEPTS AND SUMMARY

Review concepts from Chapter 2   dream interpretation

symptom   transference

free association

In this chapter and the previous one we have considered psychoanalytic theory as illustrative of a psychodynamic, clinical approach to personality. The psychodynamic emphasis is clear in the interpretation of behavior as a result of the interplay among forces, in the emphasis on anxiety and defense mechanisms, and in the interpretation of symptoms as compromises between instinct and defense. The clinical qualities of psychoanalysis are apparent in the emphasis on the individual, the attention given to individual differences, and the attempt to assess and understand the total individual. The psychoanalytic approach is highly interpretive, making use of many constructs that are not open to direct observation to account for a wide range of individual and group behavior.

In terms of emphasis on the stability of personality, it is not surprising that psychoanalytic theory places great importance on structural concepts. The main structural concepts are those of id, ego, and superego, which roughly represent drives (instincts), an orientation toward reality, and morals (values), respectively. Psychic life is also described in terms of the extent to which thoughts and memories are available to awareness—ranging from unconscious (unavailable to awareness), preconscious (available to awareness), and conscious (part of awareness).

Psychoanalytic theory also places great emphasis on the processes (dynamics) of psychological functioning. Basically, the organism seeks expression or discharge of the life (libido) and death instincts or sexual and aggressive instincts. Because of its association with a past trauma, expression of an instinct may signal danger to the ego and lead to the experience of anxiety. The individual then faces a conflict situation in which he seeks to gratify the instinct but also fears doing so. Often the result is the use of mechanisms of defense (i.e., projection, denial, isolation, undoing, reaction-formation, rationalization, repression) which attempt to give some expression to the instinct in a way that does not produce anxiety. The use of mechanisms of defense always involves some distortion of reality. Only in sublimation is the individual able to express an impulse free of anxiety and without distortion of reality. In such a case id, ego, and superego are acting in unison and with freedom from conflict.

The psychoanalytic theory of development places great emphasis on stages of development (i.e., oral, anal, phallic, latency, genital) which are rooted in the biological processes of the organism. Experiences during the first five years of life are viewed as critical for the determination of later, adult personality characteristics. This is particularly true where frustration has led to fixation at a pregenital stage of development or where, because of later frustration, the individual regresses back to an earlier mode of functioning. Oral, anal, and phallic character types illustrate how adult personality characteristics may be understood in terms of partial fixations at early stages of development.

The above concepts lay the groundwork for an understanding of psychopathology. While all pathology is believed to center in the Oedipus complex, representing fixations at the phallic stage of development, frustration and trauma can lead to regression to an earlier stage of development. Thus, the exact form taken in a neurosis or a psychosis is dependent upon the stage to which the individual regresses. In psychopathology there is a struggle between the striving of the id instincts for discharge and the efforts of the ego to prevent discharge and defend against anxiety. Behavior change in the direction of growth occurs when individuals are exposed to conditions which allow them to gratify their instincts in new, more mature ways which will neither lead to guilt nor external threat. In psychoanalysis, the free association method is used to facilitate the process of becoming aware of unconscious wishes and conflicts. The transference situation is used as an opportunity for insight and growth.

Finally, an evaluation of psychoanalytic theory must recognize the richness of observations, the range of behavior covered in a reasonably economical way, and the fertile areas for research suggested by the theory. At the same time the theory suffers from a number of scientific limitations (for example, terms are ambiguous, constructs are often far removed from observable and measurable behavior, relationships among phenomena are not always made explicit). It also has come under attack from humanists for being too far removed from the actual experiences of individuals and from that which is uniquely human, and from feminists as well as others who give greater emphasis to cultural influences relative to biological influences.

CARL R. ROGERS (1902-): A VIEW OF THE THEORIST
ROGERS' VIEW OF THE PERSON
ROGERS' VIEW OF SCIENCE, THEORY, AND RESEARCH METHODS
THE PERSONALITY THEORY OF CARL ROGERS
Structure
• The Self
• Research on the Concept of Self

Process
• Self-actualization
• Self-consistency and Congruence
• The Need for Positive Regard

Growth and Development
• Self-actualization and Healthy Psychological Development
• Research on Parent-Child Relationships and the Development of Self-Esteem
MAJOR CONCEPTS AND SUMMARY

4 A PHENOMENOLOGICAL THEORY: CARL ROGERS' PERSON—CENTERED THEORY OF PERSONALITY

Chapter Focus:

In this chapter we shall consider Rogerian theory as illustrative of a phenomenological, clinical approach to personality. The clinical emphasis will be apparent in the attention given to individual differences and the efforts to understand and assess the total individual. The phenomenological approach will be apparent in the emphasis on the phenomenal world of the individual — how the person perceives and experiences the self and the world. Assessment and research follow in their emphasis on verbal self-report and concepts such as self and experience. The theory is a part of the humanistic, human potential movement which emphasizes self-actualization and the fulfillment of an individual's growth potential.

To me such a highly personal "view from within" is not only the best source of learning, it also points the way, perhaps, toward a new and more human science . . .

ROGERS, 1972, P. 3

I see the actualizing tendency in the human organism as being basic to motivation . . . So I reaffirm, even more strongly than when I first advanced the notion, my belief that there is one central source of energy in the human organism; that it is a trustworthy function of the whole organism rather than of some portion of it; and that it is perhaps best conceptualized as a tendency toward fulfillment, toward actualization, not only toward maintenance but also toward the enhancement of the organism.

ROGERS, 1977, P. 237, PP. 242-243

In the previous chapter we discussed the psychoanalytic theory of Freud. Psychoanalytic theory was considered in light of its emphasis on individual differences, the total individual, the importance of the unconscious, and human behavior as a function of the interplay among various forces — a dynamic model.

In this second chapter on a specific theoretical position, the focus will be on the phenomenological theory of Carl Rogers. Originally, the theory was not one of personality. Rather it was a theory of psychotherapy and the process of behavior change. However, a theory of personality has been an outgrowth of the theory of therapy. The position of Rogers is presented because it is representative of the approach to personality which stresses that people can and should be understood in terms of how they view **phenomenological** themselves and the world around them — the **phenomenological**
approach   **approach**. Rogers' theory also is presented because of the attention it gives to the concept of the *self* and experiences related to the self, and because it illustrates a conscious, focused effort to combine clinical intuition with objective research. In his emphasis on human experience and the importance of being a fully functioning human being, Carl Rogers has had a tremendous impact on the training of counselors, teachers, and executive management people in business. His view of the person is frankly stated, in opposition to the one presented by Freud, and is clearly related to his views of therapy and his selection of problems for research. Finally, this view and the total spirit of the theory and the theorist have resulted in the association of Rogers with a significant part of the human potential movement.

Although the American emphasis on objective and quantitative research has influenced Rogers, the theory is derived from intensive work with individuals and, in turn, is applied to individuals. Throughout his career, Rogers has spent time in the treatment of individuals and generally has begun his research efforts by examining clinical material. Like psychoanalytic theory, Rogers' theory involves assumptions relevant to all people, but the theory has particular relevance to the study of individual differences and the total functioning of individuals. For example, Rogers is interested in therapy as a unique experience for each individual. However, although it is unique, the therapy involves a predictable *process* for all individuals. Unlike the psychoanalytic emphasis on the unconscious, the theory of Rogers places emphasis on that which is conscious. For Rogers, the phenomenological world of individuals, the world as it is experienced by them, primarily in conscious terms, contains the data necessary to understand and to predict behavior. Although the private world of the individual can be known only to the individual himself, the psychologist can, by providing a supportive atmosphere, approximate an understanding of the private world of the individual.

In summary, this chapter and the next will analyze and evaluate a theory that is significant in its emphasis on individual differences, the entire personality, and behavior as a function of the private, unique way in which individuals experience their worlds. In particular, the concern is with the importance of the concept of the *self* in personality theory, with the ways in which individuals experience themselves and others, and with the conditions under which individuals are capable of becoming fully functioning people.

CARL R. ROGERS (1902 –   ): A VIEW OF THE THEORIST

"I speak as a person, from a context of personal experience and personal learning." Thus does Rogers introduce his chapter "This Is Me" in his 1961 book *On Becoming A Person*. The chapter is a personal, very moving account by Rogers of the development of his professional thinking and personal philosophy. Rogers states what he does and how he feels about it.

This book is about the suffering and the hope, the anxiety and the satisfaction, with which each therapist's counseling room is filled. It is about the uniqueness of the relationship each therapist forms with each client, and equally about the common elements which we discover in all these relationships. This book is about the highly personal experiences of each one of us. It is about a client in my office who sits there by the corner of the desk, struggling to be himself, yet deathly afraid of being himself —striving to see his experience as it is, wanting to be that experience, and yet deeply fearful of the prospect. This book is about me, as I sit there with that client, facing him, participating in that struggle as deeply and sensitively as I am able. It is about me as I try to perceive his experience, and the meaning and the feeling and the taste and the flavor that it has for him. It is about me as I bemoan my very human fallibility in understanding that client, and the occasional failures to see life as it appears to him, failures which fall like heavy objects across the intricate, delicate web of growth which is taking place. It is about me as I rejoice at the privilege of being a midwife to a new personality —as I stand by with awe at the emergence of a self, a person, as I see a birth process in which I have had an important and facilitating part. It is about both the client and me as we regard with wonder the potent and orderly forces which are evident in this whole experience, forces which seem deeply rooted in the universe as a whole. The book is, I believe, about life, as life vividly reveals itself in the therapeutic process —with its blind power and its tremendous capacity for destruction, but with its overbalancing thrust toward growth, if the opportunity for growth is provided.

ROGERS, 1961, PP. 4-5

Carl Rogers was born on January 8, 1902 in Oak Park, Illinois. He was reared in a strict and uncompromising religious and ethical atmosphere. His parents had the welfare of the children constantly in mind and inculcated in them a worship of hard work. In behavioral terms, the religious and ethical concerns led to "no alcoholic beverages, no dancing, cards or theatre, very little social life, and much work." From his description of his early life, we see two main trends which are reflected in his later work. The first is the concern with moral and ethical matters already described. The second is the respect for the methods of science, particularly where things need to be accomplished. The latter appears to have developed out of exposure to his father's efforts to operate their farm on a scientific basis and Rogers' own reading of books on scientific agriculture.

Rogers started his college education at the University of Wisconsin in the field of agriculture, but after two years he changed his professional goals and decided to enter the ministry. During a trip to the Orient, in 1922, he had a chance to observe commitments to other religious doctrines and to observe the bitter mutual hates of French and German people, who otherwise seemed to be likable individuals. Experiences like these influenced his decision to go to a liberal theological seminary, the Union Theological Seminary in New York. Although he was concerned about questions regarding the meaning of life for individuals, Rogers had doubts about specific religious doctrines. Therefore, he chose to leave the seminary, to work in the field of child guidance, and to think of himself as a clinical psychologist.

Rogers obtained his graduate training at Teachers College, Columbia University, receiving his Ph. D. in 1931. He describes his course and clinical experience as leading to a "soaking up" of both the dynamic views of Freud and the "rigorous, scientific, coldly objective, statistical" views then prevalent at Teachers College. Again, there were the pulls in different directions, the development of two somewhat divergent trends. In his later life Rogers attempted to bring these divergent trends into harmony with one another. Indeed, these years represent an effort to integrate the religious with the scientific, the intuitive with the objective, and the clinical

CARL R. ROGERS

with the statistical. Throughout his career, Rogers has tried continually to apply the objective methods of science to what is most basically human.

Therapy is the experience in which I can let myself go subjectively. Research is the experience in which I can stand off and try to view this rich subjective experience with objectivity, applying all the elegant methods of science to determine whether I have been deceiving myself. The conviction grows in me that we shall discover laws of personality and behavior which are as significant for human progress or human relationship as the law of gravity or the laws of thermodynamics.

ROGERS, 1961, P. 14

In 1968 Rogers and his more humanistically oriented colleagues formed the Center for the Studies of the Person. The development of the Center expressed a number of shifts in emphasis in the work of Rogers — from work within a formal academic structure to work with a collection of individuals who share a perspective, from work with "disturbed" individuals to work with "normal" individuals, from individual therapy to intensive group workshops, and from conventional empirical research to the phenomenological study of people: "We are deeply interested in persons but are rather 'turned-off' by the older methods of studying them as 'objects' for research" (Rogers, 1972, p. 67). From this perspective Rogers feels that most of psychology is sterile and generally feels alienated from the field. Yet, the field continues to value his contributions — he was president of the American Psychological Association in 1946 – 1947, was one of the first three psychologists to receive the Distinguished Scientific Contribution Award (1956) from the profession, and in 1972 was the recipient of the Distinguished Professional Contribution Award. In his address in receiving this award, Rogers looked back on his 46 years as a psychologist and noted his contributions to counseling, psychotherapy research, the empirical study of emotional phenomena, the philosophy of science, and the encounter group movement. He accounted for his widespread influence in the following way: "I expressed an idea whose time had come, as though a pebble was dropped in water and spread ripples. The idea was that the individual has vast resources within himself for altering his life and these resources can be mobilized given the proper climate" (Rogers, 1973).

With Rogers, the theory, the man, and the life are interwoven. In his chapter on "This Is Me," Rogers lists fourteen principles that he has learned from thousands of hours of therapy and research. Because the man, his life, and his theory are so interwoven, the principles themselves contain much of the theory. Here are some illustrations:

1. In my relationships with persons I have found that it does not help, in the long run, to act as though I were something that I am not.

2. I find I am more effective when I can listen acceptantly to myself, and can be myself.

3. I have found it of enormous value when I can permit myself to understand another person . . .

4. I have found it highly rewarding when I can accept another person.

5. Experience is, for me, the highest authority . . . It is to experience that I must return again and again, to discover a closer approximation to truth as it is in the process of becoming in me . . .

6. The facts are friendly . . . painful reorganizations are what is known as learning . . .

7. . . . what is most personal and unique in each one of us is probably the very element which would, if it were shared or expressed, speak most deeply to others.

8. It has been my experience that persons have a basically positive direction . . . I have come to feel that the more fully the individual is understood and accepted, the more he tends to drop the false fronts with which he has been meeting life, and the more he tends to move in a direction which is forward.

9. Life, at its best, is a flowing, changing process in which nothing is fixed.

ROGERS, 1961, PP. 16-27

These, then, are the personal experiences and learnings which Rogers has gathered in his role as an individual and as a theorist. Having started with the development of a therapeutic technique, he moved to an emphasis on the full humanization of the therapist-client relationship. Maintaining and expanding on his commitment to the full realization or actualization of the human potential, Rogers has emphasized the wider applicability of his theory to virtually all aspects of human existence. What began in the arena of therapy and helping relationships now has been broadened to the arenas of education, business administration, interracial relations, and even international affairs (Holdstock and Rogers, 1977). Whereas previously Rogers referred to his theory as client-centered theory, more recently he has changed the name to person-centered theory. This change in name gives expression to his emphasis on the broader relevance of the theory of personality.

ROGERS' VIEW OF THE PERSON

Implicit in Rogers' learnings and explicit in his writings, is his view of the person. For Rogers, the core of our nature is essentially positive. The direction of our movement basically is toward self-actualization, maturity, and socialization. It is Rogers' contention that religion, particularly the Christian religion, has taught us to believe that we are basically sinful. Furthermore, Rogers contends that Freud and his followers have presented us with a picture of the person with an id and an unconscious which would, if permitted expression, manifest itself in incest, murder, and other crimes. According to this view, we are at heart irrational, unsocialized, and destructive of self and others. For Rogers, we may at times function in this way, but at such times we are neurotic and not functioning as fully developed human beings. When we are functioning freely, we are free to experience and to fulfill our basic nature as positive and social animals, ones that can be trusted and basically are constructive.

Aware that others may seek to draw parallels between the behaviors of other animals and the behavior of humans, Rogers draws his own parallels. For example, he observes that, although lions are often seen as a "ravening beasts", actually they have many desirable qualities — they kill only when hungry and not for the sake of being destructive, they grow from helplessness and dependence to independence, and they move from being self-centered in infancy to being cooperative and protective in adulthood.

For Rogers the lion is, in some basic sense, a constructive and trustworthy member of the species *felis leo*. Aware that others may call him a naive optmist, Rogers is quick to point out that his conclusions are based on more than twenty-five years of experience in psychotherapy:

I do not have a Pollyana view of human nature. I am quite aware that out of defensiveness and inner fear individuals can and do behave in ways which are incredibly cruel, horribly destructive, immature, regressive, antisocial, hurtful. Yet one of the most refreshing and invigorating parts of my experience is to work with such individuals and to discover the strongly positive directional tendencies which exist in them, as in all of us, at the deepest levels.

ROGERS, 1961, P. 27

Here is a profound respect for people, a respect that is reflected in Rogers' theory of personality and his person-centered approach to psychotherapy. Although it may appear to be a somewhat extreme position, the tone and spirit of the Rogerian position is similar to that of others. A number of theories, such as those of Goldstein, Angyal, and Maslow, emphasize the continuous striving of the organism to realize its inherent potential. These theories do not assume that there are inherent destructive drives in the organism but instead posit a natural growth toward a healthy, self-realizing, self-actualizing, personality. These assumptions are part of Rogers, part of his life, and part of his theory. It will be important to keep these assumptions in mind as we attempt to understand and to assess the theory.

ROGERS' VIEW OF SCIENCE, THEORY, AND RESEARCH METHODS

Although Rogers' theory and specific research tools have changed, he has remained a phenomenologist. According to the phenomenological posi-

phenomenal field

tion of Rogers (1951), the individual perceives the world in a unique way. These perceptions make up the individual's **phenomenal field**. Individuals react to the environment as they perceive it. This environment may or may not correspond with an experimenter's definition of the environment. The phenomenal field of the individual includes both conscious and unconscious perceptions, those of which the individual is aware and those of which he is not aware. But the most important determinants of behavior, particularly in healthy people, are the ones that are conscious or capable of becoming conscious. Although the phenomenal field is essentially a world that is private to the individuals, we can (particularly with clinical material) attempt to perceive the world as it appears to individuals, to see behavior through their eyes and with the psychological meaning it has for them:

We are admitted freely into the backstage of the person's living, where we can observe from within some of the dramas of internal changes which are often far more compelling and moving than the drama which is presented on the stage viewed by the public. Only a novelist or a poet could do justice to the deep struggle which we are permitted to observe from within the client's own world of reality.

ROGERS, 1947, P. 104

In a later paper on the subject, Rogers (1964) reiterated his commitment to phenomenology as a basis for the science of the person and as the method to be used in the development of a theory of subjective phenomena. Here Rogers distinguishes among several kinds of knowledge: subjective, objective, and interpersonal. In *subjective knowledge*, we know something from our own internal frame of reference. In *objective knowledge*, what we know has been checked against the observations of others. In interpersonal knowing, we attempt to put ourselves in someone else's shoes and to understand the phenomenal field of that person — that is, we empathize. This is called *phenomenological knowledge*. According to Rogers, it represents a legitimate and necessary part of the science of psychology. Rogers argues for the use of all three kinds of knowledge, since there is "no royal road to scientific attitude" and "no such thing as a 'scientific methodology' which will see us safely through" (Rogers, 1964, p. 117). Research in psychology must involve a persistent, disciplined effort to understand the phenomena of subjective experience. In following the path of science, these efforts need not start in the laboratory or at the calculating machine, and they should not take the advanced stages of theoretical physics as the most helpful model of science.

As has been observed, Rogers believes that clinical material, obtained during psychotherapy offers a valuable source of phenomenological data. In attempting to understand human behavior, Rogers always starts with clinical observations. He attempts to listen to recorded therapeutic interviews, as naively as possible, with as few preconceptions as possible, and to develop some hypotheses concerning the events he has observed. He attempts to steep himself in the events of the human drama, to soak up clues concerning the mystery of behavior, and then to use these observations to formulate hypotheses that can be tested in a rigorous way. Rogers believes that it is legitimate to start free of concerns for objectivity and rigor, and then to move forward to the process of empirical investigation. As previously stated, Rogers views therapy as a subjective, "letting go" experience and research as an objective effort with its own kind of elegance. He is as committed to one as a source for hypotheses as he is to the other as a tool for their confirmation.

In developing this process of a constant interplay between subjective phenomena and objective research, Rogers has made an effort to develop a theory containing explicit hypotheses and explicit statements about links among the hypotheses. Rogers has tried to define his concepts and, in most cases, to develop measures for them. Since he believes in starting with inferences that stay close to what he has observed and working toward greater elaboration and refinement, he has started with a simple theoretical model and has gradually developed a fairly complex system. In line with his belief in the possibility of change in people, he is committed to the constant refinement and elaboration of personality theory. For Rogers, both people and theories are always in a state of becoming.

Throughout his career, then, Rogers has attempted to bridge the gap between the subjective and the objective, just as in his youth he felt a need to bridge the gap between religion and science. Within this context, Rogers has been concerned with the development of psychology as a science and with the preservation of people as individuals who are not simply the pawns of science. On a number of occasions, Rogers has debated with others the questions of free will and determinism, subjective choice, and the control of human behavior. The most famous of these debates was with B. F. Skinner (Rogers, 1956), a behaviorist and learning theorist whose views will be discussed later in this book. In this debate, Rogers suggested that he and Skinner agree that people always have endeavored to understand, predict, influence, and control human behavior. Furthermore, both agree that the behavioral sciences are making progress in understanding behavior and in developing the capacity to predict and control. Both are committed to a science of human behavior. However, Rogers expresses particular concern about the following: Who will be controlled? Who will control? What type of control? Toward what end or purpose? Although Rogers argues that psychotherapy is a scientific endeavor involving efforts toward prediction, influence, and control, he stresses that the goals also involve the client becoming more self-directing, less rigid, less subject to outside influence and control, and more capable of making subjective value choices. Therapy is a lawful (determined) process in which individuals achieve greater freedom to will.

THE PERSONALITY THEORY OF CARL ROGERS

As we have stated previously, Rogers' main focus has been on the process of psychotherapy. His theory of personality is an outgrowth of his theory of therapy. Also, both the theory and the focus of the related research have changed over time, from the beginnings of a Rogerian point of view in 1942 until the extension of his efforts to the treatment of schizophrenics in 1967, and continuing through the most recent extension of his efforts to schools, industry, and the relationships between races and cultures (Rogers, 1977). Throughout, however, there is a concern with how people perceive their worlds, in particular the self, and a concern with the process of change. In contrast to the psychoanalytic emphasis on drives, instincts, the unconscious, tension reduction, and early character development, the phenomenological approach emphasizes perceptions, feelings, subjective self-report, self-actualization, and the process of change. One should keep these differences in mind as the concepts and research efforts that are part of the Rogerian theory of personality are examined.

Structure

The Self

self

ideal self

The key structural concept in the Rogerian theory of personality is that of the **self**. According to Rogers, the individual perceives external objects and experiences and attaches meanings to them. The total system of perceptions and meanings make up the individual's phenomenal field. The particular perceptions and meanings that appear to be related to us, to ourselves, make up that part of the phenomenal field known as the self. The self is an organized pattern of perceptions that includes those parts of the phenomenal field seen by the individual as "self," "me," or "I" (Rogers, 1959). A related structural concept is that of **ideal self**. The ideal self is the self-concept the individual would most like to possess. It includes the perceptions and meanings that potentially are relevant to the self and that are valued highly by the individual.

There are two interesting points in relation to the Rogerian concept of self. First, Rogers views the perception of self as following the general laws of perception. Thus, the concept of self fits within what has traditionally been a basic part of psychology. Second, the self-concept is a series of interrelated parts. The self-concept represents an organized and consistent pattern of related perceptions. Although the self is changing, it always retains a patterned, coherent, integrated, and organized quality to it. The self is not made up of thousands of conditioned responses, each having occurred independent of the others, but instead it is a patterned whole that changes with the addition of new elements and yet always retains its patterned quality. Third, the self is not a little person inside of us. The self does not "do" anything. The individual does not have a self that controls behavior. Rather there is a body of experience symbolized by the self. Finally, the pattern of experiences and perceptions known as the self is, in general, available to awareness, that is, it can be made conscious. Although individuals do have experiences of which they are unaware, the self-concept is primarily conscious. Rogers believes that such a definition of the self is accurate and a necessary one for research. A definition of the self that included unconscious material, according to Rogers, could not be studied objectively. In summary, the self is an organized body of perceptions that generally is available to awareness and follows the general rules of perception.

The concept of self has a long history in psychology and has been used in a variety of ways. Hall and Lindzey (1978) have observed that, in some cases, the self has been defined as the person's attitudes and feelings about himself and, in other cases, it has been defined as a group of psychological processes that govern behavior. The former, called *self-as-object*, is clearly related to the Rogerian concept of self, whereas the latter, called the *self-as-process*, is clearly related to the Freudian concept of ego.

Just as the concept of self has been used to refer to attitudes toward the self as an object and to the self as a doer, so the concept has been used to refer to conscious and to unconscious attitudes. This has been a continuous source of confusion among self theorists. Is it true, as Vernon (1963) suggests, that the individual has many selves — a social self that is public, a conscious, private self, a private self that is not generally realized but which we can recognize when pressed to do so, and a repressed, or depth, self that is unconscious and generally prevented from becoming conscious? If so, what are the ramifications for assessment and research on the self in psychology?

Research on the Concept of Self

Rogers maintains that he did not begin his work with the concept of the self. In fact, in his first work he thought that it was a vague, scientifically meaningless term. However, as he listened to clients expressing their problems and attitudes, he found that they tended to talk in terms of the self. The concept of self finally appeared in his 1947 description of personality.

In that paper, he reported the statements made by a client, Miss Vib, who came for nine interviews. At the outset of counseling, her conscious perception of herself was reflected in statements of this kind: "I haven't been acting like myself; it doesn't seem like me; I'm a different person from what I used to be in the past." "I don't have any emotional response to situations; I'm worried about myself." "I don't understand myself; I haven't known what was happening to me." By the ninth interview, 38 days later, the perception of self had been deeply altered: "I'm taking more interest in myself." "I do have some individuality, some interests. "I can look at myself a little better." "I realize I'm just one person, with so much ability, but I'm not worried about it; I can accept the fact that I'm not always right." Statements like these convinced Rogers, and have continued to convince him, that the self is an important element in human experience and that the goal of individuals is to become their real selves.

Q-sort

Although impressed with the self-statement of clients, and by Raimy's (1948) elaborate consideration of the utility and importance of the concept, Rogers experienced the need for an objective definition of the concept, a way to measure it, and a research tool. Rogers began his research by recording therapy interview sessions and then categorizing all words that referred to the self. After the early reasearch with recorded interviews, he made considerable use of the **Q-sort** developed by Stephenson (1953). The Q-sort involves a task in which the subject sorts a number of statements, in this case about the self, into categories ranging from most characteristic to least characteristic. The Q-sort provides for a measure of statements regarding the self and the ideal self, of discrepancies between the two, and of changes over time in the two concepts (Box 4.1). The Q-sort leads to data that represent a systematic expression of subjects' perceptions of parts of their phenomenal fields. However, it does not represent a completely phenomenological report, since subjects must use statements provided by the experimenter, instead of their own, and must sort the statements into prescribed piles, representing a normal distribution, rather than according to a distribution that makes the most sense to them.

BOX 4.1 **Measurement of the Self and Ideal Self**

HYPOTHESES   (1) Client-centered counseling results in decrease of self-ideal self discrepancies. (2) Self-ideal self discrepancies will be reduced more clearly in clients who have been judged to exhibit definite improvement than in clients judged to exhibit little or no improvement.

METHOD   The experimental group (N = 25) consists of clients who are randomly selected from the adult clients of the University of Chicago

BOX 4.1   **Measurement of the Self and Ideal Self**   *continued*

Counseling Center and who complete six or more counseling interviews. The control group (N = 16) consists of adults equivalent in age, sex, socio-economic status, and student-nonstudent status who are not applicants for treatment. The experimental group is asked to sort 100 statements on a scale ("like-me" to "unlike-me") to describe themselves and to sort the same statements on a scale ("like-ideal" to "unlike-ideal") to describe the person they would most like to be. Subjects complete this task before counseling, at the end of counseling, and at a follow-up point between six months and a year following the termination of therapy. Subjects in the control group complete the sortings at the same times to test for whether there is a change as a result of the passage of time, experience with the test, or other random influences. Also, an own-control group (N = 15) is used. This consists of members of the experimental group who undergo a 60 — day control period between the time of applying for treatment and beginning treatment.

The amount of improvement is judged according to overall ratings of success by the counselors and by analysis of psychological tests by someone other than their counselors. These judgments are independent of the Q-sort ratings.

RESULTS

MEAN SELF-IDEAL/SELF CORRELATIONS FOR CLIENT AND CONTROL GROUPS*

	Precounseling	*Postcounseling*	*Follow-up*
Experimental	−.01	.34	.31
Control	.58	**	.59

1   Although the control group shows no significant change in the self-ideal self correlation, the average correlation for the client group shows a significant increase in self-ideal congruence. The gain is maintained at the follow-up point.

2   The own-control group had an average correlation of self and ideal of — .01 at pre-wait and — .01 at precounseling, indicating no change during the waiting period.

3   The group selected as definitely improved, by criteria independent of the self and ideal sorts, was found to be significantly different from the less improved group at the follow-up point though not at the pre-counseling point.

CONCLUSION   The results indicate that client-centered counseling results in an increase in congruence between self and self-ideal concepts in the client. This change reflects a rise in the level of self-esteem and adjustment.

*   The term mean refers to the average score for the individuals tested. The term correlation refers to the extent of a relationship between two sets of scores, in this case ratings of the self and ideal self. A perfect relationship between both ratings would result in a correlation of 1.00. If the two sets of scores were exactly reversed, a correlation of — 1.00 would result. An absence of any relationship at all would result in a correlation value of .00. A frequently used illustration of a positive correlation is the relationship between height and weight. Generally, although not always, taller people weigh more than shorter people. This relationship would result in a high positive correlation between height and weight.

**   Data not presented by Butler and Haigh.

SOURCE   J. M. Butler, and G. V. Haigh, Changes in the relation between self-concepts and ideal concepts consequent on client-centered counseling. In C. R. Rogers and R. F. Dymond (Eds.). *Psychotherapy and personality change.* Chicago, Ill.: University of Chicago Press, 1954, Pp. 55-75.

Other efforts to obtain subjective reports about the self have made use of the adjective checklist, in which subjects check adjectives that they feel are applicable to them, and the semantic differential, in which the subjects rate concepts such as My Self and My Ideal Self on a series of two-sided adjective scales such as good-bad or strong-weak. The Q-sort, adjective checklist, and semantic differential all approach the Rogerian ideal of phenomenological self-report, providing data that are statistically reliable and theoretically relevant. It can be argued that there are many self-concepts rather than a single self-concept, that these tests do not get at unconscious factors, and that the tests are subject to defensive distortion. Rogers feels, however, that these tests provide useful measures for the concepts of self and ideal self (as he has defined them) and that they have been a necessary part of a productive research effort. We shall not discuss the status of the concept of self and its measurement until the critique and evaluation section of the next chapter. In the meantime, we explore its relationship to other parts of the theory and its place in the related research.

Process

Self-actualization

Freud viewed the essential components of personality as relatively fixed and stable, and he developed an elaborate theory of the structure of personality. Rogers used a view of personality that emphasizes change, and he

self-actualization

has used few concepts of structure in his theory. Freud considered the person as an energy system. Thus, he developed a theory of dynamics to account for how this energy is discharged, transformed, or "dammed up." Rogers thinks of the person as forward-moving. Therefore, he has tended to deemphasize the tension-reducing aspects of behavior, in favor of an emphasis on **self-actualization**. Whereas Freud placed great emphasis on drives, for Rogers there is no motivation in the sense of drives per se. Instead, the basic tendency is toward self-actualization: "The organism has one basic tendency and striving — to actualize, maintain, and enhance the experiencing organism" (Rogers, 1951, p. 487). "It should be noted that this basic actualizing tendency is the only motive which is postulated in this theoretical system" (Rogers, 1959, p. 196).

Rogers has chosen to postulate a single motivation to life and to stay close to that idea rather than to be tied to abstract conceptualizations of many motives. But the conceptualization of a self-actualizing tendency is highly abstract and as yet has not been measured objectively. In a poetic passage, Rogers (1963) describes life as an active process, comparing it to the trunk of a tree on the shore of the ocean as it remains erect, tough, resilient, maintaining and enhancing itself in the growth process: "Here in this palm-like seaweed was the tenacity of life, the forward thrust of life, the ability to push into an incredibly hostile environment and not only to hold its own, but to adapt, develop, become itself" (Rogers, 1963, p. 2).

The concept of actualization involves the tendency on the part of the organism to grow from a simple structure to a complex one, to move from dependence toward independence, from fixity and rigidity to a process of change and freedom of expression. The concept involves tendencies on the part of the organism toward need-reduction or tension-reduction, but emphasizes the pleasures and satisfactions that are derived from activities that enhance the organism. The concept of actualization emphasizes the creative activities of the organism emphasized by the ego psychologists in psychoanalytic theory and described by White in his concept of competence motivation: "Even when its primary needs are satisfied and its homeostatic choices are done, an organism is alive, active, and up to something" (1959, p. 315).

Self-Consistency and Congruence

**self-consistency
congruence**

The concept of an organism moving toward actualization has not been the subject of empirical investigation. Much more critical to the process aspects of the theory and to research, has been Rogers' emphasis on **self-consistency** and **congruence** between self and experience. According to Rogers, the organism functions so as to maintain consistency (an absence of conflict) among self-perceptions and congruence between perceptions of the self and experiences: "Most of the ways of behaving which are adopted by the organism are those which are consistent with the concept of the self" (Rogers, 1951, p. 507). The concept of self-consistency was developed by Lecky (1945). According to Lecky, the organism does not seek to gain pleasure and to avoid pain but, instead, seeks to maintain its own self-structure. The individual develops a value system, the center of which is the individual's valuation of the self. Individuals organize their values and functions so as to preserve the self-system. For Lecky, people can be true only to themselves. Individuals will behave in a way that is consistent with their self-concept, even if this behavior is otherwise unrewarding to them. Thus, if you define yourself as a poor speller you will try to behave in a manner consistent with this self-perception.

Does the individual ever experience inconsistencies in the self, a lack of congruence between self and experience? If so, how does the individual function in order to maintain consistency and congruence? According to Rogers, we experience a state of **incongruence** when there is a discrepancy between the perceived self and actual experience. For example, if you view yourself as a person without hate and you experience hate, you are in a state of incongruence. The state of incongruence is one of tension and internal confusion. When it exists, and the individual is unaware of it, he is potentially vulnerable to anxiety. Anxiety is the result of a discrepancy between experience and the perception of the self. For the most part, we are aware of our experiences and allow them into consciousness. However, we also are capable of making experiences unavailable to awareness. Here Rogers makes reference to the process called **subception** (McCleary and Lazarus, 1949). The individual can experience a stimulus without bringing it into awareness. The individual can discriminate an experience as threatening, as being in conflict with the self-concept, and not allow it to become conscious. In the interest of maintaining congruence between self and experience, the individual denies certain experiences to awareness. The price for this is anxiety — the "subception" of the organism that the discrepant experience may enter awareness and force a change in the self-concept. Again, the person whose self-concept is that they never hate anyone will experience anxiety whenever hateful feelings are experienced to any degree at all.

The organism seeks to maintain the self-concept. Its response to a state of incongruence — to the threat presented by recognition of experiences that are in conflict with the self — is that of **defense**. An experience is dimly perceived as incongruent with the self-structure, and the organism reacts defensively so as to deny awareness of the experience. Two defensive processes are described — **distortion** of the meaning of experience and **denial** of the existence of the experience. Denial serves to preserve the self-structure from threat by denying it conscious expression. Distor-

incongruence

subception

defense

**distortion
denial**

tion, a more common phenomenon, allows the experience into awareness but in a form that makes it consistent with the self: "Thus, if the concept of self includes the characteristic 'I am a poor student', the experience of receiving a high grade can be easily distorted to make it congruent with the self by perceiving in it such meanings as, 'That professor is a fool;' 'It was just luck' " (Rogers, 1956, p. 205). What is striking about this last example is the emphasis it places on self-consistency. What is otherwise likely to be a positive experience, receiving a high grade, now becomes a source of anxiety and a stimulus for defensive processes to be set in operation. Events do not have meanings in and of themselves. Meaning is given to events by individuals with past experiences and concerns about the maintenance of a self-system.

Research on self-consistency and congruence

Rogers is not clear as to whether he has in mind actual experiences, such as emotions, or perceptions of these experiences. That is, does a person respond defensively to the experience of hostility *per se* or to the dim perception of the self as a hostile person that is in conflict with other perceptions of the self? In any case, the related research has tended to focus on perceptions. An early study in this area was performed by Chodorkoff (1954). In a study of self-perception, perceptual defense, and adjustment, Chodorkoff found that subjects were slower to perceive words that were personally threatening than they were to perceive neutral words. This tendency was particularly characteristic of defensive, poorly adjusted individuals. The poorly adjusted individual, in particular, attempts to deny awareness to threatening stimuli.

Although the Chodorkoff study involved perceptual defense, research by Cartwright (1956) involved the study of self-consistency as a factor affecting immediate recall. Following Rogers' theory, Cartwright hypothesized that individuals would show better recall for stimuli that are consistent with the self than for stimuli that are inconsistent. He hypothesized further that this tendency would be greater for maladjusted subjects than for adjusted subjects. In general, subjects were able to recall adjectives they felt were descriptive of themselves better than they were able to recall adjectives they felt were most unlike themselves. Also, there was considerable distortion in recall, for the latter, inconsistent adjectives. For example, a subject who viewed himself as hopeful mis-recalled the word "hopeless" as being "hopeful", and a subject who viewed himself as friendly mis-recalled the word "hostile" as being "hospitable." As predicted, poorly adjusted subjects (those applying for therapy and those for whom psychotherapy had been judged to be unsuccessful), showed a greater difference in recall than did adjusted subjects (those who did not plan on treatment and those for whom psychotherapy had been judged to be successful). This difference in recall scores was due particularly to the poorer recall of the maladjusted subjects for inconsistent stimuli. In a related study, an effort was made to determine the ability of subjects to recall adjectives used by others to describe them (Suinn, Osborne, and Winfree, 1962). Accuracy of recall was best for adjectives used by others that were consistent with the self-concept of subjects and was poorest for adjectives used by others that were inconsistent with the self-concept. In sum, the degree of accuracy of recall of self-related stimuli appears to be a function of the degree to which the stimuli are consistent with the self-concept.

The two studies just discussed relate to perception and recall. What of overt behavior? Aronson and Mettee (1968) considered this question and found results that were consistent with Rogers' view that the individual behaves in ways that are congruent with the concept of the self (Box 4.2). In a study of dishonest behavior, they reasoned that if people are tempted to cheat they will be more likely to do so if their self-esteem is low than if it is high; that is, whereas cheating is not inconsistent with generally low self-esteem, it is inconsistent with generally high self-esteem. The data gathered indeed suggested that whether or not an individual cheats is influenced by the nature of the self-concept. People who have a high opinion of themselves are likely to behave in ways they can respect while people with a low opinion of themselves are likely to act in ways that are consistent with that self-image.

BOX 4.2 **Self-Consistency and Behavior**

HYPOTHESES   Individuals who are provided with self-relevant information that temporarily causes them to lower their self-esteen (but does not specifically make them feel immoral or dishonest) are more apt to cheat than are those who are made to raise their self-esteem — or those who are given no self-relevant information at all (control condition). Similarly, people who are induced to raise their self-esteem will be less likely to cheat than will controls.

METHOD   Subjects are 45 females from introductory psychology classes at the University of Texas. Subjects are led to believe that they are participating in a study concerned with the relationship between personality test scores and extrasensory perception (ESP). They are told that their personalities are to be evaluated with the self-esteem scales of the California Personality Inventory (CPI) and that their ESP ability will be ascertained with the aid of a modified game of blackjack. Before participating in the blackjack game, subjects take the personality test and receive false

BOX 4.2   **Self-Consistency and Behavior**   *continued*

feedback (either positive, negative, or neutral) about their personalities. During the blackjack game, subjects are faced with the dilemma of either cheating and winning or not cheating and losing in a situation in which they are led to believe (erroneously) that cheating is impossible to detect. The opportunity to cheat occurs when the subjects are "accidentally" dealt two cards at once instead of one. The rightful card puts the subject over 21 and ensures defeat, whereas the mistakenly dealt extra card, if kept, provides the subject with a point total that virtually assures victory. Whether the subject keeps the extra card provides a measure of dishonest behavior.

RESULTS   Subjects were divided according to whether they never cheated or cheated on at least one occasion. The table below shows how many of the low self-esteem (LSE), neutral self-esteem (NSE), and high self-esteem (HSE) subjects cheated at least once. The differences in the groups were statistically significant; that is, there was a significant difference in cheating behavior among LSE, NSE, and HSE subjects.

NUMBER OF PEOPLE CHEATING AT LEAST ONCE
AS A FUNCTION OF SELF-ESTEEM

Condition	Cheat	Never Cheat
LSE	13	2
NSE	9	6
HSE	6	9

CONCLUSION   The data indicate that whether or not an individual cheated was influenced by the nature of the self-esteem feedback received. People who learned uncomplimentary information about themselves showed a far greater tendency to cheat on at least one occasion than did individuals who received positive information about themselves. The results suggest that people behave in a way that is consistent with their opinion of themselves. The development of high-esteem may be crucial in choosing moral rather than immoral behavior.

SOURCE   E. Aronson, and D. R. Mettee. Dishonest behavior as a function of differential levels of induced self-esteem. *Journal of Personality and Social Psychology*, 1968, 9, 121-127.

A final study may be noted which attempted to explore the varied ways in which our self-concept influences our behavior (Markus, 1977). The hypothesis considered was that general conceptions of the self influence how people perceive and respond to information relevant to them. The study involved three groups of undergratuate students selected on the basis of self-ratings on personality tests. One group, Independents, consisted of individuals who rated themselves high on characteristics such as independent, individualist, and leader and who rated these characteristics as important to them. The second group, Dependents, consisted of individuals who rated themselves high on characteristics such as dependent, conformist, and follower and who rated these characteristics as important to them. The third group consisted of individuals who did not rate themselves as high on either set of characteristics and did not feel that the independence-dependence dimension was an important part of their self-concept.

In one task subjects were required to view adjectives displayed on a screen and then to indicate whether the adjective applied to them. Members of the three groups differed in the words they judged to be self-descriptive. Independents judged significantly more independent words to be self-descriptive than did Dependents, whereas the reverse was true for dependent words. In both cases the third group was in-between. Perhaps even more significant was the findng that Independents were faster in their responses to independent adjectives than to dependent adjectives whereas Dependents were faster in their responses to dependent adjectives. Members of the third group did not differ in their responses to the two sets of words. Evidently the self-concept provided a readiness to respond to a particular kind of information.

On another task the subjects were asked to rate the likelihood of their behaving in a way described in a particular social situation. Some of the descriptions presented involved independent behavior ("You speak up as soon as you have some comments on the issue being discussed") while other descriptions involved dependent behavior ("You hesitate before commenting, only to hcar someone else make the point you had in mind"). Members of the three groups differed markedly in their "likelihood of behavior" ratings for the two sets of behaviors. The Independent subjects were quite sure that they would behave in an independent way and the Dependent subjects were quite sure that they would behave in a dependent way. Whereas members of these groups were relatively certain of the behavior that would be characteristic of them, members of the third group did not show as much certainty of judgment and did not indicate a greater likelihood of independent or dependent behavior. Similar differences were found in a recall task. Independents could best recall situations where they acted independently, Dependents could best recall situations where they acted in a dependent way, and members of the third group did not differ in their recall for the two kinds of behavior.

Finally, in the last situation the subjects were given information that was incongruent or inconsistent with their self-concept. After taking a phoney "Suggestibility Test," Independent subjects were told that the results indicated that they were suggestible and good followers while Dependent subjects were told that the results indicated that they were independent and not at all suggestible. Half of the members of the third group were given each type of feedback. How did subjects respond to this information, particularly when it was incongruent with the self concept? A large portion of Independent and Dependent subjects questioned the accuracy of the test while members of the third group tended to feel that the test described them accurately. In other words, the subjects with the clear conception of themselves were unwilling to accept incongruent information. Taken together, these findings provide evidence for the importance of conceptions of the self in influencing perceptions of daily events and responses to social situations. More specifically, they support Rogers' view that people seek to function in ways that are congruent with the self-concept.

The Need for Positive Regard

need for positive regard

We have, then, a number of studies supporting the view that the individual attempts to behave in accordance with the self-concept and that experiences inconsistent with the self-concept are often ignored or denied awareness. In the earlier writings of Rogers, no mention was made of the reasons for the development of a rift between experience and self and, therefore, the need for defense. In 1959 Rogers presented the concept of the **need for positive regard**. The need for positive regard includes attitudes such as warmth, liking, respect, sympathy, and acceptance and is seen in the infant's need for love and affection. If the parents give the child unconditional positive regard, if the child feels "prized" by his parents, there will be no need to deny experiences. However, if the parents make positive regard conditional, the child will be forced to disregard its own experiencing process whenever it conflicts with the self-concept. For example, if the child feels that it will only receive love (positive regard) for always being loving, it will deny all feelings of hate and struggle to preserve a picture of the self as loving. In this case the feeling of hate not only is incongruent with the self concept but also threatens the child with loss of positive regard. Thus it is that the imposition of conditions of worth on the child lead to the denial of experiences, the rift between organism and self. The origins of inaccuracies in the self-concept, the origins of conflict between the individual's experience and the self-concept, lie in the individual's attempts to retain love.

To summarize, Rogers does not feel a need to use the concepts of motives and drives to account for the activity and goal-directedness of the organism. For him, the person is basically active and self-actualizing. As part of the self-actualizing process, we seek to maintain a congruence between self and experience. However, because of past experiences with conditional positive regard, we may deny or distort experiences which threaten the self-system. The result is a state of incongruence, in which we experience anxiety and rigidly hold on to a fixed way of perceiving and experiencing.

Before we leave this section on process, we should raise some questions that will be given detailed consideration in the critique and evaluation section of the next chapter. In his conceptualization of the process of awareness and denial to awareness, to what extent does Rogers depart from the Freudian notion of the unconscious? In his description of the development of anxiety and the processes of defensive denial and distortion, to what extent does Rogers depart from the Freudian concepts of anxiety and the mechanisms of defense? Clearly, there are differences in the two points of view. We shall keep these differences in mind as we study the rest of the theoretical network.

Growth and Development

The concept of growth includes the possible courses of development and the factors accounting for one or another type of development. Rogers has not really developed a theory of growth and development and has done no research in the area in terms of long-term studies or studies of parent-child interaction. Basically, Rogers believes that growth forces exist in all individuals. The natural growth process of the organism involves greater complexity, expansion, increasing autonomy, greater socialization — in sum, self-actualization. The self becomes a separate part of the phenomenal field and becomes increasingly complex. The self develops as a total whole, so that each element is part and parcel of the total self-concept. As the self emerges, the individual develops a need for positive regard. If the need for positive regard by others becomes more important then being in touch with one's own feelings, the individual will screen various experiences out of awareness and will be left in a state of incongruence.

Self-actualization and Healthy Psychological Development

Essentially, then, the major developmental concern for Rogers is whether the child is free to grow within a state of congruence, to be self-actualizing, or whether he will become defensive and operate out of a state of incongruence. A healthy psychological development of the self takes place in a climate where the child can experience fully, can accept itself, and can be accepted by its parents, even if they disapprove of particular pieces of behavior. This is a point that is emphasized by most child psychiatrists and psychologists. It is the difference between a parent saying to a child "I don't like what you are doing" and their saying to the child "I don't like you". In saying "I don't like what you are doing" the parent is accepting the child while not approving of the behavior.

Because the budding structure of the self is not threatened by loss of love, because feelings are accepted by his parent, the child in this instance does not need to deny to awareness the satisfactions which he is experiencing, nor does he need to distort his experience of the parental reaction and regard it as his own. He retains, instead, a secure self which can serve to guide his behavior by freely admitting to awareness . . . all the relevant evidence of his experience in terms of its organismic satisfactions, both immediate and longer range. He is thus developing a sound structural self in which there is neither denial nor distortion of experience.

ROGERS, 1951, P. 503

In contrast to this climate is one in which the parents tell the child, verbally or in more subtle ways, that they feel that its behavior is bad and that it is bad. The child then feels that recognition of certain feelings would be inconsistent with the pictures of itself as loved or lovable, leading to denial and distortion of these feelings.

Research on Parent-Child Relationships and the Development of Self-esteem

Rogers refers to the studies by Baldwin (1945) of parent-child relationships for support of his views. These studies suggest that acceptant, democratic parental attitudes are most growth-facilitating. Whereas children of parents with these attitudes showed an accelerated intellectual development, originality, emotional security, and control, the children of rejecting, authoritarian parents were unstable, rebellious, aggressive, and quarrelsome. Helper (1958) found a relationship between parental evaluations and acceptance of their children and the self-evaluations of the children. Apparently, what is most critical is the children's perceptions of their parents' appraisals. If they feel that these appraisals are positive, they will find pleasure in their bodies and in their selves. If they feel that these appraisals are negative, they will develop negative appraisals of their bodies and insecurity (Jourard and Remy, 1955). Apparently, the kinds of appraisals that the parents make of their children reflect, to a considerable degree, their own degree of self-acceptance. Mothers who are self-accepting also tend to be accepting of their children (Medinnus and Curtis, 1963).

self-esteem   An extensive study of the origins of **self-esteem** gives further support to the importance of the dimensions suggested by Rogers. Coopersmith (1967) conducted a study of self-esteem, which he defined as the evaluation an individual makes and customarily maintains with regard to the self. Self-esteem, then is a personal judgment of worthiness. It is a general personality characteristic, not a momentary attitude or an attitude specific to individual situations. Self-esteem was measured by a 50 — item Self-Esteem Inventory, with most of the items coming from scales previously used by Rogers. Children in the public schools of central Connecticut filled out the inventory, and their scores were used to define groups of high, medium, and low self-esteem. When compared to children low in self-esteem, those high in self-esteem were found to be more assertive, independent, and creative. The high self-esteem subjects were also less likely to accept social definitions of reality unless they were in accord with their own observations, were more flexible and imaginative, and were capable of more original solutions to problems. In other words, the subjective estimates of self-esteem had a variety of behaviors attached to them.

Having found this behavioral support of the self-esteem measure, Coopersmith studied the origins of self-esteem. He obtained data on the children's perceptions of their parents, ratings from staff members who interviewed the mothers, and responses from the mothers to a questionnaire relating to childrearing attitudes and practices. The results indicated that external indicators of prestige such as wealth, amount of education, and job title, did not have as overwhelming and as significant an effect on self-esteem as is often assumed. Instead, the conditions in the home and the immediate interpersonal environment had the major effect on judgments of self-worth. Apparently children are influenced in their self-judgments

reflected appraisal   through a process of **reflected appraisal** in which they take the opinions of them expressed by others who are important to them and then use these opinions in their own self-judgments.

What kinds of parental attitudes and behaviors appeared to be important in the formation of self-esteem? Three areas of parent-child interaction seemed to be particularly important. The first area concerned the degree of acceptance, interest, affection, and warmth expressed toward the child. The data revealed that the mothers of children with high self-esteem were more loving and had closer relationships with their children than did mothers with low self-esteem. The interest on the part of the mother appeared to be interpreted by children as an indication of their significance, that they were worthy of the concern, attention, and time of those who were important. The second critical area of parent-child interaction related to permissiveness and punishment. The data relevant to this area of parent-child interaction revealed the following:

The conditions that exist within the families of children with high self-esteem are notable for the demands the parents make and the firmness and care with which they enforce these demands. Reward is the preferred mode of affecting behavior, but where punishment is required it is geared to managing undesired responses rather than to harsh treatment or loss of love . . . The total amount of punishment administered in these families is no less than in others, but it is different in its expression and is perceived as justifiable by our high self-esteem subjects.

COOPERSMITH, 1967, P. 19

In contrast to this pattern, the parents of children low in self-esteem gave little guidance and relatively harsh and disrespectful treatment. The parents did not establish and enforce guidelines for their children, were apt to use punishment rather than reward, and tended to lay stress on force and loss of love.

Finally, differences were found in parent-child interactions in relation to democratic practices. Parents of children with high self-esteem established an extensive set of rules and were zealous in enforcing them, but treatment within the defined limits was noncoercive and recognized the rights and opinions of the child. Parents of children low in self-esteem set few and poorly defined limits and were autocratic, dictatorial, rejecting, and uncompromising in their methods of control. Coopersmith summarized his findings as follows: "The most general statement about the origins of self-esteem can be given in terms of three conditions: total or nearly total acceptance of the children by their parents, clearly defined and enforced limits, and the respect and latitude for individual actions that exist within the defined limits" (Coopersmith, 1967, p. 236) (Box 4.3). Coopersmith further suggested that it is the perception of the parents by the child and not necessarily the specific actions they express that is important, and that the total climate in the family influenced the child's perception of the parents and their motives.

BOX 4.3   **Origins of Self-esteem**

PROBLEM   What are the relationships between different patterns of parent-child interaction and the development of self-esteem?

METHOD   Subjects are preadolescents of middle class backgrounds who are male, white, and normal. A 50 — item Self-Esteem Inventory is used to measure self-esteem from the perspective of the subject. A Behavior

Rating Form, involving teacher ratings of the children, is used as an observer measure of theoretically related behaviors.

Information on the children's experiences and relationships is obtained from both the mothers and the children. Information from the children comes from their responses to questionnaire items relating to parental treatment and home life and from responses to a psychological test. Information from a mother comes from her responses to questionnaire items relating to childrearing attitudes and practices and responses to an interview. Information about the father is obtained from both mother and child, but there is no direct contact with the father himself.

RESULTS

1 Parent-Child Relationships: Acceptance. Mothers of children with high self-esteem are more loving and have closer relationships with their children than do mothers of children with less self-esteem.

Illustrative Item (p. 177): "Children should not annoy their parents with their unimportant problems." (Source. Mother's Questionnaire)

SUBJECTIVE SELF-ESTEEM (%)

Reply	Low	Medium	High
Disagree	26.5	68.7	54.8
Agree	73.5	31.3	45.2

2 Parent-Child Relationships: Permissiveness and Punishment. The conditions that exist within the families of children with high self-esteem are notable for the demands the parents make and the firmness and care with which they enforce those demands. In the familial conditions of children with low self-esteem, there is a lack of parental guidance and relatively harsh and disrespectful treatment.

Illustrative Item (p. 186): Care and consistency with which rules are enforced (Source. Mother's Interview)

SUBJECTIVE SELF-ESTEEM (%)

Degree of Enforcement	Low	Medium	High
Relatively careful and consistent enforcement	60.0	58.8	87.9
Moderate or little enforcement of rules	40.0	41.2	12.1

BOX 4.3 **Origins of Self-esteem**

continued

3 Parent-Child Relationships: Democratic Practices. In the families of high self-esteem children, there is a clear setting of limits, but within these limits parental treatment is non-coercive and recognizes the rights and opinions of the child. For the low esteem children, there are few and poorly defined limits and harsh and autocratic methods of control.

Illustrative Item (p. 214): Procedure generally employed to obtain child's cooperation or compliance. (Source. Mother's Interview)

SUBJECTIVE SELF-ESTEEM (%)

Procedure	Low	Medium	High
Stress discussion and reasoning	40.0	52.9	78.8
Stress force, autocratic means	60.0	47.1	21.2

CONCLUSION   The most general statement about the origins of self-esteem can be given in terms of three conditions: total or nearly total acceptance of the children by their parents, clearly defined and enforced limits, and the respect and latitude for individual action that exist within the defined limits.

SOURCE S. Coopersmith. *The antecedents of self-esteem.* San Francisco: W. H. Freeman, 1967.

Rogers' views on the parent characteristics and practices that influence the child's development of self-esteem have influenced the thinking of researchers and childcare experts. While not always referring to Rogers, in many cases their emphasis on respect for the child and protection of the child's self-esteem speaks to the influence of Rogers and other members of the human potential movement. His emphasis on the conditions that promote self-actualization and the conditions that block it will receive further attention in the next chapter when we consider the clinical applications of the theory.

MAJOR CONCEPTS AND SUMMARY

phenomenological	congruence
self	incongruence
ideal self	subception
Q-sort	defense: distortion and denial
self-actualization	need for positive regard
self-consistency	self-esteem

Before turning to the clinical applications of Rogers' theory of personality, let us take stock of the theorist and the basic theory of personality. In this chapter we have begun to see how Rogers attempted in his own life and in his theory to combine the religious and the scientific, the philosophical and the pragmatic. The emphasis by Rogers is on what is "good" and self-actualizing in people. Humans are unique among the species. Basic to this uniqueness is the awareness of a sense of self and of movement toward self-actualization.

The ways in which we experience events, in particular ourselves, is central in Rogers' theory. The sense of self represents an organized pattern or set of experiences and perceptions. In our daily functioning we seek to preserve the sense of self and, beyond this, to move toward self-actualization, a process of continuing growth and development. It is this emphasis on self-actualization as the central motivation that links Rogers with the human potential movement.

Self-actualization involves continuous openness to experience and the ability to integrate experiences into an expanded, more differentiated sense of self. Self-actualizing, "fully-functioning" people are trusting of themselves as well as others, open to their own experiences as well as those of others, spontaneous and flexible, free to be creative, and able to respond to others in a geniune, non-defensive way. We are most able to self-actualize when we have a sense of self and self-worth that is not easily threatened. During the early years it is up to the parents to provide the basic acceptance and respect for the child that facilitates the development of such a sense of self. If such conditions are not provided, if the child experiences itself as conditionally accepted or rejected, then there is not room for growth and self-actualization. Under such conditions the child, out of a fear of loss of love, must reject experiences which are incongruent with the desired sense of self and which therefore arouse anxiety.

We have here the basic elements of the theory. However, as we shall see, many of these concepts become most meaningful in relation to Rogers' discussions of the problems of his clients and the process of psychotherapy. During most of the development of the theory, Rogers' main commitment has been to psychotherapy and the process of affecting change — to understanding the conditions that provide for therapeutic change and self-actualization. The personality theory really is an outgrowth of these clinical and research efforts. Therefore, it will not be surprising to find considerable elaboration of the basic concepts when viewed within the context of psychopathology and change.

CLINICAL APPLICATIONS

Psychopathology

Change
- The History of Client-Centered Therapy
- Therapeutic Conditions Necessary for Change
- The Process of Personality Change
- Outcomes of Client-Centered Therapy

A CASE EXAMPLE — MRS. OAK

RELATED POINTS OF VIEW AND RECENT DEVELOPMENTS

The Human Potential Movement
- Kurt Goldstein
- Abraham Maslow

Rogers' Shift in Emphasis: From Individuals to Groups and Society

CRITICAL EVALUATION

Phenomenology

The Concept of Self

Conflict, Anxiety, and Defence

Growth and Development

Psychopathology and Change

Summary Evaluation

MAJOR CONCEPTS AND SUMMARY

5 A PHENOMENOLOGICAL THEORY: APPLICATIONS AND EVALUATION OF ROGERS' THEORY

Chapter Focus:

Rogers' theory of personality has followed from his work with clients. His major emphasis has been on how individuals are led to deny and distort experience and on the conditions that provide the basis for all growth and therapeutic change. Also considered in this chapter are other significant figures in the human potential movement (Goldstein and Maslow) and an overall evaluation of Rogers' theory of personality.

I wanted only to try to live in accord with the promptings which came from my true self. Why was that so very difficult?

PASSAGE FROM DEMIAN,
By H. HESSE, 1965, p. 80

It also means that if the counselor is congruent or transparent, so that his words are in line with his feelings rather than the two being discrepant—if the counselor likes the client, unconditionally, and if the counselor understands the essential feelings of the client as they seem to the client—then there is a strong probability that this will be an effective helping relationship.

ROGERS, 1961, P. 103

CLIENT   That's why I want to go, 'cause I don't care what happens.

THERAPIST   M-hm, m-hm. That's why you want to go, because you really don't care about yourself. You just don't care what happens. And I guess I'd just like to say—I care about you. And I care what happens. (Silence of 30 seconds) (Jim bursts into tears and unintelligible sobs)

THERAPIST   (*Tenderly*) Somehow that just makes all the feelings pour out.

ROGERS, 1967, P. 409

Clinical Applications

In this section on clinical applications we will consider Rogers' views on psychotherapy and personality change. These views are an important part of the theory; in fact, the major part of Rogers' professional life has involved these clinical applications. The person-centered approach developed first in counseling and psychotherapy, where it has been known as **client-centered therapy**, "meaning that a person seeking help was not treated as a dependent patient but rather as a responsible client" (Rogers, 1977, p. 5). Rather than focusing on an illness model of abnormal behavior and a medical model of a doctor treating a patient, Rogers has emphasized the individual's drive toward health, the conditions that may interfere with such growth, and the therapeutic conditions that help to remove obstacles to self-actualization.

client-centered therapy

Psychopathology

The essential elements of the Rogerian view of psychopathology have been given in the last chapter in the sections on process and growth and development. For Rogers, the healthy person does or can assimilate experiences into the self-structure. In the healthy person, there is a congruence between self and experience, an openness to experience, a lack of defensiveness. In contrast to this, the neurotic person's self-concept has become structured in ways which do not fit organismic experience. The psychologically maladjusted individual must deny to awareness significant sensory and emotional experiences. Experiences that are incongruent with the self-structure are *subceived* as threatening and are either denied or distorted. The result is a rigid, defensive maintenance of the self against experiences that threaten the wholeness of the self and frustrate the need for positive self-regard. Rogers sees no utility in diagnosing different psychopathological illnesses, viewing such diagnoses as meaningless tools. Psychotic behaviors are viewed as behaviors that are inconsistent with the self but which have broken through the defensive processes. "Thus the person who has kept sexual impulses rigidly under control, denying them as an aspect of self, may now make open sexual overtures to those with whom he is in contact. Many of the so-called irrational behaviors of psychosis are of this order" (Rogers, 1959, p. 230).

defensive behaviors

Although Rogers does not differentiate among forms of pathology, he does differentiate among types of **defensive behaviors**. The defensive behaviors described are similar to those described by Freud. For example, in *rationalization* the person distorts behavior in such a way as to make it consistent with the self. For example, if you view yourself as a person who does not make mistakes, you are likely to attribute a mistake to some other factor. Another example of defensive behavior is *fantasy*. A man who defensively believes himself to be an adequate person may fantasize that he is a prince, that all women adore him, he may deny any experiences that would be inconsistent with this image. A third example of defense behavior is *projection*. Here the individual expresses a need, but it is expressed in a form such that the need is denied to awareness and the behavior is viewed as consistent with the self. People whose self-concept involves no "bad" sexual thoughts may feel that others are making them have these thoughts. The descriptions of these defensive behaviors are quite similar to the ones given by Freud. For Rogers, however, the important aspect of these behaviors is their handling of an incongruence between self and experience by denial in awareness or distortion of perception: "It should be noted that perceptions are excluded because they are contradictory, not because they are derogatory" (Rogers, 1951, p. 506). Furthermore, the classification of the defenses is not as critical to Rogerian theory as it is to Freudian theory.

Although in his 1951 presentation of the theory Rogers interpreted psychological pathology in terms of disturbed relationships between self and experience, most of the related research has been on the relationship between the self and ideal-self concepts. For example, in the study by Butler and Haigh (1954), described in the last chapter, the discrepancy between self and ideal-self (Q-sorts) was used as a measure of maladjustment and improvement in treatment. Throughout the Rogers and Dymond book, *Psychotherapy and Personality Change* (1954), the discrepancy between self and ideal-self ratings is referred to as a measure of adjustment, and it has frequently been used as such in later research. The use of this measure would appear to date back to the observation by Raimy (1948) that, as successful personality reorganization occurs in psychotherapy, there is a shift from self-disapproval to self-approval statements. The discrepancy between self and ideal-self statements is then assumed to be a legitimate measure of self-esteem and healthy personality organization. Unfortunately, the self-ideal discrepancy does not appear to be a measure of the discrepancy between experience and self. Yet, it is this incongruence between self and experience that Rogers describes as being basic to psychopathology.

Later in his career, Rogers, along with Gendlin (1962), gave more specific attention to the experiencing process and to the measurement of this process. According to Rogers (1958, 1961, 1967), maladjusted people are likely to be unaware of feelings that they exhibit and which are obvious to an observer. They are unaware of self-contradictory statements and seek to avoid expressions that would be revealing to themselves. Close relationships are perceived as dangerous, and involvement with others is avoided. In contrast, healthy people are likely to experience and express feelings, to take responsibility for ownership of these feelings, and to "risk" themselves in relationships with others. Rogers (Walker, Rablen, and Rogers, 1960) has developed a scale to measure how individuals relate to their feelings and how they experience feelings. The scale relates to statements made by individuals, generally clients in a therapeutic interview, which are then rated by judges according to prescribed rules. For example, according to the scale maladjusted prople would express disownership of feelings or a vagueness about their feelings. Statements representative of these states would be "The symptom was—it was—just being depressed" and "I am experiencing something vague and puzzling which I do not understand." In contrast to this mode of experience, healthy people accept their feelings ("I am depressed.") and are clearer about them. The scale represents an attempt to gather data, in a systematic way, on the individual's mode of relating to the self and to others. Although still not a measure of the discrepancy between self and experience, the scale does begin to give attention to the way individuals relate to their feelings, a variable that Rogers has long felt to be critical to psychopathology.

Change

The client-centered point of view has a number of distinguishing characteristics. These include the developing hypothesis that certain attitudes in the therapist constitute the necessary and sufficient conditions of therapeutic effectiveness; the developing concept of the therapist's function as being immediately present to his client, relying on his moment-to-moment felt experience in the relationship; the continuing focus on the phenomenal world of the client; a developing theory that the therapeutic process is marked by a change in the client's manner of experiencing and an ability to live more fully in the immediate moment; a continuing stress on the self-actualizing quality of the human organism as the motivating force in therapy; a concern with the process of personality change, rather than with the structure of personality; a stress on the necessity of research to discover the essential truths of psychotherapy; the hypothesis that the same principles of psychotherapy apply to the competently functioning business executive, the maladjusted and neurotic person who comes to a clinic, and the hospitalized psychotic on the back ward; a view of psychotherapy as one specialized example of all constructive interpersonal relationships, with the consequent generalized applicability of all our knowledge from the field of therapy; and, finally, a concern with the philosophical and value issues that grow out of the practice of therapy.

ROGERS, 1966, PP. 183-184

As stated above, although a theory of personality has developed out of Rogers' experiences in client-centered therapy, his central focus has been on the therapeutic process itself. Rogers' main concern is with the manner in which personality change comes about. Although he is interested in the process of change generally, he has committed himself to a continuous subjective and objective involvement with the process of change in psychotherapy in particular. The titles of his books reflect this orientation and emphasis: *Clinical Treatment of the Problem Child* (1939), *Counseling and Psychotherapy* (1942), *Client-Centered Therapy* (1951), *Psychotherapy and Personality Change* (with R. F. Dymond, 1954), *The Therapeutic Relationship and Its Impact* (in collaboration with others, 1967). In summary, for Rogers, change and growth in therapy represent a special instance of growth and development that can occur in any human being. It is this process, the process of becoming, that is of greatest concern to him.

The History of Client-Centered Therapy

Seeman (1965), in his review of the development of client-centered therapy, observed that the theory and techniques of therapy have been just as much a part of a process of change as has therapy itself. Seeman described three phases in the history of client-centered therapy. In the first phase, Rogers placed great emphasis on the therapist's use of the technique of reflection of feeling. "As material is given by the client, it is the therapist's function to help him recognize and clarify the emotions which he feels" (Rogers, 1940, p. 162). According to this view, there is to be a minimum of therapist activity and guidance of what the client says—the nondirective view. In particular, the therapist was not to offer interpretations about unexpressed attitudes or about the unconscious. The task of the therapist was to recognize and clarify the client's expressed feelings. Research at this point tended to focus on the therapist's behavior. For example, a study by Gump (1944) compared nondirective methods of treatment with psychoanalytic methods. Gump found that psychoanalytic methods involved a greater proportion of interpretation, whereas nondirective methods emphasized more reflection of feelings. In both methods, however, the client did more than 70 percent of the talking.

Rogers believed that a misconception about his goals was developing. Some counselors who thought that they were being nondirective were merely being passive and seemingly uninterested. Also, the emphasis on "technique" led to over intellectualizing by some counselors. Rogers began to realize that the same statement on the part of the counselor could be given in a way that expresses indifference, critical judgment, or empathy and understanding. In the second phase, therefore, Rogers changed his focus from an emphasis on the counselor's being nondirective to an emphasis on his being *client-centered*. The emphasis changed from one on technique to one on attitude. The counselor was to have an attitude of interest in the phenomenal world of the client. "This formulation would state that it is the counselor's function to assume, in so far as he is able, the internal frame of reference of the client, to perceive the world as the client sees it, to perceive the client himself as he is seen by himself . . . and to communicate something of an empathetic understanding to the client" (Rogers, 1951, p. 29). Counselors were to be involved with an active experiencing of their clients' feelings. They were, in an empathic way, to get under the skin of their clients, to understand clients as the clients seem to themselves.

In this second phase, attention was given to process elements in therapy. Emphasis was placed on the client's increased awareness of previously denied attitudes, on the client's increased ability to evaluate phenomena and on reorganization of the self-concept. His 1954 book contained a variety of studies on changes in the self-concept during therapy. During this period, the Q-sort was used extensively in research, as illustrated in the Butler and Haigh study discussed in the last chapter, where clients were found to have large self-ideal discrepancies at the beginning of treatment and smaller discrepancies by the end of the treatment.

In the third phase of client-centered therapy, there has been increased emphasis on the therapeutic atmosphere. Rogerian therapists are not detached but involved. They express feelings and are involved in a relationship with their clients. There is an increased emphasis on experiencing rather than verbal self-exploration. Increasingly, there is the sense of a counselor and a client involved in a relationship. There is an emphasis in research on the therapeutic climate and the process of personality change.

Although client-centered therapy has been changing, it has retained from its inception certain distinguishing characteristics (Rogers, 1946, 1977). First, there is the belief in the capacity of the client. Since the basic strivings of the organism are toward growth, actualization, and congruence, the therapist need not control or manipulate the therapeutic process. Second, there is an emphasis on the importance of the therapeutic relationship. What is important is that the therapist attempt to understand the client and to communicate this understanding. In contrast to the psychoanalytic search for hidden meanings and insights into the unconscious, the Rogerian therapist believes that personality is revealed in what clients say about themselves. Diagnoses are not important, since they say little about peoples' view of themselves and do not help to create the necessary therapeutic relationship. Third, there is the belief that client-centered therapy involves a predictable process. Growth occurs if the therapist establishes a helping relationship and is able to help free the strong drive of the individual to become mature, independent, and productive. "Given certain conditions, the individual has the capacity to reorganize his field of perception, including the way he perceives himself, and that a concomitant, or a resultant, of this perceptual reorganization is an appropriate alteration of behavior" (Rogers, 1947, p. 361). Finally, with his research emphasis, Rogers has tried to maintain ties among theory, therapy, and research. The client-centered theory of therapy is an if-then theory. The theory states that if certain *conditions* exist, then a *process* will occur that will lead to personality and behavioral change.

Therapeutic Conditions Necessary for Change

It is Rogers' belief that the critical variable in therapy is that of the therapeutic climate (Rogers, 1966). If therapists can provide three conditions in their relationships with their clients, in a way that is phenomenologically meaningful to the clients, then therapeutic change will occur. The three conditions hypothesized by Rogers to be critical to therapeutic movement are **congruence** or genuineness, **unconditional positive regard**, and **empathic understanding**. Genuine therapists are themselves. They do not give a facade but rather are open and transparent. Therefore, clients feel that they can be trusted. Congruent or genuine therapists feel free to be what they are, to experience events in the therapeutic encounter as they occur. They can be with their clients on a person-to-person basis and be themselves. In a genuine relationship, therapists are free to share feelings with their patients, even when negative feelings toward the client are involved: "Even with such negative attitudes, which seem so potentially

congruence

unconditional positive regard

empathic understanding

damaging but which all therapists have from time to time, I am suggesting that it is preferable for the therapist to be real than to put on a false posture of interest, concern, and liking that the client is likely to sense as false" (Rogers, 1966, p. 188).

The second condition essential for therapeutic movement is that of unconditional positive regard. This means that the therapist communicates a deep and genuine caring for the client as a person; the client is prized in a total, unconditional way. The unconditional positive regard provided by the therapist provides a nonthreatening context in which clients can explore their inner selves.

Finally, the third condition of empathic understanding involves the ability of the therapist to perceive experiences and feelings and their meaning to the client during the moment-to-moment encounter of psychotherapy. It is not a diagnostic formulation of the client's experiences, or a rote reflection of what the client says, but instead a "being with" the client while being oneself. It is active listening and understanding of the feelings and personal meanings as they are experienced by the client.

A number of research studies have influenced Rogers' thinking regarding the importance of the therapeutic climate. Others have been influenced by his formulation. Essentially, Rogers is talking about factors that go beyond all forms of psychotherapy, factors that are independent of the theoretical orientation of the therapist, unless that orientation prevents the development of a helping relationship. In one important study, Fiedler (1950) had judges listen to the recorded interviews of experts and nonexperts of the psychoanalytic, nondirective (Rogerian), and Adlerian schools. The judges then sorted a number of descriptive items according to the extent to which they were characteristic of the interview. Fiedler found that, compared to nonexperts, experts were more successful in creating an "ideal" therapeutic relationship. Independent of orientation, experts were similar to one another in their ability to understand, to communicate with, and to maintain rapport with the client. In a related study, Heine (1950) investigated the relation between the theoretical orientation of therapists and therapeutic progress as viewed by clients. Clients sorted a number of statements to describe the changes they felt had occurred while in treatment and a number of statements to describe the therapeutic factors that they felt were responsible for the changes. Heine found that, according to their own reports, patients from psychoanalytic, nondirective, and Adlerian schools did not differ in the kinds of changes they reported had occurred. Furthermore, the clients who reported the greatest changes described similar factors as being responsible for these changes. A later study by Halkides (1958) found that the existence of the attitudes of genuineness, positive regard, and empathy in the therapist were related to therapeutic success.

The Process of Personality Change

Although these and other related studies lend support to the Rogerian emphasis on the importance of a therapeutic climate, they do not give us insight into the process of change or details about the kinds of changes that do occur as a result of therapy. Rogers suggests that, when the necessary therapeutic conditions are present, a specific process is set in motion. In his earliest formulations, Rogers viewed the therapeutic process as involving the release of personal feelings (emotional catharsis), followed by insight into the origin and nature of the difficulties, and concluding with the application of the insights to positive choices and decisions. Support was indeed found for this view. For example, Snyder (1945) studied the process of therapy and found that initially the client released negative feelings, after which insight emerged and, finally, active planning. However, Rogers began to feel the need to attend to the process of change in the self. After a period of emphasis on the process of self-integration, Rogers moved toward a fresh picture of the process of change. According to his most recent model of the process of change, individuals move from fixity, rigid structure, and stagnation at one end of the continuum to changingness, flow, and process at the other end. The therapeutic process involves movement from the early stages to the later stages in each of seven areas (Box 5.1).

BOX 5.1 **The Process of Personality Change**

There is a continuum that applies to all personality change and development. There are seven areas (strands) in the change process. In each area there are seven stages. At one end of the stage continuum there is fixity, rigidity, and stagnation; at the other end of the stage continuum there is changingness, flow, and process.

STRAND 1 Relationship to Feelings and Personal Meanings
Low Stage: Feelings are unrecognized or unexpressed.
High Stage: Feelings are experienced freely in the immediate moment.

STRAND 2 Manner of Experiencing
Low Stage: Individual is remote from experiencing.
High Stage: Experience is an accepted inner event.

STRAND 3 Degree of Incongruence
Low Stage: Individual is unaware of contradictory self-statements.
High Stage: Individual is able to recognize temporary moments of incongruence.

BOX 5.1   **The Process
of Personality Change** *continued*

STRAND 4   Communication of Self
    Low Stage: Individual avoids revealing himself.
    High Stage: Individual experiences his self and is able to communicate his self-awareness.
STRAND 5   Manner in which Experience is Construed
    Low Stage: Individual has rigid views which he accepts as fact.
    High Stage: Personal views are recognized to be ways of construing a moment of experiencing and are open to change.
STRAND 6   Relationship to Problems
    Low Stage: Problems not recognized or perceived to be external to self, and individual is closed to change.
    High Stage: Individual lives his problem and seeks to cope with it.
STRAND 7   Manner of Relating
    Low Stage: Close relationships avoided as dangerous.
    High Stage: Individual risks being himself in the process of relating to others.

SOURCE   C. R. Rogers. A tentative scale for the measurement of process in psychotherapy. In M. I. Stein (Ed.), *Contemporary psychotherapies.* New York: Free Press, 1961. Pp. 113-127.

The process of change in client-centered therapy involves changes in the self-concept and ways of experiencing the self. This leads to changes in behavior. The self normally resists incorporating into itself experiences that are inconsistent. But when the self is free from threat, previously rejected perceptions and feelings may be integrated into the self-concept. The unconditional positive regard of the counselor provides a safe and protective atmosphere in which individuals can examine all their experiences. The empathy of the counselor assists the clients in recognizing and labelling their feelings. The fact that positive regard is not withdrawn enables the clients to experience their worthless selves and yet accept themselves as worthwile. The fact that the therapists are congruent, that they not only accept the clients' experiences but are accepting of their own, enables the clients to internalize this attitude of the therapist and to look on experiences as something to be recognized, owned, and treasured. The operation of these forces is movingly described in the following passages from letters between Eldridge Cleaver, then a prisoner, and Beverly Axelrod, then his lawyer.

AXELROD   I'm going purely on instinct now, which is not usual for me, but somehow I know I'm right, or maybe its just that it's so important that I don't care about the risk of being wrong . . . Believe this: I accept you. I know you little and I know you much, but whichever way it goes I accept you.

CLEAVER   I share with you the awesome feeling of being on the verge of really knowing another person. (I place a great deal of emphasis on people really listening to each other, to what the person has to say, because one seldom encounters a person capable of taking either you or themselves seriously . . .) Do you know what shameless thought just bullied its way into my consciousness? That I deserve you, that I deserve to know you and to communicate with you, that I deserve to have all this happening. What have I done to merit this? I don't believe in the merit system. I Am That I Am. No. I will not hurt you.

E. CLEAVER, SOUL ON ICE,
1968, Pp. 145, 147.

Outcomes of Client-Centered Therapy

What, then, are the changes brought about by client-centered therapy? A significant number of research studies have been completed on the outcomes of client-centered therapy. In the section on therapeutic conditions, we already have noted a number of studies which support the view that, given certain therapeutic conditions, positive change does come about. The changes studied, by and large, have related to Rogerian concepts. Furthermore, the research has been done using techniques (Q-sorts, rating scales, etc.) related to these concepts. The following is illustrative of the kinds of changes that have been studied and documented by both clinical illustration and empirical evidence:

1 *Change in ability to evaluate phenomena.* In the course of therapy, there is a shift away from using the values of others toward asserting one's own evaluations (Ruskin, 1949).

2 *Change in defensiveness and manner of experiencing.* In the course of therapy, clients become less defensive, more flexible, more consciously aware of material previously unavailable to awareness, more differentiating in their perceptions, and more open to experiencing themselves (Haigh, 1949: Kessler, 1949; Rogers, 1951; Rogers, 1953; Vargas, 1954).

3 *Change in self-concept.* In the course of therapy, clients develop a clearer, more positive, and more congruent self (Butler and Haigh, 1954; Raimy, 1948; Rogers, 1951, pp. 136-141; Sheerer, 1949; Stock, 1949).

4 *Change in views of others and mode of relating to others.* In the course of therapy, clients not only develop a greater sense of their own worth but also change their evaluation of others in a positive direction. Clients also learn to accept positive feelings from others and to express their own positive feelings (Rogers, 1953; Sheerer, 1949; Stock, 1949).

5 *Change in maturity and organization of personality.* In the course of therapy, clients show an increase in the maturity of reported behavior, show greater tolerance for frustration and quicker recovery to a frustrating situation, and show personality changes on broader measures of personality than the Q-sort (Dymond, 1954; Haimowitz, 1948; Hoffman, 1949; Jonietz, 1950; Muench, 1947; Thetford, 1949; Vargas, 1954).

Many findings support the specific views presented by Rogers within the client-centered framework. In a more philosophical vein, they involve what Rogers calls being one's organism, being one's experience. In a statement that recalls the feelings expressed in the passage by Eldridge Cleaver quoted previously, Rogers summarizes his views as follows: "In therapy the individual has actually become a human organism, with all the richness which that implies. He is realistically able to control himself, and he is incorrigibly socialized in his desires. There is no beast in man. There is only man in man, and this we have been able to release" (Rogers, 1953, p. 67). Notice that most of the above studies were reported between the late 1940s and the mid–1950s. More recently, Rogers (1967) has completed a major study of the therapeutic relationship and its impact on hospitalized schizophrenic patients.

The 1967 study of therapeutic impact involved a test of the if-then hypotheses formulated by Rogers. Instruments were developed to measure therapist empathy, congruence (genuinesess), and unconditional positive regard. The relationship was evaluated by judges who listened to recorded passages from the therapy interviews, by the patients, and by the therapists. Scales were used to measure the process aspect of therapy, in terms of the seven areas and seven stages of the continuum discussed previously. The variable of the immediacy of client's experiencing was critical. Again, judges made ratings of the functioning of the patients in terms of their behavior in recorded sample interviews. The outcome was evaluated according to a variety of criteria—scores on tests, ratings by therapists, and changes in hospitalization status. The study is a difficult one to report and to evaluate because many variables were used and relationships held for some variables but not for others. Rogers himself observed that problems in the research and the design made it difficult for the study to provide for a critical test of the theory. However, a number of important developments, observations, and findings did occur in the course of the research. Some of the relevant conclusions follow:

1 It is possible to develop rating scales to measure therapy conditions and dimensions of the process of client experiencing.

2 There is evidence that positive therapeutic conditions and a patient's feeling of involvement are related to positive personality change.

3 Therapist relationship factors appear to be more crucial for schizophrenics than for neurotics. Compared to neurotics, schizophrenics are less interested in self-exploration and more concerned with the issue of trust.

4 There was evidence that competent and conscientious therapists who have been unable to establish high levels of empathy, genuineness, and unconditional positive regard in their relationship may actually worsen the condition of their schizophrenic patients.

5 The establishment of a therapeutic climate is not dependent on therapist or patient factors alone, but is a complex function of the dynamic interaction between the capacities, attitudes, and motives of patient and therapist.

This study of the therapeutic relationship continues the Rogerian tradition of research on human behavior without a movement toward neurological or biological aspects of behavior, or toward a fragmented study of isolated components of behavior. It continues the Rogerian tradition of the systematic observation of complex phenomena:

In this combining of . . . clinical intuition with hard-headed empiricism, we believe that we are groping toward a new philosophy of the behavioral sciences—one which will be freed of the rigid confines of a strict behaviorism, but which will also be free of the irresponsibility of dogmatic speculation.

ROGERS, 1967, P. 545

A CASE EXAMPLE—MRS. OAK

One of Rogers' outstanding contributions to the field of psychotherapy has been his leadership in opening it up as an area for investigation. He has made available a verbatim transcript of therapy (Rogers, 1942), films of client-centered therapy sessions and a file of recorded therapy sessions that can be used for research purposes. In his 1954 volume on psychotherapy and personality change, Rogers presented an extensive analysis of a single case, the case of Mrs. Oak. As Rogers observes, it is the individual case that makes a total research investigation come to life, which brings diverse facts together in the interrelated way in which they exist in life. The case of Mrs. Oak is presented here to illustrate the Rogerian approach to an understanding of personality.

Mrs. Oak was a housewife in her late thirties when she came to the University of Chicago Counseling Center for treatment. At that time, she was having great difficulty in her relationship with her husband and her adolescent daughter. Mrs. Oak blamed herself for the daughter's psychosomatic illness. Mrs. Oak was described by her therapist as a sensitive person who was eager to be honest with herself and deal with her problems. She had little formal education but was intelligent and had read widely. Mrs. Oak was interviewed 40 times over a period of 5½ months, at which point she terminated treatment. A battery of tests were given to her at the beginning of treatment, at the end of treatment, and seven months after the end of treatment.

In the early interviews, Mrs. Oak spent much of her time talking about specific problems with her daughter and her husband. Gradually, there was a shift from these reality problems to descriptions of feelings:

> And, secondly, the realization that last time I was here I experienced a- an emotion I had never felt before—which surprised me and sort of shocked me a bit. And yet I thought, I think it has sort of a . . . the only word I can find to describe it, the only verbalization is a kind of cleansing. I-I really felt terribly sorry for something, a kind of grief.
>
> P. 311

At first the therapist thought Mrs. Oak was a shy, almost nondescript person and was neutral toward her. He quickly sensed, however, that she was a sensitive and interesting person. His respect for her grew and he describes himself experiencing a sense of respect for, and awe of, her capacity to struggle ahead through turmoil and pain. He did not try to direct or guide her. Instead, he found satisfaction in trying to understand her, in trying to appreciate her world, in expressing the acceptance he felt toward her.

> MRS. OAK And yet the-the fact that I—I really like this I don't know, call it a poignant feeling. I mean . . . I felt things that I've never felt before. I like that, too. Uh-Uh . . . maybe that's the way to do it. I-I just don't know today.
>
> THERAPIST (M-hm.) Don't feel at all sure, but you know that you somehow have a real, a real fondness for this poem that is yourself. Whether it's the way to go about this or not, you don't know.
>
> P. 314

Given this supportive therapeutic climate, Mrs. Oak began to become aware of feelings she had previously denied to awareness. In the twenty-fourth interview, she became aware of conflicts with her daughter that related to her own adolescent development. She felt a sense of shock at becoming aware of her own competitiveness. In a later interview, she became aware of the deep sense of hurt inside of her.

> MRS. OAK   And then of course, I've come to . . . to see and to feel that over this . . ., see, I've covered it up. (*Weeps.*) But . . . and . . . I've covered it up with so much bitterness, which in turn I had to cover up. (*Weeps.*) That's what I want to get rid of! I almost don't care if I hurt.
>
> THERAPIST   *(Gently.)* You feel that here at the basis of it, as you experienced it, is a feeling of real tears for yourself. But that you can't show, mustn't show, so that's been covered by bitterness that you don't like, that you'd like to be rid of. You almost feel you'd rather absorb the hurt than to . . . than to feel bitterness. (*Pause.*) And what you seem to be saying quite strongly is, "I do hurt, and I've tried to cover it up."
>
> MRS. OAK   I didn't know it.
>
> THERAPIST   M-hm. Like a new discovery really.
>
> MRS. OAK   *(Speaking at the same time.)* I never really did know. But it's . . . you know, it's almost a physical thing. It's . . . it's sort of as though I-I-I were looking within myself at all kinds of . . . nerve endings and-and bits of-of . . . things that have been sort of mashed. (*weeping*)
>
> P. 326

At first, this increased awareness led to a sense of disorganization. Mrs. Oak began to feel more troubled and neurotic, as if she was going to pieces. She said she felt as though she were a piece of structure or a piece of architecture that had parts removed from it. In struggling with these feelings, Mrs. Oak began to recognize the dynamics of anxiety that had operated in her and to discover how, in an attempt to cope with anxiety, she had deserted her self. She described her previous inability to recognize and "sort of simply embrace" fear. She described her feeling that the problem for her and for many others is that they get away from self.

Intermittently, Mrs. Oak expressed her feelings toward the therapist. At first she felt resentful that the therapist was not being very helpful and that the therapist would not take responsibility for the sessions. During the course of therapy, she at times felt very strongly that the therapist didn't "add a damn thing." But, also, in the course of therapy, she developed a sense of relationship with the therapist and how this relationship compared with the descriptions her friends had given of the relationship in psychoanalysis. She concluded that her relationship with the therapist was different, was something she would never be casual about—was the basis of therapy.

> I'm convinced, and again I may sound textbookish, that therapy is only as deep as this combination, this relationship, as the need in the client is as deep as the need, and as deep as the willingness for the relationship to grow on the part of the therapist.
>
> P. 399

Progress did not occur in all areas. By the end of therapy, Mrs. Oak still had sexual conflicts. However, significant gains had been made in a number of areas. She began to feel free to be herself, to listen to herself, and to make independent evaluations. Mrs. Oak began to stop rejecting the feminine role and, more generally, began to become accepting of herself as a worthwhile human being. She decided that she could not continue in her marriage, and she arrived at a mutually agreeable divorce with her husband. Finally, she obtained and held a challenging job.

The positive results described above are matched by the test results on Mrs. Oak. The psychological test responses at the beginning of therapy emphasized the neurotic aspects of her functioning. Mrs. Oak was described as a dependent, passive individual. According to the first report, she was lonely, unhappy, and without affectional ties to anyone. Interpersonal ties, where they existed, were based on a sense of duty or a sense of rebellion. Daydreams were used to escape from her conflicts and feelings of being an ugly duckling. The results of the second psychological test noted a sense of hope, although considerable self-doubt, despair, and dependency remained. A greater sense of openness to trying new things was also observed. The third psychological test reported a marked change. Mrs. Oak was described as a person with self-directed goals, who felt free to make independent value judgments and who experienced little personal threat to others. In contrast to the earlier dependency and resignation, the third test emphasized the sense of interest in and possibility of independent accomplishment. The area of sex, however, continued to be filled with conflict and with views of sex as dirty or sordid.

The positive changes observed on the psychological test were matched by changes in her sortings on the Q-sort. Although the self ratings had little resemblance to the ideal self ratings at the beginning of therapy, the similarity became far greater by the end of therapy and continued to become increasingly similar through the follow-up period.

In sum, the test data indicated that both Mrs. Oak and others who knew her felt that she had become more mature and more accepting of herself and other people. The data suggested that therapy had contributed to a positive and relatively stable change in behavior and personality organization.

RELATED POINTS OF VIEW AND RECENT DEVELOPMENTS

It was noted in the previous chapter that the tone and spirit of the Rogerian position are apparent in other theories of personality, particularly in the emphasis on the continuous striving of the organism to realize its inherent potentials. Together with similar emphases by others, Rogers' position is part of the human potential movement which has been called the "third force" in psychology, offering an alternative to psychoanalysis and to behaviorism.

The Human Potential Movement

According to Riesman (1950), with rapid industrialization the prevailing American personality structure changed from an emphasis on behavior in accordance with tradition to behavior in accordance with individual initiative and an internal set of goals (for example, accumulation of money, possessions, and power). With the development of bureaucratized, large cities and a consumer orientation, there was a further change in personality structure toward conformity and an anxious concern with being popular and well-liked. In recent years, however, this emphasis on conformity and adjustment has changed to an emphasis on fulfillment. Along with Rogers, a number of personality theorists speak to this concern with fulfillment and with being human in the face of large institutions and the demands of society. While there are theoretical differences among them, many humanist theories of personality are joined together in the human potential movement. These theories respond to current concerns (for example, anxiety, boredom, and lack of meaning) with an emphasis on self-actualization, fulfillment of potential, and openness to experience. Two major figures in this tradition are Kurt Goldstein and Abraham Maslow.

Kurt Goldstein

Kurt Goldstein came to the United States in 1935, at age 57, after achieving considerable status as a neurologist and psychiatrist in Germany. During World War I he had extensive experience working with brain-injured soldiers and this work formed the foundation for his later views. He was impressed with the separation of functions that often occurs in brain-injured patients in contrast with the smooth, coordinated brain functioning of normal individuals. What he observed as differences in brain functioning and disturbances due to brain injury he extended to other aspects of personality functioning. Thus, for example, the healthy human organism is characterized by flexible functioning while the disturbed human organism is characterized by rigid functioning. The healthy organism is characterized by planned and organized functioning while the disturbed organism is characterized by mechanical functioning. The healthy organism can delay and anticipate the future while the disturbed organism is bound by the past and the immediacy of the present. Yet, at the same time, Goldstein was impressed with the tremendous adaptive powers of his brain-injured patients, the same powers that he felt were basic to all human functioning.

Like Freud, Goldstein (1939) had an energy view of the organism. How-

KURT GOLDSTEIN

ever, his views concerning the movement and direction of energy flow differed considerably from Freud: "Freud fails to do justice to the positive aspect of life. He fails to recognize that the basic phenomenon of life is an incessant process of coming to terms with the environment; he only sees escape and craving for release. He only knows the lust of release, not the pleasure of tension" (1939, p. 333). Rather then seeking tension reduction, the main motive for the person is self-actualization. All aspects of human functioning are basically expressions of this one motive—to actualize the self. It can be expressed in such simple ways as eating or in such lofty ways as our highest creative productions, but in the final analysis it is this motive that guides our behavior. Each person has inner potentials which are there to be fulfilled in the growth process. It is the recognition of this that ties Goldstein to others in the human potential movement.

The threats to self-actualization come from disturbances inside the person's bodily functioning and from some forms of interaction with the environment. For example, disease, anxiety, or excessive controls from the environment may interfere with healthy functioning and with full expression of the self-actualization drive. However, the motive remains and the growth process can be continued once these internal and environmental disturbances have been eliminated. Thus, the task of the organism always is that of regulating its internal functioning and relating to the environment in such a way that the self-actualization process can be supported.

Goldstein's work with brain-injured patients was of considerable importance for workers in that area. In addition, his views on the general nature of human functioning have had a significant influence on humanist thinkers in the field of psychology.

Abraham Maslow

Maslow (1968, 1971) perhaps has been the major theorist in the human potential movement. It was he who described this psychology as the "third force" in American psychology. He criticized the other forces, psychoanalysis and behaviorism, for their pessimistic, negative, and limited conception of humans. He proposed, instead, that people are basically good or neutral rather than evil, that there is in everyone an impulse towards growth or the fulfillment of potentials, and that psychopathology is the result of twisting and frustration of the essential nature of the human organism. Society often causes such twisting and frustration, and there is a problem when we assume that the result is the essential nature of the organism. Rather, we should recognize what could occur were these obstacles to be removed. Here we see one of the reasons for the popularity of the human potential movement on the part of those who feel excessively restricted and inhibited by their environment. Maslow both speaks

ABRAHAM H. MASLOW

to these concerns and offers encouragement for the belief that things can be better if people are free to express themselves and be themselves.

In addition to this overall spirit, Maslow's views have been important in two ways. First, he has suggested a view of human motivation which distinguishes between such biological needs as hunger, sleep, and thirst and such psychological needs as self-esteem, affection, and belongingness. While we cannot survive as a biological organism without food and water, we cannot develop fully as a psychological organism without satisfaction of our other needs as well. Far too often, Maslow suggests, psychologists have been concerned with our biological needs and have developed views of motivation which suggest that people respond only to deficiency and only seek tension reduction. While accepting that such motivation exists, Maslow calls for us to recognize as well motivation that is not based on deficiency and that often involves an increase in tension—motivation that is expressed when people are being creative and fulfilling their potential.

A second major contribution by Maslow (1954) was his intensive study of healthy, self-fulfilling, self-actualizing individuals. These were figures from the past as well as some who were living at the time. From this research Maslow concluded that actualizing people have the following characteristics: they accept themselves and others for what they are; they can be concerned with themselves but also are free to recognize the needs and desires of others; they are capable of responding to the uniqueness of people and situations rather than responding in mechanical or stereotyped ways; they can form profoundly intimate relationships with at least a few special people; they can be spontaneous and creative; and they can resist conformity and assert themselves while responding to the demands of reality. Who are such people? Illustrative figures are Lincoln, Thoreau, Einstein, and Eleanor Roosevelt. Clearly these are very special individuals and few people have all or even most of these characteristics to any substantial degree. What is suggested, however, is that all of us have it within our potential to move increasingly in the direction of these qualities.

At times the views of Maslow and other leaders of the human potential movement sound almost religious and messianic. At the same time, they do speak to the concerns of many people and do serve as a corrective influence on other views that would represent the human organism as passive, fragmented, and completely governed by tension-reducing motives from within or rewards from the environment.

Rogers' Shift in Emphasis: From Individuals to Groups and Society

Over the years, Rogers has emphasized consistently the phenomenological approach, the importance of the self, and the change process. Whereas earlier there was a clear effort to combine clinical sensitivity with scientific rigor, in recent years Rogers has appeared to move increasingly toward sole reliance on personal, phenomenological types of studies: "To my way of thinking, this personal, phenomenological type of study—especially when one reads all of the responses—is far more valuable than the traditional 'hard-headed' empirical approach. This kind of study, often scorned by psychologists as being 'merely self-reports,' actually gives the deepest insight into what the experience has meant" (Rogers, 1970, p. 133). Apparently Rogers feels that the yield of orthodox scientific studies is minute compared to the insights obtained from clinical work. At this point, Rogers defines knowledge as something that is subjectively convincing and intuitively understood. Rogers' emphasis on experience, particularly private experience, and his disappointments with graduate education in psychology have led to a certain disillusionment with current definitions of science: "I'm not really a scientist. Most of my research has been to confirm what I already felt to be true . . . Generally I never learned anything from research" (Rogers, in *Bergin & Strupp,* 1972, p. 314). What Rogers is searching for is a new view of the person and a more human science of the individual.

Another shift for Rogers, at least in emphasis, has been from the one-to-one therapy relationship to an interest in groups. In his book *On Encounter Groups* (Rogers, 1970), Rogers states that changes occur more rapidly and clearly in small, intensive groups. Of particular interest to Rogers has been the marital partnership group and alternatives to marriage (Rogers, 1972). This interest is focused on the extent to which there is openness, honesty, sharing, and movement toward awareness of inner feelings in the relationship. The interest is in the here and now, in the experiencing of one's own organism, and in the growth process. Rogers' interests as a scientist, as a therapist, and as a group leader come together in his efforts to get closer to what individuals are experiencing and in his efforts to help the individuals themselves to do so. Finally, Rogers (1977) has extended his person-centered approach to administration, minority groups, interracial, intercultural, and international relationships. Rogers expresss a revolutionary spirit in his belief that the person-centered approach may yet produce a change in the concepts, values, and procedures of our culture: ". . . it is the *evidence* of the *effectiveness* of a person-centered approach that may turn a very small and quiet revolution into a far more significant change in the way humankind perceives the possible. I am much too close to the situation to know whether this will be a minor or major event, but I believe it represents a radical change" (p. 286).

CRITICAL EVALUATION

Except for occasional comments and questions, little has been done in this and the last chapter to assess the strengths and weaknesses of Rogers' theory of personality. Until now, the theory has been presented along with supportive research. It is time, however, to take a more critical look at the theory. The phenomenological approach and various parts of the theory will be returned to in order to examine questions that can be raised and to discuss research that contradicts the theory. Three questions, each related to the other, form the basis for this evaluation: (1) To what extent does Rogers' philosophical view of the person lead to omissions or to minimal consideration of critical causes of behavior? (2) To what extent does Rogers pay a price for defining (for research purposes) the self in terms of conscious perceptions? (3) In the elaboration of his theory, in general, and in his views of the nature of anxiety and defense, in particular, to what extent does Rogers represent a departure from Freud?

Phenomenology

The phenomenological approach has been part of a significant effort by many psychologists to come to terms with human experience as it occurs. The phenomenological approach seeks to consider life as it is experienced by the person, without neglecting that which is most human, without splitting it into unrelated parts, and without reducing it to physiological principles. Two questions may be raised in relation to this approach: What are the limitations of a phenomenological approach to psychology? To what extent does the Rogerian counselor in fact take a phenomenological approach?

There are two potential major limitations to the phenomenological approach in psychology, First, it may exclude from investigation certain critical variables, and, second, it may lead to unscientific speculation. These dangers are not unique to the phenomenological approach, but they are relevant to it. As Smith (1950) has argued, a psychology of experience or consciousness has distinct explanatory limits. Smith points to the sometimes unacceptable strivings that warp our behavior (for example, aggressive drives) and to the defensive techniques of adjustment of which we are unaware (for example, repression). Furthermore, Smith argues that, in the development of a scientific psychology, the psychologist must use concepts that are abstractions and must go beyond the phenomenal field of the individual. As MacLeod (1964), himself a phenomenologist, observes, to build a science of psychology, one must go beyond the phenomenal world by developing concepts that can be related to objective measures. The study of the phenomenal self is a legitimate part of psychology as long as it is studied empirically, with a boundless curiosity that is tempered by discipline and not with irresponsible speculation.

On both of these points, Rogers appears to take a reasonable position. He does not believe that the phenomenological approach is the only approach for psychology (Rogers, 1964). He does believe in the empirical investigation of the phenomenal field, in general, and of the phenomenal self, in particular. However, although Rogers acknowledges the importance of experiences of which we are unaware and often refers to the effects of defensive efforts on the part of the individual, he does little to take these effects into consideration in his research. The definition of the self, in terms of that which is conscious, appears to be more a result of Rogers' philosophical view of the person and of Rogers' desire to be able to define the concept in a way that it can be measured, than a result of a commitment to the position that there are only conscious attitudes and experiences relevant to the self. Although Rogerians, as we shall learn, often refer to the effects of defensive sortings on the self Q-sort, little is done to investigate these effects systematically and to build them into the entire research effort.

To return to our second question, to what extent is the theory based on unbiased phenomenological investigation? In a sense, the question was well put by MacLeod (1964, p. 138) in responding to a presentation by Rogers: "On what basis are you so convinced that you have understood your client better than Mr. Freud has understood his patient?" Rogers' response was that the client-centered therapist brings fewer biases and preconceptions to therapy because of a lighter "baggage of preconceptions." The client-centered therapist is more likely to arrive at an understanding of the phenomenal world of an individual than is the Freudian analyst. In an early paper, Rogers (1947) stated that if one read the transcripts of a client-centered therapist, one would find it impossible to form an estimate of the therapist's views about personality dynamics. But we do not know that this is actually the case. Furthermore, that statement was made at a time when the theory was not very developed and therapists were being nondirective. With the development of the theory and the increased emphasis on client-centered but active involvement by the therapist, is this still true? We know that minor behaviors on the part of the interviewer, including expressions such as m-hm, may exert a profound effect on the verbalizations and behavior of the person being interviewed (Greenspoon, 1962). As one reads the transcripts of the therapy sessions, the comments of the counselor do not appear to be random or inconsequential as far as content is concerned. Counselors appear to be particularly responsive about the self and about feelings, and appear to formulate some of their statements in theory-related terms:

THERAPIST OF MRS. OAK   *I'd like to see if I can capture a little of what that means to you. It is as if you've gotten very deeply acquainted with yourself on a kind of a brick-to-brick experiencing basis, and in that sense you have become more self-ish, and the notions of really . . . in the discovering of what is the core of you as separate from all the other aspects, you come across the realization, which is a very deep and pretty thrilling realization, that the core of the self is not only without hate but is really something more resembling a saint, something really very pure, is the word I would use.*

ROGERS, 1954, P. 239

This point (of influence of the interviewer on the client) is quite critical, since so much of Rogers' data comes from clinical interviews.

In summary, the phenomenological approach has distinct merits and potential dangers associated with it. Rogers has recognized that it is not the only approach to psychology and that it must be associated with empirical investigation. However, he has not given adequate consideration to the role of unconscious forces in behavior or to the relationship between these forces and the conscious phenomenal field. Furthermore, we are still unclear about the extent to which the behavior of the client in client-centered therapy is, in fact, free of the biases and preconceptions of the counselor.

The Concept of Self

The concept of self is an important area for psychological investigation. A number of questions are relevant to the status of the concept and to its measurement. The concept of self, as developed by Rogers, assumes a constancy over time and across situations; that is, the way people view themselves at one point in time and in one situation is related to their views of themselves at other points in time and in other situations. Furthermore, the Rogerian concept of self assumes a total whole instead of a composite of unrelated parts. Is there any evidence to support these assumptions? The studies of Rogers have suggested that ratings of the self, of the ideal-self, and of the discrepancy between self and ideal-self remain fairly stable for non-therapy groups. As predicted, those ratings change during the course of successful therapy. Other studies support the view that the self-concept is fairly stable over time. Engel (1959) studied the stability of the concept in adolescents over a two-year period. Coopersmith studied the stability of self-esteem in grade school children during a three-year period and concluded that individuals arrive at a fairly stable appraisal of their worth by middle childhood: "Although the idea of self is open to change and alteration, it appears to be relatively resistant to such changes. Once established, it apparently provides a sense of personal continuity over space and time, and is defended against alteration, diminution, and insult" (1967, p. 21). Coopersmith also interpreted his data as suggesting that there is stability of the appraisal of the self across situations, and that appraisals of worth in specific situations are made within the context of an overall, general appraisal. A study by Akeret (1959), however, suggests that individuals may not have a unified view of themselves but, rather, may value themselves in some areas and not others. Stability of the self-concept may itself be a source of individual differences. Thus, a variety of studies indicate that some people show far greater change in their self-concept than do others.

Although there is evidence to support the view that the self-concept has some stability and can be measured reliably, it presents many assessment hazards. One problem with the tests used is that we do not know whether they contain a representative sample of items relevant to the self. For example, the items used by Butler and Haigh were taken from verbal statements of clients in client-centered therapy. Is that sample of items biased in favor of client-centered therapy (Crowne and Stephens, 1961)? A second assessment problem involves the questions raised with respect to the phenomenological approach. It concerns the extent to which subjects are capable of giving and are willing to give honest self-reports. To what extent do subjects report what they perceive to be socially desirable? To what extent are self-evaluative responses influenced by defensive behavior (Crowne and Stephens, 1961)? One study in this area suggests that social desirability is a powerful influence on self-ratings (Milgram and Helper, 1961). Another study suggests a relationship between being defensive and rating oneself favorably (Pervin and Lilly, 1967). We know that subjects will give different ratings in a personal setting than in an impersonal setting (Abernethy, 1954) and will give different responses according to whether they are subjects for research or candidates for employment (Davids and Pildner, 1958). It has also been found that subjects give conscious self-characterizations that are neither very favorable or very unfavorable (Huntley, 1940). As Wylie (1974) observes in her review of the literature on the concept of self, assessment problems like these leave many questions unsettled.

Because of the difficulties in conceptualization of the self, and because of the many unsettled questions concerning assessment, some psychologists have been led to conclude that the relevant research has led us toward bankruptcy: "If we attempt to assess how far these various currents and crosscurrents of opinion about self have taken us toward scientific knowledge, we must conclude that they have not taken us very far at all" (Diggory, 1966, p. 60). Still, there would appear to be little reason for abandoning interest in the concept. In spite of the many conceptual and methodological problems involved with the concept of self, it remains one of considerable importance to the layperson and to the field of psychology. It is also probably true that Rogers, more than any other theorist, has given it the attention it deserves in theory, assessment, and research.

Conflict, Anxiety, and Defense

In his formulation of the dynamics of behavior, Rogers gives particular attention to the self-actualization process and to the efforts on the part of the organism to maintain a stable, consistent, congruent picture of the self. Little attention has been given here to the actualization concept. It is an important concept to Rogers, but one that has not been measured and that has not played a role in research. On the other hand, critical attention has been given to Rogers' concepts of congruence, anxiety, and defense, and we've compared these process concepts with the Freudian model of anxiety and defense.

We can recall that, according to the theory, the individual may prevent awareness (through denial or distortion) of experiences that are "subceived" as threatening to the current structure of the self. Anxiety is the response of the organism to the subception that an experience incongruent with the self-structure may enter awareness, thus, forcing a change in the self-concept. The incongruence between self and experience remains as a constant source of tension and threat. The constant need to use defensive processes results in a restriction of awareness and freedom to respond.

We have, then, a model in which the essential ingredients are conflict (incongruence), anxiety, and defense. Both the Freudian and Rogerian theories involve conflict, anxiety, and defense. In both theories the defenses are used to reduce anxiety. However, the sources of anxiety and, therefore, the processes through which anxiety is reduced, are different in the two theories. For Freud, the conflict leading to anxiety is generally between the drives and some other part of the personality—the ego or the superego as mediated by the ego. For Freud, the defenses are used to deal with the threatening nature of the instincts. The result may be formation of symptoms—symptoms representing partial expressions of the instinct and partial drive reduction. Rogers rejects the assumption that the defenses involve forbidden or socially taboo impulses such as those that Freud describes as coming from the id. Instead, he emphasizes perceptual consistency. Experiences that are incongruent or inconsistent with the self-concept are rejected, whatever their social character. As observed previously, according to Rogers, favorable aspects of the self may be rejected because they are inconsistent or discrepant with the self-concept. Whereas Freud placed an emphasis on instincts and drive reduction, Rogers emphasizes experiences and their perceptual inconsistency with the self-concept. The ultimate goal for Freud was the proper channeling of the drives. The ultimate goal for Rogers is a state of congruence between organism and self. The description given by Rogers of possible modes of defense is similar to Freud's and was undoubtedly influenced by psychoanalytic theory. Generally, however, Rogers gives much less attention to differences in types of defense and does not try to relate the type of defense used to other personality variables, as is the case in psychoanalytic theory.

The above distinctions seem fairly clear, until Rogers attempts to account for the development of a rift between organismic experience and self and introduces the concept of the need for positive regard. According to Rogers, if parents make positive regard conditional, their children will not accept certain values or experiences as their own. In other words, children keep out of awareness experiences which, if they were to accept them, might result in the loss of love. According to Rogers, the basic estrangement in humans is between self and experience, and this estrangement has come about because humans falsify their values for the sake of preserving the positive regard of others (Rogers, 1959, p. 226). This statement complicates Rogers' position, since it suggests that the individual disregards experiences that formerly were associated with pain (loss of love). This view is not unlike that of Freud's concerning trauma and the development of anxiety. In essence, one can again see a conflict model, in which experiences which were, in the past, associated with pain later become sources of anxiety and defense.

In both the theoretical formulations of Freud and Rogers, the concepts of conflict, anxiety, and defense play a major role in the dynamics of behavior. Both view well-adjusted people as less concerned with these processes and neurotic people as more concerned with them. For Freud, the process aspects of behavior involve the interplay among drives and the efforts on the part of the defenses to reduce anxiety and to achieve drive-reduction. For Rogers, the process aspects of behavior involve the efforts of the individual toward actualization and toward self-consistency. Although at times Rogers appears to emphasize the pain associated with the loss of positive regard, his major emphasis appears to be on the maintenance of congruence, which includes disregarding positive characteristics that are inconsistent with a negative self-concept and accepting negative characteristics that are consistent with this self-concept.

Growth and Development

Clearly, Rogers has given little elaboration to a theory of growth and development. Little, if any, attention is given to the cultural, social class, and genetic causes of personality. Minor attention is given to familial causes, but this is not related to any research effort. But one finding that is relevant to the theory can be noted. A study by Katz and Zigler (1967) hypothesized that self-ideal self discrepancy is a function of developmental level. In a study of children in the fifth, eighth, and eleventh grades, self-ideal self discrepancy was found to be related to age and intelligence. A greater discrepancy in older and brighter children was accounted for by both decreased self-evaluations and increased ideal self images. As children grow older they accept many parental and societal ideals. They then also are capable of honestly considering themselves in relation to these ideals. They may begin to recognize and accept without distortion that they are not as bright, or athletic, or popular as they would like to be. In some areas they may even have to revise their glorified picture of themselves. This suggests that with maturity individuals show a greater capacity for guilt and for a clearer picture of strengths and limitations. This suggests the type of developmental research that could be done within a Rogerian framework. Although the study does not refute any Rogerian principle of growth and development, it does raise the question of the appropriateness of using self-ideal self discrepancy as a measure of psychopathology since such a discrepancy in some areas may reflect a mature holding of ideals and acceptance of where one stands in relation to these ideals.

Psychopathology and Change

In an earlier study of self-ideal self discrepancy and social competence, Zigler (Achenbach and Zigler, 1963) found that highly competent subjects showed a greater self-ideal self discrepancy than did subjects low in social competence. The Rogerian theory of psychopathology relates to a lack of congruence between experience and self, and the self-ideal self measure is not critical to the theory. On the other hand, self-ideal self discrepancies have been used consistently by Rogerians as a measure of adjustment. Thus, the above finding points to some of the problems that emerge in the use of this measure. A variety of studies have found a relationship between the size of the self-ideal self discrepancy and characteristics such as psychopathology, self-depreciation, anxiety, and insecurity. For example, Turner and Vanderlippe (1958) found that the college student who is high in self-ideal self congruence, in contrast to the student low in such congruence, participated in more extracurricular activities, had a higher scholastic average, was more popular with fellow students, and received higher adjustment ratings on personality tests. On the other hand, other studies (for example, Pervin and Lilly, 1967) have found a relationship between high self-ideal self congruence and defensiveness. For example, Havener and Izard (1962) found a relationship between high congruence and unrealisticly high self-esteem in paranoid schizophrenics. These subjects appear to be defending against a complete loss of positive self-regard. It appears that the self-ideal self relationship is far too complex to be an altogether satisfactory measure of adjustment (Vernon, 1963; Wylie, 1974).

The problems associated with using differences between self and ideal self ratings as a measure of adjustment have been recognized by Rogers and many of his followers. The problem is important both in and of itself and also in relation to evaluating the results of therapy. There is considerable evidence to suggest that different methods of therapy may lead to different kinds of change (Garfield and Bergin, 1978). Some changes may be measured by particular personality tests but not by others. For example, a psychological test developed in relation to Rogerian theory may relate well to Q-sort measures of change and to the results of client-centered therapy but not to tests developed in relation to psychoanalytic theory or to the results of psychoanalysis (Grummon and John, 1954; Vargas, 1954). The reverse might be true for tests developed in relation to psychoanalytic theory. The closer the relationship between the test and the theory, the greater the likelihood of the test being sensitive to changes produced by the therapy associated with that theory. Rogers undoubtedly would agree that there are various viewpoints from which to consider the person. Thus, it could be argued that "no single test score, no one rater's rating can be considered adequately representative of the diversity of measured changes accompanying psychotherapy" (Cartwright et al., 1963, p. 175).

Notice that a conclusion similar to this one was reached during the course of a discussion of a case by Rogers and psychoanalysts (Rogers, 1967). Rogers, Rogerian therapists, and psychoanalysts were concerned with the positive movement that occurred in a case presented for discussion. Rogers reports that, at one extreme, the analysts could see little or no progress in therapy, whereas, at the other extreme, the client-centered therapists tended to see great and consistent movement in therapy. Apparently, psychoanalysts emphasize structure, character, and fixity in human behavior. In their view they go from the twigs of a tree to the trunk of the tree, from the superficial to the core of personality. In contrast to this view, the Rogerian emphasizes process and change in human behavior. For the Rogerian, one need not go beyond what is immediately observable to encounter that which is basic to the person.

Summary Evaluation

How, then, may the theory of Rogers be evaluated? It is reasonably comprehensive, although many areas of neglect remain. The theory really says little about the course of growth and development or about the specific factors that determine one or another pattern. In a similar vein, although Rogers refuses to accept diagnostic categories, he does little to recognize the tremendous variation in symptomatology in patients or to relate this variation to previous conditions. Furthermore, one finds strikingly little mention of sex and aggression or of feelings such as guilt and depression. Yet, much of our lives seem to be concerned with these feelings. On the other hand, Rogers has attempted to develop a comprehensive theory and has given considerable attention to the process of change. Within the area that he does cover in the theory and, in particular, within the theory of the process of change, his theory is quite economical. Out of all the complexities of psychotherapy Rogers has attempted to define the few necessary and sufficient conditions for positive personality change. Furthermore, he has attempted to develop the theory in a logically consistent manner and with explicit definitions for most variables.

Much of this theory expresses a philosophical, perhaps religious, view of the person. Assumptions most related to this view, such as the drive toward actualization, have remained assumptions and have not provided the basis for research. Also, the system is still without a measure of self-experience congruence. However, it is clear that the theory has provided extremely fertile ground for research. Rogers has always kept clinical work, theory, and research in close touch with one another. Most of his work reflects a reluctance to sacrifice the rigors of science for the intuitive aspects of clinical work, and all of his work reflects an unwillingness to sacrifice the rich complexities of behavior for the empirical demands of science. As is properly the case, the development of his system has been the result of a constant interplay among gross observations, theoretical formulations, and systematic research efforts.

This chapter on Rogers is concluded by stating three major contributions. Extending beyond the discipline of psychology, Rogers has developed a point of view and an approach toward counseling that has influenced teachers, members of the clergy, and people in business. Within psychology, Rogers has opened up the area of psychotherapy for research. By recording interviews, by making interviews and transcripts available to others, by developing clinically relevant measures of personality, and by demonstrating the potential value of research in the area, Rogers has led the way in the legitimization of research on psychotherapy. Although not all of the research is supportive of client-centered therapy (Fiske and Goodman, 1965), the studies done in relation to client-centered therapy remain among the few that provide well-documented support for the effectiveness of treatment. Finally, more than any other personality theorist, Rogers has focused both theoretical and empirical attention on the nature of the self. The study of the self has always been a part of psychology, but it has, at times, been in danger of being dismissed as "mere philosophy." As MacLeod (1964) notes, you may not find many papers on the self at meetings of experimental psychologists, but clinicians find the problem staring them in the face. More than any other personality theorist, Rogers has attempted to be objective about what is otherwise left to the artists:

Slowly the thinker went on his way and asked himself: What is it that you wanted to learn from teachings and teachers, and although they taught you much, what was it they could not teach you? And he thought: It was the Self, the character and nature of which I wished to learn. I wanted to rid myself of the Self, to conquer it, but I could not conquer it, I could only deceive it, could only fly from it, could only hide from it. Truly, nothing in the world has occupied my thoughts as much as the Self, this riddle, that I live, that I am one and am separate and different from everybody else, that I am Siddartha; and about nothing in the world do I know less than about myself, about Siddartha.

H. HESSE, *SIDDARTHA*, 1951, P. 40

MAJOR CONCEPTS AND SUMMARY

self-experience discrepancy

defensive behaviors

client-centered therapy

congruence (genuineness)

unconditional positive regard

empathic understanding

human potential movement

In this chapter and the last the phenomenological theory of personality of Carl Rogers has been discussed. The theory is concerned with individual differences and the entire personality of the individual. The emphasis is on the phenomenal world of individuals—how individuals perceive and experience themselves and the world about them.

The main structural concepts in the theory are the self, representing an organized pattern of perceptions relating to "me", or "I", and the ideal self, representing the self-concept the individual would like to possess. Although structural concepts are important in terms of representing particular parts of the phenomenal field and in representing stability in an individual's functioning over time, the main focus of the theory is on process and change. The basic tendency in the individual is toward self-actualization—toward maintaining, enhancing, and actualizing the experiencing organism. Beyond this the individual is oriented toward self-consistency, interpreted as a congruence between self and experience. A state of incongruence is created when the individual perceives or subceives experiences that are contradictory with his self-image. Such experiences have been associated in the past with the loss of positive regard. The subception of such experiences is associated with tension or anxiety and leads to the use of defensive devices to remove the incongruence and reduce the anxiety. The basic defensive processes are distortion and denial, leading to a distorted representation of experience or to an unawareness of experience. This sequence of threat due to incongruence between self and experience and the consequent use of defenses forms the basis for psychopathology. There is research evidence to support the view that individuals attempt to behave in accordance with the self-concept and that experiences inconsistent with the self-concept are often ignored or denied into awareness.

Rogers has not really developed a theory of growth and development. Basically growth is seen as involving increased differentiation, expansion, and autonomy. The critical theoretical and practical questions are the circumstances that maximize the opportunity for growth. According to Rogers, it is critical that parents give their children feelings of self-worth. Presumably the conditions for growth that parents must provide for their children are the same ones that therapists must provide for their clients—congruence (genuineness), unconditional positive regard, and empathic understanding.

Rogers' view of the person and his approach to research are quite different from those of Freud. Rogers' theory emphasizes constructive forces in contrast to the psychoanalytic emphasis on that which is "innately destructive." Also, in contrast to the psychoanalytic emphasis on hidden meanings, Rogers emphasizes the usefulness of self-reports and direct sources of information. In contrast with Freud's emphasis on the past, Rogers prefers to deal with what is present or anticipated. These differences in points of view obviously translate themselves into differences in theory and research. Instead of the use of free-association and dream analysis there is the use of verbal self-report and Q-sorts. Instead of an emphasis on studies of the unconscious, there is an emphasis on studies of the conditions that promote positive change (that is, change toward self-actualization and openness to experience) and studies of the characteristics of the self.

Evaluation of Rogers' theory has brought out certain problems and limitations. (1) There has been inadequate attention given to unconscious forces, particularly given the fact that the theory recognizes the existence of such phenomena. (2) There are problems with the definitions and assessment devices for some concepts. For example, it is not clear how one studies in a systematic way the drive toward self-actualization and there are serious questions about the extent to which the self-ideal self discrepancy can be considered to be an accurate measure of psychopathology. (3) There is evidence that even in the Rogerian, client-centered therapy situation the therapist is a source of considerable bias and differentially rewards certain client behaviors (Truax, 1966).

Nevertheless, Rogers, while aware of these problems, has gone on to make a number of very significant contributions. (1) He has developed an approach to counseling that has had a significant impact upon the field. (2) He has opened up the entire area of psychotherapy for systematic research. (3) He has focused both theoretical and empirical attention on the nature of the self. (4) In his emphasis on self-actualization and openness to experience, he has provided one source of leadership for the human potential movement and has spoken to the concerns of many individuals in our society.

GEORGE A. KELLY (1905-1966): A VIEW OF THE THEORIST
KELLY'S VIEW OF THE PERSON
KELLY'S VIEW OF SCIENCE, THEORY, AND RESEARCH METHODS
THE PERSONALITY THEORY OF GEORGE KELLY
Structure
• The Role Construct Repertory Test (Rep Test)
Process
Growth and Development
MAJOR CONCEPTS AND SUMMARY

A COGNITIVE THEORY OF PERSONALITY: GEORGE A. KELLY AND HIS PERSONAL CONSTRUCT THEORY OF PERSONALITY

6

Chapter Focus:

In this chapter we shall discuss Kelly's personal construct theory as illustrative of a clinical, cognitive theory of personality. What distinguishes this theory is its emphasis on how the individual perceives, interprets, and conceptualizes events and the environment. The person is viewed as a scientist who develops a theory (construct system) to predict events. A new test, the Rep test, is presented as one means of assessing construct systems and thereby of understanding an individual's personality.

To a large degree — though not entirely — the blueprint of human progress has been given the label of "science." Let us, then, instead of occupying ourselves with man-the-biological-organism or man-the-lucky-guy, have a look at man-the-scientist.

KELLY, 1955, P. 4

Man looks at his world through transparent patterns or templets which he creates and then attempts to fit over the realities of which the world is composed . . . Let us give the name constructs to these patterns that are tried on for size. They are ways of construing the world.

KELLY, 1955, PP. 8-9

In the preceding four chapters, two clinical theories of personality have been discussed — the psychodynamic theory of Freud, and the phenomenological theory of Rogers. Both theories derived from clinical contacts with patients; both emphasize individual differences; both view individuals as having some consistency across situations and over time; and both view the person as a total system. Freud and Rogers attempted to understand, predict, influence, and conceptualize behavior without fragmenting people into unrelated parts. Although sharing these characteristics in common, the two theories were presented as illustrative of different approaches to theory and research.

personal construct theory

In this chapter, we study a third theory, one that also is expressive of the clinical approach toward understanding personality. The **personal construct theory** of George Kelly, like the theories of Freud and Rogers, was developed mostly out of considerable contact with clients in therapy. Like the theories of Freud and Rogers, Kelly's personal construct theory emphasizes the whole person. It emphasizes individual differences and the stability of behavior over time and across situations. As Kelly observes, the first consideration of personal construct theory is the individual person, rather than any part of the person, any group of persons, or any particular process in a person's behavior. The personal construct clinician cannot fragment the client and reduce the client's problem to a single issue. Instead, the clinician must view the client from a number of perspectives at one and the same time.

Although sharing these characteristics with other clinical theories, Kelly's theory is vastly different from the theories of Freud and Rogers. It is an extremely imaginative effort to interpret behavior in *cognitive* terms; that is, it emphasizes the ways in which we perceive events, the way we interpret and transform these events in relation to already existing structures, and the ways that we behave in relation to these interpretations and transformations. For Kelly a **construct** is a way of perceiving or interpreting events. For example, good-bad is a construct frequently used by people as

construct

they consider events. An individual's personal construct system is made up of the constructs, or ways of interpreting events, that are available and the relationships among these constructs. There is a strong emphasis on cognition in the theory, but Kelly insisted that his theory was not merely a theory of cognition. However, it is, primarily, a theory of efforts to conceptualize (to construe) the person's environment. Kelly's theory dares to reconstrue — that is, reinterpret — the field of psychology and he challenged others to reconstrue it with him. But, for this part of the story, let the theorist speak for himself.

TO WHOM IT MAY CONCERN

It is only fair to warn the reader about what may be in store for him. In the first place, he is likely to find missing most of the familiar landmarks of psychology books. For example, the term learning, so honorably embedded in most psychological texts, scarcely appears at all. That is wholly intentional; we are for throwing it overboard altogether. There is no ego, no emotion, no motivation, no reinforcement, no drive, no unconscious, no need. There are some brand-new psychological definitions, words like foci of convenience, preemption, propositionality, fixed-role therapy, and the credulous approach . . . Unfortunately, all this will make for periods of strange, and perhaps uncomfortable, reading. Yet, inevitably, a different approach calls for a different lexicon; and, under its influences many old terms are unhitched from their familiar meanings.

To whom are we speaking? In general, we think the reader who takes us seriously will be an adventuresome soul who is not one bit afraid of thinking unorthodox thoughts about people, who dares peer out at the world through the eyes of strangers, who has not invested beyond his means in either ideas or vocabulary, and who is looking for an ad interim, rather than an ultimate, set of psychological insights.

KELLY, 1955, PP. x-xi

GEORGE A. KELLY (1905-1966): A VIEW OF THE THEORIST

Less has been written about the life of Kelly than of Freud and Rogers, but we do know something of his background, and the nature of the man comes through in his writing. He appears to be someone who would enjoy reading his books — an adventuresome soul who is unafraid to think unorthodox thoughts about people and who dares to explore the world of the unkown with the tools of tentative hypotheses. In his review of Kelly's theory, Sechrest (1963) observes that Kelly's philosophical and theoretical positions stem, in part, from the diversity of his experience. Kelly grew up in Kansas and obtained his undergraduate education there at Friends University and at Park College in Missouri. He pursued graduate studies at the University of Kansas, the University of Minnesota, and the University of Edinburgh. He received his Ph.D. from the State University of Iowa in 1931. He developed a traveling clinic in Kansas, was an aviation psychologist

GEORGE A. KELLY

during World War II, and was a professor of psychology at Ohio State University and at Brandeis University.

Kelly's early clinical experience was in the public schools of Kansas. While there, he found that teachers referred pupils to his traveling psychological clinic with complaints that appeared to say something about the teachers themselves. Instead of verifying a teacher's complaint, Kelly decided to try to understand it as an expression of the teacher's construction or interpretation of events. For example, if a teacher complained that a student was lazy, Kelly would not look at the pupil to see if the teacher was correct in the diagnosis. Rather he would try to understand the behaviors of the child and the way the teacher perceived these behaviors — that is, the teacher's construction of them — which led to the complaint of laziness. This was a significant reformulation of the problem. In practical terms, it led to an analysis of the teachers as well as the pupils, and to a wider range of solutions to the problems. Furthermore, it led Kelly to the view that there is no objective, absolute truth, and that phenomena are meaningful only in relation to the ways in which they are construed or interpreted by the individual.

George Kelly, then, was a person who refused to accept things as black or white, right or wrong. He was a person who liked to test new experiences; a person who dismissed truth in any absolute sense and, therefore, felt free to reconstrue or reinterpret phenomena; a person who challenged the concept of "objective" reality and felt free to play in the world of "make-believe;" a person who perceived events as occurring to individuals and, therefore, was interested in the interpretations of these events by individuals; a person who viewed his own theory as only a tentative formulation and who, consequently was free to challenge views that others accepted as fact; a person who experienced the frustration and challenge, the threat and joy, of exploring the unkown.

KELLY'S VIEW OF THE PERSON

Theories of personality have implicit in them philosophical assumptions about human nature. Often, they can be uncovered only as we study why a theorist explores one phenomenon instead of another, and as we observe that different theorists go beyond the data in different ways — ways that are meaningful in relation to their own life experiences. In general, Kelly is straightforward, and his view of the person is explicit. In fact, he begins his presentation of the psychology of personal constructs with a section on his perspectives of the person. Kelly's assumption about human nature is that every person is a scientist. The scientist attempts to predict and control phenomena. Kelly believes that psychologists, operating as scientists, try to predict and control behavior, but that they do not assume that their subjects operate on a similar basis. Kelly describes this situation as follows:

It is as though the psychologist were saying to himself, "I, being a psychologist, and therefore a scientist, am performing this experiment in order to improve the prediction and control of certain human phenomena; but my subject, being merely a human organism, is obviously propelled by inexorable drives welling up within him, or else he is in gluttonous pursuit of sustenance and shelter."

KELLY, 1955, P. 5

Kelly regards himself as having theories, testing hypotheses, and weighing experimental evidence and he considers this an appropriate view of people. Not every person is a scientist in the sense of limiting attention to some specific area and of using agreed on techniques to collect and to evaluate data. However, these are matters of detail, whereas the principles of operation are the same. All people experience events, perceive similarities and differences among these events, formulate concepts or constructs to order phenomena and, on the basis of these constructs, seek to anticipate events. All people are similar in that they use constructs and follow the same psychological processes in the use of these constructs. In this respect, all people are scientists. However, individuals are unique in their use of particular constructs. Differences between individuals in the constructs that they use correspond to the differences among scientists in their theoretical points of view.

The view of the person as a scientist has a number of further consequences for Kelly. First, it leads to the view that we are essentially oriented toward the future. "Anticipation is not merely carried on for its own sake; it is carried on so that future reality may be better represented. It is the future which tantalizes man, not the past. Always he reaches out to the future through the window of the present" (Kelly, 1955, p. 49). Second, it suggests that we have the capacity to "represent" the environment, rather than merely to "respond" to it. Just as scientists can develop alternative theoretical formulations concerning phenomena, so individuals can interpret and reinterpret, construe and reconstrue, their environments. Life is a representation, or construction, of reality, and this allows us to make and remake ourselves. Some people are capable of viewing life in many different ways while others cling rigidly to a set interpretation. Those with a greater number of possible interpretations have a greater opportunity for selection and are likely to be more able to differentiate among different situations and different people. However, everyone can only perceive events within the limits of the categories (constructs) that are available to him or her. In Kelly's terms, we are free to construe events but are bound by our constructions. Thus, it is that we come to a new understanding of the issue of free will and determinism. According to Kelly, we are both free *and* determined. "This personal construct system provides him (man) with both freedom of decision and limitations of action — freedom, because it permits him to deal with the meaning of events rather than forces him to be helplessly pushed about by them, and limitation, because he can never make choices outside the world of alternatives he has erected for himself" (Kelly, 1958, p. 58). Having "enslaved" ourselves with these constructions, we are able to win freedom again and again by reconstruing the environment and life. Thus, we are not victims of past history or of present circumstances — unless we choose to construe ourselves in that way.

KELLY'S VIEW OF SCIENCE, THEORY, AND RESEARCH METHODS

constructive alternativism

Much of Kelly's thinking, including his view of science, is based on the philosophical position of **constructive alternativism**. According to this position, there is no objective reality or absolute truth to discover. Instead, there are efforts to construe events — to interpret phenomena in order to make sense of them. There are always alternative constructions available from which to choose. This is true for the scientist as it is for people who behave as scientists. In Kelly's view the scientific enterprise is not the discovery of truth or, as Freud might have suggested, the uncovering of things in the mind previously hidden. Rather, the scientific enterprise is the effort to develop construct systems that are useful in anticipating events.

Kelly was concerned about the tendency toward dogma in psychology. He thought psychologists believed that constructs of inner states and traits actually existed rather than understanding them as "things" in a theoretician's head. If someone is described as an introvert, we tend to check to see whether he *is* an introvert, rather than checking the person who is responsible for the statement. Kelly's position against "truth" and dogma is of considerable significance. It leads, for instance, to the freedom to view "make-believe" as an essential feature of science (Kelly, 1964). Kelly criticized those who view science as a way of avoiding subjective, or personal, statement and, hence, for getting down to the hard facts of reality For Kelly, subjective thinking is an essential step in the scientific process. Subjective thinking allows one to establish the "invitational mood" in which one is free to invite many alternative interpretations of phenomena, and to entertain propositions that, initially, may seem absurd. The invitational mood is a necessary part of the exploration of the world, for the professional scientist as well as for the patient in therapy. It is the mood established by the creative novelist. But where the novelist publishes his make-believe and may even be unconcerned with the evidence supporting his constructions, the professional scientist tends to minimize the world of make-believe and to focus on objective evidence. Kelly concluded his comparison of the novelist and the scientist:

But neither of these differences between the novelist and the scientist is very fundamental. Both men employ nonetheless typically human tactics. The fact that the scientist is ashamed to admit his phantasy probably accomplished little more than to make it appear that he fits a popular notion of the way scientists think. And the fact that a novelist does not continue his project to the point of collecting data in support of his portrayals and generalizations suggests only that he hopes that the experiences of man will, in the end, prove him right without anyone's resorting to formal proof.

But the brilliant scientist and the brilliant writer are pretty likely to end up saying the same thing — given, of course, a lot of time to converge upon each other. The poor scientist and the poor writer, moreover, fail in much the same way — neither of them is able to transcend the obvious. Both fail in their make-believe.

KELLY, 1964, P. 140

range of convenience focus of convenience

According to Kelly, it is the freedom to make believe and to establish the invitational mood that allows for the development of hypotheses. A hypothesis should not be asserted as a fact, but instead should be accepted as a conclusion that allows the scientist to pursue its implications *as if* it were true. Kelly viewed a theory as a tentative expression of what has been observed and of what is expected. A theory has a **range of convenience**, indicating the boundaries of phenomena the theory can cover, and a **focus of convenience**, indicating the points within the boundaries where the theory works best. For example, Freud's theory had a broad range of convenience, providing interpretations for almost all aspects of personality, but its focus of convenience was the unconscious and abnormal behavior. Rogers' theory has a narrower range of convenience and its focus of convenience is more on the self concept and the process of change. Kelly points out that different theories have different ranges of convenience and different foci of convenience. Regardless of these differences, however, there are common grounds for determining whether one has a good theory.

A good psychological theory has an appropriate focus and range of convenience . . . It should be fertile in producing new ideas, in generating hypotheses, in provoking experimentation, in encouraging inventions. The hypotheses which are deduced from it should be brittle enough to be testable, though the theory itself may be cast in more resilient terms. The more frequently its hypotheses turn out to be valid, the more valuable the theory.

KELLY, 1955, p. 44

For Kelly, theories were modifiable and ultimately expendable. A theory is modified or discarded when it stops leading to new predictions or leads to incorrect predictions. Among scientists, as well as among people in general, how long one holds on to a theory in the face of contradictory information, is partly a matter of taste and style.

Kelly's view of science is not unique, but it is important in terms of its clarity of expression and its points of emphasis. It does have a number of important ramifications. First, since there are no "facts", and since different theories have different ranges of convenience, we need not argue about whether facts are "psychological" or "physiological." There are psychological *and* physiological constructions of the same or different phenomena. Second, Kelly's approach involved criticism of an extreme emphasis on measurement. Kelly believed that such an extreme approach would mean that no theoretical statement could be made unless each concept referred to something tangible, that is, something that could be measured. Kelly felt that such an approach could lead to viewing concepts as "things" rather than as representations, and to making a psychologist into a technician rather than a scientist. On the other hand, Kelly's view of science did include the need for theories to lead to research with variables that could be measured. Third, Kelly's view of science left room for the clinical as opposed to the experimental method, which he considered useful because it spoke the language of hypothesis, because it led to the emergence of new variables, and because it focused on important questions. "When one ponders the fact that mankind has probably spent more time trying to answer poorly posed questions than figuring out sensible issues, one wonders if this feature of the clinical method should not be more widely advocated in all human enterprise" (Kelly, 1955, p. 193). Here we have a fourth significant aspect of Kelly's view of science — it should focus on important issues. In Kelly's belief, many psychologists are afraid of doing anything that might not be recognized as science, and they have given up struggling with important aspects of human behavior. His suggestion was that they stop trying to be scientific and that they get on with the job of understanding people. Kelly believed that a good scientific theory should encourage the invention of new approaches to the solution of the problems of people and society.

Finally, Kelly took a firm stand against dogma, and he argued for the language of hypothesis. It was his contention that many scholars waste time trying to disprove their colleagues' claims in order to make room for their own explanations. It is as if to be "right" one has to prove the other "wrong." In Kelly's opinion, this is a terrible waste of time. Instead, he suggested that psychologists think in less concrete terms, that they invite the formulation of new hypotheses, that they not feel the need to destroy the constructions of others on events. All theories are only part of the world of make-believe, and all are destined to be modified and abandoned. It is a tribute to Kelly's sense of perspective, sense of humor, and lack of defensiveness concerning his own work that he could describe one of his own theoretical papers as involving "half-truths" only, and that he could view his theory as contributing to its own downfall. It is this theory — the theory of personal constructs — that we now discuss.

THE PERSONALITY THEORY OF GEORGE KELLY

Structure

construct
construing

The scientist develops concepts to describe and interpret the events that are of interest to him. Kelly's key structural concept for the person as a scientist is that of the **construct**. A construct is a way of **construing**, or interpreting, the world. It is a concept that the individual uses to categorize events and to chart a course of behavior. According to Kelly, a person anticipates events by observing which events tend to follow which other events, that is, by observing patterns and regularities. A person experiences events, interprets them, and places a structure and a meaning on them. In experiencing events, individuals notice that some events share characteristics that distinguish them from other events. Individuals distinguish similarities and contrasts among events. They observe that some people are tall and some short, that some are men and some are women, that some things are hard and some are soft. It is this construing of a similarity and a contrast that leads to the formation of a construct. Without constructs, life would be chaotic. Since no two events are exactly the same, we make certain abstractions by construing events as being similar to each other and different from other events, thereby developing a construct and imposing some order and regularity on the world.

similarity pole

contrast pole

It is important to note that Kelly viewed all constructs as composed of opposite pairs. At least three elements are necessary to form a construct: two of the elements of the construct must be perceived as similar to each other, and the third element must be perceived as different from these two. The way in which two elements are construed to be similar forms the **similarity pole** of the construct; the way in which they are contrasted with the third element forms the **contrast pole** of the construct. For example, observing two people helping someone and a third hurting someone could lead to the construct kind-cruel, with kind forming the similarity pole and cruel the contrast pole. Kelly stressed the importance of recognizing that a construct is composed of a similarity-contrast comparison. This suggests that we do not understand the nature of a construct when it uses only the similarity pole or the contrast pole. We do not know what the construct *respect* means to a person until we know what events the person includes under this construct and what events are viewed as being opposed to it. Interestingly, whatever constructs one applies to others are potentially applicable to the self. "One cannot call another person a bastard without making bastardy a dimension of his own life also" (Kelly, 1955, p. 133).

A construct is not dimensional in the sense of having many points between the similarity and contrast poles. Subtleties or refinements in constructions of events are made through the use of other constructs, these being constructs of quantity and quality. For example, the construct *black-white* in combination with a quantity construct leads to the four-scale value of black, slightly black, slightly white, and white (Sechrest, 1963).

A construct is similar to a theory in that it has a range of convenience and a focus of convenience. A construct's range of convenience comprises all of those events for which the user would find application of the construct useful. A construct's focus of convenience comprises the particular events for which application of the construct would be maximally useful. Constructs can themselves be categorized in a variety of ways. For example, there are **core constructs** that are basic to a person's functioning, and there are **peripheral constructs** that can be altered without serious modification of the core structure.

core constructs
peripheral constructs

Do not assume from this discussion that constructs are verbal or that they are always verbally available to a person. Although Kelly emphasized the cognitive aspects of human functioning — the ones that Freudians would call the conscious — he did take into consideration phenomena described by Freudians as being unconscious. The conscious-unconscious construct is not used by Kelly. However, Kelly did use the verbal-preverbal construct to deal with some of the elements that are otherwise interpreted as conscious or unconscious. A **verbal construct** can be expressed in words, whereas a **preverbal construct** is one that is used even though the person has no words to express it. A preverbal construct is learned before the person developed the use of language. Sometimes, one end of a construct is not available for verbalization — it is characterized as being **submerged**. If a person insists that people do only good things, one assumes that the other end of the construct has been submerged since the person must have been aware of contrasting behaviors to have formed the "good" end of the construct. Thus, constructs may not be available for verbalization, and the individual may not be able to report all of the elements that are in the construct; but this does not mean that the individual has "an unconscious."

verbal construct
preverbal construct

submerged

The constructs used by a person in interpreting and in anticipating events are organized as part of a system. The constructs within a system are organized into groups to minimize incompatabilities and inconsistencies. There is a hierarchical arrangement of constructs within a system. A **superordinate construct** includes other constructs within its context, and a **subordinate construct** is one that is included in the context of another (superordinate) construct. For example, the constructs bright-dumb and attractive-unattractive might both be subordinate to the superordinate construct good-bad. It is important to recognize that the constructs within the person's construct system are interrelated to at least some extent. A

superordinate construct
subordinate construct

person's behavior generally expresses the construct system rather than a single construct and a change in one aspect of the construct system generally leads to changes in other parts of the system.

In terms of the above, people can be seen to differ both in the content of their constructs and in the organization of their construct systems. Individuals differ in the kinds of constructs they use, in the number of constructs available to them, in the complexity of organization of their construct systems, and in how open they are to changes in these construct systems.

To summarize, according to Kelly's theory of personal constructs, an individual's personality is his or her construct system. A person uses constructs to interpret the world and to anticipate events. The constructs used by a person define his or her world. Two people are similar to the extent that they have similar construct systems. Most important, if you want to understand a person you must know something about the constructs that person uses, the events subsumed under these constructs, the way in which these constructs tend to function, and the way in which they are organized in relation to one another to form a system.

The Role Construct Repertory Test (Rep Test)

Knowing other people, then, is knowing how they construe the world. How does one gain this knowledge of a person's constructs? Kelly's answer is direct — ask them to tell you what their constructs are. "If you don't know what is going on in a person's mind, ask him; he may tell you" (1958, p. 330). Instead of using tests that had been developed by others in relation to different theoretical systems, Kelly developed his own assessment technique — the **Role Construct Repertory Test** (Rep test). As an assessment technique the Rep test is probably more closely related to a theory of personality than is any other comprehensive personality test. The Rep test was developed out of Kelly's construct theory and was designed to be used as a way of eliciting personal constructs.

Role Construct Repertory Test

Basically the Rep test consists of two procedures — the development of a list of persons based on a *Role Title List* and the development of constructs based on the comparison of triads of persons. In the first procedure, the subject is given a Role Title List or list of roles (figures) believed to be of importance to all people. Illustrative role titles would be: mother, father, a teacher you liked, a neighbor you find hard to understand. Generally, 20 to 30 roles are presented and subjects are asked to name a person they have known who fits each role. Following this the examiner picks three specific figures from the list and asks the subject to indicate the way in which two are alike and different from the third. The way in which two of the figures are seen as alike is called the *similarity pole* of the construct while the way in which the third is different is called the *contrast pole* of the construct. For example, a subject might be asked to consider the persons named for Mother, Father, and Liked Teacher. In considering the three, the subject might decide that the people associated with the titles Father and Liked Teacher are similar in being outgoing and different from Mother, who is shy. Thus, the construct outgoing-shy has been formed. The subject is asked to consider other groups of three persons (triads), usually 20 to 30 of them. With each presentation of a triad, the subject generates a construct. The construct given may be the same as a previous one or a new construct.

One can see how the Rep test follows from Kelly's theory since it elicits people's constructs, or ways of perceiving the world, based on their consideration of the way in which two things are similar and different from the third. It is particularly attractive since subjects are completely free to express how they construe the world. At the same time, however, it makes a number of important assumptions. First, it is assumed that the list of roles presented to the subjects is representative of the important figures in their lives. Second, it is assumed that the constructs that are verbalized by the subject are, indeed, the ones used to construe the world. In turn, this assumes that the subjects can verbalize their constructs and that they feel free to report them in the testing situation. Finally, it is assumed that the words the subjects use in naming their constructs are adequate to give the examiner an understanding of how they have organized their past events and how they anticipate the future.

In a clinical interpretation of the Rep test, the examiner considers the number of different constructs, the manner in which various figures are related to the constructs and to one another, and the relationships of the constructs to one another. An illustration of the type of record that is produced on a form of the test used in group testing is given in Box 6.1. The subject, Mildred Beal, took the test as part of a classroom exercise. Since she had also applied for psychological counseling, there was an opportunity to check the interpretation of the test results against the information that was obtained independently during the course of therapy. The interpretation of the test results focused on the limited number of dimensions Mildred used to construe people and on her limited versatility in relating to people. Superficially, many constructs suggest some intellectual striving. However, on closer examination we find that there are really very few dimensions. One important dichotomy is between unhappy striving (hypersensitive, socially maladjusted, feelings of inferiority) and pleasant, comfortable quiescence (easygoing, relaxing, socially better than adequate). A second dominant dichotomy is in the construct friendly and understanding versus hypercritical.

BOX 6.1 **Role Construct Repertory Test: Raw Protocol of Mildred Beal**

RAW PROTOCOL

Sort No.	Similar Figures	Similarity Construct	Dissimilar Figure	Contrasting Construct
1	Boss Successful person	Are related to me	Sought person	Unrelated
2	Rejecting person Pitied person	Very unhappy persons	Intelligent person	Contented
3	Father Liked teacher	Are very quiet and easygoing persons	Pitied person	Nervous hypertensive
4	Mother Sister	Look alike Are both hyper-critical of people in general	Boyfriend	Friendliness
5	Ex-flame Pitied person	Feel inferior	Boyfriend	Self-confident
6	Brother Intelligent person	Socially better than adequate	Disliked teacher	Unpleasant
7	Mother Boss	Hypertensive	Father	Easygoing
8	Sister Rejecting person	Hypercritical	Brother	Understanding
9	Rejecting person Ex-flame	Feelings of inferiority	Disliked teacher	Assured of innate worth
10	Liked teacher Sought person	Pleasing personalities	Successful person	High-powered nervous
11	Mother Ex-flame	Socially maladjusted	Boyfriend	Easygoing self-confident
12	Father Boyfriend	Relaxing	Ex-flame	Uncomfortable to be with
13	Disliked teacher Boss	Emotionally unpredictable	Brother	Even temperament
14	Sister Rejecting person	Look somewhat alike	Liked teacher	Look unalike
15	Intelligent person Successful person	Dynamic personalities	Sought person	Weak personality

DESCRIPTIONS OF FIGURES
(Note: Constructs which were used as bases of similarity are italicized.)

	Figure	Constructs Used to Describe Figure
1	Mother	*Looks like sister*
		Hypercritical of people in general
		Hypertensive
		Socially maladjusted
2	Father	*Quiet*
		Easygoing
		Relaxing
		Easygoing
3	Brother	*Socially better than adequate*
		Even temperament
		Understanding
4	Sister	*Looks like mother*
		Hypercritical of people in general
		Hypercritical
		Looks like rejecting person
5	Boyfriend	*Relaxing*
		Easygoing
		Self-confident
		Self-confident
		Friendliness
6	Liked teacher	*Quiet*
		Easygoing
		Pleasing personality
		Looks unlike sister and rejecting person
7	Disliked teacher	*Emotionally unpredictable*
		Assured of innate worth
		Unpleasant
8	Boss	*Related to me*
		Hypertensive
		Emotionally unpredicable
9	Rejecting person	*Very unhappy*
		Hypercritical
		Looks like sister
		Feelings of inferiority
10	Ex-flame	*Feels very inferior*
		Feelings of inferiority
		Socially maladjusted
		Uncomfortable to be with
11	Sought person	*Pleasing personality*
		Weak personality
		Not related to me
12	Pitied person	*Very unhappy*
		Feels very inferior
		Nervous
		Hypertensive
13	Intelligent person	*Socially better than adequate*
		Dynamic personality
		Contented

BOX 6.1   **Role Construct Repertory Test:**
Raw Protocol of Mildred Beal *continued*

14	Successful person	*Related to me*
		Dynamic personality
		High-powered
		Nervous

SOURCE   G.A. Kelly, The Psychology of Personal Constructs,
New York; Norton, 1955, pp. 242-243.

The analysis of the constructs led the examiner to the following hypotheses: (1) The subject can be expected to show little versatility in handling the figures in her interpersonal world. (2) The subject can be expected to vacillate between unhappy agitation and easy self-indulgence. (3) She may be expected to intellectualize, to state insights glibly but not to retain them. (4) The therapist will initially be viewed as either friendly and understanding or hypercritical. These hypotheses tended to be confirmed by the therapist's reports. Mildred was viewed as being quite inflexible in dealing with people. The therapist observed that she perceived all social situations as forms of social pressure, in which she would win praise and social approval or be criticized and rejected. Although generally presenting herself as cheerful, she could at times become quite sad. She showed a need to be dependent on the therapist and to have him take the initiative in the interviews. On the other hand, she tended to resist all suggestions that he made. An important part of her interaction was an attempt to keep things on a superficially friendly, relaxed level, and to avoid criticism.

As has been indicated, one can describe people not only in terms of the content of their constructs but also in terms of the structure of the construct system. Both the Rep test and modifications of it have again proved to be useful in this regard. An early effort to look at structural aspects of the construct system was Bieri's (1955) study of cognitive complexity. Bieri designated the degree to which a construct system is broken down (levels in the hierarchy) or differentiated as reflecting the system's **cognitive complexity-simplicity**. A cognitively complex system contains many constructs and provides for considerable differentiation in perception of phenomena. A cognitively simple system contains few constructs and provides for poor differentiation in perception of phenomena. A cognitively complex person sees people in a differentiated way — as having a variety of qualities, whereas a cognitively simple person sees people in an

cognitive complexity-simplicity

undifferentiated way — even to the extent of using only one construct (for example, good-bad) in construing others. Using a modified Rep test, Bieri compared cognitively complex and cognitively simple subjects in relation to their accuracy in predicting the behavior of others and in relation to their ability to discriminate between themselves and others. As predicted, it was found that cognitively complex subjects were more accurate in predicting the behavior of others than were cognitively simple subjects. Furthermore, cognitively complex subjects were more able to recognize differences between themselves and others. Presumably the greater number of constructs available to complex subjects allows for both greater accuracy and greater potential for recognition of differences.

Bieri went on to construe cognitive complexity-simplicity as a dimension of personality, defining it as an information-processing variable: "Cognitive complexity may be defined as the capacity to construe social behavior in a multidimensional way" (Bieri, Atkins, Briar, Leaman, Miller, and Tripoldi, 1966). In one study of the way in which individuals process information, it was found that subjects high in complexity differed from subjects low in complexity in the way that they handled inconsistent information about a person. Subjects high in complexity tended to try to make use of the inconsistent information in forming an impression, whereas subjects low in complexity tended to form a consistent impression of the person and to reject all information inconsistent with that impression (Mayo and Crockett, 1964), (Box 6.2). Later research has also indicated that more complex individuals are more empathic, or better able to take the role of others, than are individuals who are cognitively simple (Adams-Webber, 1979).

BOX 6.2 **Cognitive Style
as a Personality Characteristic**

QUESTION   Do individuals differ in the ways in which they process information and make judgments about people? Are such differences related to a cognitive style variable?

HYPOTHESIS   Given an introductory set of information about a person leading to one impression and then a second set of information about that person which is the opposite of the first, subjects high in cognitive complexity will tend to assimilate the second set of information into a mixed final impression of the person. Given the same set of circumstances, subjects low in cognitive complexity will tend to accept the second set of

BOX 6.2 **Cognitive Style
as a Personality Characteristic** *continued*

information and reject the first. In sum, subjects high in cognitive
complexity should be more likely than subjects low in cognitive
complexity to expect the presence of both positive and negative traits in
others.

METHOD   Subjects are 44 male and 36 female undergraduate students. The
measure of cognitive complexity is taken from Kelly's Role Construct
Repertory Test. Subjects give names of people to eight role titles. Five
triads are selected and for each triad the subject is asked to say how
persons 1 and 2 are similar and different from person 3, how persons 1 and
3 are similar and different from person 2, and how persons 2 and 3 are
similar and different from person 1. Thus, for each of the five triads, the
individual gives three constructs, or 15 constructs in all.

As a measure of cognitive complexity, determine the number of different
constructs used by each subject. Establish two distributions of cognitive
complexity scores, one for each sex. From these distributions select 18 men
and 18 women so that one half of each group is in the upper third and one
half in the lower third of the relevant distribution of complexity scores.

Have subjects listen to a tape recording that presents eight descriptions of
a man named Joe. Each description illustrates two important traits of Joe
with an anecdote. Of the eight descriptions, have four describe positive
traits (considerate, intelligent, humorous, well-liked) and four describe
negative traits (immature, bad-tempered, dishonest, sarcastic). For some of
the subjects present the four positive speakers in succession and have the
subjects record their impressions on a trait checklist of 22 paired
opposites. Then present the four negative speakers, ask the subjects to add
that information to what they already know about Joe, and then have
them record their impressions of Joe on the same trait checklist. For the
rest of the subjects, follow the same procedure but present the negative
speakers first.

RESULTS   For each subject develop two scores, one for each time that the
subject completed the trait checklist. The score is the number of traits
checked that are expressive of the first set of information about Joe. The
results for subjects high and low in cognitive complexity are presented in
Table 1. There are no significant differences between the two groups of
subjects in initial impressions. Also, for all subjects, the second impression
was significantly less extreme than the first. However, the final impressions

of subjects high in complexity are almost exactly mixed between positive and negative traits and show less of an extreme reaction to the second description than do the final impressions of subjects low in complexity.

	POSITIVE FIRST		NEGATIVE FIRST	
Cognitive Complexity	First Response	Second Response	First Response	Second Response
High	18.88	13.88	15.30	9.70
Low	19.88	6.75	15.50	6.10

TABLE 1
Mean Number of Traits Checked Which Correspond to the First Set of Information for Subjects High and Low in Cognitive Complexity

CONCLUSION   The results lend support to the view that subjects differing in level of cognitive complexity differ in the manner in which they use information about others in forming impressions of them. Other expected differences such as in the degree of differentiation of perception of others and the extent to which mixed impressions are integrated into a unified, consistent impression remain to be tested in future experiments.

SOURCE   C.W. Mayo, and W.H. Crockett. Cognitive complexity and primary-recency effects in impression formation. Journal of Abnormal and Social Psychology, 1964, 68, 335-338.

Thus, the Rep test can be used to determine the content and structure of an individual's construct system as well as to compare the effects of different construct system structures. As Vernon (1963) points out, the Rep test has the advantages of arising from a theory and of allowing subjects to generate their own constructs, instead of forcing subjects to use dimensions provided by the tester. In his review of the relevant literature, Bonarius (1965) gives a generally positive appraisal of this assessment technique. Two summary statements are worthy of attention.

The research over the past decade shows that the Rep Test, if used in a standard manner, is a safe instrument providing consistent information. That is to say, the figures and constructs elicited are indeed representative of the persons who make up an individual's social world, and of the constructs he applies to them.

BONARIUS, 1965, P. 17

The constructs an individual employs in social interaction are quite stable and relatively independent of the particular persons who make up his social environment. Further, not only can an individual be identified by his personal constructs, but a knowledge of his personal constructs may lead to a different, if not a better, understanding of this individual than descriptions of him by others. Finally, the research has shown convincingly that the individual prefers to express himself and to describe others by using his own personal constructs rather than provided dimensions, such as the usual Q-sort statements . . .

BONARIUS, 1965, P. 26

In sum, Kelly posits that the structure of personality consists of the construct system of the individual. An individual is what he construes himself and others to be, and the Rep Test is a device to ascertain the nature of these constructions.

Process

In his process view of human behavior, Kelly took a radical departure from traditional theories of motivation. As we have mentioned already, the psychology of personal constructs does not interpret behavior in terms of motivation, drives, and needs. For personal construct theory, the term "motivation" is redundant. The term motivation assumes that the person is inert and needs something to get started. But, if we assume that the person is basically active, the controversy as to what prods an inert organism into action becomes a dead issue. "Instead, the organism is delivered fresh into the psychological world alive and struggling" (Kelly, 1955, p. 37). Kelly contrasted other theories of motivation with his own position in the following way:

Motivational theories can be divided into two types, push theories and pull theories. Under push theories we find such terms as drive, motive, or even stimulus. Pull theories use such constructs as purpose, value, or need. In terms of a well-known metaphor, these are the pitchfork theories on the one hand and the carrot theories on the other. But our theory is neither of these. Since we prefer to look to the nature of the animal himself, ours is probably best called a jackass theory.

KELLY, 1958, P. 50

The concept of motive traditionally has been used to explain why humans are active and why their activity takes a specific direction. Since Kelly did not feel the need for the concept of motive to account for a person's activity, how did he account for the direction of activity of this very much alive and struggling organism? Kelly's position is simply stated in his fundamental postulate: A person's processes are psychologically channelized by the ways in which he anticipates events. Kelly offers this postulate as a given and does not question its truth. The postulate implies that we seek prediction, that we anticipate events, that we reach out to the future through the window of the present. In experiencing events, the individual observes similarities and contrasts, thereby developing constructs. On the basis of these constructs, the individual, like a true scientist, anticipates the future.

As we see the same events repeated over and over, we modify our constructs so that they will lead to more accurate predictions. Constructs are tested in terms of their predictive efficiency. But what accounts for the direction of behavior? Again, like the scientist, people choose that course of behavior which they believe offers the greatest opportunity for anticipating future events. Scientists try to develop better theories, theories that lead to the efficient prediction of events, and individuals try to develop better construct systems. Thus, according to Kelly, a person chooses that alternative which promises the greatest further development of the construct system.

In making a choice of a particular construct, the individual, in a sense, makes a "bet" by anticipating a particular event or set of events. If there are inconsistencies in the construct system, the bets will not add up — they will cancel each other out. If the system is consistent, a prediction is made that can be tested. If the anticipated event does occur, the prediction has been upheld and the construct validated, at least, for the time being. If the anticipated event does not occur, the construct has been invalidated. In the latter case, the individual must develop a new construct or must loosen or expand the old construct to include the prediction of the event that took place. Maher (1966) gives the example of the child who uses the construct of reassuring-punitive in relation to his mother. The child may find that his mother is at times punitive when he had expected her to be reassuring. The child may abandon the reassuring-punitive construct for a just-unjust construct and may interpret his mother's punishment as just.

In essence, then, individuals make a prediction and consider further change in their construct systems on the basis of whether they have led to accurate prediction. Notice that individuals do not seek reinforcement or the avoidance of pain; instead, they seek validation and expansion of their construct system. If a person expects something unpleasant and that event occurs, he experiences validation regardless of the fact that it was a negative, unpleasant event that occurred. In observing individuals in a shock experiment, Pervin (1964) concluded that individuals seek to confirm their predictive strategies and will prefer the pain of an electric shock to no shock if the absence of shock would disconfirm their predictive system. One should understand that Kelly is not suggesting that the individual seeks certainty, such as would be found in the repetitive ticking of a clock. The boredom people feel with repeated events and the fatalism that comes as a result of the inevitable are usually avoided wherever possible. Rather, the individual seeks to anticipate events and to increase the range of convenience or boundaries of his construct system. Finally, this point leads to a distinction between the views of Kelly and the views of Rogers. According to Kelly, individuals do not seek consistency for consistency's sake or even self-consistency. Instead, individuals seek to anticipate events, and it is a consistent system that allows them to do this.

Thus far, Kelly's system appears to be reasonably simple and straightforward. The process view becomes more complicated with the introduction of the concepts of anxiety, fear, and threat. Kelly defined **anxiety** in the following way: Anxiety is the recognition that the events with which one is confronted lie outside the range of convenience of one's construct system. One is anxious when one is without constructs, when one has "lost his structural grip on events," when one is "caught with his constructs down." In contrast to anxiety, one experiences **fear** when a new construct appears to be about to enter the construct system. Of even greater significance is the experience of **threat**. Threat is defined as the awareness of imminent comprehensive change in one's core structure. A person feels threatened when a major shake-up in the construct system is about to occur. One feels threatened by death if it is perceived as imminent and if it involves a drastic change in one's core constructs. Death is not threatening when it does not seem imminent or when it is not construed as being fundamental to the meaning of one's life.

The experiences of anxiety and threat are critical for the functioning of the organism. People protect themselves from anxiety in various ways. Confronted by events that they cannot construe, that is, that lie outside the range of convenience, individuals may broaden a construct and permit it to apply to a greater variety of events, or they may narrow their constructs and focus on minute details. Anxiety is not the result of invalidated constructs but, rather, is the result of not having constructs to deal with a situation. On the other hand, threat is the result of a number of invalidated constructs and the resultant questioning that occurs about whether one has any constructs at all. Threat, in particular, has a wide range of ramifications. Whenever people undertake some new activity, they expose themselves to confusion and threat. Confusion may lead to something new, but it may also eventuate in a threat to the individual. Individuals experience threat when they realize that their construct system is about to be drastically affected by what has been discovered. "This is the moment of threat. It is the threshold between confusion and certainty, between anxiety and bordeom. It is precisely at this moment when we are most tempted to turn back" (Kelly, 1964, p. 141). The response to threat may be to give up the adventure — to regress to old constructs in order to avoid panic. Threat occurs as we venture into human understanding and when we stand on the brink of a profound change in ourselves.

What makes the concepts of anxiety, fear, and threat so significant is that they suggest a new dimension to Kelly's view of human functioning. The dynamics of functioning can now be seen to involve the interplay between the individual's wish to expand the construct system and the desire

anxiety

fear

threat

to avoid the threat of disruption of that system: "If one wished to state negatively Kelly's position on the psychology of personal constructs, as they relate to motivation, one might say that human behavior is directed away from ultimate anxiety" (Kelly, 1955, p. 894). Thus, we have here a model of anxiety and defense. In response to anxiety, individuals may *submerge* one end of a construct in order to keep perceiving events in a familiar, comfortable way, or they may *suspend* elements that do not fit so well into a construct. Submergence and suspension are responses to anxiety. They are viewed as being similar to the psychoanalytic concept of repression. Thus, in the face of anxiety, individuals may act in ways that will make their constructs or parts of their constructs unavailable for verbalization. In the face of threat, individuals have a choice between constricted certainty and broadened understanding. Individuals always seek to maintain and to enhance their predictive systems. However, in the face of anxiety and threat, individuals may rigidly adhere to a constricted system, instead of venturing out into the risky realm of expansion of their construct systems.

To summarize, Kelly assumes an active organism, and he does not posit any motivational forces. For Kelly, the person behaves as a scientist in construing events, in making predictions, and in seeking expansion of the construct system. Sometimes, not unlike the scientist, we are made so anxious by the unknowns and so threatened by the unfamiliar that we seek to hold on to absolute truths and become dogmatic. On the other hand, when we are behaving as good scientists, we are able to adopt the invitational mood and to expose our construct systems to the diversity of events that make up life.

Growth and Development

Kelly was never very explicit about the origins of construct systems. He stated that constructs were derived from observing repeated patterns of events. But he did little to elaborate on the kinds of events that would lead to differences like the ones between simple and complex construct systems. Kelly's comments relating to growth and development were limited to an emphasis on the development of preverbal constructs in infancy and the interpretation of culture as involving a process of learned expectations. People belong to the same cultural group in that they share certain ways of construing events and have the same kinds of expectations regarding certain kinds of behavior.

Some research has been undertaken that suggests the kinds of variables that influence the development of construct systems. In a study conducted within a slightly different but related framework, Signell (1966) found that between the ages of nine and sixteen children become more cognitively complex; that is, as children develop, they tend to become more abstract in their thinking, they tend to have a greater number of ways of interpreting the environment, and they tend to be more flexible in their interpretations of events. Two studies have been reported that are relevant to the question of the determinants of complex cognitive structures. In one study, the subjects' level of cognitive complexity was found to be related to the variety of cultural backgrounds to which they had been exposed in childhood (Sechrest and Jackson, 1961). In another study, parents of cognitively complex children were found to be more likely to grant autonomy and less likely to be authoritarian than were parents of children low in cognitive complexity (Cross, 1966). Presumably, the opportunity to examine many different events and to have many different experiences is conducive to the development of a complex structure. One would also expect to find that children who experience longstanding and severe threat from authoritarian parents would develop constricted and inflexible construct systems.

The question of factors determining the content of constructs and the complexity of construct systems is of critical importance. In particular, it is relevant to the field of education, since a part of education appears to be the development of complex, flexible, and adaptive construct systems. Unfortunately, Kelly himself made few statements in this area, and research is only now beginning to elaborate on this part of the theory.

MAJOR CONCEPTS AND SUMMARY

construct

construct system

range of convenience

focus of convenience

similarity and contrast poles

core and peripheral constructs

verbal and preverbal constructs

submerged part of a construct

superordinate and subordinate constructs

Role Construct Repertory Test (Rep test)

cognitive complexity-simplicity

anxiety, fear, and threat

In this chapter we have reviewed parts of the life of an unusual theorist and the basic essentials of his theory of personality. George Kelly developed a theory out of a diversity of clinical experiences. His theory of personality avoids many of the standard terms found in the field of psychology and invites the reader to dare to interpret the human organism in a new light — as a scientist who seeks to construe the world in a way that will permit increasingly better prediction of events. The emphasis on the invitational mood is an important part of setting the stage for perceiving phenomena in a different way. The emphasis on the person as a scientist is an important part of his approach — our personality is our theory or construct system as well as the ways in which we act and feel in accordance with our construct system.

For Kelly the essential aspect of personality is the construct — the person's way of looking at, interpreting, or construing events. Constructs are developed as a result of noticing similarities and differences in events as we live our daily lives. The Rep test was developed by Kelly to assess the construct system of a person. Following the logic of personal construct theory, in the Rep test the person is asked to consider triads of persons and to indicate how two are alike and different from the third. This leads to the definition of a similarity pole and a contrast pole. Through the use of the Rep test the psychologist can attempt an analysis of the structure of the person's construct system in terms of core and peripheral constructs, superordinate and subordinate constructs, and the overall level of complexity or simplicity.

Just as the scientist seeks to predict events, so the human organism seeks to anticipate events. The function of the construct system is the anticipation of events — a task which is always before us and which we are always seeking to master. So critical is this to our functioning that we experience anxiety when our constructs do not appear to fit the events we are observing, and experience threat when our construct system itself seems endangered. Under such circumstances one or more parts of the construct system may become submerged, new experiences may be rejected, and the individual may defensively adhere to viewing events in preconceived ways.

As a result of experience we develop a construct system with a variety of kinds of constructs, involving distinct content for each individual, and an organization that reaches varying degrees of complexity or simplicity. Some constructs are learned prior to the development of language (preverbal constructs) but for most people the vast majority of the constructs in their construct system can be expressed in words. Under supportive circumstances the child and the adult feel free to expand their construct systems to include new phenomena and to organize what has been learned in new ways. In other words, increased complexity and integration are aspects of a healthy, developing construct system. Just as scientists attempt to develop theories that will include more phenomena and predict more events, so healthy development involves increasing the range of convenience and focus of convenience of the construct system. On the other hand, if new experiences are not provided or if the person feels too threatened to construe life in a different way, then the construct system may remain fixed, rigid, and unchanged.

In sum, in Kelly's theory we act and move because we are alive, not because of urges from within or pushes from without. As the scientists we are, we seek to expand our construct systems so as to better anticipate events. The only exceptions are when we are feeling so anxious or threatened that exploration and the invitational mood are impossible. A major part of Kelly's efforts were directed toward understanding people in terms of their own construct systems and toward facilitating their developing more useful ways of construing events. In the next chapter we shall learn about his efforts to develop methods to help people to change their constructions of themselves and events around them.

CLINICAL APPLICATIONS
Psychopathology
Change
A CASE EXAMPLE—RONALD BARRETT
RELATED POINTS OF VIEW AND RECENT DEVELOPMENTS
CRITICAL EVALUATION
Kelly and Freud
Kelly and Rogers
Kelly, Freud, and Rogers
MAJOR CONCEPTS AND SUMMARY

7 A COGNITIVE THEORY OF PERSONALITY: APPLICATIONS AND EVALUATION OF KELLY'S THEORY

CHAPTER FOCUS:

In this chapter we will consider the clinical applications of Kelly's personal construct theory. Kelly felt that any significant theory of personality had to suggest ways to help people. The area of psychotherapy was a major source of interest and concern to Kelly and was held as a major aspect or focus of convenience of personal construct theory.

From the standpoint of the psychology of personal constructs, we may define a disorder as any personal construction which is used repeatedly in spite of consistent invalidation.

KELLY, 1955, P. 831

Yet we see it as the ultimate objective of the clinical psychology enterprise . . . the psychological reconstruction of life. We even considered using the term reconstruction instead of therapy. If it had not been such a mouth-filling word we might have gone ahead with the idea. Perhaps later we may.

KELLY, 1955, p. 187

CLINICAL APPLICATIONS

Psychopathology

According to Kelly, psychopathology is a disordered response to anxiety. As in the theories discussed previously, the concepts of anxiety, fear, and threat play a major role in Kelly's theory of psychopathology. However, it must be kept in mind that these concepts, although retained, have been redefined in terms relevant to personal construct theory.

For Kelly, psychopathology is defined in terms of disordered functioning of a construct system. A poor scientist is one who retains a theory and makes the same predictions despite repeated research failures. Similarly, abnormal behavior involves efforts to retain the content and structure of the construct system despite repeated incorrect predictions or invalidations. "From the standpoint of the psychology of personal constructs we may define a disorder as any personal construction which is used repeatedly in spite of consistent invalidation" (Kelly, 1955, p. 831). At the root of this rigid adherence to a construct system are anxiety, fear, and threat. Kelly stated that one could construe human behavior as being directed away from ultimate anxiety. Psychological disorders are disorders involving anxiety and faulty efforts to reestablish the sense of being able to anticipate events:

There is a sense in which all disorders of communication are disorders involving anxiety. A "neurotic" person casts about frantically for new ways of construing the events of his world. Sometimes he works on "little" events, sometimes on "big" events, but he is always fighting off anxiety. A "psychotic" person appears to have found some temporary solution for his anxiety. But it is a precarious solution, at best, and must be sustained in the face of evidence which, for most of us, would be invalidating.

KELLY, 1955, PP. 895-896

permeable
impermeable

What are some of the faulty ways in which people try to hold on to their construct systems? These efforts involve problems in the ways in which constructs are applied to new events, problems in the ways in which constructs are used to make predictions, and problems in the ways in which the overall system is organized. Let us consider an illustration of each. An example of the pathological application of constructs is that of making constructs excessively **permeable** or excessively **impermeable**. An excessively permeable construct allows almost any new content into it whereas an excessively impermeable construct admits no new elements into its context. Excessive permeability can lead to the use of just a few constructs that are very broad and the lack of recognition of important differences among people and events. Too much becomes lumped together, as in stereotypes. Excessive impermeability can lead to pigeonholing each new experience, as if everything is distinctive, and to rejecting events that cannot be pigeonholed. This pattern of response is found in people who are described as being very compulsive.

tightening
loosening

An illustration of the pathological use of constructs to make predictions is excessive **tightening** and excessive **loosening**. In excessive tightening the person makes the same kinds of predictions regardless of the circumstances. In excessive loosening, the person makes excessively varied predictions with the same construct. In neither case can prediction be very accurate since both involve ignoring circumstances that might call for shifts in the construct system — in the first case through always predicting the same and in the second case through random, chaotic predictions. Tightening may be seen in the compulsive person who rigidly expects life to be the same regardless of changes in circumstances, while loosening can be seen in the psychotic person whose construct system is so chaotic that it cannot be used to communicate with others: "They (schizophrenic clients) are not caught short of constructs. But what constructs!" (Kelly, 1955, p. 497) (Box 7.1).

BOX 7.1 **Personal Construct Theory and Psychopathology**

PROBLEM   In personal construct theory terms, schizophrenics have an overly loose and inconsistent system for construing people. In conventional terms, their ideas about people are both poorly related and unstable. Is it possible to develop a clinically economic and adequately standardized test for detecting the presence of schizophrenic thought disorder?

BOX 7.1   **Personal Construct Theory and Psychopathology**   *continued*

SUBJECTS   Test seven different groups of subjects: (a) 30 thought-disordered schizophrenics; (b) 30 nonthought-disordered schizophrenics; (c) 30 normals; (d) 30 depressives; (e) 20 neurotics; (f) 20 patients with organic brain damage; (g) 28 subnormals (i.e., patients with an IQ below 80).

METHOD   Test each subject individually. Present to the subject eight passport-type photographs and ask him which person was the most likely to be kind. Then ask the subject to select the person most likely to be kind from the remaining seven photographs, and so on until the subject has ranked all eight photographs from the most kind to the least kind. Use the same procedure to obtain from the subject a rank ordering of the eight photographs on six constructs: kind, stupid, selfish, sincere, mean, and honest. When this is done, go through the same procedure again, using the same photographs and having the subject rank them for the same qualities. Instruct the subject that this is not a test of memory and that he should take the test as if he were doing it for the first time.

SCORING   Derive two scores from the rest — one for intensity and one for consistency. The intensity score reflects how closely the subject has ranked the photographs on one construct to the rank orderings on the other constructs. A high intensity score indicate that the subject is rank ordering as if the qualities he is judging are related, whereas a low score indicates that he is treating the qualities as relatively independent. Previous studies with these six constructs indicates that they are highly interrelated for nonthought-disordered subjects and therefore one would expect the thought-disordered schizophrenics to have lower intensity scores than the subjects in the other groups. Low scores reflect loose construing.

The consistency score reflects the degree to which the subject has maintained the pattern of relationships between the first and second times that he took the test. Essentially, it is a test-retest relationship and measures the degree to which the subject on retest continues to apply the constructs in the same way that he did on the original test. Thought-disordered schizophrenics are expected to have lower consistency scores than other subjects since they tend to show radical changes in their pattern of construing events.

RESULTS

1   The population of subnormal subjects had very low intensity and consistency scores, suggesting that there is an effect of very low intelligence on these test scores. However, within the normal range of intelli-

gence, there does not appear to be a relationship between intelligence and these two test scores.

2 The means (average) for consistency and intensity for the remaining subjects are presented in the table below. On both the intensity and the consistency scores, thought disordered schizophrenics are significantly lower than the subjects in the other groups.

GROUP MEANS (AVERAGES) OF INTENSITY AND CONSISTENCY TEST SCORES FOR SIX GROUPS OF SUBJECTS

	Mean Intensity	Mean Consistency
Thought-Disordered Schiz.	728	.18
Normals	1253	.80
Nonthought Disordered Schiz.	1183	.73
Depressives	1115	.75
Neurotics	1383	.74
Organics	933	.73

CONCLUSION   The test used here is useful in detecting and measuring schizophrenic thought disorders. The value of using concepts like Intensity and Consistency is that they can be related to other aspects of the theory of schizophrenia; that is, they are not just empty empirical findings.

SOURCE   D. Bannister, and F. Fransella. A grid test of schizophrenic thought disorder. *British Journal of Social and Clinical Psychology*, 1966, *5*, 95-102.

**constriction
dilation**

Finally, we come to disordered efforts to maintain the overall organization of the construct system, as illustrated in **constriction** and **dilation**. Constriction involves a narrowing of the construct system to minimize incompatibilities. The range and focus of convenience of the construct system becomes quite small. Constriction tends to be found in people who are depressed and who limit their interests, narrowing their attention to a smaller and smaller area. In contrast to this, in dilation the person attempts to broaden the construct system and to reorganize it at a more comprehensive level. Extreme dilation is observed in the behavior of the manic person who jumps from topic to topic and who makes sweeping generalizations with few ideas. It is as if everything can now be included in the construct system of this person.

These faulty devices to prevent anxiety and avoid the threat of change in the construct system illustrate Kelly's efforts to interpret pathological behavior within the framework of person construct theory. Another illustration of his interpretation of psychopathology is the case of suicide — namely, that it represents the turning inward of hostility. According to this psychoanalytic view, every suicide is a potential homicide. Because of anxiety or guilt, the hostility that would otherwise be directed toward some other person becomes directed instead toward the self. Not so according to the psychology of personal constructs. Kelly (1961) interpreted suicide as an act to validate one's life or as an act of abandonment. In the latter case, suicide occurs because of fatalism or because of total anxiety — because the course of events is so obvious that there is no point in waiting around for the outcome (fatalism), or because everything is so unpredictable that the only definite thing to do is to abandon the scene altogether. As noted, we often must choose between immediate certainty and wider understanding. In suicide, the choice is for the former and represents ultimate constriction. "For the man of constricted outlook whose world begins to crumble, death may appear to provide the only immediate certainty which he can lay his hands on" (Kelly, 1955, p. 64).

While Kelly did not emphasize the concept of hostility in relation to suicide, he did recognize its importance in human functioning. Again, however, the concept is redefined in terms relevant to personal construct theory. Kelly made an important distinction between aggression and hostility, one that often is absent in other theories. According to Kelly, **aggression** involves the active expansion of the person's construct system. This active expansion of the construct system does not interfere with the functioning of other people. In contrast to this, **hostility** occurs when one tries to make others behave in an expected way. For example, it would be hostile for a person to intimidate someone because they expected them to behave in a submissive way. According to this view, the hostile person does not intend to do harm. Rather, injury is an accidental outcome of the effort to protect one's construct system by attempting to make people behave in expected ways. Here too the emphasis is on protection of the construct system. The opposite of hostility is curiosity and respect for the freedom of movement of others.

To summarize Kelly's view of psychophathology, we return to the analogy of the scientist. Scientists attempt to predict events through the use of theories. Scientists develop poor theories when they fear venturing out into the unknown, when they fear testing out hypotheses and making bets, when they rigidly adhere to their theory in the face of contradictory evidence, when they can account only for trivia, and when they try to say that they are accounting for things that, in fact, are outside the range of convenience of their theories. When scientists construe in these ways, we say they are bad scientists. When people construe in these ways, we refer to them as sick people. When people know how to stay loose and also tighten up, we call them creative and reward them for their efforts. When people stay too loose or too "up tight," we say they are ill and consider

aggression

hostility

hospitalization. It all depends on their constructs — and on how others construe the constructs.

Change

The process of positive change is discussed by Kelly in terms of the development of better construct systems. If sickness represents the continued use of constructs in the face of consistent invalidation, psychotherapy is the process whereby clients are assisted in improving their predictions. In psychotherapy, clients are trained to be better scientists. Psychotherapy is a process of reconstruing — a process of reconstruction of the construct system. This means that some constructs need to be replaced, some new ones need to be added; some need to be tightened while others are loosened; and some need to be made more permeable while others are made less permeable. Whatever the details of the process, *psychotherapy is the psychological reconstruction of life.*

According to Kelly's theory, three conditions exist that are favorable to the formation of new constructs. First, and perhaps most important, there must be an *atmosphere of experimentation.* This means that, for example, in therapy "one does not 'play for keeps.' Constructs, in the true scientific tradition, are seen as 'being tried on for size' " (Kelly, 1955, p. 163). In psychotherapy, one creates the invitational mood and accepts the language of hypothesis. Psychotherapy is a form of experimentation. In therapy, constructs (hypotheses) are developed, experiments are performed, and hypotheses are revised on the basis of empirical evidence. By being permissive and responsive, by providing the client with the tools of experimentation, and by encouraging the client to make hypotheses, the therapist assists in the development of the client as a scientist.

The second key condition for change is the *provision of new elements.* Conditions favorable to change include new elements that are relatively unbound by old constructs. The therapy room is a "protected environment" in which new elements can be recognized and confronted. Therapists themselves represent a new element in relation to which their clients can start to develop new constructs. It is here that the question of *transference* emerges, and the therapist must ask: "In what role is the client now casting me?" Clients may attempt to transfer a construct from their repertory that was applicable in the past and to use it in relation to their therapists. They may construe the therapist as a parent, as an absolver of guilt, as an authority figure, as a prestige figure, or as a stooge. Whatever the content of the transference, the therapist tries to provide fresh, new elements in an atmosphere of make-believe and experimentation.

Along with this, therapists provide the third condition for change — they make *validating data available.* We are told that knowledge of results facilitates learning. We know that, given a supportive atmosphere and the permeable aspects of the construct system, invalidation does lead to change (Bieri, 1953; Poch, 1952). The therapist provides new elements in a situation in which the client will at first attempt to use old constructs. It is the therapist's task to share his own perceptions of and reactions to the client, against which the client can check his own hypotheses: "By providing validating data in the form of responses to a wide variety of constructions on the part of the client, some of them quite loose, fanciful, or naughty, the clinician gives the client an opportunity to validate constructs, an opportunity which is not normally available to him" (Kelly, 1955, p. 165).

We know that there are individual differences in resistance to change (Bonarius, 1965: Diggory, 1966), and that rigidity is related to psychopathology (Pervin, 1960). However, given an atmosphere of experimentation, given new elements, and given validating data, people do change. Conversely, the conditions unfavorable for change include threat, preoccupation with old material, and the lack of a "laboratory" in which to experiment. It is within the context of the former conditions of change that Kelly developed a specific therapeutic technique — **fixed-role therapy**. Fixed-role therapy assumes that, psychologically, people are what they represent themselves to be and that people are what they do. Fixed-role therapy encourages clients to *represent themselves in new ways*, to *behave in new ways*, to construe themselves in new ways and thereby, to *become new people.*

fixed-role therapy

In fixed-role therapy, the clients are presented with a new personality sketch that they are asked to act out. On the basis of some understanding of the client, a group of psychologists get together to write a description of a new person. The task for the clients is to behave "as-if" they were that person. The personality sketch written for each client involves the development of a new personality. Many characteristics are presented in the sketch that are in sharp contrast with the person's actual functioning. In the light of construct theory, Kelly suggested that it might be easier for people to play up what they believe to be the opposite of the way they generally behave than to behave just a little bit differently. Design of the sketch involves setting in motion processes that will have effects throughout the construct system. Fixed-role therapy does not aim at the readjustment of minor parts. Instead, it aims at the reconstruction of a personality. If offers a new role, a new personality for the client in which new hypotheses can be tested out; it offers the client the opportunity to test out new ways of construing events under the full protection of "make-believe."

Just how does the process of fixed-role therapy work? After a personality sketch is drawn up, it is presented to the client. The client decides whether the sketch sounds like someone he would like to know and whether he would feel comfortable with such a person. This is done to make sure that the new personality will not be excessively threatening to the client. In the next phase of fixed-role therapy, the therapist invites the client to act as if he were that person. For a period of about two weeks, the client is asked to forget who he is and to be this other person. If the new person is called Tom Jones, then the client is told the following: "For two weeks, try to forget who you are or that you ever were. You are Tom Jones! You act like him! You think like him. You talk to your friends the way you think he would talk. You do the things you think he would do! You even have his interests and you enjoy the things he would enjoy!" The client may resist, he may feel that this is play-acting and that it is hypocritical, but he is encouraged, in an accepting manner, to try out and see how it goes. The client is not told that this is what he should eventually be, but he is asked to try it out. He is asked to temporarily give up being himself so that he can discover himself.

During the following weeks, the client eats, sleeps, and feels the role. Periodically, he meets with the therapist to discuss problems in acting the role. There may be some rehearsing of the personality sketch in the therapy session so that the therapist and client will have a chance to examine the functioning of the new construct system when it is actually in use. The therapist must himself be prepared to act as if he were various persons and to accept the invitationl mood. He must at every moment "play in strong support of an actor — the client — who is continually fumbling his lines and contaminating his role" (Kelly, 1955, p. 399). The purpose of this entire procedure is to reestablish the spirit of exploration, to establish the construction of life as a creative process. Kelly was wary of the emphasis on being oneself — how could one be anything else? He viewed remaining what one is as dull, uninteresting, and unadventuresome. Instead, he suggested that people should feel free to make-believe, to play and, thereby, to become:

What I am saying is that it is not so much what man is that counts as it is what he ventures to make of himself. To make the leap he must do more than disclose himself; he must risk a certain amount of confusion. Then, as soon as he does catch a glimpse of a different kind of life, he needs to find some way of overcoming the paralyzing moment of threat, for this is the instant when he wonders what he really is — whether he is what he just was or is what he is about to be.

KELLY, 1964, P. 147

Fixed-role therapy was not the only therapeutic technique discussed by Kelly. However, it is one that is particularly associated with personal construct theory, and it does exemplify some of the principles of the personal construct theory of change. The goal of therapeutic change is the individual's reconstruction of himself and others (Box 7.2). The individual drops some constructs, creates new ones, does some tightening and loosening, and develops a construct system that leads to more accurate predictions. The therapist encourages the client to make believe, to experiment, to spell out alternatives, and to reconstrue the past in the light of new constructs. The process of therapy is very complex. Different clients must be treated differently, and the resistance to change must be overcome. However, positive change is possible in a situation where a good director assists in the playing of the human drama or a good teacher assists in the development of a creative scientist.

BOX 7.2 ## Change in the Construct System

QUESTION   Do individuals change their preferences for particular concepts in perceiving others with whom they interact closely as a result of participation in sensitivity training? Sensitivity training involves the participation of a number of individuals in a group experience in which the goal is an increase in individuals' awareness of how others respond to them and how they feel and respond toward others. Participants are encouraged to look beyond "good-bad" interpretations of behavior to "deeper" causes of behavior in terms of attitudes and feelings.

HYPOTHESES   (1) Participants in sensitivity training will change in their description of others toward the use of more concepts dealing with feelings, attitudes, and emotions. (2) Changes in concept usage will be related to ratings of participants' behavior in the sensitivity training sessions; that is, the extent of change will be related to effective participation in the training activities.

METHOD   Take subjects who are participating in sensitivity training. Subjects are drawn from middle levels of responsibility in industry and government and in voluntary and educational organizations. In all, there are 115 participants in the study (79 men, 36 women).

Have the subjects describe themselves and 10 close associates on a modified form of Kelly's Role Repertory Test. Mail a readministration of the test to the participants three weeks after they have participated in the training experience, and again the third month following training.

Each subject gives 20 constructs on the Rep test each time the test is given. Responses are coded into two broad categories: concrete-instrumental and inferential-expressive.

Examples of concrete-instrumental constructs would be "man-woman," and "tall-short." Examples of inferential-expressive constructs would be "afraid of people-confident," "warm-cold," and "trusting-suspicious." The percentage of the constructs that are of the inferential-expressive type is calculated for each of the three times the test is given.

As a measure of effective participation in the training activities, have each participant rated by others in the group at the end of training sessions. Participants are rated on questions relating to the extent to which they were perceived by others to be involved actively in the sensitivity training process.

RESULTS   Table 1 shows the changes from presensitivity training to the first follow-up and from presensitivity training to the second follow-up in the use of inferential-expressive concepts on the modified Rep test. There is a change in the predicted direction for both follow-up tests, but it is significant only for the second administration. The change in use of constructs appears to be progressive during the post-training period.

TABLE 1
Changes in Use of Inferential Expressive (I-E) Concepts

	PRETRAINING USAGE (N = 115)	POST-TRAINING USAGE FIRST ADMINISTRATION (N = 79)	POST-TRAINING USAGE SECOND ADMINISTRATION (N = 76)
Mean number of I-E concepts (out of a maximum of 20) 10.6		Mean change .39	Mean change .95

Of the five items on which the participants were rated for involvement in the training process, three showed a positive significant relationship between active involvement and increase in use of inferential-expressive concepts. For example, high ratings on the item "Has made it easy for others to give him feedback." are related to large increases in use of inferential-expressive constructs.

CONCLUSION   There is a significant change in concept use following a sensitivity training experience. This change appears to be progressive and appears to be due to active involvement in the sensitivity training process.

SOURCE   R. Harrison, Cognitive change and participation in a sensitivity-training laboratory. *Journal of Consulting Psychology*, 1966, *30*, 517-520

A CASE EXAMPLE — RONALD BARRETT

From the phenomenological point of view, and from that of personal construct theory, the client is always right. Although clinicians may choose to construe events differently, they should never ignore the contructions of their clients. Hence, Kelly was led to say: "If you do not know what is wrong with a person, ask him: he may tell you." An approach that is construed as useful in understanding the clients is to have them write a character sketch of themselves. One client who did this was Ronald Barrett, a university student who came to a counseling service with generalized complaints regarding academic, vocational, and social adjustments.

In his self-descriptive character sketch, Ronald Barrett began by indicating that he gives others the impression that he is quiet and calm, and that he dislikes drawing unfavorable attention to himself. Aside from this quiet behavior in public, however, he reported that he was likely to flare up easily. Little anger was shown to others, but he readily became frustrated and worked up about his own errors or those of others. He thought much of his behavior was an effort to impress others and to show that he was considerate and sincere. He considered morals and ethics as guides to behavior, and guilt the result of not being sufficiently kind. Ronald described himself as striving toward being logical, accurate, and aware of minor technicalities. Finally, he described himself as relatively inflexible and as attaching too much importance to kissing a girl.

In his discussion of the sketch, Kelly observed that a conventional approach to it would emphasize its compulsive aspects. However, beyond this view, Kelly suggested an approach in which the effort is made to see the world through the client's own eyes. In his analysis of Ronald's account, Kelly emphasized the need to look at the order in which the material is presented, the way in which it is organized, the terms (inconsiderate, sincerity, conscientiousness, morals, ethics, guilt, kindhearted) that are used, the themes that are repeated, and the simlarities and contrasts that are made. In approaching the material in these ways, Kelly made reference to the following:

1 Ronald's vehement assertion that he ought to have the appearance of a quiet and calm personality suggests that he is sensitive to the public. The effort to retain a public mask seems critical.

2 The contrast between external calm and the feeling of sitting on a lid of explosive behavior seems significant. He appears to get upset by behaviors in others which he sees in himself and rejects — the loss of intellectual controls.

3 He reports inconsistencies in his behavior and appears to be aware of breakdowns in his construct system.

4 Sincerity is a key construct and is linked with consideration and kindheartedness. By implication, the characteristics of insincerity, inconsid-

eration, and unkindheartedness are also critical in his construing of events. He appears to vacillate between these poles and to find neither totally satisfactory.

5 He appears to use criticism and correction as an intellectual process through which he can avoid flare-ups. His stress upon technicalities is a way of leading a righteous life.

6 Ronald appears to think in terms of "nothing but," preemptive constructs and to think in stereotyped ways. He is concrete in his formulations of events and is not terribly imaginative.

At the time of Ronald's self-description, he had completed a number of therapy sessions. They, however, were not part of a fixed-role therapy program. Such a program was undertaken, and it began with the writing of a fixed-role sketch by a panel of clinicians. The central theme of the sketch was the effort to seek answers in the subtle feelings of others rather than in dispute with them. The sketch, given the name of Kenneth Norton, emphasized attention to feelings. Here is the sketch of "Kenneth Norton" that was presented to Ronald Barrett.

Kenneth Norton

Kenneth Norton is the kind of man who, after a few minutes of conversation, somehow makes you feel that he must have known you intimately for a long time. This comes about, not by any particular questions that he asks, but by the understanding way in which he listens. It is as if he had a knack of seeing the world through your eyes. The things which you have come to see as being important he, too, soon seems to sense as similarly important. Thus he catches not only your words but the punctuations of feeling with which they are formed and the litle accents of meaning with which they are chosen.

Kenneth Norton's complete absorption in the thoughts of the people with whom he holds conversations appears to leave no place for any feelings of self-consciousness regarding himself. If indeed he has such feelings at all, they obviously run a poor second to his eagerness to see the world through other people's eyes. Nor does this mean that he is ashamed of himself, rather it means that he is too much involved with the fascinating worlds of other people with whom he is surrounded to give more than a passing thought to soul-searching criticisms of himself. Some people might, of course, consider this itself to be a kind of fault. Be that as it may, this is the kind of fellow Kenneth Norton is, and this behavior represents the Norton brand of sincerity.

Girls he finds attractive for many reasons, not the least of which is the exciting opportunity they provide for his understanding the feminine point of view. Unlike some men, he does not "throw the ladies a line" but, so skillful a listener is he, soon he has them throwing him one — and he is thoroughly enjoying it.

With his own parents and in his own home he is somewhat more expressive of his own ideas and feelings. Thus his parents are given an opportunity to share and supplement his new enthusiasms and accomplishments.

KELLY, 1955, PP. 374-375

At first, Ronald had trouble in understanding the role he was to play and found that he was not too successful in his role-playing. In the midst of this discouragement, however, he met a former classmate at a movie and found that the role worked better with her than with anyone else. In fact, after a while she was paying him several compliments and indicated that he had changed (presumably for the better) since he had gone away to college. Some role-playing was tried in the therapy sessions. At times, Ronald would lapse back into dominating the conversation. At other times, however, he was able to draw out the therapist, who was now acting the role of various people in Ronald's life. When Ronald performed as Kenneth Norton, the therapist rewarded him with compliments.

Although the early presentations of himself as Kenneth Norton were without spontaneity or warmth, Ronald began to feel more comfortable in the role. He reported to the therapist that he felt less insecure in social situations, that he had fewer quarrels with others, and that he seemed to be more productive in his work efforts. When a difficult situation was described in the session, the therapist asked Ronald how Kenneth Norton would have handled it and then proceeded to engage Ronald in a role-playing rehearsal of the situation. Here, Ronald behaved with greater warmth and spontaneity, and the therapist congratulated him in an effort to reinforce the new behavior. In general, the therapist tried to reinforce whatever new behavior Ronald exhibited.

The therapy of Ronald Barrett was necessarily incomplete, since after only a few sessions it was time for him to leave school. We are, unfortunately, without data on the exact kinds of changes that did occur and how long they lasted. For example, it would have been interesting to have obtained Ronald's responses to the Rep test before treatment, at the end of treatment, and at some later point in time. This, of course, is the procedure Rogers used in some of his research. In any case, we do have a picture of how a Kellyian might construe an individual and how he might seek to engage a client in a creative process of change.

RELATED POINTS OF VIEW AND RECENT DEVELOPMENTS

Virtually all personality theorists today attempt to conceptualize cognitive variables, regardless of whether they interpret these variables as only part of the organism or as virtually all of the organism. Kelly's theory was presented at a relatively early stage in the development of this now vigorous trend in the study of personality. In the chapter on theory, it was pointed out that theories are influenced by the *zeitgeist* or spirit of the times. It is clear that cognition is part of the current *zeitgeist*, although we do not know whether the work of Kelly was merely a forerunner of what was yet to come or itself had an impact on the development. In either case, it is clear that Kelly's theory places great emphasis on the constructions individuals place upon the world, and research associated with the theory has developed within this general orientation.

Although Kelly's theory attracted considerable attention when it was presented in 1955, in the following decade relatively little research was conducted that was tied specifically to the theory. Since then, however, there have been efforts to explore the many leads suggested by personal construct theory. A major focus of this research effort has been the Rep test and the structure of construct systems. There have been studies of the reliability of the Rep test and the evidence to date suggests that the responses of individuals to the role title list and constructs used are reasonably stable over time (Landfield, 1971). Rep test data have been used to study the construct systems of a variety of individuals with psychological problems (for example, stutterers, an arsonist, thought-disordered schizophrenics, etc.), the construct systems of married couples and changes in construct systems of individuals participating in group psychotherapy (Bannister and Fransella, 1971). Furthermore, there have been studies of constructs relating to objects (for example, films, paintings) and situations as well as to people and interpersonal relationships (Bonarius, 1977; Honikman, 1976).

One important modification of the Rep test involved an analysis of the structural complexity of construct systems. In one variation, individuals are asked to indicate which other constructs would change if they were to shift from one end of a particular construct to another. Presumably changes in constructs higher in the hierarchy of the construct system (superordinate constructs) would have greater implications for other constructs than would constructs lower in the hierarchy (subordinate constructs). In another variation, subjects are asked to apply a construct and then are asked why they gave that response. The response to the question why represents another construct which is higher in the system hierarchy than the previous one. Each response of the individual is followed by the question why, resulting in a laddering of constructs in the system. Both variations offer insight into the hierarchical nature of construct networks (Hinkle, 1965). Further study of the complexity of organization of construct systems suggests that people with many constructs organized at different levels (high complexity) are likely to be described by others as healthy and mature whereas those with many constructs but little hierarchical organization (low complexity) are likely to be described as confused and malad-justed (Landfield, 1977).

The question of complexity of construct system structure is an important one from a developmental point of view. As has been noted, Kelly made few statements relevant to the area of growth and development of the construct system. His main points concerned the change from the use of concrete constructs (for example, like mother-not like mother) to the use of more abstract constructs (for example, sympathetic-cruel). Recent formulations of growth and development within personal construct theory terms (Adams-Webber, 1970; Salmon, 1970). emphasize the increase in complexity of the construct system that generally occurs with age and experience. According to this view, the normal course of development involves the addition of new and more abstract concepts, the progressive differentiation of the system into organized subsystems, and increasing integration of the subsystems within an overall framework. Thus, there is movement from a global, undifferentiated system to a differentiated, hierarchically arranged, integrated system. There is evidence that such developmental change does occur in construct systems (Brierly, 1967; Crockett, 1965) and that such growth occurs in relation to efforts to incorporate new elements into the construct system. Of particular importance in this regard are the recent efforts of some followers of Kelly to determine the potential role of schools in the extension and differentiation of the developing child's construct system. For example, it is suggested that the educational system may provide the child with the opportunity to experience and experiment with new constructions of the self. In particular, the school may help the child to develop self-fulfilling constructs of the nature of "I am, among other things . . ." as opposed to such self-limiting constructs as "I am nothing but . . ." — thereby allowing for the gaining of an identity which "is not also a prison" (Bannister and Agnew, 1977, p. 124). Additional research has focused on changes in the types of constructs that children use, in particular the change from an emphasis on concrete constructs to describe people (for example, in terms of their physical appearance) to an emphasis on abstract constructs (for example, in terms of their personality) (Barratt, 1977). Such research, together with research on the development of the self as a major construct subsystem, suggests considerable potential for further significant exploration in this area.

The above developmental principles suggest a number of similarities in the developmental theories of both Kelly and Piaget: (1) an emphasis on progression from a global, undifferentiated system to a differentiated, integrated system; (2) increasing use of more abstract structures so as to be able to handle more information more economically; (3) development in response to efforts to accommodate new elements into the cognitive system; (4) development of the cognitive system as a system, as opposed to a simple addition of new parts or elements. At the same time, it is clear that there are differences between the two approaches. For example, Piaget's theory is based upon considerable observation of children and is much more advanced than the growth and development views associated with personal construct theory.

Research in the area of psychotherapy has focused on factors in the construct system and factors in the therapeutic relationship that affect change. As one might expect, there is evidence that superordinate constructs are harder to change than subordinate constructs, presumably because they involve more threat of potential disruption of the construct system. It also appears that constructs must undergo some loosening before change can occur. A critical factor in the loosening process is the recognition of new elements. In this regard it is interesting to note that Landfield (1971) has found that a certain amount of similarity in therapist-client construct systems is necessary to facilitate communication but, at the same time, a certain amount of structural difference appears to facilitate the change process. The psychotherapeutic process, then, can be understood in terms of the relationship and experiences provided that facilitate the reconstruction of the construct system.

CRITICAL EVALUATION

Kelly's theory has been presented as a cognitive theory of personality. While discussing it in these terms it should be recognized that others have construed the theory in different terms and that Kelly himself refused to attach any labels to it. Kelly noted that his theory had been described as humanistic, phenomenological, psychodynamic, existential, and even behavioristic as well as cognitive. Kelly rejected the term cognitive principally because he felt that it was too restrictive and suggested an artificial division between cognition (thinking) and affect (feeling). He rejected phenomenology as being concerned only with subjective reality, and behaviorism as only concerned with objective reality, whereas personal construct theory is concerned with both. If he had to pick a label, Kelly probably would have described himself as a humanist. For Kelly, humanists emphasize what is possible rather than what is inevitable, are interested in the entire person and in novelty and the emancipation of the mind.

Despite these statements, Kelly's theory can be viewed as primarily a cognitive theory in its emphasis on the ways individuals receive and process information about the world and in its use of the Rep test as a way of determining a person's concepts. As such, Kelly's personal construct theory is certainly in the direction of taking (as far as one can) a cognitive view of behavior. The structural model, with its emphasis on constructs and the construct system, represents a significant contribution to personality theory. The interpretation of behavior in terms of the individual's construing of events is a useful one in theory and in practice. This interpretation allows one to take into consideration the unique aspects of the behavior of individuals and, also, the lawfulness or regularity of much of this behavior. To the extent that Kelly's emphasis on cognitive structures has influenced the current research efforts in cognitive style, the theory has made a significant contribution to research. The Rep test, which has the beauty of being derived from the theory, represents an important assessment device. Although it has been criticized by some as so flexible as to be unmanageable (Vernon, 1963), it is also recognized by others as an extremely imaginative technique, quite amenable to quantification (Kleinmutz, 1967; Mischel, 1968). A remaining, unresolved problem for the Rep test, as well as for the theory as a whole, is that it requires the individual to use words even though it is recognized that preverbal or submerged constructs may exist.

The process view of Kelly has a number of interesting facets to it. It clearly represents a departure from the drive-reduction or tension-reduction views of Freud and other theorists. In the suggestion that the individual dislikes both the monotony of the ticking of a clock and the threat of the completely unkown, personal construct theory is similar to other views which suggests that the individual experiences small degrees of variety as pleasurable and large degrees of variety or no variety at all as unpleasurable. However, the process view leaves open a number of issues. The basis for action of an individual is not really clear. For example, how does the individual know which construct will be the best predictor? How does one know which end of the construct (similarity or contrast) to use? Also, what determines the individual's response to invalidation (Sechrest, 1963)? As Bonarius (1965) observes, the process of construct change is not made very explicit, and there is no discussion of the question of individual differences in sensitivity to invalidation. Finally, in relation to the process view, what determines whether individuals will choose, in the face of threat, to risk change in their system or to retreat into the conservative strategies of the old system? One would guess that this choice would be dependent on the external conditions under which a prediction needed to be made, how critical the constructs involved were to the construct system, and the past experiences of the individual with the language of hypothesis. Considerations such as these are involved in Kelly's conceptualization of the process of therapy and construct change, but they are not made as explicit as would be desirable for research purposes.

In his review of Kelly's theory, Bruner (1956) referred to it as the single greatest contribution of the decade between 1945 and 1955 to the theory of personality functioning. There is clearly much to the theory that is new and worthwhile. However, there are some areas of psychology that appear to be more within the range of convenience of the psychology of personal constructs than are other areas. For example, until recently the theory has had little to say about growth and development. The theory offers an interesting analysis of anxiety, but it has almost nothing to say about the important emotion of depression. In fact, for all of its worthwhile emphasis on cognition, the theory offers a limited view of the person. Although Kelly denied the charge, the theory is noticeably lacking in emphasis on human feelings and emotions. In his review, Bruner stated that people may not be the pigs that reinforcement theory makes of them, but he wondered also whether people are only the scientists that Kelly suggests. Bruner commented further as follows: "I rather suspect that when some people get angry or inspired or in love, they couldn't care less about their systems as a whole! One gets the impression that the author is, in his personality theory, overreacting against a generation of irrationalism" (Bruner, 1956, p. 356).

The psychology of personal constructs is an important and useful theory. Within its focus of convenience, it has many contributions to make. Beyond the specific contributions of the theory, however, are the many challenges that Kelly threw out to the field of psychology. Kelly, as a theorist, and the psychology of personal constructs, as a theory, challenged traditional concepts of motivation and challenged the belief in "objective reality." The challenge is there to personality psychologists to develop functional theories, to accept the language of hypotheses, to establish the invitational mood, and to have fun at the same time. In a sense, the goal for Freud was to make life more gratifying, the goal for Rogers to make life more meaningful, and the goal for Kelly to make life more fun in the world of make-believe and as-if.

A final note in the evaluation of Kelly's theory concerns its current status as a basis for active research. Recently there has been growing interest in personal construct theory, as expressed in an important symposium (Cole and Landfield, 1976), the development of an international newsletter, the holding of yearly international meetings devoted to personal construct theory, and the publication of books reporting noteworthy research efforts (Adams-Webber, 1979; Bannister, 1977). However, for the most part, there have not been consistent efforts to test and elaborate upon essential aspects of the theory, and this remains an important weakness. As noted by one follower of Kelly, without new ideas and new research efforts provided by supportive followers, no theory of personality can survive: "The psychology of personal constructs is not currently being elaborated and tested by empirical research or clinical practice, and there are no new names associated with Kelly's in the promulgation of the theory. It is not unimaginable that the theory will simply die out . . ." (Sechrest, 1977, p.

238). Should this turn out to be the case, it will not be because of a lack of value in personal construct theory but rather because the field now is more prepared to integrate Kelly's ideas into other theoretical points of view (Tyler, 1978).

Before turning to a summary of personal construct theory, it may be useful to compare Kelly with Freud and Rogers to appreciate some of the similarities and differences among the three points of view.

Kelly and Freud

Although Kelly was extremely critical of psychoanalytic theory, he appreciated the many important observations and clinical contributions that were made by Freud. The criticisms of Freud are mainly in three areas — Freud's view of the person, the considerable dogmatism in psychoanalytic thinking, and the weaknesses of psychoanalysis as a scientific theory. Kelly was critical of Freud's view of the person-the-biological-organism, and substituted instead the view of person-the-scientist. Kelly was critical of Freud's metaphors and his emphasis on unconscious drives and instincts.

Kelly placed great reliance on understanding the individual's construction of events and on the tentativeness with which theories are put forward. Both of these reflect an open-minded attitude. Against this background, Kelly was critical of Freud's emphasis on understanding what clients meant by what they *did not* say. Kelly was critical of what he thought was the Freudian's dogmatic outlook and insistence that, if the client's own construct system did not include the appropriate "insights," they were necessarily a part of his unconscious. Furthermore, he viewed the followers of Freud as unnecessarily opposed to change.

The third area of major criticism of psychoanalysis was qualification as a scientific enterprise. Kelly observed that Freud's observations of the unconscious were difficult to explore scientifically. As far as Kelly was concerned, the psychoanalytic movement had shunned scientific methodology in favor of impressionistic observation. Hypotheses were so elastic that they could not be invalidated. They were what Kelly called "rubber hypotheses" — they could be stretched to fit any kind of evidence. This for Kelly was psychoanalysis' most vulnerable point.

Although Kelly had these many criticisms of psychoanalysis, he also believed that the psychoanalytic system of dynamics permitted the clinician to determine that something was going on inside the client. According to Kelly, Freud made many astute observations, and his adventurousness helped to open up the field of psychotherapy for exploration. What is particularly striking in reading Kelly is the number of times that he seems to be describing phenomena that were also described by Freud, even though he may interpret them in a different way. For example, Kelly placed great emphasis on the closeness of opposites, a view quite evident in Freud's thinking. In fact, in dreams, ideas were frequently represented by their opposites. Both Freud and Kelly were sensitive to the fact that the way people view others may also be expressive of views they hold about themselves; both were aware that one is threatened only by something that seems plausible and that one "protests too much" about things one does not want to acknowledge to be true; both viewed people as at times functioning in relation to principles they are unaware of, although in one case the concept of the unconscious was emphasized, while in the other the emphasis was on preverbal constructs; both noted that at times an individual may feel uncomfortable with praise, although in one case the concept of guilt was stressed, and in the other the emphasis was on the strangeness of new praise and the complex internal reorganization it could imply; both placed emphasis on the concept of transference in therapy; both believed that the clients should not get to know their therapists too well and that therapists should avoid social contacts with their clients; both felt that diagnoses could be useful in treatment; both felt that patients are resistant to change; both felt that free associations and dreams could be useful in understanding the person's functioning; and, both believed that there was a relationship between the thinking found in some forms of pathology and that found in creative people. In Freud's case, an emphasis on primary process thinking was found in both psychopathology and creativity; for Kelly, there was an emphasis on the process of construct loosening. In addition, Freud, too, saw people as scientists: "Scientific thought is, in its essence, no different from the normal process of thinking, which we all, believers and unbelievers, alike, make use of when we are going about our business in everyday life" (Freud, 1933, p. 232). It is not surprising that the theories of Freud and Kelly share a number of observations, since the foci of convenience of the two theories are somewhat similar.

Kelly and Rogers

There also are a number of similarities in the works of Kelly and Rogers. Both view the person as more active than reactive; both theories emphasize the phenomenological approach, although Kelly believed that personal construct psychology was not just phenomenology. In both, there is an emphasis on consistency, although for Rogers this is on self-consistency, per se, and for Kelly it is so that predictions can add up rather than cancel each other out. Both stress the total system functioning of the organism.

Probably, their common emphasis on the phenomenological approach and their common avoidance of a drive model of human functioning leads to the appearance of considerable similarity between Kelly and Rogers. At one point, Kelly asked a question that would be quite characteristic of Rogers: "Is the therapist ever more familiar with the client's construct system than the client is himself?" His answer was clear. "We think not" (Kelly, 1955, p. 1020). Despite these similarities, however, there are major differences between the two theories. Kelly placed considerably less emphasis on the self than does Rogers. Also, although Kelly agreed with Rogers that the present is what counts most, he refused to take a completely ahistorical approach toward behavior. Kelly was interested in the past because individuals' perception of their past gives clues to their construct system and because a reconstruing of the past could be an important element in treatment. In general, Kelly was interested in a whole range of clinical phenomena (for example, transference, dreams, diagnosis, the importance of preverbal constructs), which brought him closer to Freud than to Rogers in this regard.

Kelly viewed Rogers' position as more of a statement of philosophical convictions about the nature of the person than a true psychological theory. Kelly was critical of the Rogerian principle of growth and contrasted it with personal construct theory. Whereas the former emphasizes an unfolding of inner potential, the latter emphasizes the continuous development of a changing and ever expanding construct system. Where Rogers emphasized the importance of being and becoming, Kelly emphasized the importance of make-believe and doing. The difference has important ramifications for treatment, a point that was made explicit by Kelly:

The nondirectionist, because of his faith in the emerging being, asks the client to pay attention to himself as he reacts with his everyday world. Somewhere the mature self is waiting to be realized. The nondirective therapist is hesitant to say what the self is, so he prefers to hold a mirror before the client in which can be seen the reflections of those vague stirrings of life which are called feelings. The personal-construct psychologist, because he sees life proceeding by means of a series of hypotheses, and validating experiences, may hold the same mirror, but he sees that mirror, and the image of validating experience which it reflects, as setting up the succession of targets toward which the growth is directed. The personal-construct psychologist is probably more inclined to urge the client to experiment with life and to seek his answers in the succession of events which life unveils than to seek them within himself . . . He urges the client to see himself in terms of an ever emerging life role rather than in terms of a self which approaches a state of maturity.

KELLY, 1955, PP. 401-402

Kelly greatly emphasized the verbal fluency and acting skill of the therapist. He opposed the view that the therapist must be known as a real person and was critical of phenomenologically oriented therapists who became involved in "lovely personal relationships." The differences between Kelly and Rogers as people are important and translate themselves into views concerning therapy. Rogers (1956), in his review of Kelly's work, expressed the belief that Kelly had found an approach congenial to his personality. However, he was critical of what he thought was Kelly's interpretation of therapy as an intellectual process. Rogers was influenced by Kelly and uses the concepts of construct complexity and construct flexibility in his analysis of changes in therapy. However, Rogers was critical of the excessive amount of activity and control assumed in fixed-role therapy. For Rogers, therapy is much more a process of feeling than of thinking, and it is important that therapists be congruent and not that they be skillful in manipulating the situation. "An overwhelming impression is that, for Kelly, therapy is seen as almost entirely an intellectual function, a view which should be comforting to many psychologists. He is continually thinking about the client, and about his own procedures, in ways so complex, that there seems no time or room for entering into an emotional relationship with the client" (Rogers, 1956, p. 358).

Kelly, Freud, and Rogers

In their study of suicide, Farberow and Schneidman (1961) obtained the ratings by Kelly of a patient, along with the ratings by a Freudian, a Rogerian, and members of other schools of thought. In general, Kelly's ratings of the case, and presumably therefore his interpretation of it, were much more similar to those made by the Rogerian than to those made by the Freudian. In commenting on this study, Kelly (1963) noted that the theories could perhaps be understood in terms of their likenesses and differences. In his own analysis of the ratings, Kelly differentiated the theories according to the attention given to interpersonal relations, with construct psychology giving the most attention, psychoanalytic theory the least, and Rogerian theory something in between. Another dimension of importance was the attention given to aggression and hostility. Here, the psychoanalytic ratings indicated a considerable degree of emphasis, whereas the ratings by Kelly and the Rogerian suggested much less emphasis. A third dimension related to the attention given to the affective dimension of behavior. Here, the psychoanalytic and Rogerian ratings were quite high, while Kelly's indicated much less attention to this area.

If not the only approach toward a comparative analysis of theories, the approach emphasized by Kelly certainly is worthy of merit. Three elements represent the necessary number for the formation of a similarity-contrast construct. We now have three theories and, thus, can be on our way toward developing comparative constructs like the ones mentioned above. With the addition of new theories, we can seek to develop some new constructs and to drop some old ones, to make some more permeable and to call others so unique that no further elements can be added.

With the completion of this chapter on Kelly, we bring to a close the analysis of three clinical theories of personality. Regardless of their differences, the three theorists have in common the use of clinical material as the original source of data for their hypotheses. The three theories are different, but then each theorist grew out of a different background, was himself a different personality in interacting with his patients, and had a somewhat different patient (subject) population. It may be that, although different, the theories are not mutually exclusive — an issue that will be important for us to consider as further theories are assessed; that is, the theories are possibly expressing the same things in different terms, such as the process of anxiety and defense, or it may be that the theories have different foci of convenience.

These three clinical theories also share an emphasis on individual differences, an emphasis on qualities within the individual that result in relatively stable behavioral characteristics across situations and over time, and an emphasis on the functioning of all parts of the individual within the context of a total system. The next three chapters will examine other approaches that have quite different views of the person and science, that use different techniques of assessment, and that focus on different problems in research.

MAJOR CONCEPTS AND SUMMARY

permeable – impermeable	aggression
tightening – loosening	hostility
constriction – dilation	fixed role therapy

In this chapter and in the preceding one, we have discussed the personal construct theory of George Kelly. The theory is distinguished by its clinical approach, its emphasis on the whole person, the use of the Rep test for assessment purposes, and its emphasis on cognition — how the individual perceives, interprets, and conceptualizes events and the environment. This emphasis is further expressed in the view of people as scientists with their own theories (construct systems) and efforts to anticipate events.

The major structural concept for Kelly is that of a construct. A construct is an interpretation placed upon the world by the individual. Constructs can be described in terms of their content and in terms of their characteristic mode of functioning. An individual can be described in terms of the constructs used and in terms of the structural aspects of the construct system (for example, complex vs. simple construct system). The emphasis on the system aspects or interrelationships among constructs again points to the holistic properties of the theory which emphasize the entire person.

The Rep test, and modifications of it, represents the principal means for determining how individuals construe their worlds and thereby for describing the personalities of individuals.

In accounting for the activity of people, Kelly assumes that the person is active, and rejects concepts such as motives, drives, and needs. The direction of behavior is accounted for in terms of the fundamental postulate — an individual chooses that alternative which offers the greater possibility for expansion and definition of the system. As scientists choose to pursue research along lines that show promise of developing their theories, people choose to act in ways that will facilitate the expansion and development of the construct system. Anxiety, fear, and threat are experienced when individuals find themselves without constructs applicable to a situation or when they face the possibility of change in their construct systems. At the extremes of functioning, we can choose between confusion and certainty, between anxiety and boredom. Individuals can defend against anxiety and threat by processes such as loosening (making variable, unstable predictions) and tightening (making unvarying predictions). Essentially, the dynamics of functioning involve the interplay between the wish to elaborate the construct system and the desire to avoid the threat of disruption of the construct system.

Under favorable circumstances, the developing individual responds to new elements in the environment with the development of new constructs, more abstract constructs, and a more hierarchical construct system. There is a resemblance here to some of the views of Piaget. For growth and expansion of the construct system to occur, there must be the presence of new elements, relative consistency in the environment so that prediction is possible, and sufficient looseness in the construct system so that new predictions can be attempted. Pathological developments occur when anxiety leads to rigid construct system functioning or to chaotic system functioning in the face of repeated invalidations. This may involve making constructs excessively permeable or impermeable to new information, excessive loosening or tightening in making predictions, or excessive constriction or dilation of the overall construct system. This may also involve efforts to extort evidence in support of the construct system from others (hostility).

The psychotherapeutic process of change involves the reconstruction of an individual's construct system so that it leads to more accurate predictions. For this to occur conditions are necessary which are similar to those that facilitate growth: an atmosphere of experimentation, the provision of new elements, and the availability of validating data. Fixed-role therapy was developed as one means of encouraging clients to experience new elements and to experiment with new opportunities for obtaining validating data. The aim is the reconstruction of the construct system, that is, of the entire personality and not a minor readjustment of parts of the person. Improvement occurs because behavior change leads to cognitive change and not because of behavior change itself.

Personal construct theory represents a remarkable effort to interpret a broad range of behavior within a cognitive framework. It has led to the development of a significant assessment device (Rep test) which is more closely linked to a specific theory than almost any other assessment device. In its emphasis upon cognitive processes it is part of the current *zeitgeist* and, after a period of slow development in research activity, it recently has been associated with a number of serious research efforts. At the same time, the theory has some major weaknesses. It is difficult to test some parts of the theory and it is only with difficulty that emotions such as love, anger, guilt and depression are incorporated into its range of convenience. Finally, the Rep test suffers from its dependence upon the verbalization of constructs while the theory itself recognizes the possibility that constructs may exist at a nonverbal level and that such nonverbal constructs may be important for behavior.

THE TRAIT THEORY OF GORDON W. ALLPORT (1897-1967)

THE TRAIT-TYPE, FACTOR-ANALYTIC THEORY OF
HANS J. EYSENCK (1916-   )

THE TRAIT, FACTOR-ANALYTIC APPROACH OF
RAYMOND B. CATTELL (1905-   )

Cattell's View of the Person

Cattell's View of Science, Theory, and Research Methods

Cattell's Theory of Personality
• Structure
• Process
• Growth and Development

Clinical Applications of Cattell's Theory
• Psychopathology
• Change

A Case Example

Critical Evaluation of Cattell's Theory
• How Many Factors?
• Are the Same Factors Identified in Different Studies?
• Are There Certain Questionable Assumptions in the Factor-Analytic
  Procedure?
• How Sure Can We Be that the Factors Identified Have the Same
  Meaning?
• Scope of the Effort and Evaluation

TRAIT THEORY AND SITUATIONIST CRITICISM

MAJOR CONCEPTS AND SUMMARY

8 TRAIT APPROACHES TO PERSONALITY: ALLPORT, EYSENCK, AND CATTELL

Chapter Focus:

In this chapter we shall review theories that are significant in their efforts to identify the basic dimensions of personality. The basic conceptual unit is the trait, that is, a broad disposition to behave in a particular way. Two of the three trait theorists, Eysenck and Cattell, use a particular statistical procedure, factor analysis, to determine the basic traits that make up the human personality. The trait approach has been popular in American psychology and comes close to the layman's approach to describing someone's personality. Recently it has come under attack from psychologists who suggest that people's behavior varies much more from situation to situation than is suggested by trait theory.

Personality is that which permits a prediction of what a person will do in a given situation.

CATTELL, 1950, P. 2

It would be hard to find anything more important to the advance of psychology at the present moment than the development of a meaningful methodology for measurement.

CATTELL, 1956, P. 65

The term trait theory *is as superfluous as a two-legged man theory; for the alternative is a structureless theory of personality structure.*

CATTELL, 1977, P. 166

In the preceding chapters on theories of personality attention has been given to one major representative of each theoretical point of view. In this chapter on trait theory attention will be given to the views of three theorists, though the major emphasis will be given to one proponent of this point of view. Whereas in earlier chapters it was easy to determine the major figure representative of that school of thought, this is not nearly as easy with trait theory. For some time Gordon Allport championed trait theory, but he did relatively little empirical research to further its development. Hans Eysenck and Raymond Cattell both have made important theoretical and research contributions, with Eysenck's influence being greater in Great Britain and Cattell's greater in the United States.

Let us put aside the question of who is the leading theorist or representative of trait theory and consider, instead, the essentials of the point of view itself. As has been indicated, it is an approach to personality that has been an influential part of personality theory and research. At the same time, it is an approach that has come under attack by proponents of the social learning theory point of view (Chapter 11). The basic assumption of the trait point of view is that people possess broad predispositions to respond in particular ways. Such predispositions are called **traits**. In other words, people may be described in terms of the likelihood of their behaving in a particular way — for example, the likelihood of their being outgoing and friendly or their being dominant and assertive. People having a strong tendency to behave in these ways may be described as being high on these traits, for example, high on the traits of "extroversion" and "dominance," whereas people with a lesser tendency to behave in these ways would be described as low on these traits. While various trait theorists differ as to how to determine the traits that make up the human personality, they all agree that traits are the fundamental building blocks of the human personality.

Beyond this, trait theorists agree that human behavior and personality can be organized into a hierarchy. By this they mean that the parts of our

traits

personality and behavior have an organized quality such that there are links among the parts and some are more influential or key than others. An illustration of this hierarchical point of view comes from the work of Eysenck. Eysenck suggests that at its simplest level behavior can be considered in terms of specific responses. However, some of these responses generally are linked to one another forming more general habits. Again, we generally find that groups of habits tend to occur together to form what are called traits. For example, people who prefer meeting people to reading also generally enjoy themselves at a lively party, suggesting that these two habits can be grouped together under the trait of sociability. Or, to take another example, people who act without stopping to think things over also tend to shout back at others, suggesting that these two habits can be grouped together under the trait of impulsiveness. Finally, at an even higher level of organization, various traits may tend to be linked together to form what Eysenck calls types. How we find such traits and determine the hierarchical organization of personality will be discussed shortly. What is important to recognize here is the conceptualization of personality as organized at various levels. A representation of Eysenck's view of such organization is given in Figure 8.1.

In sum, trait theories suggest that people have broad predispositions to respond in certain ways and that there is a hierarchical organization to personality. In considering the trait theories of Allport, Eysenck, and Cattell we will see that while differences emerge, these two themes remain constant.

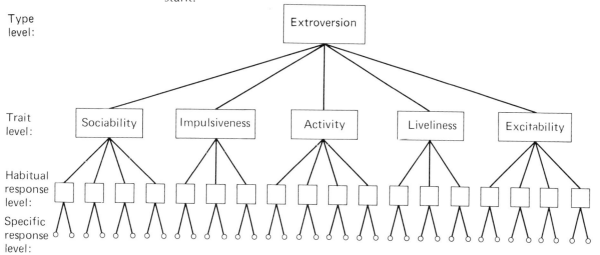

FIGURE 8.1 Diagrammatic representation of hierarchical organization of personality. (From Esyenck, 1970.)

THE TRAIT THEORY OF GORDON W. ALLPORT (1897-1967)

Gordon W. Allport, who was born in Indiana in 1897, probably will be remembered more for the issues he raised and principles he emphasized than for a particular theoretical perspective. Throughout his long and influential career, he emphasized the human, healthy, and organized aspects of our behavior. This is in contrast with other views that emphasized the animalistic, neurotic, tension-reducing, and mechanistic aspects of behavior. In this regard, he was critical of aspects of psychoanalysis and was fond of telling the following story. At the age of 22, while traveling through Europe, Allport decided that it would be interesting to visit Freud. When he entered Freud's office he was met with expectant silence as Freud waited to learn of Allport's mission. Finding himself unprepared for silence, Allport decided to start an informal conversation with the description of a 4-year-old boy with a dirt phobia, whom he had met on the train. After he completed his description of the boy and his compulsive mother Freud asked, "And was that little boy you?" Allport describes his response as follows:

"Flabbergasted and feeling a bit guilty, I contrived to change the subject. While Freud's misunderstanding of my motivation was amusing, it also started a deep train of thought. I realized that he was accustomed to neurotic defenses and that my manifest motivation (a sort of rude curiosity and youthful ambition) escaped him. For therapeutic progress he would have to cut through my defenses, but it so happened that therapeutic progress was not here an issue. This experience taught me that depth psychology, for all its merits, may plunge too deep, and that psychologists would do well to give full recognition to manifest motives before probing the unconscious" (Allport, 1967, p. 8).[1]

Allport's first publication, written with his older brother Floyd, centered on traits as an important aspect of personality theory — *Personality Traits: Their Classification and Measurement* (Allport and Allport, 1921). In 1924 he gave the first course on personality ever taught in the United States and in 1937 published a book on personality (*Personality: A Psychological Interpretation*), which for twenty-five years was a basic text in the field. In this book and in its later revision, *Pattern and Growth in Personality* (1961), Allport emphasized the importance of self-images, complex integrative functions, the mature aspects of personality, and the process of growth and becoming. Allport is known not only for his emphasis on traits but

functional autonomy   also for his emphasis on the concept of **functional autonomy** and the con-

---

1   A particularly amusing aspect of this is that Allport was indeed a person who was neat, meticulous, orderly, and punctual — possessing many of the characteristics associated by Freud with the compulsive personality. Freud may not have been as far off in his question as Allport suggested.

HANS J. EYSENCK

proprium

cept of **proprium**. The concept of functional autonomy suggests that while the motives of an adult may have their roots in the tension-reducing motives of the child, the adult grows out of them and becomes independent of these earlier tension-reducing efforts. What originally began as an effort to reduce hunger or anxiety can become a source of pleasure and motivation in its own right. Thus, adult motivation need not be reduced to the motives of childhood. In the concept of proprium, Allport gave expression to his belief in the organized quality of the functioning of the person. The proprium includes the many aspects of the self (for example bodily self, self-identity, self-esteem) which the person seeks to organize into an integrated, unified whole. For Allport the concept of the person itself involved unity or at least the striving for unity: "Personality is many things in one — a *unitas multiplex*" (Allport, 1961, p. 376).

Allport believed that traits are the basic units of personality. According to Allport, traits actually exist and are based in the nervous system. They represent generalized personality dispositions which account for regularities in the functioning of a person across situations and over time. Regularity in functioning is achieved through perceiving many stimuli as equivalent and many personal acts of behavior as equivalent expressions of the same trait. Traits can be defined by three properties — frequency, intensity, and range of situations. For example, a very submissive person would *frequently* be *very* submissive over *a wide range of situations.*

cardinal traits

central traits

secondary dispositions

Allport made a distinction among **cardinal traits**, **central traits**, and **secondary dispositions**. A cardinal trait expresses a disposition that is so pervasive and outstanding in a person's life that virtually every act is traceable to its influence. For example, we speak of the machiavellian person named after Prince Machiavelli, the sadistic person named after the Marquis de Sade, and also of the authoritarian personality who sees virtually everything in black-white, stereotyped ways. Generally people have few, if any, such cardinal traits. Central traits (for example, honest, kind, assertive) express dispositions that cover a more limited range of situations than is true for cardinal traits. Secondary traits represent dispositions that are the least conspicuous, generalized, and consistent. They can be the same personality characteristics that are central traits for other people. In other words, people possess traits of varying degrees of significance and generality. It is the central traits that we usually think of in describing someone's personality.

It is important to recognize that Allport did not say that a trait expresses itself in all situations independent of the characteristics of the situation. While consistency in behavior is necessary evidence for a trait, instances of "inconsistency" do not mean that the trait does not exist. Indeed, Allport recognized the importance of the situation and the variation of behavior across situations. A trait expresses what a person generally does over many situations, not what will be done in any one situation: "We are forced to the conclusion that while the situation may modify behavior greatly, it can do so only within the limits of the potential provided by the personality. At the same time, we are forced to concede that traits of personality must not be regarded as fixed and stable, operating mechanically to the same degree on all occasions. Rather we should think of traits as *ranges of possible behavior,* to be activated at varying points within the range according to the demands of the situation" (Allport, 1961, pp. 180-181). Thus, the trait concept was necessary to explain the consistency found in behavior; recognition of the importance of the situation was necessary to explain the inconsistency or variability of behavior.

While Allport emphasized the concept of trait and tried to clarify its relation to the situation, he did little research to establish the existence and utility of specific trait concepts. Similarly, while believing that many traits were hereditary, he did not conduct research to substantiate this. To consider illustrations of such conceptual and research efforts we must turn to the works of the two remaining trait theorists — Hans J. Eysenck and Raymond B. Cattell.

THE TRAIT-TYPE, FACTOR-ANALYTIC THEORY OF HANS J. EYSENCK (1916-   )

Hans J. Eysenck was born in Germany in 1916 and fled to England to escape Nazi persecution. His work has been influenced by methodological advances in the statistical technique of factor analysis (Charles Spearman), by the thinking of European typologists, such as Jung and Kretschmer, by the research on heredity of Sir Cyril Burt, and by the American learning theory of Clark Hull. While his work has included the sampling of both normal and pathological populations, most of it has been done at the Institute of Psychiatry, Maudsley Hospital, England.

Eysenck is strict in his standards for scientific pursuits, placing great emphasis on conceptual clarity and measurement. For this reason he consistently has been one of the harshest critics of psychoanalytic theory. While supporting trait theory, he has emphasized the need to develop adequate measures of traits, the need to develop a theory which relates performance in different areas in a conceptually meaningful way, and the importance of establishing the biological foundations for the existence of each trait. "I feel that the major, most fundamental dimensions of personality are likely to be those on which variation has had evolutionary significance, and that this evolutionary history is likely to manifest itself in strong genetic determination of individual differences along these dimensions" (Eysenck, 1977, pp. 407-408). Efforts such as these are emphasized by Ey-

GORDON W. ALLPORT

senck as being important to avoid a meaningless circularity of explanation whereby a trait is used to explain behavior that serves as the basis for the concept of the trait in the first place. For example, Jack talks to others because he is high on the trait of sociability but we know that he is high on this trait because we observe that he spends lots of time talking to others.

factor analysis

The basis for Eysenck's emphasis on measurement and the development of a classification of traits is the statistical technique of **factor analysis**. Factor analysis is a technique in which one starts with a large number of test items that are administered to a large number of persons. The question to be answered is: "To which items do groups of people respond in the same way?" Through a number of statistical procedures, clusters or factors are derived, the items within any single factor being highly related to one another and being slightly related, or not at all related, to items in the other factors. According to trait theory, there are natural, unitary structures in personality, and the logic of factor analysis allows us to detect them. If things (variables, test responses) move together, that is if they appear and disappear together, then one can infer that they have some common feature behind them, that they belong to the same unity of personality functioning. Factor analysis assumes that behaviors that function with one another are related. It is a statistical device for determining which behaviors are related to one another and thereby for determining the unities or natural elements in personality.

types

The process described leads to factors, in this case called traits, which are named in terms of the characteristic that seems common to the items or behaviors that have been found to be related to one another. Through some further statistical procedures Eysenck determines the basic dimensions that underlie the factors or traits that have been found. These basic dimensions are called **types**. Thus, for example the traits of sociability, impulsiveness, activity, liveliness, and excitability can be grouped together under the type concept of extroversion (Figure 8.1). Though the term "type" is used, it is important to recognize that in fact it is a dimension with a low end and a high end that is being considered, such that people may fall along various points between the two extremes.

Introversion-Extroversion

Neuroticism

In his earlier research Eysenck found two basic dimensions to personality which he labeled as **Introversion-Extroversion** and **Neuroticism** (stable-unstable). The relationship of these two basic dimensions of personality to the four major temperamental types distinguished by the Greek physicians Hippocrates and Galen and to a wider range of personality characteristics is presented in Figure 8.2. Since the earlier emphasis on these two dimensions, Eysenck has added a third dimension, which he calls **Psychoticism**. People high on this dimension tend to be solitary, insensitive, uncaring about others, and opposed to accepted social custom.

Psychoticism

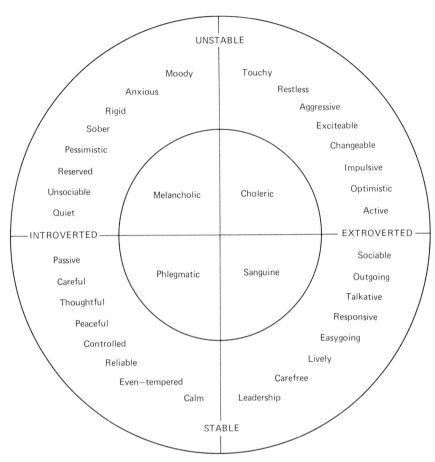

FIGURE 8.2   The Relationship of Two Dimensions of Personality Derived From Factor Analysis to Four Greek Temperamental Types (Eysenck, 1975).

A further appreciation of Eysenck's theoretical system can be gained from a more detailed consideration of one of these three dimensions, that of Introversion-Extroversion. According to Eysenck, the typical extrovert is sociable, likes parties, has many friends, craves excitement, acts on the spur of the moment, and is impulsive. As can be seen, there appear to be two aspects to this dimension, sociability and impulsiveness, which can be separated out to a certain extent but which have been found to be related sufficiently to be linked under the same concept of extroversion. In contrast to these characteristics the introverted person tends to be quiet, introspective, reserved, reflective, distrustful of impulsive decisions, and to prefer a well-ordered life to one filled with chance and risk.

Eysenck has developed two questionnaires to measure people along the dimension of Introversion-Extroversion — the Maudsley Personality Inventory and the Eysenck Personality Inventory. The typical extrovert will answer *yes* to questions such as the following: Do other people think of you as very lively? Would you be unhappy if you could not see lots of people most of the time? Do you often long for excitement? In contrast, the typical introvert will answer *yes* to these questions: Generally, do you prefer reading to meeting people? Are you mostly quiet when you are with people? Do you stop and think things over before doing anything? In addition to such questionnaires, other, more objective, measures have been devised. For example, there is some suggestion that the "lemondrop test" may be used to distinguish between introverts and extroverts. In this test a standard amount of lemon juice is placed on the subject's tongue. Introverts and extroverts differ in the amount of saliva produced when this is done.

What is the theoretical underpinning of this dimension? Eysenck suggests that individual variations in introversion-extroversion reflect differences in neurophysiological functioning. Basically introverts are more easily aroused by events and more easily learn social prohibitions than are extroverts. As a result, introverts are more restrained and inhibited. There also is some evidence that introverts are more influenced by punishments in learning whereas extroverts are more influenced by rewards. It is hypothesized that individual differences along this dimension have both hereditary and environmental origins. Indeed, several studies of identical and fraternal twins suggest that heredity plays a major part in accounting for differences between individuals in their scores on this dimension (Shields, 1976).

Previously it was suggested that Eysenck felt that an adequate trait theory should be based on careful measurement, a theory of the basis for the trait differences and their development, and a body of related, empirically determined differences in behavior between individuals high and low on the dimension. Eysenck's use of factor analysis and his theory of the nature and origin of differences in extroversion-introversion have been discussed. Are there other significant and theoretically meaningful differences in behavioral functioning associated with different scores on this dimension? A recent review of the dimension presents us with an impressive array of findings. For example, introverts are more sensitive to pain than are extroverts, they become fatigued and bored more easily than do extroverts, excitement interferes with their performance while it enhances performance for extroverts, and they tend to be more careful but less fast than extroverts (Wilson, 1978). The following are some additional differences that have been found:

1 Introverts do better in school than extroverts, particularly in more advanced subjects. Also, students withdrawing from college for

academic reasons tend to be extroverts whereas those who withdraw for psychiatric reasons tend to be introverts.

2 Extroverts prefer vocations involving interactions with other people whereas introverts tend to prefer more solitary vocations. Extroverts seek diversion from job routine while introverts have a lesser need for novelty.

3 Extroverts enjoy explicit sexual and aggressive humor whereas introverts prefer more intellectual forms of humor such as puns and subtle jokes.

4 Extroverts are more active sexually, in terms of frequency and different partners, than are introverts.

5 Extroverts are more suggestible than are introverts.

The last finding is interesting in relation to a study of an overbreathing epidemic in England (Moss and McEverly, 1966). An initial report by some girls of fainting and dizziness was followed by an outbreak of similar complaints, with 85 girls needing to be taken to the hospital by ambulance — "they were going down like ninepins." A comparison of the girls who were affected with those who were not demonstrated, as expected, that the affected girls were higher in both neuroticism and extroversion. In other words, those individuals with a predisposing personality proved most susceptible to influence by suggestions of a real epidemic. In sum, Eysenck's trait-type approach goes far beyond the principle of the formulation of a trait concept to the development of (1) questionnaire and objective measures of the concept; (2) a view of the origins of the development of the individual differences and the grounding of these differences in biological functioning; and (3) demonstration of an array of meaningful empirical relationships in a wide variety of areas of psychological functioning.

THE TRAIT, FACTOR-ANALYTIC APPROACH OF RAYMOND B. CATTELL (1905-)

Raymond B. Cattell was born in 1905 in Devonshire, England. He obtained a B.Sc. degree in chemistry from the University of London in 1924. Cattell then turned to psychology and obtained a Ph.D. degree at the same university in 1929. During these years he was a research assistant under Charles Spearman, a psychologist who pursued the view that all mental tests measure, to some extent, one basic intellectual ability. Before coming to the United States in 1937, Cattell did a number of studies in personality and acquired clinical experience while directing a child guidance clinic.

Since coming to the United States he has held positions at Columbia, Harvard, Clark, and Duke Universities. For 20 years he was Research Professor of Psychology and Director of the Laboratory of Personality Assessment at the University of Illinois. During his professional career, he has written more than 200 articles and 15 books.

Although relatively little is known of the experiences that shaped Cattell's life and work, a number of influences seem apparent. First, Cattell's interest in the use of factor-analytic methods in personaliy research and his attempt to develop a hierarchical theory of personality organization can be related to his associations with two of the same British psychologists who influenced Eysenck, Spearman and Burt. Second, Cattell's views on motivation were influenced by another British psychologist, William McDougall.

His years spent jointly in personality research and clinical experience were a third influence on Cattell. These years sensitized him to the assets and limitations of clinical and experimental research. Finally, Cattell's earlier experience in chemistry influenced much of his later thinking in psychology. In chemistry, the development of the periodic table by Mendeleef in 1869 led to renewed experimental activity. Just as Mendeleef developed a classification of the elements in chemistry, much of Cattell's work can be viewed as an attempt to develop a classification (taxonomy) of variables for experimental research in personality.

Cattell's writing conveys the sense of a person totally committed to a science of personality in general and to the factor-analytic approach in particular. In his book on *The Scientific Analysis of Personality*, Cattell (1965) opens with the following remarks:

Personalities react differently even to the study of personality. To the scientifically minded it is the supreme scientific challenge, promising formulae of fantastic and intriguing complexity. To others the notion that we will measure and predict in the field of human personality is a sacrilege and a threat. Yet in an age when we are investigating everything, how can we shut our eyes to the possibilities of scientifically studying personality?

CATTELL, 1965, P. 11

For Cattell, the understanding of personality is basic to the understanding of the more restricted and specialized disciplines in psychology, such as perception and learning. And, for Cattell, it is the factor-analytic model that will lead to the understanding of personality.

In reading Cattell there is, at times, the sense of his being unfair in underestimating the contributions of others and in overestimating the conclusiveness of his own findings. However, there is also the wonderful sense of a person who feels that he is on the path of progress and at the brink of discovery.

RAYMOND B. CATTELL

Cattell's View of the Person

Because of the way in which Cattel gathers data and formulates his concepts, there is less that can be said about his view of the person than was true for the clinical theorists. His emphasis on objective test instruments, large samples of tests and subjects, and factor analysis of the data suggest little personal bias in theoretical formulation. However, at times Cattell goes far beyond the data to formulate theoretical principles, particularly in his formulation of the principles of motivation in personality. Here it becomes apparent that Cattell views the person as an energy system functioning in accordance with the principles of reinforcement (reward and punishment) and tension reduction.

Like Freud, Cattell conceptualizes motivation in terms of energy that may be transformed from one form into another and then discharged. Thus, we have the figurative expression of one motivational component of behavior "turning the wheels" of another motivational component of behavior. According to Cattell, the organism experiences tension and then obtains reward through the reduction of this tension.

In summary, Cattell views human behavior as lawful, and understands it in terms of the relationship among structural entities. Some of these structures consist of drives. These drives are sources of energy that get behavior going and keep it going. Cattell uses the model of an energy system as a useful analogy for motivational behavior.

Cattell's View of Science, Theory, and Research Methods

An understanding of Cattell's view of science, theory, and research is critical for an understanding of his theory. Cattell ties his research method to his theory of personality more closely than perhaps any other personality theorist. For all of his exuberance, Cattell in no way minimizes the difficulties of understanding personality. Research in psychology is difficult because of the intangible and fluid quality of behavior, because of the problem of separating psychology as a science from the daily preoccupation of all humankind, and because of the unique situation in science of scientists studying themselves (Cattell, 1966b). In the face of the complexities of human behavior, Cattell argues that we must have methodological self-awareness instead of unsystematic investigation or compulsive methodology. Furthermore, he contends that we must have a close relationship between research methods and theory. Theory must be based on measurement, but measurement must be meaningful.

bivariate
multivariate
clinical

Cattell distinguishes among three methods in the study of personality: **bivariate**, **multivariate**, and **clinical**. The typical *bivariate* experiment, which follows the classical experimental design of the physical sciences, contains two variables, an independent variable that is manipulated by the experimenter and a dependent variable that is measured to observe the effects of the experimental manipulations. In contrast to the bivariate method, the *multivariate method* studies the interrelationships among many variables at once. Furthermore, in the multivariate experiment the investigator does not manipulate the variables. Instead, in multivariate research the experimenter allows life itself to make the experiments and then uses statistical methods to extract meaningful dimensions and causal connections. The method of factor analysis is illustrative of the multivariate method. Both the bivariate method and the multivariate method express a concern for scientific rigor. The difference between them is that, in the bivariate method, experimenters limit their attention to a few variables that they can manipulate in some way whereas, in the multivariate methods, experimenters consider many variables as they exist in a natural situation. The multivariate investigator can manipulate variables, but generally there is no need to do so.

Cattell is quite critical of the bivariate method. He argues that attention to the relationship between two variables represents a simplistic and piecemeal approach to personality. Human behavior is complex and expresses the interactions among many variables. Having understood the relationship between two variables, one is left with the problem of understanding how these relate to the many other variables that are important in determining behavior. Second, the fact that bivariate experimenters attempt to manipulate the independent variable means that they must neglect many matters that are of real importance in psychology. Since the more important emotional situations cannot be manipulated and therefore cannot be used in controlled experiments in humans, the bivariate researcher has been forced to attend to trivia, to look for answers in the behavior of rats, or to look for answers in physiology.

In contrast to the bivariate method, the *clinical method* has the virtues of studying important behaviors as they occur and looking for lawfulness in the functioning of the total organism. Thus, in scientific aims and in philosophical assumptions the clinical method and multivariate method are close to one another and separate from the bivariate method. Both the clinician and the multivariate researcher are interested in global events; both are interested in complex patterns of behavior as they occur in life; both allow life itself to be the source of experimental manipulation; and, both are interested in an understanding of the total personality instead of in isolated processes or fragmented pieces of knowledge. The difference between the clinician and the multivariate researcher is that while the former uses intuition to assess variables and memory to keep track of events, the latter uses experimental procedures and statistical analyses (Cattell, 1962). Thus, according to Cattell, "the clinician has his heart in the right place, but perhaps we may say that he remains a little fuzzy in the head" (1959c, p. 45). In the light of these similarities and differences, Cattell concludes that the clinical method is the multivariate method but without the latter's concern for scientific rigor.

The statistical method associated with the multivariate research is *factor-analysis*, previously described in relation to the theory of Hans Eysenck. The major difference between the two theorists is that Cattell prefers to work at the trait level whereas Eysenck further factors his data to work at the type level (Figure 8.1).

In sum, Cattell thinks the multivariate method has the desirable qualities of the bivariate and clinical methods. The multivariate method is objective and scientifically rigorous; it allows one to study what cannot be experimentally controlled; it is economical since it can consider many variables at once; it can consider variables over many subjects and situations; it can allow for a variable to be measured by many tests; and it can look at the totality of manifestations of a large number of variables at the same time and as a total influence. Indeed, Cattell has virtually unlimited praise for the multivariate approach. "That which is really new in the area of personality theory deriving from experiment is generally the offspring of the bolder multivariate experimental designs" (Cattell, 1963, p. 420).

If Cattell is right in suggesting that the multivariate method is the best method for studying personality, then many psychologists are wasting their time on the bivariate and clinical methods. If he is right in suggesting that psychologists are reluctant to try out the new instrument of factor analysis, just as scientists in the past hesitated to make use of instruments new to their times, then we need to train a new breed of psychologists. To understand and to predict behavior, we must know which units there are to measure and how to measure them. "Most sciences have made their initial progress by measurement and by the development of taxonomy" (Nesselroade and Delhees, 1966, p. 564).

The terms *measurement* and *taxonomy* are keys to understanding Cattell's efforts. We can make significant progress in research only when we have developed tools for description and measurement. Theory cannot be independent of measurement, and measurement must be related to meaningful conceptual units. Psychology is without its periodic table of the elements, but multivariate research and factor analysis *can provide* the tools for defining the basic structural elements of personality.

Cattell's Theory of Personality

Some background factors relating to Cattell's theory of personality now have been examined. The observation has been made that Cattell views behavior as complex and is committed to a multivariate, factor-analytic approach toward description and measurement. It is time now to look at the theory as it stands over 30 years of research.

Structure

Given Cattell's emphasis on taxonomy, one expects him to give considerable attention to the structure of personality. Indeed, in Kelly's terms, we may expect to find the structural aspects of personality to be the focus of convenience of Cattell's theory of personality.

trait

Surface traits and source traits   The basic structural element for Cattell is the **trait**, which was defined earlier as a predisposition. The concept of trait assumes some pattern and regularity to behavior over time and across situations. Some traits may be common to all people, others unique to an individual; some determined by heredity, others by the environment; some relate to motives (dynamic traits), and others to ability and to temperament. An important distinction among traits is that between **surface**

surface traits
source traits

traits and **source traits**. Surface traits are expressive of behaviors that on a superficial level may appear to go together but in fact do not always move up and down (vary) together and do not necessarily have a common cause. A source trait, on the other hand, expresses an association among behaviors that do vary together to form a unitary, independent dimension of personality. Whereas surface traits can be discovered through subjective methods such as asking people which personality characteristics they think go together, the refined statistical procedures of factor analysis are necessary for the discovery of source traits. These source traits represent the building blocks of personality.

L-data
Q-data
OT-data

Sources of data: L-data, Q data, OT data   How do we discover source traits that cover a variety of responses across many situations? Where do we find our building blocks? According to Cattell, there are three sources of data: life record data (**L-data**), questionnaire date (**Q-data**), and objective test data (**OT-data**). L-data relates to behavior in actual, everyday-life situations such as school grades or ratings of an individual on traits such as sociability, emotional stability or conscientiousness. Q-data depends on introspection by the subject. Subject responses to questionnaires can be considered as accurate representations of the person or pieces of behavior that do not necessarily represent accurate appraisals of the subject himself; that is, if the subject says he is conscientious, we can either consider him to be so or just treat his response as a piece of behavior elicited by a question. Because of self-deception and faking, Cattell suggests the latter approach to Q-data.

The third source of data used to get at personality structure, OT-data, is, for Cattell, the most desirable. Cattell considers an objective test to be a behavioral miniature situation in which subjects are unaware of the relationship between their response and the personality characteristic being measured.

According to Cattell, if multivariate, factor-analytic research is indeed able to determine the basic structures of personality, then the same factors or traits should be obtained from L-data, Q-data, and OT-data. This is an important, logical, and challenging commitment. Research along these lines began with L-data. The goal of the original research was to obtain data on all aspects of human behavior, what Cattell called the **personality sphere**. It seemed most possible to gather a huge mass of data covering the personality sphere through L-data sources rather than through Q-data or OT-data sources. The strategy was to find source traits in L-data and then to determine if questionnaires and objective tests could be developed to reflect and test the same traits (Cattell, 1959b).

personality sphere

The original L-data research began with the assumption that the behaviors that cover the total personality sphere have their verbal symbols in language; that is, if we take all of the words used by individuals to describe behavior, we will have covered the personality sphere. A series of related analyses and experiments, including factor analysis, led to a total of 15 L-data factors that appeared to account for most of the behaviors represented in the personality sphere.

Of the 15 L-data factors, some readily make sense in terms of categories we generally use in looking at behavior, although others are more difficult to understand. An example of the former is the source trait of Dominance versus Submissiveness. The following bipolar adjectives combined to form the Dominance versus Submissiveness factor: self-assertive-submissive, confident-unsure, vigorous-meek, and adventurous-timid. An example of a source trait that is perhaps more difficult to appreciate at a glance is that of Mollity versus Durity or, as it was later called, Premsia versus Harria. Bipolar adjectives relevant to this source trait are: impatient-emotionally mature, imaginative-unaffected by "fancies," and frivolous-responsible. This trait is interpreted in terms of a dimension going from emotional sensitivity to hard realism and toughmindedness. It is described as having the sensitivity and sudden shifts or lability of mind that goes with an "artistic temperament" or with far-ranging imagination. The labels of some of these factors are taken from Greek, and others are compound words formed from the initial letters of a phrase (for example, Premsia is taken from Protected Emotional Sensitivity). In both cases, they express Cattell's efforts to avoid labels that will lead to an incorrect interpretation of the factor.

Of the L-data traits, the one that factor analysis demonstrated to be of greatest importance in accounting for individual differences was Cyclothymia-Schizothymia. The trait elements related to this dimension are easygoing-cantankerous, adaptable-rigid, warmhearted-cool, frank-secretive, emotionally expressive-reserved, and trustful-suspicious. In an extreme form, the cyclothymic person is likely to show prolonged mood swings between elation and depression. In contrast to this, the schizothymic person tends to remain cool and aloof and to avoid affective involvement with people or situations. This source trait is also associated with differences in body build, the cyclothyme being more round-bodied than the schizothyme. Finally, research has suggested that this source trait is largely hereditary. This is not true for the Dominance-Submissiveness source trait, which is largely environmentally determined.

Sixteen Personality Factor Inventory

The second part of Cattell's research strategy in collecting data on the personality sphere was to determine whether comparable factors could be found in Q-data. The main result of work with Q-data is the **Sixteen Personality Factor** (16 P.F.) **Inventory**. In the construction of the 16 P.F., Cattell used the personality dimensions found in ratings (L-data) as a source of hypotheses for test items. Thousands of questionnaire items were written and administered to large groups of normal people. Tests were run to see which items went together. Factor analyses were completed, leading to the development of the 16 P.F. Inventory. Of the 16 factors or source traits measured by this questionnaire, 12 show considerable similarity with factors from L-data and four appear to be unique to Q-data. For example, let us return to the L-data factor Cyclothymia-Schizothymia. The following are questionnaire items to which the responses are associated with this same factor.

(1) I would rather work as:
    (a) An engineer   (b) A social science teacher
(2) I could stand being a hermit:
    (a) True   (b) False
(3) I trust strangers:
    (a) Sometimes   (b) Practically always

A very cyclothymic person will answer that he would rather work as a social science teacher, that he could not stand being a hermit, and that he practically always trusts strangers. In contrast to this pattern of response, the very schizothymic person answers that he would rather work as an engineer, that he could stand being a hermit, and that he only sometimes trusts strangers. Further illustrations of the association between L-data ratings and Q-data response are given in Box 8.1 for the source trait Ego Strength-Neurotic Emotionality.

Cattell is committed to the use of questionnaires, in particular, factor analytically derived questionnaires such as the 16 P.F. On the other hand, Cattell also has expressed concern about the problems of motivated dis-

BOX 8.1   **Correspondence Between Data from Two Different Test Domains: L-Data Ratings and Q-Data Responses**

SOURCE TRAIT C. EGO STRENGTH-VERSUS-EMOTIONALITY
AND NEUROTICISM, IN L- AND Q-DATA

Behavior ratings by observer on these elements:

Ego Strength		*Emotionality/Neuroticism*
Mature	vs	Unable to tolerate frustration
Steady, persistent	vs	Changeable
Emotionally calm	vs	Impulsively emotional
Realistic about problems	vs	Evasive, avoids necessary decisions
Absence of neurotic fatigue	vs	Neurotically fatigued (with no real effort)

Questionnaire responses on these items*:

Do you find it difficult to take no for an answer even when what you want to do is obviously impossible?
(a) yes   (b) *no*
If you had your life to live over again, would you
(a) *want it to be essentially*   (b) Plan it very differently?
    the same?
Do you often have really disturbing dreams?
(a) yes   (b) *no*
Do your moods sometimes make you seem unreasonable even to yourself?
(a) yes   (b) *no*
Do you feel tired when you've done nothing to justify it?
(a) *rarely*   (b) often
Can you change old habits, without relapse, when you decide to?
(a) *yes*   (b) no

*Answer in italic type indicates high ego strength.
SOURCE   R.B. Cattell, *The scientific analysis of personality.* Baltimore, Md.: Penguin, 1965.

tortion and self-deception in relation to questionnaire responses. Also, he feels that the questionnaire is of particularly questionable utility with mental patients. Because of problems with L-data and Q-data, and because the original research strategy itself called for investigations with objective test (OT) data, Cattell's efforts have been concerned more recently with personality structure as derived from OT-data. It is the source traits as expressed in objective tests that are the "real coin" for personality research.

The results from L-data and Q-data researches were important in guiding the development of miniature test situations; that is, the effort was to develop objective tests, as defined by Cattell, that would measure the source traits already discovered. Thus, for example, tendencies to be assertive might be expressed in behaviors such as long exploratory distance on a finger maze test, fast tempo in arm-shoulder movement, and fast speed of letter comparisons. More than 500 tests were constructed to cover the hypothesized personality dimensions. These tests included speed tasks in which the subject had to cancel out letters, a test of motor-perceptual rigidity in which the subject had to write numbers or familiar words backwards, and a test in which two dreams were reported.

The result of administering these tests to large groups of subjects and repeated factoring of data from different research situations has been the establishment of 21 OT-data source traits. The theoretical interpretation of the traits is based primarily on the tests found to be expressive of the trait, and on the relationships between performance on these tests and performance in the realms of L-data and Q-data. For example, factor analysis of OT-data suggests that there is a single anxiety factor. Individuals scoring high on this trait show the following performance characteristics: high susceptibility to annoyance and embarrassment, admission of many common frailties, a high tendency to agree, low in confidence in their skill in untried performance, and low in physical strength and endurance. Scores on this trait relate to scores on a number of scales on the 16 P.F.

As mentioned before, the source traits or factors found in L-data and Q-data could, for the most part, be matched to one another. Also observed was the fact that Cattell's theory assumes that source traits are inherent structures in personality and that it should be possible to measure the same traits by ratings, questionnaires, or objective tests. How then do the OT-data factors match up with those derived from L-data and Q-data? Several relationships have been found between L-data and Q-data factors on the one hand, and OT-data factors on the other. However, no simple "point-to-point" relationship has been found.

The issue of the matching of factors in the three kinds of observation — ratings, questionnaires, and objective tests, is highly complex. It will be returned to in the critique and evaluation section. For now, what has been said in this section can be summarized by stating the following: (1) Cattell set out to define the structure of personality in three areas of observation, called L-data, Q-data, and OT-data. (2) He started his research in L-data, constructed a personality sphere of word symbols for behavioral characteristics, and through the factor analysis of ratings came up with 15 source traits. (3) Guided in his research on Q-data by the L-data findings, Cattell developed the 16 P.F. Inventory, which contains 12 traits that match traits found in the L-data research and four traits that appear to be unique to questionnaire methods. (4) By using these results to guide his research in the development of objective tests, Cattell found 21 source traits in OT-data that appear to have a complex relationship to the traits previously found in the other data.

The source traits found in the three types of observation do not complete Cattell's formulation of the structure of personality. However, the traits presented in this section do describe the general nature of the structure of personality as formulated by Cattell. In the next section on process, some of the dynamic structures of personality will be examined. Here, however, what is conceived to be the basis for psychology's table of the elements — its classification system — has been examined. It is the basis for Cattell's answer to the question: "What units shall we employ?" (Allport, 1958).

Process

In chapter 1 the observation was made that although a useful conceptual distinction can be made between structure and process, the actual separation of structure from process often is fuzzy. This is particularly true in Cattell's theory where his efforts to determine the motivational sources of behavior continue to involve an emphasis on taxonomy and factor analysis. Cattell makes a distinction among ability, temperament, and dynamic traits, principally relating to the traditional distinction in psychology among cognition (thinking), affection (emotion), and conation (motivation). Dynamic traits are related to the why and how of behavior, and it is these traits that will be discussed in this section.

attitude

Dynamic traits: attitudes   A basic conceptual unit for Cattell in the development of a comprehensive taxonomy is that of **attitude**. An attitude expresses a strength of interest in following out a particular course of action. For example, individuals differ in their strength of interest in areas such as home, recreation, occupation, religion, politics, relationships to others, and relationship to oneself. Attitudes, or interests in these areas, are "the individual bricks in the house of the total dynamic structure. From these final measureable manifestations we must arrive, by experimental measures and statistical processes, at a picture of the total structure" (Cattell, 1965a, p. 173). An attitude, then, indicates a readiness to act in a certain direction in a given situation.

In his research on motivational processes, Cattell set out to answer two basic questions: What are the components of any single motive or attitude? What are the different kinds of motives or attitudes that exist? The first question relates to whether the strength of a motive is determined by a single component or by the combined action of many components. In the first major study along these lines, Cattell (Cattell and Baggaley, 1956) administered fifty-five objective tests on four attitudes to Air Force OCS cadets and Air Force ROTC students. The attitudes related to flying ("I want to fly an airplane,") drinking and smoking ("I want to do more drinking and smoking."), and movies ("I like to go to the movies.").

The factor analysis of the tests given to the Air Force subjects led to the discovery of five factors, suggesting that there are many components to a motive. These five components were again found in a study of the attitudes of children toward movies and religion (Cattell, Radcliffe, and Sweeney, 1973). The five factors or components to motivation have been described as follows:

1 Conscious Id — behavior that expresses an "I wish" or "I want" quality to it.
2 Ego Expression — behavior expressing a mature interest that has been brought into contact with reality.
3 Ideal Self or Superego — behavior expressing an "I ought to be interested" quality to it.
4 Physiological Need Expressions — behavior expressive of physiological reactivity.
5 Repressed Complexes — behavior expressing that which has been repressed and rendered unconscious as a result of conflict.

It is interesting to observe that, although Cattell did not start this research with any bias in favor of psychoanalysis, he found it appropriate to interpret the three major components of motivation in psychoanalytic terms — id, ego and superego.

To summarize the conceptualization of motivation presented thus far, it can be said that the factoring of many scores from tests of single attitudes suggests that any motive is made up of a variety of components. Three of the components found can be interpreted in terms of the psychoanalytic concepts of id, ego, and superego.

Attitudes: ergs and sentiments   Although this research suggests the structure of a single motive, it does not suggest an answer to the second question. Still to be determined are the kinds of motives that exist in individuals. Again, as is typical of his research strategy, Cattell tried to examine all possible attitudes and to measure each attitude by at least two devices. The result of these studies has been the discovery of a variety of factors that Cattell has separated into two categories. Some of the factors appeared to reflect the forces of innate biological drives, and other factors appeared to reflect environmentally determined patterns of behavior. The former are called **ergs**, the latter **sentiments**.

ergs
sentiments

An erg represents an innate tendency to react to goals in a specific way. The socialization process may influence the overt expression of an erg, but the innate qualities of an erg may be observed in the emotional qualities and biological goals that are associated with it and which remain constant across cultures. Ten factor patterns have been identified that appear to represent the following ergs: Mating (Sex), Security-Fear, Self-Assertion,

Gregariousness (Sociability), Parental Protection, Exploration (Curiosity), Sensuality, Appeal, and Constructiveness. The sex and fear ergs are manifest in the following attitudes.

Sex Erg Attitudes

I want to love a person I find attractive.
I want to satisfy my sexual needs.
I want to dress to impress the opposite sex.
I like a novel with love interest and a ravishing heroine.

Security-Fear Erg Attitudes

I want more protection from nuclear weapons.
I want to reduce accidents and diseases.
I want to take out more insurance against illness.
I want never to be an insane patient in a mental hospital.

Notice that these ergs range from fear and sex to curiosity and gregariousness. Notice also that, in contrast to Freud, Cattell does not indicate the presence of a destructiveness erg, although at least one presentation of the theory does list a pugnacity erg, for example, "I want to see violence in movies and television shows" (Horn, 1966).

Sentiments have their source in social institutions such as the family or school. They represent acquired attitude patterns. Examples of sentiments would be the Religious Sentiment (I want to worship God.), the Career Sentiment (I want to learn skills required for a job.), and the Self Sentiment (I want never to damage my self-respect.). The self sentiment is particularly important in Cattell's view of personality functioning.

The dynamic lattice and specification equation   How do these structures relate to the process aspects of behavior? How do ergs and sentiments translate into answers to the why of human behavior? Although the motivation component and dynamic factor structures have been discovered through systematic research and the use of factor analysis, much of Cattell's explanation of the why of human behavior is merely theoretical speculation. Cattell uses the concept of a **dynamic lattice** to represent the relationship of ergs, sentiments, and attitudes to one another. Within the dynamic lattice, an individual may express a variety of attitudes, for instance, toward a film, toward a person, or toward a principle. These attitudes may be linked to various sentiments, such as the religious, political, and career sentiments. Finally, the sentiments are understood to be linked to ergs. For example, behaviors in relation to one's career (sentiment) may be related to the gratification of the curiosity, self-assertion and protection ergs. In other words, the dynamic lattice is a way of indicating that the at-

dynamic lattice

titudes are invested with energy so as to satisfy sentiments, which themselves must be invested with energy in order to satisfy the basic ergs or biological goals. "For example, a person may study accountancy in order that he may keep his job in a big business, in order that he may earn money, in order that he may marry and have a family, and so on" (Cattell, 1965a, p. 185).

The dynamic lattice expresses Cattell's efforts to represent the complexity of motives. Behaviors are viewed as satisfying immediate and distant goals. A single behavior can be expressive of many attitudes, each of which may be related to a number of sentiments and, ultimately, to a number of ergs. In other words, one behavior may satisfy a variety of drives. Although the ultimate goal remains the satisfaction of the biological drives, the self-sentiment retains an important function within the dynamic lattice. The satisfaction of many of the ergs is viewed as dependent on what happens in relation to the self-sentiment. It is the self-sentiment that is responsible for the control of the impulses of ergs and for the integration of many lesser sentiments.

conflict

Because of the above complexity of motives, there is not only the potential for gratification of many drives through one behavior but also the potential for **conflict**, that is, for a situation in which the satisfaction of one drive is accompanied by the frustration of another. Conflict may arise between attitudes or within a single attitude. In either case, the attempt to satisfy one erg or sentiment is expressed at the cost of frustration of another erg or sentiment. In contrast to the state of conflict, in an integrated state the gratifications of the ergs or sentiments add up rather than cancel one another out. As will be discussed later, the degree of conflict is an important criterion of the degree of psychopathology within an individual.

specification equation

The various forces that Cattell believes are important in predicting behavior are expressed in the **specification equation**. Personality is that which predicts what a person will do in a defined situation. The specification equation gives expression to personality factors as they enter into specific situations. The behavior of an individual in a situation will depend on the traits of the individual that are relevant to the situation and on transient variables that may enter into a given situation (Horn, 1966). One example of a transient variable that may enter into a specific situation is that of *state*. If a person happens to be anxious at a given moment, his behavior in a situation will be influenced by the anxiety he is experiencing at that time. A second transient influence is what Cattell calls *role*. The concept of role gives expression to the fact that the very same stimulus is perceived in a different way by an individual according to his role in the situation. For example, a teacher may respond differently to a child's behavior in the classroom than to the same behavior outside of the classroom when no longer in the role of teacher. Cattell suggests that the individual is a changed person in different role situations. Therefore, the importance of personality factors will vary according to the situation. Thus, although Cattell believes that personality factors lead to a certain degree of stability to behavior across situations, he also believes that a person's mood (state) and the way he is presenting himself in a given situation (role) will influence his behavior. "How vigorously Smith attacks his meal depends not only on how hungry he happens to be, but also on his temperament and whether he is having dinner with his employer or is eating alone at home" (Nesselrode and Delhees, 1966, p. 583). The specification equation is important because it indicates that Cattell does not see behavior as due to personality factors alone, or wholly due to situational factors, but rather as due to the joint effects of both personality and situational determinants.

Summary   Before going on to the growth and development part of the theory, let us summarize the section on process. (1) Cattell started with the concept of *attitude* to represent interest in following a particular course of action. The factor analysis of single attitudes led to the discovery of *motivation components* such as Conscious Id, Ego Expression, and Super Ego. (2) The factor analysis of many attitudes led to the discovery of factors tied to biological drives, called *ergs*, and factors related to the socialization process, called *sentiments*. (3) Cattell has presented the concept of the dynamic lattice to express his belief that the basic source of energy is in the ergs. Attitudes operate in the service of sentiments that themselves act as "holding companies" for the energy which basically stems from the ergs. (4) Finally, the concept of the *specification equation* gives expression to Cattell's belief in the complexity of variables that enter into behavior in a given situation. Cattell's theory suggests that behavior expresses the individual's traits that operate in a situation, the ergs and sentiments associated with attitudes relevant to a situation, and the *state* and *role* components that may vary from time to time or situation to situation (Horn, 1966).

Growth and Development

Cattell has been concerned with two major issues relevant to the growth and development of personality — the determinants of personality and the pattern of development of the structural traits. Like most personality theorists, Cattell emphasizes the importance of both heredity and learning — of nature and nurture — in the development of personality. However, he is virtually unique among major personality theorists in that he has tried to determine the specific environmental and hereditary contributions to each trait.

Multiple Abstract Variance Analysis (MAVA) Method

Cattell has developed a method, the **Multiple Abstract Variance Analysis (MAVA) Method** to determine how much influence heredity and environment have in the development of different traits (Cattell, 1965b). This method involves administering a number of personality tests to the members of a large number of families. The data are then analyzed in relation to four kinds of influences: within-family environmental differences, between-family environmental differences, within-family hereditary differences, and between-family hereditary differences. Through the use of a number of equations, the researcher is able to determine the genetic and environmental influences on the development of a trait. The importance of these two influences has been found to vary with the trait. For example, it is estimated that heredity accounts for 80 to 90 percent of the variation found in scores on a measure of the intelligence ability trait. The genetic influence on neuroticism also has been found to be considerable, although it is only about half that found in intelligence. On the other hand, how emotionally sensitive one is and how carefree as opposed to cautious one is appear to be determined mainly by environmental influences. One estimate has been made that overall personality is about two-thirds determined by environment and one-third by heredity (Hundleby, Pawlik, and Cattell, 1965).

Cattell emphasizes the interaction between hereditary and environmental influences in pesonality development. The type of genetic endowment that individuals bring into the world will influence the responses of others to them, will influence the ways in which they learn, and will set limits on the modifiability of their personalities by environmental forces. This latter aspect of the interaction between nature and nurture is of particular importance. It is expressed in Cattell's principle of *coercion to the biosocial mean*. This suggests that society typically exerts pressure on genetically different individuals to conform to a social mean. For example, the naturally more dominant person is encouraged by society to be less dominant, and the naturally submissive person is encouraged to show more self-assertion.

The process of personality development is further complicated by maturation. Maturation may delay the full-blown appearance of genetic influences in traits. Furthermore, maturation may influence the kind of learning that occurs in relation to traits at any given time in the development of the organism. For example, learning to walk cannot occur until a certain degree of physical development has occurred. In general, it is Cattell's belief that the early years are of particular importance to personality formation. In fact, he concludes that much of the basic formation of personality occurs before the age of seven years. In relation to this complex developmental process, Cattell has conducted research on *age trends* in the formation of personality traits. This research on age trends is part of an effort to discover the personality traits that will characterize children, adolescents, and adults at every stage of their development. Age trends research also involves the study over time of the development of each trait. Much of the age trends research suggests that the same underlying factors can be found, both in number and in kind, in subjects from age four through adulthood (Coan, 1966). On the other hand, a recent study of nursery school children indicated that only about one third of the traits found in adults are found in children (Damarin and Cattell, 1968).

As with his structure and process conceptions of personality, Cattell attempts to give full attention to the complexity of growth and development. Traits are not due to heredity or environment, but to a complex interaction of both in relation to maturational factors; what is learned becomes incorporated into the developing personality structure, and this structure influences the course of future learning. Some of this complexity is expressed in Cattell's definition of personality learning as a "multi-dimensional change in response to a multi-dimensional situation" (Cattell, 1965a, p. 283). In other words, the individual responds to complex situations in ways that simultaneously affect many different parts of the personality. Experiences, especially early experiences, represent more than one-to-one associations between a stimulus and a response. Instead, experiences relate to the development of individual traits and to the overall organization of personality traits.

Clinical Applications of Cattell's Theory

Psychopathology

Development in general is viewed in terms of the interaction between heredity and environment. In accord with this view, the cause of psychopathology is considered both in terms of inherited influences that predispose the individual to experience conflict, and environmental influences in terms of history of personal trauma. Cattell's conception of the development of psychopathology is based on a conflict model. According to the model, a drive is stimulated and then blocked. The individual attempts to break the barrier but fails and is forced to give up the goal. This leads to a state of conflict and anxiety that results in neurotic symptoms. As described in the process section, a state of conflict exists when satisfaction of one drive is accompanied by frustration of another. Cattell has been able to develop a formula for computing the degree to which an individual's attitudes serve to satisfy some ergs (or sentiments) at the cost of satisfying other ergs (or sentiments). In one research effort, the resulting index of conflict was found to distinguish between mental patients and nonpatients, to relate to estimates made by psychiatrists of the amount of conflict in each patient, and to relate to the 16 P.F. scale of ego weakness (Williams, 1959).

Basic to Cattell's approach to psychopathology is his effort to find concrete differences between normal people and members of various patient groups (Cattell and Rickels, 1964; Cattell and Tatro, 1966; Rickels and Cattell, 1965). In an important study of neuroticism and anxiety, it was found that neurotics differ from normals on several factors. Furthermore, it was found that anxiety is only one of many factors contributing to neurosis, that is, anxiety is a part, but not all, of neurosis (Cattell and Scheier, 1961). Some factors appear to be important for all forms of neurosis, although other personality factors are important only to some forms of neurosis. Thus, for example, high scores on anxiety and neuroticism and low scores on ego strength appear to characterize all neurotics, while a low score on surgency, indicative of restraint and reticence, is characteristic only of depressives. Psychotics have been found to differ from normals in personality source traits, but in ways different from that of neurotics. Psychotics share with neurotics low scores on ego strength but do not deviate on anxiety in the striking way neurotics do (Cattell and Tatro, 1966).

BOX 8.2 **Differences between Normals and Neurotics on Personality Factors**

PROBLEM   Past research has indicated that neurotics can be distinguished from normals on six personality factors. The Anxiety factor and the Regression ("Neuroticism") factor seem to be particularly important. To what extent is the typical private patient consulting the general psychiatrist for nervous troubles recognizably above normals on the two dimensions of anxiety and neuroticism?

HYPOTHESIS   Neurotics will score significantly higher than normals on tests of anxiety and regression.

SUBJECTS   128 private, middle class male and female patients visiting eight general psychiatrists in urban and rural practices in the eastern United States. 54 members of the clerical staff of a large business serve as the control (normal) population. The two groups are matched for occupational level and age. Also, subgroups from the neurotic and normal populations are matched on educational level and income.

METHOD   Test patients at the time of their first visit to the psychiatrist. As measures of the anxiety factor, use two scales, one that relates to both overt anxiety (IPAT Verbal Anxiety Scale) and one that measures the regression ("neuroticism") factor (IPAT Objective-Analytic Regression Battery). Approximate time for the total battery of tests is one and one-half hours.

RESULTS

1 Neurotic patients and normal controls differ significantly in their performance on the anxiety and regression tests. Neurotic patients show significantly more anxiety and significantly more regression than do normal controls.

IPAT Anxiety and Regression Batteries for Neurotics
and Normal Controls Showing Significant Differences

| | Mean Scores | |
	Neurotics N = 128	Normal Controls N = 54
IPAT Test or Battery		
IPAT Verbal Scale (total)	44.40	26.12
IPAT Covert Anxiety	20.21	14.81
IPAT Overt Anxiety	24.19	11.81
IPAT Q-A Anxiety	0.74	−1.76
IPAT Q-A Regression	1.60	−0.67

2 Social class, as measured by educational level and income, does not significantly influence the results.

CONCLUSION   Neurotic patients show significantly more anxiety and significantly more neuroticism, as measured by the IPAT verbal and objective tests, than do normal controls.

SOURCE   R. B. Cattell, and K. Rickels, Diagnostic power of IPAT objective anxiety neuroticism tests. *Archives of General Psychiatry*, 1964, *11, 459-465.*

One of the major conclusions reached by factor-analytic research concerning the nature of neurosis is that neurosis is a special type of personality pattern which is distinct from both normal and psychotic personality patterns. Some of the factors basic to neurosis are largely hereditary, and others are largely environmentally determined. Anxiety is a contributing factor to neurosis, but it is a separate entity. Very neurotic people can show only moderately high degrees of anxiety and anxiety can exist at appreciable levels in normal people. An effort has been made to study national differences in average mental health level. Of six countries studied (the United States, England, Japan, Italy, France, India), the United States was found to have the lowest national level of neuroticism, and India the highest.

These are some of the results from factor-analytic research into psychopathology. The major aspects of this approach are the effort to define factors experimentally for the general population and, then, the effort to define various types of psychopathology in terms of their unique patterns of scores on these factors.

Change

As is characteristic, Cattell recognizes the complexity of change and therefore differentiates it according to types of change. In general, Cattell holds that personality remains more constant, over time and across situations, than is often supposed. This is particularly true of the basic personality traits, although specific attitudes and interests may be somewhat less stable. However, change is recognized and analyzed in terms of three components: maturation, reversible fluctuations and instabilities, and learning.

In maturation, there is the gradual development of a biological organism. Both the sequence of change and the timing of the changes show considerable similarity across all persons. The long-term study of age trends offers clues about the importance of maturational factors in the change of personality traits. The second change component, reversible fluctuations and instabilities, is perhaps best represented in the concept of *states*. The concept of states refers to behaviors that are reversible and that change more rapidly than the behaviors associated with traits. In their study of anxiety, Cattell and Scheier (1961) note that there are some people who characteristically have high anxiety levels and other, typically nonanxious, people who are temporarily highly anxious. They then raise the important question as to whether trait anxiety is just state anxiety held permanently high or, in fact, is a different form of anxiety than is state anxiety. Their conclusion is that there are two forms of anxiety –– **trait anxiety** and **state anxiety**. Thus, it is assumed that occasional anxiety does not represent a change in the trait structure but may be the result of changes in the physiological functioning of the organism (Nesselroade and Bartsch, 1977).

trait anxiety
state anxiety

This leaves the change that is due to learning. According to Cattell, change does not generally involve the learning of specific behaviors but instead involves changes in traits or patterns of traits as a whole. The focus in psychotherapy is on the kinds of trait changes that can be measured in relation to the therapeutic process. Changes that result from psychotherapy, for instance, in ego strength, are not due to change in a large number of specific behaviors. Rather, they represent the general changes that accompany the modification of specific behaviors. In neurosis, the whole personality pattern is defective. Thus, for psychotherapy to be effective it must involve a change in the pattern.

A Case Example

Cattell values the intensive study of the individual case. He views the individual as a representation of the universal and attempts to find the same traits and the same processes in the study of an individual that he finds in the study of many subjects. The tool Cattell uses for the study of the individual is **P technique**. In *P* technique, scores on a variety of tests are obtained for one individual on many occasions. These scores are then factor analyzed to determine the underlying structure of the individual's personality; that is, which aspects of his behavior tend to vary together and to be independent of variation in other aspects of his behavior?

The individual case reported here in detail was first presented as an illustration of *P* technique (Cattell and Luborsky, 1950), and then as an illustration of the merits of the clinical and factor-analytic approaches (Luborsky, 1953). In this study, a patient was seen for two hours each day for 54 days over a period of 12 weeks. During one hour of each session, the patient took a standard test battery including objective personality tests and physiological measures. During the second hour of each session, the patient reported dreams and resulting free associations.

The patient studied was a 25-year-old male who had completed two semesters and then had been dropped from college for low grades. Although robust and of athletic build, he had been rejected from the army with a diagnosis of peptic ulcer. He had been brought up on a farm and had been a successful farmer on his own. Then he decided to get a higher education and sold his farm. At college he was active in a variety of activities and was described by others as being friendly and self-assured. The student had gone to the Guidance Bureau for counseling after he had been dropped from school, and he then was referred for treatment and participation in the research project. He had continuous stomach trouble prior to and during treatment. This trouble was not a motive for treatment but it was often referred to during therapy, and it became one of the focal points of the clinical and factor-analytic investigations.

On the basis of clinical material gained through the dreams and free associations, the patient was described as having strong unconscious needs to be dependent and to have problems solved for him. He defended himself against recognizing these needs partly through active striving and partly through obsessive thinking. The typical context in which he reported stomach pains was when he was talking about his strivings (for example, to win his girlfriend, to get ahead in school) or when he was talking about possible consequences of his strivings (for example, losing money,

P technique

feeling weak, being taken advantage of). The stomach pains were interpreted as being particularly associated with fears of being weak, passive, or dependent. Again, competition and obsessive moral self-justification were used to defend against feelings of being weak and helpless. This pattern is consistent with the personality characteristics described as typical of patients with stomach ulcers (Alexander, 1950).

Nine factors were found through the factor analysis of data gathered on 46 variables for 54 testing sessions. Many of these factors correspond to factors found in the study of many individuals, but other factors appear to be unique to this study. The main factors relevant to the subject's personality appeared to be the ones relating to his being prudent and serious as opposed to impulsive and enthusiastic, to his being submissive and dependent as opposed to dominant, and to his being emotionally stable. The stomach pains were found to be somewhat associated with the waxing and waning of his general level of emotional stability. Even more striking, however, was the association of the stomach pains with the prudent, serious versus impulsive, enthusiastic factor. Stomach upset was greatest when he was lively and active.

During the course of treatment the changes in factor scores suggested that the patient had become less concerned about pleasing others and more resistant to treatment. The data suggested that the patient had slowed down in pushing himself and also had felt greater freedom to satisfy his needs. These changes in factor scores were found to be consistent with changes observed in relation to the content of the free associations. For example, in sessions with high scores for being prudent and serious, the patient's free associations reflected less of a need to be active and more of a "take it or leave it" attitude. On the other hand, in sessions with high scores for being impulsive and enthusiastic, the free associations tended to be hurried and to involve concerns about measuring up to others. The stomach pains were associated with the latter sessions.

This case illustrates how factor analysis can be used in relation to the study of the individual. In this case, factors were found that corresponded to factors found in studies of many individuals. Changes in factor scores could be observed during the course of treatment, and these changes could be related meaningfully to changes observed in the content of the free associations. The correspondence between clinical data and factor-analytic data is particularly noteworthy. The factor-analytic approach, as represented here, has the advantage of being objective and rigorous. On the other hand, some are of the opinion that the factor traits are too abstract and leave out the richness of personality found in the clinical material.

Critical Evaluation of Cattell's Theory

Clearly, Cattell's theory will stand or fall on the strengths and weaknesses of his use of factor analysis. We can, at this time, discuss certain questions that are relevant to this technique and that, perhaps, have been apparent in the sections already covered. For example, there are questions such as: How does one know how many factors to use in developing the theory? How sure can we be that the same factors are coming up in different studies? Are there assumptions in the use of factor analysis that one might not want to make? How does one know the "meaning" of a factor and can the scores on factors really be used to formulate an accurate picture of the personality? There is no agreed-on answer to these questions, so let us consider some of the views held in relation to each one.

How Many Factors?

Factor analysis is an objective, mathematical procedure. However, there are variations in some details of the factor-analytic procedure that leave room for judgment on the part of the investigator. Thus, although both Cattell and Eysenck use factor analysis to gain insight into the structure of personality, the factor-analytic procedure used by Eysenck results in the indentification of few factors, and the procedure used by Cattell results in the identification of many factors (Cohen, 1966). Without going into the details and the logic of each procedure, we can state that different points of view are held concerning the utility of different factor-analytic procedures, which result in the identification of different numbers of factors.

Are the Same Factors Identified in Different Studies?

This is a complex question. First, how do we know whether factors discovered in different studies are the same? Second, if the factors identified are not the same can this be because of differences in tests used or factor analytic procedures used to analyze the data? While Cattell argues that his factors have been identified in numerous studies, Howarth (1972a) reports that he has not been able to replicate Cattell's factors. Howarth asks whether Cattell's personality factors are "sensitive plants" that can be bred under certain conditions or are "hardy perennials." His conclusion is that the factors are sensitive plants. Other investigators register similar concern, particularly in terms of difficulty in replicating (reproducing) Cattell's trait factors (Eysenck, 1977; Guilford, 1975).

As was pointed out in the section on structure, a related question is whether the same factors are identified when different kinds of data (for example, ratings, questionnaires, objective tests) are used. Cattell and his associates believe that the use of different tests will influence the data to some extent but that "the results do not leave any doubt about the behavioral generality of factors found in different media" (Hundleby, Pawlik, and Cattell, 1965, p. 327; Wilde, 1977). On the other hand, there does appear to be room for doubt, for other psychologists conclude that the factors from the three media (L-data, Q-data, OT-data) do not match up well (Becker, 1960; Bouchard, 1972; Skinner and Howarth, 1973; Tyler, 1965).

A final question concerning factor matching is whether the same factors appear across different subject populations and age groups. As noted, Cattell argues that there has been good replication of factors across subject populations and age groups. However, one study of children suggests that personality factors may change drastically as children mature (Damarin and Cattell, 1968) and at least some psychologists hold reservations concerning the variations in results from subject sample to subject sample (Peterson, 1965; Sells, 1959).

In sum, in spite of Cattell's arguments to the contrary, many psychologists have concluded that the same factors are not replicated in different studies, that the nature of the test used does influence the factors found, and that there is factor variability due to subject differences. It is interesting to note that although these studies include objective tests and sophisticated mathematical techniques, the resulting data are still open to differing interpretations.

Are There Certain Questionable Assumptions in the Factor-Analytic Procedure?

Many psychologists have been critical of factor analysis on technical grounds. Many of these criticisms get into the complexities of the procedure itself. Others, however, can more easily be appreciated. One point suggests that the factor analytic procedure can not consider some complicated relationships that may exist between behaviors. For example, suppose that two behaviors are related to one another but do not necessarily *always* increase or decrease together. For example, anxiety and anger may be related to one another, but whether or not both are expressed in behavior may have to do with other influences. Since factor analysis emphasizes only the joint rise and decline of behaviors, it will not pick up this more complex relationship. Another point sometimes made is that behavior may not result from the added contributions of different traits but rather from some more complicated relationship. For example, the arousal of both sexual and aggressive drives may cause one to have an effect on the other beyond the pure addition of one drive to another. Cattell's specification equation only suggests additive relationships among traits. In sum, these and other criticisms suggest that factor analysis does not allow for more complex relationships among human behaviors. Cattell's response to these criticisms is that the simpler, additive model is adequate for the prediction of most behavior and that "one must walk before one can run" (Cattell, 1956, p. 104).

How Sure Can We Be that the Factors Identified Have Some Meaning?

The questions already raised suggest caution concerning the acceptance of factors as established personality units. Holtzman (1965) notes that people will have a hard time making sense out of Cattell's factors. This has probably already been apparent to the student. In an interesting study relevant to this problem, Overall (1964) obtained data on the physical dimensions of books and then performed a factor analysis of the data. Ordinarily, people will describe the physical characteristics of books in terms of the dimensions of height, width, and thickness. Instead of these dimensions, the factor analysis resulted in the identification of dimensions resembling size, obesity, and squareness. One interpretation of this finding is that factor analysis failed to reveal the primary dimensions of books and, therefore, cannot be counted on for the discovery of the "real" structure in nature. "The results need not and do not have inherent in them any necessary relationship to 'real' or 'primary' characteristics of the objects or persons being measured" (Overall, 1964, p. 270). However, we might also assume that the observed dimensions need not correspond to what we generally consider to be the primary physical dimensions of a book. The important point is whether the observed dimensions appear to have some meaning and can be used in further research.

Overall's conclusion is that we cannot expect factor analysis to point out to us, in a magical way, the basic structures of phenomena. However, we can expect factor analysis to help us to discover an underlying structure to a mass of data and to discover dimensions that are, in their own way, meaningful. The argument can be made that meaning is not dependent on the layperson being comfortable with the concept but instead is dependent on the usefulness of the concept in accounting for phenomena. In other words, meaning is defined here in terms of usefulness in prediction rather than in terms of familiarity.

These questions concerning number of factors, matching of factors, underlying assumptions, and meaning of factors, as well as others, must make us cautious in relation to the factor-analytic approach. In general, the main question is whether we can rely on factor analysis to discover the basic dimensions or underlying structure of personality. It is clear that Cattell remains convinced that factor analysis is an adequate, in fact, necessary, tool for the job. However, others have reservations. For example, one psychologist, in reviewing the findings, has concluded that the record of factor analysis is undistinguished, that it has not paid off, and that there is "less there than meets the eye" (Lykken, 1971). One argument frequently made is that with factor analysis you get out what you have put in (Holt, 1962). If researchers start with different principles and use different variables, the observed factors can differ substantially. Another argument made in relation to the factor analysis of ratings is that the observed factors reflect social stereotypes and the conceptual dimensions (constructs) of judges instead of underlying personality traits (Mischel, 1968). Frequently, the suggestion is made that factor analysis is useful for reducing large amounts of data to a few categories, but one should be careful about assuming that these categories reflect underlying structures. To those who are more clinically oriented and more humanistically oriented, the factor analytic method seems questionable as a method for uncovering the complexity basic to humans. Thus, Allport expresses the feeling that many of the factors identified "resemble sausage meat that has failed to pass the pure food and health inspection" (1958, p. 251). Another psychologist summarizes his views as follows:

I am supposing that a factor analysis of various measures of an operating automobile might reveal its components at the level of steering wheel, carburetor, brakes, and so on without yielding a model of the automobile as an integrated system. . .In short, it is my prejudice that factor analysis is as appropriate for the unravelling of a dynamic system as complex as man as a centrifuge might be, though the latter rotation would also yield some real and independent components of man's basic stuff.

TOMKINS, 1962, P. 287

The factor-analytic approach, then, does have its problems. And what of the multivariate method of which it is a part? The multivariate method described by Cattell appears to have the advantages of being objective, of assessing many variables at once, and of being relevant to the study of variables that do not lend themselves to experimental manipulation. It has advantages over the bivariate and clinical methods, but it receives criticism from proponents of both points of view. The psychologists who use the experimental bivariate method are critical of the use of many different tests (some of which have questionable reliabilities) to measure the same variable. Furthermore, they are critical of the method used by Cattell, since it leaves the question of causal influence ambiguous. On the other hand, as noted above, clinicians are critical of the unfamiliar, and at times unintelligible, nature of the factors identified — factors that they find of questionable utility in understanding what is going on in an individual. Sentiments along these lines were expressed by Luborsky who compared the factorial with the clinical approach in the individual case presented in this chapter:

The factor approach in personality research gives "truth" in the usual scientific sense, with more demonstrable certainty, but it is difficult to see how the statistical manipulations eventuate in clinically meaningful end products. . .The clinical approach's value, of course, is in revealing information which is more immediately understandable and usable to clinicians. The level of abstraction of the factors often bears little relationship to what a clinician wants to know. A clinician (especially psychotherapist) may or may not have any need to know what are the patient's major source traits.

LUBORSKY, 1953, P. 412

Scope of the Effort and Evaluation

Turning from considerations of Cattell's method to the work itself, we must be impressed with the scope of his efforts. The research has touched on every one of the dimensions we have outlined as relevant to personality theory — structure, process, growth and development, psychopathology, and change. Cattell has been a major force in the development of new factor-analytic techniques and in the development of new techniques for determining the genetic contribution to personality. His work covers almost all age ranges and the use of a wide variety of measurement techniques. Furthermore, he has endeavored to put his work in a cross-cultural perspective. There have been studies on levels of neuroticism in different countries and a cross-cultural comparison of patterns of extroversion and anxiety (Cattell and Warburton, 1961). Also, an effort has been made to develop a culture-free intelligence test that uses materials unfamiliar to all subjects.

How, then, is this massive effort to be evaluated? Cattell can be praised for his breadth of interests, the range of questions he has attacked, and the progress he has made in systematizing his findings. However, his work has been criticized because of problems associated with the use of factor analysis, because of the questionable validity of the tests used, and because the data collected often appear to be superficial in comparison with the wide-ranging interpretations of the findings. Indeed, a curious mixture of rigorous methodology and theoretical speculation is found in Cattell. Of particular concern is Cattell's tendency to equate theoretical speculation with fact. For example, Cattell describes the dynamic lattice as follows. "Essentially the dynamic lattice concept is at only a low level of abstraction from the facts — it is an undeniable, almost literal description of the way dynamic habit systems get organized in any organism that must learn ways to its goals" (1959b, p. 294-5). The concept of the dynamic lattice does not seem to warrant this certainty of conviction. Yet, this degree of overstatement is characteristic of Cattell. Furthermore, in being so committed to his point of view, he is at times unduly disparaging of the works of others. The gains of the clinical and bivariate approaches are minimized, and the ones of the multivariate approach are overstated.

In any case, it is strange that a man who has produced so much and who is so convinced of his being on the right path should be so ignored by many psychologists. Some reviews of Cattell's work have commented on this tendency of psychologists to respect Cattell but also to ignore him (Gordon, 1966), and for psychologists to be unaware of the scope and sophistication of Cattell's conceptions (Klein, Barr, and Wolitzky, 1967). This is in part because of the complexity of the methods he uses and because of the difficulty psychologists have in interpreting his factors. However, we can rely on Cattell to continue with his efforts in spite of his being ignored by others. Cattell knows that in the past people have been resistant to the use of new scientific techniques and have been slow to act on discoveries. "Captain Lancaster discovered the cause and cure for scurvy at sea in 1605, but sailors died of scurvy for 200 years more before naval surgeons acted on the discovery. In our time, thirteen years elapsed between Fleming's discovery of penicillin and its availability for use in clinical medicine" (Cattell, 1962, p. 265). We can rely on Cattell to pursue his work because he has an aesthetic appreciation of the complexity of human behavior and because he feels that the future of the field is with him.

TRAIT THEORY AND SITUATIONIST CRITICISM

Over the past decade trait theory has come in for considerable criticism because of the emphasis it gives to the hierarchical organization of stable and enduring properties of the person. In particular, critics of trait theory argue that behavior is much more variable from situation to situation than trait theorists suggest (Mischel, 1968). Furthermore, the critics claim that trait theory has proven to be ineffective in predicting behavior. Instead of an emphasis on broad predispositions in the *person* to respond in a certain way, many of these critics emphasize the importance of *situations*, or rewards in the environment, in the control of human behavior. Thus, for some time debate raged over whether regularities in behavior could be accounted for by aspects of the person, such as traits, or by aspects of the situation — the person-situation controversy or internal-external controversy noted in Chapter One.

It is impossible to do justice to all the various issues and evidence involved in the person-situation controversy within the context of this chapter.[2] However, before turning to a summary of the trait theories discussed, it may be useful to comment, at least briefly, on the status of trait theory relative to this issue. As was noted, critics of trait theory charge that there is more situational variability in human behavior than trait theorists suggest and that trait concepts and associated tests are not useful in the

2   A more extensive discussion of this issue is given in Pervin, L.A., *Current controversies and issues in personality.* New York: Wiley, 1978.

prediction of behavior. To a great extent these criticisms present a distorted picture of trait theory, one in which it is the person or trait alone that accounts for behavior — as if the situation has nothing to do with behavior. But it is clear that trait theory does recognize the importance of situations (Cattell, 1977). Traits represent predispositions to respond in specific ways which become manifest when behavior is considered over a wide range of situations. Traits represent aggregate measures of behavior. A trait may not be expressed on a particular occasion because of factors in the person, such as mood, or because of factors in the situation, such as strong rewards for behaving in a different way or strong punishments for behavior expressive of the trait. Trait theorists recognize the importance of the situation in influencing behavior. An illustration of this is Cattell's emphasis on the specification equation, which predicts what a person will do in a defined situation. However, trait theorists choose to emphasize the role of personal dispositions in behavior and, by and large, have neglected to work out the relationship between person and situational factors in accounting for behavior. Most simply put, trait theory does not say that a person possessing a trait will behave the same way in *all* situations or that behavior will express that trait in *all* situations. On the other hand, it has not defined the characteristics of situations which do and do not bring forth the trait.

The considerable research done by Eysenck and Cattell bear upon other criticisms of trait theory. First, it is clear that a variety of empirical and conceptual criteria are used in the development of a trait concept. Traits are not just thought up, they are based on data from a variety of tests administered to a variety of populations. Second, traits are often useful in predicting how different groups of people will behave in various situations. This is clear in the work of both Eysenck and Cattell. Cattell's specification equation goes even further in terms of attempting to predict how various combinations of traits will relate to performance in various areas. It is indeed true that prediction of individual performance in a specific situation remains a difficult task for trait psychologists. However, they are not alone in this regard! Perhaps the following statement by Eysenck best summarizes the trait position:

Altogether I feel the debate is an unreal one. You cannot contrast persons and situations in any meaningful sense, or ask which is more important, because clearly you will always have person-in-situations, and the relative importance of personality and situational factors depends on the nature of the situation, the selection of people, and in particular the selection of traits measured. No physicist would put such a silly question as: Which is more important in melting a substance — the situation (heat of the flame) or the nature of the substance!

EYSENCK, PERSONAL
COMMUNICATION, AUGUST 7, 1978

MAJOR CONCEPTS AND SUMMARY

Allport

functional autonomy

proprium

cardinal traits, central traits, secondary dispositions

Eysenck

factor analysis

types

introversion-extroversion, neuroticism, psychoticism

Cattell

bivariate, multivariate, clinical methods

factor analysis

surface traits and source traits

L-data, Q-data, OT-data

Sixteen Personality Factor Inventory (16 P.F.)

attitude

ergs and sentiments

dynamic lattice

specification equation

MAVA method

trait anxiety and state anxiety

In this chapter we have explored three theories of personality that emphasize the concept of trait, or a predisposition to respond to situations in a particular way. In addition, there is the view of personality structure as hierarchically organized (for example, habits, traits, types). One of the early proponents of trait theory was Gordon Allport. He viewed traits as the basic units of personality, characterized by the properties of frequency, intensity, and range of situations. He also distinguished among cardinal traits, central traits, and secondary dispositions. Allport suggested that most people can be described in terms of traits that represent ranges of possible behaviors or aggregate descriptions of their behavior over a wide range of situations.

Whereas Allport conducted little research on traits and the structure of personality, the personality theorist Hans Eysenck has been quite active in this regard. While finding utility in the concept of trait, and in the even more abstract concept of type, Eysenck holds to four criteria for the utility of any such personality concept: (1) It must find support in factor-analytic studies; (2) One must be able to demonstrate a biological-genetic basis for the predictions based on the theory; (3) The concept must be related to theory and to specific predictions based on the theory; (4) The concept must be related to important social events and groups. With such criteria in mind and through the factor analysis of a wide variety of data on many different subject populations, Eysenck has been led to emphasize three basic dimensions of personality: Extroversion-Introversion, Neuroticism, and Psychoticism. Major attention was given to the Extroversion-Introversion dimension. The biological-genetic basis for associated individual differences and the relationship of such individual differences to functioning in a wide variety of areas was discussed in relation to Eysenck's criteria for an adequate concept of personality.

The trait theory of Raymond Cattell has been given extended discussion. Cattell's goal is the identification of the basic dimensions of personality and the development of a set of instruments to measure these dimensions — taxonomy (classification) and measurement. Multivariate research and factor analysis are viewed as providing the tools for defining the basic structural elements of personality. These basic structural elements are called traits and represent broad dispositional tendencies. Of particular interest are source traits which represent associations among behaviors that vary (increase and decrease) together. The argument has been made that, with some few exceptions, the same source traits can be found from the analysis of life record data (L-data), questionnaire data (Q-data), and objective test data (OT-data). The Sixteen Personality Factor Inventory has been developed to measure personality using questionnaire data. However, there is a preference for the use of objective test data. Using a variety of tests and subject populations, work goes on to discover the exact number of traits necessary to describe personality and to define the nature of these traits.

Dynamic traits, relating to the why and how of behavior, are of particular interest in relation to the process aspects of behavior. The basic conceptual unit in this area is that of attitude, representing a strength of interest in following a particular course of action. Some attitudes are tied to biological drives and are called ergs. Other attitudes are related to the socialization process and are called sentiments. The dynamic lattice expresses the interplay between ergs and sentiments. Predicting behavior, as in the specification equation, means that one must take into consideration both the various traits of the individual and such situational, transient variables as states (mood) and role. Behavior, then, is a function of both personality and situational determinants.

Cattell is interested in maturational factors and in the relative influence of heredity and environment in determining traits. In relation to maturation, Cattell has studied the development of traits by age at every stage of development. This research suggests that the same underlying factors can be found, both in number and in kind, in subjects from age four through adulthood. The relative influence of heredity and environment in relation to each trait is defined by the method called Multiple Abstract Variance Analysis (MAVA).

Cattell's research in the area of psychopathology has involved the analysis of factors on which normal and patient populations differ; that is, psychopathology is defined by differences observed between groups on the same factor tests. High scores on some factors are common to all forms of psychopathology (for example, high anxiety and neuroticism scores for all neurotics) while some are specific to each form of pathology. Psychotherapy, where effective, involves a change in the pattern of traits as opposed to the change of specific behaviors.

Most of the criticism of Cattell's theory of personality relates to the use of factor analysis as a method for discovering the underlying structure of personality. In spite of some evidence and Cattell's arguments to the contrary, some psychologists have concluded that the record of factor analysis to date is undistinguished and there is little hope that in the future it will provide us with a classification structure that fits reality. At the same time, one cannot fail to be impressed with the scope of Cattell's efforts, with the progress he has made in systematizing his findings, and with his own conviction that he is on the right path.

In relation to the scope of Cattell's work, his theory serves as a useful transition between the theories already presented and the theoretical approach to be described in Chapters 9 through 11. First, we have noted already Cattell's effort to combine the advantages of the clinical approach and those of the bivariate approach. The former were represented in the earlier chapters on Freud, Rogers, and Kelly while the latter will be represented in the learning theory — behavioral view of personality that follows in the next chapter. Second, Cattell is one of the few personality theorists to have given attention both to inherited and environmental behavioral determinants. The clinical theories presented earlier emphasized individual consistency across situations and the factors within the individual that lead to this consistency. In the next chapter we shall examine a theoretical point of view that emphasizes the variability of behavior from situation to situation and the factors in the environment that lead to different behavioral responses. Cattell's theory gives recognition to both sets of variables. In the concept of trait, there is an emphasis on the personality of the individual and consistency in his behavior across situations. At the same time, the role of environmental stimuli in changing the action of personality source traits also is emphasized. According to Cattell, through factor analysis we may in the future be able to develop a catalog of situations just as we have been able to develop a catalog of personality factors. In this way, we may be able to look at the interactions between individuals and environments rather than looking at each in relative isolation from the other.

THE BEHAVIORAL VIEW OF THE PERSON

THE BEHAVIORAL VIEW OF SCIENCE, THEORY, AND
RESEARCH METHODS

EARLY INFLUENTIAL FIGURES

Pavlov's Theory of Classical Conditioning

Watson's Behaviorism

SKINNER'S THEORY OF OPERANT CONDITIONING

A View of the Theorist

Skinner's Theory of Personality
• Structure
• Process
• Growth and Development

Clinical Applications of Skinner's Theory
• Psychopathology
• Change

Case Example—Joey

Critical Evaluation of Skinner's Theory

MAJOR CONCEPTS AND SUMMARY

BEHAVIORAL APPROACHES TO PERSONALITY: UNDERPINNINGS OF LEARNING THEORY AND SKINNER'S OPERANT CONDITIONING

Chapter Focus:

In this chapter, we shall study a theory of personality based on principles of learning. The chapter begins by noting that there are many different theories of learning. These theories share a focus on learned behavior and a commitment to the experimental testing of clearly defined hypotheses. Furthermore, they all attempt to identify and manipulate the environmental variables that control behavior. This chapter focuses on Watson's behaviorist point of view and on two processes of learning — Pavlov's classical conditioning and Skinner's operant conditioning. In Chapter 10, we will consider another theory of learning and then turn to an overall critical evaluation of learning, behavioral approaches to personality.

Psychology as the behaviorist views it is a purely objective, experimental branch of natural science. Its theoretical goal is the prediction and control of behavior. Introspection forms no essential part of its methods . . . The time seems to have come when psychology must discard all references to consciousness.

WATSON, BEHAVIOR, 1914

The practice of looking inside the organism for an explanation of behavior has tended to obscure the variables which are immediately available for scientific analysis. These variables lie outside the organism, in its immediate environment and in its environmental history.

SKINNER, 1953, P. 31

The concern in this chapter is with an approach to personality that in many ways is radically different from the clinical point of view. And, although it shares with the trait, factor-analytic approaches an emphasis on empirical investigation, it involves assumptions that lead to considerable criticism of the trait approach to personalty.

In an effort to understand the learning theory approach to personality, one must be prepared to make new assumptions and to consider new strategies for research and new interpretations of old data. The learning theory approach to personality has two basic assumptions from which a number of critical points tend to follow. The first is the assumption that nearly all behavior is learned. The answer to the question of *what* psychologists should study is that they should study the processes of learning through which new behaviors are acquired. The second basic assumption is that research methodology is important — that objectivity and rigor in the testing of clearly formulated hypotheses are crucial. The answer to the question of *how* psychologists should study behavior is that they should formulate explicit hypotheses and should measure behavior in precise ways.

Notice that where Eysenck and Cattell view learning as part of the broader area of personality, the theoretical approach discussed in this chapter and the next reflects an opposite point of view: "There is no reason to assume that the study of personality offers any new or unique problems for psychology. We can consider the study of personality to be a branch of the general field of learning which investigates in particular those processes significant to human adjustment" (Lundin, 1963, p. 254). Although this may seem to be just a matter of where you cut the pie, it is of considerable importance when making decisions about where to begin the study of behavior.

Of perhaps even greater consequence, however, is the decision about methodology. The emphasis on objectivity and rigor, on testable hypotheses and the experimental control of variables, has led, for example, to an emphasis on the laboratory as the place for studying behavior. One generalizes from observations in the laboratory to real life, but only in the laboratory can one systematically study phenomena. Furthermore, the emphasis on the careful manipulation of explicitly defined variables has led to the concentration on simple, rather than complex, pieces of behavior. The assumption is that one builds toward explaining the complex through the careful study of the simple.

Although they need not have, other consequences have tended to follow from this methodological orientation. Thus, the emphasis on the careful manipulation of objectively defined variables has led to an emphasis on forces *external* to the organism as opposed to ones *internal* to it. According to the learning, or behavioral, approach, one manipulates variables in the environment and observes the consequences of these manipulations in behavior. Whereas psychodynamic theories emphasize causes of behavior that are inside the organism (for example, instincts, defenses, self-concept, constructs), learning theories emphasize causes that are in the external environment. Stimuli in the environment that can be experimentally manipulated, such as food rewards, are emphasized instead of concepts that cannot be manipulated, such as the self, the ego, and the unconscious. As Skinner argued, when we can control behavior through the manipulation of variables outside the organism, there is no need to be concerned with what goes on inside the organism.

situational specificity

The behavioral emphasis on external, environmental determinants has been associated with an emphasis on **situational specificity** in behavior and a de-emphasis on individual predispositions to behave in particular ways. In contrast with the emphasis in psychodynamic and trait theories on characteristics or traits that express themselves in a range of situations, behavior theory suggests that whatever consistency is found in behavior is the result of the similarity of environmental conditions that evoke these behaviors. "With the possible exception of intelligence, highly generalized behavioral consistencies have not been demonstrated, and the concept of personality traits as broad response predispositions is thus untenable" (Mischel, 1968, p. 146). In summary, the view that is presented here is that behavior is situation specific; that is, that behavior tends to change unless there is a similarity of environmental conditions.

functional analysis of behavior

Since behavior is situation specific and is a function of conditions in the environment, the purpose of behavioral research is to establish laws concerning behavior by relating environmental changes to changes in behavior. For example, in the **functional analysis of behavior**, one seeks to identify the conditions or *environmental stimuli* that control behavior. One is interested both in the entire range of behavior (behavioral repertoire) of the individual and in the conditions that affect the acquisition of new behaviors and the performance of previously learned behaviors. The ABC's of behavioral assessment involve an analysis of *A*ntecedent conditions (conditions that precede the behavior), *B*ehaviors exhibited (emitted) by the individual, and the *C*onsequences of these behaviors. Individual differences exist, but they are of no importance in developing behavioral laws. The same laws hold true for all individuals, and individual differences are viewed merely as blocks in the path to the discovery of these laws.

To use Cattell's term, the theoretical point of view that is discussed in this chapter and the next emphasizes the *bivariate approach* to research. There is an emphasis on simple behaviors that lend themselves to experimental control; there is an emphasis on behavior in the laboratory as opposed to behavior in the real world; and there is the use of animals, such as rats and pigeons, as subjects for the testing of laws about behavior. Although most behavioral theorists would suggest that findings with rats need to be checked against findings with humans, they are in general agreement that the same laws of behavior operate for members of different species. Similarly, they assume that the laws of learning that govern the behaviors of members of one age group also operate for members of another age group. As we shall see in Chapter 11, more recent developments in social learning theory do not necessarily make these assumptions.

Outlined here have been a number of assumptions characteristic of learning theory and the behavioral point of view. In particular, an effort has been made to begin by contrasting some of these learning theory assumptions with those made by Freud, Rogers, Kelly, and Cattell. Like the last chapter, this chapter and the next are concerned with the efforts of many individuals. There is a learning theory and behavioral point of view, but there is no one theory of learning or one behavioral theory of personality. There is a shared commitment to the importance of learning, and a shared commitment to rigorous methodology. In this chapter we will first consider some of the early influential figures and then concentrate our attention on a major theory of learning — Skinner's theory of operant conditioning. Then, in Chapter 10, we will consider Hull's instrumental learning theory. In studying these two approaches we shall see that beyond the shared commitments, there exist important differences. Before turning to these theories, however, let us consider common themes basic to the learning theory view of the person and science.

THE BEHAVIORAL VIEW OF THE PERSON

There are three broad assumptions about the nature of the person that tend to run throughout learning theory and the behavioral point of view.

1 Behavior is learned by the building up of associations.

2 People basically seek to obtain pleasure and avoid pain.

3 Behavior is basically environmentally determined.

The first characteristic suggests that complex behavior can be understood in terms of the building up and joining together of simple associative bonds between something that occurs in the environment and the organism's response to it. There is an implicit view of the brain as a huge switchboard in which incoming stimuli are connected with outgoing responses (Baldwin, 1968).

The second assumption, that is, that people seek to obtain pleasure and avoid pain, is most clearly evident in Thorndike's *Law of Effect*. "Any act which in a given situation produces satisfaction becomes associated with that situation, so that when the situation recurs the act is more likely than before to recur also. Conversely, any act which in a given situation produces discomfort becomes dissociated from that situation, so that when the situation recurs the act is less likely than before to recur" (1905, p. 203). The message here is similar to that in psychoanalytic theory — people seek rewards and strive to avoid pain. In their complex functioning, people strive to maximize gains and to minimize losses. As a result of this view, there is among behaviorists, as Rosenhan (1968) observes, a tendency to neglect altruistic phenomena such as the concern of parents for their children, charitability, and love for another person.

The third characteristic, an emphasis on environmental forces in determining behavior, in part follows from the first two characteristics and, as pointed out in Chapter 1, is in keeping with the American tradition. Watson, in particular, emphasized the importance of the environment over heredity. He claimed that, given a free hand in controlling the environment, he could train an infant to become any type of specialist he might select — doctor, lawyer, beggar-man, or thief. Since behavior is a function of stimulus-response connections developed mainly as a result of rewards and punishments in the environment, there is considerable room for optimism concerning the ability to shape human behavior. In accordance with these assumptions concerning the nature of the person, Skinner strongly supports the control of behavior. According to Skinner, we are always controlling or being controlled, although the reinforcements and punishments involved may be subtle. Since all people control or are controlled, we need a view of the person that allows for a scientific analysis of the variables involved in the control process. An emphasis on associations, reinforcements, and environmental factors allows for such a view.

THE BEHAVIORAL VIEW OF SCIENCE,
THEORY, AND RESEARCH METHODS

The theory and research that is presented in this chapter and the next can be considered to be representative of the behavioral tradition in psychology. This means that they are opposed, on theoretical grounds, to the use of certain concepts and research methods in psychology and that they are committed to other types of concepts and methods. In the original learning position, the intent was to throw out concepts such as consciousness, will, idea, thought, and intention. The argument was that these concepts tended to fall within the realm of private experience and, therefore, could not be subjected to public observation and empirical confirmation. Skinner (1963) suggests that we throw out concepts that attribute the visible behavior of an organism to another organism inside — to a little man or homunculus. He observes how students interpreting the learning behavior of a pigeon suggest that the pigeon *expected* reinforcement, or that it *hoped* to get food again, or that it *observed* that a certain behavior produced a particular result. Yet, according to Skinner, the behavior of the pigeon could be described without the use of any of these concepts.

The argument against the use of such concepts is not that they apply to phenomena that are inappropriate for psychologists to study. Rather, the objection is that they are defined in ways that make it impossible for them to be studied scientifically. Concepts that are not explicit, that are not open to empirical verification, are viewed as unscientific and useless. There is, then, at the heart of this criticism, a rejection of the methods used to study these concepts. Originally an attack on the method of self-observation or introspection, the view has been extended to include all observations that are not made in a public way and that cannot be measured.

The view of science emphasized here attaches importance to behaviors that can be observed and to methods that involve the manipulation of phenomena. "There are, of course, other legitimate interpretations of nature and man than the scientific one and each has its own right to be pursued. The behavior scientist merely asks that he be given the same opportunity to develop a scientific account of his phenomena that his colleagues in the physical and biological fields have had" (Spence, 1948, p. 70). In general, there is a strong tendency to avoid theoretical speculation and to focus instead on empirical findings. The methodological goal is to be able to manipulate the environmental (independent) variables, to use appropriate controls so that one is observing only the effects of the particular variable under study and, then, to measure the resulting behavior (dependent variable). By establishing such cause-effect relationships, one operates within the bounds of a natural science and goes on to establish relevant laws.

As was pointed out earlier in the chapter, some of the consequences of this view of science have been an emphasis on research in the laboratory, an emphasis on behavior that can be manipulated experimentally, a tendency to minimize the importance of events going on inside of the organism, and an inclination toward the use of animals in research. Again, the following arguments are used to justify these consequences: (1) It is desirable to be able to manipulate the variables and to control the experimental conditions. (2) One can start with simple behavior and go from there to the complex. In fact, science advances from the simple to the complex. (3) The basic processes discovered in animals will likely be found to have considerable relevance to the functioning of humans.

EARLY INFLUENTIAL FIGURES IN
BEHAVIORAL THEORY — PAVLOV AND WATSON

A number of people were significant in the early development of learning theory. We have noted already, for example, Thorndike's (1874-1949) Law of Effect and its emphasis on how "pleasure stamps in responses" and punishment "stamps out responses." Thorndike also is significant for his emphasis on the use of animals in the psychology laboratory. Of the various significant figures, however, two in particular stand out — Pavlov and Watson.

Pavlov's Theory of Classical Conditioning

Ivan Petrovitch Pavlov (1849–1936) was a Russian physiologist who, in the course of his work on the digestive process, developed a procedure for studying behavior and a principle of learning that had a profound effect on the field of psychology. Around the beginning of the twentieth century Pavlov was involved in the study of gastric secretions in dogs. As part of his research he would place some food powder inside the mouth of a dog and measure the resulting amount of salivation. Coincidentally he noticed that after a number of such trials a dog would begin to salivate to certain stimuli before the food was placed in its mouth. This salivation would occur in response to cues such as the sight of the food dish or the approach of a person who generally brought the food. In other words, stimuli which previously did not lead to this response (called neutral stimuli), could now elicit the salivation response because of their association with the food powder that automatically caused the dog to salivate. To animal owners this may not seem like a startling observation. However, it led Pavlov to

IVAN PETROVICH PAVLOV

**classical
conditioning**

conduct some very significant research on the process known as **classical conditioning**.

The essential characteristic of classical conditioning is that a previously neutral stimulus becomes capable of eliciting a response because of its association with a stimulus that automatically produces the same or a similar response. In other words, the dog salivates to the first presentation of the food powder. One need not speak of a conditioning or learning process at this point. The food can be considered to be an **unconditioned stimulus** (US) and the salivation an **unconditioned response** (UR). This is because the salivation is an automatic, reflex response to the food. A neu-

**unconditioned
stimulus
unconditioned
response**

tral stimulus, such as a bell, will not lead to salivation. However, if on a number of trials the bell is sounded just before the presentation of the food powder, the bell itself may take on the potential for eliciting the salivation response. Conditioning has occurred, in this case, when the presentation of the bell alone is followed by salivation. At this point, the bell may be referred to as a **conditioned stimulus** (CS), and the salivation may be considered a **conditioned response** (CR).

conditioned stimulus
conditioned response

In a similar way, it is possible to condition withdrawal responses to previously neutral stimuli. In the early research on conditioned withdrawal, a dog was strapped in a harness and electrodes were attached to his paw. The delivery of an electric shock (US) to the paw led to the withdrawal of the paw (UR), which was a reflex response on the part of the animal. If a bell was repeatedly presented just before the shock, eventually the bell alone (CS) would be able to elicit the withdrawal response (CR).

The experimental arrangement designed by Pavlov to study classical conditioning allowed him to investigate a number of important phenomena. For example, would the conditioned response become associated with the specific neutral stimulus alone or would it become associated with other similar stimuli? Pavlov found that the response that had become conditioned to a previously neutral stimulus would also become associated with similar stimuli, a process called **generalization**. In other words, the salivation response to the bell would generalize to other sounds. Similarly, the withdrawal response to the bell would generalize to sounds similar to the bell. What are the limits of such generalization? If repeated trials indicate that only some stimuli are followed by the unconditioned stimulus, the animal recognizes differences among stimuli, a process called **discrimination**. For example, if only certain sounds but not others are followed by shock and reflexive paw withdrawal, the dog will learn to discriminate among sounds. Thus, while the process of generalization leads to consistency of response across similar stimuli, the process of discrimination leads to increased specificity of response. Finally, if the originally neutral stimulus is presented repeatedly without at least occasionally being followed by the unconditioned stimulus, there is an undoing or progressive weakening of the conditioning or association, a process known as **extinction**. Whereas the association of the neutral stimulus with the unconditioned stimulus leads to the conditioned response, the repeated presentation of the conditioned stimulus without the unconditioned stimulus leads to extinction. For example, for the dog to continue to salivate to the bell, there must be at least occasional presentations of the food powder with the bell.

generalization

discrimination

extinction

The phenomena of generalization, discrimination, and extinction are important to classical conditioning theory as well as other theories of learning. In addition to his work on these phenomena, research by Pavlov was significant in terms of a possible explanation for other phenomena such as conflict and the development of neuroses. An early demonstration of what came to be known as experimental neuroses in animals was completed in Pavlov's laboratory. A dog was conditioned to salivate to the signal of a circle. A differentiation between a circle and an ellipse was then conditioned by not reinforcing the response to the ellipse. When the ellipse was gradually changed in shape to approximate the shape of a circle, the dog first developed fine discriminations but then, as it become impossible to discriminate between the circle and the ellipse, its behavior became disorganized. Pavlov described the events as follows:

After three weeks of work upon this discrimination not only did the discrimination fail to improve, but it became considerably worse, and finally disappeared altogether. The hitherto quiet dog began to squeal in its stand, kept wriggling about, tore off with its teeth the apparatus for mechanical stimulation of the skin, and bit through the tubes connecting the animal's room with the observer, a behavior which never happened before. On being taken into the experimental room the dog now barked violently, which was also contrary to its usual custom; in short, it presented all the symptoms of a condition of acute neurosis.

PAVLOV, 1927, P. 291

Pavlov's work on the conditioning process clearly defined stimuli and responses and provided an objective method for the study of learning phenomena. It therefore played an influential role in the thinking of later behaviorists such as Watson.

Watson's Behaviorism

behaviorism

John B. Watson (1878-1958) was the founder of the approach to psychology known as **behaviorism**. He began his graduate study at the University of Chicago in philosophy, and then switched to psychology. During these years he took courses in neurology and physiology and began to do a considerable amount of animal research. Some of this research consisted of the study of the increased complexity of behavior in the rat and the associated development of the central nervous system. During the year before he received his doctorate, he had an emotional breakdown and had sleepless nights for many weeks. Watson described this period as useful in preparing him to accept a large part of Freud (Watson, 1936, p. 274). The graduate work at Chicago culminated in a dissertation on Animal Education and was associated with the development of an important attitude regarding the use of human subjects.

JOHN B. WATSON

At Chicago, I first began a tentative formulation of my later point of view. I never wanted to use human subjects. I hated to serve as a subject. I didn't like the stuffy, artificial instructions given to subjects. I always was uncomfortable and acted unnaturally. With animals I was at home. I felt that, in studying them, I was keeping close to biology with my feet on the ground. More and more the thought presented itself: Can't I find out by watching their behavior everything that the other students are finding by using O's (human subjects)?

WATSON, 1936, P. 276

Watson left Chicago to become a professor at Johns Hopkins University in 1908, where he served on the faculty until 1919. During his stay there, which was interrupted by a period of service during World War I, Watson developed his views on behaviorism as an approach to psychology. These views, which emphasized the study of behavior that is observable and which excluded the study of self-observation or introspection, were presented in public lectures in 1912 and were published in 1914 in Watson's book, *Behavior*. Watson's call for the use of objective methods and the end of speculation about what goes on inside the person was greeted enthusiastically and he was elected president of the American Psychological Association for the year 1915. His views were further developed to include the work of Pavlov, and can be found in his most significant work, *Psychology From the Standpoint of a Behaviorist* (1919).

Shortly after the publication of this book, Watson reported on the conditioning of emotional reactions in an infant. The research on Albert, an 11-month-old child, has become a classic in psychology. In this research, the experimenters, Watson and Rayner (1920), trained the infant to fear animals and objects that previously were not feared. Watson and Rayner found that striking a hammer on a suspended steel bar produced a startle and fear response in the infant Albert. They then found that if the bar was struck immediately behind Albert's head just as he began to reach for a rat, he would begin to fear the rat whereas previously he had not shown this response. After doing this a number of times the experimenters found that the instant the rat alone (without the sound) was shown to Albert, he began to cry. He had developed what is called a **conditioned emotional reaction**. Albert now feared the rat because of its emotional association with the frightening sound. Furthermore, there was evidence that Albert began to fear other objects that somewhat resembled the rat. Despite some evidence that Albert's emotional reaction was not as strong or as general as expected (Harris, 1979), Watson and Rayner concluded that many fears are conditioned emotional reactions. On this basis they criticized the more complex psychoanalytic interpretations.

**conditioned
emotional
reaction**

> The Freudians twenty years from now, unless their hypotheses change, when they come to analyze Albert's fear of a seal skin coat . . . will probably tease from him the recital of a dream upon which their analysis will show that Albert at three years of age attempted to play with the pubic hair of the mother and was scolded violently for it . . . If the analyst has sufficiently prepared Albert to accept such a dream when found as an explanation of his avoiding tendencies, and if the analyst has the authority and personality to put it over, Albert may be fully convinced that the dream was a true revealer of the factors which brought about the fear.
>
> WATSON AND RAYNER, 1920, P. 14

Watson was divorced in 1919, immediately married Rayner, and was forced to resign from Hopkins. The circumstances of his departure from Hopkins led him to make his livelihood in the business world. Although he had already established a considerable reputation as a psychologist, he now was forced to do studies of potential sales markets. He found, however, "that it can be just as thrilling to watch the growth of a sales curve of a new product as to watch the learning curve of animals or men" (Watson, 1936, p. 280) and became successful in business. After 1920, Watson did write some popular articles and published his book *Behaviorism* (1924), but his career as a productive theorist and experimenter closed with his departure from Hopkins. However, his hope that instructors would begin to teach objective psychology instead of what he termed "mythology" was to be realized in the years ahead.

SKINNER'S THEORY OF OPERANT CONDITIONING

B. F. Skinner (1904—   ) is the most influential supporter of an extreme behaviorist point of view. He is perhaps the best known American psychologist and his views about psychology and society have been the source of considerable controversy.

A View of the Theorist

The scientist, like any organism, is the product of a unique history. The practices which he finds most appropriate will depend in part upon his history . . . When we have at last an adequate empirical account of the behavior of Man Thinking, we shall understand all this. Until then, it may be best not to try to fit all scientists into any single mold.

SKINNER, 1959, P. 379

In this passage, Skinner takes the point of view that has been argued in each of the theory chapters in this book; that is, that psychologists' orientations and research strategies are, in part, consequences of their own life histories and expressions of their own personalities.

B. F. Skinner was born in New York, the son of a lawyer who was described by his son as having been desperately hungry for praise, and a mother who had rigid standards of right and wrong. Skinner (1967) described his home during his early years as a warm and stable environment. He reported a love for school, and showed an early interest in building things. This common interest in building things is particularly interesting in relation to the behavioral emphasis on laboratory equipment in the experimental settings, and because it contrasts with the absence of such an interest in the lives or research of the clinical personality theorists.

At about the time that Skinner entered college, his younger brother died. Skinner commented that he was not much moved by his brother's death and that he probably felt guilty for not being moved. Skinner went to Hamilton College and majored in English literature. At that time, his

B. F. SKINNER

goal was to become a writer, and at one point he sent three short stories to Robert Frost, from whom he received an encouraging reply. After college, Skinner spent a year trying to write, but concluded that at that point in his life he had nothing to say. He then spent six months living in Greenwich Village in New York. During this time he read Pavlov's *Conditioned Reflexes* and came across a series of articles by Bertrand Russell on Watson's behaviorism. Although Russell thought that he had demolished Watson in these articles, they aroused Skinner's interest in behaviorism.

Although Skinner had not taken any college psychology courses, he had begun to develop an interest in the field and was accepted for graduate work in psychology at Harvard. He justified his change in goals as follows. "A writer might portray human behavior accurately, but he did not therefore understand it. I was to remain interested in human behavior, but the literary method had failed me; I would turn to the scientific" (Skinner, 1967, p. 395). Although he was not quite sure what it was about, psychology appeared to be the relevant science. Besides, he had long been interested in animal behavior (being able to recall his fascination with the complex behaviors of a troupe of performing pigeons). Furthermore, there would now be many opportunities to make use of his interest in building gadgets.

During his graduate school years at Harvard, Skinner developed his interest in animal behavior and in explaining this behavior without reference to the functioning of the nervous system. After reading Pavlov, he did not agree with him that, in explaining behavior, one could go "from the salivary reflexes to the important business of the organism in everyday life." However, Skinner believed that Pavlov had given him the key to understanding behavior. "Control your conditions (the environment) and you shall see order!" During these and the following years, Skinner (1959) developed some of his principles of scientific methodology: (1) When you run into something interesting, drop everything else and study it. (2) Some ways of doing research are easier than others. A mechanical apparatus often makes doing research easier. (3) Some people are lucky. (4) A piece of apparatus breaks down. This presents problems, but it can also lead to (5) serendipity — the art of finding one thing while looking for something else.

After Harvard, Skinner moved first to Minnesota, then to Indiana, and then returned to Harvard in 1948. During this time he became, in a sense, a sophisticated animal trainer — he was able to make organisms engage in specific behaviors at specific times. He turned from work with rats to work with pigeons. Finding that the behavior of any single animal did not necessarily reflect the average picture of learning based on many animals, he became interested in the manipulation and control of individual animal behavior. Special theories of learning and circuitous explanations of behavior were not necessary if one could manipulate the environment so as to produce orderly change in the individual case. In the meantime, as Skinner notes, his own behavior was becoming controlled by the positive results being given to him by the animals "under his control" (Figure 9.1).

The basis of Skinner's operant conditioning procedure is the control of behavior through the manipulation of rewards and punishments in the environment, particularly the laboratory environment. However, his conviction concerning the importance of the laws of behavior and his interest in building things have led Skinner to take his thinking and research far beyond the confines of the laboratory environment. He built a baby box to mechanize the care of a baby, developed teaching machines that used rewards in the teaching of school subjects, and developed a procedure whereby pigeons would be used militarily to land a missile on target. He has written a novel, *Walden Two*, describing a utopia based on the control of human behavior through positive reinforcement (reward). He has com-

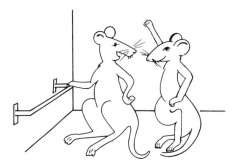

FIGURE 9.1   "Boy, have I got this guy conditioned! Everytime I press the bar down he drops in a piece of food." *Source:* Skinner, B.F. A case history in the scientific method. *American Psychologist,* 1956, 11, 221-233.)

mitted himself to the view that a science of human behavior and the technology to be derived from it must be developed in the service of humankind.

In 1971, Skinner's *Beyond Freedom and Dignity* was published and became a national best seller. In this book, Skinner spelled out the rationale for his position that a technology of behavior in which environmental conditions are manipulated to shape human behavior offers the greatest hope for solving the problems of society. The book touched off a great deal of controversy and criticism, both of Skinner and of behaviorism. Aside from outrage at the thought of a society in which virtually all behavior was systematically controlled by external forces, Skinner's work was criticized for its neglect of essential aspects of humans — innate endowment, cognitive processes, and feelings or other states within the organism. This criticism led to Skinner's book *About Behaviorism* (1974) in which he indicated acceptance of genetic endowments and internal processes, but continued to argue the importance of controlling conditions in the external environment. "The exploration of the emotional and motivational life of the mind has been described as one of the great achievements in the history of human thought, but it is possible that it has been one of the great disasters. In its search for internal explanation, supported by the false sense of cause associated with feelings and introspective observations, mentalism has obscured the environmental antecedents which would have led to a much more effective analysis" (1974, p. 165).

Before turning to Skinner's theory as it relates to personality, it may be useful to contrast its general qualities with those of theories considered in earlier chapters. Each of the theories covered in these earlier chapters has placed considerable emphasis on structural concepts. Freud used structural concepts such as id, ego, and superego; Rogers used concepts such as self and ideal self; Kelly used the concept of constructs; and Allport, Ey-

senck and Cattell used the concept of traits. The concept of structure relates to relatively enduring qualities of organization and tends to be an important element in accounting for individual differences. But the behavioral approach to personality emphasizes situational specificity and
minimizes the importance of broad response predispositions relative to
the importance of stimuli in the external environment. Therefore, it is not
surprising to find few structural concepts in learning theory. Corresponding to a lack of emphasis on structure, there is considerable emphasis on
the concepts of process and, in particular, on processes that hold true for
all individuals. In summary, because the theory is based on assumptions
that are different from the ones of other theories, the formal properties of
the theory are different from those already studied.

Skinner's Theory of Personality

Structure

response

The key structural unit for the behavioral approach in general, and Skinner's approach in particular, is the **response**. The nature of a response may
range from a simple reflex response (for example, salivation to food, startle
to a loud noise) to a complex piece of behavior (for example, solution to a
math problem, subtle forms of aggression). What is critical to the definition of a response is that it represents an external, observable piece of behavior (response) that can be related to environmental events. The learning process essentially involves the association or connection of responses
to events in the environment.

operants

In his approach to learning, Skinner distinguishes between responses
elicited by known stimuli, such as an eyeblink reflex to a puff of air, and
responses that cannot be associated with any stimuli. These responses are
emitted by the organism and are called **operants**. Skinner's view is that
stimuli in the environment do not force the organism to behave or incite it
into action. The initial cause of behavior is in the organism itself. "There is
no environmental eliciting stimulus for operant behavior; it simply occurs.
In the terminology of operant conditioning, operants are emitted by the
organism. The dog walks, runs, and romps; the bird flies; the monkey
swings from tree to tree; the human infant babbles vocally. In each case,
the behavior occurs without any specific eliciting stimulus . . . It is in the
biological nature of organisms to emit operant behavior" (Reynolds, 1968,
p. 8).

Process — Operant Conditioning

If structural units are of such minor significance to the theory, it is critical that there be considerable sophistication about the process aspects of behavior. Indeed, in the sense that a learning theory approach to personality is being considered, a process orientation is being dealt with. Before discussing some of the processes that this theory views as underlying behavior, it is important to consider the concept of reinforcer. The Skinnerians

reinforcer define a **reinforcer** as an event (stimulus) that follows a response and increases the probability of its occurrence. If a pigeon's pecking at a disc is followed by a reinforcer such as food, the probability of it pecking at the disc is increased. According to this view, a reinforcer strengthens the behavior it follows and there is no need to turn to biological explanations to determine why a stimulus reinforces behavior. Skinnerians postulate that some stimuli appear to be reinforcing for all animals and appear to be innate, while other stimuli only serve as reinforcers for some animals and appear to be based on their past association with innate reinforcers, that is, stimuli that originally do not serve as reinforcers can come to do so through their association with other reinforcers. Some stimuli, such as

generalized money, become **generalized reinforcers** because they provide access to
reinforcers many other kinds of reinforcers.

It is important to observe here that a reinforcer is defined by its effect on behavior, an increase in the probability of a response, and is not defined in a theoretical way. Often it is difficult to know precisely what will serve as a reinforcer for behavior, as it may vary from individual to individual or from organism to organism. Finding a reinforcer may turn out to be a trial and error operation. One keeps trying stimuli until one finds a stimulus that can reliably increase the probability of a certain response.

The focus of the Skinnerian approach is on the qualities of responses and their relationships to rates and intervals at which they are reinforced

schedules of or **schedules of reinforcements**. A simple experimental device, the Skinner
reinforcements box, is used to study these relationships. In this kind of box there are few stimuli, and behaviors such as a rat's pressing of a bar or a pigeon's pecking of a key are observed. It is here, according to Skinner, that one can best observe the elementary laws of behavior. These laws are discovered through the control of behavior, in this case the bar-pressing activity of the rat or the key-pecking activity of the pigeon. Behavior is understood when it can be controlled by specific changes in the environment. To understand behavior is to control it. Behavior is controlled through the choice of responses that are reinforced and the rates at which they are reinforced. Schedules of reinforcement can be based on a particular *time interval* or a particular *response interval*. In a time interval schedule, the reinforcement appears after a certain period, say every minute, regardless of the number of responses made by the organism. In response interval, or a response ratio schedule, reinforcements appear after a certain number of responses (for example, presses of a bar, pecks of a key) have been made.

Thus, reinforcements need not be given after every response, but can instead be given only sometimes. Furthermore, reinforcements can be given on a regular or a *fixed* basis, always after a certain period of time or after a certain number of responses, or they can be given on a *variable* basis, sometimes after a minute and sometimes after two minutes, or sometimes after a few responses and sometimes after many responses. Each schedule of reinforcement tends to stabilize behavior in a different way.

successive approximation

In a sense, operant learning represents a sophisticated formulation of the principles of animal training. Complex behavior is *shaped* through a process of **successive approximation**; that is, complex behaviors are developed by reinforcing pieces of behavior that resemble the final form of behavior one wants to produce.

> Operant conditioning shapes behavior as a sculptor shapes a lump of clay. Although at some point the sculptor seems to have produced an entirely novel object, we can always follow the process back to the original undifferentiated lump, and we can make the successive stages by which we return to this condition as small as we wish. At no point does anything emerge which is very different from what preceded it . . . An operant is not something which appears full grown in the behavior of the organism. It is the result of a continuous shaping process.
>
> SKINNER, 1953, P. 91

The process of shaping or successive approximation is seen most clearly in the work of animal trainers. The difficult tricks performed by circus animals are not learned as complete wholes. Rather, the trainer gradually builds up sequences of learned responses through the reinforcement of particular behaviors that are then linked to or chained to one another. What started off as the learning of individual behaviors ends up as the display of a complex series of acts before a circus audience. The animal ultimately is rewarded for its behavior, but the final reward is made dependent, or contingent, upon the performance of the series of previously learned behaviors. In a similar way, complex behaviors in humans may be developed through the process of successive approximation.

negative reinforcer

While most of the emphasis in operant conditioning is on the use of positive reinforcers such as food, money, or praise, Skinnerians also emphasize the importance of negative reinforcers. A **negative reinforcer** is an unpleasant or aversive event which when removed increases the probability of occurrence of the preceding response. Just as behavior can be conditioned and shaped through the presentation of positive reinforcers such as food, so it can be shaped by the removal of painful stimulus such as shock.

escape learning

In **escape learning**, a response is reinforced because it is associated with the termination of an aversive (unpleasant) stimulus. The experimenter can shape behavior by applying an aversive stimulus, such as a shock, and then allow the organism to terminate the shock by making the desired re-

avoidance learning

sponse. In **avoidance learning**, behaviors are reinforced because they allow the individual to avoid completely an aversive stimulus. Thus, in a situation similar to the classical conditioning of the withdrawal response, a tone may be sounded before the presentation of a shock. If the organism emits the desired response, the shock does not appear, and the tone may be turned off. The relevant response is reinforced because it is associated with the avoidance of the aversive shock stimulus and because it ends the aversive tone stimulus. In contrast with classical conditioning, the interest here is in the reinforcement of a response through escape or avoidance, rather than in the process by which the tone takes on aversive properties. In contrast with the situation of *positive reinforcement*, escape and avoidance behaviors are reinforced by the removal of a stimulus instead of by the presentation of a stimulus.

punishment

Both escape and avoidance situations can also be contrasted with the effects of another aversive situation, namely **punishment**. In punishment, an aversive stimulus is presented following the occurrence of an operant response. *The presentation of the aversive stimulus decreases the probability that a particular response will occur again.* However, the effect is temporary and it appears to be of little value in eliminating behavior. For this reason, Skinner has emphasized the use of positive reinforcement in the shaping of behavior.

Growth and Development

Although theories of learning have grown out of research with animals, considerable effort has been made to relate these theories to principles of human growth and development. In some ways, this is a natural development, since the socialization of the child is basically a learning process. Furthermore, it is a process in which parents attempt to use material and psychological rewards to shape the behavior of their children. The process by which children shape the behavior of their parents, through their own dispensation of rewards and punishments, has received less attention (Lewis and Rosenblum, 1974).

The Skinnerian view of growth and development continues to emphasize the importance of schedules of reinforcement in the acquisition and performance of behavior. As the child develops, responses are conditioned and remain under the control of reinforcement contingencies in the environment. The emphasis is on specific response patterns as they are influenced by specific environmental reinforcers (Gewirtz, 1968b). Children become self-reliant through the reinforcement of acts in which they take care of themselves, for instance, in eating and dressing. The child is reinforced immediately on the completion of those acts, both by material rewards such as food and by social rewards such as praise. The child becomes emotionally independent through the development of a stable rate of response (one that occurs at regular intervals) that required only occasional reinforcement. In learning to tolerate delay of gratification (reinforcement), the child may first be gratified after a brief period of delay and then gradually may be reinforced for longer periods of delay between request and gratification. After a while, delay behavior becomes stabilized, and one can say that the child has developed an ability to tolerate delays in gratification (Gewirtz, 1968a).

Skinnerians accept the view that behaviors can be imitated without being directly reinforced. However, this is true only where imitation itself has taken on the qualities of a reinforcer; that is, the positive reinforcement of a number of specific imitative responses can lead to a generalized imitative response tendency (Baer and Sherman, 1964; Baer, Peterson, and Sherman, 1967). Thus, whereas initially responses are reinforced because they match the ones of a model, ultimately the matching of responses per se becomes reinforcing. In this way, the child becomes generally imitative and learns many responses that are similar to those performed by the model.

In line with Skinnerian principles of reinforcement, Sherman (1971) has developed imitative language behavior in formerly nonimitative, speech-deficient children. Using bites of food as reinforcers for successively close approximations to what the experimenter did, Sherman was able to increase the probability of a child's imitating a new response from a very low level to nearly 100 percent. Children reinforced for doing as the experimenter did would imitate new behaviors even though the specific responses had never been trained. Furthermore, they would continue to exhibit these new behaviors in the absence of reinforcement for them — as long as other, different imitations were reinforced. Thus, from the Skinnerian point of view, new behaviors may be acquired in the course of growth and development through the process of successive approximations, or through the process of development of a generalized imitative repertoire. In either case, the behaviors are under the control of the reinforcement contingencies in the environment.

Clinical Applications of Skinner's Theory

Psychopathology

The general learning theory position on psychopathology may be stated as follows: the basic principles of learning provide a completely adequate interpretation of psychopathology. Explanations in terms of symptoms with underlying causes are superfluous. According to the behavioral point of view, behavioral pathology is not a disease. Instead, it is a response pattern learned according to the same principles of behavior as are all response patterns. "The specific behavior termed abnormal is learned, maintained, and altered in the same manner as is normal behavior, and normal behavior itself may be viewed as an adjustment resulting from a particular history of reinforcement" (Ullman and Krasner, 1969, p. 105). The authors of this quote go on to define abnormal behavior as the failure to make an appropriate response. This definition again points to the behavioral emphasis on observable behavior and specific responses. Furthermore, they suggest that definitions of adjustment must be situation specific. Again one can see the behavioral emphasis on the external environment and the minimization of factors inside the individual that may lead to consistency in behavior across situations.

The proponents of the learning theory point of view argue against any concept of the unconscious, against the concept of disease entities, and against the concept of a "sick personality." Individuals are not sick, they merely do not respond appropriately to stimuli. Either they have failed to learn a response or they have learned a maladaptive response. Change the response, or change the relationship of responses to stimuli, and you have removed the pathology. There is no need to interpret behavior as resulting from an Oedipus complex, a self-concept, or a construct system. One need only demonstrate the ability to account for behaviors in terms of the principles of learning theory; one needs to assess the specific inappropriate responses and the specific conditions under which they occur. The behavioral therapist seeks to know the factors (reinforcements) that are currently maintaining the responses. Diagnoses, in the sense of disease categories, are meaningless. They are unreliable and are not in accordance with the behavioral point of view. One is not interested in abstract psychiatric concepts. One is interested in knowing which behaviors are causing trouble, under what conditions the behaviors appear, and what the consequences of these problem behaviors are.

Two points are explicit. There is a continual emphasis on the question of "what," and there is a continual emphasis on measurement . . . Given the influence of Freud, much previous diagnostic work . . . centered on the question "why." Presuming unconscious motivation or disease processes, overt behavior was, by definition, only a surface manifestation, a symptom. The underlying cause, the why, was the focus of diagnostic work. *The answers to why questions are frequently beyond behavioral specification, testing, and direct modification . . . What questions are much more likely to lead to behavioral answers than why questions.*

ULLMAN and KRASNER, 1975, P. 221

The Skinnerian interpretation of abnormal behavior follows directly from the emphasis on reinforcement contingencies in the environment that shape and maintain response patterns. Behaviors that are labeled as pathological are learned in the same way as all other behaviors. A person may be labeled as neurotic or psychotic because of a faulty conditioning history. This faulty conditioning history may involve the lack of development of a response that is normally part of a person's response repertoire (the entire range of response behavior), or the development of a "healthy" response that is under the control of inappropriate reinforcers, or the development of a response that is labeled as "bad," "sick," or "neurotic" in the society.

The first of these three conditions represents a case of behavioral deficit (Bandura, 1968). For example, children and adults who are socially inadequate may have had faulty reinforcement histories in which social skills were not developed. Ordinarily a variety of social skills are learned as a result of reinforcement during the socialization process. When this fails to occur, the person is left with an inadequate response repertoire with which to respond to social situations. In the second pathological condition, a response pattern has been developed but it is "out of whack" with schedules of reinforcement in the environment. People may have "normal" responses in their repertoires, but these responses are not being reinforced by the environment. One possible result of the withdrawal of positive reinforcement in the environment is what is ordinarily called depression. Depression represents a lessening of behavior or a lowered response rate. The depressed person is often not responsive because positive reinforcement has been withdrawn (Ferster, 1973).

The situation in which a person is out of touch with the conditions of reinforcement in the environment is viewed as basic to schizophrenia, a serious thought disorder. According to Ullman and Krasner (1975), schizophrenia is a result of the failure of the environment to reinforce certain sequences of behavior. Schizophrenics attend to unusual cues in the environment because they have not been reinforced for attending to the social stimuli to which "normal" people respond. What is interpreted by the ordinary observer as a lack of attention is really an attention to unusual cues. What is labeled as lack of emotion and blandness is a lack of responsiveness to normal social stimuli. Related to this situation, is the development

superstitious behavior

of **superstitious behavior** (Skinner, 1948). Superstitious behavior develops because of an accidental relationship between a response and reinforcement. Thus, Skinner found that if he gave pigeons small amounts of food at regular intervals regardless of what they were doing, many birds would come to associate the response that was coincidentally rewarded with systematic reinforcement. For example, if a pigeon was coincidentally rewarded while walking around in a counterclockwise direction, this response might become conditioned even though it had no cause-effect relationship with the reinforcement. The continuous performance of the behavior would result in occasional, again coincidental, reinforcement. Thus, the behavior could be maintained over long periods of time. An observer looking in on this situation might be tempted to say: "Look at that crazy pigeon."

The third pathological condition involves a situation where individuals have responses they should not have. This can be either because of a history in which these responses resulted in the avoidance of punishment or they resulted in positive reinforcement. Neurotic symptoms, such as obsessions and compulsions, are learned because they remove an aversive stimulus. What is ordinarily called masochism can have a similar basis (Sandler, 1964).

According to one interpretation, in masochism individuals expose themselves to an aversive stimulus to avoid another aversive stimulus. Thus, individuals may behave in a way that suggests that it is better to hit themselves before someone else hits them harder. Another interpretation of masochism relates to the inappropriate positive reinforcement of behaviors. According to this interpretation, masochists punish themselves because they have come to associate this response with positive reinforcement. This could happen, for example, if the reinforcement history involved punishment as a condition for reward, such as when a parent praises a child for having "atoned" in some way for "bad" behavior.

Other "sick" behaviors can be similarly interpreted as a result of positive reinforcement. For example, someone could develop a fetish (unusual attraction to an object) because of a history in which the desired object has been associated with reinforcement. Bandura (1968) reports two relevant cases in the literature. In one, a ten-year-old boy developed a dress fetish because his mother had paid him attention whenever he stroked her dress. In the other, a man developed an association between sexual arousal and black shiny rubber as a result of an early experience in which a group of boys seized him, tied him up, and masturbated him.

These examples illustrate how the Skinnerian avoids an emphasis on concepts such as drive, conflict, and unconscious, and instead interprets psychopathology in terms of responses and schedules of reinforcement.

Change

The major aspects of behavior modification are the focus on overt behavior and the application of concepts drawn from learning theory to attain change . . . Despite differences in approaches and techniques, we would propose that all behavior modification boils down to procedures utilizing systematic environmental contingencies to alter the subject's response to stimuli.

ULLMAN and KRASNER, 1965, P. 29

Despite other differences among behavioral psychologists, there is a common emphasis on the importance of learning in human behavior and on the importance of a rigorous methodology in the study of this behavior.

This section on change or, as it tends to be called by learning theorists, *behavior modification* and *behavior therapy*, extends this point of view. There is no one single method of therapy that is suggested by learning theory. Different learning theorists emphasize different aspects of the learning process in their efforts to account for behavioral pathology and these explanations of behavioral pathology are associated with different treatment methods. As Krasner (1965) observed, agreement in the following areas allows us to group these approaches together:

1 All emphasize the use of concepts that can be measured, and the experimental manipulation of variables.

2 All emphasize the importance of environmental stimuli in causing and maintaining behaviors and, thus, tend to focus on these environmental stimuli in attempting to change behavior.

3 All reject the medical model of a diseased organism in favor of the psychological model of an organism that has learned certain undesirable responses.

4 In relation to this psychological model, all focus on the specific response that is to be altered by direct means rather than on the disease, neurosis, or psychosis that is to be altered through indirect means.

target behaviors

Behavior therapists deal with **target behaviors**, not with neuroses. Behavior therapists do not "cure" people, instead they act so as to modify behavior. The test of whether therapy has been successful is not whether the person has become "healthy," but rather whether there has been a change in the behavior emitted and the environmental conditions under which it is emitted.

Although not a clinician, Skinner's approach to the control of behavior has had a considerable impact on the therapeutic efforts. This has been particularly true beginning with the 1960's and with psychotic as opposed to neurotic difficulties. The Skinnerian approach to behavior change or **behavior modification** does not involve the use of a therapist. Instead, it involves the use of an expert in operant conditioning who can serve as a behavioral technician or behavioral engineer. It is the task of this technician to specify the target behaviors, to define the desired new behaviors, to determine the rewards to which the patient will respond, and to determine the schedules of reinforcement that must be used to shape the desired behaviors. As in all operant conditioning, the emphasis is on the use of reinforcement to shape the desired behaviors through a series of successive approximations.

behavior modification

Some of the details of the operant conditioning approach to behavior

modification are indicated in the following report of the successful treatment of a case of hysterical blindness (blindness without physical cause)
(Brady and Lind, 1961). The patient was a 40-year-old man who had been
blind for two years. The patient suddenly became blind in both eyes while
he was shopping with his wife and mother-in-law. Medical examinations
clearly indicated that there was no physical cause for the blindness and
this was a case of hysteria. Psychiatric and drug treatments were tried but
were unsuccessful. Finally, a program of operant conditioning was begun.
An analysis of the patient's behavior suggested that he had a need for approval and was sensitive to criticism. Therefore, praise and approval were
used as the behavior-shaping reinforcers. The patient was put in a situation where he was reinforced for responding every 18 to 21 seconds. A correctly spaced button-pressing response (18 to 21 seconds since the previous one) was reinforced with praise and approval, whereas an incorrectly
spaced response resulted in disapproval and criticism. This system of reinforcement was sometimes supplemented by special privileges and trips for
good performance and withdrawal of these rewards for poor performance.

In the first six sessions a stable response was developed. Then a light
bulb was put in the room where it could not be seen directly by the patient. The light went on after 18 seconds and off after 21 seconds. Thus, the
patient could improve his performance by using this visual cue. For the
next ten sessions the patient appeared to avoid the light and his performance fell. The light was then put at full intensity in clear view. The patient
was told that the light would help him to know when to respond properly.
Performance improved, but the patient suggested he was able to use the
heat from the bulb as a cue. Performance continued to improve as the intensity of the light was decreased. Finally, the patient exclaimed that he
could see and use his eyesight to distinguish among a number of different
cues in the testing situation. At the time of the report, the patient had re-
gained his sight for more than one year and was functioning well in a variety of situations.

As has been observed, much of the therapeutic work with operant conditioning is done with psychotic patients. An important development in
this area was the work of Ayllon in the analysis of the ward behavior of patients (Ayllon and Michael, 1959). This analysis clearly suggested that the
nurses and other staff personnel were often reinforcing the behaviors they
wished to abolish. This led to the suggestion that the nurse might be used
as a behavioral engineer; that is, the nurses could make sure that they were
only reinforcing the desired behaviors. In a further development of this
strategy, Ayllon (Ayllon and Michael, 1962) attempted to deal with feeding
problems through the use of operant conditioning techniques. An analysis
of patient behavior suggested that social reinforcements in the form of
coaxing and attention were shaping the behavior of patients so that they

would eat only with assistance. A new schedule of reinforcements was then instituted. Refusals to eat were no longer followed by social reinforcement and access to the dining room was made contingent upon the performance of a series of responses. After a while it became possible in many cases to use food or entrance into the dining room as a reinforcer for many desired behaviors. Whereas previously patients were being shaped by their social environment into rejecting food, now food became a sufficient reinforcer to control the normal eating behavior of the psychotic patients.

token economy

The logical extension of the work of Ayllon has been the development of what is called a **token economy** (Ayllon and Azrin, 1965). Under a token economy, the behavioral technician rewards, with tokens, the various patient behaviors that are considered desirable. The tokens in turn can be exchanged by the patient for desirable products, such as candy and cigarettes. Thus, for example, patients could be reinforced for activities such as serving meals or cleaning floors. In a tightly controlled environmental setting, possibly in a state hospital for long-term psychiatric patients, it is feasible to make almost anything that a patient wants contingent on the desired behaviors.

A similar token economy was set up by Atthowe and Krasner (1968). Again, attainment of the "good things in life" was made contingent on the patient's performing the desired behaviors. Here it was found that the tokens themselves became valuable to the patients and hoarding and theft started to occur. A complex system of banking and identification of tokens had to be established. In any case, we are told that the results in terms of patient behavior were quite favorable. Although "cures" did not occur, there was a definite increase in patient responsibility and activity. Figure 9.2 demonstrates, for example, how group activity level increased and decreased as a function of reward level. Also, 21 patients left the hospital, almost double the number who left in the previous year. Finally, staff morale increased, working on the token ward became a sign of prestige and two additional wards adopted similar token economies because of the usefulness of the technique for modifying patient behavior. Similar principles have been used in a patient rehabilitation program existing outside the hospital in the natural environment (Atthowe, 1973).

In sum, the Skinnerian behavioral technician seeks a straightforward application of the operant conditioning method to the problem of behavior change. Target behaviors are selected, and reinforcement is made contingent on performance of the desired responses. The psychoanalyst's attempt to explain behavior in terms of unconscious forces is criticized and ridiculed. Thus, one account is given of a patient who was reinforced for holding a broom (Haughton and Ayllon, 1965). The behavior was chosen arbitrarily by the investigators. In the course of the behavior-shaping, the

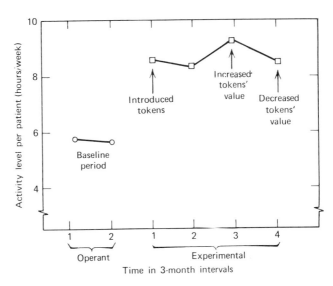

FIGURE 9.2   Group activity level as a function of tokens given for the activity (Ullmann and Krasner, 1969, p. 413. Redrawn from Atthowe and Krasner, 1968, p. 39).

patient began to pace while holding the broom. She resisted the efforts of other patients to take the broom from her and sometimes became aggressive when they tried to do so. A psychiatrist, who observed her behavior without knowing the circumstances under which it had been shaped, suggested that the broom symbolized one of three things: a child, the scepter of an omnipotent queen, or a phallic symbol. Here a psychiatrist was led to a number of complex interpretations for a response that had been conditioned and maintained by reinforcements in the environment.

A Case Example — Joey

The case example described below (Wahler and Pallio, 1968) gives us the opportunity to consider behavior modification techniques and how they produce changes in people's descriptions of themselves along with changes in deviant behavior. The argument runs that, if conditioning techniques can be used to change the target behaviors, then these changes could generalize to other learned behaviors. One such learned behavior, of particular interest to clinicians, is the individual's view of himself and his world. In other words, can changes in deviant behavior brought about by behavior therapy be demonstrated to generalize to how a person describes himself to his world?

The patient, Joey, was an eight-year-old boy who refused to go to school and was very dependent on his mother. Many of his difficulties, such as the refusal to go to school and his fears concerning his parents' safety, were characteristic of a school phobia. The investigators assumed that the parents were maintaining the dependent behavior and decided to use them as the major therapeutic agents in a program of behavior modification. The therapeutic sessions were 20 minutes long and were held twice weekly in a playroom. During a 10-minute segment of each session, Joey spent time alone with the professional behavior therapist. The therapist was used to facilitate change and to train the parents in the use of reinforcements to change behavior.

The first four sessions were used to observe Joey's behavior and to develop categories of behavior that could be used in tests of whether significant changes did occur. Five response classes were obtained: Smiling, Spontaneous Nonverbal Behavior, Spontaneous Verbal Behavior, Aggressive Behavior, and Cooperative Behavior. Cooperative behavior included following suggestions or commands from others and was expressive of Joey's dependence on others. Parent and therapist responses to these behaviors were defined as social attention stimuli. They presumably were the events that were affecting the rate of each of Joey's behaviors.

Following these sessions, there were five sessions in which observers recorded whether each of the above types of responses occurred within a 10-second interval. Twelve reinforcement sessions followed the baseline observations. In these sessions, the social attention reinforcements provided by the therapist and the parents were made contingent on specific responses. Now all responses other than the ones classified as cooperative (dependent) were to be reinforced. The parents were told that they were not to offer their attention and approval for dependent behavior and that they should offer it following the other responses from Joey. During the first 10-minute segments the parents observed the therapist attempt to shape Joey's behavior through this schedule of reinforcements. The observers continued to record the frequency of the response classes. At this point, the therapist undertook two reversal sessions in which he only reinforced the dependent behavior. These two sessions involved an effort to determine whether a change in the reinforcement contingencies would lead to a return to Joey's original behavior. The parents did not change their behavior during this period because they did not want to return to their old habits. Finally, there were five reinforcement sessions in which the professional therapist returned to a schedule of reinforcement for cooperative or nondependent behavior. The parents continued with their schedule of reinforcements.

In sum, there were five baseline observation sessions, twelve reinforcement sessions, two reversal (professional therapist) sessions, and five final reinforcements sessions. The frequency of Joey's responses in each of the five response classes were reliably recorded at 10-second intervals. The impact of the professional therapist's reinforcement schedules on Joey's behavior is shown in Figure 9.3. There is clear evidence of a change in his behavior in accordance with the schedule of reinforcements followed by the therapist. The charts of frequency counts of responses with his mother and with his father showed a very similar pattern except for the lack of significant change during the two reversal periods. This is understandable since they did not alter their behavior during these sessions. The change in response rate during the fourth session appears to have been because of an incident during the session in which Joey objected to being left alone after the meeting; Joey cried and the therapist and father felt "compelled" to offer suggestions during the session.

The frequency counts of Joey's behavior give clear evidence of change produced by changes in the reinforcement schedules followed by the

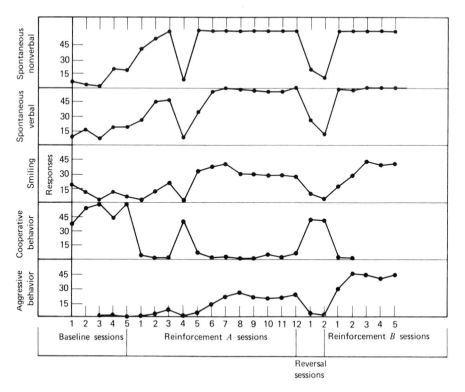

FIGURE 9.3   Frequency counts of Joey's response classes over all therapy periods with the professional therapist (Wahler and Pollio, 1968, p. 50).

therapist and parents. Furthermore, Joey's attendance at school began to increase during the second reinforcement series of sessions. This record of improvement in attendance continued for the five-month period during which follow-up data were gathered. The parents also reported considerable improvement as a result of the behavior therapy program. Joey played more frequently with his peers and worried less about his own welfare or that of his parents. However, information obtained from measures of Joey's self-concept indicated lesser change in this area.

The authors' conclusion concerning the data on the frequency counts of responses are stated as follows. "The data presented indicate much progress: progress which takes Joey from a depressed, possibly even suicidal, child at the beginning of therapy to a much less constricted and more effective child at the conclusion of twenty-four twenty-minute reinforcement sessions" (Wahler and Pollio, 1968, p. 56).

Critical Evaluation of Skinner's Theory

Since a lengthy evaluation of learning theory approaches to personality is included in the next chapter, we will only briefly consider an evaluation of the Skinnerian approach. Skinner's theory has been the basis of considerable research and controversy. "It is a movement whose controversiality has grown with its influence" (Herrnstein, 1977, p. 593). It has taken the behaviorist principles to an extreme, and perhaps herein lie its strengths and weaknesses.

The virtue of the operant approach is in its objectivity and rigor. Starting with a relatively simple research procedure, Skinnerians have investigated the development of complex behaviors and have developed a systematic understanding of the effects of various schedules of reinforcement on these behaviors. There is a very sophisticated understanding of how environmental variables can control behavior and the approach has contributed to many valuable therapeutic programs. At the same time, Skinner's approach seems limited in its point of view (Bandura, 1977; Herrnstein, 1977). In particular, the approach seems deficient in its disregard of fundamental characteristics of organisms and, in a related way, its disregard of essential aspects of humans. Implicitly, Skinner assumes that all responses can be conditioned in the organism. Yet, considerable research suggests that members of different species will learn the same response with greater or lesser ease. In other words, whereas some animals seem quite prepared to learn certain behaviors, others do not. These differences have to do with the fundamental nature of the organism and do not have to do with differences in reinforcement histories. While Skinner recognizes the importance of differences among the species and of inherited differences among humans, these variables have been neglected in operant theory and research.

Of perhaps even greater significance has been the neglect of motivational and cognitive variables. Motivational behavior is quite complex and the Skinnerian approach has shed little light on the matter. Whether one chooses to use concepts such as instinct, drive, need, or otherwise, it seems important to recognize that something goes on inside the organism that affects its response to stimuli, often guides its behavior, and influences the value of reinforcers. Similarly, it seems important to recognize that the human capacity for thought and language significantly influences the entire learning process. There is evidence that because of this capacity people can learn without reinforcement and, when influenced by reinforcers, people are affected by their expectations of future reinforcement rather than by a mechanical recording of past reinforcements. Furthermore, such capacities for cognitive functioning allow people to integrate their actions around more general plans or goals rather than around specific acts or chained sequences of acts.

Essentially, then, much of the criticism of Skinner suggests that his interpretation of the learning process is limited because of his limited view of the organism. This criticism will become increasingly meaningful when we consider other learning approaches in the next two chapters.

MAJOR CONCEPTS AND SUMMARY

functional analysis	operant conditioning
classical conditioning	positive and negative reinforcers
generalization	generalized reinforcers
discrimination	schedules of reinforcement
extinction	shaping-successive approximation
behaviorism	behavior modification
conditioned emotional reaction	token economy
emitted behaviors — operants	

This chapter has focused on an approach to personality strikingly different from the approaches previously covered. First, in contrast to the theories of Freud, Rogers, and Kelly, the learning approach comes from the laboratory rather than from the clinic. Second, in contrast with the approach of trait theorists, the learning approach emphasizes specific connections between behavior and environmental events (reinforcers), rather than broad personality dispositions. Third, in this approach, there is a much greater tendency to look for controlling conditions in the environment rather than forces within the organism.

Watson, Pavlov, and Thorndike are three significant figures who laid the foundation for the learning theory, behavioral approach to personality. Watson spelled out the rationale for a behaviorist approach to psychology. Pavlov's work on classical conditioning illustrated how a previously neutral stimulus could become capable of eliciting a response because of its association with a stimulus that automatically produces the same or similar response (for example, the dog salivates to the bell stimulus associated with the food powder). Generalization, discrimination, and extinction represent three important processes studied by Pavlov. The classical conditioning procedure suggests that many abnormal behaviors are the result of conditioning responses to inappropriate stimuli. Watson and Rayner's case of little Albert illustrated such a conditioned emotional reaction.

In Skinner's operant conditioning, there is an interest in responses (operants) that cannot be linked with known stimuli but which are learned because they are followed by reinforcement. A reinforcer increases the probability of the responses it follows. Behavior is brought under the control of the experimenter through the manipulation of schedules of reinforcement. Complex behaviors are shaped by reinforcing successive approximations to the desired, final behavior. Imitation of behaviors occurs where the person has been reinforced for specific imitative responses and thus developed a generalized imitative response tendency. The Skinnerian interpretation of psychopathology emphasizes behavioral deficits (for example, lack of speech, lack of social skills) and the development of maladaptive responses that are maintained by reinforcers in the environment. Behavior modification involves a careful, functional analysis of the behavioral repertoire of clients and the reinforcing events that maintain their behavior. Target behaviors are then selected and reinforcement is made contingent (dependent) upon the performance of the desired behaviors. The token economy represents an extension of operant principles to more general responses in an institutional setting.

Skinner's approach has been both influential and controversial. It has contributed to our understanding of how behavior can be controlled by various schedules of reinforcement and has led to important new treatment efforts. At the same time, many psychologists feel that it neglects important differences among different species and ignores important motivational and cognitive aspects of the human organism.

STIMULUS-RESPONSE THEORY

A View of the Theorists
• Clark L. Hull (1884-1952)
• John Dollard (1900-   ) and Neil E. Miller (1909-   )

The S-R Theory of Personality

Clinical Application of S-R Theory

Classical Conditioning and Wolpe's Systematic Desensitization

Summary

Case Example—A Behavioral Interpretation of Little Hans

RECENT DEVELOPMENTS IN BEHAVIORAL APPROACHES
Statement of Ideology, Utopian Planning, and Social Engineering

Interest in Self-Control and Self-Reinforcement

Increased Range of Application of Behavior Therapy Techniques

Interest in Processes at Work in Behavior Therapy

Interest in a Broader Range of Variables

CRITICAL EVALUATION OF BEHAVIORAL APPROACHES
Oversimplification of Behavior

Neglect of Important Areas

Objectivity and Rigor

Learning Theory Interpretations of Behavior Change

The Effectiveness of Behavior Therapy

Moral and Ethical Issues

Summary Evaluation

10 BEHAVIORAL APPROACHES TO PERSONALITY: STIMULUS-RESPONSE (S-R) THEORY AND OVERALL EVALUATION

Chapter Focus:

Chapter Nine considered the influences of Pavlov and Watson on the development of learning theory and the behavioral approach in psychology. Particular attention was given to Skinner's operant conditioning approach. It was indicated that while there are many different theories of learning, they share a focus on learned behavior and a commitment to the experimental testing of clearly defined hypotheses. This chapter continues with this general orientation while focusing on stimulus-response (S-R) theory, as reflected primarily in the works of Hull and Dollard and Miller. The chapter concludes with an overall evaluation of the past influence and current status of learning theory, behavioral approaches to personality.

Science has no use for unverifiable hypotheses (p. 23) . . . There is reason to believe that the relative backwardness of the behavior sciences is due not so much to their inherent complexity as to the difficulty of maintaining a consistent and rigorous objectivism (p. 28).

HULL, 1943

This book is an attempt to aid in the creation of a psychological base for a general science of human behavior. Three great traditions, heretofore followed separately, are brought together. One of these is psychoanalysis, initiated by the genius of Freud and carried on by his many able students in the art of psychotherapy. Another stems from the work of Pavlov, Thorndike, Hull, and a host of other experimentalists. They have applied the exactness of natural-science method to the study of the principles of learning. Finally, modern social science is crucial because it describes the social conditions under which human beings learn. The ultimate goal is to combine the vitality of psychoanalysis, the rigor of the natural-science laboratory, and the facts of culture.

DOLLARD AND MILLER, 1950, p. 3

STIMULUS-RESPONSE THEORY

Chapter Nine began by considering general characteristics of the learning theory, behavioral approach. It was noted that while there are many different theories of learning, they all emphasize the following: (1) The importance of understanding the fundamental principles of learning in our efforts to understand human behavior. (2) The experimental testing of clearly defined hypotheses. (3) The identification and manipulation of environmental variables that control behavior. (4) The importance of external conditions and behavior changing in accordance with changes in these conditions, leading to a greater emphasis on process relative to that on structure. These points of emphasis were quite clearly represented in the operant conditioning approach of Skinner.

This chapter will consider another, different approach to learning and personality. Stimulus-response (S-R) theory was being developed by people such as Hull and Dollard and Miller at around the same time that Skinner was developing his operant conditioning view. However, S-R theory probably reached its peak of systematization and influence earlier than did Skinner's approach. For some time the operant and S-R approaches represented competitive points of view and considerable controversy and debate existed over their relative merits. This is not quite as true today, although differences remain and, as shall be seen in the discussion of social learning theory (Chapter Eleven), often these differences do become controversial.

Perhaps the main difference between Skinner's approach and that of S-

R theorists is Skinner's commitment to a radical or extreme behaviorism which permits almost no reference to internal variables and places complete emphasis on overt behavior and environmental control of this behavior. In contrast with Skinner's operant approach, S-R theory emphasizes the following: (1) Learning as consisting of the establishment of stimulus-response associations or bonds. Whereas Skinner emphasizes emitted behaviors for which the stimulus cannot be determined, S-R theory emphasizes the experimental manipulation of stimuli that lead to responses as well as the process of reinforcement. (2) Learning involves motivational variables such as *drives*. The organism has *primary or innate drives*, such as pain or hunger, as well as *learned or secondary drives*, such as the desire for money, and particular fears and guilts learned during the course of development. Thus, while there is an emphasis on internal processes such as drives, S-R theorists insist that such concepts be tied to specific conditions that control the amount of drive (for example, number of hours of food deprivation determining the strength of the hunger drive) and to specific consequences in overt behavior. In other words S-R theorists accept a role for internal processes or variables between the stimulus and the response (intervening variables) so long as they can be defined objectively and measured. (3) Overt human behavior often is a result of *thought or the action of higher mental processes*. In other words, learning does not just consist of reflexive action. Dollard and Miller (1950) contrast two "levels" of learned behavior as follows: "A great deal of human behavior is made up of simple automatic habits. We respond directly to the cues in our environment and to our internal drives without taking time to think first . . . In a second type of behavior people do not respond immediately and automatically to cues and drives. The final overt response follows a series of internal responses, commonly called a train of thought . . . Many acts are a complex blend of both types of behavior. Man has a much greater capacity for the second, or thoughtful, type called the higher mental process" (p. 98). Again, there is an emphasis on internal processes with an effort to study these processes in an objective and rigorous manner.

Having considered what is shared in common with the Skinnerian approach, an emphasis on learned behavior and experimental rigor, and what is different about S-R theory, an emphasis on defined stimuli, drives, and higher mental processes, let us turn to more detailed consideration of the theorists and the theory itself.

A View of the Theorists

As has been indicated, several theorists have made significant contributions to the development of stimulus-response learning theory. Among these, however, three figures are of particular significance. The first, Clark

CLARK L. HULL

Hull, made a major effort to develop a systematic, comprehensive theory of learning. The second two, John Dollard and Neil Miller, are particularly well-known for their efforts to bring together the remarkable accomplishments of Freud and Hull.

Clark L. Hull (1884-1952)

Hull was born in New York, but early in his life he and his family moved to a farm in Michigan. There was a considerable emphasis on religion in his family. Although at one point he had a religious conversion experience at an evangelist revival meeting, Hull began to have considerable doubt about religion and abandoned his beliefs in it.

During his early school years, Hull was very interested in mathematics and described the study of geometry as the most important event of his intellectual life. At college, he began studying math, physics, and chemistry with the goal of becoming a mining engineer. However, after two years at school, he became ill with polio and was forced to consider a new life occupation. His interest in theory and in the design of automatic equipment led him to the study of psychology. After a difficult and incomplete recovery from polio, Hull returned to college to concentrate in psychology at the University of Michigan.

After a brief stint as a teacher in Kentucky, Hull went on to graduate work in psychology at the University of Wisconsin. He first developed an interest in finding a scientific basis for aptitude testing and then systematically studied what takes place during hypnosis. During the time that he was at the University of Wisconsin, word was spreading of Watson's views of behaviorism and Hull found himself sympathetic to this new emphasis on objectivity.

In 1929, Hull went to Yale as a professor of psychology. He had just read a translation of Pavlov's *Conditioned Reflexes* and was interested in comparisons between Pavlov's research and the experiments that were being conducted in this country. Also, he was forced to end his research on hypnosis because of an attitude of fear of hypnosis. The following years witnessed a coming together of his interests in math, geometry, theory, apparatus construction, and psychology as a natural science. In 1940, he published his *Mathematico-Deductive Theory of Rote Learning*, and, in 1943, his *Principles of Behavior*. Of particular importance was Hull's emphasis on a systematic theory of the process of instrumental learning.

Hull's emphasis on a systematic theory of learning, careful experimentation, the development of habits (stimulus-response associations) as a result of reward, and on the many facets of the instrumental learning process laid much of the ground-work for a learning theory approach to social psychology and to the study of personality. Out of Hull's framework developed attempts to understand attitude change from an instrumental learning model (Hovland and Janis, 1959), and attempts to relate the behavioral laws of learning theory to psychoanalytic phenomena (Dollard and Miller, 1950).

John Dollard (1900-   ) and Neil E. Miller (1909-   )

John Dollard was born in Wisconsin and received his undergraduate degree from the University of Wisconsin in 1922. He obtained his graduate degree (Ph.D., 1931) in sociology from the University of Chicago. Following this he taught sociology, anthropology, and psychology at Yale University. An unusual aspect of Dollard's professional development, and one that significantly influenced his later thinking, was his training in psychoanalysis at the Berlin Psychoanalytic Institute. His interest in psychoanalysis, clinical work, and the social sciences has continued throughout his professional career.

JOHN DOLLARD

Neil Miller also was born in Wisconsin. He received his undergraduate degree from the University of Washington and his Ph.D from Yale University in 1935. During this time he came into contact with Hull and Dollard, and also obtained training in psychoanalysis at the Vienna Institute of Psychoanalysis. He continued to spend the major part of his professional career at Yale until 1966 when he joined the faculty at Rockefeller University. During his time at Yale, Miller made many significant experimental and theoretical contributions to stimulus-response theory. These were particularly in the area of motivation and learned drives. Subsequently he has become a major figure in the area of biofeedback or the learning of voluntary

NEIL E. MILLER

control over bodily processes such as heart rate and blood pressure (Miller, 1978). In 1951 Miller was elected president of the American Psychological Association.

The collaborative work of Dollard and Miller is expressed in three major books. In the first, *Frustration and Aggression* (1939), completed with colleagues at Yale's Institute of Human Relations, there was an attempt to develop a scientific theory of aggressive behavior based on the assumption that aggression is a response to frustration. In the second, *Social Learning and Imitation* (1941), Dollard and Miller attempted to apply Hull's theory to personality and social psychology. Finally, in the third book, *Personality and Psychotherapy* (1950), Dollard and Miller attempted to integrate the achievements of learning theory, as expressed in the works of Pavlov, Hull, and others, with the achievements of psychoanalysis, as expressed in the works of Freud, and the achievements of other figures in the social sciences. In this book they attempted to apply the basic principles of learning to complex personality functioning, neurotic phenomena, and psychotherapy. This was significant in that it directed attention to the application of learning theory to clinical phenomena. However, in contrast with the approaches of current behavior modificationists and behavior therapists, the use of learning theory did not itself lead to the development of new therapeutic techniques.

The S-R Theory of Personality

The helpless, naked, human infant is born with primary drives such as hunger, thirst, and reactions to pain and cold. He does not have, however, many of the motives that distinguish the adult as a member of a particular tribe, nation, social class, occupation, or profession. Many extremely important drives, such as the desire for money, the ambition to become an artist or a scholar, and particular fears and guilts are learned during socialization.

DOLLARD AND MILLER, 1950, P. 62

Structure

As in Skinner's operant theory, the key structural concept for S-R theory is the *response*. However, whereas Skinner places little importance on the stimulus that leads to and becomes associated with the response, the S-R view is that stimuli become connected to responses to form stimulus-response bonds. According to Hullian theory, an association between a stimulus and a response is called a **habit**; personality structure is largely composed of the habits, or S-R bonds, that are learned by the organism and of the relationships among these habits.

habit

drive

Another structural concept used by the followers of Hull is that of **drive**. A drive is broadly defined as a stimulus strong enough to activate behavior. Using the Hullian model, it is drives that make the individual respond. A distinction is made between *innate, primary drives,* and *learned, secondary drives.* The primary drives, such as pain and hunger, are generally associated with physiological conditions within the organism. "One of these is pain. Pain can reach stabbing heights of greater strength than probably any other single drive. The parching sensation of thirst, the pangs of extreme hunger, and the sore weight of fatigue are other examples of powerful innate drives. The bitter sting of cold and the insistent goading of sex are further examples" (Dollard and Miller, 1950, p. 30).

Secondary drives are drives that have been acquired on the basis of their association with the satisfaction of the primary drives. "These learned drives are acquired on the basis of the primary drives, represent elaborations of them, and serve as a facade behind which the functions of the underlying innate drives are hidden. These learned drives are exceedingly important in human behavior" (Dollard and Miller, 1950, pp. 31-32). An acquired drive of considerable importance is that of anxiety or fear. Based on the primary drive of pain, the secondary drive of anxiety is important because it can be learned quickly and become strong. Anxiety can lead the organism toward a variety of behaviors and is of particular importance in relation to abnormal behavior.

In contrast with the psychoanalytic emphasis on drives, the S-R emphasis on drives is associated with specific environmental conditions and has more to do with the question of motivation than with differences among individuals. One studies drives in relation to the process of learning rather than in terms of the kinds of drives that characterize different individuals.

Process

instrumental learning

According to S-R theory, learning consists of the association of stimuli with responses as a result of the reinforcement that follows these connections. In **instrumental learning** there is an emphasis on learned responses being instrumental in bringing about a desirable situation (for example, reward, escape from pain, avoidance of pain). The Hullian model of instrumental conditioning is derived from an interest in more complex forms of learning (for instance problem solving) than is classical or operant conditioning, and is interested also in motivation or goal-directed activity. In the Hullian model, there is an emphasis on drives that lead to internal stimuli, these stimuli then leading to responses that result in rewards. The rewards represent a reduction of the drive stimuli. The theory attempts to derive lawful relationships among environmental influences on the organism, such as the number of hours of food deprivation, the responses on the part of the organism, and the consequences of these responses for an assumed internal drive state in the organism, in this case, hunger.

The typical experiment in instrumental learning might involve the variables affecting a rat's learning to run a maze. The experimenter changes the number of hours of food deprivation, assumes that this is related to the strength of internal drive (hunger) stimuli, and then observes the behavioral consequences of the rat's having been rewarded for making certain turns in the maze. If a hungry rat receives food for making a response or series of responses in the maze, then the probability is increased that he will make the same responses on further trials in the maze. The responses are reinforced through the reduced strength of hunger drive stimuli.

Another type of experiment is conducted in relation to instrumental escape learning. In this type of experiment (Miller, 1951), a rat is put into a box with two compartments: a white compartment with a grid as a floor, and a black compartment with a solid floor. The compartments are separated by a door. At the beginning of the experiment, the rats are given electric shocks while in the white compartment and are allowed to escape into the black compartment. Thus, a fear response is conditioned to the white compartment. A test is then made as to whether the fear of the white compartment can lead to the learning of a new response. Now, in order for the rat to escape to the black compartment, it must turn a wheel placed in the white compartment. The turning of the wheel opens the door to the black compartment and allows the rat to escape. After a number of trials, the rat begins to rotate the wheel with considerable speed.

The interpretation is that the rat has acquired a fear drive in relation to the white compartment. This drive operates to activate the organism and to set the stage for reinforcement, just as the hunger drive did in the maze experiment. Escape from the white into the black compartment involves the learning of a new response — the turning of a wheel. This instrumental learning is based on the consequences of the response, escape from the white compartment, and on the associated reduction in the strength of the fear drive stimuli.

As is true of other theories of learning, S-R theory emphasizes concepts such as generalization, discrimination, and extinction. Although there are many phenomena that are similar in classical, operant, and instrumental conditioning, a number of differences can be observed. First, there is a different emphasis on the timing of events. Put another way, different events in the learning process are chosen for investigation. For example, in classical conditioning the interest is in the way in which stimuli lead to responses (bell leads to salivation), while in instrumental conditioning the emphasis is on how a response leads to, or is associated with, a consequent reinforcing stimulus (turning the wheel leads to escape from fear). In relation to this, in classical conditioning there is an interest in the pairing of the conditioned and unconditioned stimuli, and not in the effects of a response or in the motivational state of the organism. In instrumental conditioning there is an emphasis on the association of the response with reinforcement. The response is specified in terms of its consequences for the organism. Another difference is that although the responses of interest in classical conditioning tend to be automatic (reflex responses), those of interest in instrumental conditioning tend to be more varied. In the latter case, the response of interest may not initially be linked to any particular stimulus in the environment. This leads to the last point. In classical conditioning, the response of the organism is controlled by the experimenter through the presentation of a stimulus — first the unconditioned stimulus and then the conditioned stimulus. In instrumental conditioning, the response comes out of the trial and error behavior of the organism. In this latter kind of conditioning, therefore, the response becomes contingent on reinforcers, but it is not initially provoked by the experimenter.

Growth and Development

In general, S-R theory interprets growth and development as consisting of the accumulation of habits, which are then related to one another in a hierarchical arrangement or order of importance. Within this general conceptualization the development of higher mental processes and imitative behavior are of particular importance.

Initially the behavior of the infant is largely a reflexive response to ex-

higher mental processes

ternal stimuli and internal drives. In the course of development, however, behavior reflects the central role of thought or **higher mental processes**. Language is of particular importance in the functioning of our higher mental processes and in enabling us to go beyond simple, reflexive responses to stimuli. Language helps us to make important discriminations and generalizations. Words can be attached to drives and, through their symbolic function, themselves lead to drives being aroused. Language enables us to anticipate the future, and thus to go beyond reinforcers in the immediate situation.

imitative behavior

In 1941 Miller and Dollard attempted a social learning interpretation of **imitative behavior**. They suggested that there were different kinds of imitative behavior but that all such behavior could be derived from a Hullian theory of learning. Most attention was given to a process called matched-dependent behavior. The matched-dependent form of imitative behavior was assumed to occur when one person was aware of important cues in the environment while the other was not. In the socialization of children, there are many times when children are dependent on parents for the recognition of cues and, therefore, match their behavior to that of the parents. The matching of behavior then leads to rewards to the child.

The following illustrates matched-dependent behavior. Two children were playing. One child heard the father's footsteps indicating he was home from work. This child ran to the father and received some candy, which the father generally brought home for the children. The second and younger child was not aware of the footsteps as a cue for the father's return. He generally did not run when the older brother did but, on one occasion, by chance ran behind his brother. This behavior was rewarded by candy from the father and led to an increase in the running of the younger at the sight of the running of the older brother. The younger brother had been rewarded for matching the behavior of the older brother, but he was not aware of the cue for running being used by the other brother.

In an experiment to test this interpretation, Miller and Dollard rewarded one group or rats for going in the same direction in a maze as the leader and another group of rats for going in the opposite direction. Whereas the leader had been trained to make use of a cue for finding food, the other rats were without this cue. As a result, the rats reinforced for imitating the leader learned to use the response of the leader as their cue. Put in other situations, the rats continued to imitate the behavior of the leader. The rats in the other group did not show imitative behavior. In sum, the rats reinforced for following the behavior of a leader learned the response of imitating, and this learned response generalized from the original learning situation to other situations. Similar results were found in research on the learning of imitation by children.

The essential aspects of the imitative process described by Miller and

Dollard are that it develops out of trial and error or random behavior and that it is based on the positive reinforcement of matching behavior. Individuals learn to imitate because they are rewarded in the course of doing so. Once such learning has occurred in relation to specific acts, it may generalize to a tendency to imitate other acts in the same person or to the imitation of other people. Thus, the child may develop a generalized tendency toward imitation.

Other efforts have been made to translate Hullian theory into principles of gowth and development. Such efforts generally have emphasized the importance of rewards in parental child rearing practices. For example, in one research program the pattern of child rearing found to be most likely to result in "high conscience" development in children was one in which the mother is generally warm and loving but also uses the threat of withdrawal of affection as a method of control (Sears, Rau, and Alpert, 1965). Later research has suggested that the concept of "conscience" is complex and involves many possible behaviors. Furthermore, the relationship of child rearing practices to personality development is very complicated. As a result, there have tended to be fewer such studies relating early patterns of parental reward to the later development of broad personality characteristics.

Clinical Applications of S-R Theory

Psychopathology

If a neurosis is functional (i.e., a product of experience rather than of organic damage or instinct), it must be learned (p. 8) . . . The dynamics of conflict behavior are systematically deduced from more basic principles. Thus, a fundamental fact of neurosis — that of conflict — is tied in with general learning theory (p. 10).

DOLLARD AND MILLER, 1950

The Hullian theory of learning emphasizes the importance of drives and the reinforcement that comes from the reduction of drive stimuli. One drive that is critical in the learning of abnormal behaviors is that of anxiety. Although the details of various Hullian explanations of abnormal behavior differ, and some are supportive of psychoanalytic theory while others are not, they all state that abnormal behaviors are learned because they result in the reduction of anxiety drive stimuli.

Dollard and Miller (1950) were among the first to relate the principles of learning theory to personality phenomena, in general, and to abnormal behavior, in particular. In this effort they emphasized the concepts of drive, drive conflict, anxiety, and reinforcement through the reduction of anxiety.

According to Dollard and Miller, a neurosis represents the expression of learned conflicts that are inaccessible to verbal awareness. Neuroses are caused by conflict. In the course of development, children must learn socially accepted outlets for their drives. Particularly critical learning situations are the ones involving feeding, toilet training, and sexual and aggressive behavior. As children grow, they may wish to express certain drives but be punished for doing so by their parents. Or, children may wish to express aggression toward the parents, but be punished for this. The result of punishment is the development of an acquired fear drive in relation to certain stimuli. As we illustrated earlier in this chapter, Miller demonstrated that the response of fear could be conditioned to a previously neutral stimulus (white compartment) and then, itself, take on the properties of a drive stimulus. In some cases, the same stimulus may come to elicit both the original drive and the acquired fear drive. At this point, the individual experiences an **approach-avoidance conflict**. Thus, the individual may be torn between making sexual advances toward a girl (approach) and the fear of doing so (avoidance). Another example would be of the individual who wishes to express his anger (approach) but is afraid of doing so (avoidance).

approach-avoidance conflict

Thus, the approach-avoidance conflict between two drives is the basic ingredient for the development of neurotic behavior. As a result of the conflict and the anxiety involved, the individual develops a symptom. The symptom reduces the anxiety and relieves the pressure of the conflict. For example, Dollard and Miller described the case of a 23-year-old married woman who had developed a number of fears, one of which was that her heart would stop beating if she did not concentrate on counting the beats. The difficulties started with her feeling faint in a store, then developed into a fear of going out alone, and then into a fear of heart trouble. Dollard and Miller interpreted the symptom as involving a sex-fear conflict. When on the streets alone, the woman was afraid of sexual temptation. She felt that someone might try to seduce her and that she would be vulnerable to the seduction. The increased sex desire accompanying the fantasied seduction touched off anxiety and guilt, leading to the sex-anxiety conflict. Going home and avoiding being alone on the streets were reinforced because they reduced the anxiety and relieved the conflict. The counting of heartbeats was similarly reinforcing because it preoccupied her and did not allow her to think of possible seductions. The counting habit was reinforced by the drop in anxiety.

The case illustrates how Dollard and Miller made use of the concepts of drive, drive conflict, anxiety, and reinforcemnt through drive reduction to account for the development of a neurosis. Although the details are only sketchy, the case also illustrates how Dollard and Miller attempted to use Hullian theory in a way that was consistent with psychoanalytic theory. In a similar way, they were led to interpret repression as a response inhibiting thought (that is, a "not-thinking" response).

While most attention has been given to approach-avoidance conflicts in the development of neuroses, Dollard and Miller also emphasized the importance of approach-approach and avoidance-avoidance conflicts. In an **approach-approach conflict** the person is torn between two desirable alternatives. Should the person date one or another attractive individual, watch this great movie or the other great movie, buy this car or that car? In an **avoidance-avoidance conflict** the person is torn between undesirable, unpleasant alternatives. Should the person pay the bill now and be without money or pay a larger bill later, is divorce or living in an unpleasant situation worse, should the child tell the parent and risk punishment or stay silent and feel guilty?

There have been other efforts to use Hullian theory to explain abnormal behavior. Although they have emphasized the concepts of anxiety as a drive, and symptoms as responses that are drive-reducing, they have used neither the conflict model nor psychoanalytic theory. In fact, other efforts along Hullian lines have been hostile to psychoanalytic interpretations (Eysenck and Rachman, 1965; Mednick, 1958; Wolpe and Lazarus, 1966). For example, Wolpe suggests that neurotic behaviors are learned reponses. At the time of onset of neurosis, the individual is exposed to a threatening situation and experiences anxiety. The anxiety then generalizes so that now it can be elicited by a variety of stimuli. Neurotic responses express anxiety-reducing efforts on the part of the individual. Finally, Mednick interprets the development of schizophrenia (an extreme thought disorder) in terms of anxiety, generalization, and anxiety-reduction. According to Mednick (1958), schizophrenia begins with a state of intense anxiety. This leads to generalization, so that many stimuli in the environment become threatening. Responses formerly found to be useful in reducing anxiety are used, although, in many cases, this now involves the use of irrelevant responses and preoccupations. Finally, irrelevant responses and preoccupations dominate the patient's life because they are reinforced through anxiety reduction. As in Wolpe's explanation of neurotic phenomena, there is no mention of concepts such as instinctual impulses, the unconscious, or mechanisms of defense. The emphasis is on the reinforcing effects of anxiety drive reduction. Whereas Dollard and Miller, in their application of learning theory to psychoanalytic concepts, continued to use a term such as symptom, current learning approaches reject such concepts. As noted in Chapter Nine, they are viewed as part of a disease-medical model which is rejected in favor of a behavioral-psychological model.

approach-approach conflict

avoidance-avoidance conflict

Change

In this section on change we will consider a variety of approaches to change and the principles of learning on which they are based. As noted previously, Dollard and Miller used S-R theory to interpret the process of change and hoped that the theory would provide a clear framework for therapeutic practice. However, their work itself did not lead to new therapeutic efforts. Thus, in this section we will be considering a variety of individuals who use the principles of classical conditioning and S-R learning theory to develop new approaches to personality change. These approaches have been called **behavior therapy** and the individuals who use them are called **behavior therapists**.

behavior therapy
behavior therapists

Before discussing the major systems of change that have been developed, it will be useful to point out the major processes of learning on which they are based. Five such processes have been suggested (Bandura, 1969; Bandura and Walters, 1963). The first is based on the process of **extinction**. Where an undesirable trait is being maintained by positive reinforcement, the withdrawal of this reinforcement leads to the extinction of the response. One illustration of this process is the extinction of psychotic talk about delusions through nonreinforcement (Ayllon and Michael, 1959). A decrease in psychotic talk was found when nurses did not respond to this behavior and instead reinforced, with sympathetic listening, sensible talk. A second relevant process is **discrimination learning**. As a result of discrimination learning, individuals are able to distinguish between behaviors that are being reinforced and those that are not being reinforced, or between stimuli that they need to be afraid of and stimuli that do not represent punishment. According to Dollard and Miller (1950), much of therapy consists of learning new discriminations. Through the process of discrimination learning, the individual is able to distinguish between past experiences of reinforcement and punishment and current realities.

extinction

discrimination learning

Although extinction and discrimination learning are important processes, they have not been as critical to the development of behavior therapy as have three other processes: **counterconditioning, positive reinforcement**, and **imitation**. In counterconditioning, a desirable response that is incompatible with an undesirable response is conditioned to the same environmental stimulus. Thus, relaxation can be conditioned to a stimulus and inhibit an anxiety response (you can't be relaxed and anxious at the same time). In an early use of this method by Jones (1924), a boy was relieved of his fear of furry animals through counterconditioning of positive, pleasurable responses associated with eating to the same stimuli. As shall be demonstrated, the counterconditioning procedure is critical to Wolpe's system of behavior therapy.

counterconditioning
positive reinforcement
imitation

As has been seen, the use of positive reinforcement is particularly relevant to the Skinnerian operant conditioning procedure. By using this procedure as a model, efforts have been made to develop social behavior in disturbed, aggressive children (Bijou, 1965) and to develop appropriate speech patterns in schizophrenic children (Lovaas, Berberich, Perloff, and Schaeffer, 1966). The new behaviors are conditioned through rewarding successive approximations to the desired behavior. Finally, behavior can be changed through the process of imitation or modeling. New behaviors can be acquired through the observation of models, and inappropriate fears can be lost through the observation of models who are not harmed by the feared stimulus. (See Chapter 11 for a more complete discussion of modeling.)

Having considered the processes of change associated with learning theory and behavior therapy, let us now consider one of the systems that has been developed as a direct outgrowth of learning theory.

Classical conditioning and Wolpe's systematic desensitization   Behavioral therapy based on the classical conditioning model emphasizes the conditioning of new responses to stimuli that elicit undesired behaviors. The effort of Jones (1924) to countercondition a pleasurable response to the previously fear-provoking animal stimulus has been noted already. Another early procedure that gained considerable attention was one developed by Mowrer and Mowrer (1928) for the treatment of bed-wetting. In general, bed-wetting in children occurs because the child does not respond to stimuli from the bladder so as to awaken and urinate in the bathroom. To deal with this condition, Mowrer and Mowrer developed a device based on the classical conditioning model. This consisted of an electrical device in the bed of the child. If the child urinated, the device activated a bell which awakened the child. Gradually stimuli from the bladder became associated with the awakening response. Eventually, the response was anticipated so that bed-wetting no longer took place.

The classical conditioning procedure also has been used in the treatment of alcoholics. For example, an aversive stimulus such as shock or a nausea-inducing agent is applied immediately after the alcoholic takes a drink. The aversive stimulus acts as an unconditioned stimulus, and the avoidance response is conditioned to the alcohol.

systematic desensitization

By far the most influential development in this area has been that of Joseph Wolpe's method of **systematic desensitization**. Interestingly, this method of therapy was developed by a psychiatrist rather than a psychologist, and by someone who originally practiced within a psychoanalytic framework. After a number of years of practice, however, Wolpe read and was impressed by the writings of Pavlov and Hull. He came to hold the view that a neurosis is a persistent, maladaptive learned response that is almost always associated with anxiety. Therapy, then, involves the inhibition of anxiety through the counterconditioning of a competing response. "If a response inhibitory to anxiety can be made to occur in the presence of anxiety-evoking stimuli so that it is accompanied by a complete or partial suppression of the anxiety response, the bond between these stimuli and the anxiety response will be weakened" (Wolpe, 1961a, p. 189). In other words, therapy involves the conditioning of responses that are antagonistic to or inhibitory of anxiety. A variety of anxiety-inhibiting responses can be used for counterconditioning purposes. However, the one that has received most attention is that of deep muscle relaxation. Through a process called systematic desensitization, the patient learns to respond to certain previously anxiety-arousing stimuli with the newly conditioned response of relaxation.

The therapeutic technique of sytematic desensitization involves a number of phases (Wolpe, 1968; Wolpe 1961a; Wolpe and Lazarus, 1966). First, there is a careful assessment of the therapeutic needs of the patient. A detailed history is taken of every symptom and of every aspect of life in which the patient experiences undue difficulty. A systematic account of the patient's life history also is obtained. After having determined that the patient's problems lend themselves to systematic desensitization, the therapist trains the patient to relax. A detailed procedure is described for helping the patient to first relax one part of the body and then all parts of the body. Whereas, at first, patients have limited success in their ability to feel free of muscle tension, by the end of about six sessions most are able to relax the entire body in seconds. The next phase of treatment involves the construction of an anxiety hierarchy. This is a difficult and complex procedure in which the therapist tries to obtain from the patient a list of stimuli that arouse anxiety. These anxiety-arousing stimuli are grouped into themes such as fear of heights, or fear of rejection. Within each group or theme, the anxiety-arousing stimuli are then ordered from the most disturbing to the least disturbing. For example, a theme of claustrophobia (fear of closed spaces) might involve placing the fear of being stuck in an elevator at the top of the list, an anxiety about being on a train in the middle of the list, and an anxiety in response to reading of miners trapped underground at the bottom of the list. A theme of death might involve being at a burial as the most anxiety-arousing stimulus, the word death as somewhat anxiety-arousing, and driving past a cemetery as only slightly anxiety-arousing. Patients can have many or few themes, and many or few items within each anxiety hierarchy.

With the construction of the anxiety hierarchies completed, the patient is ready for the desensitization procedure itself. The patient has attained the capacity to calm himself by relaxation, and the therapist has established the anxiety hierarchies. Now the therapist encourages the patient to achieve a deep state of relaxation and then to imagine the least anxiety-arousing stimulus in the anxiety hierarchy. If the patient can imagine the stimulus without anxiety, then he is encouraged to imagine the next stimulus in the hierarchy while remaining relaxed. Periods of pure relaxation are interspersed with periods of relaxation and imagination of anxiety-arousing stimuli. If the patient feels anxious while imagining a stimulus, he is encouraged to relax and return to imagining a less anxiety-arousing stimulis. Ultimately the patient is able to relax while imagining all stimuli in the anxiety hierarchies. Relaxation in relation to the imagined stimuli generalizes to relaxation in relation to these stimuli in everyday life. "It has consistently been found that at every stage a stimulus that evokes no anxiety when imagined in a state of relaxation will also evoke no anxiety when encountered in reality" (Wolpe, 1961a, p. 191).

A number of reports of clinical studies of the success of Wolpe's method have been published. The first such report by Wolpe (1958) indicated that almost 90 percent of his 210 patients were rated as cured or much improved in an average of about 30 therapeutic sessions. This is an extremely high rate of therapeutic success. Furthermore, according to Wolpe (1961b), follow-up studies of these patients suggest that in most cases the therapeutic gains have been maintained. Proponents of this point of view have been led to question the psychoanalytic view that, as long as the underlying conflicts remain untouched, the patient is prone to develop a new symptom in place of the one removed (symptom substitution) (Lazarus, 1965). According to the behavior therapy point of view, there is no symptom that is caused by unconscious conflicts. There is only a maladaptive learned response, and once this response has been eliminated there is no reason to believe that another maladaptive response (symptom) will be substituted for it.

Along with these uncontrolled clinical studies of the success of systematic desensitization, there have been some carefully designed laboratory investigations. One such early study was carried out by Lang and Lazovik (1963). In this study, college students who were intensely afraid of nonpoisonous snakes were randomly assigned to one of two groups. Subjects in the experimental group experienced desensitization therapy, whereas the subjects in the control group did not. Subjects in the experimental, desensitization group were found to be more able to hold or to touch a snake and reported less fear of snakes than did subjects who did not experience the desensitization therapy. Furthermore, at a six-month follow-up evaluation, subjects in the experimental group were found to hold or to increase their gains, and there was no evidence of symptom substitution.

Some important research also has been done on the comparative effectiveness of systematic desensitization and other forms of treatment. In one important study, Paul (1966) compared the effectiveness of systematic desensitization in the treatment of public-speaking situation anxiety with that of short-term, insight-oriented treatment and with a form of treatment that only emphasized therapist interest and a "fast-acting tranquilizer," which in reality was sodium bicarbonate. Subjects treated by systematic desensitization showed a significantly greater reduction in anxiety than did subjects treated by the other two forms of therapy. These gains were also significant relative to a group of subjects who had similar interpersonal performance anxieties but who received no treatment at all. In further research, Paul (Paul and Shannon, 1966) found that a group desensitization procedure also could be effective in the treatment of social-evalutive anxiety (Box 10.1). These studies and other clinical reports suggested that the effectiveness of systematic desensitization need not be limited to the treatment of specific fears. Furthermore, a two-year follow-up of the individuals treated by the individual and group systematic desensitization techniques indicated that the therapeutic gains had been maintained and extended. Although specifically sought, there was no evidence of relapse or symptom substitution (Paul, 1967; Paul 1968).

BOX 10.1 ## Counterconditioning, Systematic Desensitization, and Behavior Change

HYPOTHESES   (1) Compared with a control group of untreated, wait-period subjects, a group of "chronically" anxious college students treated with a group systematic desensitization procedure will show more improvement on personality and anxiety scales and on college grade point average. (2) The effects of this group treatment procedure will be comparable to the ones found with individual systematic desensitization with similar subjects.

SUBJECTS   Select 50 highly anxious male subjects who are college undergraduates. Selection is based on motivation for treatment and high scores on performance anxiety scales. Subjects report a general anxiety in dealing with other people, but are particularly anxious in public speaking situations.

PROCEDURE   Distribute subjects into five groups of ten subjects each. Subjects in three groups receive one of the following kinds of individual treatment: systematic desensitization, insight-oriented psychotherapy, attention-placebo. The attention-placebo group was included to determine general effects of any kind of treatment. Attention consisted of warmth and interest of the therapist. The placebo was a tablet of sodium

BOX 10.1 **Counterconditioning,
Systematic Desensitization,
and Behavior Change**   *continued*

bicarbonate that the subjects were told was a "fast-acting tranquilizer."
This was used to see the effects of suggestion and faith. One group of ten
subjects remains as an untreated control group and the final group of ten
subjects receives group desensitization. Administer the personality and
anxiety scales prior to treatment and after the completion of treatment.
Similarly, determine the grade point averages (GPA) at these two points in
time. All forms of therapy are conducted by highly experienced psychoth-
erapists. In the group desensitization procedure, have the members
construct hierarchies of situations from the least to the most anxiety
producing and then have them repeatedly visualize these situations while
deeply relaxed. Explain to the subjects how relaxation inhibits the anxiety
response. Direct the initial treatment sessions to the anxiety provoked by a
public speech situation. Two years after the completion of the treatment
procedures, conduct a follow-up study by readministering the personality
and anxiety scales.

RESULTS

1 There is evidence that the group desensitization procedure produced
   significant reductions in interpersonal anxiety (the treatment target) for
   "chronically" anxious males. Pre-post scores showed a greater reduction in anxiety for members of the group treatment than for members
   of the wait-period, untreated control group.

2 The members of the group desensitization showed a significant
   improvement in GPA when compared with members of the untreated
   control group.

TABLE 1
Mean Pre-Post Grade
Point Averages for
Subjects Treated by Group
Desensitization and
Matched Controls

	SEMESTER GPA	
Group	*Pretreatment*	*Posttreatment*
Treatment (N = 10)	3.152	3.562
Control (N = 10)	3.532	2.573

3 When the effects of group desensitization are evaluated against the
   results obtained through individual treatment with comparable

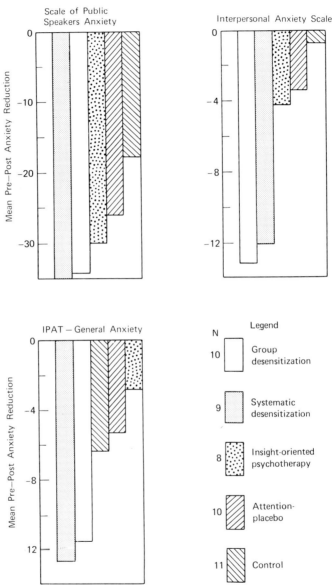

FIGURE 10.1   Mean reduction on scales relating to anxiety in public speaking situations, interpersonal anxiety, and more general anxiety (IPAT-anxiety) from pretreatment to two-year follow-up for subjects in various groups.

BOX 10.1   **Counterconditioning,
Systematic Desensitization,
and Behavior Change**   *continued*

subjects, the group method is found to be as effective as the individual application of systematic desensitization and significantly better than insight-oriented psychotherapy and attention-placebo treatments.

4 Follow-up data indicate a maintenance of improvement for subjects who received the group desensitization procedure, with additional improvement over the long term, follow-period.

5 There was no evidence of symptom substitution.

CONCLUSION   The group desensitization procedure offers an efficient and effective treatment for interpersonal anxiety.

SOURCE   G. L. Paul, and D. T. Shannon. Treatment of anxiety through systematic desensitization in therapy groups. *Journal of Abnormal Psychology, 1966,* 71, 124-135.
G. L. Paul, A two-year follow-up of systematic desensitization in therapy groups. *Journal of Abnormal Psychology,* 1968, *73,* 119-130.

To summarize, there is considerable evidence to support the effectiveness of Wolpe's counterconditioning, systematic desensitization method of treatment. The psychoanalytic suggestion that the relief from "symptoms" would be followed by a relapse or the appearance of other symptoms (symptom substitution) has been challenged, if not rejected. At the same time, recent reviews of the literature raise questions concerning Wolpe's interpretation of the causes of changes resulting from systematic desensitization (Kazdin and Wilcoxon, 1976). Whereas initially systematic desensitization played the major role in behavior therapy, it now is seen as one among many devices to be used to accomplish and maintain behavior change. Modern clinical behavior therapy goes beyond relaxation training and systematic desensitization to include training in specific skills, such as assertiveness training and problem-solving skills, and the elimination of irrational beliefs held by the person (Goldfried and Davison, 1976).

Summary   The varied approaches to behavior change used by behavior therapists suggest that there is no pure school. However, these approaches do share common features. In each method of therapy there is an emphasis on specific responses, on the relationships of these responses to environmental events, and on the model of a controlled laboratory experiment.

The aims and procedures of these systems have been contrasted with the ones of psychoanalysis (Eysenck, 1959; London, 1964). Psychoanalysis was derived from clinical observations and emphasizes symptoms as outward manifestations of underlying conflicts and mechanisms of defense. Furthermore, a treatment of the individual as a whole is required, and the transference relationship is encouraged. In behavior therapy, techniques are derived from experimental studies in the laboratory, and "symptoms" are described as maladaptive, learned responses. It is the response that needs to be affected, and personal relationships need not be part of the process. As London (1964) pointed out, there is a distinction between an insight therapy and an action therapy. Whereas the psychoanalyst attempts to help patients to understand their problems and thereby to gain freedom, the action therapist attempts to influence the problem in a more direct way. In the case of behavior therapy, one does not worry about growth, empathy, positive regard, and healthy constructs. The behavior therapist is an engineer, and seeks to alter the ways in which individuals respond to their environmental stimuli. In support of their approach, behavior therapists present evidence relevant to learning theory and to observed changes under controlled conditions.

Case Example — A Behavioral Interpretation of Little Hans

In this section the application of the learning theory approach will be observed in a case presented by Wolpe and Rachman (1960) which gives us the excellent opportunity to continue the comparison of the behavioral approach with that of psychoanalysis. In fact, it is not a case in the same sense as other cases that have been presented. Rather, it is a critique and reformulation of Freud's case of Little Hans.

As we learned in Chapter 3, the case of Little Hans is a classic in psychoanalysis. In this case, Freud emphasized the importance of infantile sexuality and Oedipal conflicts in the development of a horse phobia, or fear. Wolpe and Rachman are extremely critical of Freud's approach to obtaining data and of his conclusions. They make the following points. (1) Nowhere is there evidence of Hans' wish to make love to his mother. (2) Hans never expressed fear or hatred of his father. (3) Hans consistently denied any relationship between the horse and his father. (4) Phobias can be induced in children by a simple conditioning process and need not be related to a theory of conflicts or anxiety and defense. The view that neuroses occur for a purpose is highly questionable. (5) There is no evidence that the phobia disappeared as a result of his resolution of his Oedipal conflicts. Similarly, there is no evidence of "insight" or that information was of therapeutic value.

Wolpe and Rachman feel handicapped in their own interpretation of the phobia because the data were gathered within a psychoanalytic framework. They do, however, attempt an explanation, and this is based on Hullian learning theory. A phobia is regarded as a *conditioned anxiety reaction.* As a child, Hans heard and saw a playmate being warned by her father that she should avoid a white horse lest it bite her: "Don't put your finger to the white horse." This incident sensitized Hans to a fear of horses. Also, there was the time when one of Hans' friends injured himself and bled while playing horses. Finally, Hans was a sensitive child who felt uneasy about seeing horses on the merry-go-round being beaten. These factors set the condition for the later development of the phobia. The phobia itself occurred as a consequence of the fright Hans experienced while watching a horse fall down. Whereas Freud suggested that this incident was an exciting cause that allowed the underlying conflicts to be expressed in terms of a phobia, Wolpe and Rachman suggest that this incident was *the* cause.

Wolpe and Rachman see a similarity here to Watson's conditioning of a fear of rabbits in Albert. Hans was frightened by the event with a horse and then generalized his fear to all things that were similar to or related to horses. The recovery from the phobia did not occur through the process of insight, but probably through a process of extinction or through a process of counterconditioning. As Hans developed, he experienced other emotional responses that inhibited the fear response. Or, it is suggested that, perhaps, the father's constant reference to the horse within a nonthreatening context helped to extinguish the fear response. Whatever the details, it appears that the phobia disappeared gradually, as would be expected by this kind of learning interpretation, instead of dramatically, as might be suggested by psychoanalytic, insight interpretation. The evidence in support of Freud is not clear, and the data, as opposed to the interpretations, can be accounted for in a more straighforward way through the use of a learning theory interpretation.

RECENT DEVELOPMENTS IN
BEHAVIORAL APPROACHES TO PERSONALITY

The behavioral approach to personality is at a very active and productive stage of development. Numerous journals are devoted exclusively to behavioral reports from the laboratory and clinic, while other journals include behavioral reports along with those expressive of different points of view. With so much current activity, it may be difficult to separate the main strands of development — in particular, those strands that are likely to have long-term consequences. However, an effort to do this would suggest the following five major areas of development: (1) statement of the ideology, utopian planning, and social engineering; (2) interest in self-control and self-reinforcement; (3) increased range of application of behavior therapy techniques; (4) interest in processes at work in behavior therapy; (5) interest in a broader range of variables, including cognition. In discussing many of these developments, particularly in areas such as cognition and self-control, we will be involved with contributions that could just as well be covered in the next chapter on social learning theory. In fact, the dividing line between social learning theory and other learning approaches is not always clear. Understanding that this is the case, it will nevertheless be useful to consider these developments here, and then return to them again in the next chapter. It is important to be aware that in this section we will be considering developments in behavioral approaches generally, including both the approaches discussed in Chapter 9 and the approaches discussed in this chapter.

Statement of Ideology, Utopian Planning, and Social Engineering

As has been noted in each of the theory chapters, implicit in each theory is a view of the person and, in some, a view of the relationship between the individual and society. To a certain extent, Skinner has always been prepared to consider the societal implications of his theory. In his 1948 novel, *Walden Two*, he described in detail how a society based on the principles of positive reinforcement would function. The use of operant conditioning techniques has become an increasing reality and has stirred concern about the possibility of people becoming robots in an operant technology society. Within this context, Skinner has presented the rationale for an emphasis on reinforcement contingencies in the environment as opposed to feeling states within individuals.

In *Beyond Freedom and Dignity*, Skinner argues a position similar to that of Darwin. According to Skinner, the environment, in a role similar to that in evolution and natural selection, selects the behavior that will be maintained over time. The selective role of the environment in shaping and maintaining behavior is the psychological equivalent of the environment's effect upon the development of genetic stuctures. People do not act on the basis of feelings such as freedom and dignity, but rather on the basis of contingencies of reinforcement in the environment. Rather than focusing on such internal and abstract concepts as freedom and dignity, one should seek to change the environment. "As a science of behavior adopts the strategy of physics and biology, the autonomous agent to which behavior has traditionally been attributed is replaced by the environment — the environment in which the species evolved and in which the behavior of the individual is shaped and maintained" (Skinner, 1971, p. 184). We do not look for explanations in terms of character traits such as "industrious" or "lazy" but rather in terms of environmental histories of reinforcement.

It is interesting that a view which emphasizes how the environment acts upon people, as opposed to how people act upon the environment, has resulted in a group of social engineers who are committed to acting upon the environment. Watson suggested that through control of the environment he could train an infant to become any type of specialist he might select. Skinnerian social engineers take this principle one step further. They seek to design environments that will control broad aspects of human behavior. Currently, these efforts are seen most clearly in the token economies that have been developed in hospitals and prisons. According to a 1970 report, there are over 100 token economies in existence in over 50 different institutions (Krasner, 1970). By now these numbers may well have doubled. There is evidence in support of the effectiveness of token economies with severely disturbed patients and with mentally retarded individuals in increasing such behaviors as social interaction, self-care, and job performance. Token economies also have been used effectively to decrease aggressive behavior in children and to decrease marital discord (Kazdin, 1977). These programs together with reports of communes based on Skinnerian principles, suggest the widespread influence of the social engineering-utopian planning point of view.

Interest in Self-Control and Self-Reinforcement

The potential for individuals to develop control over reinforcement contingencies in the environment, and over their own behavior, was recognized some time ago by Skinner. However, it is only recently that there has been a surge of research in this direction. Basically, self-control involves a process through which individuals become able to influence the variables that determine their behavior — they become their own teacher, therapist, or social engineer. For example, individuals may establish self-control over their eating behavior by rewarding themselves for not eating and penalizing themselves for overeating (Krasner and Ullman, 1973). Another example would be individuals gaining control over their behavior by training themselves to make only certain self-statements. Thus, Meichenbaum (1973) reports that test-anxious college students can be taught to talk to themselves in ways that will facilitate performance on exams. This suggests that not only overt behavior but also what people say to themselves may be brought under self-control. Apparently behavior can be maintained over an extended period of time and generalize to a variety of situations through self-administered rewards (Mahoney and Bandura, 1972).

A variety of factors appear to account for the recent surge of research on self-control. First, many researchers involved in behavior modification programs have been frustrated by the lack of stability of positive behavioral changes when the treated individual is put into a different environment. The potential for individuals to control their own behavior and reinforcements offers a possible solution to this problem. Second, the Skinnerian ideology brings to the mind of many the image of authoritarian control and robot-like functioning. The development of self-control mechanisms would appear to hold some hope for relieving such anxieties. Finally, developments in biofeedback research have suggested the possibility that individuals may be able to gain control over aspects of their own physiological functioning. For example, there now is evidence that individuals can learn to control their heart rate, blood pressure, and sweat gland activity (Lang, 1971). There is some hope that the development of self-control mechanisms in relation to what was previously thought to be involuntary activity may be useful in treating a variety of conditions (for example, heart disease). The use of self-control as a treatment device still remains a hope for the future (Blanchard and Young, 1973). But this research is impressive not only because it covers three areas of functioning — overt behavior, speech and thought processes, and physiologic functioning — but also because it gives learning theory a means for accounting for behaviors that remain stable over a long period of time in the absence of external reinforcers.

Increased Range of Application of Behavior Therapy Techniques

Within behavior therapy there is a freedom of movement between research and treatment, and between the laboratory and the natural environment. The result has been considerable variety in the behavioral techniques applied to problem behaviors, considerable range of application in terms of types of problems and types of patients treated, and considerable diversity in types of setting in which the therapy is done.

For the most part, the major behavioral treatment techniques continue to be those reported earlier — systematic desensitization and operant conditioning. What is impressive here is the tremendous increase in the use of these techniques. Along with this increased use one finds modifications of the techniques and new techniques which also are based on learning theory principles. Thus, for example, the process of implosive therapy developed by Stampfl (Morganstern, 1973; Stampfl, 1970) is based on learning theory, yet it moves in a direction opposite to that of systematic desensitization. In an effort to extinguish fears, Stampfl presents patients with imagined scenes that are very frightening to them. The goal is to reproduce the anxiety associated with the original conditioning event, but this time in the absence of negative consequences. In contrast with Wolpe's approach, the effort is to produce a maximum level of anxiety. With the repetition of the scenes, the anxiety response is extinguished.

The efforts of Meichenbaum (1977), mentioned in the preceding section, to directly influence what clients say to themselves, represents another new behavioral technique. Although some investigators support staying close to a learning theory base, others suggest the broad application of behavior techniques — even when the exact theoretical basis for the technique remains unclear (Lazarus, 1971; London, 1972).

Behavioral techniques have been used with almost every conceivable problem behavior. The list of behaviors viewed as products of social learning and treated with behavioral techniques includes obesity, asthma, stuttering, phobias, delusional speech, antisocial acts, marital difficulties, depression, alcoholism, smoking, drug addiction, fetishism, and auditory hallucinations (Craighead, Kazdin, and Mahoney, 1976). In a particularly striking illustration of the application of behavioral techniques, Lang (1970) reported on the treatment of a nine-month-old infant with chronic vomiting. After the failure of a series of medical treatments, the infant remained malnourished and in danger of dying. As at last resort, behavior modification was tried. The treatment selected was based on avoidance conditioning. A brief, intense electric shock was administered to the infant's leg coincident with the first sign of vomiting. Shocks were repeated at one-second intervals until vomiting ceased. Success in inhibiting vomiting was achieved in the first treatment session and shocks were administered on only five treatment days. The child ceased vomiting, increased body weight, and was discharged from the hospital. A follow-up study two years later indicated that the child was developing normally, both physiologically and psychologically.

The Lang study suggests not only the potential power of behavioral techniques but also the range of patients that can be treated with them. In contrast with the focus of traditional treatment programs on young, attractive, verbal, intelligent, and successful patients, many behavior modification programs started by treating individuals on whom almost everyone else gave up — the chronic schizophrenic, the autistic child, the retarded, etc. Work with these populations continues, but along with this there has been a movement toward treating the patients typically treated by analysts, and by dynamically oriented therapists.

Finally, these treatments occur in a wide variety of settings, including the school, the home, the office, and the hospital ward. Particularly significant have been efforts to train teachers in the use of token reinforcement programs (O'Leary and Drabman, 1971) and to train families in the ABC's of assessment (Antecedent conditions — Behaviors — Consequences) and the application of reinforcement principles (Patterson, 1971). Rather than altering underlying family conflicts, family reinforcement schedules are altered.

Interest in Processes at Work in Behavior Therapy

In the back-and-forth movement between the laboratory and the clinic, behavior therapists have attempted to determine the therapeutic factors at work in various techniques. Perhaps the greatest amount of work in this area has been directed toward understanding the processes at work in systematic desensitization. As noted earlier in the chapter, Wolpe emphasized the pairing of anxiety-inhibiting relaxation with aversive imaginary stimuli in a graded hierarchy. However, further research by other investigators brings into question the necessity of all three elements in systematic desensitization (that is, graded hierarchy, muscle relaxation, imagination with relaxation) and suggests alternative explanations for the success of the method. Thus, for example, in one study there was no difference in success between systematic desensitization with relaxation or without relaxation (Cooke, 1968). In another study, relaxation alone and cognitive rehearsal alone (imagining scenes) were as effective as the complete desensitization program in reducing stress (Folkins, Lawson, Opton, and Lazarus, 1968). Finally, the necessity of using a graded hierarchy has been brought into question by an experiment in which therapeutic effects could be achieved by starting at the top of the hierarchy as well as at the bottom (Wolpin and Raines, 1966).

Results such as these have led to the development of alternative explanations for the success of systematic desensitization. One explanation suggests that therapeutic gains are a result of extinction while another suggests an operant conditioning interpretation for the success of the procedure — the client receives verbal positive reinforcement from the therapist for reports of no anxiety and for approach responses toward previously feared objects (Leitenberg, Agras, Barlow, and Oliveau, 1969). The interpretations that have received the greatest attention, however, have been those that emphasize cognitive and social influence variables. A recent review of the literature suggests that patient expectancies of therapeutic change are an important element in systematic desensitization (Kazdin and Wilcoxon, 1976). Thus, at this point the evidence seems to suggest that systematic desensitization can be an extremely effective therapeutic technique, but Wolpe's theory of counterconditioning does not provide a satisfactory explanation for the therapeutic effects.

As time goes on, early and simple explanations for the success of various behavioral techniques are being challenged. In addition, where alternative techniques are compared with one another there are conflicting reports of comparative success. It is a credit to this theoretical approach and to the investigators committed to it that so much attention is being directed toward establishing the effective ingredients in behavior therapy. At the same time, there appears to be enough evidence to suggest that the phenomena are far more complex than the originators of the techniques ever conceived (Krasner, 1971a).

Interest in a Broader Range of Variables

Whereas almost all of the early behavioral research was on overt behavior, the research reported in the above sections suggests the extent to which this approach has been broadened to include other variables. While primary attention is still given to overt behavior, cognitive and emotional variables are also now recognized as important. A number of years ago it would not have appeared likely to hear a Skinnerian recognize the importance of cognitive variables and express the view that "it makes no sense to attempt a study with a human being that approaches him as a stupid animal who cannot understand English" (Krasner, 1971b, p. 646). The interest in cognitive variables is particularly striking in social learning theory (Chapter Eleven).

CRITICAL EVALUATION OF BEHAVIORAL APPROACHES TO PERSONALITY

Clearly, learning theory is an approach that is distinct from the others previously studied and one that has a lot to offer. The behavioral approach to personality is based on a considerable body of literature on the psychology of learning. Although there is a behavioral, learning theory point of view, there is no one school. Differences in specific theoretical orientations have led to lively conroversy and significant research. The approach tends to be characterized by a respect for scientific methodology and a respect for evidence in support of a new point of view. Theoretical biases are not given up easily, but there is a sense of commitment to discovery as opposed to dogma.

    Also impressive is the way in which learning concepts have been used to explain a variety of phenomena. Thus, for example, learning theory has been used to explain the development of the self-concept (Helper, 1955), to explain self-critical behavior (Aronfreed, 1964), and to account for masochism (Sandler, 1964). Learning theory rejects the concept of self as a determinant of behavior (as a little man inside the individual that controls behavior), but it accepts the idea that the individual may learn to use a variety of adjectives in association with the concept of self. It rejects an evaluative and punitive agency such as "conscience" or "superego", but accepts that self-criticism may be a learned response that is reinforced by anxiety drive reduction. That is, through a self-critical response the child reduces the anxiety associated with anticipated punishment from an external source. Finally, in relation to masochism, the pairing of an aversive stimulus with reward can result in the aversive stimulus taking on its own reward qualities. Or, punishment can be perceived to be a necessary step prior to reward; that is, punishment may be a learned contingency for reward. Thus, there is no need to turn to such abstract concepts as guilt, superego conflicts, and libidinal strivings to understand masochistic behavior. One can understand this behavior through extensions of the laws of learning.

Although learning theory has much to offer, it has many properties that are open to serious criticism. The learning theory approach to personality may be criticized on three broad grounds: (1) It tends to oversimplify behavior. (2) It tends to neglect important areas. (3) If often is not as objective and rigorous as is claimed.

Oversimplification of Behavior

There are many components to the criticism that learning theorists oversimplify behavior. One component is the claim that the principles of learning used are derived from research on rats and other subhuman animals, and there is a quesiton as to whether the same principles are involved in human learning. In other words, can rat laws be applied to human behavior? A second component of this criticism is the claim that the behaviors studied by the learning theorists are superficial. In their effort to gain experimental rigor and control over relevant variables, learning theorists have limited themselves to simple, specific responses and have avoided complex behaviors. We may recall here Cattell's argument that the bivariate method limits investigators to the study of a few variables, and this means that they must ignore behaviors that cannot be produced in the laboratory.

A third and critical component of the criticism regarding oversimplification is concerned with cognitive behavior. Cognitive behavior involves the way in which the individual receives, organizes, and transmits information. The work of many psychologists gives clear evidence of the importance of an understanding of cognitive behavior. Yet, for a long time behaviorists avoided considering these phenomena. Whether because of a reluctance to look at internal processes or because of a reluctance to consider complex processes, learning theorists stuck fast in their attempts to understand all behavior in terms of stimulus-response bonds or in terms of operants and successive approximation.

There have been some attempts to understand cognitive behavior within a learning framework. As we shall see in the next chapter, social learning theorists place considerable emphasis on cognitive variables, though other learning theorists have been critical of this emphasis. Experiments emphasizing attitudinal and belief variables, together with increased work with intelligent and highly articulate clients, have apparently forced some learning psychologists into the "lion's den" of verbal, imaginal, and other cognitive processes (Kanfer and Karoly, 1972). It remains to be seen just how far these efforts will be taken, and the extent to which these subject variables will lend themselves to the same analyses as do environmental variables.

Neglect of Important Areas

The criticism concerning cognitive behavior is relevant to the second category of criticism — the neglect of important areas of human behavior. The behavioral psychologists have focused on environmental determinants of behavior and general laws. They have tended to neglect the importance of genetic factors and internal motivational processes, both of which are relevant to understanding individual differences (Herrnstein, 1977). The emphasis on simple stimulus-response units tends to be associated with an outmoded switchboard model of the brain and runs into difficulty when it must deal with the question of how responses are organized into larger units. The assumption is that an understanding of the laws involving simple units will readily lead to an understanding of the laws of complex behavior. Within the past decade there have been attempts to understand complex thinking processes, language, and interpersonal relations in terms of a learning theory model. However, these efforts have been late in coming and, generally, have run into difficulty.

Interestingly, those who criticize the learning theory model for its neglect of important areas also at times question whether, in fact, there is a learning theory of personality. Theories of personality traditionally have been concerned with individual differences, with complex behaviors, and with the whole personality. Yet learning theory has grown out of the observations of specific responses, under controlled conditions, in subhuman animals. In other words, if learning theory neglects areas traditionally considered to be critical parts of personality, can it accurately be considered a theory of personality?

Objectivity and Rigor

The question of the relevance of learning theory to the study of personality has merit. However, the discussion in this chapter and the last would certainly suggest that learning theory can hold its own in relation to other theories of personality when it comes to criteria such as comprehensiveness, economy, and internal consistency. But it is also true that as learning theory is extended into the realm of personality, it often becomes less objective and rigorous than is claimed. Thus, Taylor, a proponent of the learning theory approach to behavior, commented that "the further one gets from simple laboratory situations, the greater the numbers of assumptions that must be made" (Taylor, 1963, p. 5). Even within the laboratory environment there are problems in obtaining agreement as to what constitutes a drive, a response, or a reinforcement. Various measures of the same variable, such as response strength, often do not agree, and the relationships among the variables used often will vary according to the test used as a measure of performance. Unfortunately, the aura of the laboratory too often has led to the assumption that because something is associated with laboratory study, it must of necessity be objective and rigorous.

Learning Theory Interpretations of Behavior Change

The question of objectivity and rigor becomes critical in relation to learning theory approaches to behavior change. In fact, all three of the criticisms discussed above are relevant. For example, consider the problems of oversimplification and neglect of important areas. Although Wolpe and others claim that systematic desensitization is appropriate for a great variety of difficulties, almost all of the cases reported relate to specific phobias or to cases in which a specific environmental stimulus arouses anxiety. When laboratory studies are conducted, again, the most frequently studied problem is a specific phobia, typically a fear of snakes. Furthermore, all too often the subjects are college students, usually females. Depressions, obsessive disorders, interpersonal difficulties, and existential problems concerning the meaning of life are minimized or ignored (Breger and McGauch, 1965; Rosenhan and London, 1968). London (1964), who is equally critical of the insight therapies, observes that the behavioral therapies are far too limited in the phenomena they attend to. "Whether life has meaning or not, there are men who think it does, or can, or should; for these, perhaps the search alone or lack of it brings despair or suffering. Such miseries, by their nature, take the Actionist (Behaviorist) off guard; his system is geared to lesser aches and pains" (p. 39).

Returning to the question of rigor, there are many ways in which the behavioral approaches, particularly Wolpe's systematic desensitization, fall down. There is, for example, a question as to the extent to which the techniques are actually based on or logically deduced from learning theory (Breger and McGaugh, 1965; Feldman, 1966; Locke, 1971). Although Wolpe's theory of pathology reportedly is based on Hullian learning theory, there is little of Hull in the systematic desensitization procedure. Furthermore, there are so many things done in most of these treatments that it is hard to say just what the effective component is.

There are further problems. At times the definitions given to concepts cause us to wonder about the relationship of the clinic to the laboratory. Lazarus, for example, suggests that "a depressed person is virtually on an extinction trial. Some significant reinforcer has been withdrawn. There is loss and deprivation — loss of money or love, status or prestige, recognition or security, etc." (1968, pp. 81-85). Such an interpretation of depression gives great latitude and hardly represents an objective, easily measurable definition. Yet, this is not atypical of work in the field. Anything can be a reinforcer — giving praise, or hitting a child — the latter presumably representing attention which is interpreted as a reinforcer. In systematic desensitization the patient is asked to imagine a scene and to feel relaxed. Are they to be taken as definitions of a stimulus and a response? Do we in fact know whether the patient is imagining a scene? Do we know that the patient can make the scene (that is, the stimulus) appear and disappear on command from the therapist? It is questions like these that lead to the following criticism.

> . . . counterconditioning is no more objective, no more controlled, and no more scientific than classical psychoanalysis, hypnotherapy, or treatment with tranquilizers. The claim to scientific respectability rests on the misleading use of terms such as stimulus, response, and conditioning, which have become associated with some of the methods of science because of their place in experimental psychology. But this implied association rests on the use of the same words and not on the use of the same methods.
>
> BREGER AND McGAUGH, 1965, P. 340

Comments such as these do not come only from psychologists who are basically critical of the learning theory approach to personality. They also come from those who are basically supportive. Thus, for example, London (1972) views behavior modification as a technique rather than a theory-based scientific procedure: "When you eliminate the polemics and politics and gratuities, however, what remains of theory to define the field and to tell you what it is about? Not a whole lot" (p. 916). Finally, Lazarus (1977), a founder of behavior therapy, questions whether behavior therapy has outlived its usefulness since it cannot explain events that arise in the course of treatment.

The Effectiveness of Behavior Therapy

The questions raised concerning behavior theory also relate to behavior therapy. There are, in addition, questions concerning the effectiveness of behavior therapy. These questions may be phrased as follows: (1) To what extent is there, in behavior therapy, successful generalization from one situation to another and from one response to another? (2) To what extent are the results durable or stable over time? (3) Are the originally published success rates accurate and are behavioral techniques equally successful with all patients? (4) Where behavioral techniques are successful, do we understand the processes involved? Essentially, we are asking whether behavioral techniques induce desirable changes, whether these changes generalize and are maintained over time, and whether we can account for the successes and failures of the application of these techniques.

1   *To what extent is there successful generalization from one situation to another and from one response to another?* A distinguishing characteristic of behavior therapy is the focus on specific responses, often within the context of a specific environmental setting. Ideally, however, one hopes for therapeutic change beyond the specific situation or the specific response. In relation to the response, the effects of systematic desensitization may be limited to behavioral responses. That is, even though there may be no behavioral signs of the problem, the individual may still show physiological signs of anxiety and report fear. The results of operant conditioning also suggest some problems in this area. Lovaas has had significant success in treating autistic children with behavior therapy (Bucher and Lovaas, 1979; Lovaas, Koegel, Simmons, and Lang, 1973). Inappropriate behaviors were decreased during treatment and appropriate behaviors increased. In some cases the children even began to look more alert and happier. At the same time, in most cases, there were no generalized changes in behavior. Particularly noteworthy was the fact that many children had difficulty in using their newly acquired verbal response in a conversational, information-seeking manner. Lovaas himself notes as a major weakness in the treatment the failure to isolate a "pivotal" response which when altered would produce a profound "personality" change.

Similar kinds of problems arise in relation to generalization of effects from one environment to another. Bandura, for example, has suggested that in systematic desensitization there may be an inability to transfer therapeutic effects from symbolic to real-life stimuli: "It is not at all uncommon for clients to respond fearfully when confronted with intimidating situations after imaginal counterparts have been neutralized" (Bandura, 1972). Similar, and perhaps even more striking, problems have arisen in relation to operant conditioning. For example, reducing delusional speech and increasing rational speech in an interview situation may not generalize to other social situations (Liberman, Teigen, Patterson, and Baker, 1973). The generalization of behavior gains in token economy situations to other situations remains an open question (Kazdin and Bootzin, 1972).

Practitioners of behavior modification would suggest that the generalization of behavior changes depends on the continuity of reinforcements from one situation to another. Thus, in working with children, there often is a simultaneous effort to train parents in the use of reinforcement principles in the home setting. Although there are many reports of success with this procedure, there also are some reports of failures (Herbert, Pinkston, Hayden, Sajwaj, Pinkston, Cordua, and Jackson, 1973). Generalization of changes appears to remain a problem for behavior therapy and has led to the recent efforts to develop ways that treated individuals can reinforce themselves.

2 *To what extent are the results durable or stable over time?* The question of maintenance of therapeutic gains over time is related to that of generalization of results since, over time, an individual is generally exposed to a variety of environmental circumstances. Wolpe originally reported that his patients maintained their gains for a long time. However, some studies of the effects of systematic desensitization since then have suggested that in many patients the improvement is eventually lost (Eysenck and Beech, 1971).

As noted before,behavior therapists using an operant model are interested in the continuity of reinforcers over time. In his follow-up study of the treatment of autistic children, Lovaas found large individual differences in the extent to which children maintained their improvement. These differences appeared to depend upon the post treatment environment. When children were returned to a home environment where the parents had been trained to reinforce certain behaviors, the improvement was maintained. When children were sent to institutions, there was considerable relapse. His conclusion from this study is worthy of note: "In other words, generalization across environments is a process that can be manipulated, and it seems pointless to ask about permanence of behavior change unless the post-treatment environment is controlled, or somehow assessed. With a different model of psychopathology and health, postulating relatively permanent personality constructs not closely tied to environmental contingencies, as in psychodynamic theories, it seems more reasonable to expect global and permanent change" (Bucher and Lovaas, 1970, p. 55).

3 *Are the originally published success rates accurate and are behavioral techniques equally successful with all patients?* Often, the original publication of some therapeutic technique will report success with all treated patients. However, such a report usually contains inadequate data upon which to fully evaluate the technique. For example, in the original reports

by Wolpe, patients who left early in treatment were excluded from the analyses of the results. Further reports by other therapists may give support to the utility of a particular technique but similarly fail to meet critical assessment standards. With time, a number of careful studies may be completed which suggest more limited success and generally a more complex picture. At this point there remains considerable evidence in support of the effectiveness of various behavioral techniques. However, evaluative studies of behavioral techniques such as systematic desensitization, aversion therapy, and Stampfl's implosion therapy suggest that their success rates do not even begin to approach 100 percent (Eysenck and Beech, 1971; Feldman, 1966; Morganstern, 1973). Later reports of success rarely suggest the success rates originally reported.

Of considerable significance in evaluating the success of a therapeutic technique is the population involved. A particular technique that works with one population may not work with another. For example, it has been suggested that systematic desensitization is appropriate for introverted individuals but not for extroverts (Eysenck and Beech, 1971). Many psychologists have questioned the relevance of studies of the systematic desensitization of snake phobias to the treatment of serious clinical anxieties. Lazarus, an early follower of Wolpe, argues that few phobias are the result of a single traumatic experience and that most phobias require more than a simple systematic desensitization treatment. In arguing for the use of more than one technique, Lazarus has suggested that behavior therapy is not the only technique but rather an effective treatment approach when used with carefully selected cases by informed practitioners (Lazarus, 1971; Lazarus, 1972).

Given the frequency of initial reports of success in the history of therapy, it is not unwise to view these reports with some skepticism and to insist upon supportive data that can stand the test of scientific credibility. Also, given the complexity of human behavior and the vast variety of maladaptive behaviors, it seems reasonable to ask whether the technique is effective in the treatment of all behaviors or just in the treatment of some, and whether it is effective with all people or just effective with some.

4   *What are the effective therapeutic processes in behavior therapy?* It has been noted already that considerable research on the therapeutic processes at work in behavior therapy is now going on. It also has been noted that there is a question concerning the processes at work in systematic desensitization. At one point these therapeutic processes seemed to be easily understood within a traditional learning framework. Thus, most therapeutic gains could be accounted for in terms of extinction, counterconditioning, positive reinforcement, and modeling. What we now see is a recognition that some results cannot currently be explained and that a broader view of the therapeutic processes may be at work.

In recognition of the limitations of our current understanding, Lovaas has indicated that often he cannot understand the difficulty in getting a child to use speech in the conventional way. Furthermore, he has trouble understanding the significant gains in appearance and interpersonal relations that some autistic children make as a result of the reinforcement of speech responses. Both the former difficulty and the latter success remain puzzling. Perhaps we will indeed have to look to variables and processes that were not formerly considered. Krasner has suggested that it would be pure "operant jingoism" to claim credit for all behavioral successes and that the operant approach itself makes use of a variety of "behavior influence" techniques. Included under the rubric of behavior influence techniques are interpersonal variables, the therapist as a social reinforcer, and cognitive changes.

In sum, the processes at work in successful behavior therapy are complex and incompletely understood. In this regard, it is important to recognize that reports of therapeutic success are not supportive of a theory unless the technique is clearly derived from the theory. Furthermore, it must be demonstrated that the technique itself is the therapeutic agent. As we have learned, in most instances it is difficult to demonstrate that this is the case. The history of therapy is filled with modes of treatment that apparently effected genuine cures but which were based on superstitions, faith, and suggestion (Frank, 1961; London, 1964).

Moral and Ethical Issues

Before leaving behavior therapy, some consideration should be given to certain moral and ethical issues. These issues are relevant to any social influence program, and thus to any form of psychotherapy, but because of the behavioral emphasis on the control of behavior, they are particularly critical to behavior therapy. In Skinner's words, "the trick is not to free oneself from control but to improve control . . . It is a mistake to suppose that the whole issue is how to free man. The issue is how to improve the way in which he is controlled" (1972, p. 64). Unfortunately, there are incidents that have occurred that give cause for considerable concern about how behavioral control will be exercised.

In one incident, at a midwestern state hospital, physical restraints were reintroduced to make a token economy more effective. Patients were rewarded with tokens for desirable behavior and could then cash in their tokens in return for being released from the restraints. In another incident, this one taking place in a Vietnamese mental hospital, patients were given their choice between shock therapy three times a week or working for their living in the hospital. In another program, patients were given the choice of work or no food. Both programs were successful in getting the patients to work and were mistakenly presented as successful applications of operant conditioning.

Although these efforts already have been condemned by behavior modifiers, they point to the dangers of which we must be aware. The potential for behavior control, and legitimization of this control, suggested by behavior modification can give license to the efforts of individuals who understand neither the techniques involved nor the underlying social philosophy.

Summary Evaluation

In conclusion, it must be observed that the criticisms of the learning, behavioral approach to personality do not go unchallenged. To the charge of oversimplification, the behaviorists suggest that one must start somewhere and that it makes sense to start with simple events. These events can be understood through objective measurement and control. As understanding progresses, there is movement from the simple to the complex, but it is based on a solid foundation of knowledge. In the same way, the use of animals such as rats and pigeons is justified. The behavior of these animals is controlled more easily that that of humans, and we know that the basic principles of learning apply to both. It is true that by using these methods, certain processes of "thinking," "imagining," and "feeling" may be neglected. However, these realms of behavior can be understood only when they are studied as public rather than as private events and when they are interpreted in the light of a solid foundation of knowledge. Similarly, individuals can be understood in terms of the application of basic general laws of behavior and cannot be understood in isolation from these laws.

To questions concerning the effectiveness of behavior therapy, the argument is made that in most comparative studies behavior therapy is more significant than alternative therapies (for example, verbal psychotherapy). A recent review of the literature found no evidence that behavior therapy produces less general or substantial forms of change than other therapies (Kazdin and Wilson, 1978). Finally, those committed to a broadened approach to behavior therapy suggest that it need not be mechanistic, manipulative, or superficial (Goldfried and Davison, 1976).

The articles published in the professional journals indicate that the momentum at this time is with those who follow the learning and behavior modification approach to behavior. Disenchantment exists with the theoretical and applied failings of other approaches. The qualities of rigor, objectivity, and measurability of concepts have appeal for those in academia who have accepted the values of the scientist. Successes in applied efforts have buoyed hopes and created a sense of optimism about the future.

When taken together, the various learning theories are thought to be capable of accounting for a wide range of behavior in a reasonably economical way. It now remains to be determined whether these theories can be integrated into a single, consistent framework and, then, whether the valued scientific objectivity can be retained in the course of studying complex behavior.

MAJOR CONCEPTS AND SUMMARY

habit   approach—avoidance conflict
drives (primary & secondary)   behavior therapy
instrumental learning   systematic desensitization
higher mental processes   counterconditioning
imitation

There is no one learning theory of personality. Instead, there is a learning theory-behavioral approach to personality. Included here are proponents of different theories of learning who share certain assumptions. A major shared assumption is that nearly all behavior is learned. An understanding of personality is, for the most part, an understanding of learned behavior. A second shared assumption is that objectivity and rigor in the testing of clearly formulated hyoptheses are essential for the development of psychology as a science.

In this chapter we have focused on the S-R, instrumental learning approach of Hull and Dollard and Miller. In instrumental learning, habits are learned through the reinforcement of stimulus-response connections. Reinforcement consists of the reduction of drive stimuli, either of primary, innate drives, or of secondary, learned drives, such as anxiety. The emphasis in growth and development is on the development of higher mental processes and imitation. The S-R interpretation of psychopathology places major emphasis on the role of approach-avoidance conflicts and the role of anxiety drive stimuli. As with other learning approaches, the basic principles of learning are seen as adequate for an understanding of the development of abnormal behavior. Psychopathology is viewed in terms of learned maladaptive responses and adaptive responses that have not been learned adequately. In other words, a behavioral-psychological model is used rather than a medical-disease model.

In behavior therapy there is an attempt to apply experimentally established principles of learning to the treatment of problem behaviors. The major processes involved in behavioral interpretations of personality change are extinction, discrimination learning, counterconditioning, positive reinforcement of new behaviors, and imitation. In Wolpe's systematic desensitization treatment, anxiety responses are inhibited through the counterconditioning of competing relaxation responses. There is considerable evidence to support the effectiveness of systematic desensitization as a therapeutic technique, but there is also considerable question as to whether it is effective because of a counterconditioning process. A variety of studies suggest that cognitive and social influence variables may play a major role in the effectiveness of the procedure.

In the past, criticism of the learning approach to personality has focused on three major points: there is an oversimplification of behavior, important areas of behavioral functioning are neglected, and it is not as objective and rigorous as is claimed. In addition, the effectiveness of behavior therapy has been questioned and serious moral issues raised. While undoubtedly there is much validity to these criticisms, it is also true that recent research within the behavioral framework has shown an increasing recognition of the complexity of behavior and an interest in a broader range of variables. In particular, this relates to recognition of and research into cognitive variables. In addition, although we are not in a position to evaluate fully the results of behavior therapy, the approach has succeeded in challenging long-standing assumptions of other therapies (for example, psychoanalysis) and has resulted in an interest in the treatment of individuals formerly considered to be beyond assistance.

Although the ideology and enthusiasm of Skinnerian social engineers indeed give cause for concern, it is at least somewhat reassuring that followers of this orientation have themselves been outspoken in their criticism of unethical efforts at behavioral control.

A VIEW OF THE THEORISTS
Albert Bandura (1925-   )
Walter Mischel (1931-   )
VIEW OF THE PERSON
VIEW OF SCIENCE, THEORY, AND RESEARCH METHODS
SOCIAL LEARNING THEORY OF PERSONALITY
Process
• Observational Learning
• Self-regulation
Structure
Growth and Development
CLINICAL APPLICATIONS
Psychopathology
Change
A CASE EXAMPLE
CRITICAL EVALUATION
Strengths of the Theory
Limitations of the Theory
MAJOR CONCEPTS AND SUMMARY

11

SOCIAL LEARNING THEORY: BANDURA AND MISCHEL

Chapter Focus:

In this chapter we will consider a personality theory that shares many features with earlier learning approaches, but remains distinctive. Social learning theory focuses attention on the conditions that affect the acquisition, performance, and maintenance of behavior. We give particular attention to observational learning or modeling, in which people may acquire complex patterns of behavior even without being rewarded. We also examine cognitive processes as they affect learning, self-control, and the perception of self-efficacy or the perceived ability to cope with situations in the environment.

This conception of human functioning then neither casts people into the role of powerless objects controlled by environmental forces nor free agents who can become whatever they choose. Both people and their environments are reciprocal determinants of each other.

BANDURA, 1977a, p. vii

I would conceptualize observational learning as essentially a cognitive process, and our theories of learning are moving in a more cognitive direction.

BANDURA, 1976, p. 245

Behavior is generated by the person, not by a self, ego or other agent distinct from the individual. And "self-control" refers to the powers of the person to regulate or control his own actions, thus overcoming the power of "stimulus [situational] control."

MISCHEL, 1977, p. 50

In the social learning view, psychological changes, regardless of the method used to achieve them, derive from a common mechanism. . . . Psychological procedures, whatever their form, alter expectations of personal efficacy.

BANDURA, 1977a, p. 79

Social learning theory has for some time been presented as part of learning theory, but it now warrants separate consideration. In the academic community social learning theory is probably the most popular personality theory, and it is gaining increasing numbers of adherents in the clinical community as well. The theory has been most clearly represented in the works of two psychologists, Albert Bandura and Walter Mischel.

Social learning theory is distinct from the other theories we have studied in a number of ways. First, in contrast to most, if not all, of the other theories, it is questionable whether a specific social learning theory exists. Many would argue that social learning theory is a point of view based on some general principles rather than a fully developed theory. A theory has nevertheless been evolving and there has been a recent attempt by Bandura (1977) to systematize it. Second, as it has evolved, social learning theory has attempted to integrate and go beyond some of the earlier points of view. It has attempted to go beyond such divisions in the field as the relative importance of internal and external determinants of behavior and a behavioral "as opposed to" humanist view of the person. As will be seen, according to social learning theory there always is a process of interaction between the organism and its environment, a process Bandura calls **reciprocal determinism**

reciprocal determinism

Through the development of cognitive structures and mechanisms of self-control, the person influences the environment as well as being influenced by it. Finally, social learning theory is distinct from other theories in that it is currently advancing the most and receiving the most attention.

Given this state of evolution of theory and current popularity, how can it be differentiated further from the theories previously considered? As noted in Chapter 8, Mischel has been critical of traditional trait and psychoanalytic theory. His influential book *Personality and Assessment* (1968) took such views to task for their emphasis on internal dispositions that presumably lead to consistency in behavior across situations. Instead, Mischel presented a social learning view that emphasized the significant influence of varying contingencies of reinforcement in the environment. Thus, in contrast to trait and psychoanalytic positions, social learning theory places less emphasis on structure (dispositions) and greater emphasis on the organism's ability to respond to a changing environment.

Such a view might fit neatly within traditional learning theory (see Chapters 9 and 10). However, while social learning theory developed out of earlier learning points of view, its suggestion that learning occurs in the absence of rewards represented the beginnings of a major break with tradition. Whereas both Hullian and Skinnerian theories of learning emphasize reward, Bandura suggests that rewards are far more important in the *performance* of learned behaviors than in their acquisition. Indeed, Bandura's emphasis on learning in the absence of reinforcement continues to be a major point of contention between him and Skinnerians.

Finally, in its most recent forms social learning theory is distinctive in its emphasis on cognition within the framework of learning theory. Cognitive processes were emphasized by Kelly in his personal construct theory (Chapters 6 and 7), but he threw out many traditional concepts in psychology generally and in studies of learning in particular. In contrast, social learning theory emphasizes the role of cognitive operations within the person in the context of general principles of learning.

This chapter will consider a theory that is still evolving and growing in popularity and influence. It is different from traditional trait and psychoanalytic views in its emphasis on the variability of behavior in response to changing circumstances in the environment. It is different from traditional Hullian and Skinnerian learning theory in its emphasis on learning independent of reinforcement and in its emphasis on cognitive processes.

A VIEW OF THE THEORISTS

Albert Bandura (1925-   )

Little is known about the early life of Bandura other than that he grew up in northern Alberta, Canada. He went to college at the University of British Columbia. On graduation he chose to do graduate work in clinical psy-

ALBERT BANDURA

chology at the University of Iowa because it was known for the excellence of its research on learning processes. Even then Bandura was interested in the applications of learning theory to clinical phenomena. In a recent interview Bandura indicated that he "had a strong interest in conceptualizing clinical phenomena in ways that would make them amenable to experimental tests, with the view that as practitioners we have a responsibility for assessing the efficacy of a procedure, so that people are not subjected to treatments before we know their effects" (quoted in Evans, 1976, p. 243). At Iowa, he was influenced by Spence, a follower of Hull, and by the general emphasis on careful conceptual analysis and rigorous experimental investigation. During that time he was also influenced by the writings of Miller and Dollard.

After obtaining his Ph.D. at Iowa in 1952, Bandura went to Stanford and began his work on interactive processes in psychotherapy and on family patterns that lead to aggressiveness in children. The work on familial causes of aggression, with Richard Walters, his first graduate student, gave rise to the emphasis on the central role of modeling influences (learning through observation of others) in personality development. These findings and consequent laboratory investigations of modeling processes resulted in the books *Adolescent Aggression* (1959) and *Social Learning and Personality Development* (1963). Since then he has continued with research on aggression, modeling and observational learning, and the processes of behavior change. Bandura describes himself as conducting a multifaceted research program aimed at clarifying aspects of human capability that should be emphasized in a comprehensive theory of human behavoir. The emphasis on human capabilities is an important aspect of Bandura's recent thinking and research. It is related to his interest in processes of development and therapeutic change and is associated with what some perceive as a humanist emphasis in his work. Professor Bandura has received a number of distinguished scientific achievement awards and in 1974 was president of the American Psychological Association.

Walter Mischel (1930-   )

As with Bandura, there are only sketchy details concerning Mischel's early life and his roots in psychology. He was born in Vienna and lived his first nine years "in easy playing distance of Freud's house." He describes the possible influence of this period as follows:

When I began to read psychology Freud fascinated me most. As a student at City College (in New York, where my family settled after the Hitler-caused forced exodus from Europe in 1939), psychoanalysis seemed to provide a comprehensive view of man. But my excitement fizzled when I tried to apply those ideas as a social worker with "juvenile delinquents" in

WALTER MISCHEL

New York's Lower East Side: somehow trying to give those youngsters "insight" didn't help either them or me. The concepts did not fit what I saw, and I went looking for more useful ones.

MISCHEL, 1978, PERSONAL COMMUNICATION

The experience with "juvenile delinquents" is of particular interest for two reasons. First, it probably relates to Mischel's long-standing interest in the psychological mechanisms underlying delay of gratification and self-control. Second, there is a similarity to Bandura in that both did their early clinical work with aggressive youngsters.

Mischel did his graduate work at Ohio State University where he came under the influence of two significant figures: "George Kelly and Julian Rotter were my dual mentors and each has enduringly influenced my thinking" (Mischel, 1978, personal communication). The work of George Kelly has already been discussed. The thinking of Julian Rotter (1954) has only lately become popular in the field of personality, primarily because of his concept of internal-external locus of control (Chapter 15). However, Rotter's views were developed much earlier and had a number of distinguishing elements. First, Rotter emphasized learning theory in relation to important human social (interpersonal) phenomena; second, he emphasized the importance of situational factors as well as person factors in behavior. Rotter was critical of personality theories and measurement devices that ignored the contribution of situational factors to the variability in any person's behavior. Third, Rotter emphasized the importance of cognitive processes in learning as opposed to mechanical stimulus-response connections. In particular, he emphasized the importance of individual *expectancies* concerning reinforcements for various behaviors in particular situations. These concepts, together with those emphasized by Kelly, have increasingly played a major role in Mischel's thinking in particular and social learning theory in general. Mischel describes his work in relation to that of his dual mentors as follows: "I see my own work both with cognition and with social learning as clearly rooted in their contributions, a focus on the person both as construer and actor, interacting with the vicissitudes of the environment, and trying to make life coherent even in the face of all its inconsistencies" (Mischel, 1978, personal communication).

After completing his graduate work at Ohio State, Mischel spent a number of years at Harvard University and then joined Bandura at Stanford. His current work focuses on how people categorize events and on how they can and do overcome "stimulus control" through cognitive self-control. An example of the latter is his work on how people use thought to delay gratification more easily by refocusing their attention or by changing their interpretation of the situation altogether. In 1978 he received the Distinguished Scientist Award from the Clinical Psychology Division of the American Psychological Association.

VIEW OF THE PERSON

Both Bandura and Mischel recognize the relationship of a general view of the person to a theory of personality and have attempted to be explicit concerning this view. In a statement very much in tune with a point made throughout this book, Bandura notes that "views about human nature influence which aspects of psychological functioning are studied most thoroughly and which remain unexamined. Theoretical conceptions similarly determine the paradigms used to collect evidence which, in turn, shape the particular theory" (1977, p. vi). In other words, there is a back-and-forth or reciprocal relationship between a view of the person, a program of research, and a theory of personality.

Current social learning theory emphasizes a view of the person as active, using symbolic (cognitive) processes to represent events and communicate with others, and capable of choice and self-regulation. Social learning theory rejects the view that the person is either a passive victim of unconscious impulses and past history or a passive respondent to environmental events. Theories of personality that emphasize internal factors to the exclusion of environmental events are rejected because of their disregard for the individual's responsiveness to varying situations. At the same time, theories that emphasize external factors to the exclusion of internal factors also are rejected because of their failure to consider the role of cognitive functioning and self-regulation in behavior. "Theories that explain human behavior as solely the product of external rewards and punishments present a truncated image of people because they possess self-reactive capacities that enable them to exercise some control over their own feelings, thoughts, and actions" (Bandura, 1977, p. 129).

Rejecting both the view that people are driven by inner forces and that they are buffeted by environmental stimuli, social learning theory suggests that behavior can be explained in terms of a reciprocal interaction between personal and environmental determinants. People are influenced by environmental forces but they also choose how to behave. The person is both responsive to situations and actively constructs and influences situations. Through the use of thought and symbols people can go beyond immediate experience and anticipate the future. However, such cognitive processes themselves are largely determined by experience. Furthermore, plans for the future generally are, to some extent, influenced by expectations concerning rewards and punishments. In a view that recalls Kelly, social learning theory suggests that the person is both free and determined:

"Within the process of reciprocal determinism lies the opportunity for people to influence their destiny as well as the limits of self-direction" (Bandura, 1977, p. vii).

Basically, social learning theory sees the person, when functioning properly, as a well-tuned organism capable of adapting to changing conditions in the environment. The ongoing process of reciprocal determinism involves valuing certain environmental events (outcomes), discriminating among situations in terms of their potential to result in these valued outcomes, judging one's ability to cope, deciding which situations to enter into and how to behave in them, and using feedback information concerning the results of these decisions. The feedback information concerning behavioral outcomes is then used to form further discriminations, expectancies, and decisions. In a sense, the person is a problem-solving organism seeking to behave in ways that will maximize both rewards in the environment and internal rewards in the form of self-praise. Mischel describes the emerging image of the human being as follows:

This image is one of the human being as an active, aware problem-solver, capable of profiting from an enormous range of experiences and cognitive capacities, possessing great potential for good or ill, actively constructing his or her psychological world, and influencing the environment but also being influenced by it in lawful ways—even if the laws are difficult to discover and hard to generalize. . . . It is an image that has moved a long way from the instinctual drive-reduction models, the static global traits, and the automatic stimulus-response bonds of traditional personality theories. It is an image that highlights the shortcoming of all simplistic theories that view behavior as the exclusive result of any narrow set of determinants, whether these are habits, traits, drives, reinforcers, constructs, instincts, or genes and whether they are exclusively inside or outside the person. It will be exciting to watch this image change as new research and theorizing alter our understanding of what it is to be a human being.

MISCHEL, 1977, P. 253

This current view of the person suggests a shift from what earlier appeared to be a more passive view of the organism. While a social learning view of the person was not spelled out in earlier papers, there certainly was much more of an emphasis on how contingencies in the environment regulate, influence, guide, and direct behavior. The emphasis on cognitive control and self-regulation is a later development in social learning theory. One can only speculate why this should have occurred. Probably there were both scientific and personal reasons. In terms of the former, Bandura and Mischel recognized that the same situation could lead to very different behaviors in people. Furthermore, a variety of experiments were suggesting the importance of cognitive factors in learning. In terms of the latter, the Skinnerian view of an organism shaped by environmental events probably did not sit well with their own personal beliefs. Thus, the view of a reciprocal relationship between person and environment allowed for the integration of earlier work on the importance of reinforcement with later work on cognitive control and with personal beliefs and values.

VIEW OF SCIENCE, THEORY, AND RESEARCH METHODS

Both Bandura and Mischel are committed to the use of theory and empirical research. There is a strong commitment to concepts that are clear and based on systematic observations. Theories that emphasize motivational forces in the form of needs, drives, and impulses are criticized for being vague and inferred from the behavior they supposedly caused. In other words, too often it is said that a person has an aggressive impulse or trait because they behave aggressively and that they behave aggressively because of their instinct or motive for aggression.

Whereas extreme behaviorism rejects the study of cognitive processes because of a distrust for introspective data, Bandura and Mischel feel that such inner processes must be studied and that the use of some types of self-report is both legitimate and desirable. They suggest that self-reports which are general, based on long-term recall, and involve anxiety that can lead to defensiveness are *not* likely sources of reliable information. However, self-reports that are specific, given as events occur and under conditions that do not arouse evaluative apprehensions, can be valuable aids in understanding cognitive processes. In defense of the use of verbal self-reports, Bandura notes that "vast numbers of people are outfitted by ophthalmologists with suitable corrective eyeglasses on the basis of verbalized discriminations of printed and pictorial stimuli. They can be easily outfitted with defective eyeglasses by reporting that the blurred stimuli are the clearer ones. However, this would hardly constitute justification for renouncing the optometric enterprise. Rather than decrying the limitations of verbal probes of thought, we should be improving the tools for measuring it" (Bandura, 1978, p. 15).

In sum, social learning is concerned with both a broad variety of aspects of human behavior and with scientific rigor. There is a concern both with conceptual clarity and with theoretical formulation, with important inner processes and with systematic observations. In all likelihood it is this blend of concern with important human events and scientific respectability that most accounts for the theory's current popularity.

SOCIAL LEARNING THEORY OF PERSONALITY

The stage has been set for considering the details of the social learning theory of personality. In tune with the learning theories presented earlier, there is an emphasis on responses and learning processes and much less emphasis on structures or organization. For this reason we will begin with a consideration of processes and then briefly move to the question of personality structure.

Process

Social learning theory emphasizes two processes distinct from other learning theories of personality—observational learning and self-regulation. Observational learning involves the ability to learn complex behaviors by watching others. "Because people can learn from example what to do, at least in approximate form, before performing any behavior, they are spared needless errors" (Bandura, 1977, p. 22). Self-regulation involves the ability of individuals to exercise influence over their own behavior rather than reacting mechanically to external influences. Both observational learning and self-regulation involve considerable use of thought (cognitive) processes. Both are influenced by rewards and punishments, but they are not determined by them.

Observational Learning

observational learning

modeling

The theory of **observational learning** suggests that people can learn merely be observing the behaviors of others. The person being observed is called a model. There is evidence to suggest that an individual can learn behaviors by observing a model perform these behaviors. Thus, for example, the child may learn language by observing parents and other people speaking, a process called **modeling**. The types of behaviors under consideration are often included under the terms *imitation* and *identification*. However, imitation has the very narrow connotation of response mimicry and, at the other extreme, identification implies an incorporation of entire patterns of behavior. Modeling involves something broader than imitation but less diffuse than identification. In addition, these terms are rejected because they have been associated with stimulus-response reinforcement theories and with psychoanalytic theory. These theories are considered inadequate in accounting for the observed data.

The theories of Hull and Skinner are viewed as inadequate in the following ways: (1) They do not account for the appearance of new, or novel, behaviors. (2) In particular, they do not account for the appearance of new, large segments of behavior in their entirety; that is, they do not account for the fact that, with a model, full patterns of behavior can be acquired that would be difficult to account for in terms of a slow, gradual conditioning process. (3) The acquisition of these response patterns appears to occur independent of reinforcement variables. (4) The first appearance of the behaviors learned may not occur for days, weeks, or months after the model has been observed. The importance of the process of observational learning is well described by Bandura:

> The provision of social models is also an indispensable means of transmitting and modifying behavior in situations where errors are likely to produce costly or fatal consequences. Indeed, if social learning proceeded exclusively on the basis of rewarding and punishing consequences, most people would never survive the socialization process. . . . In fact, it would be difficult to imagine a socialization process in which language, mores, vocational and avocational patterns, the familial customs of a culture, and its educational, social, and political practices were shaped in each new member by selective reinforcement without the response guidance of models who exhibit the accumulated cultural repertoires in their own behavior.
>
> BANDURA, 1969, P. 213

Observational learning, then, accounts for the learning of new, complex patterns of behavior independent of reinforcements.

acquisition
performance

An important part of the theory of modeling is the distinction made between **acquisition** and **performance**. The early research suggested that children who observed a model rewarded for aggressive behavior would reproduce these behaviors, and those who observed the model punished would not. Since learning is expressed in performance, this might suggest that reinforcements to the model are critical for the learning process. However, many of the children who did not reproduce the model's aggressive behavior in the test situation were able to describe it with considerable accuracy. This led to an experiment in which children observed a model express aggressive behavior with either rewarding consequences, punishing consequences, or no consequences. Although in the initial test situation, the children who observed the punished model performed fewer imitative acts than the children observing other models, this difference could be wiped out by offering the children attractive incentives for reproducing the model's behavior (Bandura, Ross, and Ross, 1963) (see Box 11.1). In other words, the consequences to the model for the aggressive acts had an effect on the children's performance of these acts but not on the learning of the aggressive behaviors.

BOX 11.1 **Observational Learning:
Acquisition Versus Performance**

HYPOTHESIS   Reinforcements administered to a model influence the performance but not the acquisition of matching (imitative) responses.

SUBJECTS   33 boys and 33 girls of nursery school age. 2 adult males served as models.

METHOD   Randomly divide the children up into three groups of 22 subjects each. Bring all children into a room and let them watch a film on a television set. The film begins with a scene in which a model walks up to an adult-size plastic Bobo doll and orders the doll to clear the way. When the doll does not comply, the model exhibits four novel aggressive responses each accompanied by a distinct verbalization. For example, the model sits on the doll, punches it in the nose, says "Pow, right in the nose, boom, boom," and then hits it on the head with a mallet. Make the closing scene in the film different for the children in the three groups.

For children in a Model-Rewarded Condition, have a final scene in which a second adult appears with candy and soft drinks and gives the model considerable praise for his aggressive behavior. For children in a Model-Punished Condition, have a final scene in which a second adult appears, shakes his finger menacingly, criticizes the model for his aggressive behavior, and finally hits the model while reminding him of his aggressive behavior. For children in a No Consequences Condition, have the film end after the model is finished being aggressive to the doll.

After the children have watched the film, escort them to a room in which there is a Bobo doll and other toys. Leave the child free to play in the room alone for 10 minutes while observing the child's behavior through a one-way mirror. Record the child's behavior in terms of predetermined imitative response categories. Use the number of different physical and verbal imitative responses emitted spontaneously by the children as a measure of their performance.

After measuring their performance, tell the children in all three groups that they will receive treats (positive incentive) for reproducing the physical and verbal responses that they observed in the film. The number of different physical and verbal imitative responses reproduced by a child serves as a measure of learning.

RESULTS   The figure below shows the average number of different matching responses reproduced by children in each of the three treatment conditions during the no-incentive and the positive-incentive phases of the experiment. The analysis of these data reveals the following:

1 When the model was rewarded there was a significant increase in the number of matching responses that the children spontaneously reproduced.

BOX 11.1 **Observational Learning:
Acquisition Versus Performance** *continued*

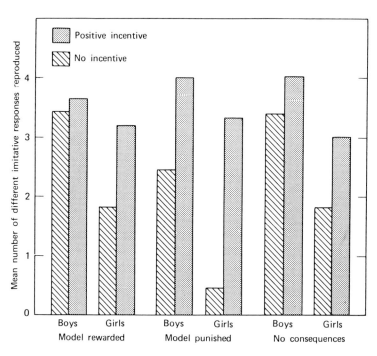

Figure 11.1 Mean number of different imitative responses reproduced by children as a function of response consequences to the model and positive incentives.

2 Boys performed more imitative responses than girls. Girls were more influenced by whether or not the model was rewarded.

3 The introduction of positive incentives completely wiped out the previously observed performance differences. Under the positive-incentive conditions there was evidence of an equivalent amount of learning for children in the three groups.

CONCLUSION   Reinforcements administered to a model influence the performance but not the acquisition of matching (imitative) responses.

SOURCE   A. Bandura, Influence of models' reinforcement contingencies on the acquisition of imitative responses. *Journal of Personality and Social Psychology*, 1965, 1, 589-595.

A number of other studies have since demonstrated that the observation of consequences to a model affects performance but not acquisition. The difference between acquisition and performance suggests, however, that in some way the children were being affected by what happened to the model; that is, either on a cognitive basis or on an emotional basis, or both, the children were responding to the consequences to the model. The suggestion here is that the children learned certain emotional responses by sympathizing with the model; that is, vicariously by observing the model. Not only can behavior be learned through observation, but emotional reactions (fear responses) can also be conditioned on a vicarious basis. The effects of **vicarious conditioning** were demonstrated in an experiment by Berger (1962) in which subjects who observed a model being shocked after the signal of a buzzer developed, vicariously, conditioned emotional reactions to the buzzer. The process of vicarious conditioning was demonstrated further in a study by Bandura and Rosenthal (1966). Here again it was found that emotional reactions would be conditioned to a previously neutral stimulus if the subjects observed a model who appeared to be shocked after the appearance of the stimulus.

vicarious conditioning

The discussion above has indicated that behavioral responses and emotional reactions can be acquired through the process of observational learning. In addition to specific responses, rules or general plans for action can be learned through observation. For example, by observing models people may acquire rules concerning language and grammar as well as standards for evaluating their own behavior and that of others. In other words, modeling involves the acquisition of abstract principles as well as the acquisition of discrete responses.

Although at first glance observational learning may appear a simple process, in reality it is not. Not all observers appear to acquire the model's behavior patterns. Apparently this has something to do with the characteristics of the model (for example, prestige) and characteristics of the observer (for example, dependence on others). The current interpretation of the process of observational learning is that it is governed by four major subsystems (Bandura, 1971a; Bandura, 1971b). The first subsystem involves **attention processes**. Here the individual attends to, recognizes, and differentiates among distinctive features of the model's responses. Second, there are **retention processes**. For the individual to be able to reproduce the model's behavior without the continued presence of external modeling cues, the original observational inputs must be retained in some symbolic form. In other words, the observer sees the model perform some behaviors and these modeling stimuli become coded into images. Short-lived perceptual phenomena thereby result in relatively enduring, retrievable images of modeled sequences of behavior. These visual images also may be represented in verbal forms for long-term retention. What is important

attention processes

retention processes

to recognize is that according to the theory the individual is actively thinking about and expanding on external stimuli. "In social learning theory observers function as active agents who transform, classify, and organize modeling stimuli into easily remembered schemes rather than as quiescent cameras or tape recorders that simply store isomorphic representations of modeled events" (Bandura, 1971a, p. 20). Retention processes are followed by **morotic reproduction processes** in which the individual uses the symbolic representations of modeled patterns to guide his actions. Finally, there are **reinforcement and motivational processes**. In order for learning to be used there must be positive incentives. Reinforcement is not essential for the acquisition of behavior but it is for the overt performance of learned responses. For observational learning and performance to occur, then, a person must attend to a model's behavior, register the relevant stimuli and transform them into appropriate representational forms, and then be sufficiently motivated to retrieve the relevant images and verbal symbols so as to transform them into overt behavior.

Performance of observed behaviors may, initially, only roughly approximate these behaviors. Skills are developed as the person progressively matches overt behavior against the conception of the desired behavior. It is the symbol or generalized conception that guides corrective adjustments in the process of continuous skill refinement.

Self-regulation

Banduaira distinguishes between the acquisition of responses and the maintenance, regulation, or performance of responses. Learning, response acquisition, occurs through observation and through the positive and negative effects that actions produce (response consequences). Among the responses learned are **standards** for expecting reinforcement from others and standards for reinforcing oneself. We learn to set appropriate goals for ourselves and to reward ourselves with self-praise or punish ourselves with self-criticism by observing models engaged in such behavior and by being reinforced directly for such behavior. If responses are thus acquired through observation and direct reinforcement, how are they maintained or regulated? According to Bandura, "Behavior is, in fact, extensively regulated by its consequences. Responses that result in unrewarding or punishing effects tend to be discarded, whereas those that produce rewarding outcomes are retained. Human behavior, therefore, cannot be fully understood without considering the regulatory influence of response consequences" (1977, p. 96).

That statement would appear to put social learning theory in agreement with other reinforcement theories as far as performance is

morotic reproduction processes

reinforcement and motivational processes

standards

concerned—reinforcement contingencies determine whether behavior appears. However, this is not the case. First, social learning theory does not view reinforcers as establishing stimulus-response connections. Rather, what is being established are certain expectations concerning the results of various actions and the development of general rules of action. Rather than an automatic, mechanical connection between behavior and reinforcement there is a complex cognitive process. Rather than being maintained by its immediate consequences, behavior is maintained by **expectancies** or anticipated consequences. In addition, rather than behavior being regulated exclusively by external reinforcers there is the process of **self-reinforcement** through which individuals reward themselves for attaining standards they set for themselves. These performance standards serve as motivators for behavior. It is the anticipation of satisfactions for desired accomplishments and dissatisfactions with insufficient accomplishments that provides the incentive for our efforts. Performance standards and anticipated consequences thus explain goal-directed behavior.

expectancies

self-reinforcement

The emphasis on the development of standards for self-reinforcement and on cognitive processes are of critical importance for social learning theory. Through them the emphasis is shifted from a purely external, environmental locus of control to an emphasis on both internal and external factors. In other words, it is true that behavior is affected by its consequences. However, since the consequences result in expectancies in the person and since many consequences or reinforcements are self-generated (self-reward or self-punishment), one cannot say that behavior is maintained by the environment alone. People experience consequences directly, they experience consequences vicariously through the observation of others, and they experience consequences that they create for themselves. All three kinds of consequences affect behavior. The person integrates information from these sources over a period of time and thereby is led to certain general conclusions and rules of action. Thus, behavior is not maintained by the person or by the situation but by the back-and-forth reciprocal relationship between the two: "To the oft-repeated dictum, 'change contingencies and you change behavior,' should be added the reciprocal side, 'change behavior and you change the contingencies' " (1977, p. 203). Through the development of such cognitive mechanisms people not only are able to exercise some control over their lives but also are able to establish plans or goals for the future. In other words, people can change the environmental contingencies that eventually will affect their behavior. The capacities to anticipate the future, to set standards, and to experience self-satisfaction and self-criticism are critical in permitting us to engage in endeavors over long periods of times. Human behavior is regulated by cognitive processes that integrate information coming from external and self-generated consequences. Expectancies of reward from external and internal sources serve as incentives and guides for action.

Structure

goals
plans

Personality structures, to the extent that social learning theory emphasizes them, can be seen as based on the cognitive and self-regulatory processes explained above. Two concepts which are most recent to social learning theory should be noted here. First is the concept of **goals** or **plans**. This concept accounts for behavior that is maintained for extended periods of time in the absence of (sometimes in spite of) external consequences (Mischel, 1973). The concept of goals or plans also suggests an organization to personality processes that would not otherwise be present. In other words, our goals or plans guide us in establishing priorities among rewards and in selecting among actions that might otherwise seem of equal value. Goals-plans enable us to go beyond momentary influences and to organize our behavior over extended periods of time.

self

The second concept worthy of note is that of the **self**. The self is not a structure per se but a structural concept used to explain cognitive processes such as self-conceptions, self-praise, self-criticism, and self-control (Bandura, 1977; Mischel, 1977). People's self-conceptions and self-regulatory mechanisms are critical for understanding what goes on between environmental inputs and behavior. As the organism develops it increasingly uses the processes of self-control and self-regulation to direct behavior. However, it should be clear that this concept of self is not identical to other concepts of the self. For example, the social learning concept of self does not suggest "an extra causal agent that dwells in the person and somehow generates or causes behavior in ways that are separable from the organism in which 'it' resides" (Mischel, 1977, pp. 4950). The social learning concept of self refers to processes that are part of the person's psychological functioning. In a sense, the person does not have a structure called "the self," but rather self-processes that are part of the person. In addition, earlier concepts of the self are criticized for being too global. Rather than having a self-concept, social learning theory suggests that a person has self-conceptions and self-control processes which may vary from time to time and from situation to situation.

It can be seen that the emphasis on cognitive processes and the interplay between external and internal sources of influence is critical to the understanding of social learning theory. It is these processes which increasingly have been emphasized by social learning theory and increasingly have set it apart from other theories of learning.

Growth and Development

cognitive competencies

The social learning theory of growth and development follows from the principles already established. A behavioral repertoire and skills in processing information, or **cognitive competencies**, are developed through observational learning and direct experience. In addition, the development of expectancies, plans, and self-regulatory functions are important. These developing competencies are greatly influenced by experience, but biological factors do enter in. Bandura describes the interplay between experiential and biological factors as follows:

> Human competencies are not fashioned solely through experience. Biological factors, of course, set constraints on behavioral development, and evolved biological systems predispose organisms to perceive and to learn critical features of their immediate environment. . . . The specific forms that behavior takes, the frequency with which it is expressed, and the situations in which it is displayed are largely determined by social learning factors. Because of the limited inborn programming of action patterns, human nature is characterized as a vast potentiality that can be fashioned by direct and vicarious experiences into a variety of forms within biological limits.
>
> BANDURA, 1979 (IN PRESS)

While social learning theory recognizes the importance of biological factors, it does not emphasize maturational factors in the way that is done by stage theorists such as Piaget or Freud. Stage theorists assume that a structure emerges in the course of maturation and that the acquisition of cognitive skills and rules at one stage is dependent upon the person having passed through previous stages. Social learning theory emphasizes social influence variables and suggests that individuals need not learn various skills in a fixed, sequential fashion. Furthermore, the suggestion is made that the person's cognitive functioning is not uniform at a particular level but may vary from issue to issue and from situation to situation (Rosenthal and Zimmerman, 1978). Bandura suggests that a major problem with stage theories is that it is hard to find people who fit them well. Most people exhibit a mixture of thought patterns that span several "stages." Rather than viewing people in terms of stages or categories, it is suggested that we view them in terms of the individuality of their thought and action.

Finally, the suggestion is made that stage doctrines underestimate human capabilities and accept as unchangeable certain limitations which otherwise might be modified. In contrast, social learning theory suggests that earnest teaching efforts may eradicate deficiencies formerly attributed to shortcomings in children: "Greater progress can be achieved in identifying the developmental determinants of complex abilities, by analyzing the prior competencies needed to master them, than by categorizing people into ill-fitting types" (Bandura, 1977, p. 47).

The social learning theory view of growth and development can be illustrated further by consideration of three areas: aggression, moral judgments, and delay of gratification. In terms of the development of aggressive behavior, a distinction is made among the acquisition of aggressive responses, the events that instigate these behaviors, and the processes that regulate and maintain aggression (Bandura, 1977). In other words, social learning theory seeks to explain how aggressive patterns are developed, what provokes people to behave aggressively, and what sustains such actions once they have begun.

In general, aggression is learned through observation of aggressive models and learning by direct experience. Aggressive styles of behavior are learned from observation of family models ("Familial violence breeds violent styles of conduct."), from observation of peer behavior ("The highest incidence of aggression is found in communities in which aggressive models abound."), and from observation of models through mass media such as television ("Both children and adults today have unlimited opportunities to learn the whole gamut of violent conduct from televised modeling within the comfort of their homes").

In terms of the activation of aggression, social learning theory emphasizes how aggressive behaviors can be provoked by painful stimulation, by expectations of reward for such behavior, or by both. What is emphasized is that when a person is aroused by painful or aversive events it may or may not lead to an aggressive response. Whether or not the person responds aggressively depends both on the interpretation of the conditions of arousal and the expectations of consequences for aggressive behavior. Such a view is distinct from an instinct view, which focuses on an automatic buildup of aggressive energy, and from other learning theories which view aggressive behavior as a response to frustration (Figure 11.2). According to social learning theory, frustration may or may not lead to aggression, and aggression can occur in the absence of frustration. Thus, whether or not frustration leads to aggression depends on how the person interprets the arousal, the alternative modes available for response, and the expectations of consequences for these various responses given the particular situation.

Finally, aggressive behavior is sustained or ended depending on its consequences. As with other behaviors, aggressive behavior is regulated by its consequences, which can come from three sources—**direct external consequences**, **vicarious experiencing of consequences to others**, and

direct external consequences

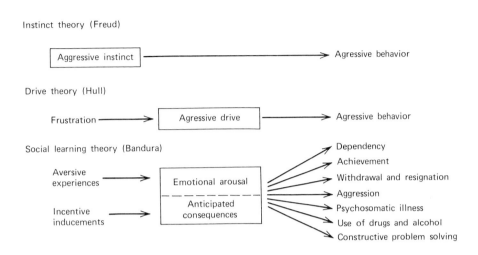

Figure 11.2   Comparison of Social Learning Theory of Aggression with Instinct and Drive Theories of Aggression.

vicarious experiencing of consequences to others

self-produced consequences

discrimination

self-produced consequences. The first two are social consequences while the third are personal consequences. Aggressive behavior may be stopped through threats of external punishment or through expectations of self-condemnation, otherwise known as control through fear and guilt, respectively. Guilt involves the learning of ethical and moral standards of behavior. But these standards may be dropped or used in a way to justify aggressive behavior. Thus, through such processes a "reprehensible," aggressive act can be considered "honorable": "Over the years much destructive and reprehensible conduct has been perpetrated by decent, moral people in the name of religious principles and righteous ideologies. Acting on moral or ideological imperative reflects not an unconscious defense mechanism, but a conscious offense mechanism" (Bandura, 1977, p. 43).

The observation of models and the development of standards and self-control mechanisms are important not only in aggression but in moral judgments and in toleration of delays in gratification as well. Social learning theory views moral judgments as complex, multidetermined social decisions (Rosenthal and Zimmerman, 1978). General rules are formed from a wide range of experience. At the same time, considerable **discrimination** may be involved in invoking different moral judgments in different circumstances. Since people vary their judgments depending on circumstances, it is hard to fit them into moral judgment types. And, because many more factors begin to be considered in moral judgments and greater discrimination is used in the application of various moral criteria to specific situations, moral judgment processes do become more complex with age. In addition, as children mature there is a shift from external to internal control. Initially parents use punishment and the threat of punishment to discourage certain behaviors. In successful socialization, however, there is a "gradual substitution of symbolic and internal controls for external sanctions and demands. After moral standards of conduct are established by instruction and modeling, self-evaluative consequences serve as deterrents to transgressive acts" (Bandura, 1977, p. 43). Obviously, both the development of more complex rules of moral judgment and the increased use of internal controls depend on the development of increasingly complex cognitive skills and abilities.

Considerable research has been done on the effects of models in the acquisition of moral standards and rules for moral judgments. For example, it has been demonstrated that children can be influenced in the kinds of judgments they make by exposure to different models. Thus, children who judge behavior in terms of the intent of the act (whether harm or injury was intended), and who are exposed to models judging behavior in terms of consequences (whether harm or injury actually occurred), come to modify their behavior toward making the latter kinds of moral judgment. The opposite kind of shift in moral judgment is made by children who judge behavior in terms of consequences and then are exposed to models who judge behavior in terms of intentions (Bandura and McDonald, 1963).

delays in gratification

Research also has demonstrated the importance of modeling and observational learning in the development of performance standards for success and reward which may then serve as the basis for **delays in gratification**. Children exposed to models setting high standards of performance for self-reward tend to limit their own self-rewards to exceptional performance to a greater degree than do children who have been exposed to models setting lower standards or to no models at all (Bandura and Kupers, 1964). Children will model standards even if they result in self-denial of available rewards (Bandura, Grusec, and Menlove, 1967) and will also impose learned standards on other children (Mischel and Liebert, 1966). Children can be made to tolerate greater delays in receiving gratification if they are exposed to models exhibiting such delay behavior. Furthermore, these effects of exposure to a model may be maintained well beyond the time of the original test situation (Bandura and Mischel, 1965) (Box 11.2).

BOX 11.2 **Modeling and Delay of Gratification**

HYPOTHESIS   Modeling procedures can be used to alter children's delay-of-reward behavior. This effect will be more evident with live models than with symbolic models.

SUBJECTS   60 boys and 60 girls from the fourth and fifth grades of school.

METHOD   Take approximately 250 children and give them a series of 14 paired rewards. In each pair ask the child to select either a small reward that can be obtained immediately or a more valued item that they must wait for from 1 to 14 weeks. For example, the child must choose between $.25 today and $.35 in 1 week. For each child, compute a delay of gratification score based on the number of items for which the child preferred an immediate reward and the number for which a larger delayed reward was preferred. From the total pool of subjects, select those falling in the extreme top and bottom 25 percent of the delay-score distribution, computed separately for boys and girls. The *low-delay* group consists of the 30 boys and 30 girls who displayed a marked preference for immediate reward, and the *high-delay* group consists of the 30 boys and 30 girls who displayed a marked preference for the larger delayed rewards.

Randomly assign the children to one of three treatment conditions with 10 boys and 10 girls in each. In the *live-model* condition, have each child individually observe a testing situation in which an adult model is asked by the experimenter to choose between an immediate reward and a more valued object at a later date. With high-delay children, have the model consistently select the immediately available rewards, frequently comment on the benefits (monetary) of immediate reward, and occasionally express the virtues of immediate gratification. With low-delay children, have the model select the delayed rewards, comment on the benefits of delay, and express the (moral) virtues of postponement of gratification.

In the *symbolic-model condition*, describe to each child the choices faced by the adult model and have the child read the verbal accounts of the model's behaviors. Match the verbal accounts to be read with the opposite of the child's patterns of responding, so that low-delay children read accounts of high-delay models and vice versa.

BOX 11.2   **Modeling and Delay of Gratification** *continued*

In the *no-model-present* condition, just show the children the choices that were given the adults. This controls for the effects of mere exposure to a set of reinforcers.

After a child is exposed to one of these three procedures, give a new set of 14 paired items involving a choice between an immediate reward and a more valuable delayed reward. To test for the stability of any altered delay patterns, readminister the initial set of items 4 to 5 weeks after the experimental treatments.

RESULTS   Analysis of the responses indicates the following:

1   High-delay children in all three conditions significantly altered their delay-of-reward behavior in favor of immediate gratification and maintained the response changes over a period of time. (See figure below.)

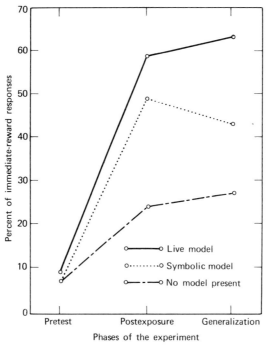

Figure 11.3   Mean percentage of immediate-reward responses by high-delay children on each of three test periods for each of three experimental conditions.

2 High-delay children who had been exposed to live or symbolic models differed substantially in their postexposure delay behavior from the no-model controls. The live condition produced the greatest effect, and this condition produced the most stable effect over time.

3 The data for low-delay children indicate that both forms of modeling produced highly significant temporary and long-term increases in self-imposed delay of reward. These children, however, were not differentially affected by the live as compared to the symbolic model.

CONCLUSION   Both live and symbolic models can produce substantial modifications in children's delay-of-reward behavior.

SOURCE   A. Bandura and W. Mischel, Modification of self-imposed delay of reward through exposure to live and symbolic models. *Journal of Personality and Social Psychology*, 1965, 2, 698-705.

As was mentioned previously, the performance of observed behaviors clearly is influenced by the observed consequences to the model. For example, children who watch a film in which a child is not punished for playing with toys that were prohibited by the mother are more likely to play with prohibited toys than are children who see no film or see a film in which the child is punished (Walters and Parke, 1964). The old saying "Monkey see, monkey do" is not completely true. It would be more appropriate to say "Monkey sees rewarded or not punished, monkey does." After all, the monkey is no fool.

cognitive and behavioral competencies

The ability to delay gratification involves the development of **cognitive and behavioral competencies**. Relevant behaviors are acquired through the observation of others and through direct experience. The ability to delay gratification is determined by the outcomes expected, as influenced by past direct personal experience, observation of consequences to models such as parents and peers, and self-reactions. Delay decisions are influenced by context and circumstances. Thus, people who exhibit control in some circumstances may act impulsively in others. Gratification may not be delayed because the person lacks the necessary skills for delay or because the rewards expected for delay do not outweigh those expected for nondelay. The discriminations people make among situations and the variability found in their behavior are such as to reject stage theories as well as trait and psychoanalytic theories of conscience or superego: "Rather than acquiring a homogeneous conscience that determines uniformly all aspects of their self-control, people develop subtler discriminations that depend on many moderating variables and involve complex interactions" (Mischel, 1977, p. 39).

CLINICAL APPLICATIONS

Psychopathology

To a certain extent the social learning view of psychopathology is in accord with the view presented in Chapter 10. For example, the earlier views and social learning theory share these points of emphasis: (1) Rejection of the disease model in favor of a model emphasizing the learning of maladaptive behaviors. (2) An emphasis on the present as opposed to the past: "Instead of asking 'why did he become this kind of person?,' behavioral approaches ask 'what is *now* causing him to behave as he does?' " (Mischel, 1976, p. 252). (3) An emphasis on overt behavior rather than underlying dynamics. (4) An emphasis on therapy as the learning of new patterns of thinking and behaving rather than therapy as cure to some underlying cause. What differentiates social learning theory from the Hullian and Skinnerian views is the emphasis on cognitive variables, particularly as they enter into self-evaluative processes.

According to social learning theory, maladaptive behavior is the result of dysfunctional learning. As with all learning, maladaptive responses can be learned as a result of direct experience or as the result of exposure to inadequate or "sick" models. Thus, Bandura (1968) suggests that the degree to which parents themselves model forms of aberrant behavior is often a significant causal factor in the development of psychopathology. Again, there is no need to look for traumatic incidents in the early history of the individual or for the underlying conflicts. Nor is there necessarily the need to find a history of reinforcement for the initial acquisition of the pathological behavior. On the other hand, once the behaviors have been learned through observational learning, it is quite likely that they have become manifest and that they have been maintained because of direct and vicarious reinforcement.

dysfunctional expectancies and self-conceptions

While the learning of specific overt behaviors is important in psychopathology, increasingly social learning theory has come to emphasize the role of **dysfunctional expectancies** and **self-conceptions**. People may erroneously expect painful events to follow some events or pain to be associated with specific situations. They then may act so as to avoid certain situations or in a way that creates the very situation they were trying to avoid. An example would be the person who fears that closeness will bring pain and then acts in a hostile way, resulting in rejection by others and presumed confirmation of the expectancy that closeness leads to disappointment and rejection. Cognitive processes not only enter into such dysfunctional expectancies but also into **dysfunctional self-evaluations**. One example would be the person who fails to develop standards for self-reward and thus experiences boredom or almost complete dependence on

dysfunctional self-evaluations

momentary, external pleasures. Even more common are the problems associated with the development of overly severe standards. Such developments lead to excessive self-punishment and depression: "In more extreme forms, harsh standards for self-evaluation give rise to depressive reactions, chronic discouragement, feelings of worthlessness, and lack of purposefulness. Excessive self-disparagement, in fact, is one of the defining characteristics of depression" (Bandura, 1977, p. 141).

The social learning view of psychopathology may be contrasted with the psychoanalytic and other views of anxiety and defense. According to Bandura, the social learning view differs on two counts. First, there is a different view of anxiety. In social learning theory anxiety results from **perceived inefficacy** in coping with potentially aversive events rather than from the threat of unconscious impulses. Second, anxiety is not seen as leading to **defensive** (avoidance) **behaviors**. Rather, anxiety *and* defensive, avoidance behavior both are seen as resulting from expectancies of injury. It is this expectation and the perceived inability to cope that leads to both anxiety and defensive behaviors.

perceived inefficacy

defensive behaviors

Defensive behaviors, as responses to threat or the signal of the potential for a painful outcome, are difficult to unlearn because they remove the person from the circumstances. This is a phenomenon that in the past has been called the "neurotic paradox" and which Bandura describes as the problem of "subjective confirmation" of the utility of defensive behavior: " . . . avoidance prevents the organism from learning that the real circumstances have changed. The failure of anticipated hazards to materialize reinforces the expectation that the defensive maneuvers forestalled them. This process of subjective confirmation is captured in the apocryphal case of a compulsive who, when asked by his therapist why he snapped his fingers ritualistically, replied that it kept ferocious lions away. When informed that obviously there were no lions in the vicinity to ward off, the compulsive replied 'See, it works!' " (Bandura, 1977, p. 62).

The social learning theory of psychopathology emphasizes the acquisition of maladaptive, dysfunctional behaviors and expectancies as the result of direct experience and observational learning. Such behaviors and expectancies are then maintained by their consequences, either external or internal. Particularly important is the role of learned expectancies of harm or injury and the sense of inefficacy or inability to cope with a perceived threat. Such expectancies and self-evaluations lead to defensive behaviors that are difficult to unlearn because their value is subjectively confirmed when harm does not occur. The social learning theory view of therapy consequently emphasizes the importance of changes in the sense of inefficacy and in the exposure to situations previously feared and avoided. Throughout, the emphasis is on specific learned expectancies and behaviors rather than on "underlying dynamics" or generalized defensive styles.

Change

Therapeutic work within the social learning framework is relatively recent, though it has become an important area of theory and research. Bandura's efforts increasingly have been directed toward developing methods of therapeutic change and toward working out a unifying theory of behavioral change (Bandura, 1976; 1977). In many ways the emphasis given to developments in this area is quite remarkable. Indeed, Bandura goes so far as to suggest that "the worth of a theory is ultimately judged by the power of the change procedures it produces" (1976, p. 253). While emphasizing the importance of the development of such procedures, Bandura is extremely cautious in his approach. He suggests that therapeutic procedures should be applied clinically only after there is understanding of the basic mechanisms by which change is effected and there has been adequate testing of the effects of preliminary methods.

According to Bandura, the change process involves not only the acquisition of new patterns of thought and behavior, but also their generalization and maintenance. The treatment approach emphasized is the acquisition of cognitive and behavioral competencies through **modeling** and **guided participation**. In the former, desired activities are demonstrated by various models who experience positive consequences or at least no adverse consequences. Generally, the complex patterns of behavior that are to be learned are broken down into subskills and increasingly difficult subtasks so as to ensure optimal progress. In guided participation the individual is assisted in performing the modeled behaviors.

modeling

guided participation

Much of the research on therapeutic modeling and guided participation has been carried out in the laboratory using severe snake phobias and children's avoidance of dogs as targets of behavior change. In one early study the modeling technique was compared with systematic desensitization and with a no-treatment control condition (Bandura, Blanchard, and Ritter, 1967). The subjects were people who answered a newspaper advertisement offering help to people with a snake phobia. Subjects were tested for how much contact they could stand to have with a snake both before and after they participated in one of the following four conditions: (1) *Live modeling with participation* (a model demonstrated the desired behavior and then assisted the subject to learn increasingly more difficult responses). (2) *Symbolic modeling* (subjects observed a film that showed children and adults engaged in progressively more threatening interactions with a large king snake. Subjects were also trained to relax while watching the film). (3) *Systematic desensitization.* (4) *Control—No treatment.* The results were that the control subjects remained unchanged in their avoidance behavior, the symbolic modeling and systematic desensitization subjects showed substantial reductions in phobic behavior, and the live modeling combined with guided participation subjects showed the most substantial improvement. Live modeling with guided participation proved to be a superior and unusually powerful treatment that eliminated the snake phobia in virtually all of the subjects. As an illustration, all of the subjects in this group progressed to the point where they were able to sit in a chair with a snake in their laps for 30 seconds.

A study of nursery school children who were afraid of dogs found that observation of another child playing with a dog helped to remove much of the fear and avoidance behavior (Bandura, Grusec, and Menlove, 1967). Of particular importance is the fact that these gains were maintained at a follow-up test one month later. In another study, Bandura and Menlove (1968) demonstrated that watching films of models playing with dogs could be helpful in reducing children's avoidance behavior. A particularly interesting finding was the possibility that the real-life models themselves were afraid of dogs. Whereas only one parent in a group of bold children reported any fear of dogs, in the group of avoidant children many of the parents were found to have such a fear.

These studies relate to the reduction of fear and avoidance behavior through the observation of models. What is the process that underlies such changes? Bandura's most recent explanation of the change process is a marked shift from his earlier views but is in accordance with his current emphasis on cognitive processes. In his earlier interpretations of psychotherapy as a learning process, Bandura (1961) emphasized such therapeutic processes as extinction, discrimination learning, counterconditioning, and reinforcement. However, his most recent statement suggests that psychological procedures, whatever their form, alter the level and strength of **self-efficacy** or the perceived ability to cope with specific situations. Cognitive processes are part of psychopathology in that these processes involve dysfunctional expectancies and perceptions of self-inefficacy. Such expectancies and self-perceptions lead to anxiety and the defensive avoidance of threatening situations. Therefore, it makes sense that an effective therapeutic procedure would alter such expectancies and self-perceptions. Procedures such as modeling and guided participation help to effect such changes and thereby enable the person to reduce anticipatory fears and avoidance behaviors. At the root of such procedures, as well as other diverse therapeutic procedures, is a cognitive process involving changed expectations of personal efficacy.

Is there evidence to support this theory of psychological change? A number of studies have been conducted in which individuals with phobias have received treatment while their efficacy expectations and behav-

self-efficacy

iors were measured (Bandura and Adams, 1977; Bandura, Adams, and Beyer, 1977) (Box 11.3). As predicted, subject statements of self-efficacy consistently predicted performance on tasks of varying levels of difficulty or threat. In other words, as therapeutic procedures led to improvement in perceived self-efficacy individuals were increasingly able to confront previously feared objects. Individuals who at first were frightened at the sight of a snake and would not enter a room with a caged snake in it would now sit and hold a snake.

BOX 11.3   **Behavioral Change and Perceived Self-Efficacy**

HYPOTHESES   (1) Treatment based on participant modeling will produce higher, stronger, and more generalized self-efficacy expectations than will treatment relying solely on vicarious experience. (2) Level of self-efficacy will be related directly to performance.

SUBJECTS   33 subjects (7 males, 26 females), recruited through advertisements in newspapers, whose lives were affected adversely by chronic snake phobias. Virtually all were plagued by intrusive thoughts and nightmares.

METHOD   Randomly assign subjects to one of the following three treatment conditions: (1) *Participant Modeling* (Performance-Based Treatment): To weaken subject inhibitions the therapist models the threatening activities and then introduces increasingly difficult subtasks. Where necessary the therapist performs the task along with the subjects. The subjects then perform the task alone, proving to themselves that they can cope. (2) *Modeling.* Subjects observe the therapist perform the same graduated set of activities but do not engage in them themselves. (3) *Control Condition.* Subjects receive assessment procedures (Behavioral Avoidance Test and Efficacy Expections, see below) at same time as other subjects but with no intervening treatment.

Use the following as measures of change in behavior and self-efficacy expectations. (1) Test subjects on a *Behavioral Avoidance Test* before (pretest) and after (posttest) treatment. The test of avoidance behavior consists of 29 performance tasks requiring increasingly more threatening interactions with a red-tailed boa constrictor. The final task involves letting the snake crawl in their lap while their hands are held passively at their sides. To gauge the generality of change after treatment first test the subjects with a dissimilar corn snake and then with the snake used in the pretest. (2) Obtain *Efficacy Expectations* three times: (a) after the behavioral avoidance pretest; (b) before the posttest which is administered after the conclusion of treatment; (c) after the posttest. Subjects rate the level and strength of their expectations in coping successfully with an unfamiliar snake (dissimilar threat) as well as with a boa constrictor similar to the one used in treatment. (3) As further measures of the generalization of perceived self-efficacy, subjects rate the degree to which they are afraid of confrontations with snakes in various situations, how effectively they could cope with snake encounters in everyday life, and their self-efficacy expectations in coping with other animal and social threats. (4) To evaluate the durability of change and the relationship of earlier self-efficacy judgments to such changes, assess the subjects again one month following the completion of treatment.

RESULTS

1 Participant modeling and modeling produced significant increases in approach behavior toward both threats (decrease in avoidance of snakes). Controls improved slightly in coping with the familiar threat (boa constrictor) but not with the dissimilar threat (corn snake) (Figure 11.4 below).

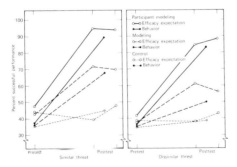

Figure 11.4   Level of self-efficacy and approach behavior displayed by subjects toward different threats after receiving vicarious (modeling) or performance-based participant modeling treatments or no treatment. (In the posttest phase, level of self-efficacy was measured prior to and after the behavioral avoidance tests with the two subjects.)

BOX 11.3   **Behavioral Change and Perceived Self-Efficacy** *continued*

2 Participant modeling resulted in higher self-efficacy expectations than did modeling which, in turn, surpassed the control condition (Figure 11.4).

3 Self-efficacy judgments are uniformly accurate predictors of individual task performance in subjects from the three treatment conditions and with the two snake threats. The probability of successful performance of a task was found to be a function of the strength of the efficacy expectation; that is, the stronger the self-efficacy, the more likely a particular task would be completed successfully. Furthermore, efficacy expectations clearly have superior predictive power over past performance.

4 In terms of generalization, both participant modeling and modeling reduced anticipatory fear and enhanced self-efficacy in coping with snakes in natural conditions whereas controls showed no change on either measure.

5 After completion of the formal experiment, control subjects and those in the modeling condition who achieved only partial improvement were given the participant modeling treatment. Therefore, the follow-up data reflect the enduring effects of treatment for all subjects. The subjects not only maintained their gains in self-efficacy and approach behavior but achieved some further improvements on measures of generalization.

CONCLUSIONS

1 Participant modeling produced higher, more generalized, and stronger expectations of personal efficacy than did modeling alone.

2 Self-efficacy, in turn, proved to be a consistently accurate predictor of performance on tasks varying in difficulty, with dissimilar threats, and for diverse modes of treatment.

3 The data support the social learning view that treatments improve performance because they raise expectations of personal efficacy. It is presumed that such expectations influence level of performance by encouraging subjects to try harder and longer.

SOURCE   A. Bandura, Adams, N. E., and Beyer, J. Cognitive processes mediating behavioral change. *Journal of Personality and Social Psychology*, 1977, *35*, 125-139.

A variety of criticisms have been made of Bandura's work and theory of change, especially by behaviorists who take the view that cognitions cannot be causes of behavior. His responses give further clarification of his thinking. First, some psychologists have argued that therapy consists of the acquisition of skills, not changes in self-efficacy. Bandura, however, notes that people with equal skill perform differently depending on the level and intensity of their self-efficacy perceptions. People who have been desensitized to the same extent show varying levels of behavioral performance when confronting feared objects. Whereas desensitization level may be a weak predictor of performance, self-efficacy judgments are excellent predictors. Second, some psychologists argue that therapy consists of the reduction of anxiety. Here Bandura argues that defensive behavior can occur with or without anxiety and, whereas anxiety levels may show little relationship to behavioral change, personal self-efficacy statements show a strong relationship. In the social learning analysis, anxiety is reduced by enhancing perceived ability to cope (self-efficacy). Third, some psychologists argue that the verbal self-reports of efficacy may themselves affect behavior and, in any case, are unreliable. Bandura argues that there is no evidence of this and that the argument against such self-reports has more to do with conceptual orthodoxy than with their usefulness in prediction. Finally, some psychologists have argued that Bandura's work in this area has been limited to laboratory studies and snake phobias, suggesting limited generalizability to clinic situations and broader difficulties. Bandura (1978) counters that laboratory investigations of behavioral change do not involve artificially created situations. The behavioral dysfunctions and processes of change are identical to the clinical situation. Furthermore, the results of the treatment for snake phobias have profound consequences for the people involved: "To contend that because phobics completely avoid a threatening object it has no impact on their daily living is to miss the point that it is the avoidance maneuvers that constrict and impair the phobic's life. . . . The treatments being analyzed in these laboratory investigations enable people burdened with such phobias to master their fears and to engage in activities they formerly avoided, and it eliminates their ruminative thoughts and nightmares" (1978, pp. 9394). Furthermore, modeling procedures now are being applied widely to diverse psychological conditions (Rosenthal and Bandura, 1978).

Social learning theory emphasizes the importance of changes in cognitive processes, particularly those concerning self-judgments. Modeling and guided participation are not viewed as the only means of effecting such change. Some investigators, such as Meichenbaum (1977), have been developing procedures to influence people's self-appraisals, and generally

there has been a trend toward emphasis on influencing cognitive processes in therapeutic efforts. Some such efforts follow directly from social
learning theory; others do not. What they hold in common with earlier
learning approaches is an emphasis on specific dysfunctional behavioral
processes which can be modified through training procedures. Where
they differ from earlier learning approaches is in their emphasis on cognitive processes.

BOX 11.4 **Summary of Social Learning Therapy**

GENERAL VIEW   Psychological procedures, whatever their format, serve as
ways of creating and strengthening expectations of personal effectiveness.
Social learning therapy emphasizes the acquisition of cognitive and
behavioral competencies through modeling and guided participation.

ATTRIBUTES OF GOOD MODELS: RELEVANCE AND CREDIBILITY   Models who
compel attention, who instill trust, who appear to be realistic figures for
self-comparison, and whose standards seem reasonable to the learner will
be good sources for therapeutic modeling effects. These attributes may be
summarized in terms of the positive functions of relevance and credibility.

SOME ILLUSTRATIVE RULES FOR INDUCING AND MAINTAINING DESIRED CHANGES

1 Structure the tasks to be learned in an orderly, stepwise sequence.

2 Explain and demonstrate general rules or principles. Check client's
understanding and provide opportunities for clarification.

3 Provide guided simulated practice with feedback concerning success
and error.

4 Once the desired behavior is established, increase opportunities for
self-directed accomplishment.

5 Test newly acquired skills in the natural environment under conditions
likely to produce favorable results.

6 Test skills in increasingly more demanding situations until a satisfactory
level of competence and self-efficacy has been obtained.

7 Provide opportunity for therapist consultation and feedback during
periods of increased independent mastery.

THERAPEUTIC EFFECTS OF MODELING

1 *Development of New Skills.* Through observing models and through
guided participation people acquire new patterns of behavior and new

coping strategies. For example, submissive clients learn to model assertive behavior.

2 *Changes in Inhibitions About Self-expression.* As a result of modeling,
responses already available to the person may be weakened or
strengthened. For example, inhibitory effects can occur as a result of
observing models receive negative consequences for certain behaviors.
Disinhibitory effects, which are more common in therapy, result from
observing models perform behaviors without adverse consequences or
with positive consequences. Fears may be overcome in this way.

3 *Facilitation of Pre-existing Patterns of Behavior.* Behaviors already available to the person and which are not associated with anxiety may
occur more often as a result of modeling influences. For example,
learners may be aided to become more skillful conversationalists.

4 *Adoption of More Realistic Standards for Judging One's Own
Performance.* Observing models reward themselves for varying levels
of performance can affect the learner's self-standards. For example,
rigid self-demands characteristic of depressed people can be relaxed as
a result of modeling.

CONCLUSION   "A burgeoning literature confirms the value of modeling
treatments for redressing deficits in social and cognitive skills, and for
helping to remove defensive avoidance behavior" (Rosenthal and
Bandura, 1978, p. 622).

A CASE EXAMPLE

It is interesting and perhaps significant that few, if any, in-depth individual
cases have been reported by proponents of social learning theory. One extended case illustration of a behavior therapy approach to treatment illustrates that such therapy is not simple and straightforward. In this case the
treatment of a depressed and anxious woman involved *51* sessions over a
period of *two* years (Goldfried and Davison, 1976). It is related to social
learning theory in its emphasis on modeling, self-monitoring, and feelings
of self-adequacy. However, many other therapeutic techniques were used
as well and it cannot be seen strictly as illustrative of social learning theory.

Mischel (1968, 1976) has taken a case previously reported in the literature and interpreted it from a social learning standpoint. Originally reported by two psychiatrists-psychoanalysts in a book on the psychological
trauma experienced by servicemen during World War II (Grinker and Spiegel, 1945), the case involved a bombardier who, during one of his missions,

experienced psychological and physical trauma. His plane was damaged by flak and, although it began to dive, was pulled out of the dive just before crashing. However, the bombardier was hurled against the bombsight. Upon return to flight duty, he found that he would become faint whenever the plane reached an altitude of about 10,000 feet. This, of course, interfered with his continuation on active duty.

Mischel notes that the analysts concluded that the bombardier's fainting was related to deep, underlying anxieties rooted in his childhood experiences. Instead of such a dynamic explanation Mischel suggests a social behavior analysis according to which the emotional trauma probably was conditioned to the altitude the plane reached at about the time of the mishap. When he went on a flight and reached that altitude he would re-experience the cues connected with the accident and become emotionally helpless. Therefore, the causes of the problem lie in the current conditions rather than in early childhood antecedents. Rather than needing insight therapy Mischel suggests that "the treatment implications seem clear for social behavior theory: render the traumatic cues neutral by desensitizing him to them through slow, graded exposure under conditions that prevent arousal and that, instead, insure incompatible responses such as relaxation" (1968, p. 267). Mischel is critical of the approach which emphasizes events in childhood, defenses against feelings, dynamic explanations, and the value of insight. Instead, he argues for an emphasis on the conditions precipitating the difficulty, the situational factors maintaining the problem, and the kinds of structured tasks or situations that will facilitate new kinds of learning.

CRITICAL EVALUATION

Strengths of the Theory

Social learning theory is probably the current favorite among academic personality psychologists, and a good number of clinicians would also probably label themselves social learning psychologists. The term *social learning* has been in use at least since 1941 and, as noted, in 1954 Rotter suggested a social learning position that emphasized expectancies, the subjective value of reinforcers, and the situational variability of behavior. Yet, it is only during the past decade that a social learning theory has evolved and achieved widespread popularity and influence. How can we account for this growth in popularity and influence? Probably the major factors have been the attention given to experimentation and evidence and a parallel consideration of important human phenomena. Beyond this there is an impressive openness to change and development as well as a continuing concern with other points of view and more general social issues. These strengths of social learning theory will be considered in greater detail.

Concern with Experimentation and Evidence

Developments in social learning theory have been grounded in careful experimental research. Bandura and Mischel, as well as other social learning theorists, have been concerned with defining concepts in ways that leave them open to empirical verification and have always conducted active research programs. The record of phenomena investigated and the ways in which they have been investigated is impressive. For example, the research on modeling indicates that the observation of models can lead to the acquisition of new responses and to changes in the frequency of occurrence of behaviors already learned. The range of behaviors investigated includes aggression, moral judgments, setting of standards, vicarious conditioning of fears, delay of gratification, and helping behavior. Children and adults have been found to be influenced by a wide range of models— live humans, filmed humans, verbally presented models of behavior, and cartoons. The process of modeling has been studied in terms of the influences of model characteristics, observer characteristics, and observed consequences to the model of the demonstrated behavior—an impressive record of research.

Importance of Phenomena Considered

Most social learning research has been conducted with the social behaviors of humans. Thus, in considering the evidence, we are not asked to make large extrapolations from animal research to humans and from simple behaviors to complex human processes. Social learning theory investigates and attempts to account for the very phenomena that are of interest to most people—aggression, the effects of parents and mass media on children, the change of dysfunctional behaviors, the development of self-regulatory capacities, and the increase of control over one's life.

A Theory Open to Change

Social learning theory has changed and evolved over the years. A comparison of *Social Learning and Personality Development* (1963) by Bandura and Walters with Bandura's *Social Learning Theory* (1977) gives ample testimony to the changes that have come about. The emphasis on behavior, observational learning, and the importance of maintaining behavior has been continued. However, with time there has been an increased emphasis on cognitive processes and self-regulation. Not only are external events emphasized, but internal ones are emphasized as well. In the process of reciprocal determinism we not only have environmental contingencies shaping people but also people shaping environmental contingencies. Not only is there an emphasis on behavior but one on cognition and emotion as well. Furthermore, there is an emphasis on the relationships among thought, feeling, and overt behavior. Social learning theorists have tried to remain informed about developments in other areas of psychology and to adjust their position so that it remains consistent with these developments. Beyond this, social learning theory itself has influenced and contributed to other parts of psychology. While social learning theory draws on advances in fields such as cognition and development, it also contributes to these advances.

Focus of Attention on Important Issues

Social learning theorists have played a valuable role in criticizing other theoretical positions (psychoanalytic, trait, Skinnerian) and in bringing critical issues to the forefront, among them the role of reinforcement in the acquisition and performance of behavior. Mischel, in particular, has been influential in drawing attention to the problems associated with views that overemphasize trait factors. The person-situation controversy has led in some wasteful directions, such as examining whether persons *or* situations are more important in determining behavior. Generally, however, it has led to a more realistic assessment of the complex, interacting causes of behavior.

View of the Person and Social Concern

Social learning theory offers a view of the person that is more reasonable than a robot or telephone switchboard and suggests possible solutions to problems of genuine social concern. Social learning approaches are used to help people with common problems of life. Yet they are also considered in relation to larger problems of social change. Bandura (1977) considers the soundness of a legal system of deterrence, the potential for creating environments conducive to learning and intellectual development, and the interplay between personal freedom and limits on conduct that must exist in every society. Interestingly enough, he concludes his book: "As a science concerned with the social consequences of its applications, psychology must promote public understanding of psychological issues that bear on social policies to ensure that its findings are used in the service of human betterment" (p. 213).

Limitations of the Theory

Given these significant strengths, what are the limitations of social learning theory? Some of these are associated with new developments and the fact that many of the approaches are recent. Social learning theory has shown a constructive openness to change but has not followed a path that has led to a carefully integrated network of theoretical assumptions. Many of the concepts, findings, and therapeutic procedures have been challenged by proponents of alternative points of view. Finally, social learning theory would appear to continue to ignore phenomena of importance which are recognized by other approaches. Again, these points will be considered in greater detail:

Social Learning Theory Is Not a Systematic, Unified Theory

Social learning theory is not a theory in the sense of a network of assumptions tied together in a systematic way leading to specific predictions. More recent efforts at systematic formulation have been made. However, occasionally diverse concepts are merely lumped together and sometimes opposing findings would appear to fit equally well into the theory. An example of the former would be the concepts emphasized by Mischel (1973) in his cognitive social learning reconceptualization of personality. In this paper Mischel emphasizes the importance of such personality variables as competencies, personal constructs, expectancies, and plans. These variables appear to be important but how they relate to one another in a consistent, organized, integrated way is unclear.

New Problems Have Arisen with New Developments

Perhaps not unexpectedly, each new development in social learning theory creates new criticism and new difficulties. Social learning theory's emphasis on the learning of complex acts in the absence of reinforcement has been attacked consistently by Skinnerians, who suggest, for example, that observational learning may, in fact, illustrate a generalized imitative response that is sometimes, but not always, reinforced (Gewirtz, 1971). Skinnerians suggest that while the individual may learn, without being reinforced, a response performed by a model, this does not mean that reinforcement was not a necessary part of the overall learning process; one cannot determine this without knowing the reinforcement history of the individual. Other psychologists, working within a strict behaviorist framework are critical of the recent emphasis on internal variables and verbal self-report. Developments here have occurred with an eye toward past pitfalls of research on the self and the use of verbal reports. It is strange, perhaps welcome, to see social learning psychologists emphasizing what people have to report about themselves. However, it remains to be seen whether detailed verbal report procedures and supportive reporting conditions can take care of the fact that people often are unaware of processes in themselves. Years of research on the concept of self have left us with a host of major unresolved problems (Wylie, 1974). Can social learning theory find a way to overcome them?

Social Learning Theory Neglects or Gives Minimal Emphasis to Some Important Areas

It undoubtedly is impossible for a theory of personality to be truly encompassing at this time. In addition, a new theory of personality may interpret phenomena described by another theory in different terms. For example, social learning theorists may interpret what Freudians call repression as an illustration of overly learned response suppression. Accepting such qualifications, it would still appear that social learning theorists ignore or give minimal emphasis to significant aspects of human functioning. Without accepting all of the viewpoint of stage theorists, maturational factors would appear to be important in the feelings people experience and in the way that they process information. Sexual feelings do become increasingly important at particular times in the life cycle and the thinking of a child is fundamentally different from that of an adult in a variety of ways. Beyond this, while social learning theory recognizes the importance of motivational factors and conflict, it gives relatively little attention to these processes. Recently the concept of incentives has been used, and the concepts of standards and plans do have motivational properties, but this remains an area in need of further development. Conflict, which would seem to be such an important part of our lives, particularly the part that distresses us, does not even appear as a separate heading in the subject index of Bandura's most recent work. Finally, there remains in social learning theory a lack of concern with the system aspects of human personality functioning. The human functions as both a biological and a psychological system. The parts of the system are important not only for themselves but also in terms of their implications for other parts of the system. Whether one speaks in terms of concepts such as wholeness, organization, Gestalt qualities, or other concepts, it would appear to be important for a theory to recognize the links that occur among different processes and the implications they have for one another.

Many Developments Are Recent and Findings Should Be Regarded as Preliminary Rather than Conclusive

Throughout its history, psychology generally, and the field of psychotherapy in particular, has been beset with fads. Therefore one must be cautious in distinguishing between actual progress and overzealous commitment to a new idea. Whereas at one time theories that emphasized cognitive processes were viewed with skepticism, today such theories are adopted readily: "1976 could well be designated the year of cognition for both theoretician and practitioner. Like the activities of Superman and the Scarlet Pimpernel, cognition is in the air, it is here, there, and everywhere" (Franks and Wilson, 1977, p. vii). Without minimizing their importance in human behavior, we should be careful about prematurely accepting cognitive processes as our basic explanatory concepts.[1]

While the results of guided participation and modeling are significant, these therapeutic processes remain to be tested by other therapists, with different patients and with different problems. Bandura has answered critics who suggest that his results are of limited generalizability. However, the history of psychotherapy is filled with methods that were introduced as solving the problems of those in psychological distress. Most recently, evaluation of efforts in the area of behavior modification and behavior therapy should make us aware of the complexities of the problem and the work that remains to be done.

In sum, there are good grounds both for enthusiasm about social learning theory and for caution and even skepticism. Social learning theory represents a major development. It is still evolving, and its further efforts are worthy of careful attention.

MAJOR CONCEPTS AND SUMMARY

reciprocal determinism

observational learning

modeling

acquisition, performance, and maintenance of behaviors

vicarious conditioning

discrimination among situations

delay of gratification

cognitive and behavioral competencies

dysfunctional expectancies

self-conceptions

---

[1]   Bandura's response to a draft of this section is noteworthy: "[It] portrays the development of social learning theory as an expedient, faddish activity. I am more interested in gaining a deeper understanding of human behavior than in hustling popularity points by adopting whatever catches the popular fancy. In many respects, the research on observational learning and self-regulatory processes ran counter to the fashions of the day which emphasized the shaping and regulation of behavior through the effects of one's actions. These lines of theorizing opened up new areas of experimentation rather than simply reflected current fashions." He also suggests that social learning theory concepts serve an integrative function rather than merely being lumped together. These points are valid. Social learning theory is the work of serious investigators and clearly is more than a passing fad. The comments in the text are intended to draw attention to the potential problems associated with an excessive or near-exclusive emphasis on cognitive processes.

self-regulation

expectancies

goals-plans

self

direct, vicarious, and self-produced
consequences

dysfunctional self-evaluation

self-efficacy and inefficacy

defensive behaviors

guided participation

self-efficacy expectations

Social learning theory is an evolving, influential, and popular theory of personality. It shares with the Hullian and Skinnerian positions an emphasis on the central importance of learned patterns of behavior. However, its emphasis on learning independent of reinforcement and the importance of cognitive processes results in a different view of the human organism. The human organism is one that affects the environment as well as is affected by it, one that responds to information from the environment in an organized and selective way rather than in a mechanical way, and one that is capable of responding to self-reward and self-punishment as well to external forms of reinforcement. Instead of emphasizing internal (person) factors *or* external (environment) factors, social learning theory stresses the process of reciprocal determinism between person and environment.

Social learning theory distinguishes between response acquisition and response performance. As is evident in observational learning, reinforcement is not necessary for response acquisition; people can learn complex behaviors through the observation of others performing such behaviors. Emotional reactions as well can be conditioned vicariously through the observation of others. Such learning processes have functional, adaptive value since we are thereby spared the inefficiency and hazards of trial-and-error learning. Learning from observing others, modeling, involves something broader than imitation but less diffuse and global than identification. Considerable attention has been directed to the factors that influence the modeling process (for example, consequences to the model) and to the components of this process. Observational learning is governed by four subsystems: attention processes, retention processes, motoric reproduction processes, and reinforcement and motivational processes.

While reinforcement is not critical for the acquisition of responses, it is critical for the performance and maintenance or regulation of behavior. According to social learning theory, behavior is regulated by its consequences—which can come from the person (self-praise and self-criticism) as well as from the environment. Among the responses an individual learns are standards of goal attainment and standards for self-reinforcement. These standards permit the person to continue working toward a goal in the absence of outside reward or despite outside interference and punishment. They form the basis for self-regulation and self-control. While behavior is regulated by internal and external consequences, it is the expectation of these consequences that is important rather than the mechanical linking of behavior with reinforcement. Here too there is an emphasis on cognitive processes and reinforcement as representing information from the environment.

While the main focus remains on processes explaining the acquisition and maintenance of behavior, social learning theory has recently also emphasized structural concepts such as goals-plans and the self. Goals-plans are derived from learned standards for reinforcement and help to establish priorities among alternative patterns of behavior, particularly over long periods of time. The concept of self does not represent a little person inside the organism controlling behavior but rather a set of cognitive processes involved in self-conception, self-reinforcement, and self-regulation. Self-concepts and self-control processes are viewed as relatively specific and as varying from situation to situation and from time to time.

Social learning theory views growth and development as resulting from the interplay of biological and experiential factors. It is critical of stage theories that suggest a fixed order of development and a single level for a person's cognitive processes. Instead, social learning theory emphasizes the potential for cognitive development and the processes through which cognitive functioning varies from issue to issue and situation to situation. Considerable research attention has been directed toward an understanding of the development of aggressive behavior, moral judgments, and tolerance for delay of gratification. Similar principles are stressed throughout. For example, a distinction is made between the factors that determine the acquisition of responses, those that instigate these responses, and those that regulate and maintain the responses. Behavioral responses are acquired through observational learning or direct experience. Behavior is activated by internal or external stimuli and/or expectations of reward. Behavior is then sustained or terminated, depending on its consequences. Expectancies concerning consequences arise from three sources—direct external consequences, vicarious experiencing of consequences to others, and self-produced consequences. Information from these three sources is combined to lead both to discriminations among situations in terms of their potential for various consequences and to the formation of general rules of behavior.

Social learning theory rejects the disease model of psychopathology and sees abnormal behavior as being on a continuum with normal behavior. According to social learning theory maladaptive, pathological behavior represents the result of dysfunctional learning of behaviors, expectancies, and standards for self-reward. Such maladaptive responses are learned, as are other behaviors, either directly or through the observation of inadequate models. A central role in the interpretation of psychopathology is given to the feeling of inefficacy. This is experienced when the person perceives the self as unable to cope with a threat or a situation expected to lead to pain or injury and leads to defensive behaviors. Anxiety, in this view, does not lead to defensive behaviors. Anxiety and defensive behaviors both are seen as resulting from perceived inefficacy in coping with potentially aversive events rather than as causing one another.

Defensive behaviors are difficult to unlearn because they remove the person from the threatening circumstances and prevent one from revising one's expectancies. The task in psychotherapy, then, is to increase the sense of self-efficacy so that previously avoided situations may be confronted and new expectancies learned. According to social learning theory, all psychological procedures, whatever their form, alter the level and strength of self-efficacy or the perceived ability to cope with specific situations. Modeling and guided participation have been used in therapeutic efforts. Recent research has suggested that self-efficacy expectations are excellent predictors of performance and are superior in this regard to past performance itself.

Interest in and support for social learning theory is probably largely influenced by its dual emphasis on experimentation and important personality and social phenomena. In addition, proponents of the theory have shown a striking willingness to revise the theory as new evidence emerges. At the same time, it has been criticized for not being a truly systematic theory and for ignoring or giving minimal attention to important areas such as maturation, motivation, conflict, and the holistic (system) properties of the organism. In addition, while the recent developments in social learning theory are noteworthy, they have created new conceptual and methodological difficulties. It is too early to evaluate fully the potential of therapeutic efforts based on social learning theory. The theory represents a significant effort and has already been associated with noteworthy research accomplishments. How much it can be extended and systematized in the future remains to be seen.

GOALS OF TESTS, MEASURES, AND ASSESSMENT TECHNIQUES

Reliability

Validity

CLASSIFICATION OF TESTS

Projective Techniques
• The Rorschach Inkblot Test
• The Thematic Apperception Test (TAT)

Subjective Techniques
• Interviews
• Measures of the Self-concept

MAJOR CONCEPTS AND SUMMARY

12 ASSESSMENT: PROJECTIVE AND SUBJECTIVE TESTS

Chapter Focus:

In this chapter and the next we shall examine techniques of assessment—procedures for systematically gaining information about the personality of individuals. We shall discuss the goals assessment methods share and the advantages and disadvantages of alternative approaches. The main focus is on the association of personality theories with assessment techniques and how this leads to different kinds of observations about people. In this chapter we discuss the concepts of reliability and validity and projective and subjective assessment techniques.

It is the assessment philosophy that it is the total picture, a formulation of what is relatively central and enduring in the person, that offers the soundest basis for prediction.

OFFICE OF STRATEGIC SERVICES STAFF, *ASSESSMENT OF MEN*, 1948, P. 118

The most distinct contribution that projective tests continue to make, however, probably is in revealing aspects of motivation and personality that do not fit neatly into either the self-concept or behavioral category.

KLOPFER AND TAULBEE, 1976, P. 563

All theories of personality assume that individual differences exist and can be measured. This assumption is critical to personality assessment. An assessment procedure is a way of gaining information about a person. More specifically, assessment involves the systematic observation of behavior under specified conditions and relative to specific stimuli. We gain insight into the nature of personality and gather data relevant to a personality theory through observing the responses of individuals to defined conditions.

Many variables are potentially relevant to a particular person, so it is easy to see why there is so much variation in modes of personality assessment. At least four properties of assessment lend themselves to variation: nature of the situation, nature of the stimulus, nature of the instructions given, and nature of the response required. Then there is variation in how the data gathered are to be scored, analyzed, and interpreted. Because this process is highly complicated, the observations of differences among human beings must be meaningful, as they are when they have been gathered systematically and when they are relevant to concepts defined by a theory. They are meaningless when the data have been gathered unsystematically and show no relation to theoretical assumptions. The interplay between theory of personality, assessment technique, and observations recorded is central to this chapter. Different theories of personality lead to different techniques of personality assessment and different kinds of observations about individuals. In terms of theories and assessment devices already considered, we can contrast the information gained by Freud through free association and dream analysis with that obtained by Rogers with the Q-sort, that obtained by Kelly with the Rep rest, that obtained by Cattell with the 16 P.F. questionnaire, and that obtained by behaviorists through the functional analysis of behavior. It is important, then, to understand not only theories and techniques of assessment, but also their intimate relationship. A theory of personality that does not relate to any mechanism for obtaining information about people is useless, and data that cannot be related to a theory are irrelevant and often meaningless.

Throughout this chapter and the next, the terms *assessment technique, test,* and *measure* are used interchangeably, all standing for a procedure by which personality data about one or many individuals are obtained systematically. The word *measure* means the recording of a specific and limited piece of behavior. A *test* is an instrument for gaining a wider variety of information about behavior. *Assessment* is a procedure for gathering many kinds of information about individuals in order to obtain an understanding of their personalities. The meanings of these terms are of interest in relation to the ways in which psychologists approach the entire field of personality. Clinicians for example, tend to associate themselves with assessment procedures, whereas laboratory investigators tend to associate themselves with measures of personality. The basis for such associations will become clear as various approaches available for observing personality are analyzed. All personality tests, measures, and techniques nevertheless share certain common characteristics. They all attempt to result in meaningful observations about personality, and they share certain scientific goals in relation to these observations.

GOALS OF TESTS, MEASURES, AND ASSESSMENT TECHNIQUES

Our task here has already been defined as the systematic gathering of meaningful observations. The emphasis on systematic observation suggests that observation needs to be free of error and bias. When obtaining data a situation must be presented, information (individual responses) must be recorded, and the information must be interpreted or analyzed. There is an enormous potential for error and bias at every phase of the data-gathering process. In addition, we want to develop measures that are sensitive to the things in which we are interested and that result in data relevant to our theory. Ideally, our method for observing behavior should be very sensitive to the phenomenon or variable of interest to us and completely unaffected by all other factors. If our method is sensitive to a number of variables, we must have ways of distinguishing among them. What is critical is that when we gather data we know exactly what we are observing. Another way of stating our goal is to say that we are after reliable and valid observations about behavior.

Reliability

The reliability of a test is a measure of the consistency of scores derived from a test or their freedom from chance error. If we have developed a reliable measure of personality, then different observers should arrive at the same observations: they should see the same things, score or record them in the same way, and come up with the same analyses and interpretations. Also, if one assumes that the personality characteristic being measured is relatively stable, one would expect observations of individuals on two different test occasions to correspond to one another.

A reliable measure of personality, then, reflects true and systematic variation in the subject rather than error, bias, or unsystematic variation. Without reliability in personality measures, we cannot be sure of the nature of the differences among individuals and we cannot begin to relate findings from different studies in a meaningful way.

Validity

Although high reliability indicates that there has been a systematic gathering of data and that the observations can be replicated, it in no way indicates that what is being measured is meaningful. Many tests in psychology have satisfied the requirements of reliability and yet measured personality characteristics other than those they were designed to measure.

A valid test is one that measures what it claims to measure. There have been cases where a number of tests presented as measuring the same thing were found to show little relationship to one another. For example, different tests of a person's self-concept and ideal self do not always agree in their picture of the person's self or level of adjustment (Wylie, 1974). A variety of tests measure cognitive style—how people process information from their environment. In spite of the fact that each of these tests has been associated with a number of interesting findings and all appear relevant to the same personality characteristic, scores of individuals on one test do not correspond to those on the others (Vannoy, 1965). Which test, if any, is the true test of that personality characteristic?

Although it might not seem so, the process of validating a test is an extremely difficult one, but a process crucial to the development of personality psychology. Developments in any science depend on the adequacy of measures of relevant phenomena. For research in personality to progress, our measures must not only be reliable, they also must be valid.

content validity

experimental criterion-oriented validity

concurrent validity predictive validity

Just as there are many kinds of reliability, there are many kinds of validity. One type—**content validity**—concerns whether the test is measuring what it claims to be measuring. For example, does a test of values have items relevant to values, and does an intelligence test have items relevant to intelligence? Of even greater consequence is **experimental** or **criterion-oriented validity**. A criterion is a standard or measure of behavior to which one attempts to relate performance on a particular test. For example, do scholastic aptitude tests relate to current grades and predict future academic performance? Criterion-oriented validity may be of two types—**concurrent validity** and **predictive validity**. In concurrent validity, the criterion either has already been obtained or can be obtained at the same time and the test's utility is mainly that of convenience. It is easier to use a Block Design Test (the subject must arrange blocks to fit a design pictured on a card) than a neurological examination to assess brain damage (Cronbach, 1960). If the scores on the Block Design Test relate very well to scores on the neurological examination, one would be justified in saying that the test has validity, in this case concurrent validity.

In predictive validity we are interested in predicting to a criterion (such as achievement), that will be evident in the future. In this case the validity of the test is measured by the extent to which scores from the test relate to the criterion obtained at a later date. For example, scores on the Strong Vocational Interest Blank are used to predict success in various occupations. If the scores relate well to data obtained at a subsequent time (grades, success in occupation), the test may be said to have predictive validity.

In concurrent validity the utility of the test is convenience and in predictive validity it is predictive power. In both cases the concern is with the relationship of a test score to a clearly defined criterion.

These types of test validity are of considerable importance when considering the practical utility of a test but of limited theoretical significance. The relationship between personality theory and test validity becomes **construct validity**   quite critical, however, in relation to **construct validity**. While in criterion-oriented validity a definite criterion (grades, brain damage, vocational success) can be established, in many areas of personality this is not the case. Some theories use constructs that are merely postulated attributes of people or theoretical conceptions as to the qualities people possess (motives, drives, traits). Here there are no absolute criteria for the constructs; they are defined in relation to the theory of which they are a part. For example, there are no absolute criteria for the concept of introversion–extroversion, but the relevant criteria are part of the theory in which the construct is embedded. Similar comments could be made about the drive toward self-actualization, the mechanisms of defense, and many other major theoretical concepts reviewed in this book.

The construct validity of a test becomes more and more certain as the test is found to be useful in confirming relationships derived from a theory (Cronbach and Meehl, 1955). Just as a theory postulates a construct, such as anxiety, and assumes that this attribute can be found in people, so a test such as Eysenck's test of neuroticism is assumed to measure that construct. If the test is useful in research in relation to the theory, it gains construct validity. If two or more tests claim to be measuring the same thing, the one most useful in relation to the development of a theory is the one with the most construct validity. The notion of construct validity is critical to an appreciation of the use of assessment techniques of personality.

The requirement that a test result in the systematic accumulation of meaningful data has now been defined further in terms of the concepts of reliability and validity. From an analysis of these concepts. it should be clear that a test can be reliable without being valid, but it cannot be valid if it is unreliable. We can obtain theoretically inconsequential results that can be replicated, but we cannot obtain results that are theoretically significant but cannot be confirmed by other investigators. The subtleties involved in the concepts of reliability and validity indicate that tests are not either reliable or unreliable, valid or invalid, but that they have degrees of various kinds of reliability and validity. These concepts are important because they provide the guidelines for judging the scientific merit of various assessment techniques.

CLASSIFICATION OF TESTS

Assessment procedures can involve many stimuli or a single stimulus, stimuli that are ambiguous or clearly defined, the recording of many responses or a single response, a verbal report or a physiological response, objective scoring by a machine or subjective ratings by a judge, computer-programmed interpretations or clinical interpretations of single scores. With so much variation possible, can assessment techniques be classified in any meaningful way? An excellent effort to define categories for the classification of personality tests has been made by Campbell (1950, 1957). In his first attempt at classification, Campbell (1950) described two polar (opposite) dimensions along which tests could be classified. The first dimension is that of **structured-nonstructured**. This involves the degree of freedom the subject has to respond in varied ways. In a structured test, subjects are confronted with a limited array of alternatives, whereas in a nonstructured test subjects are free to respond as they choose. The second dimension is that of **disguised-nondisguised**. This involves the degree of the subject's awareness of the purpose of the test. In a disguised test, the psychologist interprets the test in a way other than that the subject assumed it would be when responding to it. For example, a test is disguised if presented to the subject as a test of perceptual ability when it will be used by the investigator as a measure of psychopathology. In a nondisguised test, both the experimenter and the subject have the same understanding of the purpose of the test. An interview or intelligence test to be used for assignment to a job or admission to a school have the qualities of a nondisguised test. Since these two polar dimensions are independent a test can be classified in one of four ways: structured-nondisguised, structured-disguised, nonstructured-nondisguised, nonstructured-disguised.

In his later attempt at a typology of tests, Campbell (1957) used dimen-

structured-nonstructured.

disguised-nondisguised

voluntary-objective

sions similar to the two outlined above and added a third dimension: **voluntary-objective**. In a voluntary test subjects can give their own response whereas in an objective test subjects are asked to give a correct response. In both, subjects are presented a limited number of defined alternatives, as in a structured test, but on the voluntary test subjects indicate whether they like or dislike something or whether something is or is not characteristic of them, whereas on the objective test subjects attempt to give a correct response rather than one that involves a self-report. A personality inventory that ask subjects to indicate their preference among given alternatives is a voluntary test. A test that asks subjects to provide the correct solution to a problem is an objective test. Adding a third polar dimension provides three sets of two alternatives, or eight categories for the classification of personality tests.

While these and other dimensions are useful, and while at least eight categories for the classification of all personality tests are probably necessary, some dimensions appear more basic than others. This becomes increasingly clear when the relationship between theory and assessment technique is analyzed. Viewed in this light, the nonstructured-structured dimension is crucial to our understanding of alternative ways of assessing personality. This dimension can be related to a representation of personality theories on a clinical-empirical basis. Clinical types of theories, which place great emphasis on the variability of human behavior and the importance of individual differences, tend to be associated with nonstructured tests. Empirical theories, which emphasize consistencies across individuals and use rigorous experimental procedures, are associated with structured tests. The disguised-nondisguised dimension is most relevant to nonstructured tests, while the voluntary-objective dimension is most relevant to structured tests. Therefore, if the number of categories of tests is reduced to four, there remain:

projective

1 Tests that are nonstructured and disguised and tend to be associated with clinically oriented theories that emphasize unconscious factors. The clinical orientation is associated with the variability in response emphasized in nonstructured tests. The emphasis on the unconscious is associated with the need for disguise. **Projective** tests are an example of this approach.

subjective

2 Tests that are nonstructured and nondisguised and tend to be associated with clinically oriented theories that emphasize a phenomenological approach. The clinical emphasis is the same as in the first catergory, but here the interest is in subjects' perceptions of the external environment and of themselves. Interviews are illustrative of this approach, which can be called **subjective**.

3 Tests that are structured and voluntary and tend to be associated with empirical theories that accept verbal reports as useful data. Standard questionnaires, often derived through factor analysis, reflect this **psychometric** approach and may be designated as **psychometric**.

4 Tests that are structured and objective and tend to be associated with empirical theories that rely on behavioral data. Data-gathering procedures that require subject behavior in a controlled situation may be **objective-behavioral** designated as **objective-behavioral**.

These four categories do not exhaust all possibilities and each tends to have characteristics associated with it beyond those described. What is important at this point, however, is to appreciate the relationships among types of theories, assessment techniques, and kinds of data recorded in attempting to understand human behavior. The rest of this chapter will consider the relationship between theory and technique in the first two of these four categories—projective and subjective tests. Chapter 13 will consider psychometric and behavioral tests.

Projective Techniques

The relationship between projective techniques, particularly the Rorschach Inkblot Test, and psychodynamic theory can be seen in the rationale for the Rorschach and the history of its development. Psychodynamic theories emphasize:

1 Individual differences; behavior as a result of the interplay among complex forces (motives, drives, needs, and conflicts).

2 Personality structure as involving layers of organization, as in the conscious and unconscious.

3 Personality as a process through which the individual imposes organization and structure on external stimuli in the environment.

4 A holistic understanding of behavior in terms of relationships among parts, rather than the interpretation of behavior as expressive of single parts or personality traits.

The relationship of projective techniques of assessment to psychodynamic theories of personality can be seen in these characteristics:

1 Their emphasis on allowing individuals to choose their own response or responses among an infinite number of alternatives (nonstructured, voluntary).

2 Their use of directions and stimuli that provide few guidelines for responding and in which the purposes of the test are partially or completely hidden (disguised).

3 The tendency for clinicians who use these techniques to make clinical and holistic interpretations in relation to the data gathered.

Lindzey has given this definition:

A projective technique is an instrument that is considered especially sensitive to covert or unconscious aspects of behavior, it permits or encourages a wide variety of subject responses, it is highly multidimensional, and it evokes unusually rich or profuse response data with a minumum of subject awareness concerning the purpose of the test.

LINDZEY, 1961, P. 45.

The term *projection* in relation to assessment techniques was first used in 1938 by Henry A. Murray, who developed the Thematic Apperception Test, but emphasis on the importance of projective techniques was first most clearly stated by L. K. Frank in 1939, almost 20 years after the development of the Rorschach Inkblot Test. Frank argued against the use of standardized tests, which he felt classified people but did not tell much about them as individuals. He argued for the use of tests that would offer insight into the private world of meanings and feelings of individuals. Such tests would allow individuals to impose their own structure and organization on stimuli and would thereby be expressive of a dynamic conception of personality. Frank suggested the use of stimuli relatively free of structure and cultural patterning:

a projection method for the study of personality involves the presentation of a stimulus-situation designed or chosen because it will mean to the subject, not what the experimenter has arbitrarily decided it should mean (as in most psychological experiments using standardized stimuli in order to be "objective"), but rather whatever it must mean to the personality who gives it, or imposes upon it, his private, idiosyncratic meaning and organization.

FRANK, 1939, P. 403.

The Rorschach Inkblot Test

The Rorschach Inkblot Test was developed by Hermann Rorschach, a Swiss psychiatrist. Although inkblots had been used earlier to elicit responses from individuals, Rorschach was the first to grasp fully the potential for the use of these responses for personality assessment. Rorschach developed stimuli through putting ink on paper and folding the paper so that symmetrical but ill-defined forms were produced. These inkblots were then shown to hospitalized patients. Through a process of trial and error, those inkblots that elicited different responses from different psychiatric

HERMANN RORSCHACH

groups were kept, while those that did not were discarded. Rorschach experimented with thousands of inkblots and finally settled on ten.

Rorschach was well acquainted with the work of Freud, the concept of the unconscious, and a dynamic view of personality. The development of his test certainly seems to have been influenced by this view. Rorschach felt that the data from the inkblot test would have relevance for an understanding of the unconscious and psychoanalytic theory in general, and he used psychoanalytic theory in his own interpretations of subjects' responses.

The Rorschach test consists of ten cards with inkblots on them. When showing the cards the experimenter tries to make the subjects relaxed and comfortable while providing them with sufficient information to complete the task. Thus, the test is presented as "just one of many ways used nowadays to try to understand people" and the experimenter volunteers as little information as possible—"It is best not to know much about the procedure until you have gone through it." Subjects are asked to look at each card and tell the examiner what they see—anything that might be represented on the card. Individuals are free to select what they will see, where they will see it, and what determines their perceptions. All responses offered by the subjects are given on the test record. It also records *where* on the inkblot the subjects saw each response and *what* about the blot made it look like it did. In this way the examiners are able to determine more exactly the basis for each subject's responses.

In interpreting the Rorschach one is interested in the way in which the responses or percepts are formed, the reasons for the response, and its content. The basic assumption is that there is a correspondence between the way individuals form their perceptions and the way they generally organize and structure stimuli in their environments. Perceptions that match the structure of the inkblot suggest a good level of psychological functioning that is well oriented toward reality. On the other hand, poorly formed responses that do not fit the structure of the inkblot suggest unrealistic fantasies or bizarre behavior. The content of subject responses (whether they see mostly animate or inanimate objects, humans or animals, and content expressing affection or hostility) makes a great deal of difference in the interpretation of the subject's personality. For example, compare the interpretations we might make of two sets of responses, one where animals are seen repeatedly as fighting and a second where humans are seen as sharing and involved in cooperative efforts.

Beyond this, content may be interpreted symbolicly. An explosion may symbolize intense hostility; a pig, gluttonous tendencies; a fox, a tendency toward being crafty and aggressive; spiders, witches, and octopuses, negative images of a dominating mother; gorillas and giants, negative attitudes toward a dominating father; and an ostrich as an attempt to hide from conflicts (Schafer, 1954). General categories of content such as food and nurturant animals (cows, mother hen), hostile figures and devouring animals (beasts of prey, vultures, animals clawing), and figures of power and authority (kings, queens, generals) are interpreted in relation to symbolism.

It is important to recognize that interpretation is not made on the basis of one response alone, but in relation to the total sum of responses. However, each response is used to suggest hypotheses or possible interpretations about the individual's personality. Such hypotheses are checked against interpretations based on other responses, on the total response pattern, and on the subject's behavior while responding to the Rorschach. In relation to the latter, the examiner takes note of all unusual behavior and uses this as a source of data for further interpretation. For example, a subject who constantly asks for guidance may be interpreted as dependent. A subject who seems tense, asks questions in a subtle way, and looks at the back of the cards may be interpreted as suspicious and possibly paranoid. An illustration of the interpretive process used in relation to a response is given in Box 12.1 and illustrates the effort made to capture the many properties of a single piece of behavior.

BOX 12.1   **Projective
Techniques —
The Rorschach**

RATIONALE   Provide subject with ambiguous stimuli, using disguised instructions, and try to elicit voluntary responses. These responses will best reflect the interplay of motives and organizing principles in that individual's personality.

STIMULI   Ten inkblots.

SCORING   1. Each response scored for location, (the part of the blot used), the determinants of the response (form, color, shading), content, and originality. 2. Summary scores determined for the various categories are plotted to form a profile or distribution of scores; some ratios between scores computed.

INTERPRETATION   Attempt to present a multidimensional, holistic, dynamic interpretation of personality on the basis of the following: the content of individual responses and how the percepts are formed, the profile of scores, qualitative aspects of the individual's behavior while responding.

SCORING   (Illustration No. 1) Large detail of the blot used (location), form used in relation to animal movement and color in relation to blood (determinants), animal content, and a popular response (percept of two bears is a popular response to that part of the card).

INTERPRETIVE HYPOTHESES   Subject starts off with popular response and animals expressing playful, "childish" behavior. Response is then given in terms of hostile act with accompanying inquiry. Pure color response and blood content suggest he may have difficulty controlling his reponse to the environment. Is a playful, childlike exterior used by him to disguise hostile, destructive feelings that threaten to break out in his dealings with the environment?

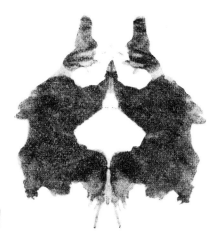

RESPONSE
"Two bears with their paws touching one another playing pattycake or could be they are fighting and the red is the blood from the fighting."

ILLUSTRATION
NO. 1

RESPONSE
"Two cannibals. Supposed to see something in this? African natives bending over a pot. Possibly cooking something–hope they're not maneaters. I shouldn't make jokes–always liking humor. (Are they male or female?) Could be male or female. More female because of breasts here. But didn't impress me at first glance as being of either sex."

ILLUSTRATION
NO. 2

SCORING   Large detail of the blot used (location), form used in relation to human movement (determinant), human content, and a popular response (percept of humans a popular response to that part of the card).

INTERPRETIVE HYPOTHESES   Subject starts off with primitive, orally aggressive characters—cannibals. Does this express some of his own drives? He then asks a question as is characteristic of him throughout the session and then makes a joke. Does this express a tendency to deal with hostility through an attempt to be dependent on others (ask questions) and to look at the funny side of everything—a polyannaish kind of denial of his hostile feelings? The lack of indication of sex of the figures and then confusion as to their sexual identity suggests some confusion of sexual identity in him.

CAUTIONARY NOTE   Final interpretations are never made on the basis of

BOX 12.1 **Projective Techniques—
The Rorschach** *continued*

single responses such as those illustrated here. The profile of scores, pattern of responses, and behaviorial qualities are all considered before arriving at a final interpretation.

SOURCE   Inkblot illustrations are from the Rorschach location chart and are printed here by permission of Hans Huber Publishers. The actual inkblot cards contain color.

The Thematic Apperception Test (TAT)

Probably the most widely used projective test is the Thematic Apperception Test (TAT) developed by Henry Murray and Christina Morgan. The test represents an extension of Murray's longstanding interest in the needs or underlying motives of individuals, fantasy behavior, and the intensive study of the individual. The TAT consists of cards with scenes on them. Most of the cards depict one or two people in some important life situation, though some of the cards are more abstract. The subject is asked to make up a story based on the scene on the card, with the story to include what is going on, the thoughts and feelings of the participants, what led up to the scene, and the outcome of what is going on. Since the scenes often are ambiguous, they leave considerable room for individuality in the content of stories made up by the subjects: "The test is based on the well-recognized fact that when a person interprets an ambiguous social situation he is apt to expose his own personality as much as the phenomenon to which he is attending" (Murray, 1938, P. 530.)

Some TAT cards are shown to both male and female subjects; others are shown to members of one sex only. An illustrative card and responses given to it by four different individuals is in Box 12.2. The card is given to female subjects and is described by Murray as: "The portrait of a young woman. A weird old woman with a shawl over her head is grimacing in the background". Common themes given in response to this card are stories of disappointment with a parent, parental pressure, and sad thoughts about the past. In addition, some women appear to see the younger woman as having a vision of her evil self or of herself in old age (Holt, 1978).

BOX 12.2 **Illustrative TAT Card and Responses to It**

ILLUSTRATION 1   This is the picture of a woman who all of her life has been a very suspicious, conniving person. She's looking in the mirror and she sees reflected behind her an image of what she will be as an old woman—still a suspicious, conniving sort of person. She can't stand the thought that

SAMPLE CARD FROM THE THEMATIC APPERCEPTION TEST

BOX 12.2   **Illustrative TAT Card and Responses to It** *continued*

HENRY MURRAY

that's what her life will eventually lead her to and she smashes the mirror and runs out of the house screaming and goes out of her mind and lives in an institution for the rest of her life.

ILLUSTRATION 2   This woman has always emphasized beauty in her life. As a little girl she was praised for being pretty and as a young woman was able to attract lots of men with her beauty. While secretly feeling anxious and unworthy much of the time, her outer beauty helped to disguise these feelings from the world and, sometimes, from herself. Now that she is getting on in years and her children are leaving home, she is worried about the future. She looks in the mirror and imagines herself as an old hag—the worst possible person she could become, ugly and nasty—and wonders what the future holds for her. It is a difficult and depressing time for her.

ILLUSTRATION 3   I think of a young man who's a dancer—I know it's supposed to be a woman, but it—I think of someone I know who's a dancer and looks like this and is, has what I think of as a basic disdain for women, although he's married. I , I think of him because I think that he is *so* beautiful—that's him right up there [pointing to a photograph]. I think he is so beautiful as a person, as a—*physically* he is so beautiful that I feel that women, and maybe I relate to myself, couldn't possibly be that beautiful, physically beautiful. He also happens to be nice inside, which is unusual. That's all I get out of that. (What about the figure behind?) I think I—this represents Woman . . . just "woman" in quotes, who just can't seem to be as beautiful as John.

ILLUSTRATION 4   The old crone is the mother to the daughter—uh, illegitimate daughter, and she brought up the girl to be a prostitute and expected the daughter to always support the mother. The daughter isn't quite sure that she wants to stick to that kind of a life. And yet, what else does she have? The old gal is thinking, "I've got her. There's nothing she can do about it now. If she tries to step out of this, I can report her to the police. She's got to stay by me and take care of me." She's a nasty old lady.

The thinking behind the TAT clearly shows its relation to the psychodynamic view. According to Murray (1938), the TAT is used to discover unconscious and inhibited tendencies. The assumption is that subjects are not aware that they are talking about themselves and that thereby the defenses can be bypassed: "If the procedure had merely exposed conscious fantasies and remembered events it would have been useful enough, but it did more than this. It gave the experimenter excellent clues for the divination of unconscious thematic formations!' (p. 534).

TAT responses of subjects can be scored systematicaly according to a scheme developed by Murray or on a more impressionistic basis. It is used both in clinical work and in experimental studies of human motivation (McClelland, 1961). The TAT assumes a close relationship between the expressed fantasy (story about the TAT card) and underlying motivation as well as a relationship between such fantasy and behavior. Efforts to test these assumptions have met with mixed results. Fantasy can both be associated with the expression of motives in behavior and also serve as a substitute for the expression of motives in behavior. Thus, for example, a person with a strong motive to be aggressive with others may express this motive both in fantasy (TAT) and behavior, but the person may also express it in fantasy and block it from expression in overt behavior.

Evaluation of Projective Tests   How can we evaluate projective tests? Since comments made in relation to the Rorschach are generally applicable to other projective tests and the approach to theory associated with them, discussion here focuses on the Rorschach.

The attempt to use the richness of Rorschach responses to assess most, if not all, dimensions of an individual's personality creates problems in determining the test's reliability and validity. There is no substantial evidence to support the reliability of the Rorschach, but it is difficult to know whether this is because of unreliability or because of the difficulty in making appropriate reliability studies. Because Rorschach interpretation involves the use of so many sources and combinations of data, and because it is hard to separate individual interpretive statements from the total description of the individual's personality, there is no conclusive evidence concerning the reliability of interpretation on the Rorschach. One study has found contradictions in interpretations given by clinical psychologists (Little and Shneidman, 1959), while another found high agreement among analyzed psychologists but less agreement among psychologists who had not been analyzed and who had less professional experience (Silverman, 1959).

The validity of the Rorschach is a quite complex matter. The literature is filled with contradictory findings, and there is considerable disagreement about an appropriate test of its validity. One procedure for determining the validity of the Rorschach has been to check the extent to which interpretations based on Rorschach protocols match interpretations based on other kinds of data. Some studies show good agreement between Rorschach interpretations and clinical descriptions (Benjamin and Ebaugh, 1938; Krugman, 1942); others find little agreement between Rorschach interpretations and interpretations based on other projective tests (Little and Schneidman, 1959). In general, efforts to use the Rorschach to predict behavior have been quite unsuccessful.

The difficulty in assessing the reliability of the Rorschach alone would make the determination of its validity difficult. As has been noted, if the test is not reliable it can hardly be valid. Beyond this, however, are a variety of issues that complicate efforts to validate the test and reflect the clinical aspects of the test and its use. One problem in validation is that of agreement on an appropriate criterion for the accuracy of interpretations. Furthermore, according to Piotrowski (1966), the Rorschach provides a better measure of how a person might act than of actual behavior. If this is

so, how do we validate mere potentials? The situation is further complicated by the view that the Rorschach measures a level of personality "below the surface behavior" (Stone, 1960). What kinds of criteria can be used
to check on Rorschach interpretations of these deeper levels of behavior?

These difficulties in Rorschach validation are related to the clinical and
psychodynamic aspects of the test, which attempt to give a multidimensional picture of the total personality. Overemphasis on any one aspect of
the subject's responses may distort the entire interpretation, resulting in
the loss of much that was otherwise accurate. It is difficult, if not impossible, to locate such sources of error where the interpretation is global and
holistic.

What we have, then, after years of research on the Rorschach, is a mass
of contradictory information. For those psychologists who have an invest-
ment in measurement properties of tests and emphasize the usual measurement criteria of objectivity, reliability, and validity, the Rorschach
hardly seems an adequate measure of personality. Other psychologists are
impressed with the clinical utility of the Rorschach in the assessment of
personality but also take seriously the equivocal nature of the research
findings. Such psychologists find themselves in a dilemma:

> We exhibit faith in the Rorschach and in our own clinical skills by continuing to use it in the
> face of strong professional admonitions to the contrary. We recognize that adequate use of
> the test is dependent upon the clinician; a function of training, experience, and unknown
> personality variables. Simultaneously, there is continual pressure to demonstrate that the test
> meets the usual . . . criteria of objectivity, reliability, validity . . . which in fact it does not.
>
> DANA 1965, P. 494

For those psychologists who respect the need for validity but question the
adequacy of current procedures for establishing such validity, the data
gained in the clinic far outweigh those data gained in research. The clinician who uses the Rorschach and other projective techniques is convinced
that such tests are necessary to capture the total personality. "The outcome is a formalized, yet alive, picture of the complete personality" (Rickers-Ovsiankina, 1960, p. 3). The data from other tests are looked upon as
being trivial and fragmented compared to the richness of a Rorschach interpretation. The Rorschach is seen as being the psychologist's "microscope," "stethoscope," or "fluoroscope," and "X-ray" able to penetrate to
the depths of the individual's personality. Although its critics assess the
evidence and conclude that the Rorschach is invalid, its advocates conclude that "the most stable instrument so far developed for probing into
the human personality at its several levels is that made up by Rorschach's

ten ink-blot figures" (Beck, 1951, p. 103). The controversy is unresolved. A recent study of the testing practices of clinical psychologists criticizes them for their disregard of negative research evidence (Wade and Baker, 1977), while a clinician responds that "the clinical practitioner is wise to reject inappropriate experimental investigations of phenomena of importance to him or her" (Karon, 1978, p. 765).

This discussion of the Rorschach has not been intended to make the student an expert in the use of this instrument. Similarly, the discussion of its reliability and validity is not presented as one that leads to a conclusion about the utility of the test or of a psychodynamic model of personality. It does, however, help the reader to get a glimpse of the relationship between an approach toward the conceptualization of personality and an assessment technique. The assets and limitations, strengths and weaknesses, contributions and problems of the theory become an integral part of the assessment technique.

In sum, we have a model of personality that is clinical in its emphasis on the individual and dynamic in its emphasis on behavior as a result of the interplay among forces, drives, conflicts, and layers of personality. In relation to this model, we have an assessment technique, the projective test, that in its administration, scoring, and interpretation reflects a dynamic orientation to the analysis of personality. Questionnaires, such as the ones described below, are viewed as being of limited use because many people are too insecure to admit to some personality characteristics, vary in how they interpret the meaning of questions, and do not know themselves. More focused and objective samples of behavior lead to fragmented and trivial conceptualizations of personality.

Those who use projective techniques emphasize that only these tests are capable of capturing the richness of personality. Ambiguous stimuli elicit individual, idiosyncratic responses. Each response given by the individual expresses his or her personality. This "projective hypothesis" assumes that each response is projected out from within and that, through the freedom to respond, the personality of the individual comes through. "Every act, expression, response bears the stamp of this personality" (Mayman, Schafer, and Rapaport, 1951, p. 542). Responses that are most idiosyncratic and most deviant from the stimulus are assumed to be of particular significance. Every response is presumed to have ramifications for behavior outside the testing situation; there is a parallel between the way subjects handle the test stimuli and the way in which they characteristically deal with their environment in vital matters (Piotrowski, 1966). The unstructured, disguised, and voluntary qualities of projective tests are seen as providing the best opportunity for assessing the interplay of motives and organizing principles in an individual's personality.

Subjective Techniques

Interviews

This category includes assessment techniques that are nonstructured, non-disguised, and voluntary. Techniques in this category emphasize individuality in response by allowing people to choose their own response among a considerable number of nonstructured, voluntary alternatives. In this way they are similar to projective tests. However, whereas the purpose of projective tests is disguised, the purpose of subjective tests is apparent. In these tests, examiner and subject are in agreement as to purpose, since disguise is assumed to be unnecessary or actually a barrier to obtaining the desired information. Scoring and interpretation correspondingly tend to be closely related to the data obtained, as opposed to highly symbolic interpretations. Unstructured, direct interviews and autobiographies are most illustrative of these techniques.

Personality theories that use data from subjective assessment techniques tend to emphasize individual differences and place less emphasis on unconscious layers of organization in personality functioning, correspondingly emphasizing the actual content of verbal report in the terms in which it is given. The approach here, then, is highly phenomenological; the data of interest to the psychologist are the perceptions, meanings, and experiences of the subjects as they report them. Emphasis is on the subjectivity and uniqueness of the individual's response to his phenomenal field. What is real for the individual, how he interprets phenomena in terms of his own frame of reference, is what is important in understanding behavior.

The interview represents a mixed bag as an assessment technique, since there are many different types of interviews which are used for varied purposes. A broad definition of the interview is a "face-to-face verbal interchange in which one person, the interviewer, attempts to elicit information or expressions of opinion or belief from another person or persons" (Maccoby and Maccoby, 1954, p. 449). A major distinction among types of interviews is whether they are standardized and fixed in format or unstandardized and open in format. In standardized interviews the questions to be asked are decided in advance so that the same questions are asked in the same phrasing and order for all subjects. In the unstandardized interview, the content and order of questions are dependent upon the answers given by the subject. The standardized interview facilitates measurement and quantification of responses, permitting comparisons of different subjects. Data obtained are also apt to be more reliable than data obtained from the more free-wheeling, open-format interview. On the other hand, the open-format interview allows the interviewer to develop content areas that seem significant for the individual and could not have been anticipated in the planning of a structured interview. Such an interview gives greater emphasis to the uniqueness of each subject and facilitates a detailed phenomenological analysis, though perhaps at the price of rigor and potential for quantitative comparisons across subjects.

content analysis

Whether the interview is standardized or unstandardized, the potential for systematic, objective scoring of interview data is particularly noteworthy because of a process known as **content analysis**, a procedure through which data from an interview are systematically categorized. The nature of the categories can vary according to the content of the interview and the goals of the investigator. For example, an interest in the mood of subjects can lead to scoring the content of an interview in terms of categories such as positive, neutral, or negative mood.

The interview clearly represents a significant technique for gathering a wealth of information about a subject. "If you want to know about a person's private experiences, perhaps the most direct method is to ask the person himself" (Kleinmutz, 1967, p. 20). On the other hand, there are many problems involved. A face-to-face verbal exchange between two people is a highly complex event and rarely involves mere verbal exchange. The interviewer can influence the subjects' responses in a variety of subtle ways. The appearance and manner of the interviewer will have different meanings for different subjects, and the data may vary accordingly. A dramatic example is the "Greenspoon effect." In some early research on verbal conditioning, Greenspoon (1951) found that a subject's verbal behavior (use of plural nouns) could be significantly influenced by the experimenter responding with "mmm-hum!' or "uh-huh" to specific verbal responses. What is particularly significant here is that the subject is likely to be unaware of this influence. And, if such interviewer responses are not part of the research design, the interviewer may also be unaware of this source of bias. The issue is particularly complex since the source and nature of the influence of the experimenter may vary from subject to subject (Greenspoon, 1962).

The Greenspoon effect represents only one source of potential bias. The interviewer's appearance, manner, style, expectations, and habits in recording data all may be sources of bias. Such factors lead to different interviewers eliciting different information and to low interviewer reliability. The reliability of interpretations based on interview data also remains a question. In research on psychiatric diagnoses and personality evaluations on the basis of interviews, Raines and Rohrer (1955) found that two psychiatrists interviewing the same man were likely to observe and report different personality characteristics. A given psychiatrist appeared to have a preferred personality classification. Thus, while one psychiatrist would report anxiety, another would report depression. Later research suggested that distortions in interviewer perception of subject characteristics was a

result of the interviewer's own life experiences and personality characteristics (Raines and Rohrer, 1960). In making highly subjective judgments on
the basis of verbal reports, interviewers constantly face the danger of pro-
jecting their own personalities into ambiguous data. The interview, then,
provides for the gathering of a wealth of clinical, phenomenological data,
but its reliability and validity remain to be demonstrated (Matarazzo,
1965): "The point is rarely, if ever made, but [each innovator's] approach
to the interview . . . is very much a reflection of his own highly personal
philosophy of life. In interviewing, as in all other behavior, the man himself cannot be divorced from his method" (Mattarazzo, 1965, p. 408).

The Freudian, psychoanalytic interview exphasizes free association,
conflicts, and an exploration of the unconscious. According to Deutsch
and Murphy (1955), the analytic interview attempts to determine the nature of the person's conflicts, how they motivate his life, and how they developed in relation to early family relationships. The interviewer remains
aware of the "manifold meanings, intentional and unintentional ones,
conscious and unconscious ones" in the subject's vocabulary. The goal of
the interviewer is "the intensification and continual guidance of the associations" in preparation for insight into unconscious connections that
have been suppressed.

This transcript of a psychoanalytic interview represents abstracted passages from a first interview by the doctor (D) of a patient (P). The patient
was a 26-year-old male who entered the hospital shortly after becoming
engaged to marry. He presented complaints of pains in his feet. The comments in brackets indicate the thoughts of the interviewer during the interview process.

Early in the Interview

P: I can't stand on my feet. They sent me down to the foot doctor. I
sweat all day.

D: Can't stand on your own feet?

P: I've got no strength in my feet. I've got no strength in my body.
[Feet are paramount in the body image.]

D: It isn't a nice position to be in, not to be able to stand on your own
feet. You weren't always like that? [It was decided to take the
symbolism of "standing on one's own feet" as the core of the sector.]

P: What I'd like to do. I don't know. It might be me; it might be my
doctor. I don't know why I don't seem to get anywhere.

D: You mean you're not getting anywhere on your feet? [Connecting
his own words; he needs feet to get somewhere.]

P: Getting anywhere! I got a certain problem. I go in there and tell him. It hurts me a little, maybe I start to cry. I still don't get anywhere. I don't understand it. I want to go back to Dr. B. ["It (feet) hurts him." and he cries] p. 77

D: What do you mean, a certain problem? [Dr. B. was kind and sympathetic and allowed him barbiturates. The patient is pinned down to the key word relating to feet.]

P: I'd like to get back to Dr. B.

D: What problem are you talking about? [His plea is ignored. It is important to remain consistent.]

P: Well, like the other day, I go in to talk to him and I told him how I felt. I started talking about the Army and how they used to drag me, and how I'd start crying. So I cry. Then I go off and I feel just as bad, and I still don't understand it any more.

D: You went in the Army and they started to drag you? [He was dragged when his feet gave way.]

P: That's right. They used to drag me and things, and so I'd tell him. ["And things" seems to contain the important material.]

D: They used to drag you?

P: That's right. Two people, one on each side. I want to go back to Dr. B.

D: Two people dragged you, you mean like you'd drag a kid along? ["Kid" is used here to get ready for splitting the ego into a childlike part that faces an adult portion, and to stimulate thoughts connected with the past. Was he ever "dragged" before? It is assumed that his problem is not knowing how to "walk and to stand like a man" without fear.] p. 78 (Deutsch and Murphy, 1955)

These interview sequences give some indication of the attempts by the interviewer to focus on conflicts and to draw the patient back into the past for an appreciation of the origin of the conflicts. The interviewer goes beyond the information provided by the subject and relies on his assumptions concerning the nature of the psychological forces that govern human behavior. In guiding the interview on the basis of theoretical assumptions, and in making interpretations in relation to them, the psychoanalyst is interested in more than mere self-reports of perceptions, meanings, and experiences.

    The directed and guiding aspects of the psychoanalytic interview are in contrast with the more clearly phenomenological approach of other interviews. For example, in the nondirective or client-centered approach to interviewing associated with Rogers, the interviewer asks few direct questions and avoids making interpretations that go far beyond the data. The fragments of the previous interview can be constrasted with the following fragments from an interview with a student who was having academic and personal difficulties and who expressed feelings of inferiority. He is small in stature and in his boyhood was ridiculed for having "sissy" interests. The interviewer is designated as the counselor (C) and the subject as the student (S).

BOX 12.3   **Subjective Techniques—
the Nondirective,
Client-Centered Interview**

C: You feel that you'd be a lot happier if you were just like the other fellows and not emotional.

S: That's right. Of course, I'd like to be—not, not experience these fears [Pause.] I'd like to be calm and be clear-thinking in all situations.

C: Instead of those things you find yourself to be somewhat emotional.

S: I go haywire. [Laugh, followed by pause.]

C: You've thought a lot about that. What is your ideal person?

S: Uh, well, some scientist. That is what I consider an ideal person, preferably a physical scientist, in chemistry or physics or an engineer, one who—one who serves society by making things more convenient. I like everything modern.

C: Someone who deals only in things, and not in emotions.

S: That's right, something tangible.

C: So you'd really like to solve this difficulty by being someone very different from yourself.

S: Yes. That's why I'm in engineering college. I have an opportunity to —well, just to experiment with myself and see actually what talents I do have in that direction. They're not so bad, but I lack some—some of the very fundamental things that a good engineer should have: that is, being calm, sticking right to it, and forgetting about things that have come up. A good engineer is not emotional, that's about one of the worst things he could—No person who is emotional is a good engineer.

C: So that in some respects you've gone into engineering because you felt it would be awfully good discipline for you, is that right? Make you stop being emotional?

BOX 12.3 **Subjective Techniques —
the Nondirective, Client-Centered Interview** *continued*

S: That's right.

C: It was that, perhaps, rather than being interested in engineering.

S: Well, it was mingled with a certain genuine interest. There was some that's true. But it was largely due to that, exactly what I said, to a considerable extent.

C: You don't suppose that part of your trouble is that now you're wondering whether you want to be your real self. Could that be part of it?

S: Uh, what's that?

C: Well, I just wondered. You're trying so hard to be some other fellow aren't you?

S: Yeah, because I'm not satisfied with myself.

C: You feel that the self that you are isn't worth being.

S: Yeah, that's right, and unless you can change my mind about that, then I'll continue thinking along the same line.

C: [Laughing.] Why, that almost sounds as though you were wishing that somebody would change your mind about it.

S: [Very soberly.] Yeah. Because I don't know how I can solve it the other way.

C: In other words, you're finding it a pretty rough proposition to try to be a calm, unemotional engineer when really you're something quite different.

S: Right. Yeah, that is a very tough position. I find it impossible, and I hate the idea that it's impossible.

C: And you have it partly because you feel there's nothing worthwhile about this real self of yours.

S: Yes.

C: What are some of the things your real self would like to do?

S: Oh, let's see. Well—uh, I told you I was interested in mathematics. That's one thing. Also, I was interested in anthropology. At the same time, I was interested in music and in —well, now, I used to like novels, but I don't care for them anymore, but—I would like—I think I have a gift for writing, too, and I'm ashamed of those gifts.

SOURCE   C. R. Rogers, *Counseling and Psychotherapy.* Boston: Houghton-Mifflin, 1942, pp. 201–203.

In this interview fragment, the interviewer does a great deal of restating and offers encouragement for the subject to go on. The one semi-interpretive statement about whether the student wants to be his real self is out of character with the rest of the interview. This interview is more characteristic of the phenomenological approach than the psychoanalytic interview, both in terms of the relative avoidance of structuring, interpretive comments, and in the attention paid to the way the student views himself. Interviews vary, then, in terms of stimuli (questions) presented and interpretations made. The phenomenological approach is most apparent in those interviews where the questions asked do not overly restrict the freedom of the individual to respond and where the subject's viewing of phenomena are taken at their own face value.

Measures of the Self-Concept

The phenomenological approach was discussed earlier independent of specific content. The passage in Box 12.3 from a Rogerian interview is significant in relation to the attention given to the way the individual feels about himself. Phenomenology is not limited to views about the self, but phenomenologically oriented theories of personality have tended to emphasize the self-concept: "The self is composed of perceptions concerning the individual and this organization of perceptions in turn has vital and important effects upon the behavior of the individual" (Combs, 1957, p. 470). The interview is one major method for obtaining data relevant to the self-concept, but it is not the only one. Although other methods are more structured than the interview, they are worthy of discussion within this framework.

In the interview, subjects can be asked to describe themselves or the way in which they view themselves. Under more structured conditions, the subjects can be asked to check adjectives they feel apply to them (*adjective checklist*), they can be asked to select among a variety of statements those that most apply to them and those that least apply to them (*Q-sort*), or they can be asked to rate themselves on a series of scales containing polar adjectives (*semantic differential*).

The *Q-sort* technique discussed in relation to Rogers' theory of personality (Chapter 5) has been used frequently to measure the self-concept. In this approach the experimenter gives the subject a pile of cards, each containing a statement concerning some personality characteristic. One card might say "Makes friends easily," another might say "Has trouble expressing anger," and so on for each of the cards. Subjects are asked to read these statements (generally about a hundred) and then sort the cards according to which statements they feel are most descriptive of them and which are least descriptive. The subjects are asked to arrange the cards into a certain distribution of which one end represents "Most characteristic of me" and the other "Least characteristic of me." Subjects are told how many piles of cards are to be used and how many cards are to go into each pile. For example with 100 cards the subject might be asked to sort the cards into eleven piles as follows: 2–4–8–11–16–18–16–11–8–4–2. The distribution is a normal one and expresses the subjects' comparative estimates of how descriptive each characteristic is.

The Q-sort technique is structured in that the subject must respond to the statements provided by the experimenter and must sort them into the predetermined piles. On the other hand, as Vernon (1964) points out, the items chosen by the experimenter are generally derived from statements made by similar subjects and individuals are free to distribute the items in terms of the relative applicability to them of each characteristic. Also, in contrast to standardized tests, the Q-sort technique allows for flexibility in determining the items according to the specific assessment goals of the experimenters and the specific subjects with which they are engaged. Thus there is a potential for obtaining complex descriptions about single individuals.

The *semantic differential* (Osgood, Suci, and Tannenbaum, 1957) also represents a structured test that is useful in obtaining data relevant to the self-concept and the ways in which individuals perceive the environment. Developed as a measure of attitudes and the meanings of concepts, rather than as a specific test of personality, the semantic differential has potential as a useful technique for personality assessment. In filling out the semantic differential, the individual rates a concept on a number of seven-point scales defined by polar adjectives such as good-bad, strong-weak, active-passive. Thus, a subject would rate a concept such as "my self" or "my ideal self" on each of the polar adjective scales. A rating on any one scale would indicate whether the subject felt one of the adjectives was very descriptive of the concept or somewhat descriptive, or whether neither adjective was applicable to the concept. The ratings are made in terms of the meaning of the concept for the individual.

Like the Q-sort, the semantic differential is a structured technique in that the subject must rate certain concepts and use the polar adjective scales provided by the experimenter. This structure provides for the gathering of data suitable for statistical analysis but, also like the Q-sort, the semantic differential does not preclude flexibility in decision as to the concepts and scales to be used. There is no single standardized semantic differential. A variety of scales can be used in relation to concepts such as father, mother, and doctor to determine the meanings of phenomena for the individual. Certainly the meanings an individual attaches to phenomena about him, including his self-concept, are basic to personality.

One example of the way in which the semantic differential can be used to assess personality is its application to a case of multiple personality. In the 1950's two psychiatrists, Corbett Thigpen and Harvey Cleckley, made famous the case of "The Three Faces of Eve." This was the case of a woman who possessed three personalities, each of which predominated for a period of time, with frequent shifts back and forth. The three personalities were called Eve White, Eve Black, and Jane. As part of a research endeavor, the psychiatrists were able to have each of the three personalities rate a variety of concepts on the semantic differential. The ratings were then analyzed both quantitatively and qualitatively by two psychologists (C. Osgood and Z. Luria) who did not know the subject. The analysis by the psychologists included both descriptive comments and interpretations of the personalties that went beyond the objective data. For example, Eve White was described as being in contact with social reality but under great emotional stress, Eve Black as out of contact with social reality but quite self-assured, and Jane as superficially very healthy but quite restricted and undiversified. The analysis on the basis of the semantic differential turned out to fit quite well the descriptions offered by the two psychiatrists.

BOX 12.4 **A Measure of the Self-Concept— The Semantic Differential**

RATIONALE   Determine the meaning of concepts for people by having them rate the concept on a variety of polar adjective scales.

SUBJECT   A case of triple personality, labeled as "Eve White, "Eve Black," and "Jane."

STIMULI   Fifteen concepts (for example, Me, My Father, My Mother, Love, Child), each rated on ten scales (for example, valuable-worthless, active-passive, strong-weak, tense-relaxed).

PROCEDURE   Each personality rates the 15 concepts on the ten scales.

RESULTS   The following are partial descriptions of each personality.

EVE WHITE   Perceives the world in an essentially normal fashion, is well socialized, but has an unsatisfactory attitude toward herself. The chief evidence of disturbance in the personality is the fact that ME (the self-concept) is considered a little bad, a little passive, and definitely weak.

EVE BLACK   Eve Black has achieved a violent kind of adjustment in which she perceives herself as literally perfect, but, to accomplish this break, her way of perceiving the world becomes completely disoriented from the norm. If Eve Black perceives herself as good, then she also has to accept HATRED and FRAUD as positive values.

BOX 12.4 **A Measure of the Self-Concept —
The Semantic Differential** *continued*

JANE   Jane displays the most "healthy" meaning pattern, in which she accepts the usual evaluations of concepts by her society yet still maintains a satisfactory evaluation of herself. The self concept, ME, while not strong (but not weak, either) is nearer the good and active directions of the semantic space.

CONCLUSION   "The analyses of these personalities and their changes given so far have been descriptive rather than interpretive for the most part. In a sense, we have merely put into words what this woman herself, in her several personalities, has indicated by her check marks."

SOURCE   C.E. Osgood and Z. Luria A blind analysis of a case of multiple personality using the semantic differential. *Journal of Abnormal and Social Psychology,* 1954, *49,* 579–591.

Note should also be made here of George Kelly's (1955) Role Construct Repertory (REP) Test, which was discussed in Chapter 6 and shares some similarities with the semantic differential. The REP test aims at determining the constructs people use to define, interpret, or construe their environment. Whereas the semantic differential uses scales defined by the experimenter, the REP test elicits scales from the subject. By presenting subjects successive triads of persons, including the self (self, mother, father), the tester is able to come up with polar adjective scales, or in Kelly's term constructs. It is assumed that the number and content of the constructs, and the relationships among them, offer insight into how individuals interpret their worlds, including themselves. The REP test technique is structured in the sense that it starts off with fixed roles to which the subjects assign people from their lives, but it clearly allows for maximum freedom for the individuals to then come up with their own unique assortment of similarity-contrast dimensions.

Self-report data are easy to obtain and generally relate to important aspects of how the person views the relationship between the self and the surrounding environment. If taken purely at the level of expressions of the person's phenomenal world and cognitive functioning, there is no problem with such data. However, we are in trouble when we regard self-report data as accurate reflections of the self or of life's events. Whether because of psychological defenses or of faulty memory and observation systems, reports about the self are often filled with error when checked against actual records or the observations of others (Burton, 1970). Not only is the current construction of the self influenced by past experiences, but the recall of such experiences is influenced by current constructions of the self. In addition, in our efforts to summarize our behavior in an integrated way we make many errors of judgment (Taversky and Kahneman, 1974). Tendencies to exaggerate important and consistent events and to minimize less important and inconsistent events lead to distortions in the validity of self-report data. Such problems in recall and observation are greater or less for different individuals and for different kinds of self-report data. However, they remain a serious problem if one wishes to conclude that actual events and behavior are being measured as opposed to the person's constructions and experiencing of such events and behaviors.

MAJOR CONCEPTS AND SUMMARY

reliability	disguised-nondisguised
validity	voluntary-objective
criterion-oriented validity	projective test
concurrent validity	subjective test
predictive validity	psychometric test
construct validity	objective-behavioral test
structured-nonstructured	

This chapter has considered some of the ways in which psychologists assess personality functioning. The goal of assessment is the systematic gathering of accurate and relevant data concerning the individual, translated into the concepts of reliability and validity. In assessment we seek reliable observations, information free of error or bias in recording, scoring, or interpretation. We also seek valid observations, information related to what we hope to be measuring and to other present data (concurrent validity) or useful in making predictions concerning the future (predictive validity). Another kind of validity is construct validity, in which there is no definitive criterion and the validity of the concept and test are established together in the course of extensive research.

Campbell's three dimensions of tests (structured-nonstructured, disguised-nondisguised, voluntary-objective) were used to develop a scheme for classifying tests. Throughout the chapter it was suggested that different theories of personality tend to lead to different techniques of personality assessment and to different kinds of observations about individuals. Thus, for example, projective tests such as the Rorschach and TAT were seen as being associated with clinical, psychodynamic theories of personality. Such tests emphasize maximum freedom of response, the uniqueness of each individual, the holistic aspects of personality, and the role of defenses in psychological functioning. Researchers generally question the reliability and validity of data from such tests, but many clinicians continue to find them useful in their practice and suggest that these research studies do not adequately reflect the complexity of the issues involved.

The discussion of subjective tests (nondisguised, nonstructured) focused on their association with theories that emphasize the phenomenlogical functioning of the individual generally and the self-concept in particular. The interview is a valuable tool in this area. In addition, tests such as the Q-sort, semantic differential, and Rep test were considered as illustrative of tests that provide some structure but focus on the person's perception of the self and surrounding world and generally leave some room for individuality of response. Data from such tests were seen as providing valuable information about the persons' perception of the self and life but as suffering from serious flaws when considered as accurate statements of what existed in the past or exists in the present. Self-report data are subject to serious errors and bias due to psychological defenses and/or human errors in recall and observation. Here, too, the magnitude of such error or bias may be found to vary according to the individual and area of personality functioning involved.

In the next chapter we will consider other assessment devices associated with different theoretical points of view. Such tests will be found to have different qualities and different strengths and limitations from those discussed in this chapter. Discussion of these additional tests will provide the basis for an overview of the field of personality assessment.

CLASSIFICATION OF TESTS

Psychometric Techniques
• Cattell 16 Personality Factor Inventory
• Minnesota Multiphasic Personality Inventory
• Self-Report Questionnaires: Final Comments

Objective Techniques: Standardized Performance
Tests and Behavioral Assessment
• Sign and Sample Approaches to Assessment

CLINICAL VERSUS STATISTICAL PREDICTION

The Statistical Approach

The Clinical Approach

Evidence and Controversy

Strengths and Limitations of the Two Approaches

A SUMMARY OVERVIEW OF THE ASSESSMENT FIELD

MAJOR CONCEPTS AND SUMMARY

13 ASSESSMENT: PSYCHOMETRIC TESTS AND BEHAVIORAL OBSERVATIONS

Chapter Focus:

In this chapter we continue our examination of assessment techniques —procedures for systematically gaining information about individual personality. Continuing to focus on the association between personality theory and techniques of assessment, we consider psychometric tests based on factor analysis and associated with trait theories, and techniques of behavioral observation associated with learning theories of personality. A discussion of the controversy concerning how we should organize information to make predictions about behavior is followed by an overview of the assessment field.

It appears, however, that ratings and self-report measures lend themselves better to trait identification than performance tests. . . . The riches of rating and self-rating as mining grounds for the uncovering of personality traits seem to be real despite the accompanying unwanted rocks and dust.

WILDE, 1977, P. 72

Another characteristic of behavioral approaches to assessment is that their data are often direct samples of behavior in specific situations, instead of indirect and generalized indicants of behavioral predispositions.

KANFER AND PHILLIPS, 1970, P. 509

CLASSIFICATION OF TESTS

In the preceding chapter we discussed nonstructured tests. Such tests give considerable freedom to the individual to respond in a personal way. While scoring systems can be applied to such data, the emphasis is generally on the richness of detail obtained about the person. In this chapter we concentrate on *structured* tests—tests that limit or restrict the individual's responses. The stimuli presented in these tests generally are unambiguous and explicit. Options for response tend to be fewer and to focus much more on specific aspects of behavioral functioning. Usually investigators using structured tests are more concerned with reliability and validity than are those who use projective and subjective techniques.

Psychometric Techniques

Psychometric techniques utilize structured and voluntary personality tests. Such tests tend to consist of questionnaires associated with the empirical development of a personality theory. Self-report questionnaires fall into this category because they consist of a limited number of specific items and a limited number of response options (agree-disagree, yes-no). The subjects choose the options they most agree with or feel are most descriptive of themselves. Such tests are thus both structured and voluntary. It should be noted that while self-report questionnaires in this category involve voluntary responses, they are treated differently than are responses to subjective tests. Whereas responses to subjective tests (such as interview and self-concept scales) are viewed as true statements concerning the person, this is not assumed to be the case with responses to psychometric tests. The significance of self-ratings on these tests is determined through the investigation of their relationships with other questionnaire responses or other nontest behavior. In other words, if a man says he thinks highly of himself, the researcher does not assume that this is necessarily so but, instead, is interested in how the response relates to other questionnaire responses and overt behavior. The accuracy of a self-statement then, is not important; what is important is the extent to which self-reports can be meaningfully related to other aspects of behavior.

Personality questionnaires in this category can be developed through one of three methods: rational-theoretical, factor analytic, and empirical-criterion. In **rational-theoretical** test development, the constructor starts out with a personality concept or set of concepts defined in terms of the behaviors, attitudes, values and so on that are expected to be associated with it. For example, the concept of anxiety might lead us to believe that anxious people will report that they often feel jittery, worried, tense, and have a variety of physiological symptoms. A test of anxiety developed on the basis of a rational approach might then use appropriate items in a questionnaire and ask subjects to indicate whether each is characteristic of them. This kind of process, in fact, was used by Taylor (1953) to develop the Manifest Anxiety Scale. She first defined the construct of anxiety, had clinical psychologists pick out from a list of 200 items those that appeared to fit the definition of the construct, and used those items on which there was agreement to construct her test of manifest anxiety. She then conducted many research studies to see if scores on the Manifest Anxiety Scale related to other behaviors in a way that would be expected according to her theory of anxiety.

A second method of test development uses the statistical technique of **factor analysis**, discussed in Chapter 8. The psychologist starts off with a large assortment of test items, administered to a large number of subjects. Items to which groups of subjects respond in a similar way are related to one another and form a cluster or factor. Factor analysis is a means for finding clusters or factors, the items within any single cluster being highly related to one another and slightly or not at all related to items in the other clusters. Cattell's 16 Personality Factor Inventory (page 250) illustrates this approach to test development.

In the **empirical-criterion** method of test construction, the investigator begins with groups of people known to be different in some particular way (intelligence, psychopathology, business success, criminal record, and so forth). A series of items is then given to these groups and those that discriminate between the members of the different groups are retained to form the test. For example, in the development of the Strong Vocational Interest Blank, members of different occupational groups indicated their preferences among activities and items were chosen on the basis of the degree to which the responses differentiated among successful members of the various occupational groups. The Minnesota Multiphasic Personal-

(margin labels)
rational-theoretical

factor analysis

empirical-criterion

ity Inventory (MMPI), to be considered later in this chapter, also illustrates the empirical-criterion approach to test development.

There are important differences among the three methods, but all three use empirical procedures to develop structured, voluntary, self-report questionnaires.

Cattell 16 Personality Factor Inventory

Cattell uses the concept of trait to account for regularities and consistencies in behavior (see Chapter 8). He identifies personality traits through factor analysis, and the 16 P.F. represents his major effort to develop a personality questionnaire. The manual describes the test:

The 16 P.F. is the psychologist's answer, in the questionnaire realm, to the demand for a test giving fullest information in the shortest time about most personality traits. It is not merely concerned with some narrow concept of neuroticism or "adjustment," or some special kind of ability, but sets out to cover planfully and precisely all the main dimensions along which people can differ, according to basic factor analytic research.

HANDBOOK FOR THE 16 P.F. TEST, 1957

This test is an example of the use of factor analysis to develop both a theory and an assessment technique. The original 16 P.F. followed a survey of all well-known self-report personality questionnaires and scales. As of 1946 about 20 factors could be discerned and were the basis for the development of questionnaire items "directly designed to measure the concepts better than by any existing tests" (Cattell, 1956, p. 206). Items were also based on new personality factors from nonquestionnaire sources. Factor analysis of these items gave twenty factors that showed good agreement with the factors derived from the survey of questionnaire and nonquestionnaire findings.

Some of the twenty were ambiguous; they were dropped from the further development of the personality inventory and Cattell was left with 15 personality and one general intelligence factor. According to the manual: "At this point it suffices to summarize that these are the main dimensions that have been found necessary and adequate to cover all kinds of individual differences of personality found in common speech and psychological literature. They leave out no important aspect of the total personality" (1962 Edition Manual, p. 2).

What does such a comprehensive personality questionnaire look like? The 16 P.F. has two forms, each of which contains 187 items. Each item is a statement, such as "I like to watch team games," that is responded to in terms of three possible answers—yes, occasionally, no. Subjects are told not to spend time pondering and to "give the first, natural answer" as it comes to them: "Answer as honestly as possible what is true of *you*. Do not merely mark what seems 'the right thing to say' to impress the examiner" (1962 Edition).

The 16 P.F. is, in a sense, a standardized, systematic, impersonal interview. It is *structured* in that there are only three alternative responses to each item. It is *voluntary* in that subjects are free to choose their own response rather than give a correct response or "impress the examiner." The test is direct and nondisguised in the sense that subjects know that it is a test of personality. Furthermore, in some cases they may be able to recognize the significance of an individual item, though in many cases the relevance to personality characteristics is not apparent.

The test yields scores for the subject on 16 personality dimensions, the psychological meaning of which are defined in a test manual. Taken together, these are assumed to encompass the personality in all its main dimensions. For interpretive purposes the scores are plotted on a profile sheet (See Box 13.1). Interpretations, diagnosis, and prediction can then proceed, with objective detachment, on the basis of a statistical analysis of profile scores.

The scales on the 16 P.F. appear to have adequate, though not exceptionally high, reliability. The main evidence for validity lies in the factor analytic construction of the test. Many of the factors correspond to those derived from rating and experimental data, which lends support to their validity. Proponents of the technique cite many potential applications of the test (in clinical, educational, and industrial settings) and describe it as being preferable to the "crystal ball" guesses of "unreliable" projective methods. Validity in these areas nevertheless remains to be demonstrated. According to one reviewer, "No other test covers such a wide range of personality dimensions and never before have the dimensions been so meticulously determined" (Adcock, 1965, p. 197). Other psychologists are critical of the factor analytic approach in general and still others, while using factor analysis, dispute the specific scales derived by Cattell (Guilford, 1975).

Minnesota Multiphasic Personality Inventory [MMPI]

The Minnesota Multiphasic Personality Inventory or MMPI (Hathaway and McKinley, 1943), is another example of a self-report personality questionnaire developed on statistical or empirical grounds. The MMPI—used in many industrial, business, educational, and mental health settings—is the most frequently used personality questionnaire.

The MMPI was originally constructed as part of an effort to develop a **criterion** practical screening device for psychiatric settings. The construction **empirical keying** method used is known as **criterion** or **empirical keying**: items are included

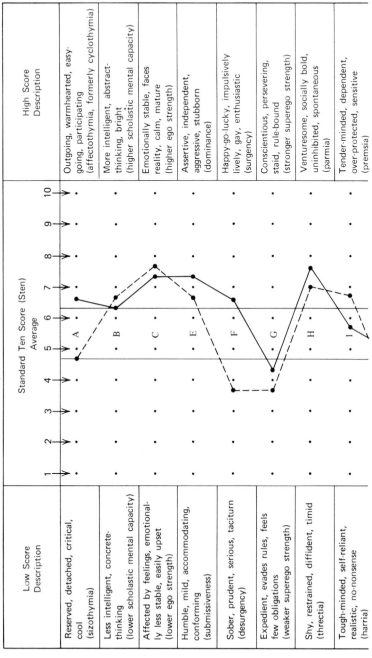

BOX 13.1 **Psychometric Test—
Cattell 16 Personality Factor Inventory**

Illustration of Profiles on the 16 P.F. for College Undergraduate (Solid Line, Based on 1128 Cases) and Administrator in University (Broken Line. Based on 69 Cases)

Low Score Description	Standard Ten Score (Sten) Average										High Score Description
	1	2	3	4	5	6	7	8	9	10	
Reserved, detached, critical, cool (sizothymia)						A					Outgoing, warmhearted, easy-going, participating (affectothymia, formerly cyclothymia)
Less intelligent, concrete-thinking (lower scholastic mental capacity)						B					More intelligent, abstract-thinking, bright (higher scholastic mental capacity)
Affected by feelings, emotionally less stable, easily upset (lower ego strength)						C					Emotionally stable, faces reality, calm, mature (higher ego strength)
Humble, mild, accommodating, conforming (submissiveness)						E					Assertive, independent, aggressive, stubborn (dominance)
Sober, prudent, serious, taciturn (desurgency)						F					Happy-go-lucky, impulsively lively, gay, enthusiastic (surgency)
Expedient, evades rules, feels few obligations (weaker superego strength)						G					Conscientious, persevering, staid, rule-bound (stronger superego strength)
Shy, restrained, diffident, timid (threctia)						H					Venturesome, socially bold, uninhibited, spontaneous (parmia)
Tough-minded, self-reliant, realistic, no-nonsense (harria)						I					Tender-minded, dependent, over-protected, sensitive (premsia)

	Suspicious, self-opinionated, hard to fool (protension)
	Imaginative, wrapped up in inner urgencies, careless of practical matters, bohemian (autia)
	Shrewd, calculating, worldly, penetrating (shrewdness)
	Apprehensive, worrying, depressive, troubled (guilt proneness)
	Experimenting, critical, liberal, analytical, free-thinking (radicalism)
	Self-sufficient, prefers own decisions, resourceful (self-sufficiency)
	Controlled, socially-precise, following self-image (high self-concept control)
	Tense, frustrated, driven, overwrought (high ergic tension)

Factors: L, M, N, O, Q_1, Q_2, Q_3, Q_4

	Trusting, adaptable, free of jealousy, east to get on with (alaxia)
	Practical, careful conventional, regulated by external realities, proper (praxernia)
	Forthright, natural, artless, sentimental (artlessness)
	Placid, self-assured, confident, serene (untroubled adequacy)
	Conservative, respecting established ideas, tolerant of traditional difficulties (conservatism)
	Group-dependent, a "joiner" and sound follower (group adherence)
	Undisciplined self-conflict, follows own urges, careless of protocol (low integration)
	Relaxed, tranquil, torpid, unfrustrated (low ergic tension)

A sten of	1	2	3	4	5	6	7	8	9	10	is obtained
by about	2.3%	4.4%	9.2%	15.0%	19.1%	19.1%	15.0%	9.2%	4.4%	2.3%	of adults

SOURCE   R.B. Cattell, and G.F. Stice, *Handbook for the Sixteen Personality Factor Questionnaire.* Champaign, Ill: Institute for Personality and Ability Testing, 1962.

if they differentiate between known groups. In the clinical scales of the MMPI, the items selected differentiated between normal people and patients receiving a particular diagnosis. For example, the Hypochondriasis (H_s) Scale consists of 33 items on which the responses of 50 patients with the diagnosis of psychoneurosis–hypochondriasis were significantly different from the responses of the normal subjects. Patients here answered false to the question "I wake up fresh and rested most mornings" significantly more often than did normals, and the empirical keying of the item was on the basis of differentiation between patients with hypochondriacal symptoms and normals. The same procedure was used for the eight remaining clinical scales in the test.

The MMPI also contains four validity scales, developed to detect test-taking attitudes and efforts to falsify test responses in a particular direction that might serve to distort results on the clinical scales. One validity scale serves to check on whether subjects are trying to present themselves in a socially acceptable or favorable light (Lie Scale). Another serves to check on whether subjects are responding in a careless manner or are trying to make themselves look seriously disturbed for some reason (F Scale). The emphasis on empirical validation and validity scales was a significant advancement over self-report questionnaires developed earlier.

Currently the MMPI consists of 550 items to which the subject responds "true," "false," or "cannot say." The profile of scores based on answers to these items can be interpreted on an impressionistic basis, or by checking the profile in an atlas that describes typical personalities with such score profiles, or by sending the results to one of the machine-scoring companies that provide a computer print-out of the scale scores and a suggested personality description (see Box 13.2).

The MMPI is *structured* in that subjects respond to specific stimuli or questionnaire items and are given a limited number of alternative answers. It is *voluntary* in that subjects choose the response they prefer or feel is most applicable to them. It is psychometric in that it is based on the criterion-keying of items. Although originally developed primarily as a diagnostic screening device, its use has been broadened to include personality descriptions. While not associated with a trait theory, the original classificatory scheme had typological elements and the personality descriptions derived from the score profiles generally consist of traitlike adjectives.

Many of the scales show poor test-retest reliability, but this is perhaps to be expected because of the type of personality functioning being tested. More serious is the evidence of social and racial bias in the interpretation of responses to many items. The test was developed in the late 1930s

BOX 13.2 **Illustration of a Personality Description That Might Be Obtained from a Computer Analysis of MMPI Responses**

AGE 21 FEMALE

SHE SEEMS TO BE ATTEMPTING TO MINIMIZE OR DENY FAULTS IN HERSELF. SHE IS HESITANT TO ADMIT TO PSYCHOLOGICAL PROBLEMS, PERHAPS BECAUSE SHE PERCEIVES THEM AS WEAKNESSES. IN SOME NORMALLY FUNCTIONING INDIVIDUALS THIS APPARENT DEFENSIVENESS MAY REPRESENT SELF-ASSURANCE AND A GOOD SELF-CONCEPT. IN AN INDIVIDUAL WITH CURRENT DIFFICULTIES, HOWEVER, IT IS MORE LIKELY TO REPRESENT RESISTANCE AND RELUCTANCE TO ENTER TREATMENT.

THIS PATIENT IS LIKELY TO BE AN EXTROVERTED, SOMEWHAT OVERACTIVE PERSON WHO TENDS TOWARD IMPULSIVENESS. SHE MAY BE A LIVELY CONVERSATIONALIST AND ABLE TO ENTER SOCIAL EVENTS ENTHUSIASTICALLY, BUT HER POOR JUDGMENT, AND LACK OF TACT AND CONSIDERATION FOR OTHERS MAY RESULT IN HURT FEELINGS AND ALIENATION FROM OTHERS. SHE MAY EXPEND GREAT AMOUNTS OF ENERGY AND EFFORT TO SATISFY HER DESIRES, BUT SHE FINDS IT DIFFICULT TO STICK TO DUTIES IMPOSED BY OTHERS. AMONG ADOLESCENTS, COLLEGE STUDENTS, AND SOME LOW SOCIOECONOMIC GROUPS THIS PATTERN APPEARS FAIRLY FREQUENTLY WITHOUT SERIOUS IMPLICATIONS, ALTHOUGH RESTLESSNESS AND IMPULSIVENESS MAY STILL BE ANTICIPATED.

THIS PERSON IS CHARACTERIZED BY A DENIAL OF ANXIETY OR WORRY. SHE EXPRESSES SELF-CONFIDENCE, AFFABILITY AND SELF-ACCEPTANCE.

and early 1940s and used patients in the University of Minnesota hospitals as the patient population and visitors to the hospitals as the normal population. Since that time, norms and values have changed and the applicability of the test to members of minority groups has been challenged (Gynther, 1972). We would no longer expect the answer of "False" by a male subject to the question "I like mechanics magazines" to be associated with effeminate interests and homosexuality. The answer "True" to the question "People say insulting and vulgar things about me" does not necessarily have the same personality implications for black and white subjects. Despite questions such as these, many psychologists feel that the MMPI remains a valuable tool for selection and a potential basis for useful insights into personality functioning.

Self-Report Questionnaires: Final Comments

Self-report questionnaires have come under attack for a variety of reasons. First, a fact emphasized by psychologists who favor the use of projectives, people often do not know themselves, are unconsciously defensive or consciously fake responses to questionnaires. Others point out that the items in the questionnaire may be interpreted differently by different people. Supporters of questionnaires argue that they do not assume that people are capable and willing to describe themselves accurately but that the established empirical relationship of test responses to other personality characteristics is what is important. In this view the response is a piece of behavior to be related to other behaviors and not necessarily an accurate statement concerning the self (Wilde, 1977).

response style   Another criticism of questionnaires is that the responses are susceptible to particular biases. Research suggests that subjects often respond to qualities in the items other than content or have a consistent tendency to respond in one or another way to a test—**response style**. There is, for example, considerable variation in the way individuals use the "like" response category on a questionnaire. Some subjects use "like" to mean all activities they do not dislike while others use the category to refer to those activities they enjoy very much.

acquiescence   Another response-style problem is **acquiescence**. The "tendency to acquiesce" is a tendency to agree or disagree with items regardless of content (Jackson and Messick, 1958). Subjects may respond to the format of items and the way they are phrased rather than to their content. Thus, for example, subjects may have a preference for responses such as "Like" and "Agree" (yea-sayers) or for responses such as "Dislike" and "Disagree" (nay-sayers). Finally, there is the potential for bias in responses to ques-

social desirability tionnaires in terms of the relative **social desirability** of the items (Edwards 1953, 1959). Instead of responding to the intended psychological meaning of a test item, a subject may respond in terms of whether it is perceived as suggesting a socially acceptable or socially desirable personality characteristic. According to one view, people who generally tend to respond in a socially desirable way on self-report tests are conventional, cautious, and greatly in need of self-protection (Crowne and Marlowe, 1964).

The 16 P.F. and MMPI attempt to deal with these problems. The instructions encourage the subject to be honest. Items on the 16 P.F. were chosen so that an equal number of "yes" and "no" responses contributes to the total score, and the MMPI validity scales were developed to deal with related problems. Ultimately, however, those who support the use of questionnaires fall back on the empirical procedures used to develop these tests. In the final analysis, the question is one of validity—and we have not yet been able to come to a clear conclusion concerning the current or potential validity of such tests as the 16 P.F. and MMPI.

Objective Techniques: Standardized Performance Tests and Behavioral Assessment

The tests included in this section are *structured*, in that subjects are given a limited number of alternative responses, and *objective*, in that the subject is called on to give the correct response. Unlike the tests previously considered, measures of behavior that do not rely on voluntary responses from the subject are obtained—various measures of physiological activity (for example, heart rate, sweat gland activity, muscle potential) and of conditioning used in personality assessment. Objective tests are performance tests—subjects are put into a situation and an objective performance score expresses their behavior. Generally the effort is made to present exactly the same stimulus to all subjects. Direct laboratory observation is used to obtain precise and dependable information. To control the situation, these tests are generally limited in kind and number of stimuli presented to the subject and in the personality characteristics assumed to be measured. Variation in subject response is limited to the behavior of interest to the experimenter. The goal is to obtain information about specific behaviors under controlled conditions.

The use of objective tests can be contrasted with the use of tests previously considered. Psychometric tests involve self-report; objective tests generally do not. Psychologists who use objective tests tend to feel that questionnaires take too broad a sweep of behaviors. Questionaire items are usually related to general attitudes, beliefs, and motives. Performance measures generally are associated with very specific situations. A questionnaire obtains information by general questions and with the hope that the subject's responses will permit inferences to specific situations. The structured performance test starts with a specific artificial situation and the hope that the responses will permit inferences to a variety of situations with very different surface characteristics. These differences can be related to the differences between a trait or type theory and a learning theory of personality (Hull's habit or stimulus-response theory, for example).

Theories of personality associated with structured, objective tests can also be contrasted with those that emphasize projective and subjective techniques. Theories that use projective and subjective tests emphasize individual differences and focus on the total functioning of the individual personality. Theories that make major use of structured, objective tests emphasize processes common to individuals and reflect the view that a science of personality can best progress through the study of performance characteristics in well-defined situations.

Some of the earliest work on the objective assessment of personality was done by Hartshorne and May (1928) as part of the Character Education Inquiry. In this study, subjects were put in situations where they were tempted to violate moral standards and where detection appeared to be impossible. Subjects were allowed to play with boxes containing money and then asked to return the boxes. They did not know that the boxes had been marked and many kept some of the money. Observations were also made of cheating on tests, honesty in work done at home, honesty in reporting scores, and other behavior associated with the "traits" of truthfulness and honesty. These tests were used to obtain quantitative, objective indices of particular personality characteristics and illustrate measures of overt behavior in well-defined situations. Hartshorne and May also found that children who cheated in one situation often did not cheat in another, findings subsequently used to support the view that much of human behavior is situation-specific.

behavioral assessment

target behaviors target responses

The emphasis on specific behaviors tied to defined situational characteristics forms the basis for what has come to be known as **behavioral assessment**. Heavily influenced by the thinking of Skinner, the behavioral approach to assessment emphasizes three things: (1) Identification of specific behaviors, often called **target behaviors** or **target responses**; (2) identification of specific environmental factors that elicit, cue, or reinforce the target behaviors; (3) identification of specific environmental factors that can be manipulated to alter the behavior. Thus a behavioral assessment of a child's temper tantrums would include a clear, objective definition of temper tantrum behavior in the child, a complete description of the situation that sets off the tantrum behavior, a complete description of the reactions of parents and others that may be reinforcing the behavior,

functional analysis of behavior

ABC assessment

and an analysis of the potential for eliciting and reinforcing other nontantrum behaviors (Kanfer and Saslow, 1965; O'Leary, 1972). This **functional analysis of behavior**, involving the effort to identify the environmental conditions that control behavior, sees behavior as a function of specific events in the environment. The approach has also been called the **ABC assessment**—one assesses the *A*ntecedent conditions of the behavior, the *B*ehavior itself, and the *C*onsequences of the behavior (Box 13.3).

BOX 13.3 **Behavioral Assessment**

ISSUE   Investigation of the feasibility of treatment in the natural setting (the home) where the child's behavior problem appeared, with the mother serving as the therapeutic agent. The child (C), a four-year-old boy, was brought by his mother (M) to the university clinic because she felt helpless to deal with his frequent tantrums and general disobedience.

OBSERVATIONS   Experimenters (Es) observed M and C in the home and noted that many of C's undesirable behaviors appeared to be maintained by attention from his mother. If C behaved objectionably M would try to explain to him why he shouldn't do something or would try to distract him by offering him toys or food. Observation in the home indicated that the following responses made up a large portion of C's repertory of undesirable behavior: (1) biting his shirt or arm, (2) sticking out his tongue, (3) kicking or biting himself, others, or objects, (4) calling someone or something a derogatory name, (5) removing or threatening to remove his clothing, (6) saying "NO!" loudly and vigorously, (7) threatening to damage objects or persons, (8) throwing objects, (9) pushing his sister. These nine responses collectively are called Objectionable Behavior (OB). The frequency of occurrence is measured by recording, for each ten-second interval, whether or not an OB occurred. Observations are made during one-hour sessions conducted two to three times a week. Two Es are used as observers on eight occasions and three on one occasion to check the reliability of the response scoring. Reliability is found to range from .70 to 1.00 with an average of .88, indicative of high observer reliability.

TREATMENT   After an initial Baseline Period of 16 sessions during which C and M interact in their usual way, the First Experimental Period is begun. Every time C emits an OB, M is either signaled by E to tell him to stop or to put him in his room by himself without toys. (This isolation period is viewed as a period of "time out" from stimuli associated with positive reinforcement). When E notices that C is playing in a particularly desirable way the M is signaled to give C attention and approval. During the Second Baseline Period M is told to interact with C as she did prior to the experi-

BOX 13.3 **Behavioral Assessment** *continued*

mental period. This is followed by the Second Experimental Period which is the same as that in the first except that special attention for desirable play is excluded, save for one accidental instance. Finally, there is a Follow-up Period after 24 days without contact between E and M.

RESULTS   During the Baseline Period OB varied between 18 and 113 per session (one hour). During the First Experimental Period the rate of OB ranged from 1 to 8 per session. Special attention was given ten times. During the Second Baseline Period the rate of OB varied between 2 and 24 per session. M reported that she had trouble responding in her previous way because she now felt more "sure of herself." She now gives C firm commands and does not give in after denying a request. She also gives more affection, mostly in response to an increase in affectionate overtures from C. During the Second Experimental Period the rate of OB varied between 2 and 8 per session. The rate of OB remains low after the 24-day interval (Follow-up Period) and M reports C is well-behaved and less demanding.

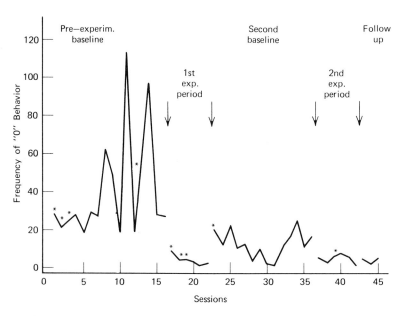

FIGURE 13.1   Number of 10-second intervals per 1-hour session, in which objectionable behavior occurred. Asterisks indicate sessions in which reliability was tested.

SUMMARY   The results of this study show that it is possible to observe and treat behavioral problems in the home, with the parent as the therapeutic agent. Since it is widely held that many of the child's problems originate in the home environment, direct modification of this environment (including the behavior of other family members) may arrest the difficulty at its source.

SOURCE   R. P. Hawkins, R. F. Peterson, Edda Schweid, and S. W. Bijou. Behavior therapy in the home: Amelioration of problem parent-child relations with the parent in a therapeutic role. *Journal of Experimental Child Psychology*, 1966, *4*, 99–107.

It is important to recognize in behavioral assessment that there is emphasis on single variables (specific target behaviors) and the gathering of reliable and objective data. There is also an association between such assessment and theories tied to empirical research. What is different about behavioral assessment in comparison to some other objective personality measures is that the behavior itself is of interest, not some theoretical construct (ego strength, extroversion) presumed to be expressed in the behavior. "Another characteristic of behavioral approaches to assessment is that their data are often direct samples of behavior in specific situations, instead of indirect and generalized indicants of behavioral predispositions" (Kanfer and Phillips, 1970, p. 509). In behavioral assessment one is not bothered by observations that performance varies with the situation since it is assumed that behavior is specific to situations and in good part is determined by situational variables. The problem of making inferences from controlled, laboratory situations to behavior in real-life situations is addressed by making every possible effort to observe and measure the target behavior in situ—in exactly the situations in which they ordinarily occur. The problem of prediction from test behavior to other situations (predictive validity) is thus minimized by assuming that one can only predict from one situation to other comparable situations. The problem of establishing a relationship between test behaviors and a theoretical construct (construct validity) is dealt with by emphasizing the importance of observable behaviors themselves rather than underlying constructs (Goldfried and Kent, 1972).

An even clearer feeling for behavioral assessment can be obtained by contrasting it and its associated theoretical assumptions with the theoretical assumptions and assessment devices described in the projective category. Projective test data are associated with theories that emphasize: (1) unique aspects of individuals; (2) behavior as a result of the interplay among complex internal forces (motives, drives, needs, and conflicts); (3) personality structure as involving layers of organization (as in the conscious and unconscious); (4) personality as a process through which the individual imposes organization and structure upon external stimuli in the environment; (5) a holistic understanding of behavior in terms of relationships among parts, rather than the interpretation of behavior as expressive of single parts or personality traits.

The behavioral assessment method also emphasizes behaviors specific to individuals. However, in contrast with projective tests, behavioral assessment is associated with theories having these emphases: (1) behavior as a result of external environmental forces that have eliciting and reinforcing value for the specific behaviors in question; (2) the avoidance of assumptions concerning personality dimensions (conscious, unconscious) that cannot be defined in clear behavioral terms; (3) personality as consisting of the organization of specific behavioral responses determined by environmental variables. Projective tests emphasize factors inside the individual that regulate behavior and provide for the stability of behavior across many different types of situations. Behavioral assessment emphasizes factors external to the individual that regulate behavior and provide for behavior varying according to situational characteristics.

Sign and Sample Approaches to Assessment

sign and sample approaches to assessment

These theoretical differences are associated with assessment differences between the two positions. Mischel (1968, 1971) has contrasted these differences in terms of **sign and sample approaches to assessment**. In the sign approach, traits are inferred from test behavior. Test items are assumed adequate to reflect personality characteristics and interpretations are made of test behavior relative to assumed underlying traits. There is, in other words, a high level of inference from test behavior to interpretations concerning personality characteristics. In the sample approach, interest is in the behavior itself and how it is affected by alterations in environmental conditions. Interest is in overt behavior and it is assumed that one must understand the surrounding stimulus conditions to understand the relevant behavior. There is, in other words, a low level of inference from test behavior to other similar behaviors in the individual. The sign approach asks about motives and traits that act together to result in observed behavior; the sample approach asks about environmental variables that affect behaviors in terms of their frequency, intensity, and duration. A summary of many of these differences is given in Table 13.1.

As noted, the main sample approach to assessment includes the analysis of specific behaviors in terms of the relevant eliciting and reinforcing environmental conditions. Often this requires a period of observation of behavior as it occurs in the daily life of the individual (naturalistic observa-

	BEHAVIORAL ASSESSMENT	TRADITIONAL ASSESSMENT
Assumptions		
1 Personality concept	Behavior as a function of the environment	Behavior as a function of underlying causes
2 "Test" interpretation	Behavior as sample	Behavior as sign
3 Situations sampled	Varied and specific	Limited and ambiguous
Primary Functions	Description in behavioral-analytic terms	Description in psycho-dynamic terms
	Treatment selection	Diagnostic labeling
	Treatment evaluation	
Practical aspects		
1 Relation to treatment	Direct	Indirect
2 Time of assessment	Continuous with treatment	Prior to treatment

TABLE 13.1
A Comparison of Traditional and Behavioral Assessment Strategies

SOURCE: Cimenero, 1977, p. 7

tion); at other times there may be efforts to set up experimental conditions that resemble real-life situations (analogs). It would be difficult through naturalistic observation to observe an individual's fear of snakes, for example, and therefore it is necessary to observe such behavior within the context of a laboratory situation. In one of the classic efforts to use behavioral assessment within the laboratory situation, Lang and Lazovik (1963) measured changes in subjects' fears of snakes in terms of the extent of approach or avoidance behavior in relation to an actual snake. This was tested in the laboratory both before and after treatment. Although there are many categories of subject behavior in such a Behavioral Avoidance Test (BAT), basically there is an assessment of whether the subject can progress through the "Look-Touch-Hold" steps in relation to the snake. Such BATs are frequently used with the assumption that they provide clear behavioral data that are less biased than self-report ratings. Recently, however, evidence has indicated that subject behavior in such a situation may be influenced by such subtle sources of bias as instructions, subject assumptions concerning expectations of the experimenter, and a variety of contextual cues. For example, if subjects identify themselves as being afraid of snakes, they may be reluctant to fail to show their fear during a BAT. Similarly, after treatment a subject may feel obligated to show less fear than before (Bernstein, 1973).

While observation and assessment in the natural environment are desirable, other approaches are at times necessary and may even include the use of self-report responses. For example, a questionnaire has been developed concerning specific fears that the individual may have (Fear Survey Schedule, Wolpe and Lang, 1964). Another questionnaire has been developed to determine which things in the environment are pleasurable for and therefore reinforcing to the individual (Reinforcement Survey Schedule, Cautela and Kastenbaum, 1967). A third questionnaire has been developed to assess how college students respond to specific problematic situations in adjusting to college (A Behavioral-Analytic Model for Assessing Competence, Goldfried and D'Zurilla, 1969). Although these assessment devices do rely on self-report, they follow the behavioral model in terms of their emphasis on specific behaviors (fears, pleasurable things to do, responses to specific situations at college), in the attention given to environmental variables, and in the limiting of interpretations to the behaviors noted rather than interpreting these behaviors in relation to other possible personality characteristics. To the extent possible, the effort is to ask questions and make interpretations that are expressive of the sample approach to assessment. At the same time, such questionnaires elicit data that do not always agree with observations derived from other behavioral techniques. For example, responses on the Fear Survey Schedule do not always match actual behavior on a BAT. One study found that up to 64 percent of the "high fear" subjects on the questionnaire would actually touch a snake while up to 16 percent of the "low fear" questionnaire subjects would not (Bernstein, 1973).

To summarize this section on behavioral assessment, we have a variety of assessment techniques which (1) share certain assumptions that distinguish them from other assessment techniques, (2) tie them to personality theories that differ from theories associated with other assessment techniques, and (3) result in the accumulation of different kinds of data than would be accumulated through the use of other assessment devices. Those who favor the use of these tests emphasize that they are objective and do not depend on the accuracy of self-report of the subject. Those who criticize the exclusive use of such tests suggest that they give a very restricted view of human behavior and have yet to demonstrate their predictive utility.

CLINICAL VERSUS STATISTICAL PREDICTION

An attempt has been made to examine the relationships between types of personality theory and types of assessment technique. Probably the most basic tendency (not a rule) is for more "clinical" theories of personality to be associated with unstructured tests and for more "statistical" theories of personality to be associated with structured tests. Although our discussion of these types of tests has given little attention to their usefulness for predictive purposes, prediction is a significant dimension of each test. One issue highlights the differences in the tests, in the ways they are used, and in the commitments and views of the psychologists who use them.

TABLE 13.4 **Illustrative Items From Behavioral Assessment Questionnaire Inventories**

1 FEAR SURVEY SCHEDULE (FSS-III)
   J. WOLPE AND P. J. LANG

	Not at all	A little	A fair amount	Much	Very much
1 Noise of vacuum cleaners					
2 Open wounds					
3 Being alone					
10 Falling					
12 Being teased					
14 Thunder					
18 High places					
19 People with deformities					
22 Receiving injections					
48 Dogs					
72 Looking foolish					

2 REINFORCEMENT SURVEY SCHEDULE
   J. R. CAUTELA AND R. KASTENBAUM
   (SUBJECTS CHECK HOW MUCH PLEASURE EACH GIVES)

	Not at all	A little	A fair amount	Much	Very much
Section A.					
1 Eating					
a. ice cream					
b. candy					
c. pastry					
4 Beautiful Women					
5 Handsome Men					
11 Watching Sports					
a. football					
b. baseball					
54 Peace & Quiet					

SECTION C SITUATIONS I WOULD LIKE TO BE IN
1 You have just led your team to victory. An old friend comes over and says, "You played a terrific game. Let me treat you to dinner and drinks."

not at all □   a little □   a fair amount □   much □   very much □

SECTION D
List things you do or think about more than:

5   10   15   20 times a day

_____   _____   _____   _____

_____   _____   _____   _____

The issue here, clinical versus statistical prediction, has a long history in the field of psychology (Gough, 1962) but gained greatest clarity and aroused most controversy as a result of a book by Paul Meehl (1954). This important work discussed the problem of the prediction of behavior from test data. It did not deal with the merits of different kinds of data or how they can be used to understand the individual personality. Rather, it explained alternative methods for predicting behavior. Meehl distinguished between two types of prediction: (1) **statistical** or **actuarial** described as formal, mechanical, and objective, and (2) **clinical**, described as informal, nonmechanical, and subjective.

statistical
actuarial
clinical

The Statistical Approach

In the statistical or actuarial approach to prediction, the investigator follows three steps: (1) A relationship between various tests scores and the criterion behavior to be predicted is established. (2) A single subject is classified on the basis of test scores. (3) A prediction is made concerning the behavior of this particular subject in relation to the criterion based on a table indicating the test-score behavior of people in the past. This type of prediction is a simple, straightforward application of a mathematical formula or table. Prediction does not rest on any theory of personality and is made solely on the basis of statistical considerations.

The Clinical Approach

In contrast, clinical prediction entails the formulation of hypotheses regarding the individual's structure or dynamics. The prediction (derived with the use of these hypotheses) can be based on intuition, hypothesis, or individual judgment and reflection but not on pure statistical relationships. At one extreme, clinical prediction is based purely on intuition, so that the clinician cannot even state the basis for the "hunch" or prediction. In a less extreme clinical approach the clinician uses general principles derived from a theory of personality to apply to the individual case. An example of an interpretation (prediction) made by psychoanlayst Wilhelm Reik during a therapy session illustrates this approach:

Our session at this time took the following course. After a few sentences about the uneventful day, the patient fell into a long silence. She assured me that nothing was in her thoughts. Silence for me. After many minutes she complained about a toothache. She told me that she had been to the dentist yesterday. He had given her an injection and then had pulled a wisdom tooth. The spot was hurting again. New and longer silence. She pointed to my bookcase in the corner and said, "There's a book standing on its head." Without the slightest hesitation and in a reproachful voice I said, "But why did you not tell me that you had an abortion?"

REIK, 1948, P. 263

Reik's interpretation was accurate. It was made on the basis of psychoanalytic theory and what he knew about the patient, and not through a mechanical process.

Evidence and Controversy

Meehl's treatise involved conclusions drawn from 20 studies in which both kinds of prediction were made and compared with one another. For example, in a study by Wittman (1941), the condition of schizophrenic patients after shock therapy was predicted on the basis of scores on a 30-item scale weighted according to findings in past applications of the scale (statistical prediction), and on the basis of psychiatric staff subjective judgments (clinical prediction). Meehl concluded that in all but one of the studies the actuarial predictions were either approximately as good as or superior to those made by the clinician. In the Wittman study, for example, the scale used for actuarial predictions predicted accurately in 81 percent of the cases; the psychiatric judgments were accurate in 45 percent. Meehl pointed out that the actuarial method takes less time, less effort, and costs less than the clinical method. For him, the clinician spends time doing jobs that can be done more efficiently by machines or by less skilled personnel using statistical methods.

It is important to note again that Meehl's argument was limited to prediction, not the kinds of data to be used in prediction. The distinction between clinical and statistical prediction was in terms of how the data, once obtained, were combined for predictive purposes. Thus, interview data or Rorschach data could be scored and the scores used for actuarial prediction. In the Wittman study, the scale used for actuarial prediction was based on many judgmental variables. Similarly, data from structured tests could be interpreted and used for predictive purposes in a clinical way. In spite of this description of the problem, the ensuing controversy encompassed both the kinds of data and methods for combining data. Many of the examples of the actuarial approach used data from structured tests while examples of the clinical approach used data from unstructured techniques such as the interview.

The clinical-statistical issue was further complicated by Meehl (1956) when he contrasted "rule-of-thumb" methods of personality description with "cookbook" methods. The former involved clinical descriptions; the latter involved mechanical transitions from patterns of scores on tests to personality description. In the "cookbook" method the clinician is discarded as unnecessary and, instead, a clerk-typist or computer reads the subject's profile scores, enters an atlas (cookbook) of profiles and personality descriptions, and comes up with a "modal description" for subjects with such a profile. (Such an approach was described in connection with the MMPI.) The pragmatic implication is that "for a rather wide range of clinical problems involving personality description from tests, the clinical interpreter is a costly middleman who might best be eliminated. An initial layout of research time could result in a cookbook whose recipes would encompass the great majority of psychometric configurations seen in daily work" (Meehl, 1956, p. 271). Meehl described this cookbook procedure as a check against "contemporary forms of tea-leaf reading," a critique that added fuel to an already brisk fire. Clinicians felt challenged not only as predictors of behavior (the original focus in the clinical versus statistical prediction treatise) but also as practitioners of a technique they use to assess personality and in their more general operating assumptions. In many cases, there was polarization. Statisticians described their procedures as objective, rigorous, scientific, empirical, and precise whereas the clinical procedures were viewed as mystical, unscientific, crude, intuitive, and muddleheaded. On the other hand, clinicians defended their method as being dynamic, global, sensitive, subtle, and meaningful while the statistical method was viewed as mechanical, atomistic, artificial, oversimplified, and superficial (Meehl, 1954). The polarization between statisticians and clinicians reflected differences not only in prediction methods but also in strongly held positions on personality theory and assessment techniques.

Robert Holt has been a staunch defender of clinical prediction and a proponent of clinical techniques. Holt (1958, 1969) argues that Meehl pitted crude clinical prediction against tried and tested actuarial prediction; the clinicians did not have past evidence of the accuracy of their judgments, but the data used in actuarial prediction had already been tested against the relevant behavior. Holt argues that clinicians cannot attempt to predict until they know the qualities of the behavior to which they are predicting, unless they know the variables that relate to performance on the criterion, and unless they know how to measure these variables. Holt sees the clinician as being useful in gathering data and in making judgments on the basis of data that bear known relationships to the criterion. He opts for "sophisticated" clinical prediction as opposed to "naive" clinical prediction. "No matter how remarkable clinical judgment may sometimes be, it can never create information where there is none" (Holt, 1958, p. 2). However, a survey of studies of clinical and statistical modes of measurement along with clinical and statistical modes of prediction showed mechanical modes to be superior in both data collection and in the combining of data for predictive purposes (Sawyer, 1966). Furthermore, there is evidence that a majority of clinicians use test data on an impressionistic, personalized basis.

Clinicians run into a number of problems in trying to predict behavior. Generally they are "naive" in Holt's sense and do not really know the variables that are critical to performance on a criterion. The data they use are often of questionable reliability, and in combining data they often are forced to arrive at some intuitive weighting of the variables. As a result they may consistently weight some variables more than they should, underestimate the importance of others or mistakenly change their weighting from case to case. Often clinicians are faced with predicting infrequent events, such as in Reik's interpretation about the abortion. Occasional "hits" on such infrequent events may be enough to make clinicians feel they are on the right track, but they are not adequate justification for the clinical process. In this respect, both Holt and Meehl would agree that clinicians need to keep track of their predictions. To the extent that they make predictive decisions under conditions of uncertainty and thereby function intuitively, they will be subject to a variety of biases found in human thinking generally (Tversky and Kahneman, 1974).

Strengths and Limitations of the Two Approaches

At this point, the clinical and statistical approaches are becoming more differentiated instead of continuing a trend toward distorted opposites. Clinicians appear not to be as good as machines at processing information. Even if some clinicians do have an intuitive grasp of situations and are able to use certain tests to predict effectively there seems to be little hope for more general clinical predictive efforts. An assessment technique that depends on the skill of the examiner has limited general utility—and is in particular difficulty when the qualities of exceptional examiners are hard to define and few rules can be developed for formalizing their assessment and prediction procedures. Some clinicians have also attempted predictions on the basis of insufficient data.

On the other hand, clinical observation can contribute valuable predictive information. Only an interview, for example, can clarify ambiguities concerning a particular individual. Clinicians generally try to do something other than an actuarial job—they are trying to form a conception of a person that will help them to understand that person and, often, to treat an individual therapeutically. The clinician can suggest hypotheses that cannot come from machines. Finally, the clinician is necessary where there is new or inadequate information. As Gough (1962) notes, how could the actuarian tell us who should be in the first rocket to the moon? The clinician may be able to extrapolate from some hypotheses concerning personality differences in reaction to stress, but the machine is helpless when it is without information or instructions about the use of the information. A balanced view of the clinical and statistical approaches requires an appreciation of the assets and limitations of each mode of measurement and each mode of prediction. Such a view is well expressed by Cronbach:

> The two approaches to observation and interpretation are suited to different purposes. When clinical testers answer questions for which their methods and theory are badly suited, their answers are next to worthless or at best are costly beyond their value. When psychometric testers are faced with a clinical problem calling for understanding rather than simple evaluation (e.g., what lies behind a given child's anxious withdrawal?) they are unable to give any answer at all. Each in his own proper province will surpass the other and each outside his province is nearly impotent.

CRONBACK, 1960, P. 606

A SUMMARY OVERVIEW OF THE ASSESSMENT FIELD

In this and the preceding chapter we have examined a variety of techniques of assessment or procedures for systematically gaining information relevant to the personality of individuals. Based on the use of three dimensions for the classification of tests (structured-nonstructured, disguised-nondisguised, voluntary-objective), the tests considered have been categorized as projective, subjective, psychometric, and objective-behavioral.

The first chapter in this book discussed the nature of theory and emphasized the current situation, in which there are alternative theories of personality or alternative paradigms. In these two chapters the emphasis has been on the relationship between personality theories and assessment techniques. Thus it is that different personality theories tend to lead to and be influenced by different kinds of data. A summary of the relationship between the assessment techniques discussed in this chapter and the theories of personality covered in the book can be found in Table 13.2.

All assessment techniques share certain goals. Chapter 12 emphasized the importance of obtaining *reliable* and *valid* data, the importance of observations that can be replicated, and the importance of observations that can be related to defined criteria. From the discussion of the various tests it should be clear that all tests are influenced by situational factors that may limit the reliability of our observations. Thus, the sex of the examiner, subtle differences in instructions, and minor changes in the physical environment may all affect the data obtained. What is most critical is that these effects can occur without the awareness of the examiner. We may eliminate the problem of situational bias by completely standardizing test pro-

TABLE 13.2
Some suggested relationships among assessment techniques and theories of personality.

TEST CATEGORY	TEST CHARAC-TERISTICS	ILLUSTRA-TION	DATA OBTAINED OR INFERRED	THEORETICAL APPROACH	ILLUSTRATIVE THEORY AND THEORIST
Projective	Nonstructured, disguised	Rorschach, TAT	Organization of conscious and uncon-scious motives and conflicts	Psycho-dynamic	Psychoanalysis—Freud
Subjective	Nonstructured or semi-structured, undisguised	Interview, Q-sort, Rep Test	Individual perceptions of self and world	Phenome-nological	Self-Rogers, Personal construct—Kelly
Psychometric	Structured, voluntary	16 P.F. MMPI	Personality traits	Trait—Type, factor analytic	Trait—Cattell
Objective-Behavioral	Structured, objective	Behavioral assessment	Behaviors (responses) in specific situations	Learning	Learning theory —Skinner, Bandura and Mischel

cedures, by including situational factors as sources of relevant data, or by studying variables that are so powerful that only major situational changes would be likely to influence the data. There are differences of opinion as to whether the emphasis in measuring and interpreting behavior should be on factors internal to the individual (psychodynamic view) or on factors in the environment external to the individual (behavioral view). Such differences of opinion lead to different strategies in the effort to cope with the potential problem of situational bias.

We have also discussed, in relation to validity, the problem of finding an appropriate criterion against which to measure test results. This is less of a problem for measures of physiological responses or of performance on learning tasks, since little is assumed beyond the data. For tests that make such assumptions, however, the problem is a difficult one. The task is difficult enough when the test is assumed to measure only one personality characteristic and where construct validity may be the challenge. But what if the test is assumed to measure many personality characteristics or all of personality? The assessment may be valid and yet not predictive of performance because we may not know how to integrate the results for performance or because performance is also dependent on unknown, nonpersonality variables. Or parts of the assessment results may be valid, but there may be no way of separating out the valid from the nonvalid, that which is gold from that which is but fool's gold.

There are, then, a variety of approaches to assessment, each following from certain assumptions about the nature of personality and how measurement should take place. All those who develop tests seek the goals of reliability and validity but do not always agree about the appropriate measures and what constitutes adequate evidence. All seek to obtain differences that reflect individual variation rather than error, whether the error be due to response style or to situational influence. However, psychologists disagree as to how closely each test approximates the ideal. All would like test behavior to be meaningfully related to other test behavior and to nontest behavior. Again, however, there is disagreement about which behavior test results should be related to or about what constitutes satisfactory evidence of such a relationship.

Proponents of each assessment technique or group of techniques point out the virtues of their own approach and the limitations of the alternatives. Those who favor projective techniques, the Rorschach in particular, argue that other tests present fragmented pictures of the individual and rely on observed behavior in unnatural situations or on untrustworthy self-report. They say that the Rorschach is a flexible instrument that makes faking difficult, allows for the study of the private world of the individual ("a psychological microscope"), and results in a picture of the total personality.

Proponents of nonprojective approaches argue that the Rorschach has questionable reliability and validity, and that it operates on the questionable assumption of a parallel between the way test stimuli are handled and the handling of interpersonal relationships. It cannot be assumed that responses to ten cards reflect the total personality and there is, in fact, a strong bias in the Rorschach toward psychopathology and the weaker, less healthy parts of the individual (Cronbach, 1960; Samuels, 1952). In spite of the potential problems in relying on self-report, some feel that "the best vantage point for understanding behavior is from the internal frame of reference of the individual himself" (Rogers, 1951, p. 494).

Structured self-report inventories such as Cattell's 16 P.F. have the advantage of being explicit, easy to administer, easy to score, and suitable for quantitative analysis. Such psychometric tests, however, come under attack both from those who favor projective techniques (for reasons already mentioned) and from those who favor objective tests and mistrust self-report. Opponents of psychometric tests also argue that, in tests based on factor analysis, the factors are not always stable from study to study. These tests nevertheless explore many dimensions of personality and responses to them have been related to many other variables, which is more than can be said for the results from most objective tests.

Objective tests are free of bias from response styles and the problems of self-report and in many ways exemplify the scientific ideal. They are objective, standardized, quantitative, and generally rigorous in design. However, they make the questionable assumption that because a test is presented in the same way to all individuals, it means the same thing to all of them. Furthermore, these tests only measure single dimensions of personality, and the relationship of this characteristic to the rest of the person's functioning is left unexplored.

At this point the assessment situation may appear to be frightfully complex and terribly discouraging. One response may be to give up in despair, another to defend one test or another, a third to recognize the assets and limitations of each approach and to clarify the task ahead. The third alternative suggests that we go beyond the question of which technique of assessment is "right" or "best" and take a more differentiated view of the situation.

Tests reflect theories of personality. This is not to say that there is, in all cases, a direct relationship between personality theory and assessment technique or that the proponents of the position will use only techniques associated with that view. Rather, there tend to be relationships between assumptions about the nature and measurement of personality. Each assessment technique tends to give a glimpse of human behavior; no one test gives, or can hope to give, a picture of the total personality of each individual. Performance on projective, subjective, psychometric, and objective tests all represent behavior and are expressive of the individual's personality. The data may not be expressive in exactly the way suggested by the experimenter, but this means that the task ahead involves clarification of the relationship between test behavior and personality. Furthermore, it seems likely that different tests are able to capture the personality of different individuals and that there also is variability in the effectiveness of each test in predicting performance in different situations.

Similarly, a more differentiated view of the clinical and statistical approaches to prediction allows us to realize that neither has a record of outstanding success. The predictive process involves gathering, organizing, and using data to generate predictions. It is possible to gather a variety of kinds of data, to organize them additively or in terms of profiles, and to generate predictions actuarially, clinically, or through a combination of the two. Decisions concerning the data to be collected, how they should be organized, and the predictive strategy to be used all depend on the behavior to be predicted, the individuals involved, and the state of our understanding of the behavior involved. Cronbach (1960) points out that as the science of psychology develops we can expect an evolution from naturalistic observation to highly structured techniques, from impressionistic description to quantitative measurement. But humans are very complex. Techniques for personality assessment will have to be tied to a theory of personality that reflects this complexity. Such tests will provide us with significant insights into personality without being speculative. They will be precise and systematic without being trivial or needlessly artificial.

MAJOR CONCEPTS AND SUMMARY

rational-theoretical approach	target behaviors
factor analysis	functional analysis of behavior
empirical-criterion keying approach	ABC approach to assessment
response style	sign and sample approaches
acquiescence	actuarial prediction
social desirability	clinical prediction
behavioral assessment	

This chapter has continued an analysis of the alternative assessment devices available to psychologists and the relationship of these devices to theoretical points of view. Following the discussion of projective and subjective tests in the previous chapter, the focus here has been on psychometric and objective-behavioral tests. Both kinds of test are structured and emphasize empirical studies of personality. Beyond this there are important differences.

The psychometric category consists of structured, voluntary tests developed through statistical procedures and often linked with trait and type theories of personality. The Cattell 16 P.F. inventory illustrates the use of factor analysis to define clusters of items that go together and thereby define a test factor (trait). The MMPI illustrates the criterion-keying approach to test development and was developed on the basis of different responses of normal and patient populations to test items. It was based on a typological classification of psychiatric disorders, and current personality descriptions derived from it use many trait terms. Both the 16 P.F. and the MMPI assume that a test item has value because it is related to some criterion or goal and not necessarily that the responding subjects are giving an accurate portrayal of themselves. Such self-report questionnaires are able to cover many aspects of personality functioning but are subject to error in terms of responses due to response style, faking, and changes in the meaning of various items resulting from changes in society.

Objective-behavioral measures focus on specific, clearly defined aspects of the person's behavior in well-defined situations. Generally there is no attempt to cover broad aspects of personality functioning and it is not assumed that behavior necessarily will show much similarity from situation to situation. Attention in this chapter was given to behavioral assessment: functional analysis of behavior or the ABC approach to assessment —Antecedent conditions, Behavior, Consequences. An important distinction between such approaches and projective techniques was made in terms of a contrast between sample and sign approaches to assessment. In sample approaches, as in behavioral assessment, interest is in the sample of behavior itself and in the environmental conditions that affect such behavior. In sign approaches, as with projective tests, the interest is in test behavior as a sign of other underlying personality characteristics.

Some of the issues discussed in this chapter and the preceding one have been formulated in terms of the issue of clinical versus statistical prediction. This issue raised the question of how test data could best be used to make predictions about behavior—through formal, mechanical procedures or on the basis of clinical judgment and intuition. Unfortunately, this very specific issue became confused with controversy over which types of tests are better and whether clinicians are necessary at all. The evidence suggests that careful, systematic studies are necessary to make predictions of behavior and that often clinicians make systematic errors of judgment when predicting under conditions of uncertainty. At the same time, the clinical and statistical approaches to observation and interpretation are suited to different purposes; each may have a different contribution to make to our understanding of personality.

THE CASE OF JIM HERSH

Rorschach and TAT: Psychoanalytic Theory

Semantic Differential: Phenomenological Theory

REP Test: Personal Construct Theory

Sixteen Personality Factor Inventory: Trait, Factor-Analytic Theory

JIM HERSH: FIVE YEARS LATER

Life Experiences Since Graduation — as Told by Jim Hersh

Brief Personality Description and
Changes Since Graduation — as Told by Jim Hersh

Behavioral Assessment:
Reinforcement Survey Schedule and Fear Survey Schedule

PERSONALITY THEORY AND ASSESSMENT DATA:
THE CASE OF JIM HERSH

14 THEORY AND ASSESSMENT IN THE STUDY OF THE INDIVIDUAL: THE CASE OF JIM HERSH

Chapter Focus:

In this chapter, we shall study the personality of an individual from the perspective of the preceding theories and assessment.

Jim Hersh

Rorschach: Card 5

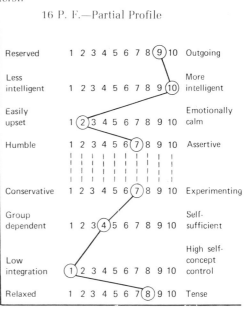

"Sort of brings to mind a dancing girl, sort of a stripper. Could almost be a ballet dancer on toes. Gypsy Rose Lee. Type that comes out with a magnificent gown. Sort of bow-legged. Body hidden by stuff to be discarded. A stripper (Stripper?) Nobody wears this unless it is to be taken off subsequently. Arms outstretched."

16 P. F.—Partial Profile

Reserved	1 2 3 4 5 6 7 8 ⑨ 10	Outgoing
Less intelligent	1 2 3 4 5 6 7 8 9 ⑩	More intelligent
Easily upset	1 ②3 4 5 6 7 8 9 10	Emotionally calm
Humble	1 2 3 4 5 6 ⑦ 8 9 10	Assertive
Conservative	1 2 3 4 5 6 ⑦ 8 9 10	Experimenting
Group dependent	1 2 3 ④5 6 7 8 9 10	Self-sufficient
Low integration	①2 3 4 5 6 7 8 9 10	High self-concept control
Relaxed	1 2 3 4 5 6 7 ⑧ 9 10	Tense

A variety of approaches to personality have now been examined: Freud's psychoanalytic theory, Rogers' self-concept theory, Kelly's construct theory. Allport's, Eysenck's, and Cattell's trait approach, learning theory, and social learning theory. Each has been studied as an outgrowth of certain kinds of theorists as well as in relation to the data available to them and on which they could base their theories. In particular, it has been emphasized that each theory tends to be associated with a different technique of assessment and with a different emphasis in research. *Beginning with different assumptions and styles of investigation, the theorists were led to use different tools to unravel the secrets of personality functioning. These different tools in turn led to the different observations that served as the basis for the theories examined here.*

In Chapter 1 it was suggested that theories of personality can be compared in terms of such criteria as comprehensiveness, parsimony or economy, logical consistency, and productivity in research. In this chapter we shall deal with another question: Are the observations obtained similar when assessment techniques associated with the different theories are applied to the same individual? Recall here the story of the wise blind men and the elephant. Each wise man examined a part of the elephant and assumed that he knew what it was. None knew that it was an elephant and each came to a different conclusion on the basis of his observations. One felt the tail and thought it was a snake, another a leg and thought it was a tree, another a trunk and thought it was a hose, and another the body and thought it was a wall. The study of one individual through the use of different techniques of assessment may provide us with a useful analogy: Do the theories refer to different parts of the same person, each representing an incomplete picture of the whole and each describing some of the same qualities in different terms, or do the theories refer to different people? When applied to an individual, are the theories talking about different parts of the individual, about the same parts but in different terms, or are they basically in conflict with one another?

THE CASE OF JIM HERSH

Jim Hersh was a student at Harvard when he agreed to serve as a subject for a project involving the intensive study of college students. He participated in the project mainly because of his interest in psychology. He also hoped that the tests given to him would give him a better understanding of himself. His autobiography reveals some of the essentials of his life. Jim was born in New York City after the end of the second world war, the first child in a Jewish family, and received considerable attention and affection. Jim's father is a college graduate who owns an automobile sales business;

his mother is a housewife who also does volunteer reading for the blind. He has a four-year-younger sister and two brothers, one five years younger and one seven years younger. The main themes in his autobiography concerned his inability to become involved with women in a satisfying way, his need for success and his relative failure since high school, and his uncertainty about whether to go on to graduate school in business administration or in clinical psychology.

Rorschach and TAT: Psychoanalytic Theory

The Rorschach Inkblot Test and Thematic Apperception Test, both projective, were administered to Jim by a professional clinical psychologist. On the Rorschach, which was first, Jim gave relatively few responses — 22 in all. This is surprising in the light of other evidence of his intelligence and creative potential. It may be of interest here to follow along his responses to the first two cards and to consider the hypotheses formulated by the psychologist, who also is a practicing psychoanalyst.

CARD 1

>   JIM: The first thing that comes to mind is a butterfly.
>
>   COMMENT: Initially cautious and acts conventionally in a novel situation.
>
>   J. This reminds me of a frog. Not a whole frog, like a frog's eyes. Really just reminds me of a frog.
>
>   C. He becomes more circumspect, almost picky, and yet tends to overgeneralize while feeling inadequate about it.
>
>   J. Could be a bat. More spooky than the butterfly because there is no color. Dark and ominous.
>
>   C. Phobic, worried, depressed, and pessimistic.

CARD 2

>   J. Could be two headless people with their arms touching. Looks like they are wearing heavy dresses. Could be one touching her hand against a mirror. If they're women, their figures are not good. Look heavy.
>
>   C. Alert to people. Concern or confusion about sexual role. Anal-compulsive features. Disparaging of women and hostile to them — headless and figures not good. Narcissism expressed in mirror image.
>
>   J. This looks like two faces facing each other. Masks, profiles — more

masks than faces — not full, more of a façade, like one with a smile and one with a frown.

C. He presents a façade, can smile or frown, but doesn't feel genuine. Despite façade of poise, feels tense with people. Repeated several times that he was not imaginative. Is he worried about his productivity and importance?

A number of interesting responses occurred on other cards. On the third card he perceived women trying to lift weights. Here again was a suggestion of conflict about his sexual role and about a passive as opposed to an active orientation. On the following card he commented that "somehow they all have an Alfred Hitchcock look of spooky animals," again suggesting a possible phobic quality to his behavior and a tendency to project dangers into the environment. His occasional references to symmetry and details suggested the use of compulsive defenses and intellectualization while experiencing threat. Disturbed and conflicted references to women come up in a number of places. At the beginning of this chapter we quoted his response to Card 5, involving a stripper. On Card 7, he perceived two women from mythology who would be good if they were mythological but bad if they were fat. On the next-to-last card he perceived "some sort of a Count, Count Dracula. Eyes, ears, cape. Ready to grab, suck blood. Ready to go out and strangle some woman." The reference to sucking blood suggested tendencies toward oral sadism, something which also appeared in another percept of vampires that suck blood. Jim followed the percept of Count Dracula with one of pink cotton candy. The tester interpreted this response as suggesting a yearning for nurturance and contact behind the oral sadism; that is, the subject uses his oral aggressive tendencies (for example, sarcasm, verbal attacks) to defend against more passive oral wishes (for example, to be fed, taken care of, and to be dependent).

The examiner concluded that the Rorschach suggested a neurotic structure in which intellectualization, compulsivity, and hysterical operations (irrational fears, preoccupation with his body) are used to defend against anxiety. However, it was suggested that Jim continues to feel anxious and uncomfortable with others, particularly authority figures. The report from the Rorschach concluded as follows. "He is conflicted about his sexual role. While he yearns for nurturance and contact from the motherly female, he feels very guilty about the cravings and his intense hostility toward women. He assumes a passive orientation, a continual role playing and, behind a façade of tact, he continues his rage, sorrow, and ambition."

What kinds of stories did Jim tell on the Thematic Apperception Test? Most striking about these stories was the sadness and hostility involved in all interpersonal relationships. In one story a boy is dominated by his mother, in another an insensitive gangster is capable of gross inhumanity, and in a third a husband is upset to learn that his wife is not a virgin. In particular, the relationships between men and women constantly involve one putting down the other. Consider this story.

Looks like two older people. The woman is sincere, sensitive, and dependent on the man. There is something about the man's expression that bespeaks of insensitivity — the way he looks at her, as if he conquered her. There is not the same compassion and security in her presence that she feels in his. In the end, the woman gets very hurt and is left to fend for herself. Normally I would think that they were married but in this case I don't because two older people who are married would be happy with one another.

In this story we have a man being sadistic to a woman. We also see the use of the defensive mechanism of denial in Jim's suggestion that these two people cannot be married since older married people are always happy with one another. In the story that came after the one above again there is the theme of hostile mistreatment of a woman. In this story there is a more open expression of the sexual theme along with evidence of some sexual-role confusion.

This picture brings up a gross thought. I think of Candy. The same guy who took advantage of Candy. He's praying over her. Not the last rites, but he has convinced her that he is some powerful person and she's looking for him to bestow his good graces upon her. His knee is on the bed, he's unsuccessful, she's naive. He goes to bed with her for mystical purposes. [Blushes] She goes on being naive and continues to be susceptible to that kind of thing. She has a very, very sweet compassionate look. Could it possibly be that this is supposed to be a guy wearing a tie? I'll stick with the former.

The psychologist interpreting these stories observed that Jim appeared to be immature, naive, and characterized by a gross denial of all that is unpleasant or dirty, the latter for him including both sexuality and marital strife. The report continued: "He is vacillating between expressing sadistic urges or experiencing a sense of victimization. Probably he combines both, often in indirect expressions of hostility while feeling unjustly treated or accused. He is confused about what meaningful relationships two people can have. He is ambivalently idealistic and pessimistic about his own chances for a stable relationship. Since he sees sex as dirty and as a mode for using or being used by his partner, he fears involvement. At the same time he craves attention, needs to be recognized, and is often preoccupied with sexual urges."

Between the Rorschach and the Thematic Apperception Test a number of important themes come out. One theme involves a general lack of warmth in interpersonal relationships, in particular a disparaging and at times sadistic orientation toward women. In relation to women, there is conflict between sexual preoccupation and the feeling that sex is dirty and involves hostility. The second theme involves experiencing tension and anxiety behind a façade of poise. A third theme involves conflict and confusion about his sexual identity. Although there is evidence of intelligence and creative potential, there also is evidence of rigidity and inhibition in relation to the unstructured nature of the projective tests. Compulsive defenses, intellectualization, and denial are only partially successful in helping him deal with his anxieties.

What can be said about the data from the projective tests, particularly since these tests relate to psychoanalytic theory? The unstructured quality of these tests led to many personal responses which presumably relate to unique aspects of Jim's personality. Furthermore, the unstructured quality of these tests allows for the development of a rich and varied response pattern that presumably allows for some understanding of many different aspects of Jim's personality. Finally, the disguised quality of the tests presumably allows us to penetrate the façade of his personality (in psychoanalytic terms his defenses) to be able to view his underlying needs, motives, or drives. We have a test that allows for considerable uniqueness of response and a theory of personality that is clinical in its emphasis on the individual. We have a test that disguises its true purpose and a theory of personality that is dynamic in its emphasis on behavior as a result of the interplay among forces, drives, conflicts, and layers of personality.

The picture of Jim given in the Rorschach and Thematic Apperception tests is quite different from that presented in the autobiography. In his autobiography Jim indicated that he received unlimited affection from his parents and was quite popular and successful through high school. He described himself as having a good relationship with his father. He described his mother as having "great feeling for other people — she is a totally 'loving' woman." At the same time, we know that Jim feels he is troubled. In his autobiography he wrote that people had a high estimate of him because they could use only superficial criteria and that inwardly he was troubled. We thus have support for the interpretation in the Rorschach that he hides his tension and anxiety behind a façade of poise. There also is evidence in his autobiography of a conflicted relationship with women.

My relationships with women were somewhat better in high school than they are now, but they weren't really satisfying then either. I was operating in a small subculture then, and I was very respected by everyone, so that probably made me more popular than I would have been otherwise. I have never had a really long-term, intimate relationship with a girl and I think those are the only kind that are meaningful. I had a number of superficial relationships, but there was always a barrier set up against my really becoming involved, and that barrier has been reinforced and made stronger over the last four years. Once a girl starts liking me a great deal I start liking her less — this has obvious implications about my lack of feelings of self-worth. It's a vicious and self-defeating circle: I like a girl only until she starts to to like me. Thus in high school I was much sought after, but I managed to remain safely uninvolved.

Jim did not like the Rorschach. He felt that he had to see something and that whatever he perceived would be interpreted as evidence that he was neurotic. He suggested that he didn't feel defensive about his troubles since he was willing to accept having them but he didn't want them overstated. When he read over some of the comments made by the psychologist, he observed that he himself believed that there was a sexual problem and that this would be the major issue if he went into therapy. Jim said that he had fears about ejaculating too quickly, his potency, and his ability to satisfy the female. It is interesting that the fear of losing control, or premature ejaculation, occurs in an individual who uses compulsive defenses and who strives to be in complete control of most situations.

What can be said about the relationship between the projective data and psychoanalytic theory? Clearly some of the importance of the data from the Rorschach and the TAT lies in the theoretical interpretations given to the responses, in particular the use of psychoanalytic symbolism. However, aside from this, it is difficult to determine how other theories of personality could make as much use of the data as psychoanalytic theory can. As we shall see, the data from the projectives are of a qualitatively different sort than those found in the other tests. It is only on the Rorschach that we obtain content such as "a stripper," "women trying to lift weights," "Count Dracula . . . ready to grab, suck blood. Ready to go out and strangle some woman," and "pink cotton candy." And only on the TAT are there repeated references to themes of sadness and hostility in interpersonal relationships. It is the content of the responses and the way in which the tests are handled that allows for the psychodynamic interpretations.

Obviously, Jim is not a Count Dracula and there is little overtly to suggest that he is a sadist. But the content of the projectives allows for the interpretation that an important part of his personality functioning involves a defense against sadistic urges. Obviously Jim does not still drink out of a milk bottle, but the references to sucking blood and to cotton candy, together with the rest of his responses, allow for the interpretation that he is partially fixated at the oral stage. It is interesting to observe in relation to this that Jim has an ulcer, which involves the digestive tract, and that he must drink milk to manage this condition.

Perhaps the point here is that if you let people's imaginations wander, you will be led to the world of the irrational. Freud not only allowed this but, indeed, encouraged it. He encouraged his patients to dream, to fantasize, to associate freely. He studied his subjects intensively and was exposed to the world of the individual and to the world of drives, conflicts, guilt, sex, and aggression. Encouraged to do so, Freud's patients reported feelings and memories they were previously unaware of. Similarly, in Jim's Rorschach and TAT we have content and themes that seem out of character with the rest of his responses to other personality tests. Having access to these feelings and memories, Freud was able to draw certain relationships between them and the problems that first brought his patients to treatment. In Jim's case we can guess in the same way that it is his sexual confusion and latent hostility that make him feel anxious or insecure and that prevent him from becoming involved with women. Finding himself making discoveries in the world of the irrational and basing his theory on observations with patients, Freud was led to overemphasize the importance of the unconscious and to overemphasize the pathological in individuals. Similarly, Jim's performance on the projectives gives little indication of the skills, talents, and resources he has used to make some significant achievements.

Semantic Differential: Phenomenological Theory

How do these observations compare with those obtained from other assessment techniques? Jim filled out the semantic differential, rating the concepts Self, Ideal Self, Father, and Mother on 104 scales. Typical scales were authoritarian-democratic, conservative-liberal, affectionate-reserved, warm-cold, and strong-weak. Each of the four concepts was rated on the same scales so that comparisons could be made of the meanings of these concepts for Jim. The test is clearly different from the Rorschach in being undisguised rather than disguised but shares with it the quality of being voluntary rather than objective. The semantic differential test does not immediately follow from Rogerian theory. However, we can interpret data from the test in relation to Rogerian theory, since there is a phenomenological quality to the data and we are assessing the individual's perception of his Self and his Ideal Self.

First, we look at the ways in which Jim perceives his Self. Jim perceives himself as intelligent, friendly, sincere, kind, and basically good. The ratings suggest that he sees himself as a wise person who is humane and interested in people. At the same time, other ratings suggest that he does not feel free to be expressive and uninhibited. Thus he rates himself as reserved, introverted, inhibited, tense, moral, and conforming. There is a curious mixture of perceptions of being involved, deep, sensitive, and kind while also being competitive, selfish, and disapproving. There is also the interesting combination of perceiving himself as being good and masculine while at the same time he perceives himself to be weak and insecure. One gets the impression of an individual who would like to believe that he is basically good and capable of genuine interpersonal relationships at the same time that he is bothered by serious inhibitions and high standards for himself and others.

This impression comes into sharper focus when we consider the Self ratings in relation to those for the Ideal Self. In general, Jim did not see an extremely large gap between his Self and his Ideal Self. However, large gaps did occur on a number of important scales. In an arbitrary way, we can define a gap of three or more positions on a seven-point scale as considerable and important. Thus, for example, Jim rated his Self as 2 on the weak-strong scale and his Ideal Self as 7 on the same scale — a difference of five positions. In other words, Jim would like to be much stronger than he feels he is. Assessing his ratings on the other scales in a similar way, we find that Jim would like to be more of each of the following than he currently perceives himself to be: warm, active, equalitarian, flexible, lustful, approving, industrious, relaxed, friendly, and bold. Basically two themes appear. One has to do with *warmth*. Jim is not as warm, relaxed, and friendly as he would like to be. The other theme has to do with *strength*. Jim is not as strong, active, and industrious as he would like to be.

Jim's ratings of his mother and father give some indication of where he sees them in relation to himself in general and these qualities in particular. First, if we compare the way Jim perceives his Self with his perception of Mother and Father, clearly he perceives himself to be much more like his father than his mother. Also, he perceives his father to be closer to his Ideal Self than his mother, although he perceives himself to be closer to his Ideal Self than either his mother or his father. However, in the critical areas of warmth and strength, the parents tend to be closer to the Ideal Self than Jim is. Thus, his mother is perceived to be more warm, approving, relaxed, and friendly than Jim and his father is perceived to be stronger, more industrious, and more active than Jim. The mother is perceived as having an interesting combination of personality characteristics. On one hand, she is perceived as affectionate, friendly, spontaneous, sensitive, and good. On the other she is perceived as authoritarian, superficial, selfish, unintelligent, intolerant, and uncreative.

With the autobiography and the semantic differential we begin to get another picture of Jim. We learn of his popularity and success through high school and of his good relationship with his father. We find support for the suggestions from the projective tests of anxiety and difficulties with women. Indeed, we learn of Jim's fears of ejaculating too quickly and not being able to satisfy the female. However, we also find an individual who believes himself to be basically good and is interested in doing humane things. We become aware of an individual who has a view of his Self and a view of his Ideal Self, and of an individual who is frustrated because of the feelings that leave a gap between the two.

Given the opportunity to talk about himself and what he would like to be, Jim talks about his desire to be warmer, more relaxed, and stronger. We feel no need here to disguise our purposes, for we are interested in Jim's perceptions, meanings, and experiences as he reports them. We are interested in what is real for Jim — in how he interprets phenomena within his own frame of reference. We want to know all about Jim, but all about Jim as he perceives himself and the world about him.

When using the data from the semantic differential, we are not tempted to focus on drives and we do not need to come to grips with the world of the irrational. In Rogers' terms, we see an individual who is struggling to move toward self-actualization, from dependence toward independence, from fixity and rigidity to freedom and spontaneity. We find an individual who has a gap between his intellectual and emotional estimates of himself. In Rogers' terms, we observe an individual who is without self-consistency, who lacks a sense of congruence between self and experience.

REP Test: Personal Construct Theory

Jim took the group form of Kelly's Role Construct Repertory Test (REP test) on an occasion separate from the other tests. Here again we have an undisguised test that also is voluntary. It is structured in terms of the roles that are given to the subject and in terms of the task of formulating a similarity-contrast construct. However, the subject is given total freedom in the content of the construct formed. As we noted in Chapter 7, the Rep test is derived quite logically from Kelly's theory of personal constructs. Two major themes appear in these constructs. The first theme has to do with that of the *quality of interpersonal relationships*. Basically this involves whether people are warm and giving or cold and narcissistic. This theme is expressed in constructs such as Gives love–Self-oriented, Sensitive-Insensitive, and Communicates with others as people–Uninterested. A second major theme concerns *security* and is expressed in constructs such as Hung up–Healthy, Unsure–Self-confident, and Satisfied with life–Unhappy. The frequency with which constructs relevant to these two themes appear suggests that Jim has a relatively constricted view of the world; that is, much of Jim's understanding of events is in terms of the Warm-Cold and Secure-Insecure dimensions. Although not evident in the data, there may be a relationship between the two dimensions. The Warm-Cold theme has a dependency quality, and it may be that he feels more secure when he is receiving love from others. Notice here that Jim did rate himself as slightly dependent on the semantic differential and on the Rorschach gave responses that suggested passivity and oral dependency.

How do the constructs given relate to specific people? On the sorts that involved himself, Jim used constructs expressing insecurity. Thus, Jim views himself as being like his sister (so hung up that their psychological

The constructs formed by Jim are:

CONSTRUCT	CONTRAST
Self-satisfied	Self-doubting
Uninterested in communicating with students as people	Interested in communicating with students as people
Nice	Obnoxious
Sensitive to cues from other people	Insensitive to cues
Outgoing–gregarious	Introverted–retiring
Introspective–hung up	Self-satisfied
Intellectually dynamic	Mundane and predictable
Outstanding, successful	Mediocre
Obnoxious	Very likeable
Satisfied with life	Unhappy

CONSTRUCT	CONTRAST
Shy, unsure of self	Self-confident
Worldly, open-minded	Parochial, close-minded
Open, simple to understand	Complex, hard to get to know
Capable of giving great love	Somewhat self-oriented
Self-sufficient	Needs other people
Concerned with others	Oblivious to all but his own interests
So hung up that psychological health is questionable	Basically healthy and stable
Willing to hurt people in order to be "objective"	Unwilling to hurt people if he can help it
Close-minded, conservative	Open-minded, liberal
Lacking in self-confidence	Self-confident
Sensitive	Insensitive, self-centered
Lacking social poise	Secure and socially poised
Bright, articulate	Average intelligence

health is questionable) in contrast to his brother, who is basically healthy and stable. In two other sorts, he sees himself as lacking self-confidence and lacking genuine social poise. These ways of construing himself are in contrast with the constructs used in relation to the father. The father is construed as being introverted and retiring, but he also is construed as being self-sufficient, open-minded, outstanding, and successful.

The constructs used in relation to the mother are interesting and again suggest conflict On one hand, the mother is construed to be outgoing, gregarious, and giving of great love, while on the other she is construed to be mundane, predictable, close-minded, and conservative. The close-minded, conservative, construct is particularly interesting since, in that sort, mother is paired with the person with whom he, Jim, feels most uncomfortable. Thus mother and the person with whom he feels most uncomfortable are contrasted with father, who is construed to be open-minded and liberal. The combination of sorts for all persons suggests that Jim's ideal person is someone who is warm, sensitive, secure, intelligent, open-minded, and successful. The women in his life — mother, sister, girlfriend, and previous girlfriend are construed as having some of these characteristics but also as missing others.

The REP test gives us valuable data about how Jim construes his environment. With it we continue the phenomenological approach discussed in relation to Rogers, and again find that Jim's world tends to be perceived in terms of two major constructs: Warm Interpersonal Relationships–Cold Interpersonal Relationships, and Secure, Confident People–Insecure, Unhappy People. Through the REP test we gain an understanding of why Jim is so limited in his relationships to others and why he has so much difficulty in being creative. His being restricted to only two constructs hardly leaves him free to relate to people as individuals and instead forces him to perceive people and problems in stereotyped or conventional ways. A world filled with so little perceived diversity can hardly be exciting, and the constant threat of insensitivity and rejection can be expected to fill Jim with a sense of gloom.

The data from the REP test are tantalizing, much like Kelly's theory. What is there seems so clear and valuable, but one is left wondering about what is missing. Both figuratively and literally, there is the sense of the skeleton for the structure of personality, but one is left with only the bones. Jim's ways of construing himself and his environment are an important part of his personality. Assessing his constructs and his construct system helps us to understand just how he interprets events and how he is led to predict the future. But where is the flesh to go along with the bones — the sense of an individual who cannot be what he feels, the sense of an individual struggling to be warm amid feelings of hostility and struggling to relate to women although confused about his feelings toward them and confused about his own sexual identity?

Sixteen Personality Factor Inventory: Trait, Factor-Analytic Theory

Let us now move to the data from structured tests, in particular the 16 Personality Factor Inventory (16 P.F.) developed by Cattell. Jim completed both forms (A and B) of the 16 P.F. His profiles for each of these forms and for the composite of the two forms are given in Figure 14.1. First, notice that although in most cases the scores on Form A and Form B are quite close, in a number of cases they are quite different (for example, A, B, C, N, Q_2). The following brief descriptions of Jim's personality were written by a psychologist who assessed the results on the 16 P.F. but was unaware of any of the other data on Jim.

FORM A

Jim appears as a very bright yet conflicted young man who is easily upset and quite insecure. His profile indicates he is somewhat cynical and introspective. His identity confusion is shown by the fact that he appears to be outgoing while he feels shy and restrained, and he evades responsibilities and obligations and then experiences the consequent guilt, anxiety, and depression.

FORM B

Jim presents himself as a very outgoing young man who is really quite shy, approval-seeking, dependent, and tense. Brighter than average, he is quite confused about who he is and where he is going. His profile indicates that Jim is shrewd, introspective, tends to be overly sensitive, and pays for his impulsivity with guilt and depression.

COMPOSITE: FORMS A AND B

Jim presents himself as a very bright and outgoing young man although he is insecure, easily upset, and somewhat dependent. Less assertive, conscientious, and venturesome than he may initially appear, Jim is confused and conflicted about who he is and where he is going, tends toward introspection, and is quite anxious. His profile suggests that he may experience periodic mood swings and may also have a history of psychosomatic complaints.

Since the 16 P.F. has been administered to college students throughout the country, we can compare Jim with the average college student. Compared to other students, Jim is higher on the following traits: outgoing, intelligent, affected by feelings — easily upset, sensitivity, depression, poor self-sentiment, anxiety.

Let us turn to the factor analytic method in an effort to reduce the number of traits necessary to describe Jim's personality. Four second-order factors have been derived from the 16 first-order factors: Low Anxiety–High Anxiety, Introversion-Extroversion, Tenderminded Emotionality-Alert Poise, and Subduedness (Group-dependent, Passive)-Independence. Jim's scores are extreme on two of these factors. First, Jim is extremely high on anxiety. This suggests that he is dissatisfied with the degree to which he is able to meet the demands of life and to achieve what he desires. The high level of anxiety also suggests the possibility of physical disturbances. Second, Jim is very low on alert poise or, conversely, he is high on tenderminded emotionality. This suggests that he is not an

FIGURE 14.1 16 P.F. Test Profile of Jim Hersh.

16 P.F. TEST PROFILE

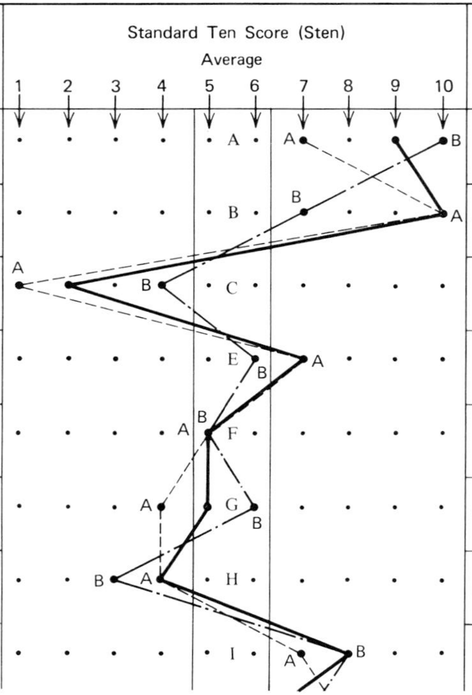

	Low-pole description				Sten	High-pole description
L	Trusting, adaptable, free of jealousy, easy to get on with (alaxia)	13	9	22	7	Suspicious, self-opinionated, hard to fool (protension)
M	Practical, careful, conventional, regulated by external realities, proper (praxernia)	16	14	30	8	Imaginative, wrapped up in inner urgencies, careless of practical matters, bohemian (autia)
N	Forthright, natural, artless, sentimental (artlessness)	10	14	24	7	Shrewd, calculating, worldly, penetrating (shrewdness)
O	Placid, self-assured, confident, serene (untroubled adequacy)	14	18	32	8	Apprehensive, worrying, depressive, troubled (guilt proneness)
Q_1	Conservative, respecting established ideas, tolerant of traditional difficulties (conservatism)	12	10	22	7	Experimenting, critical, liberal, analytical, free-thinking (radicalism)
Q_2	Group-dependent, a "joiner" and sound follower (group adherence)	12	5	17	4	Self-sufficient, prefers own decisions, resourceful (self-sufficiency)
Q_3	Undisciplined self-conflict, follows own urges, careless of protocol (low integration)	0	7	7	1	Controlled, socially-precise, following self-image (high self-concept control)
Q_4	Relaxed, tranquil, torpid, unfrustrated (low ergic tension)	15	19	34	8	Tense, frustrated, driven, overwrought (high ergic tension)

A sten of   1   2   3   4   5   6   7   8   9   10   is obtained
by about   2.3%   4.4%   9.2%   15.0%   19.1%   19.1%   15.0%   9.2%   4.4%   2.3%   of adults

enterprising and decisive personality. Instead it is suggested that Jim is troubled by emotionality and often becomes discouraged and frustrated. Although sensitive to the subtleties of life, this sensitivity sometimes leads to preoccupation and to too much thought before he takes action. Jim's other two scores indicate that he is neither introverted nor extroverted and is neither excessively dependent nor independent. The outstanding characteristics are the anxiety, the sensitivity, and the emotionality.

Before we leave the 16 P.F., it should be noted that two important features came out in sharper focus on this test than on any of the other assessment devices. The first is the frequency of mood swings in Jim. In reading over the results on the 16 P.F. Jim stated that he has frequent and extreme mood swings, ranging from feeling very happy to feeling very depressed. During the latter periods, he tends to take his feelings out on others and becomes hostile to them in a sarcastic, "biting,. or "cutting" way. The second feature of importance concerns psychosomatic complaints. As was mentioned previously, Jim has had considerable difficulty with an ulcer and frequently must drink milk for the condition. Notice that, although this is a serious condition that gives him considerable trouble, Jim did not mention it at all in his autobiography.

From the data on the 16 P.F. we can discern many important parts of Jim's personality. The concept of trait, expressing a broad reaction tendency and relatively permanent features of behavior, appears to be a useful one for the description of personality. We learn from the 16 P.F. that, although Jim is outgoing, he is basically shy and inhibited. Again, the characteristic of being anxious, frustrated, and conflicted comes through. But one is left wondering about whether sixteen dimensions are adequate for the description of personality, particularly when these can be reduced further to four dimensions. And one is left wondering whether a score in the middle of the scale means that the trait is not an important one for the individual or simply that he is not extreme on that characteristic. The latter appears to be the case. Yet, when one writes up a personality description based on the results of the 16 P.F., the major emphasis tends to fall on scales with extreme scores.

Perhaps most serious, however, is the fact that Cattell has failed to retain the virtues of the clinician in spite of his efforts to do so. The results of the 16 P.F. have the strengths and the limitations of being a trait description of personality. The results are descriptive, but they are not interpretive or dynamic. Although Cattell has attempted to deal with the individual as a whole, the results of the 16 P.F. leave one with only a pattern of scores — not a whole individual. Although the theory takes into consideration the dynamic interplay among attitudes (motives), sentiments, and ergs, the results of the 16 P.F. appear unrelated to this portion of the theory. Jim is described as being anxious and frustrated, but anxious about what and why frustrated? Why is Jim both outgoing and shy? Why does he find it so hard to be decisive and enterprising? The theory recognizes the importance of conflict in the functioning of the individual, but the results of the 16 P.F. tell us nothing about the nature of Jim's conflicts and how he tries to handle them. As pointed out in Chapter 8, the factor traits appear to have some degree of validity, but they also tend to be abstract and to leave out the richness of personality found in data from other assessment devices.

JIM HERSH: FIVE YEARS LATER

The material on Jim Hersh presented so far was written at approximately the time of his graduation from college. The revised edition of this book allows not only for a review of recent developments relevant to each theory but also for a review of developments in the life of our individual case study. Here we can try to follow trends established on the basis of earlier test results and see whether current patterns of behavior follow from earlier patterns. In other words, we can attempt to assess how stable and consistent Jim has been in his personality functioning. In noting and attempting to account for significant changes, we can ask about earlier hints of potential change and about the role of changes in environmental events. We can ask about which theories facilitated our understanding of Jim Hersh at the time of graduation and which facilitate our understanding of his functioning during the period of time since then.

Five years after graduation Jim was contacted and asked to: (1) Indicate whether there had been significant life experiences for him since graduation and, if so, to describe how they had affected him, (2) give a brief description of his personality and to describe the ways, if any, in which he had changed since graduation, and (3) complete the Reinforcement Survey Schedule and the Fear Survey Schedule, two questionnaires expressive of the behavioral approach to assessment. His responses in each of these three areas should help us answer some of the questions raised above.

Life Experiences Since Graduation — As Told by Jim Hersh

After leaving Harvard, I entered business school. I only got into one graduate school in psychology; it was not particularly prestigious, whereas I got into a number of excellent business schools, and so on that basis I chose to go to business school. I did not really enjoy business school, though it was not terribly noxious either, but it was clear to me that my interest really was in the field of psychology, so I applied to a couple of schools during the academic year, but did not get in. I had a job in a New York import-export firm over the summer, and disliked it intensely enough to once more write to graduate schools over the summer. I was accepted at two, and then went into a very difficult decision-making process. My parents explicitly wanted me to return to business school, but I eventually decided to try graduate school. My ability to make that decision in the face of parental opposition was very significant for me; it asserted my strength and independence as nothing else in my life ever had.

Going through graduate school in the midwest in clinical psychology was extremely significant for me. I have a keen professional identification as a clinician which is quite central to my self-concept. I have a system of thinking which is well-grounded and very central to the way I deal with my environment. I am entirely pleased with the decision I made, even though I still toy with the idea of returning to business school. Even if I do it, it would be to attain an adjunct degree; it would not change the fact that my primary identification is with psychology. I also fell in love during my first year in graduate school, for the first and only time in my life. The relationship did not work out, which was devastating to me, and I've not gotten completely over it yet. Despite the pain, however, it was a life-infusing experience.

During graduate school, I took up the guitar. I play and sing fairly seriously now, and it gives me some of my happiest hours. I see it as a long-term avocation for me. I have a lot of desire to get better and better with it, and frequently fantasize about getting to the point where I could play at coffee houses and the like. I've gotten enough positive feedback from enough different sources to know it is within the range of possibility. It is a very important part of my life.

Last year I lived in a communal setting and it was a watershed experience for me. We worked a lot on ourselves and each other during the year, in our formal once-a-week groups and informally at any time, and it was a frequently painful, frequently joyful, and always growth-producing experience. I am convinced that I would like to live communally as my basic style of life, though I need a very special group of people to do it with and would rather live alone or with one or two other people than with just any group. Our group is thinking about getting together again in a more permanent arrangement, and I may very well decide to live with them again beginning next year. Whether or not this happens, last year's experience was very significant for me, and therapeutic in every respect.

Toward the end of last year, I began a relationship which has now become primary for me. I am living with a woman, Kathy, who is in a master's program in social work. She has been married twice. It is a sober relationship with problems involved; basically, there are some things about her that I am not comfortable with. I do not feel "in love" at this point, but there are a great many things about her that I like and appreciate, and so I am remaining in the relationship to see what develops, and how I feel about continuing to be with her. I have no plans to get married, nor much immediate interest in doing so. The relationship does not have the passionate feeling that my other significant relationship had, and I am presently trying to work through how much of my feeling at that time was idealization and how much real, and whether my more sober feelings for Kathy indicate that she's not the right woman for me or whether I need to come to grips with the fact that no woman is going to be "perfect" for me. In any event, my relationship with Kathy also feels like a wonderful growth-producing experience, and is the most significant life experience I am currently involved in.

I think these constitute my significant life experiences since leaving Harvard.

Brief Personality Description and Changes Since Graduation — As Told by Jim Hersh

I do not think I've changed in very basic ways since leaving college. As a result of going into psychology, I think of myself as somewhat more self-aware these days, which I think is helpful. As I remember your interpretation of the tests I took back then, you saw me as primarily depressive. At this point, however, I think of myself as being primarily obsessive. I think I am prone to depression, but on balance see myself as happier these days — less frequently depressed. I see my obsessiveness as a deeply engrained characterological pattern, and have been thinking for some time now about going into analysis to work on it (amongst other things, of course). Though I consider my thinking about this serious, I am not yet very close to actually doing it. This is at least in part because I expect to be leaving Michigan at the end of this academic year, and so entering analysis at this point obviously makes no sense. On the other hand, it's a frightening proposition requiring a serious commitment, so there is some resistance to overcome over and above the geographic issue. Nevertheless, I see it as a definite possibility for myself in the next couple of years.

Let me say a word about my history with psychotherapy as a patient. I have made a number of abortive efforts to become involved, only one of which was even moderately successful. I saw someone at college a handful of times, but as I remember it, it was very superficial in every sense. I did nothing my year at business school. During my first year in graduate school, I saw an analytically oriented psychiatrist for three "evaluative sessions," after which he recommended: (1) analysis; (2) group therapy; (3) analytically oriented individual therapy. I was not ready to either enter analysis or a group, and did not want to continue with what he considered a third alternative, so I stopped. My second year in graduate school, I saw an analytically oriented psychiatrist for between six and eight sessions, but became very frustrated with his giving me so little, so that when he recommended increasing the frequency of visits from once to twice a week, I terminated. A big issue for me was how good a therapist he was: I saw him as pretty average, and felt I wanted someone special. This is clearly a form of resistance, I know, though I still feel there was some reality to my impressions of him. During my third year in graduate school, I saw a non-traditional psychiatrist about 10 times. He used a mixed bag of techniques: cathartic, gestalt, behavioral, and generally folksy and friendly (very anti-analytic). At the end of our relationship, which I thought was somewhat useful at the time, we both felt I'd had enough therapy, and that what I needed were "therapeutic" life experiences: e.g., a relationship with a woman, some time to play, etc. Since then I have had some important therapeutic life experiences, the most significant of which was living in the house I lived in last year. As a result, I feel less immediate pressure to get help, and think of going into analysis to work through basic characterological issues (like my obsessiveness). In other words, I feel in less acute pain these days.

As I said previously, I see myself as more similar to, than different from, the way I was five years ago. I think of myself as a witty, aware, interesting and fun-loving person. I continue to be quite moody, so sometimes none of these characteristics are in evidence at all. My sexual relationship with my girl friend has put to rest my concerns about my sexual adequacy (especially about premature ejaculation).

I still see myself as having an "authority" issue — i.e., being quite sensitive and vulnerable to the way in which those who have authority over me treat me. However, I see myself as having a number of important professional skills, and as being in the field I want to be in. I still have money issues — i.e., I am concerned about being paid fairly for what I do, I resent psychiatrists making more than me, I am vigilant around making sure I am not "ripped off," etc. I still have not fully come to grips with my father having money, and the fact that I will be getting some of that, but on the other hand I'm not terribly concerned about it, and it feels more like an intellectualized concern about the future than an emotional concern in the present. I am extremely compulsive, I very efficiently get done what needs to be done, and experience considerable anxiety when I am not on top of things. My life must be very well ordered for it to be possible for me to relax and enjoy myself. Unfortunately, the compulsiveness spills over into my personal life, so that my room must be orderly, my books stacked appropriately, etc., or else I experience anxiety. Again, this feels like a deeply engrained pattern which would not be easy to overcome.

Behavioral Assessment: Reinforcement Survey Schedule and Fear Survey Schedule

Ideally we would have had an opportunity to do a complete behavioral analysis of Jim's functioning, including both direct observation and self-reports of behavior, antecedent conditions, and consequent events. Although this was not possible, we were able to obtain his responses to the Reinforcement Survey Schedule and the Fear Survey Schedule. As noted in Chapter 13, the former involves the assessment of reinforcers in the life of the individual while the latter involves the assessment of anxiety-arousing stimuli. Both relate to events in the environment, as viewed by the individual, which shape his behavior.

In the Reinforcement Survey Schedule, Jim responded to a wide variety of items in terms of the extent to which each gives him pleasure. The items in the schedule related to eating, drinking, women, men, sports, reading, being praised, and other activities. In addition, Jim indicated the extent to which he liked to be in various situations and the things he frequently did or thought about each day. According to the Reinforcement Survey Schedule, the following are very reinforcing for Jim: music (listening, singing, playing a musical instrument), nude women, TV and movies, watching sports, winning a bet, being right, and expressions of praise and interest from others. The latter two reinforcers seem particularly significant since Jim indicated that being right about a wide variety of things (about his work, in an argument) and being praised for almost anything (appearance, work, physical strength, personality) gave him considerable pleasure. In another part of the questionnaire, Jim indicated that he frequently thinks about his relationship with others and whether he is liked by them. His responses to how much he would like to be in various situations again confirm the reinforcing value for him of praise. It is particularly interesting that whereas Jim indicated that he would very much enjoy being in a situation where a woman says that she appreciates what he has done for her and will remember him in her prayers, he reported that he would derive only a fair amount of pleasure from being in a tender situation with a loved one and thinking about how wonderful it is to care for that person and have her care for him.

In his responses to the Fear Survey Schedule, Jim expressed a great deal of anxiety about open wounds and the prospect of a surgical operation, and considerable anxiety about failure and being rejected by others. In general, his responses did not suggest that many things caused fear or resulted in unpleasant feelings. Among those things that might create such feelings for others but which Jim reported led to little anxiety for him were the following: being alone, speaking in public, being teased, feeling angry, people in authority, and cemeteries.

Jim's general response to the reinforcement and fear surveys is perhaps as interesting as the individual responses themselves:

I do not believe there are specific fears or rewards not mentioned in the respective question-naires which are salient for me. My experience of myself is that most of the fears and rewards which are powerful for me are so-called "secondary' [second-order]. The most powerful rewards for me are praise and recognition from significant others, and self-reinforcement (when I feel good about myself for something I have done). The most powerful fear is a generalized existential fear about the future, being alone rather than with a woman and children, not ending up with an ideal job in a place I want to be, etc. My general sense is that the questionnaires do not yield a great deal of significant information about me.

PERSONALITY THEORY AND ASSESSMENT DATA: THE CASE OF JIM HERSH

By presenting the case of James Hersh we have been able to review the data gathered from a variety of assessment techniques. The attempt here has not been to learn all about any one instrument or to prove the validity of one or another instrument but to explore the personality of a single individual through the use of a variety of assessment devices and to compare the impressions gained from these devices. Our goal is further to appreciate differences in personality theories as they relate to the different kinds of data on which the theories are based.

What of the data that we have available to us? Clearly, there are important similarities but also significant differences. We began with the data from the projectives (Rorschach, TAT) and then moved to consideration of some phenomenological data (autobiography, semantic differential). How does what we have learned from one set of data compare with what we have learned from another set? The Rorschach suggested tension and anxiety behind a façade of poise. The semantic differential suggested tension and anxiety but not a façade of tact and poise. The projectives suggested considerable difficulty with women and a conflict between sexual preoccupation and hostility. The data were far less clear in the semantic differential, although we did observe what appears to be an ambivalent attitude toward the mother. There is some further suggestion of this in the autobiography, along with some defensiveness. "My relationship with my mother is superficial but mutually satisfactory. There is no depth of understanding on her part — she wants me to succeed in a very conventional way. I understand her for what she is — a loving, lovable woman. I hope this doesn't sound like I look down on her, because I respect her very much."

Although the projectives clearly suggest some confusion in sexual identity, the ratings on the semantic differential indicate that Jim perceives himself to be masculine and more identified with his father than with his mother. In his autobiography he writes. "My father and I have achieved a great deal more rapport. I have great, almost unlimited respect for him and I think he feels the same toward me. . . . I am much more like my father than my mother." Also, the semantic differential data indicate that Jim perceives himself to be weak and somewhat passive whereas the father and Ideal Self are perceived to be strong and active. In relation to the parents, one is tempted to ask why Jim was not able to identify with the warm, outgoing aspects of mother or with the strong, active aspects of father.

There is evidence in both the projectives and semantic differential of a lack of warmth in interpersonal relationships. However, what is clear is that percepts such as vampires and Count Dracula sucking blood do not appear on the semantic differential. These data, which have a clear primitive, oral quality to them, cannot be obtained from the semantic differential. In addition, the projectives gave far less suggestion of an individual who perceives himself as being deep, sensitive, kind, thoughtful, and basically good. Perhaps it is out of fear of expressing hostility that Jim remains inhibited. Perhaps he also confuses activity and assertiveness with hostility and thereby feels unable to be a strong man. In any case, he often is unable to *be* what he *feels*. This is something that is basic to Rogerian theory and is well expressed by Jim in the conclusion of his autobiography: "All in all, there is a great chasm between my intellectual and emotional estimates of myself, and I think this chasm must be closed before I can reach some kind of peace with myself.'

The data from the semantic differential and the autobiography are not inconsistent with those from the projectives, but they are different. In both cases, there are expressions of anxiety and problems of warmth in interpersonal relationships. However, whereas in the projectives there are expressions of sadism and confusion in sexual identify, in the autobiography and semantic differential there are expressions of an individual who is not quite what he would like to be and who feels that he is not free to be himself. Thus he cannot be at peace with himself.

The data from the Kelly REP test and from the Cattell 16 P.F. continue to tell the story of information obtained from other assessment devices that is not inconsistent with previous data and theoretical interpretations but is distinct and different from them. The trait of anxiety appears on the 16 P.F., and on the Kelly REP test the construct insecurity was associated with the self. Similarly, both the 16 P.F. and the REP test data suggest problems in interpersonal relationships. The projectives and semantic differential suggested a difficulty in being uninhibited with people or becoming involved. On the REP test, Jim indicated that constructs such as Gives Love–Self-oriented, Sensitive-Insensitive, and Interested in People–Uninterested in People are important to him in interpreting his environment. The meaning of the construct Sensitive-Insensitive may be particularly critical since, in reading over the results of the 16 P.F., Jim noted that the reference to his being overly sensitive was fundamental to understanding his personality.

The use of the term *sensitive* is ambiguous. One can be a sensitive person in terms of being sensitive to the feelings and needs of others. This kind of sensitivity would suggest an empathic and warm individual. One can also be sensitive to art and music, which may or may not be related to an interpersonal, empathic sensitivity. Finally, one can be sensitive to others in terms of being dependent on them. Thus the individual who is buoyed by compliments and depressed by criticism is sensitive to others. Or the individual who is always searching to find out whether he has hurt someone's feelings may be viewed as sensitive to others. This type of sensitivity involves a concern with others but is not expressive of warmth. This distinction is of interest in relation to Jim's high score on the Tender-minded-Emotionality factor. The score suggests that Jim is easily discouraged and frustrated, sensitive to the subtleties of life, and often thinks too much. The score suggests that Jim is sensitive to people in that he is concerned with them but not necessarily that he is a warm individual. This helps us to understand how a "sensitive" individual can show signs of rigidity and inhibition on the projectives and on the 16 P.F. and still construe himself as being warm on the semantic differential and the REP test.

The behavioral assessment data were different from the previous data in two ways. First, they were obtained five years later than the previous data. Second, a full functional analysis was not possible and it was necessary to rely on Jim's responses to two questionnaires. His responses to the Reinforcement Survey Schedule and the Fear Survey Schedule indicated that being right and expressions of praise and interest by others are important reinforcers for him while injury to the body, failure, and rejection by others are particularly unpleasurable for him. The data from the other assessment devices are not in conflict with these results. In fact, there were indications of the importance of such reinforcers for Jim in the earlier data. However, what is significant is that the emphasis here is on the situational variables that control Jim's behavior. Although these data give us a general appreciation of such variables, to understand Jim's behavior in a particular situation we would want to know more about the controlling stimuli in that environment and more about his reinforcement history in comparable situations. The emphasis on such controlling environmental stimuli is in contrast with an emphasis on his personality-trait pattern, his constructs, his self-concept, or his internal psychodynamics.

What, then, is the value of these comparisons of data from different tests of Jim Hersh? The attempt here has been to demonstrate, in an individual case, a theme that has been repeated throughout this book: Different theories of personality are based on different sets of observations and in turn lead to the investigation of different phenomena. Is Jim Hersh a Dracula, a person unable to be what he feels, a person "hung-up" on security and warmth, a person characterized by the scores on 16 factor scales, or a respondent to reinforcers in the environment? Is Jim Hersh fixated at a pregenital stage of development, limited in his efforts toward self-actualization, limited by a constricted construct system, bothered by high ergic tension, or inhibited in his responses by fears of failure and rejection by others? There is evidence that he is each of these, but also evidence that he is more than any one of them. Because of the nature of the theories and the data gained in relation to each, at various points Jim Hersh appears to be one more than the other. As Kelly (1963) has observed, the bias of the investigator influences the behavior he will look at, the observations he will be sensitive to, the questions he will ask, and how important he feels it is to report various kinds of data.

At the beginning of this chapter we asked: Are the observations obtained similar when techniques of assessment associated with the different theories are applied to the same individual? I think the answer can be that the observations obtained are different in striking and important ways, but they are not inconsistent with one another. To conclude that one knows Jim or understands his personality from just one set of observations would undoubtedly put one in the same position as the blind man who examined a small portion of the elephant and was led to a wrong conclusion on the basis of his limited observations. In part the data suggest that at times the theories talk about the same phenomena in different terms. However, the data also strongly suggest that each set of observations and each theory represents an incomplete picture of the whole individual. In a certain sense, each represents a glimpse of the total complexity of human personality.

What is needed in the future is the study of the same individuals by psychologists of different orientations. In Kelly's terms, this would permit us to assess the likenesses and differences of personality theories and to determine each one's range and focus of convenience.

TWO DISCIPLINES OF SCIENTIFIC PSYCHOLOGY

Experimental Approach

Correlational Approach

Summary

TACTICS OF RESEARCH AND THE CONCEPTS OF STRESS, HELPLESSNESS, AND CONTROL

Naturalistic Observation

Laboratory Research

Correlational Research and the Use of Personality Questionnaires: Locus of Control

Action Research and Clinical Analogues

Overlapping Research Efforts and Conclusions Concerning Stress, Control, and Helplessness

THE SCIENCE AND SOCIAL PSYCHOLOGY OF RESEARCH

Demand Characteristics

Experimenter Expectancy Effects

Additional Pitfalls in Human Research

Research and Public Policy

Summary

MAJOR CONCEPTS AND SUMMARY

15 PERSONALITY RESEARCH

Chapter Focus:

In this chapter we will consider the nature of the process of personality research. In earlier chapters research was considered in relation to personality theories. Here it is considered in terms of research goals and the factors that influence the process. There is discussion of alternative approaches as exemplified by research on the concepts of stress, helplessness, and control. There is also discussion of the strengths and limitations of each approach and the commitments of various investigators to one approach or another. The chapter concludes with a discussion of the human and social forces that influence research, from conceptualization of a problem to influences on public social policy.

The well-known virtue of the experimental method is that it brings situational variables under tight control. It thus permits rigorous tests of hypotheses and confident statements about causation. The correlational method, for its part, can study what man has not learned to control or can never hope to control. . . . The correlator's method is to observe and organize the data from Nature's experiments.

CRONBACH, 1957, P. 672

Different kinds of data and differing levels of information are obtained in the laboratory and the clinic. Each is necessary, useful, and desirable.

LAZARUS AND DAVISON, 1971, P. 197

Research has to do with the systematic study of observed relationships among events. It involves the gathering of data in the search for facts or principles that can be interpreted in a broader theoretical framework. Research forms a connecting link with theory and assessment techniques; the three form a triad basic to the field of personality—or, any scientific discipline. Theory without research is mere speculation but unending research without theory is meaningless fact-gathering.

A personality theory attempts to answer the questions of what, how, and why, to provide formulations to explain structure, dynamics, development, psychopathology, and change. A personality theory suggests that certain relationships should exist among specific phenomena. Research involves the use of data-gathering techniques to observe relevant phenomena; it attempts to determine whether the suggested relationships do in fact exist. Where there are two competing theories of personality, we look for a crucial test—a place where the two theories predict different relationships among phenomena and research can determine which relationships exist. This is not to say that our understanding of personality is never advanced by research unrelated to theory or even by "chance" findings; it suggests that the general course of an increase in our understanding is through a relationship between theory and research. This chapter will describe some systematic efforts in personality research, outline some of the issues and problems, and illustrate how personality research tends to reflect differences in theoretical assumptions and styles.

Personality researchers vary in the types of issues they investigate, how they define variables (the sources of variation they consider important for investigation), and their general styles of research. Some choose to work with global, wide-range variables such as types, need for achievement or cognitive style. Others choose to work with such more specific and focused variables as trait, habit, or learned stimulus-response bond. Some researchers use concepts that are defined in relation to a theory and are intangible—again, such as need for achievement and cognitive style. Others choose variables that are defined in relation to measurement procedures and thought to be tangible, such as anxiety defined in terms of physiological response or habit defined in terms of a learned stimulus-response bond. Some researchers study how individuals vary in their responses to the same situation while others examine how situations influence behavior in a systematic way. Some study a few individuals intensively while others feel comfortable with large numbers; some use one statistical technique, such as factor analysis, whereas others avoid it completely; some "go inside the person's mind" while others stay out of "the black box;" some study behavior in the clinic, others in the laboratory; some value "flexibility" and "freedom to explore" while others value "rigor" and "sharpness of focus." This is not to say that all psychologists are of one type or the other or that there is one consistent position on all such issues, but rather that there is individual variation in the strategies psychologists use in their research. While psychological research in general, and personality research in particular, are part of science, they involve humans whose research behavior is at least partly determined by personality characteristics.

At times for logical reasons, and at times for reasons of temperament, in personality research there are relationships among type of theory, data-gathering technique, and research strategy. For example, "clinical" theories of personality tend to be associated with unstructured personality tests and frequently make use of clinical situations where the investigator (clinician) cannot exercise control over the relevant variables. "Empirical" theories are likely to be associated with structured personality tests and with direct control or manipulation of the variables by the experimenter. It is possible, in fact, desirable, to study the same variables from different theoretical viewpoints and in relation to different sources of data. More typically, however, indepedent lines of pursuit develop, each expressing its own link between theory, assessment, and research.

TWO DISCIPLINES OF SCIENTIFIC PSYCHOLOGY

Humans are complex animals and research on them is a complex pursuit. It has been stressed that there are alternative approaches to or styles of personality theory, assessment, and research. Early note was taken of these differences by Dashiell (1939), who made a distinction between the *experimental* attitude and the *clinical* attitude in his presidential address to the American Psychological Association. The experimental attitude he described as one of science, enabling the investigator, through careful experimentation, to gain control over variables and to understand the conditions under which phenomena occur. Dashiell described the clinical attitude as one of speculation, wherein the peculiar makeup of the individual person is the primary subject matter. The experimental approach is to hold everything constant except for the few variables of interest, the goal to isolate the factors that influence a typical human being. The purpose of the experimental approach is to isolate the phenomenon; the goal of the clinical approach is to isolate the individual.

Dashiell described the differences as not primarily of subject matter but of attitude, viewpoint, and ultimate aim. He also noted that while methodological differences did not necessarily follow logically, they in fact tended to occur. The issues Dashiell described are now familiar—(1) one aspect of the individual ("behavior-segment level") versus the total individual ("person-level"); (2) all persons versus the single individual; (3) situational determinants of behavior versus personality factors as leading to consistency over situation and time; and (4) "making things happen" in research versus studying what has occurred. What is significant about the Dashiell paper is not that he noted these "serious cleavages" in the field or that he attributed them to fundamental differences in motivation and attitudes among psychologists, but that he saw clear evidence of a coming together of the experimental and clinical attitudes. In 1939 he saw experimentalists and clinicians joining in common efforts leading to a broadening of each other's viewpoint.

Fifteen years later, Bindra and Scheier (1954) drew attention to a related problem—the relation between (as they called them) the *experimental* and *psychometric* approaches in psychology. Again, in the experimental approach, the experimenters are interested in how they can produce phenomena as a result of control over the experimental conditions. In the psychometric approach, researchers study differences among individuals on tests rather than differences in experimental conditions or those produced by experimental conditions. For example, the psychometric approach might define anxiety in terms of scores on a personality inventory whereas the experimental approach might define anxiety in terms of intensities of electric shock or, more generally, in terms of experimentally induced stress. Although Bindra and Scheier saw the advocates of each approach going their own ways, they proposed the combined use of the experimental and psychometric approaches. For example, we might study the experimental conditions that influence test scores or how different kinds of individuals, as defined by test scores, respond to various experimental conditions.

experimental
correlational

Cronbach (1957) also pointed to similar issues. He characterized two streams of "method, thought, and affiliation"—the **experimental** and the **correlational**. Cronbach's view of the experimental approach is similar to that described previously. In the experiment, the goal is to produce consistent variation in behavior as a result of certain treatments of the independent variables. The experimenter changes conditions to observe consequences but, most critically, it is the consequences uniform for all subjects that are of interest. The method has the virtues of permitting tight control over variables, rigorous tests of hypotheses, and confident statements about causation. It is described by Cronbach in its extreme form:

Individual differences have been an annoyance rather than a challenge to the experimenter. His goal is to control behavior, and variation within treatments is proof that he has not succeeded. Individual variation is cast into that outer darkness known as "error variance." For reasons both statistical and philosophical, error variance is to be reduced by any possible device. You turn to animals of a cheap and short-lived species, so that you can use subjects with controlled heredity and controlled experience. You select human subjects from a narrow subculture. You decorticate (cut nerve pathways to the brain) your subject by cutting neurons or by giving him an environment so meaningless that his unique responses disappear. You increase the number of cases to obtain stable averages, or you reduce N to 1, as Skinner does. But whatever your device, your goal in the experimental tradition is to get those embarrassing differential variables out of sight.

CRONBACH, 1957, P. 674.

Experimental Approach

Much of the work on the effects of conflict and stress on behavior illustrates the experimental approach. As noted in Chapter 9, Pavlov (1928) was able to produce breakdowns in behavior and "experimental neuroses" in dogs by setting up a conflict situation. As noted in Chapter 9, Pavlov first conditioned the responses of dogs to two signals, a circle and an ellipse, with one signal always reinforced by food and the other never reinforced. The two signals were made more and more similar, approximating an oval, so that eventually the dog could not tell the difference between the signals and behavioral disorganization took place. A fascinating example of the experimental production of stress is the work of Brady (1958) on ulcers in "executive" monkeys (see Figure 15.1). Brady noted that earlier experiments had suggested a relationship between stress and ulcers but had not demonstrated such a relationship conclusively. Thus, for example, ulcers were produced in rats by subjecting them to a conflict situation (food and water obtained by standing on a grid, which resulted in a shock), but it was not demonstrated that the emotional stress of having to make a decision was the critical variable (Sawrey and Weisz, 1956). In his research, Brady placed two monkeys in chairs that restrained them. A conditioning experiment was conducted during which both monkeys received shocks, but only one monkey could prevent them. The "executive" monkey could prevent shocks to himself and to his partner by pressing a lever at least every 20 seconds. If the "executive" monkey did not press the lever within

20 seconds, both he and his partner received a shock. Thus, both animals experienced the same physical stress (number of shocks), but only the "executive" monkey experienced the psychological stress of having to press the lever. The executive monkeys developed ulcers while their partners did not. Later research suggested that the schedule of trial and rest periods

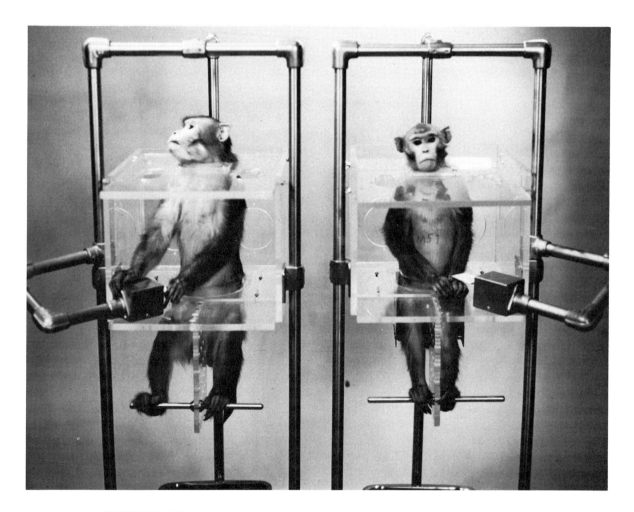

FIGURE 13.1   The "executive" monkey (left) has learned to press the lever in its left hand, which prevents shocks to both animals. The monkey (right) has lost interest in its lever, which is a dummy.

in the experiment was also critical—intermittent emotional stress (periods of stress alternating with periods of rest) caused ulcers, but continuous emotional stress did not. (Other factors, discussed later in this chapter, were also found to influence the results and their interpretation.)

The research described shows how, by using the experimental approach, the researcher is able to gain control over situational variables and determine the effect of so doing on the behavior of interest. An interesting variant of the experimental method is the Skinnerian **own-control** or **ABA research design** (Krasner, 1971). Some of the principles of this research method follow from the principles of behavioral assessment described in Chapter 13. Basically the ABA, own-control research design involves the experimental manipulation of a specific behavior and the demonstration that changes in behavior can be attributed directly to specific changes in environmental events. One subject is used and serves as his own control relating to variations in experimental conditions. In the first or baseline phase (A) of this design, the current rate of occurrence of the behavior of interest is recorded. In the second or reinforcement phase (B), a reinforcer following the behavior of interest is introduced in an effort to increase the frequency of that behavior. Once the behavioral response has been established at the desired frequency, the reinforcer may be withdrawn (A phase) to see whether the behavior returns to the original (baseline period) rate. This is called the nonreinforcement period. For example, the experimenter might be interested in increasing rational talk in a schizophrenic patient. First, a baseline period of recording speech during interviews would be established. Then, during the reinforcement phase, the patient might be reinforced with social approval, snacks, or cigarettes for talking rationally. One would expect to find an increase in rational talk as a result of the reinforcement. If the reinforcement were then terminated, establishing the nonreinforcement period, one would expect an increase in nonrational talk, indicating that the rational speech was contingent on the reinforcer and under the control of the experimenter (Liberman, Teigen, Patterson, and Baker, 1973). Instead of comparing a subject who is reinforced with one who is not, the subject is treated differently in the various phases—he is his own control. In some research, a fourth phase is also included in which the reinforcer is reintroduced to reestablish the desired behavior. Also, some experiments may begin with the reinforcement phase and then move to nonreinforcement and then reintroduction of reinforcement to demonstrate that the behavior is under the control of the reinforcer. This approach is typical when it does not make sense to begin with a baseline period, as when a new behavior is being taught (see Box 15.1).

own-control
ABA research design

BOX 15.1 **The Experimental Approach —
Behavioral ABA Design**

EXPERIMENTAL GOAL   Investigate variables that control self-destructive behavior (for example, head and arm banging, pinching and slapping self, setting hair on fire) in a nine-year-old schizophrenic girl. Attempt to establish other behaviors that will interfere with self-destructive behavior.

METHOD   Provide a table in a room with a bar-pressing apparatus on it and seats on opposite sides. When the girl (S) enters the room, experimenter (E) tells her to press the bar and praises her when she does so (reinforcement). E remains inattentive unless S presses the bar. When S does so, E looks up at S, smiles, and for five seconds says things such as: "That's a good girl; I love you very much; you are a sweetheart." Then E resumes an inattentive position until S again presses the bar. This constitutes the first acquisition period. Sessions are ten minutes daily, five days a week, for six weeks.

After a steady rate of bar-pressing has been established, begin the extinction or nonreinforcement phase. Here E no longer attends to and reinforces S for bar-pressing responses but remains inattentive throughout the sessions. This is done for seven sessions.

For the third period, the second acquisition period, E reintroduces attention and approval contingent upon S's bar press. This is done for four sessions.

During the sessions in the three different periods record the number of times S presses the bar and the number (frequency) of self-destructive acts.

RESULTS   The frequency of self-destructive behavior during the three periods is presented below. (Only the first sixteen days are represented for the first acquisition period.) Also represented is the frequency of bar-pressing (Total Rs on bar) in the same session. The data clearly indicate an increase in bar-pressing activity in the two acquisition (reinforcement) periods and a decrease in activity during the middle, extinction (nonreinforcement) phase. Self-destructive behavior declines when bar-pressing behavior increases and self-destructive behavior increases when bar-pressing behavior decreases. (see Figure 15.1, p. 497.)

CONCLUSION   The frequency of self-destructive behavior is a function of the presentation and withdrawal of reinforcement for other behaviors in the same situation. The result illustrates the lawfulness and regularity of self-destructive behavior and how such behavior is related to very specific environmental events. Therefore, self-destructive behavior can be considered to be a learned, operant behavior.

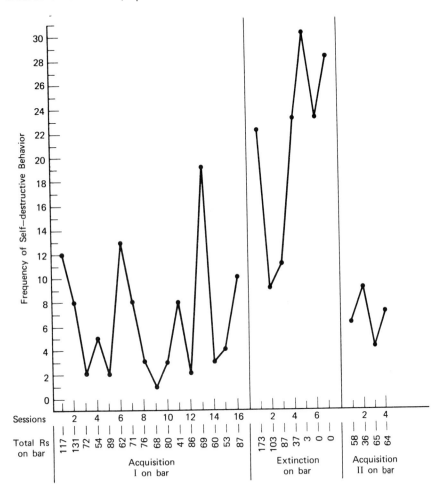

FIGURE 15.1 Frequency of self-destructive behavior over sessions where attention and approval were presented (Aquisition 1 and 2) and removed (Extinction 1) for bar-pressing behavior. Frequency of bar-pressing in the various sessions immediately below session numbers on the horizontal axis.

SOURCE   O. I. Lovaas, G. Freitag, V. J. Gold, and I. C. Kassorla Experimental studies in childhood schizophrenia: Analysis of self-destructive behavior. *Journal of Experimental Child Psychology*, 1965, *2*, 67-84.

Correlational Approach

In the experimental method, as illustrated in the studies above, there is little investigation of individual differences—in sources of emotional stress or in response to conflict. Yet it is precisely these differences in response to a situation that are significant in the correlational approach. In contrast to the experimental approach, where treatments (situations) are varied and individual differences are minimized, the correlational approach takes existing individual differences as the crux of the matter and regards treatment or situational factors a source of annoyance. In correlational research the investigator measures subjects on a variety of personality variables and then examines the relationships among the variables in the light of personality theory. As in Cattell's multivariate approach, the interest is in the correlation among personality variables that cannot readily be manipulated experimentally.

An example of the correlational approach is the classic work done on the authoritarian personality (Adorno, Frenkel-Brunswick, Levinson, and Sanford, 1950). The original research was directed toward an understanding of widespread prejudice against Jews during the 1940s. Scales were developed to measure individual differences in anti-Semitism, prejudice against blacks, and dislike of foreigners. Scores on the scale were then related to information obtained from interviews, Rorschachs, questionnaires, and other personality tests. The strategy was to develop scales to measure the personality construct of authoritarianism and to relate or correlate individual differences in scores on these tests with scores on other personality tests. After considerable research the investigators observed a complex of related personality characteristics they labeled the authoritarian personality. According to the theory, the authoritarian personality shows itself in values held, interpersonal relations, and thinking or cognitive functioning. The values express conventionalism or commitment to traditional values and uncritical submission to idealized authorities. The interpersonal relations emphasize dominance-submission, strong-weak, leader-follower issues and avoidance of feelings of sympathy and tenderness. Cognitive functioning is characterized by rigid rules and intolerance of ambiguity. Basically, the assumed underlying feelings of helplessness are seen as being defended against and a generalized hostility is expressed in prejudice and cynicism.

The correlational research conducted suggested a complex of personality variables which together made up the authoritarian personality. Situational variables were given some attention, but the major emphasis was on individual differences in personality organization. Whereas an experimental approach to authoritarianism might have emphasized situational factors as associated with authoritarian opposed to nonauthoritarian behavior, the correlational approach emphasized the complex of personality characteristics that could be found to be related to one another. Whereas in the experimental approach the investigator would have tried to create the conditions that would influence the amount of authoritarianism expressed, in the correlational approach the investigators attempted to relate individual differences in behavior to differences found on other personality tests.

Summary

This section has examined the alternative approaches to research taken by different psychologists. Dashiell emphasized the distinction between the experimental interest in uniformities across individuals and the clinical interest in the individuals themselves. Bindra and Scheier emphasized the distinction between the experimental approach, in which variation was produced by the experimenter, and the psychometric approach, in which variation was obtained by selecting individuals who differed on tests. Cronbach emphasized the distinction between the experimental approach, where interest is in uniformities produced as a result of situational variation, and the correlational approach, where interest is in individual differences that are stable across situations. We have, then, differences in research strategies. The proponents of the experimental view seek laws that are uniform across individuals and are critical of psychologists who choose another research strategy for their lack of rigor and for the inconsistencies in results they so often obtain. The latter group of psychologists argues for the complexity of human behavior, as exemplified by individual differences, and criticizes those investigators who choose another research strategy for concerning themselves with trivia and for disregarding the orderly way in which individual personalities manifest themselves across diverse situations.

Dashiell felt that the two groups would be coming together soon. Bindra and Scheier and Cronbach stressed the need for personality research that combines both methods. Such research would look at how situational variations have different effects on different types of individuals. To put it another way, such research would look at how different types of individuals are affected by situational factors. Thus, instead of looking at the effects of threatening and nonthreatening situational conditions on personality assessment data for defensive and nondefensive subjects, we would look at the effects of threatening and nonthreatening conditions on the discrepancies between subjective and projective data for defensive and nondefensive subjects. The focus would not be on situations alone or on individual differences alone but on the interactions between situations and individual differences.

TACTICS OF RESEARCH AND THE
CONCEPTS OF STRESS, HELPLESSNESS, AND CONTROL

The discussion of the two principles of scientific psychology suggests that psychologists have differing views about the best way to proceed in uncovering basic personality processes. There are rules about research that psychologists would agree on, but beyond these rules are questions about tactics of research—the utility of studying nonhuman species, the relative usefulness of naturalistic observation and laboratory research, the extent to which we can generalize from findings with college students, and so on (Pervin, 1978). The question of tactics suggests that in many areas there are neither right nor wrong answers as to how phenomena should be studied. Rather, there are decisions each investigator must make concerning alternative research strategies and the advantages and disadvantages of each. Following from the earlier discussion of the experimental and correlational approaches, and keeping in mind the issue of alternative strategies or tactics of research, we can now consider four approaches to the study of personality: naturalistic observation, laboratory research, correlational research, and clinical manipulation. We shall consider each, as well as illustrations of overlapping approaches, in relation to similar phenomena and concepts—stress, helplessness, and control.

Stress, helplessness, and control were chosen because they have been researched in a variety of ways and there is at least some overlap in findings. In one form or another they are also significant areas of current empirical investigation. Personality and other psychologists are interested in the nature and causes of stress, causes and consequences of helplessness, and human efforts at self-control, self-regulation, and self-maintenance. Considerable research has been directed toward understanding each separately as well as toward understanding relationships among stress, the experience of helplessness, and progress toward self-control.

Why there should be such a surge of interest in these phenomena is itself an interesting question. The concepts are not new and, in one form or another, they have been emphasized many times. Yet today hardly an issue of a major journal in the field of personality appears without a number of articles related to these concepts. Perhaps, as many have suggested, people today are more concerned with feelings of helplessness in relation to complex political and economic events. This view is supported somewhat by research which found that between 1966 and 1970 college students at one university increasingly expressed beliefs that events were controlled by factors they were powerless to influence (Schneider, 1971). Whatever the reason, these concepts are receiving increasing attention; thus, consideration of them can serve the dual function of allowing us to learn more about both current research and alternative strategies for gathering personality-relevant data.

Naturalistic Observation

naturalistic observation

Naturalistic observation has to do with the study of phenomena as they occur in their own environment, without any efforts on the part of the researcher to control what occurs. Biologists use naturalistic observation as a primary mode of research. Animals are studied in their natural habitats as inquiry is made into patterns of behavior characteristic of the members of the species. In psychology, psychologists have studied the play behavior of children, patterns of mother-infant interaction, aggressive behavior in adolescents, and many other phenomena through naturalistic observation. Central to each of these investigations is that the behavior is examined in its natural setting and the researcher does not influence when, where, or how the behavior occurs. The advantage of naturalistic observation is that one examines the behavior of interest directly and does not have to extrapolate from a somewhat artificial setting to the real world. At the same time, it generally does not allow the investigator to untangle the many factors that may be covering the complex behavior of interest. Naturalistic observation is the only feasible means for the study of some phenomena (for example, war-time stress), but many psychologists defend its usefulness in other areas as well.

Somewhat related to naturalistic observation in clinical research is the use of verbal reports of what occurred in the natural setting. In other words, rather than observing the behavior directly the investigator uses reports from individuals who experienced the phenomena. The material gathered by Freud and most other therapists engaged in verbal psychotherapy illustrates this approach. Interviews of people after they have experienced a trauma (physical injury, loss of a home or loved one) would be another example. The advantages and disadvantages of this method are obvious. On one hand, one can inquire about phenomena it might be impossible to observe directly and, through verbal report, learn about psychological processes that might not be apparent through the observation of overt behavior. On the other hand, one may be led astray by problems of recall and the reporter's faulty conception of what occurred.

How have naturalistic observation and clinical research been used in relation to stress, helplessness, and control? The concept of anxiety, related to that of stress, has received considerable clinical attention. The noted psychoanalyst Rollo May, in an early review of the literature, concluded that "the special characteristics of anxiety are the feelings of uncertainty and helplessness in the face of danger" (1950, p. 191). Uncertainty, or lack of cognitive structure, and a sense of helplessness, or lack of control, are mentioned repeatedly in the clinical literature. The former often is expressed in the "fear of the unknown" and is often seen as related to a sense of powerlessness or helplessness—an unknown danger creates a situation where activity cannot be directed toward any one goal, with a resultant feeling of mental paralysis and helplessness (Kris, 1944). Among the many valuable naturalistic and clinical investigations of responses to stress have been the studies by Grinker and Spiegel (1945) of the reactions of World War II flying personnel to battle stress and the studies by Janis (1965) of reactions of individuals to loss and illness.

After the second world war, two psychoanalysts (Grinker and Spiegel, 1945) reported on their experiences interviewing and treating individuals engaged in the air battle. Their book, *Men under Stress*, is a fascinating account of the stress that is common for all combatants and the varied reactions that occur among different individuals. After describing the kinds of dangers to which the airmen are exposed and their use of group morale to deal with the constant threats facing them, the authors raise the question: Of what is the airman afraid? Their description of the relationship between helplessness and anxiety runs:

Although the fear of the aircraft and of human inefficiency are a constant source of stress, the greatest fear is attached to enemy activity. The enemy has only two forms of defense against our combat aircraft: fighter planes and flak [antiaircraft guns]. The enemy's fighter aircraft are efficient and highly respected by our combat crew members. But they are not as great a source of anxiety as flak. Enemy planes are objects that can be fought against. They can be shot down or outmaneuvered. Flak is impersonal, inexorable, and as used by the Germans, deadly accurate. *It is nothing that can be dealt with*—a greasy black smudge in the sky until the burst is close.

GRINKER AND SPIEGEL, 1945, P. 34

Grinker and Spiegel similarly describe the response of ground forces to enemy air and mortar attack. What is so stressful is that "there is nothing in the environment which can be used to anticipate the approach of danger . . . any stimuli may actually mean the beginning of an attack. Inhibition of anxiety becomes increasingly difficult" (1945, p. 52). According to these psychoanalysts, the initial reaction to such stress is heightened tension and alertness. The person becomes mentally and physically prepared for trouble so as to counteract the threat and avoid loss of control. A variety of means can be used to deal with the threat but, in the final analysis, "mastery, or its opposite, helplessness, is the key to the ultimate emotional reaction" (p. 129). Confidence is lessened by near-misses, physical fatigue, and the loss of friends. Efforts to see the self as invulnerable (incapable of being harmed), become increasingly difficult: "Out of the ensuing helplessness is born the intense anxiety" (p. 129). Some strive to hold on to ideas of personal invulnerability ("It can't happen to me"), while others hold on to a faith in magical or supernatural powers ("God is my co-pilot").

Whatever the nature of the efforts, they can be viewed as attempts to deal with the threatened loss of control and experience of helplessness. With prolonged stress, the development of almost any type of neurotic and psychosomatic (psychologically induced illness) reaction is possible. These reactions are grouped under the term *operational fatigue* and generally include a mixture of anxiety, depression, and psychosomatic reaction. The depression that is so common in such cases is associated with a sense of failure ("I've let my buddies down") and wounded pride. In sum, the main component of the anxiety is the sense of helplessness in the presence of a perceived danger. Prolonged stress of this sort leads to a psychological and physical breakdown expressed in a variety of neurotic reactions that are often accompanied by fatalism and depression.

Observation of patients' responses to illness similarly illustrates this approach to the study of stress. Individuals about to be examined by a physician are bothered by the uncertainty as to what will be found. During the examination they wonder and worry about each step in the examination and search for clues about what is going on. Psychologist Irving Janis has been interested in how people attempt to master stress. Among his many studies has been research on the responses of patients to long-term illness. Through observation and interview of cancer victims, he has developed some hypotheses concerning the process of the response to their form of stress. The typical process involves a sense of shock and numbness upon being informed of the bad news. Preoccupation with their "doomed" status may then alternate with blaming of others and denial of the implications of the fatal illness. Where a reasonably healthy process is in action, there follows a period of grieving or "working through" of the loss and a gradual readaptation to the life that remains.

Janis has been particularly concerned with the process of "working through" and the anticipatory preparation for the difficulties that will follow some painful event. In one of his early studies he compared the postoperative responses of three groups of patients: those who had extremely high preoperative fear, those who had moderate anticipatory fear, and those who had extremely low anticipatory fear. He found that people who were extremely fearful before the operation were more likely than others to be anxiety-ridden after the operation. However, people who were not afraid before the operation had more than minimal distress after the operation. These individuals were found to be more likely than others to express extreme postoperative anger and resentment. The patients who expressed the least postoperative emotional disturbance were those who had displayed a moderate degree of preoperative fear. Janis' conclusion was that the arousal of anticipatory fear prior to confronting the actual stressful situation is necessary for effective psychological coping with stress. Such anticipatory fear and the "working through" process allow for mental rehearsal and inner preparation for the dangers that follow. Such rehearsal and preparation are valuable in precluding an overwhelming sense of helplessness when the full impact of the surgery and illness must be recognized. They are useful in making plans for future action which can greatly reduce feelings of helplessness. In contrast, the person who denies the threat and at first experiences little apparent stress may later experience rage and/or gloom as actual consequences are recognized: "Thus the work of worrying is conceived as increasing the level of tolerance for subsequent threat or danger stimuli. The more thorough the work of worrying, the more reality-tested the person's self-delivered reassurances are likely to be and hence, the more emotional control he will have under conditions of subsequent danger or deprivation" (Janis, 1965, p. 238). One implication is that preparatory communications to patients about to undergo stressful experiences are extremely important in the process of "emotional inoculation" against overwhelming stress.

To summarize the work of Grinker and Spiegel and that of Janis, we may note that in both cases there is the use of firsthand observation and interview material from individuals undergoing periods of extreme stress. Also, both sets of investigations have emphasized the process through which individuals attempt to cope with threat. Finally, in both cases there has been an emphasis on the person's efforts at control and responses to a perceived sense of helplessness.

Laboratory Research

laboratory research

In many ways the limitations of naturalistic observation are the virtues of laboratory research, and vice versa. In **laboratory research** there is the opportunity to define, measure, and manipulate variables. With control over the relevant variables one can sort out what is going on and begin to establish if-then, causal relationships.

learned helplessness

Are there illustrations of the utility of laboratory research in relation to the concepts under consideration? Two independent series of recent studies have generated considerable research and speak directly to the issues. The first relates to the important work of Seligman (1975) and the concept of **learned helplessness**. In the course of some early work on fear conditioning and learning, Seligman and his co-workers observed that dogs who had experienced uncontrollable shocks in one situation transferred their sense of helplessness to another situation where shock was avoidable. In the first situation, dogs were put in a situation where no response they made could affect the onset, offset, duration, or intensity of the shocks.

When placed in a second, different situation where jumping over a barrier could lead to escape from shock, most of the dogs seemed to give up and accept the shock passively. They had learned in the first condition that they were helpless to influence the shocks and transferred this learning to the second condition. Note that this was true for most of the dogs (about two-thirds), but not for all—an important difference among individuals that will be returned to later.

The behavior of the dogs who had learned that they were helpless was particularly striking in contrast with that of dogs who received no shock or shock under different conditions. Given the situation where escape and avoidance were possible, the latter dogs would run frantically until they accidentally stumbled on the response that led to escape. Thereafter they would progressively learn to move to that response more quickly until, finally, they were able to avoid the shock altogether. In contrast to such "healthy " dogs, the learned helplessness dogs would similarly first run frantically but then they would stop, lie down, and whine. With succeeding trials the dogs would give up more and more quickly and accept the shock more passively—the classic learned helplessness response. The depth of their despair would become so great that it became extremely difficult to change the nature of their expectations. The experimenters tried to make it easier for the dogs to escape and tried to get them to come to safety by attracting them with food—to no avail. By and large, the dogs would just lie there. Even outside that situation, the behavior of the helpless dogs was different from that of the nonhelpless dogs: "When an experimenter goes to the home cage and attempts to remove a nonhelpless dog, it does not comply eagerly: it barks, runs to the back of the cage, and resists handling. In contrast, helpless dogs seem to wilt; they passively sink to the bottom of the cage, occasionally even rolling over and adopting a submissive posture; they do not resist" (Seligman, 1975, p. 25).

Further research demonstrated that the same phenomena found in dogs could be produced in humans (Hiroto, 1974). In this research one group of college students heard a loud noise that they could turn off by pushing a button, a second group of students heard the same noise but could not stop it, while a third (control) group did not hear a noise. All three groups of subjects were then put in another situation where in order to escape the noise they had to move their hand from one side of the box to the other. The members of the first and third groups quickly learned to escape the noise by moving their hands while the members of the learned-helplessness group failed to escape the noise; most sat passively and accepted the painful noise. Further research demonstrated that such learned helplessness could generalize beyond the initial task to a broad range of behaviors (Hiroto and Seligman, 1975). More recently, some studies have related this work to that of Bandura and have demonstrated that learned helplessness can occur through vicarious or direct modeling (Brown and Inouye, 1978; DeVellis, DeVellis, and McCauley, 1978). Individuals will give up more easily if they see themselves as similar to a helpless model than if they observe a successful model or if they perceive themselves as more competent than the observed model.

Seligman's explanation of the learned helplessness phenomenon was that the animal or person learns that outcomes are not affected by its behavior. The expectation that outcomes are independent of the organism's response then has motivational, cognitive, and emotional implications: (1) Uncontrollable events undermine the organism's motivation to initiate other responses that might result in control. (2) As a result of uncontrollability of previous events, the organism has difficulty learning that its response can have an effect in other events. (3) Repeated experiences with uncontrollable events eventually lead to an emotional state similar to that identified in humans as depression.

This is the theory of helplessness, a theory that also leads to suggestions concerning prevention and cure. First, to prevent an organism from expecting events to be independent of its behavior one should provide it with experiences where it can exercise control. In particular, the experience of controlling trauma protects the organism from the effects caused by experiences of unescapable trauma. Here Seligman notes that the dogs in the original research who did not become helpless even when exposed to inescapable shock probably had histories of controllable trauma prior to coming to the laboratory. This hypothesis was, in fact, tested and it was found that dogs with little experience in controlling anything were particularly susceptible to helplessness. Finally, in terms of therapy, the depressed person who suffers from expectations of uncontrollability needs to be directed toward experiences that will result in recovery of the belief that responding produces reinforcement. In therapy this involves games and tasks of increasing difficulty, starting with those that ensure success (Beck, 1976).

The learned helplessness model and associated research are indeed impressive. It has been so important and generated so much research that in 1978 a complete issue of the *Journal of Abnormal Psychology* was devoted to the learned helplessness model of depression. In this special issue Seligman modified his earlier view to take into consideration distinctions humans make concerning causality and control (Abramson, Seligman, and Teasdale, 1978). According to this reformulation people may attribute the cause of their helplessness to themselves or to the nature of the situation. Helplessness may be perceived to be personal or universal and general or specific. Which attribution is chosen then influences whether expectations of future helplessness are chronic or acute, broad or narrow, and whether or not self-esteem is lowered.

And what about the executive monkey who developed the ulcers while in control? Some later research found a serious flaw in the earlier study. The monkeys who acted as executives had been selected for that position on the basis of their faster, more active responses to a shock-escape situation in comparison to the monkeys who were then placed in the nonexecutive position. However, speed of response in such a situation is apparently related to emotionality. The selection procedure, therefore, resulted in the more emotional monkeys being put in the "executive" position while the less emotional monkeys were put in the "subordinate" position. Perhaps the former developed ulcers because of their emotionality, not because of their control. Indeed, in some later research in which monkeys were randomly assigned to each position it was found that the executive monkeys got fewer and less severe ulcers than did the monkeys who were helpless and out of control (Weiss, 1968). Other further research demonstrated that, under conditions of no control, unpredictable shocks are far more likely to lead to stomach ulcers than are predictable shocks (Weiss, 1970). These data are interesting not only in that they fit Seligman's theory, whereas the earlier data did not, but they also illustrate the sensitivity of many findings in laboratory experiments to subtle influences. Of course, the later data do not necessarily contradict the oft-noted relationship between people in executive positions and the presence of stomach disorders. Such people are in positions of power but also are in situations of repeated stress with many threats to their power and a great deal of uncertainty. The long-term effects of such stress can be serious.

The second example of laboratory research also concerns the effects of stress. In the first part of this research two psychologists, Glass and Singer (1972), were concerned with the consequences of adaptation to stress generally and urban stress in particular. They made use of the laboratory because they felt that this was the best way to sort out the effects of different variables. Noise was used as the source of stress, rather than such urban problems as crowding, garbage, crime, and so on, because it could be clearly defined and manipulated in the laboratory. Thus their studies of the problem of urban stress came to focus largely on the consequences of adaptation to unpredictable and uncontrollable high-intensity noise. Prior naturalistic research had suggested that the effects of such stresses as noise depend on cognitive factors associated with unpredictability and uncontrollability. Glass and Singer set out to investigate the relationship between these factors and performance. Two basic questions were asked: Is adaptation to a stress such as noise achieved at some cost to the individual such that behavioral aftereffects are observed? Do such consequences vary with the meanings attributed to the noise?

In a number of laboratory studies Glass and Singer manipulated the intensity, predictability, and controllability of noise and examined the effects on performance in tasks of varying complexity. Initially they found that subjects could adapt to the noise under almost all of the conditions and that, by and large, performance was disrupted only when subjects had to perform highly complex tasks under conditions of unpredictable or uncontrollable noise. However, other observations led them to believe that the negative effects of noise were more important after termination of the stress than during the process of adaptation or coping itself. Further investigations of the effects of noise on performance clearly indicated that behavioral problems occurred after the noise stopped. Noise was found to have an aftereffect on tasks such as solving puzzles and proofreading even if there was no effect when the noise itself was heard.

The authors speculated that unpredictable noise was particularly stressful because the individual experienced not only the aversiveness of the noise itself but also the anxiety of not being able to do anything to prepare for it because they did not know when it would occur. Was this true and why the aftereffect phenomenon? In some further research, the authors found that the perception of control reduced the negative aftereffects of unpredictable noise. Stating their view at about the time Seligman was conducting his research, they concluded that uncontrollable noise (stress) results in a sense of helplessness: "Consider first what an organism experiences during inescapable or unavoidable stress. Nothing he can do will affect the occurrence of the stressor, for there are no available resources that will enable him to counter it. If the aversive event is also unpredictable, there cannot even be preparation for stimulation. The individual is at the mercy of his environment, in which case we may describe his psychological state as one of helplessness" (Glass and Singer, 1972, p. 86). The authors referred to the clinical work of Grinker and Spiegel and of Janis in support of their view that uncontrollable stress results in a sense of helplessness. The authors also viewed their work as fitting in with Seligman's emphasis on uncontrollability and helplessness in animal research. The various lines of research were seen as converging on the view that it is not only the stressful event that is significant, but also the experience of lack of control or helplessness that may be associated with it. What Glass and Singer demonstrated was that the perception of control alone was enough to make a difference: the individual does not actually have to exert control!

Glass and Singer extended their research to other stresses, such as electric shock and social stress (harassment by an administrative assistant). In each case they found that the negative aftereffects of stress were a function of unpredictability and perceived lack of control. They reasoned that the perception of control reduces the aversive impact of the stress and thereby the behavioral aftereffects. As demonstrated in their studies, belief in actual or potential control reduces feelings of helplessness and thereby the magnitude of the stress response (tension) and the adverse after-effects. The sequence suggested runs:

> unpredictable stress⟶ increased sense of helplessness⟶ greater magnitude of stress response (attempt to cope)⟶ greater negative behavioral aftereffects

Addressing themselves to the questions raised initially, Glass and Singer concluded that adaptation to stress may be achieved at considerable cost to the individual resulting in negative behavioral aftereffects; that is, the cumulative effects of the responses to the stress may go beyond the effects of any single response. Furthermore, the consequences of stress appear to vary with the meanings attributed to the stress. In particular, the perception of lack of control or helplessness seems to result in negative aftereffects. The unpredictability of stress appears to be a critical variable influencing the perception of helplessness. The findings indicated that psychological factors, not simply the physical characteristics of stimuli, are the principle determinants of the adverse aftereffects of aversive stimuli.

The experimental research by Seligman on learned helplessness and that by Glass and Singer on the effects of noise resulted in similar conclusions through somewhat different lines of attack. In contrast with the research done in naturalistic settings, in this research there has been the careful manipulation and control of the relevant variables and, by and large, focus on systematic influences that are independent of individual differences. Both naturalistic observation and laboratory experimentation seek an understanding of basic aspects of human functioning and, as has been seen, can result in similar observations and conclusions. However, the points emphasized and characteristics of research valued tend to be different.

Correlational Research and the Use of Personality Questionnaires: Locus of Control

The earlier discussion of research on the authoritarian personality illustrates both the correlational approach to research and the use of personality questionnaires, which are generally used when the investigator desires to survey simultaneously a number of different personality characteristics. They also are used when the intent is to differentiate among individuals on a particular personality characteristic and then to explore the relationships between these differences and other aspects of personality functioning. An illustration of the latter is the development of the **Internal-External Scale** (I-E Scale) for measurement of individual differences on the concept of **locus of control**. The concept of locus of control is part of Rotter's

Internal-External Scale
locus of control

(1966) social learning theory and represents a generalized expectancy concerning the determinants of rewards and punishments in one's life. At one extreme are the people who believe in their ability to control life's events; that is, internal locus of control. At the other extreme are the people who believe that life's events, such as rewards and punishments, are the result of external factors such as chance, luck, or fate; that is, external locus of control. The concept is defined by Rotter in these terms:

> When a reinforcement is perceived by the subject as following some action of his own but not being entirely contingent upon his action, then, in our culture, it is typically perceived as the result of luck, chance, fate, as under the control of powerful others, or as unpredictable because of the great complexity of the forces surrounding him. When the event is interpreted in this way by an individual we have labeled this a belief in *external control*. If the person perceives that the event is contingent upon his own behavior or his own relatively permanent characteristics, we have termed this a belief in *internal control*.

> ROTTER, 1966, P. 1

Individuals vary along a continuum between the two extremes of internal and external locus of control. Also, it is believed that individuals vary their expectations concerning control depending upon characteristics of the situation. Individual differences in generalized expectations nevertheless remain. For example, while a person may generally believe in internal control there may be situations perceived as outside such control. Beyond this, the concept is important because it relates to a broad variety of social phenomena and findings from empirical research. For example, according to Rotter, the effects of rewards and punishments on behavior will vary according to whether these consequences are perceived as being under the person's control as opposed to their being random or due to luck. In accordance with such a belief, a number of studies have demonstrated differing effects of reward and punishment when the person believes the consequences relate to skill (internal control) as opposed to chance (external control). The effects of these consequences (learning) are generally much greater where internal control is believed to exist. An interesting clinical vignette related to such findings concerns the behavioral treatment of a person with the goal of increasing expectations for fulfillment in work, education, and social relationships (Phares, 1978). The treatment appeared to be working—the patient was increasingly successful in his efforts in each of these areas. However, the successes did not seem to result in any significant change. The progress was very slow and puzzling until it was discovered that the patient did not perceive any causal relationship between his behavior and the positive events that followed. He perceived them as all due to luck or other factors beyond his control.

    What does the scale to measure this concept look like and how has it

FIGURE 15.2   **Illustrative Items From Rotter's Internal-External Locus of Control Scale**

1a. Many of the unhappy things in people's lives are partly due to bad luck.

1b. People's misfortunes result from the mistakes they make.

2a. One of the major reasons why we have wars is because people don't take enough interest in politics.

2b. There will always be wars, no matter how hard people try to prevent them.

3a. Sometimes I can't understand how teachers arrive at the grades they give.

3b. There is a direct connection between how hard I study and the grades I get.

4a. The average citizen can have an influence in government decisions.

4b. This world is run by the few people in power and there is not much the little guy can do about it.

been used in research? The I-E Scale consists of 29 items. Each item consists of a pair of statements. The subject is asked to indicate the statement within the pair that is more strongly believed or felt to be more true. Twenty-three items directly relate to the concept of locus of control and six are unrelated, filler items. Examples of the relevant items are given in Figure 15.2. As can be seen, the items cover a variety of specific areas including personal experiences as well as more general political beliefs. Since its publication, the scale has been used in over a thousand published and unpublished studies.

It is impossible to review all the relevant literature. What can be done, however, is to consider some of the literature that examines the relationship between perceived locus of control and aspects of how the person copes with stress. The research reported under the categories of naturalistic observation and laboratory experimentation suggests that people who experience a lack of personal control over events will experience more stress. On the other hand, it may be that people who believe in external locus of control experience less stress because they just don't worry about things; they take the attitude that it's all chance and fate anyway. The literature suggests that internals do take a more active role in attempting to cope with the environment. They more actively seek and use information relevant to the control of their environment than do externals. Similarly, internals are more oriented toward positions of power and control than are externals. In general, internals also have been found to be better adjusted and to experience less anxiety than externals. Of perhaps even greater significance are differences in how individuals at the two extremes cope with failure. Whereas internals are much more likely to blame themselves for failure, externals are much more likely to blame others or take a "sour grapes" approach by devaluing goals that were not achieved.

This description of differences between internals and externals suggests a relationship to Seligman's concept of learned helplessness. The externals' belief that events are unrelated to their behavior sounds very much like the situation in learned helplessness. In both cases, perception of the control of reinforcement is a critical variable. Earlier it was noted that Seligman's findings with dogs was duplicated in humans. Another part of that study was the investigation of differences between internals and externals in learned helplessness (Hiroto, 1974). Groups of internal and external subjects were presented with two different sets of conditions. The first group of internal and external subjects heard a loud noise they could neither escape nor avoid and then was tested for learned helplessness on a task in which the noise could be avoided through the appropriate response. The other group of internal and external subjects was first put in a situation where the noise could be escaped and then were put in an escape situation identical to the second situation given to the no-escape group. As indicated earlier in the chapter, experience with the first no-escape situation produced the learned-helplessness effect. Beyond this, externals were found to be significantly more helpless than were internals (See Box 15.2). Hiroto concluded that since uncontrollability of the aversive stimulus (noise) and belief in external control led to similar effects, they probably are related to one another. The study is of particular interest not only because it related Seligman's learned-helplessness model to Rotter's concept of locus of control but also because it used both the laboratory experimentation and personality questionnaire, both situational differences and individual differences, approaches to research.

BOX 15.2 **Locus of Control and Learned Helplessness**

HYPOTHESES   Individuals first exposed to a no-escape situation will show less escape behavior in a subsequent situation than will subjects first exposed to a situation where escape is possible. This is the learned helplessness phenomenon. In addition, external locus of control subjects will show greater evidence of learned helplessness than will internal locus of control subjects.

METHOD   Give subjects a test of internal-external locus of control. Put members at both extremes into two groups, an escape group and a no-escape group. In the first treatment phase, subjects listen to an aversive tone. For the escape group, a button is available that can stop the noise. For the no-escape group, the button has no effect on the aversive tone. The testing of helplessness occurs in a second situation that is identical for members of both groups. A light signal is followed by another aversive tone. If the subject moves a knob on top of the apparatus, the noise stops. If the knob is moved during the light signal and prior to the onset of the tone, the noise is avoided altogether. As a measure of differences in learned helplessness in this second situation, the average duration between onset of the light signal and the response of moving the knob (response latency) is calculated for each subject.

RESULTS

1 As in the animal research, subjects who were first in the no escape treatment condition took longer to respond and failed to escape more often in the test situation than did subjects who were first in the escape condition (Figure 15.3 below).

2 External locus of control subjects, regardless of their pretreatment, were slower to escape or avoid than were internal locus of control subjects (Figure 15.4, p. 514).

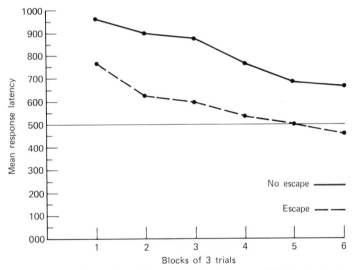

FIGURE 15.3   Mean response latencies of the 6 escape-avoidance trial blocks for the 2 treatment groups.

CONCLUSIONS

1 Learned helplessness can be experimentally produced in humans. Both animals and humans take longer to respond and fail to escape more often following inescapable aversive events than following escapable events.

2 The personality variable of externality appears to function like the pretreatment variable of inescapability.

BOX 15.2 **Locus of Control and Learned Helplessness** *continued*

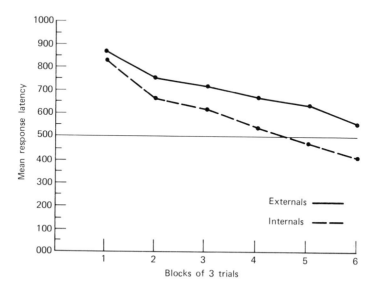

FIGURE 15.4 Mean response latencies of the 6 escape-avoidance trial blocks for internal and external control.

3 In view of the parallel effects created by inescapability and externality it is likely that the same underlying process exists in each, that is, the expectancy that responding and reinforcement are independent.

SOURCE   D. S. Hiroto, Locus of control and learned helplessness. *Journal of Experimental Psychology,* 1974, *102* 187-193.

To summarize this brief discussion of the concept of locus of control, it can be seen how efforts have been directed toward the measurement of a personality concept and then toward relating individual differences to other aspects of personality functioning. In this case individual differences in belief concerning internal and external control have been related to the extent to which individuals will seek to acquire control over their environment and to differences in response to stress and failure. The internal person takes a more active approach to life, seeking mastery and control over its pleasures and frustrations. The external person perceives the self as more helpless in influencing the course of life's events and therefore attributes consequences to luck, chance, and fate. The evidence to date suggests that externals are generally more anxious than internals.

Action Research and Clinical Analogues

In many ways the fourth approach to research represents a compromise between the first two. In naturalistic observation one examines the actual phenomena of interest but, since there is no control over the relevant variables, it is often hard to determine what is controlling them. In laboratory research the experimenter may demonstrate very exacting control over the behavior of interest but not be sure that the same principles would hold in the natural environment. In **action research**, which takes place in the natural environment, and **clinical analogues**, which generally take place in a more restricted setting in which there tends to be greater control over variables, there is an attempt to demonstrate a change in the behavior of interest under conditions approximating those occurring naturally or without experimental control. Action research may involve, for example, programs to change the attitudes or behaviors of staff or patients. Control is exercised over the change program and care is taken with regard to measurement, but the population receiving the "treatment" is not otherwise influenced by the researchers.

action research
clinical analogues

A recent effort to reduce psychological stress in a field setting is an illustration of such a program (Langer, Janis, and Wolfer, 1975). Patients about to undergo major surgery were given a stress-reducing strategy of interpreting the events as less dangerous, telling themselves to remain calm, and diverting their attention from the anxiety-provoking events to other thoughts. These patients experienced less preoperative stress and less postoperative stress than patients given preparatory information and reassurance. Preoperative stress was measured by the number of pain relievers requested and the proportion of patients requesting sedatives. Both sets of measures indicated that a program of teaching patients coping devices would be effective in reducing stress.

In a related program of action research in a field setting, two psychologists tried to determine whether the decline in functioning generally found among the aged in nursing-home settings could be slowed if these individuals experienced a greater sense of choice and control over their lives (Langer and Rodin, 1976). To study whether such was the case, they obtained the assistance of the administrator of a nursing home. Following the experimental design of the psychologists, the administrator gave a talk to residents in an "experimental, responsibility-induced group" that emphasized their responsibility for themselves. To further emphasize their control over events, patients in this group were given plants to take care of. In contrast, the talk to residents of the "comparison group" emphasized the staff's responsibility for them as patients. Members of a third, control, group received no communication. The major manipulation involved a talk emphasizing increased choice and self-control.

The effects of the responsibility-induction talk were examined in a number of ways: self-ratings by the subjects in the three groups, ratings by nurses who were unaware of the experimental manipulation, and behavioral measures of involvement in various activities. The data indicated that residents in the experimental, responsibility-induced group became more active and reported feeling happier than the comparison group of residents. In addition, members of the former group became more alert and were more sociable relative to members of the other group. Apparently the decline in functioning could be slowed or even reversed.

Even more impressive than the immediate results were the follow-up results 18 months later (Rodin and Langer, 1977). On the average, patients in the responsibility-induced group were judged to be significantly more interested in the environment, more sociable and self-initiating, and more vigorous than residents in the comparison and control groups. Even more striking were death-rate differences between members of the different groups. Over the 18 months the death rate in the experimental group was about *half* that of the comparison group! Although members of the groups did not differ in length of time they had been hospitalized or in their overall health status when the study began, significant differences did appear soon after the experimental manipulation and continued to be present 18 months later. The authors noted that in a field study it is difficult to control all variables and thereby to pinpoint the exact critical ingredients in the improvement process. However, it was demonstrated that a manipulation involving the perception of choice and self-control could produce strong and lasting effects.

In clinical analogues there is an effort to duplicate aspects of a regular therapeutic treatment program while still maintaining control over the relevant variables. Experiments that try to evaluate total treatment programs as well as contributions of specific parts under highly controlled conditions have been extremely popular in the area of behavior therapy. The work on systematic desensitization (Chapter 10) illustrates such efforts to compare treatment programs and untangle the critical ingredients of a specific treatment program. Such research typically involves college students, a specific problem such as a well-circumscribed fear (snakes, rats), and a standardized treatment format (Kazdin and Rogers, 1978). This is in contrast with the more general practice of psychotherapy or behavior therapy, where a greater range of patients and patient problems is encountered and treatment is varied accordingly.

An illustration of clinical analogue research is Meichenbaum's (1972) program of cognitive modification with test-anxious college students. In this program Meichenbaum attempted to demonstrate the therapeutic effectiveness of combining "insight", with training in the use of thoughts and images of coping with the task (a test), and positive self-statements—

all cognitive processes. Meichenbaum concluded from the relevant literature that the problem with high test-anxious people is that they attend to aspects of the situation that are irrelevant to the task, that irrelevant thoughts intrude into consciousness, and that high emotional arousal interferes with performance. Therefore, he reasoned, a treatment approach should be directed toward treating both the "worry" or irrelevant and distracting thought problem and the "emotionality" problem. The problems could, it seemed, be treated by making test-anxious subjects aware of their interfering thoughts and self-verbalizations ("insight") and then training them to handle anxiety through relaxation and task-relevant self-instructions. In sum, a **cognitive modification treatment** program was designed to treat the problem of test anxiety and its effectiveness was compared with another treatment program as well as with no treatment program.

cognitive modification treatment

Meichenbaum assigned subjects who were found to be high in test anxiety to one of three conditions: group cognitive modification, group systematic desensitization, and a waiting-list control group. After completing a questionnaire relevant to test-taking anxiety the subjects were told that tests would be given that measured general intelligence and could be used to predict college grades. These ego-involving, stress-inducing instructions were followed by two self-report measures of anxiety and two measures of performance found to be affected by anxiety. For the two treatment groups this was followed by eight therapy sessions. In these eight sessions the *cognitive modification* group was made aware of how anxiety-provoking thoughts and self-statements interfere with performance. They were trained to make incompatible self-statements ("I can do well on this exam. I am competent") that would facilitate attending to the task and were trained to make incompatible relaxation behaviors. The *systematic desensitization group* followed the traditional use of progressive relaxation training and hierarchy construction described in Chapter 10. Finally, the subjects in the two treatment groups and in the *waiting control group* were readministered the previous tests to measure the effectiveness of the treatments—the two self-report measures of anxiety, the two performance tests found to be affected by anxiety, and the original measure of test-taking anxiety. Academic performance was also measured.

The results of the research indicated that cognitive modification was most effective in significantly reducing test anxiety as assessed by test performance in analogous test situations, self-report, and grade point average. The procedure used by Meichenbaum is noteworthy in that careful measurement (self-report and objective performances) was made of the effects of two carefully controlled treatment programs. The conditions of treatment were not identical to the general clinical situation and the major measures of improvement in performance were *analogous* to test situations rather than *actual test* situations. Meichenbaum concluded that cognitive modification procedures, as illustrated in this study, can be useful therapeutic devices. He has since gone on to develop the use of such techniques with other problems and, more generally, in training people to cope with stress (Meichenbaum, 1977; Meichenbaum, Turk and Burstein, 1975). Clinical analogue research has continued, led to some action programs, and influenced the work of clinicians in their daily practices.

BOX 15.3   **Clinical Analogue Research:
Cognitive Modification of Test Anxious
College Students**

GOAL   Compare the relative effectiveness of a group cognitive modification treatment procedure with that of group systematic desensitization and no treatment.

METHOD   Randomly assign individuals found to be equally anxious on a measure of test-taking anxiety to one of three groups: cognitive modification group, systematic desensitization group, waiting list control group. Give all subjects ego-involving, stress-inducing instructions prior to administering two performance tests. Following the instructions, and prior to administering the performance tests, assess the subjects on two self-report measures of anxiety (adjective checklist and anxiety differential). Then administer the two tests (digit symbol test and Raven Matrices Test), performance on which is negatively affected by anxiety. Following these tests, schedule eight sessions of group treatment for the two treatment groups and a waiting period for the third. The *cognitive modification group* first is given "insight" into how test anxiety is the result of thoughts and verbalizations which interfere with attending to the actual task and with performance. The members of this group are then trained to make task-relevant self-statements and to use imagery of coping and mastery behaviors (such as imagining themselves studying for an exam or performing well on an exam) in otherwise anxiety-arousing situations. In other words, members of the cognitive modification group are trained to develop behaviors and thoughts which are incompatible with the previously interfering thoughts and behaviors. The *systematic desensitization group* is given the standard training involving progressive relaxation training and graduated hierarchies. Finally, the members of all three groups again are given the two self-report measures of anxiety and the two performance tests. In addition, their academic performance is measured at the end of the semester and a month after the completion of treatment (or waiting) they again fill out the questionnaire on test-taking anxiety.

RESULTS

1 The cognitive modification group showed the most significant improvement in grade point average and on the two self-report measures of anxiety (Figure 15.5). The members of this group also showed a significant improvement in the effects of test-taking anxiety on the questionnaire administered one month later.

2 The waiting-list control group showed significantly less improvement than did the two treatment groups on grade point average and on one performance measure (Figure 15.5).

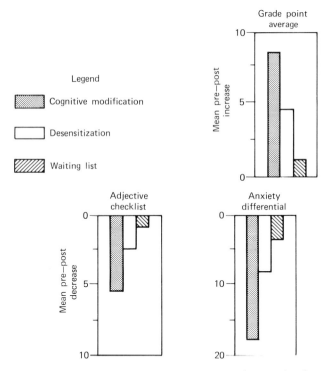

FIGURE 15.5 Mean reduction and increase in manifestations of test anxiety from pretreatment to posttreatment.

CONCLUSION   The results indicate that the cognitive modification procedure was most effective in reducing test anxiety. The superiority of the cognitive modification program was apparent immediately after treatment and at one-month follow-up. Less consistent but general improvement was evidenced by the desensitization treatment group. Further research

BOX 15.3   **Clinical Analogue Research:**
Cognitive Modification of Test Anxious
College Students *continued*

will be necessary to determine the exact elements of the cognitive modification procedure that were most effective in reducing anxiety.

SOURCE   D. Meichenbaum. Cognitive modification of test anxious college students. *Journal of Consulting and Clinical Psychology*, 1972, *39*, 370-380.

Like controlled action research and experimental research generally, clinical analogue research involves control over the relevant variables. Some critics of analogue research have suggested that it deviates from traditional therapy in such fundamental ways (limited range of problems and control of therapist behavior) that its relevance is questionable. Others suggest that such analogue research is crucial for the development of effective treatment programs. Bandura (1978) in particular has argued forcefully that such laboratory investigations involve conditions of behavior change that are not *analogous* to actual treatment. He argues that they are the *real* conditions and mechanisms of change. Bandura argues that many laboratory studies, such as his own, involve maladaptive behaviors of people who are seriously distressed. Furthermore, the treatment used is identical to that which can and should be used in outpatient settings. In other words, such laboratory investigations involve treatments that are every bit as real as those conducted in other settings. At the same time, others suggest that by defining the treatment situation as an experiment and by restricting what goes on to variables that can be carefully controlled, one *may* be limiting the generalizability of the findings. Researchers in this area are thus faced with the choice between programs that maximize experimenter control but may have less relevance to ordinary clinical practice, and programs that sacrifice some experimental controls but duplicate the conditions generally found in clinical situations (Kazdin and Rogers, 1978).

Overlapping Research Efforts and
Conclusions Concerning Stress, Control, and Helplessness

Four approaches to research have been considered in this section. They do not cover all possible approaches, and it should be clear that some research efforts involve aspects of more than one approach. In some cases this is done in the course of one experiment, illustrated in the study of locus of control and learned helplessness in which both individual differences on a personality questionnaire and the effects of experimental manipulations were considered. In other cases the mixture of approaches is evident in the course of a continuous program of investigation. For example, there has recently been investigation of the relationships among personality patterns, stress, and the development of heart disease (Glass, 1977). Many difficult studies were done that involved determining individual differences in coronary-prone behavior patterns on the basis of questionnaires, demonstrating that such individuals differ in the way they function on laboratory tasks involving stress and helplessness, and investigating reports of life stress events in patients with and without coronary disease. During the course of this research personality questionnaires, laboratory experiments, and interviews in the natural setting were used. The research concluded that individuals who attempt to control stressful events are more prone to the development of heart disease than individuals who are not concerned with the issue of control. The research also concluded that "the impact of behavior on coronary heart disease can, in our view, best be understood through systematic psychological research with small numbers of subjects in both laboratory and field settings" (Glass, 1977, p. x).

The research reviewed clearly suggests converging lines of evidence concerning the relationships among stress, control, and helplessness. The extent to which events are predictable and outcomes are experienced as controllable clearly influences the amount of stress that is experienced and the long-term effects of such stress. In addition, the research reviewed suggests that the various approaches to personality research have separate, at times complementary, contributions to make. Each approach has its own strengths and limitations. The choice is not necessarily between studying a few individuals or many subjects, individual differences or basic processes, laboratory research or naturalistic observation, correlational research or direct control research. It is both possible for alternative programs of research to proceed independently and for alternative procedures to be used together in a single program of research.

THE SCIENCE AND SOCIAL PSYCHOLOGY OF RESEARCH

In this chapter on research, some examples of personality research and some of the issues involved in developing a research program have been examined. Even though the attempt has been to illustrate personality research accurately, the accounts have failed to tell the whole story of research. What has been left out is the account of repeated frustration due to equipment failures and negative results, the repeated sense of uselessness in the effort to isolate the impact of the variable of interest, and the continuing sense of personal involvement and excitement the psychologist feels in relation to research. Students often are shocked to learn that research does not always follow the neat path described in articles in the professional journals.

Demand Characteristics

social psychology of research

The complexities and dynamics of research are such that an area of investigation that might be called the **social psychology of research** has developed. This area incorporates the study of factors influencing the behavior of subjects and experimenters during the course of an experiment as well as factors influencing the types of research performed by different investigators. The former may be labeled the social psychology of the experiment and the latter the social psychology of the researcher. Research on the social psychology of the psychological experiment suggests that generally there are factors influencing the behavior of human subjects that are not part of the experimental design (Orne, 1962; Weber and Cook, 1972). In psychological research, the focus often is on what is being done to the subject rather than whether the same experimenter behavior has the same meaning and impact on different subjects. For example, such characteristics of the experimenter as sex, age, race, manner, and prestige may affect different subject responses in different ways. In a significant paper on this topic, Orne has called attention to the effects of the **demand**

demand characteristics

characteristics of an experiment. Demand characteristics are cues implicit in the experimental setting which influence the subject's behavior. In contrast to "experimental variables," which are controlled and made explicit by the experimenter, there may be factors that are implicit in the "experimental setting" and not under the control or awareness of the investigator. For example, the subject assumes that the experimenter has a certain hypothesis and, "in the interest of science," behaves in a way that will confirm it.

What Orne points out is that the subject is not a passive respondent to experimental manipulation but has a stake in making the experiment a success or, in some cases, making sure that it fails. Subjects wonder whether they did a good job, whether they ruined the experiment, whether they responded as most subjects did. Often they are unaware of their concerns along these lines and of responses to the demand characteristics of the experimental setting.

Experimenter Expectancy Effects

Orne's point is that the psychological experiment is a form of social interaction. Subjects give purpose and meaning to things that experimenters do not. In analyzing the experiment as a form of social interaction, Orne's main emphasis is on the subject. Complementing this research is that of Rosenthal (1964), who studied the effects of the experimenter in psychological research. Rosenthal suggests that experimenters may be unintended sources of influence or bias in experiments. They may, without realizing it, affect the results of research by making errors in recording and analyzing data or by emitting cues to the subjects that influence their behavior in a particular way. Using the classic case of Clever Hans (Pfungst, 1911), Rosenthal describes the subtle cues that can be involved. Hans was a horse who by tapping his foot could add, subtract, multiply, and divide. A mathematical problem would be presented to the horse and, incredibly enough, he was able to come up with the answer. In attempting to discover the secret of Hans' talents, a variety of situational factors were manipulated. If Hans could not see the questioner or if the questioner did not know the answer, Hans was not able to come up with the correct answer. On the other hand, if the questioner knew the answer and was visible, Hans could tap out the answer with his foot. Apparently the questioner unknowingly signaled Hans when to start and stop tapping his hoof. The tapping would start when the questioner inclined his head forward, increase in speed when the questioner bent forward more, and stop when the questioner straightened up.

experimenter expectancy effects

Rosenthal's research suggests that, just as the questioner unwittingly behaved in a way that helped Hans to get the right answer, the experimenter may behave in ways that lead subjects to behave in accordance with the hypothesis. These may be called **experimenter expectancy effects**. In one experiment, five experimenters were told that subjects would tend to give positive ratings to photographs, and another group of five experimenters was told that subjects would tend to give them negative ratings. With all other facts held constant, the two groups of experimenters obtained significantly different sets of ratings, the former obtaining generally positive ratings and the latter generally negative ratings. "It seems clear from the data that experimenters' expectancies or hypotheses can be partial determinants of the results of their experiments. Since experimenters were not permitted to say anything to their subjects other than the standard instructions, the communication of experimenter's biases must have been by some subtle paralinguistic (e.g. tone) or kinesic (e.g. facial expressions, gestures) signals" (Rosenthal, 1964, p. 94).

In other research, Rosenthal demonstrated that the subtle effects of experimenter bias also can occur in research on rats. Experimenters who believe their rats to be bright obtain better performances from their animal subjects than do experimenters who believe their rats to be dull, even though the two groups of rats come from the same population. Apparently experimenters who believe that they have bright rats handle their animals more than do experimenters who believe they have dull rats, and such handling facilitates learning. Further research has suggested that it is possible to obtain comparable effects in the classroom. Teachers tend to get more from the students they expect the most from (Rosenthal and Jacobson, 1968). The point made in both Orne's and Rosenthal's research is that to the extent that psychological research involves human beings, it leaves itself open to complications, errors, and biases. These biases result from the human's ability to express and recognize unintended and subtle communications.

Additional Pitfalls in Human Research

In the social psychology of the experiment there is the observation that experimenter and subject are in a social interaction situation, the former emitting and the latter responding to cues that neither may be aware of but which may play a significant part in an experiment. In the social psychology of the researcher there is a variety of factors that influence the problems the experimenters decide to investigate and the methodological approach they choose. Why is an experiment done? Ideally, a problem is chosen because it represents a "natural" outgrowth of an important theory, because it is the next "logical" step in the gradual increase in knowledge and the resultant formulation of laws. But these are not the only reasons problems are chosen. They also are chosen because something touches the curiosity of the researcher, because a technique is available to do research on the problem, because the researcher has learned in professional training that certain problems are important while others are not, or because it is more fashionable to do research on some problems than on others (Webb, 1961).

The effects, then, of individual and social variables extend far beyond the conduct of the experiment itself (Pervin, 1978). Indeed, one psychologist concerned with pitfalls in human research suggests that the problems associated with research design, data analysis, and data interpretation are of greater significance than those associated with the conduct of the experiment itself (Barber,1976). Such researcher or investigator effects include stubbornly holding to certain views despite evidence to the contrary, missing phenomena that don't fit one's assumptions, and dismissing "negative" results and only reporting "positive" results. The ways in which questions are posed and then studied may themselves bias the results. There is evidence of such processes, for example, in earlier research on psychological differences between men and women (Shields, 1975) and in research on lesbianism and male homosexuality (Morin, 1977). Beyond this is the frequent error of assuming the results extend far beyond the actual population studied. For example, American college students often are subjects in experiments, but the results are generalized to all humans. Or, to take another example, results may be generalized to both males and females, even if only one sex is used or where both sexes are represented but the findings are not considered separately for each sex (Carlson, 1971).

Research and Public Policy

The question of the relationship between research results and public policy should also be considered briefly. One illustration of this issue is the role played by intelligence tests in the setting of American immigration quotas in the 1920s. Kamin (1974) suggests that the results of unfair, biased tests used to measure the intelligence of Eastern Europeans led to a discriminatory immigration policy favoring individuals from northern Europe. Another illustration is the influence of reports concerning the value of Head Start programs. Poorly designed studies leading to inconclusive results are used as a basis for rejecting further support for the program. Finally, there is the example of the effects on public policy of research on the viewing of television aggression. Despite the findings of a committee that television viewing of aggression could lead to increases in aggressive behavior in some viewers, there was no effect on public law or policy (Rubinstein, 1976). In other words, society may use the results of psychological research in accordance with the beliefs that are held independent of the research findings.

SUMMARY

Human factors enter at all points along the research process. Research is the process through which scientists attempt to establish lawful relationships among phenomena. As a scientific enterprise, it has the qualities of being logical, rational, rigorous, and objective. But because it is also a human enterprise and deals with many degrees of uncertainty, much that is involved is personal and subjective. By and large there is agreement concerning the goals of research, but there is considerable disagreement concerning the route to achievement of these goals. This lack of accord revolves around the nature of the variables to be studied and how they are to be studied. It reflects alternative philosophies of science, varying temperaments, and different strategies for research that are expressive of the investigators involved in the research enterprise. There are those researchers who prefer to study variation in individuals and those who prefer to study variation in situations, those who study the whole individual and those who emphasize piecemeal examination, those who emphasize the individual observation and clinical insight and those who emphasize mathematical manipulations of large samples of data on the computer, those who consider social action-oriented research "as inelegant and inefficient as trying to push a piece of cooked spaghetti across the table from the back end" (McGuire, 1967, p. 138) and those who consider much of laboratory research flashy and flamboyant, but essentially trivial fun and games (Ring, 1967). In considering research enterprises, then, we need to be able to distinguish between what is fad and what is part of a program of systematic inquiry, between what is likely to be of broad relevance and what is likely to be of limited consequence, between what is critical to theory and what is unrelated to theory, between what is due to experimental variables and what is due to setting variables, and between what is fundamental to good scientific enterprise and what reflects personal bias.

In evaluating research efforts, we must be aware of the experimenter and the subject variables discussed here under the heading of the social psychology of research. Also, in interpreting results we must be careful to avoid overgeneralizing from limited data. In particular, we must avoid a major danger in research—overgeneralization from findings based on a select population. Furthermore, when drawing conclusions from data presented, we must be aware of the potential experimenter sources of error and bias.

MAJOR CONCEPTS AND SUMMARY

experimental research

correlational research

own-control or ABA research

naturalistic observation

laboratory research

learned helplessness

behavioral aftereffects

locus of control

Internal-External Scale

action research

clinical analogue

cognitive modification treatment

demand characteristics

experimenter expectancy effects

This chapter has concerned itself with how psychologists conduct research on important personality phenomena. The goal of research is to establish facts and principles that can be interpreted within a broader theoretical framework. While sharing certain goals in research and certain standards for evaluating research, psychologists differ in the problems they choose for investigation and in the methods they favor in conducting research. Particular attention has been given to the distinction between two disciplines of scientific psychology—the experimental approach and the correlational approach. Whereas the experimental approach emphasizes consistent variation in behavior as a result of manipulations of situational conditions, the correlational approach emphasizes individual differences in response to the same situational conditions. One emphasizes variation in treatments, the other variation in people.

Discussion of the two disciplines and the potential utility of combining both approaches was followed by a more detailed analysis of the major alternative approaches to research. Four were emphasized (naturalistic observation, laboratory experimentation, correlational research using questionnaires, and action research/clinical analogues) and considered in relation to the concepts of stress, helplessness, and control. Naturalistic observation involves the study of phenomena as they occur naturally without any efforts on the part of the researcher to manipulate or control what occurs. The research cited emphasized the roles played by unpredictability and lack of control or helplessness in the experience of stress and in the aftereffects of the stress experience.

Laboratory research involves the manipulation of specific variables and the ability to state if-then causal relationships. The research cited suggests that animals and people who experience conditions where events (reinforcements) are not contingent on their behavior are likely to develop feelings of helplessness and expect that they will be unable to influence the outcomes of events in the future. The expectation that outcomes are independent of responding is seen as having motivational, cognitive, and emotional implications. Also cited was research that demonstrated that stress (noise) may have effects on performance once the stress is removed, even if there are no observable effects during the period of stress itself. Furthermore, the consequences of stress are influenced by the meanings the person attributes to the stress. If a person experiences a lack of control or sense of helplessness as a result of unpredictability, there will likely be negative behavioral aftereffects.

Work on the concept of locus of control illustrated the use of personality questionnaires in correlational research. The Internal-External Scale was developed to measure generalized expectancies concerning the control of reinforcers. Internals have a generalized belief in their ability to control events whereas externals believe in chance, luck, and fate. Individual differences in this generalized expectancy or belief have been found to be related to differences in effort on tasks, differences in anxiety and maladjustment, and differences in the attribution of blame for failure. It has been demonstrated that there is a relationship between external locus of control and the phenomenon of learned helplessness, both of which probably are related to the same causal factors.

Finally, action research and clinical analogue research were used to illustrate change programs wherein control is exercised over some variables but where there also is an effort to duplicate many of the conditions existing in the natural environment. Action research was illustrated by a program to reduce psychological stress in patients about to undergo surgery by teaching them various cognitive coping devices (cognitive reappraisal of anxiety-provoking events, calming self-talk, selective attention). In another study it was found that a program emphasizing freedom of choice and personal responsibility could reduce the sense of helplessness and improve the sense of well-being in the aged. The study used to illustrate clinical analogue research reported that a cognitive behavior modification program in which subjects were given "insight" and training in coping imagery could be effective in reducing test anxiety. These research efforts again illustrated the importance of perceptions of control-helplessness (the adequacy of coping resources) in relation to the experience and effects of stress.

The final section of the chapter concerned the ways in which personal and social forces enter into the history of a research effort. The social psychology of research concerns the unintended effects of experimenter on subject. Work on demand characteristics and experimenter expectancy effects illustrated the complexity of factors that influence the behavior of subjects and experimenters during the course of an experiment. Additional potential pitfalls in human research involve experimenter commitments to a particular point of view and neglect of contradictory evidence, as well as the generalization of findings beyond the subjects and conditions actually studied. Human factors and sources of bias also enter into the translation of research results into public policy.

This chapter has suggested that we consider the merits of alternative research strategies, as well as combined strategies, and that we remain aware of the pitfalls described in our efforts to evaluate research findings.

A RETURN TO SOME ISSUES THAT DIVIDE PERSONALITY THEORISTS
Philosophical View of the Person
Internal and External Causes of Behavior
The Unity of Behavior and the Concept of the Self
Varying States of Awareness and the Concept of the Unconscious
Influences of the Past, Present, and Future on Behavior
PERSONALITY THEORY AS AN ANSWER
TO THE QUESTIONS OF WHAT, HOW, AND WHY
Personality Structure
Process
Growth and Development
Psychopathology
Change
RELATIONSHIPS AMONG THEORY, ASSESSMENT, AND RESEARCH
A FINAL SUMMING UP

16 AN OVERVIEW OF PERSONALITY THEORY, ASSESSMENT, AND RESEARCH

Chapter Focus:

In this chapter we return to some of the major points covered in this book and consider the different theories of personality in relation to them. Our goal is a deeper understanding of the issues and, through the process of contrast and comparison, a greater appreciation of the theories. First, there is a return to some of the issues that divide personality theorists. Second, there is an overview of the concepts emphasized by each theory as it attempts to explain the what, how, and why of human behavior. Finally, attention is again drawn to relationships among theory, assessment, and research. Throughout the emphasis is on recognizing the distinctive contributions each approach can make toward a more complete understanding of human behavior.

Views about human nature influence which aspects of psychological functioning are studied most thoroughly and which remain unexamined. Theoretical conceptions similarly determine the paradigms used to collect evidence which, in turn, shape the particular theory. Limiting the scope of scientific inquiry to certain psychological processes to the neglect of other important ones can reinforce a truncated image of the human potential.

BANDURA, 1977, P. vi

This book has been an adventure into a greater understanding of why people behave as they do and how we may, in the future, proceed toward a clearer understanding of this behavior. The major focus has been on how different theories of personality conceptualize human behavior. There has been, as well, discussion of alternative approaches to assessment and research. Finally, we have considered relationships among types of theories, assessment techniques, and styles of conducting research; in other words, how different theories of personality may lead to the study of different aspects of personality functioning and the use of different means for gathering data. In this final chapter, let us take stock of some of the ground that has been covered and consider some of the issues that remain open.

A RETURN TO SOME ISSUES THAT DIVIDE PERSONALITY THEORISTS

In the first chapter we considered some issues that divide personality theorists. It was suggested that personality theorists repeatedly have confronted certain basic issues. Their solutions to these issues in part reflected their own life experiences as well as social and scientific trends current at the time of their work. Beyond this, it was suggested that theoretical positions on these issues affected which aspects of human functioning were chosen for investigation and how these aspects of human functioning were investigated. Let us briefly return to these issues in the light of previous study of the major theoretical orientations current today.

Philosophical View of the Person

We have seen that implicit in most theories of personality is a general, philosophical view of human nature. Periodically an article or book appears in the literature that addresses this issue in clear and forthright terms. For example, one distinguished psychologist recently called for an increased emphasis on a view of humans as active, selecting, choosing organisms as opposed to a view of humans as passive organisms responding in a mechanical way to stimuli: "Individuals create themselves . . . it is development we must study, but it is the development of the shaper rather than the shaped" (Tyler, 1978, pp. 233-234).

The theorists covered in this text present a diversity of views: Freud's view of the person as an energy system; Rogers' view of the person as a self-actualizing organism; Kelly's view of the person as a scientist; the Skinnerian view of the person as responding to environmental reinforcement contingencies; the cognitive social learning view of the person as a problem-solving organism. Of course, other views are possible—and within any single orientation, such as trait theory, different views can emerge. Furthermore, such labels or capsule descriptions fail to do justice to the complexity inherent in each view. At the same time, these capsule descriptions capture a distinctive element in each theoretical perspective and help to make us aware of the differing views that do exist. Of particular interest here is the emphasis on cognition found in so many recent theoretical developments (psychoanalytic ego psychology, cognitive behavior modification, and cognitive social learning theory).

Each view of the organism opens up certain avenues of thought, research, and analysis. Each also potentially closes off other important lines of emphasis and investigation. The early S-R view of the person inhibited the recognition of the importance of higher-order cognitive functions. The current cognitive emphasis may serve to correct this imbalance, but it may also lead us to ignore other important areas of experience such as motivation and emotion. The point here is not that one view is right or wrong but that such views exist and that it is important to be aware of them in understanding each theory as well as in assessing its strengths and limitations.

Internal and External Causes of Behavior

A second, related issue, is whether the causes of behavior are inside the person or in the environment. In Chapter 1 Freud and Skinner were contrasted as representing extreme positions on this issue. There was also discussion of how in recent years attention was first directed to *whether* behavior is caused by the "person" or the "situation," then to *how much* behavior was caused by person and situation factors, and finally to *how* person and situation factors interact with one another to determine behavior.

In the theories covered, this issue came out most clearly in relation to trait theory and social learning theory. At one extreme, trait theory has been characterized as suggesting that people are consistent or stable in their behavior over time and across situations. Psychoanalytic theory, with its similar emphasis on personality structure, has been seen as emphasizing internal causes of behavior and general stability in personality functioning. At the other extreme, learning theory has been characterized as emphasizing environmental determinants of behavior and the variability or situational specificity of behavior. Such characterizations are to some extent accurate and useful in highlighting important theoretical differences. At the same time, it should be clear that none of these theories emphasizes only one set of causes. To a certain extent, they are all interactionist in their emphasis; they all emphasize the interaction between individual and environment, or person and situation, in determining behavior. Trait theory, for example, does recognize the importance of situational factors in affecting which traits are activated as well as affecting the moods of the individual. It is inconceivable that a trait theorist or a psychoanalytic theorist would expect a person to behave the same way in all situations. On the other hand, social learning theory recognizes the importance of person factors in terms of concepts such as plans-goals and self-regulation. Indeed, most recently the concept of reciprocal determinism or the mutually causal relationship between person and situation has become a cornerstone of social learning theory.

As with other issues in the field, emphasis often shifts in one direction or another—in this case in terms of relative emphasis on internal, person factors or on external, environmental factors. At one point considerable evidence was presented to suggest that human behavior is quite variable over time and across situations. Such evidence was used to challenge traditional trait and psychodynamic views of personality structure and personality dispositions (Mischel, 1968). More recently, evidence has been presented to suggest that human behavior is more consistent, both over time and across situations, than had been suggested previously (Epstein, 1979; Olweus, 1979). Such consistency does not seem to be explained by unchanged environmental circumstances. Indeed, we often are impressed with how resistant some behavior is to change despite dramatic changes in environmental circumstances. Thus, whereas at one point situational determinants were emphasized, many psychologists are again emphasizing "dispositions or reaction tendencies within the individuals, however conceptualized" (Olweus, 1979, p. 14).

While important differences remain in the relative emphasis on internal (person) and external (situation) causes, all theories of personality recognize that both are important in understanding behavior. Perhaps we can now expect to find theorists who increasingly will address questions in terms of both sets of causes rather than with an almost exclusive emphasis on one or another set of causes.

The Unity of Behavior and the Concept of the Self

There is movement in human organisms, as living systems, toward integrated functioning and the reduction of conflict. Personality theories differ in the extent to which they emphasize the patterned, unified, system aspects of human functioning and efforts toward the reduction of conflict. An emphasis on the unity of behavior may be seen to be greatest in the clinical theories of Freud, Rogers, and Kelly. With the exception of Allport, it is much less present in trait theories and learning theories. Why should this be? Undoubtedly the reasons are complex and varied, but a number of points can be considered. First, clinical theories are based on observations of many behaviors of a single individual. The theories of Freud, Rogers, and Kelly evolved out of these clinical observations. Their efforts were directed toward understanding relationships among thoughts, behaviors, and feelings. Almost of necessity, they were struck with the issues of conflict and threats to the coherence of the system as reported to them by their patients. While clinical approaches based on learning theory exist and are important, they evolved out of theories rather than initially serving as the basis for them. In fact, it is probably true that as clinical approaches based on learning theory have developed they have increasingly emphasized the complexity and system aspects of human functioning.

A second point to be considered is the emphasis in trait theories, at least those based on factor analysis, and in learning theories on the systematic exploration of particular variables. The belief here is that an understanding of human behavior can come through the systematic study of particular variables or processes and then consideration of complex relationships among variables and processes. The strategy is to study phenomena systematically and to build from the simple to the complex. Pattern and organization become important when one has a clear enough grasp of the parts that constitute the pattern or organization.

The concept of self traditionally has been used to give expression to the patterned, organized aspects of personality functioning. In psychoanalytic theory, the concept of ego gives expression to the person's self-experiencing as well as to the "executive" or integrative aspects of system functioning. While sometimes portrayed as a person or homunculus inside the individual ("The ego seeks to reduce conflict"), it really is descriptive of processes going on within the person. For both Rogers and Kelly the concept of self played an important integrative function. For Rogers, the person seeks self-actualization and to make the self and experience congruent with one another. For Kelly, the constructs associated with the self and how they are organized play a central role in the person's functioning. The emphasis on the concept of self as an organizing entity is perhaps most clearly expressed in the view of Allport. The concept of self, or proprium as he called it, gave testimony to the complex, organized aspects of the mature human system.

In their efforts to avoid the vague, romantic, and fanciful, learning theorists traditionally have avoided the concept of self. In particular, the self as a homunculus within the person that determines action has been criticized. Still, as we have witnessed, recent developments in social learning theory place heavy emphasis on the concept of self. This is a somewhat different concept of self, however, involving standards for self-praise and self-criticism as well as other self-regulatory functions. Nevertheless, it is a self concept. The concept of efficacy, or ability to perform the behavior necessary for certain outcomes, an increasingly important part of Bandura's theory, involves cognitions or beliefs about the self. It is seen as a broadly integrative concept that can account for diverse findings. Thus, at this point cognitive social learning theory also has come to emphasize both the organized aspects of the human personality and the importance of the self concept in such organization.

While the utility and necessity of the concept of self continues to be debated, theories of personality appear to be drawn to it continuously. Interpretations of it clearly differ from theory to theory, and theories differ in their emphasis on it. At the same time, in one form or another, the concept of self enters into most theories and attests to the importance of the ways in which we experience ourselves, to the ways in which we understand ourselves, and to the organized aspects of our functioning.

Varying States of Awareness and the Concept of the Unconscious

Interest in varying states of awareness and altered states of consciousness has been increasing in psychology. This probably is due in part to interest in "mind-expanding" drugs during the 1960s and to the broader interest in brain functioning. Such phenomena are fascinating, yet they represent complex problems for theory, assessment and research.

As noted at the outset, many theorists are uncomfortable with the concept of the unconscious as formulated by Freud. The notion of things "buried in the unconscious" or of "unconscious forces striving for expression" is too metaphorical for most systematic thinkers. Yet, if we accept the view that we are not always aware of factors affecting our behavior, how are we to conceptualize such phenomena? Is it merely that we do not attend to them and that focusing of our attention "brings them into awareness?" Is it the case, as some learning theorists suggest, that what others view as unconscious processes actually consist of rehearsed behaviors that flow automatically or that they consist of overlearned inhibited responses (Mischel, 1976, p. 434)? In other words, is there no need to consider special processes and label them as unconscious; rather, we can say that we do not think of certain things because there are stronger responses inhibiting such thoughts?

As we have seen, both Rogers and Kelly avoided the concept of the unconscious. Instead, they developed other concepts that involve important aspects of the person's functioning which are not available to awareness.

Rogers stated the view that experiences incongruent with the self concept may be distorted and/or denied. Threatening feelings may be unavailable to awareness but experienced through the process of subception. Kelly suggested that one or both poles of a construct may be submerged and unavailable to awareness. Each of these theories describes a defensive process resulting in important aspects of personality functioning being unavailable to awareness. Though learning theorists such as Dollard and Miller accepted such processes and attempted to interpret them within the framework of Hullian theory, other learning theorists reject such concepts as vague and unnecessary.

The problem of evaluating the importance of such phenomena and conceptualizing them continues to be with us. If much of our behavior is governed by reinforcements, both from within ourselves as well as from others, are we always aware of what these reinforcers are? If not, why not? Is it because some of them were learned in infancy, prior to the development of verbal labels? Is it because some are so much a part of our daily lives that we no longer attend to them? Or is it because often we "choose" not to be aware of things that make us anxious and uncomfortable? How much attention is paid to these phenomena and how they are interpreted continue to be important issues upon which theories of personality differ.

Influences of the Past, Present, and Future on Behavior

When we think of Freud we almost automatically think of behavior being governed by the past. When we think of Kelly we think of the person as striving to anticipate the future. Prediction becomes the key to understanding behavior. Skinner's emphasis on past reinforcement contingencies can be contrasted with social learning theory's emphasis on expectancies. Is behavior regulated by the past or by our expectations of the future? Is there a difference between the two?

This is yet another issue that divides personality theorists. Often the differences among theorists are subtle but important in their implications. For example, Bandura's suggestion that past reinforcements are important for what has been *learned* but expectancies about future reinforcement are important for what is *performed* is a subtle but important distinction. It involves not only the important distinction between the acquisition and performance of behavior but also an important emphasis on cognitive functioning. In fact, there appears to be a close relationship between an emphasis on the future and an emphasis on cognitive processes. This is not surprising, since the development of higher mental processes and the capacity for language are necessary for an organism to be able to construct a future world.

FIGURE 16.1
SUMMARY OF MAJOR
THEORETICAL CONCEPTS

THEORIST OR THEORY	STRUCTURE	PROCESS	GROWTH AND DEVELOPMENT
FREUD	Id, ego, superego; unconscious, preconscious, conscious.	Life and death instincts; cathexes and anticathexes; anxiety and the mechanisms of defense.	Erogenous zones; oral, anal, phallic stages of development; Oedipus complex.
ROGERS	Self; ideal self	Self-actualization; congruence of self and experience; incongruence and defensive distortion and denial.	Congruence and self-actualization versus incongruence and defensiveness.
KELLY	Constructs	Processes channelized by anticipation of events.	Increased complexity and definition to construct system.
CATTELL	Traits	Attitudes; motives; ergs; sentiments; specification equation.	Integrative learning; multiple abstract variance analysis (MAVA); age trends.
LEARNING THEORY	Response	Classical conditioning; instrumental conditioning; operant conditioning	Imitation; schedules of reinforcement and successive approximations.
SOCIAL LEARNING THEORY	Expectancies; standards; goals-plans.	Observational learning; vicarious conditioning; symbolic processes.	Social learning through observation and direct experience; development of standards for self-regulation.

In reality, of course, past events and our anticipation of future events affect one another as well as our experiences in the present. How we anticipate the future is inevitably linked to our past. However, it is probably also the case that how we view the future influences our construction of the past. For example, if we are depressed about the future we may feel bound by our past, whereas if we are optimistic about the future we may perceive the past as having been liberating. Our views of the past, present, and future are all parts of our experience. An understanding of the relationships among these views, then, becomes the task of each theory of personality.

PERSONALITY THEORY AS AN ANSWER TO THE QUESTIONS OF WHAT, HOW, AND WHY

In Chapter 1 it was stated that a theory of personality should answer the questions of *what, how*, and *why*. In the chapters on Freud, Rogers, Kelly, trait theory, learning theory, and social learning theory, the concepts and principles used by each theorist to account for human personality were considered. A summary of some of the major concepts relevant to each theory is given in Figure 16.1. At this point, let us review some of these

PATHOLOGY	CHANGE	ILLUSTRATIVE CASE
Infantile sexuality, fixation, and regression; conflict; symptoms.	Transference; conflict resolution; "Where id was, ego shall be."	Little Hans
Defensive maintenance of self; incongruence.	Therapeutic atmosphere: congruence, unconditional positive regard, empathic understanding.	Mrs. Oak
Disordered functioning of construct system.	Psychological reconstruc-tion of life; invitational mood; fixed-role therapy.	Ronald Barrett
Heredity and environment; conflict; anxiety.	Integration learning.	Male college student
Maladaptive learned response patterns.	Extinction; discrimina-tion learning; counter-conditioning; positive reinforcement; imitation; systematic desensitiza-tion; behavior modification.	Reinterpretation of little Hans; Joey
Learned response patterns; excessive self-standards; problems in self-efficacy.	Modeling; guided participation; increased self-efficacy.	Reinterpretation of bombardier case.

concepts, consider the similarities among the theories, and raise some remaining questions.

Personality Structure

Each theory that has been studied here suggests concepts relevant to the structure of personality; each theory presents conceptual units that can be used to describe individuals. The theories differ not only in the content of these units but also in their level of abstraction and in the complexity of the structural organization. Freud's structural units are at a very high level of abstraction. One cannot observe an id, ego, or superego, or a conscious, preconscious, or unconscious. Somewhat less abstract are the structural units used by Rogers and Kelly. Many problems remain in current defini-tions of the self, but the definitions offered by Rogers do suggest some methods of systematic investigation. Similarly, although the defining prop-erties of constructs need to be clarified further, a technique for assessing the construct system of an individual is available to us.

The structural units of Cattell vary in their level of abstraction, with source traits being more abstract than surface traits. At the lowest level of abstraction is the major structural unit used by learning theorists to describe behavior—the response. Whether it refers to a simple reflex or a complex behavior, the response is always external and observable. It is defined by the behavior. In this case, one does not go from the specific act to an abstract structural unit. The act itself is the structural unit. Instead of being internal to the organism and only indirectly observable, the response is part of the observable behavior of the organism.

Social learning theory started with a similar emphasis on the overt, behavioral response. The units of the person were concrete, clearly defined, and objectively measured. Variations in response were tied to equally clearly defined and objectively measured variations in the environment. With the development of an emphasis on cognitive activities and self-regulatory behavior, however, there was a shift toward emphasis on more abstract structural units. Concepts such as standards, self-efficacy judgments, and goals or plans tend to be more abstract than the concept of a response. Furthermore, they require different tools of measurement and this has resulted in a defense of the use of verbal reports on the part of social learning theorists. At the same time, it should be clear that this movement toward an emphasis on different kinds of units has not lessened the concern for rigor, objectivity, and measurement. Social learning theorists continue to emphasize concepts that are clear in their meaning and specific in the appropriate method of measurement.

In addition to differences in their level of abstraction, theories also differ in the complexity of structural organization. This complexity may be considered in terms of the number of units involved and whether they are formed in some kind of *hierarchial arrangement* in relation to one another. Cattell's theory clearly involves a complex structural organization of personality. Not only are there many units but there also is a hierarchical arrangement of these units into surface traits, source traits, and second-order factors (types). Similarly, Eysenck emphasizes a hierarchical organization of structural units, starting with responses at the lowest level and progressing on up to habits, traits, and types. Kelly's system allows for a complex system of constructs—one in which there are many constructs, some superordinate and others subordinate. However, the complexity of organization is viewed as varying considerably with the individual personality. The psychoanalytic framework includes many structural units and almost unlimited possibilities for interrelationships among the units. Although no clear hierarchical structure is set forth, the concept of personality types clearly indicate layers of organization beyond that of specific behaviors.

In contrast to such a complexity of personality structure is the fairly simple structure described by most learning theorists. There are few categories of responses, no suggestion that behavior generally involves the expression of many units at the same time, and a definite bias against the concept of personality types, which implies a stable organization of many different responses. Indeed, it may again be noted that the social learning theorist Mischel was particularly critical of trait and psychoanalytic theories for their emphasis on a hierarchical organization of personality.

These differences in levels of abstraction and complexity of structural organization can be related to differences in the general importance attached to structure in behavior. The concept of structure generally is used to account for the more stable aspects of personality and for the consistency of individual behavior over time and over situations. To consider two extremes: psychoanalytic theory places great emphasis on the stability of behavior over time, whereas learning theory does not; psychoanalytic theory places great emphasis on the consistency of behavior across situations whereas learning theory does not; psychoanalytic theory places great emphasis on individual differences, whereas learning theory does not. At one extreme, psychoanalytic theory involves abstract units and a complex structural organization. At the other extreme, learning theory involves concrete units and little emphasis on the organization of these units. In other words, there appears to be a relationship between the importance attributed to structure by a theory and the theory's emphasis on stability and consistency in human behavior.

Process

In our review of theories of personality, the major conceptions in psychology concerning the "why" of behavior have been identified. As indicated in Chapter 1, many theories of motivation emphasize the efforts on the part of the individual to *reduce tension*. The push toward tension reduction is clearly indicated in psychoanalytic theory, in Cattell's theory, and in Hull's approach to learning theory. For Freud, the individual's efforts are directed toward expressing the sexual and aggressive instincts and, thereby, toward the reduction of the tension associated with these instincts. For Cattell, the individual is directed toward the expression of attitudes, at the basis of which are the ergs and the energy associated with them. For Hull, and for Dollard and Miller, reinforcement is associated with the satisfaction of primary or secondary drives and, thereby, with the reduction of drive-induced tension.

Rogers' theory gives expression to the motivational model suggesting that individuals often *seek tension*. Rogers suggests that individuals seek self-actualization, that they want to grow and to realize their inner potentials even at the cost of increased tension. However, Rogers also places emphasis on a third motivational force—*consistency*. The particular kind of consistency emphasized by Rogers is a congruence between self and experience. For Kelly, who also emphasizes consistency, the relevant variables are different. According to Kelly, it is important that the individual's constructs be consistent with one another, so that the predictions from one do not cancel out the predictions from another. It is also important that predictions be consistent with experiences, or, in other words, that events confirm and validate the construct system.

While operant learning theory and social learning theory both emphasize the importance of reinforcement, they do not do so in terms of drive reduction as happens in Hullian stimulus-response theory. For Skinner reinforcements affect the probability of a response, but there is no use of an internal concept of drive or tension. In social learning theory the emphasis is on cognitive processes and the development of expectancies. Reinforcers are critical for performance but not for the acquisition of behavior. Expectancies concerning reinforcement guide and direct behavior. In this way they serve a motivational function. In a sense, the person is oriented toward accurate prediction, in Kelly's terms, but it is specifically the fulfillment of expectancies concerning positive reinforcement.

Notice that these motivational models are only in conflict with one another if we assume that all behavior must follow the same motivational principles. In relation to structure, we need not assume that the individual only has drives, that one only has a concept of the self, or that one only has personal constructs. In the same way, we need not assume that the individual is always reducing tension, or always striving toward actualization, or always seeking consistency. It may be that all three models of motivation have something to say about human behavior. An individual may at some points be functioning so as to reduce tension, at other times so as to actualize the self, and at other times to achieve cognitive consistency. Another possibility is that, at one time, two kinds of motivation are operating, but they are in conflict with one another. For example, the individual may seek to relieve aggressive urges through hitting someone but also have fond feelings for the person involved and view this behavior as "out of character." A third possibility is that two kinds of motivation may combine to operate in support of one another. Thus, to make love to someone can represent the reduction of tension from sexual urges, an actualizing expression of the self, and an act consistent with the self-concept and with predictions from one's construct system. If room is left for more than one process model, it becomes the task of psychologists to define the conditions under which each type of motivation will occur and the ways in which the different types of motivation can combine to determine behavior.

Growth and Development

In Chapter 1 we considered the causes of personality—cultural, social class, familial, and genetic. None of the theories studied really gives adequate attention to the variety of factors that determine growth and development. Cattell has done important work on the influences of heredity and environment, and on age trends in personality development. Psychoanalytic theory gives attention to the role of biological and environmental factors in personality development, but in most cases this remains speculative. It is disappointing that Rogers and Kelly have so little to say in this area. Finally, although the learning theorists have done a great deal to interpret the processes through which cultural, social class, and familial influences are transmitted, there has been a serious neglect of biological factors. Also, until recently learning theorists tended to give insufficient attention to the important area of cognitive growth and development. Important contributions are, however, now being made by social learning theorists. For example, Bandura has been doing research on the development of memory codes or symbols in observational learning and Mischel has been researching how children develop methods for tolerating increased delays in reinforcement.

In considering the theorists covered in the text, differences concerning two questions about development become apparent. The first concerns the utility of the concept of stages of development and the second concerns the importance of early experiences for later personality development. Psychoanalytic theory attaches great importance to the concept of stages of development, and Cattell's work on age trends suggests that certain periods are critical for the formation of different traits. It is also true that psychoanalytic theory places the greatest emphasis on the early years of growth and development. There is impressive evidence that the early years are important for many personality characteristics. More specifically, the research suggests that the effects of the environment are greatest at the time of rapid change in a personality characteristic (Bloom, 1964; Scott, 1968). Since change and development are most rapid for many personality characteristics during the early years, it is during these years that environmental forces exert their greatest impact. This is not to say that the early years are critical for every characteristic. Different characteristics have different developmental curves and for some the period of most rapid development may be during the teens or even later in life. Nor is this to suggest that the effects of early experiences are permanent. However, generally, the early environment is of critical importance. This is true because often it is a period of rapid growth and because what is learned during these years sets the stage for later learning.

An understanding of the critical ages for different developments in personality is essential for theoretical progress and for progress in our efforts to correct various arrests in growth. Since, generally, it is not possible to make resources available to children over the course of many years, it would be extremely valuable to know at which ages the commitment of human resources would most make a difference. For example, if we are interested in the development of certain cognitive skills that develop most rapidly in prepuberty, the commitment of human resources to preschool children may be wasteful. On the other hand, if we know that the initial period for the development of an ability is between the ages of six and eight, the commitment of resources to children of a later age will not represent the most effective use of these resources.

Psychopathology

The forces producing psychopathology are interpreted differently by the theorists. However, the concept of conflict is essential to a number of them. This is most clearly the case in psychoanalytic theory. According to Freud, psychopathology occurs when the instinctive urges of the id come into conflict with the functioning of the ego. Cattell holds a similar view, emphasizing the importance of conflict between a drive that has been stimulated and some force that is blocking it. It already has been observed that, although Rogers does not emphasize the importance of conflict, one can interpret the problem of incongruence in terms of a conflict between experience and the self-concept. Although learning theory offers a number of explanations for psychopathology, at least one of these explanations emphasizes the importance of approach-avoidance conflicts.

The concept of conflict makes sense as a relevant variable in pscyhopathology. However, there is a need for a greater distinction between frustration and conflict. A drive being blocked does not represent conflict, although this may lead to a conflict situation. A state of conflict exists where two or more incompatible forces are striving for expression at the same time. The parts of a system are in conflict if the gratification of one part is achieved at the cost of frustration of another part of the system. In contrast, in an integrated system the parts are either functioning independently of each other or are in harmony with one another. In the latter case, the achievement of a goal leads to a variety of kinds of gratification.

Many complex questions concerning psychopathology remain unanswered. For example, we know that cultures vary in the incidence of various forms of psychopathology. Depression is rare in Africa, but is common in the United States. Why? Conversion symptoms, such as hysterical paralysis of the arm or leg, were quite common in Freud's time but are observed much less frequently today. Why? Are there important differences in the problems that people in different cultures face? Or do they face the same problems but cope with them differently? Or is it just that some problems are more likely to be reported than others and that this varies with the individual culture? If people today are more concerned with problems of identity than with problems of guilt, if they are more concerned with the problem of finding meaning than of relieving sexual urges, what are the implications for psychoanalysis and the other theories of personality? Although each of the theories of personality can offer some explanation for suicide, do all seem equally plausible? Can any of the theories account for the fact that the suicide rate for college students is higher than that for individuals of comparable age who are not in college and higher than the one for any other age group?

We are at a point at which the whole question of the nature of psychopathology is under reexamination. Questions are being raised concerning the disease model of mental illness, the responsibilities of the person who is ill, and illness in society as opposed to illness in the individual. Whereas psychoanalytic theory suggests that someone is ill with a "sick personality," learning theory suggests that the individual has learned a maladaptive response. But how, within the scope of either of these theories, do we account for the prevalence of psychological disorders in current society? And how, within the scope of either of these theories, do we account for the situation wherein some seemingly maladaptive responses have, in reality, adaptive qualities? Thus, for example, in their book *Black Rage*, Grier and Cobbs (1968) describe how the mistrustful, almost paranoid behavior of many blacks is based on reality and has adaptive qualities. The answers to questions like these go beyond the theories of personality we have considered, but they are relevant to them.

Change

An analysis of the change concepts of the theorists suggests that, in some cases, the point of focus for one is different from that for another. For example, the following questions concerning change are given varying amounts of attention by each theorist: What is changed? What are the conditions for change? What is the process to change?

Psychoanalytic theory, in its emphasis on changes in the relationship between the unconscious and the conscious and between the ego and the id, is particularly concerned with structural change. Kelly, in his analysis of psychotherapy as the psychological reconstruction of life, is also concerned with structural change. In contrast, Rogers is most concerned with the conditions that make change possible. Although in his research he has attended to structural change (for example, changes in self-ideal self discrepancy), this has been for the purpose of having a criterion against which he could measure the effectiveness of different variables (for example, congruence, unconditional positive regard, empathic understanding). Kelly pointed out the importance of an atmosphere of experimentation and invitational mood, but there is little research to suggest the variables critical in establishing this atmosphere or mood. Psychoanalysts have been quite concerned with the quality of the transference relationship as it affects change, but this has been, for the most part, from a practical standpoint and has had little impact on the theory as a whole.

The process of change is a particular focus of convenience for learning theory. The following learning processes are used to account for a wide range of changes related to a variety of forms of psychotherapy: extinction, discrimination learning, counterconditioning, positive reinforcement, imitation. Whereas, initially, learning concepts were used to explain treatment effects associated with other theories, more recently these concepts have been used in the development of learning-based treatment methods. This development of technique out of a theory of the process of change is healthy. A clear illustration of therapeutic technique as an outgrowth of theory is Bandura's work on modeling and guided participation. It is also interesting to note here that while therapy or psychological change has not been a major aspect of social learning theory, it is becoming an increasingly important part of it. In fact, Bandura suggests that developments in this area may well serve as a test of the theory generally. In constrast, many aspects of psychoanalysis and Rogerian therapy are based on earlier developments in these theories and do not represent direct outgrowth from them. For example, the basic structure of psychoanalysis and emphasis on free association and dream interpretation remained the same despite major changes in the theory itself.

There are, of course, basic and important differences in the theories concerning the potential for change. At one extreme would be psychoanalytic theory, which suggests that fundamental personality change is quite difficult. This view is related to the psychoanalytic emphasis on structure and the importance of early experiences. If structure is important and is developed early in life, it follows that basic change later in life is difficult. Many of the early learning theorists (for example Hull, Dollard, and Miller), particularly those who attempted to relate learning theory to psychoanalytic theory, were similarly pessimistic about the potential for change. However, the more recent developments in operant conditioning and social learning theory have led to much greater optimism for change. These theorists place little emphasis on structure and great emphasis on the ability to change behavior. With faith in their ability to shape behavior through the manipulation of external rewards, the behavior modificationists are at the other extreme from psychoanalysts. Part of this difference in point of view is a function of the relative emphasis on holistic aspects of personality functioning. If you emphasize the total personality, change should be more difficult than if you emphasize a single, isolated response. On the other hand, Rogers emphasizes the holistic aspects of behavior and in addition remains optimistic about the potential for substantial change in personality functioning.

In considering the question of how people change we again recognize the extent to which theories of personality emphasize different processes of change, different conditions for change, and change in different aspects of personality functioning. Some of these differences may well represent competing and conflicting points of view, others different terms for similar processes, and, finally, some differences may result from attending to different aspects of the person. Sorting out these differences represents a task for both students and professionals in the field.

RELATIONSHIPS AMONG THEORY, ASSESSMENT, AND RESEARCH

At various times in this book theory, assessment, and research have been considered separately. However, throughout, the attempt has been made to keep in mind the intimate relationships among the three. Indeed, this has been a major theme throughout the book.

In Chapter 1, theory as an attempt to fit together and explain a wide variety of facts with a few assumptions was considered. In Chapters 12 and 13 the tools that personality psychologists use to observe and measure behavior in a systematic way were discussed. Campbell's scheme for the classification of tests was presented (structured-unstructured, disguised-nondisguised, voluntary-objective), and four types of tests were presented in detail: projective (Rorschach, TAT), subjective (interview, self-report), psychometric (Cattell 16 P.F., MMPI), and objective (performance tests, behavioral assessment). Finally, in the chapter on research (Chapter 15) the alternative ways in which personality phenomena can be studied were considered. In viewing research as part of a triad it was suggested that research involves the use of assessment techniques to develop and test theory.

What of the relationships among theory, assessment, and research? In the assessment chapter we noted a relationship between the assumptions basic to theories and the techniques of assessment generally associated with these theories. Here it was noted that a psychodynamic theory such as psychoanalysis tends to be associated with the Rorschach, a phenomenological theory such as that of Rogers with the interview and measures of the self-concept, a factor analytic theory such as that of Cattell with psychometric tests, and a learning theory approach with objective tests. Do different theories of personality tend to lead to different techniques of assessment and to different kinds of observations about individuals? Are such differences in theory and assessment then also related to strategies for research, leading to clinical and experimental attitudes? To what extent are these disciplines associated with a greater or lesser emphasis on naturalistic observation, questionnaire research, or laboratory experimentation?

The clinical approach emphasizes dynamics, individual differences, the entire personality, the history of the individual, flexibility in observation, prediction from an understanding of the individual, and theory which postulates internal processes and allows for concepts which cannot be verified directly. "Theoretical issues require the retention of some variables that cannot be quantified with any elegance whatsoever. Similarly, if we in psychology turn away from the attempt to measure unconscious motives, for example, because of the fact that this can't be done today with demonstrable reliability or validity, this vitally important area of personality will be neglected" (Holt, 1962, p. 274). The experimental approach emphasizes consistency across individuals, changes in one or two responses under various experimental conditions rather than the pattern of many responses, tends to be ahistorical, emphasizes rigor in experimental design and theoretical conceptualization, and allows for the use of animals as subjects. "We cannot attribute a principle learned from the study of rats to human conduct until we have also observed it operating in the human species. However, once we have done so, our rat experiment may have given us a more precise understanding of the principle involved because of the more adequate controls imposed" (Lundin, 1961, p. 47).

Do differences such as these exist among psychologists generally? In a study of the psychological value systems of psychologists, Thorndike (1954) obtained ratings from 200 psychologists on the contributions made by a number of outstanding people to psychology. An analysis of these ratings suggested two major dimensions along which the psychologists made their judgments. The first factor was labeled laboratory versus clinic, and indicated that some psychologists valued laboratory research, while others valued the clinical study of the individual. The second factor located by Thorndike was labeled psychometric versus verbal approach and distinguished between psychologists who value analytic study with psychometric (statistical) techniques and psychologists who value a global and typological approach to the study of behavior.

If indeed such a theme runs throughout the study of personality, to what can it be attributed? In his review of the history of psychology, Boring (1950) notes that over time the experimentalists became more technical and electronically oriented, while the clinicians did not. He goes on to suggest that clinicians usually liked other people, whereas "the experimentalists often did not, preferring rats for subjects as being less embarrassing socially or at any rate more pliant, convenient and exploitable than human subjects" (Boring, 1950, p. 578). Boring concludes that the split may be a result of personality differences between members of the two orientations.

Clearly the emphasis here is not on whether one or another approach to theory, assessment, and research is right or wrong. Rather it is on the strengths and limitations of each and the relationships among the three. Is it not possible that different aspects of one's personality may be studied with greater or lesser accuracy with different assessment devices? Is it not possible that some phenomena can be observed quite easily in the laboratory while others cannot? Is it not possible that each assessment device and research approach has its own potential sources of error or bias? Should we not be aware that limiting ourselves to one approach to assessment and research may restrict our observations to phenomena directly relevant to a specific theoretical position? In such circumstances we may be led to confuse accuracy in a few predictions with more general aspects concerning the quality of a theory. It may be useful to be aware of restrictive relationships among theory, assessment, and research and also appreciative of the contributions that different theories, assessment devices, and research procedures can make to our understanding of human behavior.

A FINAL SUMMING UP

In a certain sense, every person is a psychologist. Every person develops a view of human nature and a strategy for predicting events. The theory and research presented in this book represent the efforts of psychologists to systematize what is known about human personality and to suggest areas for future exploration. The attempt has been to focus on similarities in what these psychologists have been trying to do and on differences in what they view as being the best mode of operation. Although psychologists as a group are more explicit about their view of the person than is the average layperson, and are more systematic in their efforts to understand and predict human behavior, there are individual differences among them. In this book the theories of many psychologists have been considered in detail. They represent major theories in the field today although not the only theories, and they are representative of the diversity of approach that can be considered reasonable and useful.

An effort has been made in this text to demonstrate that theory, assessment, and research are related to one another. In most cases some consistency can be found in the nature of the theory proposed, the types of tests used to obtain data, and the problems suggested for investigation. A distinction was drawn between the psychologists who emphasize individual differences and those who emphasize general principles, between the correlational approach and the experimental approach, between the psychologists who use unstructured tests and those who use structured tests, between those who emphasize stability and consistency in behavior and those who emphasize change and situational specificity, and between those who emphasize individuals and those who emphasize environments. Finally, we proposed that the theories of personality covered need not be considered mutually exclusive. In a very real sense, each represents a glimpse of the total picture. Human behavior is like a very complex jigsaw puzzle. The theories of personality considered have offered us many possible pieces for solution of the puzzle. Although some pieces may have to be discarded as not fitting the puzzle at all, and many remain outstanding, undoubtedly many of the pieces offered will be there when the final picture is put together.

GLOSSARY

ABA RESEARCH. A Skinnerian variant of the experimental method consisting of one subject exposed to three experimental phases: (A) a baseline period, (B) introduction of reinforcers to change the frequency of specific behaviors, and (A) withdrawal of reinforcement and observation of whether the behaviors return to their earlier frequency (baseline period).

ABC APPROACH. In behavioral assessment, an emphasis on the identification of antecedent (A) events and the consequences (C) of behavior (B); a functional analysis of behavior involving identification of the environmental conditions that regulate specific behaviors.

ACTION RESEARCH. An approach to research that involves the effort to change behaviors or events in the real world (i.e., under natural conditions).

ACQUIESCENCE. A kind of response style or bias in which there is a tendency to agree with test items regardless of their content.

ACQUISITION. The learning of new behaviors, viewed by Bandura as independent of reward and contrasted with performance — which is seen as dependent on reward.

ACTUARIAL PREDICTION. An approach to prediction described by Meehl in which predictions are based on previously established relationships between test scores and the criterion behavior of interest, in contrast to clinical prediction.

AGGRESSION (KELLY). In Kelly's personal construct theory, the active expansion of the person's construct system.

AGGRESSIVE INSTINCTS. Freud's concept for those drives directed toward harm, injury, or destruction.

ANAL CHARACTER. Freud's concept for a personality type that expresses a fixation at the anal stage of development and relates to the world in terms of the wish for control or power.

ANAL STAGE. Freud's concept for that period of life during which the major center of bodily excitation or tension is the anus.

ANXIETY. An emotion expressing a sense of impending threat or danger. In Kelly's personal construct theory anxiety occurs when the person recognizes that his or her construct system does not apply to the events being perceived.

APPROACH-AVOIDANCE CONFLICT. In S-R theory, the simultaneous presence of opposing drives to move toward an object and away from it.

ATTITUDE. In Cattell's theory, a strength of interest in following a particular course of action; a readiness to act in a certain direction in a given situation.

BEHAVIOR MODIFICATION. The approach to therapeutic treatment (behavior change) based on Skinner's operant conditioning theory.

BEHAVIOR THERAPY. An approach to therapeutic treatment (behavior change) based on learning theory and focusing on specific behavioral difficulties.

BEHAVIORAL AFTEREFFECTS. Behavioral effects that are a result of environmental conditions that do not show up during exposure to a condition but at some later point (e.g., Glass and Singer's conclusions regarding the consequences of adaptation to stress).

BEHAVIORAL ASSESSMENT. The emphasis in assessment on specific behaviors that are tied to defined situational characteristics (e.g., ABC approach).

BEHAVIORAL COMPETENCIES. Abilities to behave in particular ways, particularly emphasized in social learning theory in relation to performance, as in delay of gratification.

BEHAVIORISM. An approach within psychology, developed by Watson, that restricts investigation to overt, observable behavior.

BIVARIATE METHOD. Cattell's description of the method of personality study that follows the classical experimental design of manipulating an independent variable and observing the effects on a dependent variable.

CARDINAL TRAIT. Allport's concept for a disposition that is so pervasive and outstanding in a person's life that virtually every act is traceable to its influence.

CASTRATION ANXIETY. Freud's concept for the boy's fear, experienced during the phallic stage, that the father will cut off the son's penis because of their sexual rivalry for the mother.

CENTRAL TRAIT. Allport's concept for a disposition to behave in a particular way in a range of situations.

CLASSICAL CONDITIONING. A process, emphasized by Pavlov, in which a previously neutral stimulus becomes capable of eliciting a response because of its association with a stimulus that automatically produces the same or a similar response.

CLIENT-CENTERED THERAPY. Rogers' term for his earlier approach to therapy in which the counselor's attitude is one of interest in the ways in which the client experiences the self and the world.

CLINICAL ANALOGUE. An approach to research in which there is an attempt to demonstrate a change in the behavior of interest under conditions that approximate, but are not identical to, conditions

found in the natural environment (e.g., efforts to duplicate aspects of a regular therapeutic treatment program while still maintaining control over the relevant variables).

CLINICAL METHOD. Cattell's description of the method of personality study in which there is an interest in complex patterns of behavior as they occur in life but variables are not assessed in a systematic way.

CLINICAL PREDICTION. An approach to prediction, described by Meehl, in which predictions are based on hypotheses concerning the relationship between personality and performance rather than being based on established statistical relationships (actuarial prediction).

COGNITION. The person's thought processes, including perception, memory, and language. The term is used to refer to the ways in which the organism processes information concerning the environment and the self.

COGNITIVE COMPETENCIES. Abilities to think in a variety of ways, particularly emphasized in social learning theory in relation to the ability to delay gratification.

COGNITIVE COMPLEXITY-SIMPLICITY. An aspect of a person's cognitive functioning which at one end is defined by the use of many constructs with many relationships to one another (complexity) and at the other end by the use of few constructs with limited relationships to one another (simplicity).

COGNITIVE MODIFICATION. An approach to therapeutic treatment (behavior change) in which there is an emphasis on change in specific aspects of the person's thinking processes.

COMPETENCE MOTIVATION. White's concept for motivation that emphasizes behavior directed toward dealing competently or effectively with the environment, even if this involves an increase in tension.

CONCURRENT VALIDITY. A measure of the extent to which a test measures what it claims to measure in terms of the agreement between test scores and another measure that has already been obtained or can be obtained at the same time.

CONDITIONED EMOTIONAL REACTION. Watson and Rayner's term for the development of an emotional reaction to a previously neutral stimulus, as in Little Albert's fear of rats.

CONGRUENCE. Rogers' concept expressing an absence of conflict between the perceived self and experience.

CONSCIOUS. Those thoughts, experiences, and feelings of which we are aware.

CONSTRICTION. In Kelly's personal construct theory, the narrowing of the construct system so as to minimize incompatibilities.

CONSTRUCT. In Kelly's theory, a way of perceiving, construing, or interpreting events.

CONSTRUCT SYSTEM. In Kelly's theory, the hierarchical arrangement of constructs.

CONSTRUCT VALIDITY. The extent to which a test measures what it claims to measure, and the utility of the concept associated with the test, in terms of the results of studies using the test to investigate predictions based on a theory. Positive findings help to establish the validity of the concept and test whereas negative findings bring into question the validity of test, concept, or both.

CONTRAST POLE. In Kelly's personal construct theory, the contrast pole of a construct is defined by the way in which a third element is perceived as different from two other elements that are used to form a similarity pole.

CORE CONSTRUCT. In Kelly's personal construct theory, a construct that is basic to the person's construct system and cannot be altered without serious consequences for the rest of the system.

CORRELATIONAL RESEARCH. An approach to research, described by Cronbach, in which existing individual differences are measured and related to one another, in contrast with the experimental approach to research.

COUNTERCONDITIONING. The conditioning or learning of responses that interfere with previously learned responses to stimuli, as in the counterconditioning of a pleasurable response to a previously fear-provoking stimulus.

CRITERION-ORIENTED VALIDITY. A measure of the extent to which a test measures what it claims to measure in terms of the agreement between test scores and some independent measure.

DEATH INSTINCT. Freud's concept for drives or sources of energy that are directed toward death or a return to an inorganic state.

DEFENSE MECHANISMS. Freud's concept for those devices used by the person to reduce anxiety that result in the exclusion from awareness of some thought, wish, or feeling.

DEFENSIVE BEHAVIORS. Efforts on the part of the person, emphasized both by Freud and Rogers, to ward off anxiety.

DELAY OF GRATIFICATION. The postponement of pleasure until the optimum or proper time, a concept particularly emphasized in social learning theory in relation to self-regulation.

DEMAND CHARACTERISTICS. Cues that are implicit (hidden) in the experimental setting and influence the subject's behavior.

DENIAL. A defense mechanism, emphasized both by Freud and Rogers, in which threatening feelings are not allowed into awareness.

DILATION. In Kelly's personal construct theory, the broadening of a construct system so that it will be more comprehensive

DIRECT CONSEQUENCES. In social learning theory, the external events that follow behavior and influence future performance, contrasted with vicarious consequences and self-produced consequences.

DISCRIMINATION. In conditioning, the differential response to stimuli depending on whether they have been associated with pleasure, pain, or neutral events.

DISGUISED TESTS. Tests in which the subject is unaware of the purpose of the test and the ways in which responses will be interpreted.

DISTORTION. According to Rogers, a defensive process in which experience is changed so as to be brought into awareness in a form that is consistent with the self.

DREAM INTERPRETATION. In psychoanalysis, the use of dreams to understand the person's unconscious wishes and fears.

DRIVE, PRIMARY. In Hull's theory, an innate internal stimulus that activates behavior (e.g., hunger drive).

DRIVE, SECONDARY. In Hull's theory, a learned internal stimulus, acquired through association with the satisfaction of primary drives, that activates behavior (e.g., anxiety).

DYNAMIC LATTICE. Cattell's concept to represent the relationship of ergs, sentiments, and attitudes to one another.

DYSFUNCTIONAL EXPECTANCIES. In social learning theory, maladaptive expectations concerning the consequences of specific behaviors.

DYSFUNCTIONAL SELF-EVALUATION. In social learning theory, maladaptive standards for self-reward that have important implications for psychopathology.

EGO. Freud's structural concept for the part of personality that attempts to satisfy drives (instincts) in accordance with reality and the person's moral values.

EMITTED BEHAVIORS. In Skinner's theory, behaviors or responses that cannot be associated with known preceding stimuli.

EMPATHIC UNDERSTANDING. Rogers' term for the ability to perceive experiences and feelings and their meanings from the standpoint of another person. One of three therapist conditions essential for therapeutic progress.

EMPIRICAL-CRITERION KEYING. An approach to test construction in which the psychologist begins with groups of people known to be different on some personality characteristic and items are chosen on the basis of their ability to discriminate among members of the different groups (e.g., MMPI).

ENERGY SYSTEM. Freud's view of personality as involving the interplay among various forces (e.g., drives, instincts) or sources of energy.

ERG. Cattell's concept for innate biological drives that provide the basic motivating power for behavior.

EROGENOUS ZONES. According to Freud, those parts of the body that are the sources of tension or excitation.

EXPECTANCIES. In social learning theory, what the individual anticipates or predicts will occur as the result of specific behaviors in specific situations (anticipated consequences).

EXPERIMENTAL RESEARCH. An approach to research, described by Cronbach, in which the experimenter manipulates the variables and is interested in general laws, in contrast with the correlational approach to research.

EXPERIMENTER EXPECTANCY EFFECTS. Unintended experimenter effects involving behaviors that lead subjects to respond in accordance with the experimenter's hypothesis.

EXTINCTION. In conditioning, the progressive weakening of the association between a stimulus and a response; in classical conditioning because the conditioned stimulus is no longer followed by the unconditioned stimulus; and in operant conditioning because the response is no longer followed by reinforcement.

EXTROVERSION. In Eysenck's theory, one end of the introversion-extroversion dimension of personality characterized by a disposition to be sociable, friendly, impulsive, and risk-taking.

FACTOR ANALYSIS. A statistical method for determining those variables or test responses that increase and decrease together. Used in the development of personality tests and of some trait theories (e.g., Cattell and Eysenck).

FEAR (KELLY). In Kelly's personal construct theory, fear occurs when a new construct is about to enter the person's construct system.

FIXATION. Freud's concept expressing a developmental arrest or stoppage at some point in the person's psychosexual development.

FIXED ROLE THERAPY. Kelly's therapeutic technique that makes use of scripts or roles for people to try out, thereby encouraging people to behave in new ways and to perceive themselves in new ways.

FOCUS OF CONVENIENCE. In Kelly's personal construct theory, those events or phenomena that are best covered by a construct or by the construct system.

FREE ASSOCIATION. In psychoanalysis, the patient's reporting to the analyst of every thought that comes to mind.

FUNCTIONAL ANALYSIS. In behavioral approaches, particularly Skinnerian, the identification of the environmental stimuli that control behavior.

FUNCTIONAL AUTONOMY. Allport's concept that a motive may become independent of its origins; in particular, motives in adults may become independent of their earlier basis in tension reduction.

GENERALIZATION. In conditioning, the association of a response with stimuli similar to the stimulus to which the response was originally conditioned or attached.

GENERALIZED REINFORCER. In Skinner's operant conditioning theory, a reinforcer that provides access to many other reinforcers (e.g., money).

GENUINENESS. Rogers' term for the ability of a person to be himself or herself and honest in relation to another person. One of three therapist conditions necessary for therapeutic progress.

GOALS-PLANS. In social learning theory, desired future events that motivate the person over extended periods of time and enable the person to go beyond momentary influences.

GUIDED PARTICIPATION. A treatment approach emphasized in social learning theory in which a person is assisted in performing modeled behaviors.

HABIT. In Hull's theory, an association between a stimulus and a response.

HIERARCHY. The organization of things in a graded order or according to rank (e.g., Eysenck's conceptualization of personality and Kelly's view of the personal construct system).

HIGHER MENTAL PROCESSES. In S-R theory, the central role of thought in behavior that allows organisms to go beyond reflexive responses to stimuli.

HOSTILITY (KELLY). In Kelly's personal construct theory, making others behave in an expected way to validate one's own construct system.

HUMAN POTENTIAL MOVEMENT. A group of psychologists, represented by Rogers and Maslow, who emphasize the actualization or fulfillment of individual potential, including an openness to experience.

ID. Freud's structural concept for the source of the instincts or all drive energy in people.

IDEAL SELF. The self-concept the individual would most like to possess. A key concept in Rogers' theory.

IDENTIFICATION. The acquisition, as characteristics of the self, of personality characteristics perceived to be part of others (e.g., parents).

IMITATION. Behavior that is acquired through the observation of others. In S-R theory, the result of the process called matched-dependent behavior in which, for example, children match their behavior to that of their parents and this is followed by reward.

IMPERMEABLE CONSTRUCT. In Kelly's personal construct theory, a construct that does not allow new elements into it.

INCONGRUENCE. Rogers' concept for the existence of a discrepancy or conflict between the perceived self and experience.

INEFFICACY. In social learning theory, the inability to cope with a perceived threat or other important situation.

INSTRUMENTAL LEARNING. In S-R theory, the learning of responses that are instrumental in bringing about a desirable situation.

INTERACTIONISM. The view within psychology that behavior can be understood in terms of relationships between variables that affect one another, as in person and situation variables, or interact to determine behavior.

INTERNAL-EXTERNAL (I-E) SCALE. The personality scale developed by Rotter to measure the extent to which the person has developed a generalized expectancy that he or she has the ability to control life's events (i.e., internal locus of control) as opposed to the generalized expectancy that life's events are the result of external factors such as chance, luck, or fate (i.e., external locus of control).

INTROVERSION. In Eysenck's theory, one end of the introversion-extroversion dimension of personality characterized by a disposition to be quiet, reserved, reflective, and risk-avoiding.

L-DATA. In Cattell's theory, life-record data relating to behavior in everyday-life situations or to ratings of such behavior.

LEARNED HELPLESSNESS. Seligman's concept expressing an animal's or person's learning that outcomes are not affected by his or her behavior.

LIBIDO. Freud's concept for the energy of the life instincts directed toward sexual gratification and pleasure.

LIFE INSTINCT. Freud's concept for drives or sources of energy (libido) directed toward the preservation of life and sexual gratification.

LOCUS OF CONTROL. Rotter's concept expressing a generalized expectancy or belief concerning the determinants of rewards and punishments. (*See* Internal-External Scale.)

LOOSENING. In Kelly's personal construct theory, the use of the same construct to make varied predictions.

MAINTENANCE. Bandura's concept for the conditions that regulate behavior once it has been initiated.

MAVA METHOD (MULTIPLE ABSTRACT VARIANCE ANALYSIS). Cattell's method for determining the relative influence of heredity and environment in the development of specific personality traits.

MECHANISMS OF DEFENSE. *See* Defense Mechanisms.

MODELING. Bandura's concept for the process of reproducing behaviors learned through the observation of others.

MULTIVARIATE METHOD. Cattell's description of the method of personality study, favored by him, in which there is study of the interrelationships among many variables at once.

NATURALISTIC OBSERVATION. An approach to research that involves the study of phenomena as they occur naturally (in their own environment) and without efforts toward experimental manipulation and control.

NEED FOR POSITIVE REGARD. *See* Positive regard.

NEGATIVE REINFORCER. In Skinner's operant conditioning theory, the removal of an unpleasant or aversive event that results in an increase in the probability of occurrence of the preceding response.

NEUROTICISM. In Eysenck's theory, a dimension of personality defined by stability and low anxiety at one end as opposed to instability and high anxiety at the other end.

OBJECTIVE TESTS. Tests in which the subject is asked to give a correct response.

OBSERVATIONAL LEARNING. Bandura's concept for the process through which people learn merely by observing the behavior of others, called models.

OEDIPUS COMPLEX. Freud's concept for the mixture of wishes and fears surrounding the sexual attraction to the parent of the opposite sex during the phallic stage of development.

OPERANT CONDITIONING. Skinner's term for the process through which the characteristics of a response are determined by its consequences.

OPERANTS. In Skinner's theory, behaviors that appear (are emitted) without being specifically associated with any prior (eliciting) stimuli and are studied in relation to the reinforcing events that follow them.

ORAL CHARACTER. Freud's concept for a personality type that expresses a fixation at the oral of development and who relates to the world in terms of the wish to be fed or to swallow.

ORAL STAGE. Freud's concept for that period of life during which the major center of bodily excitation or tension is the mouth.

OT-DATA. In Cattell's theory, objective test data or information about personality obtained from observing behavior in miniature situations.

OWN-CONTROL DESIGN. A Skinnerian variant of the experimental method in which one subject is used and serves as his own control while experimental conditions are varied (*see* ABA design).

PARADIGM. Kuhn's concept for a model that is commonly accepted by scientists in a field and that defines the field of observations and the methods to be used in research.

PERFORMANCE. The production of learned behaviors, viewed by Bandura as dependent on rewards, in contrast to the acquisition of new behaviors, which is seen as independent of reward.

PERIPHERAL CONSTRUCT. In Kelly's personal construct theory, a construct that is not basic to the construct system and can be altered without serious consequences for the rest of the system.

PERMEABLE CONSTRUCT. In Kelly's personal construct system, a construct that allows new elements into it.

PERSON-SITUATION CONTROVERSY. A controversy between those psychologists who emphasize the importance of personal (internal) variables in determining behavior and those who emphasize the importance of situational (external) influences.

PERSONALITY. Those characteristics of the person, or of people generally, that account for consistent patterns of response to situations.

PHALLIC CHARACTER. Freud's concept for a personality type that expresses a fixation at the phallic stage of development and who strives for success in competition with others.

PHALLIC STAGE. Freud's concept for that period of life

during which excitation or tension begins to be centered in the genitals and during which there is an attraction to the parent of the opposite sex.

PHENOMENOLOGY. An approach within psychology that focuses on how the person perceives and experiences the self and the world.

PLEASURE PRINCIPLE. According to Freud, psychological functioning based on the pursuit of pleasure and the avoidance of pain.

POSITIVE REGARD, NEED FOR. Rogers' concept expressing the need for warmth, liking, respect, and acceptance from others.

POSITIVE REINFORCER. In Skinner's operant conditioning theory, a stimulus that results in an increase in the probability of occurrence of the response that preceded it.

PRECONSCIOUS. Freud's concept for those thoughts, experiences, and feelings of which we are momentarily unaware but can readily bring into awareness.

PREDICTIVE VALIDITY. A measure of the extent to which a test measures what it claims to measure in terms of the agreement between test scores and scores obtained on an independent measure of performance at some later date.

PREVERBAL CONSTRUCT. In Kelly's personal construct theory, a construct that is used but cannot be expressed in words.

PROCESS. In personality theory, the concept of process refers to the motivational aspects of personality.

PROJECTIVE TEST. A test that generally involves vague, ambiguous stimuli and allows subjects to reveal their personalities in terms of their distinctive responses (e.g., Rorschach, TAT).

PROPRIUM. Allport's concept expressing the organized functioning of the person and including the self.

PSYCHOMETRIC TEST. A test that is structured and voluntary, such as a questionnaire, in which test responses are related to a criterion in an objective, systematic fashion (e.g., 16 P.F., MMPI).

PSYCHOTICISM. In Eysenck's theory, a dimension of personality defined by a tendency to be solitary and insensitive at one end as opposed to accepting social custom and being caring about others at the other end.

Q-DATA. In Cattell's theory, personality data obtained from questionnaires.

Q-SORT. An assessment device in which the subject sorts statements into categories following a normal distribution. Used by Rogers as a measure of statements regarding the self and ideal self.

RANGE OF CONVENIENCE. In Kelly's personal construct theory, those events or phenomena that are covered by a construct or by the construct system.

RATIONAL-THEORETICAL APPROACH. A method of test construction that bases the test on some rational or theoretical understanding of the personality characteristic of interest to the psychologist (e.g., Manifest Anxiety Scale).

REALITY PRINCIPLE. According to Freud, psychological functioning based on reality in which pleasure is delayed until an optimum time.

RECIPROCAL DETERMINISM. The mutual effects of variables on one another, emphasized by Bandura, as in person factors and environmental factors continuously affecting one another.

REGRESSION. Freud's concept expressing a person's return to ways of relating to the world and self that were part of an earlier stage of development.

RELIABILITY. In test construction, a measure of the consistency of scores derived from the test; a measure of the freedom from chance error of the obtained scores.

REP TEST (ROLE CONSTRUCT REPERTORY TEST). Kelly's test to determine the constructs used by person, the relationships among constructs, and how the constructs are applied to specific people.

RESPONSE STYLE. The tendency of some subjects to respond to test items in a consistent, patterned way that has to do with the form of the questions and/or answers rather than with their content.

SAMPLE APPROACH. Mischel's description of assessment approaches in which there is an interest in the behavior itself and its relation to environmental conditions, in contrast to sign approaches that infer personality from test behavior.

SCHEDULE OF REINFORCEMENT. In Skinner's operant conditioning theory, the rate and interval of reinforcement of responses (e.g., response ratio schedule and time intervals).

SECONDARY DISPOSITION. Allport's concept for a disposition to behave in a particular way that is relevant to few situations.

SELF. A concept many psychologists use to express pattern, organization, and consistency in personality functioning; in social learning theory, cognitive processes (schema) associated by the person with the I or Me.

SELF-ACTUALIZATION. The fundamental tendency on the part of the organism to actualize, maintain, and enhance itself. A concept emphasized by Rogers and other members of the human potential movement.

SELF-CONCEPT. The perceptions and meaning associated with the self, Me or I.

SELF-CONCEPTIONS. In social learning theory, cognitive evaluations of the self. Dysfunctional self-evaluations, for example, are viewed as being important in psychopathology.

SELF-CONSISTENCY. Rogers' concept expressing an absence of conflict among perceptions of the self.

SELF-EFFICACY. In social learning theory, the perceived ability to cope with specific situations.

SELF-EFFICACY EXPECTATIONS. In social learning theory, the expectations on the part of the person concerning his or her ability to perform specific behaviors in a situation.

SELF-ESTEEM. The person's evaluative regard for the self or personal judgment of worthiness.

SELF-EXPERIENCE DISCREPANCY. Rogers' emphasis on the potential for conflict between the concept of self and experience — the basis for psychopathology.

SELF-PRODUCED CONSEQUENCES. In social learning theory, the consequences to behavior that are produced personally (internally) by the individual and that play a vital role in self-regulation and self-control.

SELF-REGULATION. Bandura's concept for the process through which the person regulates his or her own behavior.

SENTIMENT. Cattell's concept for environmentally determined patterns of behavior that are expressed in attitudes (i.e., readiness to act in a certain direction) and are linked to underlying ergs (i.e., innate biological drives).

SEXUAL INSTINCTS. Freud's concept for those drives directed toward sexual gratification or pleasure.

SHAPING. In Skinner's operant conditioning theory, the modification of behavior in a specific direction through the reinforcement of specific responses.

SIGN APPROACH. Mischel's description of assessment approaches that infer personality from test behavior, in contrast with a sample approach to assessment.

SIMILARITY POLE. In Kelly's personal construct theory, the similarity pole of a construct is defined by the way in which two elements are perceived to be similar.

SIXTEEN PERSONALITY FACTOR INVENTORY (16 P.F.). Cattell's personality questionnaire, derived from the use of factor analysis, measuring personality on sixteen dimensions.

SOCIAL DESIRABILITY. The perceived social value of a response to a test item that may lead to a subject responding in terms of the perceived acceptability (desirability) of a response rather than in terms of its actual relevance to the self.

SOURCE TRAIT. In Cattell's theory, behaviors that vary together to form an independent dimension of personality, which is discovered through the use of factor analysis.

SPECIFICATION EQUATION. Cattell's formula, based on scores on personality factors, for predicting behavior in specific situations (e.g., success in a particular career).

STATE ANXIETY. In Cattell's theory, a temporary state of anxiety, distinguished from trait anxiety.

STRUCTURE. In personality theory, the concept of structure refers to the more enduring and stable aspects of personality.

STRUCTURED TESTS. Tests in which the subject has a limited choice among alternative responses.

SUBCEPTION. A process emphasized by Rogers in which a stimulus is experienced without being brought into awareness.

SUBJECTIVE TEST. A test that is unstructured and non-disguised and allows for subjects to describe themselves in a relatively open-ended fashion (e.g., interview).

SUBMERGED CONSTRUCT. In Kelly's personal construct theory, a construct that once could be expressed in words but now either one or both poles of the construct cannot be verbalized.

SUBORDINATE CONSTRUCT. In Kelly's personal construct theory, a construct that is lower in the construct system and is thereby included in the context of another (superordinate) construct.

SUCCESSIVE APPROXIMATION. In Skinner's operant conditioning theory, the development of complex behaviors through the reinforcement of behaviors that increasingly resemble the final form of behavior to be produced.

SUPEREGO. Freud's structural concept for the part of personality that expresses our ideals and moral values.

SUPERORDINATE CONSTRUCT. In Kelly's personal construct theory, a construct that is higher in the construct system and thereby includes other constructs within its context.

SURFACE TRAIT. In Cattell's theory, behaviors that appear to be linked to one another but do not in fact increase and decrease together.

SYMPTOM. In psychopathology, the expression of psychological conflict or disordered psychological functioning. For Freud, a disguised expression of a repressed impulse.

SYSTEMATIC DESENSITIZATION. A technique in behavior therapy in which a competing response (relaxation) is conditioned to stimuli that previously aroused anxiety.

TARGET BEHAVIORS. In behavioral assessment, the identification of specific behaviors to be observed and measured in relation to changes in environmental events.

TENSION-REDUCTION MODEL. A view of motivation which suggests that behavior is directed toward the reduction of tensions associated with drives or needs.

THEORY. A set of assumptions and concepts used to explain existing empirical findings and suggest findings that are expected in the future.

THREAT (KELLY). In Kelly's personal construct theory, threat occurs when the person is aware of an imminent, comprehensive change in his or her construct system.

TIGHTENING. In Kelly's personal construct theory, the use of constructs to make the same predictions regardless of circumstances.

TOKEN ECONOMY. Following Skinner's operant conditioning theory, an environment in which individuals are rewarded with tokens for desirable behaviors.

TRAIT. A disposition to behave in a particular way as expressed in a person's behavior over a range of situations.

TRAIT ANXIETY. In Cattell's theory, a generalized tendency to have a high anxiety level, distinguished from state anxiety.

TRANSFERENCE. In psychoanalysis, the patient's development toward the analyst of attitudes and feelings rooted in past experiences with parental figures.

TYPE. The classification of people into a few groups, each of which has its own defining characteristics (e.g., introverts and extroverts).

UNCONDITIONAL POSITIVE REGARD. Rogers' term for the acceptance of a person in a total, unconditional way. One of three therapist conditions suggested as essential for growth and therapeutic progress.

UNCONSCIOUS. Those thoughts, experiences, and feelings of which we are unaware. According to Freud this unawareness is the result of repression.

VALIDITY. In test construction and evaluation, the extent to which a test measures what it claims to measure.

VERBAL CONSTRUCT. In Kelly's personal construct theory, a construct that can be expressed in words.

VICARIOUS CONDITIONING. Bandura's concept for the process through which emotional responses are learned through the observation of emotional responses in others.

VICARIOUS CONSEQUENCES. In social learning theory, the observed consequences to the behavior of others that influence future performance.

VOLUNTARY TESTS. Tests in which the subject gives his or her own preferred response.

ZEITGEIST. The prevailing mood or spirit within a field at a particular time.

BIBLIOGRAPHY

ABERNETHY, Ethel M. The effect of sorority pressures on the results of a self-inventory. *Journal of Social Psychology*, 1954, **40**, 177–183.

ABRAHAM, K. A short study of the development of the libido, viewed in the light of mental disorders. 1924, In *On character and libido development: Six essays by Karl Abraham*. New York: Norton, 1966.

ABRAMSON, L. Y., Seligman, M. E. P., and Teasdale, J. D. Learned helplessness in humans: Critique and reformulation. *Journal of Abnormal Psychology*, 1978, **87**, 49–74.

ACHENBACH, T., and Zigler, E. Social competence and self-image disparity in psychiatric and nonpsychiatric patients. *Journal of Abnormal and Social Psychology*, 1963, **67**, 197–205.

ADAMS-WEBBER, J. R. Actual structure and potential chaos: Relational aspects of progressive variations within a personal construct system. In D. Bannister (Ed.), *Perspectives in personal construct theory*. New York: Academic Press, 1970. Pp. 31–46.

ADAMS-WEBBER, J. R. *Personal construct theory: Concepts and applications*. New York: Wiley, 1979.

ADCOCK, C. J. Review of the MMPI. In O. K. Buros (Ed.), *The sixth mental measurements yearbook*. Highland Park, N. J.: Gryphon, 1965. Pp. 313–316.

ADORNO, T. W., Frenkel-Brunswik, Else, Levinson, D. J., and Sanford, R. N. *The authoritarian personality*. New York: Harper, 1950.

AKERET, R. U. Interrelationships among various dimensions of the self concept. *Journal of Counseling Psychology*, 1959, **6**, 199–201.

ALEXANDER, F. *Psychosomatic* medicine. New York: Norton, 1950.

ALEXANDER, F., and French, T. M. *Psychoanalytic* therapy. New York: Ronald, 1946.

ALKER, H. A. Is personality situationally specific or intrapsychically consistent? *Journal of Personality*, 1972, **40**, 1–16.

ALLPORT, F. H., and Allport, G. W. Personality traits: Their classification and measurement. *Journal of Abnormal & Social Psychology*, 1921, 16, 1–40.

ALLPORT, G. W. *Personality*: A psychological interpretation. New York: Holt, Rinehart and Winston, 1937.

ALLPORT, G. W. The trend in motivational theory. *American Journal of Orthopsychiatry*, 1953, **23**, 107–119.

ALLPORT, G. W. *Becoming*. New Haven, Conn.: Yale, 1955.

ALLPORT, G. W. European and American theories of personality. In H. P. David and H. von Bracken (Eds.), *Perspectives in personality theory*, New York: Basic Books, 1957. Pp. 3–26.

ALLPORT, G. W. What units shall we employ? In G. Lindzey (Ed.), *Assessment of human motives*. New York: Holt, Rinehart and Winston. 1958. Pp. 239–260.

ALLPORT, G. W. *Pattern and growth in personality.* New York: Holt, Rinehart and Winston, 1961.

ALLPORT, G. W. The general and the unique in psychological science. *Journal of Personality,* 1962, **30**, 405–421.

ALLPORT, G. W. Autobiopgraphy. In E. G. Boring and G. Lindzey (Eds.), *A history of psychology in autobiography.* New York: Appleton-Century-Crofts, 1967. Pp. 3–25.

ARONFREED, J. The origin of self-criticism. *Psychological Review,* 1964, **71**, 193–218.

ARONSON, E., and Carlsmith, J. M. Performance expectancy as a determinant of actual performance. *Journal of Abnormal and Social Psychology,* 1962, **65**, 178–182.

ARONSON, E., and Mettee, D. R. Dishonest behavior as a function of differential levels of induced self-esteem. *Journal of Personality and Social Psychology,* 1968, **9**, 121–127.

ARONSON, M. L. A Study of the Freudian theory of paranoia by means of the Rorschach test. *Journal of Projective Techniques,* 1952, **16**, 397–411.

ATTHOWE, J. M., Jr. Behavior innovation and persistence. *American Psychologist,* 1973, **28**, 34–41.

ATTHOWE, J. M., Jr., and Krasner, L. A. A preliminary report on the application of contingent reinforcement procedures and token economy on a "chronic" psychiatric ward. *Journal of Abnormal Psychology,* 1968, **73**, 37–43.

AYLLON, T., and Azrin, H. H. The measurement and reinforcement of behavior of psychotics. *Journal of the Experimental Analysis of Behavior,* 1965, **8**, 357–383.

AYLLON, T., and Michael, J. The psychiatric nurse as a behavioral engineer. *Journal of the Experimental Analysis of Behavior,* 1959, **2**, 323–334.

AYLLON, T., and Michael, E. Control of the behavior of schizophrenic patients by food. *Journal of the Experimental Analysis of Behavior,* 1962, **5**, 343–352.

BAER, D. M., Peterson, R.F., and Sherman, J. A. The development of imitation by reinforcing similarity to a model. *Journal of the Experimental Analysis of Behavior,* 1967, **10**, 405–416.

BAER, D.M., and Sherman, J. A. Reinforcement control of generalized imitation in young children. *Journal of Experimental Child Psychology,* 1964, **1**, 37–49.

BALDWIN, A. L. The effect of home environment on nursery school behavior. *Child Development,* 1949, **20**, 49–61.

BALDWIN, A. L. *Behavior and development in childhood.* New York: Dryden, 1955.

BALDWIN, A. L. *Theories of child development.* New York: Wiley, 1967.

BANDURA, A. The Rorschach white space response and "oppositional" behavior. *Journal of Consulting Psychology,* 1954, **18**, 17–21. (a)

BANDURA, A. The Rorschach white space response and perceptual reversal. *Journal of Experimental Psychology,* 1954, **48**, 113–117. (b)

BANDURA, A. Psychotherapy as a learning process. *Psychological Bulletin,* 1961, **58**, 143–159.

BANDURA, A. Social learning through imitation. In M. R. Jones (Ed.), *Nebraska symposium on motivation.* Lincoln: University of Nebraska Press, 1962. Pp. 211–215.

BANDURA, A. Influence of models' reinforcement contingencies on the acquisition of imitative responses. *Journal of Personality and Social Psychology,* 1965, **1**, 589–595.

BANDURA, A. A social learning interpretation of psychological dysfunctions. In P. London and D. Rosenhan (Eds.), *Foundations of abnormal psychology.* New York: Holt, Rinehart and Winston, 1968. Pp. 293–344.

BANDURA, A. Social-learning theory of identificatory processes. In D. A. Goslin (Ed.), *Handbook of socialization theory and research.* Chicago: Rand McNally, 1969. Pp. 213–262. (a)

BANDURA, A. *Principles of behavior modification.* New York: Holt, Rinehart and Winston, 1969. (b)

BANDURA, A. Analysis of modeling processes. In A. Bandura (Ed.), *Psychological modeling.* Chicago: Aldine-Atherton, 1971. Pp. 1–62. (a)

BANDURA, A. Psychotherapy based upon modeling principles. In A. E. Bergin and S. Garfield (Eds.), *Handbook of psychotherapy and behavior change.* New York: Wiley, 1971. Pp. 653–708. (b)

BANDURA, A. The process and practice of participant modeling treatment. Paper presented at the Conference on the Behavioral Basis of Mental Health, Ireland, 1972.

BANDURA, A. Social learning perspective on behavior

change. In A. Burton (Ed.), *What makes behavior change?* New York: Brunner/Mazel, 1976. Pp. 34–57.

BANDURA, A. *Social learning theory.* Englewood Cliffs, N. J.: Prentice-Hall, 1977. (a)

BANDURA, A. Self-efficacy: Toward a unified theory of behavioral change. *Psychological Review,* 1977, **84**, 191–215. (b)

BANDURA, Psychological mechanisms of aggression. Paper presented at the Werner-Reimers-Stiftung Conference on Human Ethology: Claims and Limits of a New Discipline. Bad Homburg, West Germany, October 1977. (c)

BANDURA, On paradigms and recycled ideologies. *Cognitive Therapy and Research,* 1978, **2**, 79–103. (a)

BANDURA, A. The self system in reciprocal determinism. *American Psychologist,* 1978, **33**, 344–358. (b)

BANDURA, A. Psychological mechanisms of aggression. In M. Von Cranach, K. Foppa, W. LePenies, and D. Ploog (Eds.), *Human ethology: Claims and limits of a new discipline.* Cambridge: Cambridge University Press, 1979.

BANDURA, A., and Adams, N. E. Analysis of self-efficacy theory of behavioral change. *Cognitive Therapy and Research,* 1977, **1**, 287–310.

BANDURA, A., Adams, N. E., and Beyer, J. Cognitive processes mediating behavioral change. *Journal of Personality and Social Psychology,* 1977, **35**, 125–139. (Copyright 1977 by the American Psychological Association. Reprinted by permission.)

BANDURA, A., and Barab, P. G. Conditions governing nonreinforced imitation. *Developmental Psychology,* 1971, **5**, 244–255.

BANDURA, A., Blanchard, E. B., and Ritter, B. J. The relative efficacy of modeling therapeutic approaches for producing behavioral, attitudinal and affective changes. Unpublished manuscript, Stanford University, 1967.

BANDURA, A., Grusec, Joan E., and Menlove, Frances L. Some social determinants of self-monitoring reinforcement systems. *Journal of Personality and Social Psychology,* 1967, **5**, 449–455.

BANDURA, A., and Kupers, Carol J. Transmission of patterns of self-reinforcement through modeling.

Journal of Abnormal and Social Psychology, 1964, **69**, 1–9.

BANDURA, A., and McDonald, F. J. Influence of social reinforcement and the behavior of models in shaping children's moral judgments. *Journal of Abnormal and Social Psychology,* 1963, **67**, 274–281.

BANDURA, A., and Menlove, Frances L. Factors determining vicarious extinction of avoidance behavior through symbolic modeling. *Journal of Personality and Social Psychology,* 1968, **8**, 99–108.

BANDURA, A., and Mischel, W. Modification of self-imposed delay of reward through exposure to live and symbolic models. *Journal of Personality and Social Psychology,* 1965, **2**, 698–705.

BANDURA, A., and Rosenthal, T. L. Vicarious classical conditioning as a function of arousal level. *Journal of Personality and Social Psychology,* 1966, **3**, 54–62.

BANDURA, A., Ross, Dorothea, and Ross, Sheila. Imitation of film-mediated aggressive models. *Journal of Abnormal and Social Psychology,* 1963, **66**, 3–11. (a)

BANDURA, A., Ross, Dorothea, and Ross, Sheila. Vicarious reinforcement and imitative learning. *Journal of Abnormal and Social Psychology,* 1963, **67**, 601–607. (b)

BANDURA, A., and Walters, R. H. *Social learning and personality development.* New York: Holt, Rinehart and Winston, 1963.

BANNISTER, D. The nature and measurement of schizophrenic thought disorder. *Journal of Mental Science,* 1962, **108**, 825–842.

BANNISTER, D. (Ed.), *New perspectives in personal construct theory.* New York: Academic Press, 1977.

BANNISTER, D., and Agnew, J. The child's construing of self. *Nebraska symposium on motivation,* 1977, 24, 99–126.

BANNISTER, D., and Fransella, Fay. A grid test of schizophrenic thought disorder. *British Journal of Social and Clinical Psychology,* 1966, **5**, 95–102.

BANNISTER, D., and Fransella, Fay. *Inquiring man: The theory of personal constructs.* Baltimore: Penguin, 1971.

BANNISTER, D., and Fransella, F. *A manual for repertory grid technique.* New York: Academic Press, 1977.

BARBER, T. X. *Pitfalls in human research.* New York: Pergamon, 1976.

BARBU, Z. Studies in children's honesty. *Quarterly Bulletin of the British Psychological Society*, 1951, **2**, 53–57.

BARRATT, B. The development of peer perception: A content analysis with children from 8 to 14 years. Unpublished manuscript, Harvard University, 1977.

BATESON, G. A., Jackson, D. D., Haley, J., and Weakland, Jr. Toward a theory of schizophrenia. *Behavioral Science*, 1956, **1**, 251–264.

BECK, A. T. *Cognitive therapy and the emotional disorders.* New York: International Universities Press, 1976.

BECK, S. J. The Rorschach test: A multi-dimensional test of personality. In H. H. Anderson and Gladys L. Anderson (Eds.), *An introduction to projective techniques.* Englewood Cliffs, N.J.: Prentice-Hall, 1951. Pp. 101–122.

BECKER, W. C. The matching of behavior rating and questionnaire personality factors. *Psychological Bulletin*, 1960, **57**, 201–212.

BECKER, W. C. Consequences of different kinds of parental discipline. In M. L. Hoffman and L. W. Hoffman (Eds.), *Review of Child Development Research*, Vol. 1. New York: Russell Sage Foundation, 1964, 169–208.

BENDER, M. P. Does construing people as similar involve similar behavior towards them? A subjective and objective replication. *British Journal of Social and Clinical Psychology*, 1976, **15**, 93–95.

BENJAMIN, J. D., and Ebaugh, F. G. The diagnostic validity of the Rorschach test. *American Journal of Psychiatry*, 1938, **94**, 1163–1178.

BERGER, S. M. Conditioning through vicarious investigation. *Psychological Review*, 1962, **69**, 450–466.

BERGIN, A. E., and Strupp, H. H. *Changing frontiers in the science of psychotherapy.* New York: Aldine-Atherton, 1972.

BERGMANN, G., and Spence, K. W. Operationism and theory in psychology. *Psychological Review*, 1941, **48**, 1–14.

BERNSTEIN, D. A. Situational factors in behavioral fear assessment: A progress report. *Behavior Therapy*, 1973, **4**, 41–48.

BIERI, J. Changes in interpersonal perceptions following social interaction. *Journal of Abnormal and Social Psychology*, 1953, **48**, 61–66.

BIERI, J. Cognitive complexity—simplicity and predictive behavior. *Journal of Abnormal and Social Psychology*, 1955, **51**, 263–268.

BIERI, J. Complexity—simplicity as a personality variable in cognitive and preferential behavior. In D. W. Fiske and S. R. Maddi (Eds.), *Functions of varied experience.* Homewood, Ill.: Dorsey, 1961. Pp. 355–379.

BIERI, J., Atkins, A., Briar, S., Leaman, R. L., Miller, H., and Tripoldi, T. *Clinical and social judgment.* New York: Wiley, 1966.

BIJOU, S. W. Experimental studies of child behavior, normal and deviant. In L. Krasner and L. P. Ullmann (Eds.), *Research in behavior modification.* New York: Holt, Rinehart and Winston, 1965. Pp. 56–81.

BIJOU, S. W. *Child development: The basic stage of early childhood.* Englewood Cliffs, N.J.: Prentice-Hall, 1976.

BINDRA, D., and Scheier, I. H. The relation between psychometric and experimental research in psychology. *American Psychologist*, 1954, **9**, 69–71.

BLANCHARD, E. B., and Young, L. D. Self-control of cardiac functioning: A promise as yet unfulfilled. *Psychological Bulletin*, 1973, **79**, 145–163.

BLOOM, B. S. *Stability and change in human characteristics.* New York: Wiley, 1964.

BLUM, G., and Miller, D. R. Exploring the psychoanalytic theory of the "oral character." *Journal of Personality*, 1952, **20**, 287–304.

BONARIUS, J. C. J. Research in the personal construct theory of George A. Kelly: Role construct repertory test and basic theory. In B. A. Maher (Ed.), *Progress in experimental personality research.* New York: Academic Press, 1965. Pp. 1–46.

BONARIUS, H. The interaction model of communication: Through experimental research toward existential relevance. In A. W. Landfield (Ed.), *Nebraska Symposium on Motivation.* Lincoln: University of Nebraska Press, 1977. Pp. 291–343.

BORING, E. G. *A history of experimental psychology.* New York: Appleton-Century-Crofts, 1950.

BOUCHARD, T. J. Jr. Sixteen PF questionnaire. In O. K. Buros (Ed.), *Seventh mental measurements yearbook.* Highland Park, N.J.: Gryphon Press, 1972. Pp. 329–332.

BRADY, J. V. Ulcers in "executive" monkeys. *Scientific American*, 1958, 95–100.

BRADY, J. P., and Lind, D. L. Experimental analysis of hysterical blindness. *American Medical Association Archives of General Psychiatry*, 1961, **4**, 331–339.

BRAMEL, D. Some determinants of defensive projection. Unpublished doctoral dissertation, Stanford University, 1960.

BREGER, L., and McGaugh, J. L. Critique and reformulation of "learning-theory" approaches to psychotherapy and neurosis. *Psychological Bulletin*, 1965, **63**, 338–358.

BRIERLY, D. W. The use of personality constructs by children of three different ages. Unpublished Ph.D. thesis, London University, 1967.

BROGDEN, H. E. A factor analysis of 40 character traits. *Psychological Monographs*, 1940, **52**, (3, Whole No. 234).

BROWN, I. B., Jr., and Inouye, D. K. Learned helplessness through modeling: The role of perceived similarity in competence. *Journal of Personality and Social Psychology*, 1978, **36**, 900–908.

BROWN, J. S. A comparative study of deviations from sexual mores. *American Sociological Review*, 1952, **17**, 138.

BROWN, N. O. *Life against death.* New York: Random House, 1959.

BRUNER, J. S. You are your constructs. *Contemporary Psychology*, 1956, **1**, 355–356.

BUCHER, B., and Lovaas, O. I. Operant procedures in behavior modification with children. In D. J. Levis (Ed.), *Learning approaches to therapeutic behavior change.* Chicago: Aldine, 1970. Pp. 36–64.

BURTON, R. V. Generality of honesty revisited. *Psychological Review*, 1963, **70**, 481–499.

BURTON, R. V. Validity of retrospective reports assessed by the multitrait-multimethod analysis. *Developmental Psychology Monographs*, 1970, **3**, No. 3, Part 2.

BUTLER, J. M. The use of a psychological model in personality testing. *Educational and Psychological Measurements*, 1954, **14**, 77–89.

BUTLER, J. M., and Haigh, G. V. Changes in the relation between self-concepts and ideal concepts consequent upon client centered counseling. In C. R. Rogers and Rosalind F. Dymond (Eds.), *Psychotherapy and personality change.* Chicago: University of Chicago Press, 1954. Pp. 55–75.

CAMPBELL, D. T. The indirect assessment of social attitudes. *Psychological Bulletin*, 1950, **47**, 15–38.

CAMPBELL, D. T. A typology of tests, projective and otherwise. *Journal of Consulting Psychology*, 1957, **21**, 207–210.

CARLSON, E. R., and Carlson, Rae. Male and female subjects in personality research. *Journal of Abnormal and Social Psychology*, 1960, **61**, 482–483.

CARLSON, Rae. Where is the person in personality research? *Psychological Bulletin*, 1971, **75**, 203–219.

CARR, A. C. An evaluation of nine nondirective psychotherapy cases by means of the Rorschach. *Journal of Consulting Psychology*, 1949, **13**, 196–205.

CARTWRIGHT, D. S. Self-consistency as a factor affecting immediate recall. *Journal of Abnormal and Social Psychology*, 1956, **52**, 212–218.

CARTWRIGHT, D. S., Kirtner, W. L., and Fiske, D. W. Method factors in changes associated with psychotherapy. *Journal of Abnormal and Social Psychology*, 1963, **66**, 164–175.

CATTELL, R. B. The main personality factors in questionnaire, self-estimated material. *Journal of Social Psychology*, 1950 **31**, 3–38.

CATTELL, R. B. Personality and motivation theory based on structural measurement. In J. L. McCary (Ed.), *Psychology of personality.* New York: Logos, 1956. Pp. 63–120.(a)

CATTELL, R. B. Validation and interpretation of the 16 P.F. questionnaire. *Journal of Clinical Psychology*, 1956, **12**, 205–214.(b)

CATTELL, R. B. The dynamic calculus: Concepts and crucial experiments In M. R. Jones (Ed.), *Nebraska symposium on motivation.* Lincoln: University of Nebraska Press, 1959. Pp. 84–134.(a)

CATTELL, R. B. Personality theory growing from multivariate quantitative research. In S. Koch (Ed.), *Psychology: the study of a science.* New York: McGraw-Hill, 1959. Pp. 257–327.(b)

CATTELL, R. B. Foundations of personality measurement theory in multivariate expressions. In B. M. Bass and I. A. Berg (Eds.), *Objective approaches to personality assessment.* Princeton, N.J.: Van Nostrand, 1959. Pp. 42–65.(c)

CATTELL, R. B. Personality measurement functionally related to source trait structure. In S. Messick and J. Ross (Eds.), *Measurement in personality and cognition.* New York: Wiley, 1962. Pp. 249–267.

CATTELL, R. B. Personality, role, mood, and situation perception: A unifying theory of modulators. *Psychological Review,* 1963, **70**, 1–18.(a)

CATTELL, R. B. The nature and measurement of anxiety. *Scientific American,* 1963, **208**, 96–104.(b)

CATTELL, R. B. *The scientific analysis of personality.* Baltimore: Penquin, 1965.(a)

CATTELL, R. B. Methodological and conceptual advances in the evaluation of hereditary and environmental influences and their interaction. In S. G. Vandenberg (Ed.), *Methods and goals in human behavior genetics.* New York: Academic Press, 1965. Pp. 95–130.(b)

CATTELL, R. B. Psychological theory and scientific method. In R. B. Cattell (Ed.), *Handbook of multivariate experimental psychology.* Chicago: Rand McNally, 1966. Pp. 1–18.

CATTELL, R. B. The principles of experimental design and analysis in relation to theory building. In R. B. Cattell (Ed.), *Handbook of multivariate experimental psychology.* Chicago: Rand McNally, 1966. Pp. 19–66.

CATTELL, R. B. A more sophisticated look at structure: Perturbation, sampling, role, and observer trait-view theories. In R. B. Cattell, and R. M. Dreger (Eds.), *Handbook of modern personality theory.* Washington: Hemisphere, 1977. Pp. 166–220.

CATTELL, R. B., and Baggaley, A. R. The objective measurement of motivation. I. Development and evaluation of principles and devices. *Journal of Personality,* 1956, **24**, 401–423.

CATTELL, R. B., Blewett, D., and Beloff, J. The inheritance of personality: A multiple variance analysis of nature-nurture ratios for personality factors in Q-data. *American Journal of Human Genetics,* 1955, **7**, 122–146.

CATTELL, R. B., and Child, D. *Motivation and dynamic structure.* New York: Wiley 1975.

CATTELL, R. B., and Cross, P. Comparison of the ergic and self-sentiment structures found in dynamic traits by R- and P-techniques. *Journal of Personality,* 1952, **21**, 250–270.

CATTELL, R. B., and Delhees, K. H. Seven missing normal personality factors in the questionnaire primaries. *Multivariate Behavioral Research,* 1973, **8**, 173–194.

CATTELL, R. B., and Dreger, R. M. (Eds.), *Handbook of modern personality theory.* Washington: Hemisphere, 1977.

CATTELL, R. B., and Eber, H. W. *Handbook for the Sixteen Personality Factor Questionnaire: The 16 PF Test.* Champaign, Ill.: Institute for Personality and Ability Testing. 1957, 1962.

CATTELL, R. B., Eber, H. W., and Tatsuoka, M. M. *Handbook for the 16 PF Questionnaire.* Champaign, Ill.: IPAT, 1970.

CATTELL, R. B., and Luborsky, L. B. P-technique demonstrated as a new clinical method for determining personality and symptom structure. *Journal of General Psychology,* 1950, **42**, 3–24.

CATTELL, R. B., and Nichols, K. E. An improved definition, from 10 researchers, of second order personality factors in Q data (with cross-cultural checks). *Journal of Social Psychology,* 1972, **86**, 187–203.

CATTELL, R. B., Radcliffe, J. A., and Sweeney, A. B. The nature and measurement of components of motivation. *Genetic Psychology Monographs,* 1963, **68**, 49–211.

CATTELL, R. B., Radcliffe, J. A., and Sweeney, A. B. Components in motivation strength in children compared with those in adults. *Journal of Genetic Psychology,* 1964, **70**, 65–1112.

CATTELL, R. B., and Rickels, K. Diagnostic power of IPAT objective anxiety neuroticism tests. *Archives of General Psychiatry,* 1964, **11**, 459–465.

CATTELL, R. B., Rickels, K., Weise, C., Gray, B., and Yee, R. The effects of psychotherapy upon measured anxiety and regression. *American Journal of Psychotherapy,* 1966, **20**, 261–269.

CATTELL, R. B., and Scheier, I. H. *The meaning and measurement of neuroticism and anxiety.* New York: Ronald, 1961.

CATTELL, R. B., and Stice, G. F., *Handbook for the sixteen personality factor questionnaire.* Champaign, Ill.: Institute for Personality and Ability Testing, 1962.

CATTELL, R. B., and Tatro, D. F. The personality factors, objectively measured, which distinguish psychotics from normals. *Behavior Research and Therapy*, 1966, **4**, 39–51.

CATTELL, R. B., and Warburton, F. W. A cross-cultural comparison of patterns of extraversion and anxiety. *British Journal of Psychology*, 1961, **52**, 375.

CAUTELA, J. R., and Kastenbaum, R. A reinforcement survey schedule for use in therapy, training and research. *Psychological Reports*, 1967, **20**, 1115–1130.

CHODORKOFF, B. Self perception, perceptual defense, and adjustment. *Journal of Abnormal and Social Psychology*, 1954, **49**, 508–512.

CIMINERO, A. R. Behavioral assessment: An overview. In A. R. Ciminero, K. S. Calhoun, and H. E. Adams (Eds.), *Handbook of behavioral assessment*. New York: Wiley, 1977. Pp. 3–14.

CIMINERO, A. R., Calhoun, K. S., and Adams, H. E. (Eds.), *Handbook of behavioral assessment*. New York: Wiley, 1977.

CLEAVER, E. *Soul on ice*. New York: Dell, 1968.

COAN, R. W. Child personality and developmental psychology, In R. B. Cattell (Ed.), *Handbook of multivariate experimental psychology*. Chicago: Rand McNally, 1966. Pp. 732–752.

COAN, R. W. Dimensions of psychological theory. *American Psychologist*, 1968, **23**, 715–722.

COHEN, J. The impact of multivariate research in clinical psychology. In R. B. Cattell (Ed.), *Handbook of multivariate experimental psychology*. Chicago: Rand McNally, 1966. Pp. 856–875.

COHEN, Y. A. A study of interpersonal relations in a Jamaican community. Unpublished doctoral dissertation, Yale University, 1953.

COLE, J. K., Landfield, A. W. (Eds.), *Personal construct psychology. Nebraska symposium on motivation*. Lincoln: Univ. of Nebraska Press, 1976.

COMBS, A. W., and Super, D. W. The self, its derivative terms, and research. *Journal of Individual Psychology*, 1957, **13**, 134–145.

COOKE, G. Evaluation of efficacy of the components of reciprocal inhibition psychotherapy. *Journal of Abnormal Psychology*, 1968, **73**, 464–467.

COOPERSMITH, S. *The antecedents of self-esteem*. San Francisco: W. H. Freeman, 1967.

CRAIGHEAD, W. E., Kazdin, A. E., and Mahoney, M. J. *Behavior modifications: Principles, issues, and applications*. Boston: Houghton Mifflin, 1976.

CROCKETT, W. H. Cognitive complexity and impression formation. In B. A. Maher (Ed.), *Progress in experimental personality research*. New York: Academic Press, 1965. Pp. 47–90.

CRONBACH, L. J. The two disciplines of scientific psychology. *American Psychologist*, 1957, **12**, 671–684.

CRONBACH, L. J. *Essentials of psychological testing*. New York: Harper, 1960.

CRONBACH, L. J., and Meehl, P. E. Construct validity in psychological tests. *Psychological Bulletin*, 1955, **52**, 281–302.

CROWNE, D. P. Review of R. B. Cattell, the scientific life, analysis of personality. *Comtemporary Psychology*, 1967, **12**, 40–41.

CROWNE, D. P., and Marlowe, D. *The approval motive: Studies in evaluative dependence*. New York: Wiley, 1964.

CROWNE, D. P., and Stephens, M. W. Critique of self-concept methodology. *Psychological Bulletin*, 1961, **58**, 104–121.

DAMARIN, F. Personal communication, 1969.

DAMARIN, F. L., and Cattell, R. B. Personality factors in early childhood and their relation to intelligence. *Monographs of the Society for Research in Child Development*, 1968, **33**, 1–95.

DANA, R. H. Review of the Rorschach. In O. K. Buros (Ed.), *The sixth mental measurements yearbook*. Highland Park, N.J.: Gryphon Press, 1965. Pp. 492–495.

DASHIELL, J. F. Some rapproachments in contemporary psychology. *Psychological Bulletin*, 1939, **36**, 1–24.

DAVIDS, A. Comparison of three methods of personality assessment: Direct, indirect and projective. *Journal of Personality*, 1955, **23**, 423 440.

DAVIDS, A., and Pildner, H., Jr. Comparison of direct and projective methods of personality assessment under differing conditions of motivation. *Psychological Monographs*, 1958, **72**, (11, Whole No. 464).

DAVISON, G. C. Systematic desensitization as a counterconditioning process. *Journal of Abnormal Psychology*, 1968, **73**, 91–99.

DAVISON, G. C., and Wilson, T. Critique of desensitization: Social and cognitive factors underlying the effectiveness of Wolpe's procedure. *Psychological Bulletin*, 1972, **78**, 28–31.

DAVISON, G. C., and Wilson, G. T. Processes of fear-reduction in systematic desensitization: Cognitive and social reinforcement factors in humans. *Behavior Therapy*, 1973, **4**, 1–21.

DEUTSCH, F., and Murphy, W. F. *The clinical interview*. New York: International Universities Press, 1955.

DEUTSCH, M., and Krauss, R. M. *Theories in social psychology*. New York: Basic Books, 1965.

DE VELLIS, R. F., DeVellis, B. M., and McCauley, C. Vicarious acquisition of learned helplessness. *Journal of Personality and Social Psychology*, 1978, **36**, 894–899.

DIGGORY, J. C. *Self-evaluation*. New York: Wiley, 1966.

DIVEN, K. Certain determinants in the conditioning of anxiety reactions. *Journal of Psychology*, 1937, **3**, 291–308.

DOLLARD, J., Doob, L. W., Miller, N. E., Mowrer, O H., and Sears, R. R. *Frustration and aggression*. New Haven, Conn.: Yale, 1939.

DOLLARD, J., and Miller, N. E. *Personality and psychotherapy*. New York: McGraw-Hill, 1950.

DYMOND, Rosalind F. Adjustment changes over therapy from self-sorts In C. R. Rogers and Rosalind F. Dymond (Eds.), *Psychotherapy and personality change*. Chicago: University of Chicago Press, 1954. Pp. 76–84. (a)

DYMOND, Rosalind F. Adjustment changes over therapy from thematic apperception test ratings. In C. R. Rogers and R. F. Dymond (Eds.), *Psychotherapy and personality change*. Chicago: University of Chicago Press, 1954. Pp. 109–120. (b)

EAGER, Joan, and Smith, M. B. A note on the validity of Sanford's Authoritarian-Equalitarian scale. *Journal of Abnormal and Social Psychology*, 1952, **47**, 265–267.

EAGLE, M., Wolitzky, D. L., and Klein, G. S. Imagery: Effect of a concealed figure in a stimulus. *Science*, 1966, **18**, 837–839.

EDUCATIONAL AND INDUSTRIAL TESTING SERVICE. 1967 catalog of tests, books, and guidance materials. San Diego, California, 1967.

EDWARDS, A. L. The relationship between the judged desirability of a trait and the probability that the trait will be endorsed. *Journal of Applied Psychology*, 1953, **37**, 90–93.

EDWARDS, A. L. Social desirability and personality test construction. In B. M. Bass and I. A. Berg (Eds.), *Objective approaches to personality*. Princeton, N.J.: Van Nostrand, 1959. Pp. 101–116.

ENDLER, N. S., Hunt, J. McV., and Rosenstein, A. J. An S-R inventory of anxiousness. *Psychological Monographs*, 1962, **76**, (17, Whole No. 536).

ENDLER, N. S., and Magnusson, D. (Eds.), *Interactional psychology and personality*. Washington, D.C.: Hemisphere (Halsted-Wiley), 1976.

ENGEL, Mary. The stability of the self-concept in adolescence, *Journal of Abnormal and Social Psychology*, 1959, **58**, 211–215.

EPSTEIN, S. The stability of behavior: I. On predicting most of the people most of the time. *Journal of Personality and Social Psychology*, 1979, in press.

ERIKSON, E. *Childhood and society*. New York: Norton, 1950.

EVANS, R. I. *The making of psychology*. New York: Knopf, 1976.

EYSENCK, H. J. *Dimensions of personality*, London: Routledge & Kegan Paul, 1947. (Reprinted by permission.)

EYSENCK, H. J. The organization of personality. *Journal of Personality*, 1951, **20**, 101–117.

EYSENCK, H. J. *The scientific study of personality*. London: Routledge & Kegan Paul, 1952.

EYSENCK, H. J. A dynamic theory of anxiety and hysteria. *Journal of Mental Science*, 1955, **101**, 28–51.

EYSENCK, H. J. The inheritance of extraversion-introversion. *Acta Psychologica*, 1956, **12**, 429–432.

EYSENCK, H. *Sense and nonsense in psychology*. Baltimore: Penguin, 1957.

EYSENCK, H. J. Learning theory and behavior therapy. *Journal of Mental Science*, 1959, **105**, 61–75.

EYSENCK, H. J. (Ed.). *Handbook of abnormal psychology*. New York: Basic Books, 1961.

EYSENCK, H. J. *The structure of human personality*. London: Methuen, 1970. (Reprinted by permission.)

EYSENCK, H. J. *Eysenck on extraversion*. London: Crosby, Lockwood, Staples, 1973.

EYSENCK, H. J. *The inequality of man.* San Diego: Edits Publishers, 1975.

EYSENCK, H. J. Personality and factor analysis: A reply to Guildord. *Psychological Bulletin*, 1977, **84**, 405–411.

EYSENCK, H. J., and Beech, H. R. Counter conditioning and related methods. In A. E. Bergin and S. Garfield (Eds.), *Handbook of psychotherapy and behavior change.* New York: Wiley, 1971. Pp. 543–611.

EYSENCK, H. J., and Rachman, S. *The causes and cures of neurosis.* San Diego, Calif.: Knapp, 1965.

EYSENCK, H. J., and Wilson, G. D. *The experimental study of Freudian theories.* London: Methuen, 1973.

FELDMAN, M. P. Aversion therapy for sexual deviations: A critical review. *Psychological Bulletin*, 1966, **65**, 65–79.

FERSTER, C. B. Classification of behavioral pathology. In L. Krasner and L. P. Ullman (Eds.), *Research in behavior modification.* New York: Holt, Rinehart and Winston, 1965. Pp. 6–26.

FERSTER, C. B. A functional analysis of depression. *American Psychologist*, 1973, **28**, 857–870.

FESHBACH, S. The stimulating effects of a vicarious aggressive activity. *Journal of Abnormal and Social Psychology*, 1961, **63**, 381–385.

FESTINGER, L. *A theory of cognitive dissonance.* Evanston, Ill.: Row, Peterson, 1957.

FESTINGER, L., and Bramel, D. The reactions of humans to cognitive dissonance. In A. J. Bachrach (Ed.), *Experimental foundations of clinical psychology.* New York: Basic Books, 1962. Pp. 254–279.

FIEDLER, F. E. A comparison of therapeutic relationships in psychoanalytic, non-directive, and Adlerian therapy. *Journal of Consulting Psychology*, 1950, **14**, 436–445.

FIEDLER, F. E. Engineer the job to fit the manager. *Harvard Business Review*, 1965, **43**, 115–122.

FISHER, A. E. Unpublished doctoral dissertation. Pennsylvania State University, 1955.

FISHER, S. Rorschach patterns in conversion hysteria. *Journal of Projective Techniques*, 1951, **15**, 98–108.

FISHER, S., and Greenberg, R. P. *The scientific credibility of Freud's theories and therapy.* New York: Basic Books, 1977.

FISKE, D. W., and Maddi, S. R. (Eds.). *Functions of varied experience.* Homewood, Ill.: 1961.

FISKE, D.W. *Strategies for personality research.* San Francisco: Jossey-Bass, 1978.

FISKE, D. W., and Goodman, G. The post therapy period. *Journal of Abnormal Psychology*, 1965, **70**, 169–179.

FOLKINS, C., Lawson, Karen D., Opton, E. M., Jr., and Lazarus, R. S. Desensitization and the experimental reduction of threat. *Journal of Abnormal Psychology*, 1968, **73**, 100–113.

FORD, D. H., and Urban, H. B. *Systems of psychotherapy.* New York: Wiley, 1963.

FORER, B. R. The fallacy of personal validation: a classroom demonstration of gullibility. *Journal of Abnormal and Social Psychology*, 1949, **44**, 118–123.

FRANK, L. K. Projective methods for the study of personality. *Journal of Psychology*, 1939, **8**, 389–413.

FRANKS, C. M. Reflections upon the treatment of sexual disorders by the behavioral clinician: An historical comparison with the treatment of the alcoholic. *Journal of Sex Research*, 1967, **3**, 212–222.

FRANKS, C. M., and Wilson, G. T. (Eds.), *Annual review of behavior therapy, theory, and practice.* New York: Brunner/Mazel, 1978.

FREUD, S. *Three essays on sexuality.* London: Hogarth, 1953. Original edition, 1905.

FREUD, S. Psycho-analytic notes upon an autobiographical account of a case of paranoia (dementia paranoides). In *Collected Papers*, Vol. III. New York: Basic Books, 1959. Originally published in 1911.

FREUD, S. *A general introduction to psychoanalysis.* New York: Permabooks, 1953. Boni & Liveright edition, 1924.

FREUD, S. *Civilization and its discontents.* London: Hogarth, 1949. Original edition, 1930.

FREUD, S. *New introductory lectures on psychoanalysis.* New York: Norton, 1933.

FREUD, S. An outline of psychoanalysis. *International Journal of Psychoanalysis*, 1940, **21**, 27–84.

FROMM, E. *Sigmund Freud's mission.* New York: Harper, 1959.

GARDNER, R. W., Jackson, D. N., and Messick, S. J. Personality organization in cognitive controls and intellectual abilities. *Psychological Issues*, 1960, Monograph No. 8.

GARFIELD, S. L., and Bergin, A. E. *Handbook of psycho-*

therapy and behavior change, 2d ed. New York: Wiley, 1978,

Geer, J. H., and Turteltaub, A. Fear reduction following observation of a model. *Journal of Personality and Social Psychology*, 1967, **6**, 327–331.

GENDLIN, E. T. Client-centered developments and work with schizophrenics. *Journal of Counseling Psychology*, 1962, **9**, 205–211.

GEWIRTZ, J. L. The role of stimulation in models for child development. In Laura L. Dittmann (Ed.), *Early child care: The new perspectives*. New York: Atherton, 1968. Pp. 139–168. (a)

GEWIRTZ, J. L. On designing the functional environment of the child to facilitate behavioral development. In Laura L. Dittmann (Ed.), *Early child care: The new perspectives*. New York: Atherton, 1968, Pp. 169–213.(b)

GEWIRTZ, J. L. Conditional responding as a paradigm for observational, imitative learning and vicarious imitative learning and vicarious reinforcement. In H. W. Reese (Ed.), *Advances in child development and behavior*. New York: Academic Press, 1971. Pp. 274–304.

GILMORE, J. Toward an understanding of imitation. In E. C. Simmerl, R. A. Hoppe, and G. A. Milton (Eds.), *Social facilitation and imitative behavior*. Boston: Allyn and Bacon, 1968. Pp. 217–238.

GLASS, D. C. *Behavior patterns, stress, and coronary disease*. Hillsdale, N.J.: Lawrence Erlbaum, 1977.

GLASS, D. C., and Singer, J. E. *Urban stress*. New York: Academic Press, 1972.

GLUCKSBERG, S., and King, L. J. Motivated forgetting mediated by implicit verbal chaining: A laboratory analog of repression. *Science*, October 27, 1967, 517–519.

GOFFMAN, E. *The presentation of self in everyday life*. Garden City, N.Y.: Doubleday, 1959.

GOLDFRIED, M. R., and Davison, G. C. *Clinical behavior therapy*. New York: Holt, Rinehart and Winston, 1976.

GOLDSTEIN, K. *The organism*. New York: American Book Co., 1939.

GORDON, J. E. Review of R. B. Cattell's Personality and social psychology. *Contemporary Psychology*, 1966, **11**, 236–238.

GOTTESMAN, I. I., and Shields, J. Schizophrenia in twins: 16 years' consecutive admissions to a psychiatric clinic. *British Journal of Psychiatry*, 1966, **112**, 809–818.

GOUGH, H. G. Clinical versus statistical prediction in psychology. In L. Postman (Ed.), *Psychology in the making*. New York: Knopf, 1962. Pp. 526–584.

GREENE, M.A. Client perception of the relationship as a function of worker-client cognitive styles. Unpublished doctoral dissertation, Columbia University School of Social Work, 1972.

GREENSPAN, S. I. A consideration of some learning variables in the context of psychoanalytic learning perspective. *Psychological Issues*, 1975, **9**, Monograph No. 33.

GREENSPOON, J. The reinforcing effects of two spoken sounds on the frequency of two responses. *American Journal of Psychology*, 1955, **68**, 409–416.

GREENSPOON, J. Verbal conditioning and clinical psychology. In A. J. Bachrach (Ed.), *Experimental foundations of clinical psychology*. New York: Basic Books, 1962. Pp. 510–553.

GRINKER, R. R., and Spiegel, J. P. *Men under stress*. Philadelphia: Blakiston, 1945.

GRODDECK, G. *The book of the it*. New York: Vintage, 1961. Original edition 1923.

GRUMMON, D. L., and John, Eve S. Changes over client-centered therapy evaluated on psychoanalytically based TAT scales. In C. R. Rogers and R. F. Dymond (Eds.), *Psychotherapy and Personality Change*. Chicago: University of Chicago Press, 1954. Pp. 121–144.

GUILFORD, J. P. Factors and factors of personality. *Psychological Bulletin*, 1975, **82**, 802–814.

GUMP, P. V. A statistical investigation of one psychoanalytic approach and a comparison of it with nondirective therapy. Unpublished M.A. thesis, Ohio State University, 1944.

GUR, R. C., and Sackeim, H. A. Self-deception: A concept in search of a phenomenon. *Journal of Personality and Social Psychology*, 1979, **37**, 147–169.

GYNTHER, M. D. White norms and black MMPIs: A prescription for discrimination? *Psychological Bulletin*, 1972, **78**, 386–402.

HAIGH, G. Defensive behavior in client-centered therapy. *Journal of Consulting Psychology*, 1949, **13**, 181–189.

HAIMOWITZ, Natalie R. An investigation into some personality changes occurring in individuals undergoing client-centered therapy. Unpublished Ph.D. dissertation, University of Chicago, 1948.

HALKIDES, G. An experimental study of four conditions necessary for therapeutic change. Unpublished doctoral dissertation, University of Chicago, 1958.

HALL, C. S. *A primer of Freudian psychology.* New York: Mentor, 1954.

HALL, C. S., and Lindzey, G. *Theories of personality.* New York: Wiley, 1957.

HARLOW, H. F. Mice, monkeys, men, and motives. *Psychological Review*, 1953, **60**, 23–32.

HARLOW, H. F. The nature of love. *American Psychologist*, 1958, **13**, 673–685.

HARLOW, H. F. The heterosexual affectional system in monkeys. *American Psychologist*, 1962, **17**, 1–9.

HARRIS, B. Whatever happened to Little Albert? *American Psychologist*, 1979, **34**, 151–160.

HARRIS, J. G., Jr. Validity: The search for a constant in a universe of variables. In M. A. Rickers-Ovsiankina (Ed.), *Rorschach psychology.* New York: Wiley, 1960. Pp. 380–439.

HARRISON, R. Cognitive change and participation in a sensitivity-training laboratory. *Journal of Consulting Psychology*, 1966, **30**, 517–520.

HARTSHORNE, H., and May, M. A. *Studies in the nature of character: Studies in deceit.* New York: Macmillan, 1928.

HATHAWAY, S. R., and McKinley, J. C. *Manual for the Minnesota Multiphasic Personality Inventory.* New York: Psychological Corporation, 1943.

HAUGHTON, E., and Ayllon, T. Production and elimination of symptomatic behavior. In L. P. Ullmann and L. Krasner (Eds.), *Case studies in behavior modification.* New York: Holt, Rinehart and Winston, 1965, Pp. 94–98.

HAVENER, P. H., and Izard, C. E. Unrealistic self-enhancement in paranoid schizophrenics. *Journal of Consulting Psychology*, 1962, **26**, 65–68.

HAVENS, L. Review of D. Wyss, Psychoanalytic schools from the beginning to the present. *Psychotherapy and the Social Science Review*, July 13, 1973.

HAWKINS, R. P., Peterson, R. F., Schweid, E., and Bijou, S. W. Behavior therapy in the home: Amelioration of problem parent-child relations with the parent in a therapeutic role. *Journal of Experimental Child Psychology*, 1966, **4**, 99–107.

HEBB, D. O. The role of neurological ideas in psychology. *Journal of Personality*, 1951, **20**, 39–55.

HEINE, R. W. An investigation of the relationship between change in personality from psychotherapy as reported by patients and the factors seen by patients as producing change. Unpublished doctoral dissertation, University of Chicago, 1950.

HELPER, M. M. Learning theory and the self concept. *Journal of Abnormal and Social Psychology*, 1955, **51**, 184–194.

HELPER, M. M. Parental evaluations of children and children's self-evaluations. *Journal of Abnormal and Social Psychology*, 1958, **56**, 190–194.

HENDRICK, I. *Facts and theories of psychoanalysis.* New York: Knopf, 1934.

HENDRICK, I. The discussion of the "instinct to master." *Psychoanalytic Quarterly*, 1943, **12**, 561–565.

HERBERT, E. W., Pinkston, E. M., Hayden, M. L., Sajwaj, T. E., Pinkston, S., Cordua, G., and Jackson, C. Adverse effects of differential parental attention. *Journal of Applied Behavior Analysis*, 1973, **6**, 15–30.

HERRNSTEIN, R. J. The evolution of behaviorism. *American Psychologist*, 1977, **32**, 593–602.

HESSE, H. *Siddhartha.* New York: New Directions, 1951.

HESSE, H. *Demian.* New York: Harper, 1965. Originally published in 1925.

HILGARD, E. R. Human motives and the concept of self. *American Psychologist*, 1949, **4**, 374–382.

HILL, W. F. Learning theory and the acquisition of values. *Psychological Review*, 1960, **67**, 317–331.

HINKLE, D. N. The change of personal constructs from the viewpoint of a theory of implications. Unpublished doctoral dissertation, Ohio State University, 1965.

HIROTO, D. S. Locus of control and learned helplessness. *Journal of Experimental Psychology*, 1974, **102**, 187–193. (Copyright 1974 by the American Psychological Association. Reprinted by permission.)

HIROTO, D. S., and Seligman, M. E. P. Generality of learned helplessness in man. *Journal of Personality and Social Psychology*, 1975, **31**, 311–327.

HITT, W. D. Two models of man. *American Psychologist*, 1969, **24**, 651–658.

HOFFMAN, A. E. A study of reported behavior changes in counseling. *Journal of Consulting Psychology*, 1949, **13**, 190–195.

HOLDSTOCK, T. L., and Rogers, C. R. Person-centered theory. In R. J. Corsini (Ed.), *Current personality theories.* Itasca, Ill.: Peacock, 1977, Pp. 125–152.

HOLMES, D. S. Projection as a defense mechanism. *Psychological Bulletin*, 1978, **85**, 677–688.

HOLT, R. R. Clinical and statistical prediction: A reformulation and some new data. *Journal of Abnormal and Social Psychology*, 1958, **56**, 1–17.

HOLT, R. R. A clinical-experimental strategy for research in personality. In S. Messick and J. Ross (Eds.), *Measurement in personality and cognition.* New York: Wiley, 1962. Pp. 269–283. (a)

HOLT, R. R. Individuality and generalization in the psychology of personality: An evaluation. *Journal of Personality*, 1962, **30**, 377–402. (b)

HOLT, R. R. Assessing personality. In I. L. Janis, G. F. Mahl, J. Kagan, and R. R. Holt (Eds.), *Personality.* New York: Harcourt, Brace, 1968. Pp. 577–801.

HOLT, R. R. *Methods in clinical psychology.* New York: Plenum, 1978.

HOLTZMAN, W. H. Methodological issues in P technique. *Psychological Bulletin*, 1962, **59**, 248–256.

HOLTZMAN, W. H., and Sells, S. B. Prediction of flying success by clinical analysis of test protocols. *Journal of Abnormal and Social Psychology*, 1954, **49**, 485–490.

HOLZMAN, P. S., and Gardner, R. W. Leveling and regression. *Journal of Abnormal and Social Psychology*, 1959, **59**, 151–155.

HONIKMAN, B. Construct theory as an approach to architectural and environmental design. In P. Slater (Ed.), *Explorations of intrapersonal space.* New York: Wiley, 1976. Pp. 167–182.

HORN, J. L. Motivation and the dynamic calculus concepts from multivariate experiment. In R. B. Cattell (Ed.), *Handbook of multivariate experimental psychology.* Chicago: Rand McNally, 1966. Pp. 611–641.

HORNEY, K. *The neurotic personality of our time.* New York: Norton, 1937.

HORNEY, K. *Feminine psychology.* New York: Norton, 1973.

HORNEY, Karen. *Our inner conflicts.* New York: Norton, 1945.

HOWARTH, E. Factor analysis has only just begun to fight — a reply to Lykken. *Journal of Experimental Research in Personality*, 1972, **6**, 268–272. (a)

HOWARTH, E. A factor analysis of selected markers for objective personality factors. *Multivariate Behavioral Research*, 1972, **7**, 451–476.(b)

HULL, C. L. *Mathematico-deductive theory of rote learning.* New Haven, Conn.: Yale, 1940.

HULL, C. L. *Principles of behavior.* New York: Appleton, 1943.

HULL, C. L. Autobiography. In E. G. Boring, H. S. Langfeld, H. Werner, and R. M. Yerkes (Eds.), *A history of psychology in autobiography.* Worcester, Mass.: Clark University Press, 1952, Pp. 143–162.

HUNDLEBY, J. D., Pawlik, K., and Cattell, R. B. *Personality factors in objective test devices: A critical integration of a quarter of a century's research.* San Diego, Calif.: Knapp, 1965.

HUNT, J. McV. Effects of infant feeding-frustration upon adult hoarding in the Albino rat. *Journal of Abnormal and Social Psychology*, 1941, **36**, 338–360.

HUNT, J. McV. Traditional personality theory in the light of recent evidence. *American Scientist*, 1965, **53**, 80–96.

HUNT, J. McV. Psychological development: Early experience. *Annual Review of Psychology*, 1979, **30**, 103–144.

HUNTLEY, C. W. Judgments of self based upon records of expressive behavior. *Journal of Abnormal and Social Psychology*, 1940, **35**, 398–427.

ICHHEISER, G. Misinterpretation of personality in everyday life and the psychologist's frame of reference. *Character and Personality*, 1943, **12**, 145–152.

JACKSON, D. N., and Messick, S. Content and style in personality assessment. *Psychological Bulletin*, 1958, **55**, 243–252.

JANIS, I. L. Psychodynamic aspects of stress tolerance. In S. Z. Klausner (Ed.), *The quest for self-control.* New York: Free Press, 1965. Pp. 215–247.

JASPARS, J. M. F. Individual cognitive structures. *Proceedings of the seventeenth international con-*

gress of psychology. Amsterdam: North-Holland, 1964.

JENSEN, A. R. Personality. *Annual Review of Psychology,* 1958, **9**, 295–322.

JENSEN, A. R. Review of the Maudsley Personality Inventory, In O. K. Buros (Ed.), *Sixth mental measurements yearbook.* Highland Park, N.J.: Gryphon Press, 1965. Pp. 288–291.

JONES, E. *The life and work of Sigmund Freud,* Vol. 1. New York: Basic Books, 1953; Vol. 2, 1955; Vol. 3, 1957.

JONES, Mary C. A laboratory study of fear. The case of Peter. *Pedagogical Seminar,* 1924, **31**, 308–315.

JONIETZ, Alice K. A study of the phenomenological changes in perception after psychotherapy as exhibited in the content of Rorschach percepts. Unpublished Ph.D. dissertation, University of Chicago, 1950.

JOURARD, S. M., and Remy, R. M. Perceived parental attitudes, the self, and security. *Journal of Consulting Psychology,* 1955, **19**, 364–366.

JUNG, C. G. *The integration of the personality.* New York: Farrar & Rinehart, 1939.

KAGAN, J. Personality development. In P. London and D. Rosenhan (Eds.), *Foundations of abnormal psychology.* New York: Holt, Rinehart and Winston, 1968. Pp. 117–173.

KAGAN, J. Emergent themes in human development. *American Scientist,* 1976, **64**, 186–196.

KAGAN, J., and Moss, H. A. *Birth to maturity.* New York: Wiley, 1962.

KAHN, M. W. Clinical and statistical prediction revisited. *Journal of Clinical Psychology,* 1960, **26**, 115–118.

KAHN, M., and Baker, B. Desensitization with minimal therapist contact, *Journal of Abnormal Psychology,* 1968, **73**, 198–200.

KALISH, H. I. Behavior therapy, In B. B. Wolman (Ed.), *Handbook of clinical psychology.* New York: McGraw-Hill, 1965.

KALLMANN, F. J. The genetic theory of schizophrenia. *American Journal of Psychiatry,* 1946, **103**, 309–322.

KAMIN, L. J. *The science and politics of I.Q.* Hillsdale, N.J.: Erlbaum, 1974.

KANFER, F. H., and Karoly, P. Self-control: A behavior-

istic excursion into the lion's den. *Behavior Therapy,* 1972, **3**, 398–416.

KANFER, F. H., and Phillips, J. S. *Learning foundations of behavior therapy.* New York: Wiley, 1970.

KANFER, F. H., and Saslow, G. Behavioral analysis: An alternative to diagnostic classification. *Archives of General Psychiatry,* 1965, **12**, 519–538.

KARON, B. P. Projective tests are valid. *American Psychologist,* 1978, **33**, 764–765.

KATAHN, M., and Koplin, J. H. Paradigm clash. *Psychological Bulletin,* 1968, **69**, 147–148.

KATZ, Phyllis, and Zigler, E. Self-image disparity: a developmental approach. Journal of Personality and Social Psychology, 1967, **5**, 186–195.

KAZDIN, A. E. *The token economy: A review and evaluation.* New York: Plenum, 1977.

KAZDIN, A. E., and Bootzin, R. R. The token economy: An evaluative review. *Journal of Applied Behavior Analysis,* 1972 **5**, 343–372.

KAZDIN, A. E., and Rogers, T. On paradigms and recycled ideologies: Analogue research revisited. *Cognitive Therapy and Research,* 1978, **2**, 105–117.

KAZDIN, A. E., and Wilcoxon, L. A. Systematic desensitization and nonspecific treatment effects: A methodological evaluation. *Psychological Bulletin,* 1976, **83**, 729–758.

KAZDIN, A. E., and Wilson, G. T. *Evaluation of behavior theory: Issues, evidence, and research strategies.* Cambridge, Mass.: Ballinger, 1978.

KELLY, E. L. Consistency of the adult personality. *American Psychologist,* 1955, **10**, 659–681.

KELLY, E. L., and Fiske, D. W. *The prediction of performance in clinical psychology.* Ann Arbor: University of Michigan Press, 1951.

KELLY, G. A. *The psychology of personal constructs.* New York: Norton, 1955.

KELLY, G. A. Man's construction of his alternatives. In G. Lindzey (Ed.), *Assessment of human motives.* New York: Holt, Rinehart and Winston, 1958. Pp. 33–64. (a)

KELLY, G. The theory and technique of assessment. *Annual Review of Psychology,* 1958, **9**, 323–352. (b)

KELLY, G. A. Suicide: The personal construct point of view. In N. L. Faberow and E. S. Schneidman (Eds.), *The cry for help.* New York: McGraw-Hill, 1961. Pp. 255–280.

KELLY, G. A. Non-parametric factor analysis of personality theories. *Journal of Individual Psychology*, 1963, **19**, 115–147.

KELLY, G. A. The language of hypothesis: Man's psychological instrument. *Journal of Individual Psychology*, 1964, **20**, 137–152.

KESSLER, Carol. Semantics and non-directive counseling. Unpublished M. A. thesis, University of Chicago, 1947.

KLEIN, G. S. The personal world through perception. In R. R. Blake and G. V. Ramsey (Eds.), *Perception: An approach to personality*. New York: Ronald, 1951. Pp. 328–355.

KLEIN, G. S. Need and regulation. In M. R. Jones (Ed.), *Nebraska symposium on motivation*. Lincoln: Nebraska University Press, 1954. Pp. 224–274.

KLEIN, G. S. *Perception, motives and personality*. New York: Knopf, 1970.

KLEIN, G. S. *Psychoanalytic theory: An exploration of essentials*. New York: International Universities Press, 1976.

KLEIN, G. S., Barr, Harriet L., and Wolitzky, D. L. Personality. *Annual Review of Psychology*, 1967, **18**, 467–560.

KLEIN, G. S., and Krech, D. The problem of personality and its theory. Journal of Personality, 1951, **20**, 2–23.

KLEINMUNTZ, B. *Personality measurement*, Homewood, Ill.: Dorsey, 1967.

KLINE, P. *Fact and fantasy in Freudian theory*. London: Methuen, 1972.

KLOPFER, W. G., and Taulbee, E. S. Projective tests. *Annual Review of Psychology*, 1976, **27**, 543–

KLUCKHOHN, C. *Mirror for man*. New York: McGraw-Hill, 1949.

KLUCKHOHN, C. Culture and behavior. In G. Lindzey (Ed.), *Handbook of social psychology*. Cambridge, Mass.: Addison-Wesley, 1954. Pp. 921–976.

KLUCKHOHN, C., and Morgan, W. Some notes on Navaho dreams. In G. B. Wilbur and W. Muensterberger (Eds.), *Psychoanalysis and culture*. New York: International Universities Press, 1951. Pp. 120–131.

KOHUT, H. *The analysis of the self*. New York: International Universities Press, 1971.

KOHUT, H. *The restoration of the self*. New York: International Universities Press, 1977.

KRASNER, L. The behavioral scientist and social responsibility: No place to hide. *Journal of Social Issues*, 1965, **21**, 9–30.

KRASNER, L. Token economy as an illustration of operant conditioning procedures with the aged, with youth, and with society. In D. J. Levis (Ed.), *Learning approaches to therapeutic behavior change*. Chicago: Aldine, 1970. Pp. 74–101.

KRASNER, L. Behavior therapy. *Annual Review of Psychology*. Palo Alto, Calif.: Annual Reviews, 1971, Pp. 483–532. (a)

KRASNER, L. The operant approach in behavior therapy. In A. E. Bergin and S. L. Garfield (Eds.), *Handbook of psychotherapy and behavior change*. New York: Wiley, 1971. Pp. 612–652. (b)

KRASNER, L., and Ullmann, L. P. *Behavior influence and personality*. New York: Holt, Rinehart and Winston, 1973.

KRECH, D., and Crutchfield, R. S. *Elements of psychology*. New York: Knopf, 1958.

KRIS, E. Danger and morale. *American Journal of Orthopsychiatry*, 1944, **14**, 147–155.

KUHN, T. S. *The structure of scientific revolutions*, 2d ed. Chicago: University of Chicago Press, 1970.

LACEY, J. I. The evaluation of autonomic responses: Toward a general solution. *Annals of the New York Academy of Science*, 1956, **67**, 123–164.

LAMBERT, M. J. DeJulio, S. S., and Stein, D. M. Therapist interpersonal skills: Process, outcome, methodological considerations and recommendations for future research. *Psychological Bulletin*, 1978, **85**, 467–489.

LANDFIELD, A. W. *Personal construct systems in psychotherapy*. Chicago: Rand McNally, 1971.

LANDFIELD, A. W. (Ed.), *1976 Nebraska symposium on motivation*. Lincoln: University of Nebraska Press, 1977.

LANG, P. J. Stimulus control, response control, and the desensitization of fear. In D. J. Levis (Ed.), *Learning approaches to therapeutic behavior change*. Chicago: Aldine, 1970. Pp. 148–173.

LANG, P. J. The application of psycho-physiological methods to the study of psychotherapy and behavior modification. In A. E. Bergin and S. Garfield (Eds.), *Handbook of psychotherapy and behavior change*. New York: Wiley, 1971, Pp. 75–125.

LANG, P. J., and Lazovik, A. D. Experimental desensitization of a phobic. *Journal of Abnormal and Social Psychology*, 1963, **66**, 519 525.

LANGER, E. J., Janis, I. L., and Wolfer, J. A. Reduction of psychological stress in surgical patients. *Journal of Experimental Social Psychology*, 1975, **11**, 155–165.

LANGER, E. J., and Robin, J. The effects of choice and enhanced personal responsibility for the aged: A field experiment in an institutional setting. *Journal of Personality and Social Psychology*, 1978, **34**, 191–198.

LANGNER, T. S., and Michael, S. T. *Life stress and mental health*. New York: Free Press, 1963.

LAZARUS, A. A. Behavior therapy, incomplete treatment and symptom substitution. *Journal of Nervous and Mental Disease*, 1965, **140**, 80–86.

LAZARUS, A. A. Learning theory and the treatment of depression. *Behavior Research and Therapy*, 1968, **6**, 83–89.

LAZARUS, A. A. *Behavior therapy and beyond*. New York: McGraw-Hill 1971.

LAZARUS, A. A. Has behavior therapy outlived its usefulness? *American Psychologist*, 1977, **32**, 550–554.

LAZARUS, A. A., and Davison, G. C. Clinical innovation in research and practice. In A. E. Bergin and S. L. Garfield (Eds.), *Handbook of psychotherapy and behavior change*. New York: Wiley, 1971. Pp. 196–213.

LAZARUS, R. S., and McCleary, R. A. Autonomic discrimination-stimulus awareness: A study of subception. *Psychological Review*, 1951, **58**, 113–122.

LECKY, P. *Self-consistency: a theory of personality*. New York: Island, 1945.

LEDWIDGE, B. Cognitive behavior modification: A step in the wrong direction? *Psychological Bulletin*, 1978, **85**, 353–375.

LEITENBERG, H., Agras, W. S., Barlow, D. H., and Oliveau, D. C. Contribution of selective positive reinforcement and therapeutic instructions to systematic desensitization therapy. *Journal of Abnormal Psychology*, 1969, **74**, 113–118.

LEVINE, R. A. *Culture, behavior, and personality*. Chicago: Aldine, 1973.

LEVY, L. H., and Orr, T. B. The social psychology of Rorschach validity research. *Journal of Abnormal and Social Psychology*, 1959, **58**, 79–83.

LEWIN, K. *Field theory in social science*. New York: Harper, 1951.

LEWIS, M., and Rosenblum, L. A. (Eds.), *The effect of the infant on its caregiver*. New York: Wiley, 1974.

LEWIS, M., Young, G., Brooks, J., and Micholson, L. The beginning of friendship. In M. Lewis and L. A. Rosenblum (Eds.), *Friendship and peer relations*. New York: Plenum, 1975. Pp. 27–66.

LIBERMAN, R. P., Teigen, J., Patterson, R., and Baker, V. Reducing delusional speech in chronic, paranoid schizophrenics. *Journal of Applied Behavior Analysis*, 1973, **6**, 57–64.

LIDDELL, H. S. Conditioned reflex method and experimental neurosis. In J. McV. Hunt (Ed.), *Personality and the behavior disorders*. New York: Ronald, 1944. Pp. 389–412.

LIFTON, R. J. *Thought reform and the psychology of totalism*. New York: Norton, 1963.

LINDZEY, G. *Projective techniques and cross-cultural research*. New York: Appleton-Century-Crofts, 1961.

LINDZEY, G., Lykken, D. T., and Winston, H. D. Infantile trauma, genetic factors and adult temperament. *Journal of Abnormal and Social Psychology*, 1960, **61**, 7–14.

LITTLE, K. B. Problems in the validation of projective techniques. *Journal of Projective Techniques*, 1959, **23**, 287–290.

LITTLE, K. B., and Shneidman, E. S. Congruencies among interpretations of psychological tests and anamnestic data. *Psychological Monographs*, 1959, **73** (6, Whole No. 476).

LOCKE, E. A. Is "behavior therapy" behavioristic? (An analysis of Wolpe's psychotherapeutic methods.). *Psychological Bulletin*, 1971, **76**, 318–327.

LONDON, P. *The modes and morals of psychotherapy*. New York: Holt, Rinehart and Winston, 1964.

LONDON, P. The end of ideology in behavior modification. *American Psychologist*, 1972, **27**, 913–920.

LOVAAS, O. I., Berberich, J. P., Perloff, B. F., and Schaeffer, B. Acquisition of imitative speech by schizophrenic children. *Science*, 1966, **151**, 705–707.

LOVAAS, O. I., Freitag, G., Gold, Vivian J., and Kassorla, Irene C. Experimental studies in childhood schizophrenia: Analysis of self-destructive behavior.

Journal of Experimental Child Psychology, 1965, **2**, 67–84.

LOVAAS, O. I., Koegel, R. Simmons, J. Q., and Long, G. S. Some generalization and follow-up measures on autistic children in behavior therapy. *Journal of Applied Behavior Analysis*, 1973, **6**, 131–166.

LUBORSKY, L. Intra-individual repetitive measurements (P techniques) in understanding psychotherapeutic change. In O. H. Mowrer (Ed.), *Psychotherapy: Theory and research*. New York: Ronald, 1953. Pp. 388–413.

LUNDIN, R. W. *Personality: an experimental approach*. New York: Macmillan, 1961.

LYKKEN, D. T. Multiple factor analysis and personality research. *Journal of Experimental Research in Personality*, 1971, **5**, 161–170.

MACKINNON, D. W. Violations and prohibitions. In H. A. Murray (Ed.), *Explorations in personality*. New York: Oxford, 1938.

MACKINNON, D. W. Personality. *Annual Review of Psychology*, 1950 **2**, 113–136.

MACKINNON, D. W. The nature and nurture of creative talent. *American Psychologist*, 1962, **17**, 484–494.

MACKINNON, D. W. and Dukes, W. Repression. In L. Postman (Ed.), *Psychology in the making*. New York: Knopf, 1962. Pp. 662–744.

MACLEOD, R. B. The place of phenomenological analysis in social psychological theory. In J. H. Rohrer and M. Sherif (Eds.), *Social psychology at the crossroads*. New York: Harper, 1951. Pp. 215–241.

MACLEOD, R. B. Phenomenology: A challenge to experimental psychology. In T. W. Wann (Ed.), *Behaviorism and phenomenology*. Chicago: University of Chicago Press, 1964. Pp. 47–73.

MACCOBY, E. E., and Maccoby, N. The interview: A tool of social science. In G. Lindzey (Ed.), *Handbook of social psychology*. Cambridge, Mass.: Addison-Wesley, 1954. Pp. 449–487.

MADISON, P. *Freud's concept of repression and defence: Its theoretical and observational language*. Minneapolis: University of Minnesota Press, 1961.

MAGNUSSON, D., and Endler, N. S. (Eds.), *Personality at the crossroads: Current issues in interactional psychology*. Hillsdale, N.J.: Erlbaum, 1977.

MAHER, B. *Principles of psychopathology*. New York: McGraw-Hill, 1966.

MAHER, B. *Clinical psychology and personality: The selected papers of George Kelly*. New York: Wiley, 1969.

MAHONEY, M. J. *Cognition and behavior modification*. Cambridge, Mass.: Ballinger, 1974.

MAHONEY, M. J. Publication prejudices: An experimental study of confirmatory bias in the peer review system. *Cognitive Therapy and Research*, 1977, **1**, 161–175.

MAHONEY, M. J., and Bandura, A. Self-reinforcement in pigeons. *Learning and motivation*, 1972, **3**, 293–303.

MAHONEY, M. J., Kazdin, A. E., and Kenigsberg, M. Getting published. *Cognitive Therapy and Research*, 1978, **2**, 69–70.

MAIER, N. R. F. *Frustration: The study of behavior without a goal*. New York: McGraw-Hill, 1949.

MAIER, N. R. F. Maier's Law. *American Psychologist*, 1960, **15**, 208–212.

MALLER, J. B. General and specific factors in character. *Journal of Social Psychology*, 1934 **5**, 97–102.

MALMO, R. B., and Shagass, C. Physiological studies of reaction to stress in anxiety and early schizophrenia. *Psychosomatic Medicine*, 1949, **11**, 9–24.

MALMO, R. B., Shagass, C., and Smith, A. A. Responsiveness in chronic schizophrenics. *Journal of Personality*, 1951, **19**, 359–375.

MARCIA, J. E., Rubin, B. M., and Efran J. S. Systematic desensitization: Expectancy change or counterconditioning? *Journal of Abnormal Psychology*, 1969, **74**, 382–387.

MARKS, J., Sonoda, Beverly, and Schalock, R. Reinforcement versus relationship therapy for schizophrenics. *Journal of Abnormal Psychology*, 1968, **73**, 397–402.

MARKUS, H. Self-schemata and processing information about the self. *Journal of Personality and Social Psychology*, 1977, **35**, 63–78.

MASLING, J. Role-related behavior of the subject and psychologist and its effects upon psychological data. In D. Levine (Ed.), *Nebraska symposium on motivation*. Lincoln, Nebraska: University of Nebraska Press, 1966. Pp. 67–103.

MASLOW, A. H. *Motivation and personality.* New York: Harper, 1954.

MASLOW, A. H. *Toward a psychology of being.* Princeton, N.J.: Van Nostrand, 1968.

MASLOW, A. H. *The farther reaches of human nature.* New York: Viking, 1971.

MATARAZZO, J. D. The interview. In B. Wolman (Ed.), *Handbook of clinical psychology.* New York: McGraw-Hill, 1965. Pp. 403–450.

MAY, M. A. Foreword. In J. W. Dollard, L. W. Doob, N. E. Miller, O. H. Mowrer, and R. R. Sears, *Frustration and aggression.* New Haven, Conn.: Yale, 1939.

MAY, R. *The meaning of anxiety.* New York: Ronald, 1950.

MAYMAN, M., Schafer, R., and Rapaport, D. Interpretation of the Wechsler Bellevue Intelligence Scale in personality appraisal. In H. H. Anderson and Gladys L. Anderson (Eds.), *An introduction to projective techniques.* Englewood Cliffs, N.J.: Prentice-Hall, 1951. Pp. 541-580.

MAYO, C. W., and Crockett, W. H. Cognitive complexity and primacy; recency effects in impression formation. *Journal of Abnormal and Social Psychology,* 1964, **68,** 335–338.

MCARTHUR, C., Waldron, E., and Dickinson, J. The psychology of smoking. *Journal of Abnormal and Social Psychology,* 1958, **56,** 267–275.

MCCLEARY, R. A., and Lazarus. R. S. Autonomic discrimination without awareness. *Journal of Personality,* 1949, **18,** 171–179.

MCGINNIES, E. Emotionality and perceptual defense. *Psychological Review,* 1949, **56,** 244–251.

MCGUIRE, W. J. Some impending reorientations in social psychology: Some thoughts provoked by Kenneth Ring. *Journal of Experimental Social Psychology,* 1967, **3,** 124–139.

MCNEMAR, Q. At random: Sense and nonsense. *American Psychologist,* 1960, **15,** 295–300.

MEDINNUS, G. R., and Curtis, F. J. The relation between maternal self-acceptance and child acceptance. *Journal of Consulting Psychology,* 1963, **27,** 542–544.

MEDNICK, S. A. A learning theory approach to research in schizophrenia. *Psychological Bulletin,* 1958, **55,** 316–327.

MEEHL, P. E. The dynamics of "structured" personality tests. *Journal of Clinical Psychology,* 1945, **1,** 296–303.

MEEHL, P. E. *Clinical versus statistical prediction.* Minneapolis: University of Minnesota Press, 1954.

MEEHL, P. E. Wanted—a good cookbook. *American Psychologist,* 1956, **11,** 263–272.

MEEHL, P. E. The cognitive activity of the clinician. *American Psychologist,* 1960, **15,** 19–27.

MEEHL, P. E. Schizotaxia, schizotypy, schizophrenia. *American Psychologist,* 1962, **17,** 827–838.

MEICHENBAUM, D. Cognitive modification of test anxious college students. *Journal of Consulting and Clinical Psychology,* 1972, **39,** 370–380. (Copyright 1972 by the American Psychological Association. Reprinted by permission.)

MEICHENBAUM, D. H. Cognitive factors in behavior modification: Modifying what clients say to themselves. In C. M. Franks and G. T. Wilson (Eds.), *Annual review of behavior therapy.* New York: Brunner/Mazel, 1973. Pp. 416–431.

MEICHENBAUM, D. *Cognitive-behavior modification: An integrative approach.* New York: Plenum, 1977.

MEICHENBAUM, D., Turk, D., and Burstein, S. The nature of coping with stress. In I. G. Sarason and C. D. Spielberger (Eds.), *Stress and anxiety.* Washington, D.C.: Hemisphere, 1975. Pp. 337–360.

MESSICK, S. Personality Structure. *Annual Review of Psychology.* Palo Alto: Annual Reviews, 1961. Pp. 93–128.

MIGLER, B., and Wolpe, J. Automated self-desensitization: A case report. *Behavior Research and Therapy,* 1967, **5,** 133–135.

MILGRAM, N.A., and Helper, M. M. The social desirability set in individual and grouped self-ratings. *Journal of Consulting Psychology,* 1961, **25,** 91.

MILLER, N. E. Theory and experiment relating psychoanalytic displacement to stimulus-response generalization. *Journal of Abnormal and Social Psychology,* 1948, **43,** 155–178.

MILLER, N.E. Comments on theoretical models: Illustrated by the development of a theory of conflict behavior. *Journal of Personality,* 1951, **20,** 82–100.

MILLER, N. E. Biofeedback and visceral learning. *Annual review of psychology,* 1978, **29,** 373–404.

MILLER, N. E., and Dollard, J. *Social learning and imitation.* New Haven, Conn.: Yale, 1941.

MISCHEL, W. Delay of gratification, need for achievement, and acquiesence in another culture. *Journal of Abnormal and Social Psychology*, 1961, **62**, 543–552.

MISCHEL, W. *Personality assessment.* New York: Wiley, 1968.

MiSCHEL, W. *Introduction to personality.* New York: Holt, Rinehart and Winston, 1971.

MISCHEL, W. Toward a cognitive social learning reconceptualization of personality. *Psychological Review*, 1973, **80**, 252–283.

MISCHEL, W. *Introduction to personality.* New York: Holt, Rinehart and Winston, 1976.

MISCHEL, W. Self control and the self. In T. Mischel (Ed.), *The self: Psychological and philosophical issues.* Totowa, N.J.: Rowman & Littlefield, 1977. Pp. 31–64.

MISCHEL, W., and Grusec, Joan. Determinants of the rehearsal and transmission of neutral and aversive behaviors. *Journal of Personality and Social Psychology*, 1966, **3**, 197–205.

MISCHEL, W., and Liebert, R. M. Effects of discrepancies between observed and imposed reward criteria on their acquisition and transmission. *Journal of Personality and Social Psychology*, 1966, **3**, 45–53.

MISCHEL, W., and Liebert, R. M. The role of power in the adoption of self-reward patterns. *Child Development*, 1967, **38**, 673–683.

MORGAN, C. D., and Murray, H. A. A method for investigating fantasies. *Archives of Neurology and Psychiatry*, 1935, **34**, 289–306.

MORGAN, W. G. Non-necessary conditions or useful procedures in desensitization: A reply to Wilkins. *Psychological Bulletin*, 1973, **79**, 373–375.

MORGANSTERN, K. P. Implosive therapy and flooding procedures: A critical review. *Psychological Bulletin*, 1973, **79**, 318–334.

MORIN, S. F. Heterosexual bias in psychological research on lesbianism and male homosexuality. *American Psychologist*, 1977, **32**, 629–637.

MOSS, P. D., and McEvedy, C. P. An epidemic of overbreathing among schoolgirls. *British Medical Journal* Nov. 26, 1966, 1295–1300.

MOWRER, O. H., and Mowrer, W. A. Enuresis: A method for its study and treatment. *American Journal of Orthopsychiatry*, 1928, **8**, 436–447.

MUENCH, G. A. An evaluation of non-directive psychotherapy by means of the Rorschach and other tests. *Applied Psychology Monographs*, 1947 (13), 1–103.

MUNROE, Ruth L. *Schools of psychoanalytic thought.* New York: Dryden, 1955.

MURRAY, E. J. A case study in a behavioral analysis of psychotherapy. *Journal of Abnormal and Social Psychology*, 1954, **49**, 305–310.

MURRAY, E. J., and Berkun, M. M. Displacement as a function of conflict. *Journal of Abnormal and Social Psychology*, 1955, **51**, 47–50.

MURRAY, E. J., and Jacobson, L. I. The nature of learning in traditional and behavioral psychotherapy. In A. E. Bergin and S. Garfield (Eds.), *Handbook of psychotherapy and behavior change.* New York; Wiley, 1971. Pp. 709–747.

MURRAY, H. A. *Explorations in personality.* New York: Oxford University Press, 1938.

MURRAY, H. A., and Kluckhohn, L. A conception of personality. In C. Kluckhohn, H. Murray, and D. M. Schneider (Eds.), *Personality in nature, society, and culture.* New York: Knopf, 1956. Pp. 3–49.

NEISSER, U. *Cognitive psychology.* New York: Appleton-Century-Crofts, 1967.

NESSELROADE, J. R., and Bartsch, T. W. Multivariate perspectives in the construct validity of the trait-state distinction. In R. B. Cattell and R. M. Dreger (Eds.), *Handbook of modern personality theory.* Washington, D.C.: Hemisphere, 1977. Pp. 221–238.

NESSELROADE, J. R., and Delhees, K. H. Methods and findings in experimentally based personality theory. In R. B. Cattell (Ed.), *Handbook of multivariate experimental psychology.* Chicago: Rand McNally, 1966. Pp. 563–610.

NEWCOMB, T. M., Koening, K. E., Flachs R., and Warwick, D. P. *Persistence and change.* New York: Wiley, 1967.

O'LEARY, K. D. The assessment of psychopathology in children. In H. C. Quay and J. S. Werry (Eds.), *Psychopathological disorders of childhood.* New York: Wiley, 1972. Pp. 234–272.

O'LEARY, K. D., and Drabman, R. Token reinforcement programs in the classroom: A review. *Psychological Bulletin*, 1971, **75**, 379–398.

OLWEUS, D. The consistency issue in personality psychology revisited. Unpublished manuscript, 1978.

OPLER, M. K., and Singer, J. L. Ethnic differences in behavior and psychopathology. *International Journal of Social Psychiatry*, 1956, **2**, 11–23.

ORNE, M. T. On the social psychology of the psychological experiment: With particular reference to demand characteristics and their implications. American Psychologist, 1962, **17**, 776–783.

ORNE, M. T., and Schreibe, K. E. The contribution of nondeprivation factors in the production of sensory deprivation effects: The psychology of the "panic button." *Journal of Abnormal and Social Psychology*, 1964, **68**, 3–13.

OSS Assessment Staff. *Assessment of men*. New York: Rinehart and Co., 1948.

OVERALL, J. E. Note on the scientific status of factors. *Psychological Bulletin*, 1964, **61**, 270–276.

PATTERSON, G. R. Behavioral intervention procedures in the classroom and in the home. In A. E. Bergin and S. L. Garfield (Eds.), *Handbook of psychotherapy and behavior change*. New York: Wiley, 1971. Pp. 751–775.

PAUL, G. L. *Insight vs desensitization in psychotherapy*. Stanford, Calif.: Stanford University Press, 1966.

PAUL, G. L. Insight versus desensitization in psychotherapy two years after termination. *Journal of Consulting Psychology*, 1967, **31**, 109–118.

PAUL, G. L. Two year follow-up of systematic desensitization in therapy groups. *Journal of Abnormal Psychology*, 1968, **73**, 119–130.

PAUL, G. L., and Shannon, D. T. Treatment of anxiety through systematic desensitization in therapy groups. *Journal of Abnormal Psychology*, 1966, **71**, 124–135.

PAVLOV, I. P. *Conditioned Reflexes*. London: Oxford University Press, 1927.

PERVIN, L. A. Rigidity in neurosis and general personality functioning. *Journal of Abnormal and Social Psychology*, 1960, **61**, 389–395.

PERVIN, L. A. Predictive strategies and the need to confirm them: Some notes on pathological types of decisions. *Psychological Reports*, 1964, **15**, 99–105.

PERVIN, L. A. A twenty-college study of Student x College interaction using TAPE (Transactional Analysis of Personality and Environment): Rationale, reliability, and validity. *Journal of Educational Psychology*, 1967, **58**, 290–302. (a)

PERVIN, L. A. Satisfaction and perceived self-environment similarity: A semantic differential study of student-college interaction. *Journal of Personality*, 1967, **35**, 623–634. (b)

PERVIN, L.A. Performance and satisfaction as a function of individual-environment fit. *Psychological Bulletin*, 1968, **69**, 56–68.

PERVIN, L. A. *Current controversies and issues in personality*. New York: Wiley, 1978.

PERVIN, L. A., and Lewis, M. (Eds.), *Perspectives in interactional psychology*. New York: Plenum, 1978.

PERVIN, L. A., and Lilly, R. S. Social desirability and self-ideal self on the semantic differential. *Educational and Psychological Measurement*, 1967, **27**, 845–853.

PERVIN, L. A., and Rubin, D. B. Student dissatisfaction with college and the college dropout: A transactional approach. *Journal of Social Psychology*, 1967, **72**, 285–295.

PESKIN, H. Unity of science begins at home: A study of regional factionalism in clinical psychology. *American Psychologist*, 1963, **18**, 96–100.

PETERSON, D. R. Scope and generality of verbally defined personality factors. *Psychological Review*, 1965, **72**, 48–59.

PFUNGST, O. *Clever Hans: A contribution to experimental, animal, and human psychology*. New York: Holt, Rinehart and Winston, 1911.

PHARES, E. J. Locus of control. In H. London and J. E. Exner, Jr. (Eds.), *Dimensions of personality*. New York: Wiley, 1978. Pp. 263–304.

PIOTROWSKI, Z. A. Theory of psychological tests and psychopathology. In J. D. Page (Ed.), *Approaches to Psychopathology*. New York: Columbia University Press, 1966. Pp. 165–194.

POCH, Suzanne M. A study of changes in personal constructs as related to interpersonal prediction and its outcomes. Unpublished doctoral dissertation, Ohio State University, 1952.

POHL, R. L., and Pervin, L. A. Academic performance as a function of task requirements and cognitive style. *Psychological Reports*, 1968, **22**, 1017–1020.

POLLACK, J. M. Obsessive-compulsive personality: A review. *Psychological Bulletin*, 1979, **86**, 225–241.

RAIMY, V. C. Self-reference in counselling interviews. *Journal of Consulting Psychology*, 1948, **12**, 153–163.

RAINES, G. N., and Rohrer, J. H. The operational matrix of psychiatric practice. I. Consistency and variability in interview impressions of different psychiatrists. *American Journal of Psychiatry*, 1955, **111**, 721–733.

RAINES, G. N., and Rohrer, J. H. The operational matrix of psychiatric practice. II. Variability in psychiatric impressions and the projection hypothesis. *American Journal of Psychiatry*, 1960, **117**, 133–139.

RAPAPORT, D. A critique of Dollard and Miller's "Personality and Psychotherapy." *American Journal of Orthopsychiatry*, 1953, **23**, 204–208.

RASKIN, N. J. Analysis of six parallel studies of the therapeutic process. *Journal of Consulting Psychology*, 1949, **13**, 206–220.

REIK, T. *Listening with the third ear.* New York: Farrar, Straus, and Giroux, 1948.

REYNOLDS, G. S. *A primer of operant conditioning.* Glenview, Ill.: Scott, Foresman, 1968.

RICKELS, K., and Cattell, R. B. The clinical factor validity and trueness of the IPAT verbal and objective batteries for anxiety and repression. *Journal of Clinical Psychology*, 1965, **21**, 257–264.

RICKERS-OVSIANKINA, Maria A. Psychological premises underlying the Rorschach. In Rickers-Ovsiankina, Maria A. (Ed.), *Rorschach psychology.* New York: Wiley, 1960. Pp. 3–24.

RIESMAN, D. *The lonely crowd.* Garden City, N.Y.: Doubleday, 1950.

RING, K. Experimental social psychology: Some sober questions about some frivolous values. *Journal of Experimental-Social Psychology*, 1967, **3**, 113–123.

RODIN, J., and Langer, E. Long-term effects of a control-relevant intervention with institutionalized aged. *Journal of Personality and Social Psychology*, 1977, **35**, 897–902.

ROGERS, C. R. *Clinical treatment of the problem child.* Boston: Houghton Mifflin, 1939.

ROGERS, C. R. The process of psychotherapy. *Journal of Consulting Psychology*, 1940, **4**, 161–164.

ROGERS, C. R. *Counseling and psychotherapy.* Boston: Houghton Mifflin, 1942.

ROGERS, C. R. Some observations on the organization of personality *American Psychologist*, 1947, **2**, 358–368.

ROGERS, C. R. *Client-centered therapy.* Boston: Houghton Mifflin, 1951.

ROGERS, C. R. Some directions and end points in therapy. In O. H. Mowrer (Ed.), *Psychotherapy: Theory and research.* New York: Ronald, 1953. Pp. 44–68.

ROGERS, C. R. The case of Mrs. Oak: A research analysis. In C. R. Rogers and R. F. Dymond (Eds.), *Psychotherapy and personality change.* Chicago: University of Chicago Press, 1954. Pp. 259–348.

ROGERS, C. R. A process conception of psychotherapy. *American Psychologist*, 1958, **13**, 142–149.

ROGERS, C. R. A theory of therapy, personality, and interpersonal relationships as developed in the client-centered framework. In S. Koch (Ed.), *Psychology: A study of a science.* New York: McGraw-Hill, 1959. Pp. 184–256.

ROGERS, C. R. *On becoming a person.* Boston: Houghton Mifflin, 1961. (a)

ROGERS, C. R. A tentative scale for the measurement of process in psychotherapies. In M. P. Stein (Ed.), *Contemporary Psychotherapies.* New York: Free Press, 1961. Pp. 113–127. (b)

ROGERS, C. R. The process equation in psychotherapy. *American Journal of Psychotherapy*, 1961, **15**, 27–45. (c)

ROGERS, C. R. The actualizing tendency in relation to "motives" and to consciousness. In M. R. Jones (Ed.), *Nebraska symposium on motivation.* Lincoln: University of Nebraska, 1963. Pp. 1–24.

ROGERS, C. R. Toward a science of the person. In T. W. Wann (Ed.), *Behaviorism and phenomenology.* Chicago: University of Chicago Press, 1964. Pp. 109–133.

ROGERS, C. R. Significant aspects of client-centered therapy. In H. M. Ruitenbeek (Ed.), *Varieties of personality theory.* New York: Dutton, 1964. Pp. 168–183. Originally presented in 1946.

ROGERS, C. R. Client-centered therapy. In S. Arieti (Ed.), *American Handbook of Psychiatry.* New York: Basic Books, 1966. Pp. 183–200.

ROGERS, C. R. *On encounter groups.* New York: Harper, 1970.

ROGERS, C. R. *Becoming partners: Marriage and its alternatives.* New York: Delacorte, 1972 (a)

ROGERS, C. R. My personal growth. In A. Burton (Ed.), *Twelve therapists.* San Francisco: Jossey-Bass, 1972. Pp. 28–77. (b)

ROGERS, C. R. In retrospect: Forty-six years. Distinguished professional contribution award address. American Psychological Association Convention, Montreal, August 1973.

ROGERS, C. R. *Carl Rogers on personal power.* New York: Delacorte, 1977.

ROGERS, C. R., and Dymond, Rosalind F. (Eds.), *Psychotherapy and personality change.* Chicago: University of Chicago Press, 1954.

ROGERS, C. R., Gendlin, E. T., Kiesler, D. J., and Truax, C. B. *The therapeutic relationship and its impact: A study of the psychotherapy of schizophrenics.* Madison: University of Wisconsin Press, 1967.

ROGERS, C. R., and Skinner, B. F. Some issues concerning the control of human behavior: A symposium. *Science,* 1956, **124**, 1057–1066.

RORSCHACH, H. *Psychodiagnostics.* Bern: Huber, 1921.

ROSEN, E. Differences between volunteers and non-volunteers for psychological studies. *Journal of Applied Psychology,* 1951, **35**, 185–193.

ROSENBLATT, A. D., and Thickstun, G. T. Modern psychoanalytic concepts in a general psychology. *Psychological Issues,* 1977, **11**, Monograph No. 42–43.

ROSENHAN, D. Some origins of concern for others. M. P. Mussen (Ed.), *New directions in child psychology.* New York: Holt, Rinehart and Winston, 1969. Pp. 134–154.

ROSENHAN, D., and London, P. Character. In P. London and D. Rosenhan (Eds.), *Foundations of abnormal psychology.* New York: Holt, Rinehart and Winston, 1968. Pp. 251–290.

ROSENTHAL, R. The effect of the experimenter on the results of psychological research. In B. A. Maher (Ed.), *Progress in experimental personality research,* Vol. 1 New York: Academic Press, 1964. Pp. 80–114.

ROSENTHAL, R., and Jacobson, Lenore. *Pygmalion in the classroom.* New York: Holt, Rinehart and Winston, 1968.

ROSENTHAL, R., and Rosnow, R. L. (Eds.) *Artifact in behavioral research.* New York: Academic Press, 1969.

ROSENTHAL, T., and Bandura, A. Psychological modeling: Theory and practice. In S. L. Garfield and A. E. Bergin (Eds.), *Handbook of psychotherapy and behavior change.* New York: Wiley, 1978. Pp. 621–658.

ROSENTHAL, T. L., and Zimmerman, B. J. *Social learning and cognition.* New York: Academic Press, 1978.

ROSENZWEIG, S. Need-persistive and ego-defensive reactions to frustration as demonstrated by an experiment on repression. *Psychological Review,* 1941, **48**, 347–349.

ROTTER, J. B. *Social learning and clinical psychology.* Englewood Cliffs, N.J.: Prentice-Hall, 1954.

ROTTER, J. B. Generalized expectancies for internal versus external control of reinforcement. *Psychological Monographs,* 1966, **80** (Whole No. 609).

RUBINSTEIN, E. A. Warning: The surgeon general's research program may be dangerous to preconceived notions. *Journal of Social Issues,* 1976, **32**, 18–34.

RUDIN, S. A., and Stagner, R. Figure-ground pheonomena in the perception of physical and social stimuli. *Journal of Psychology* 1958, **45**, 213–225.

SACKEIM, H. A. and Gur, R. C. Self-deception, other-deception, and self-reported psychopathology. *Journal of Consulting and Clinical Psychology,* 1979, **47**, 213–215.

SALMON, Phyllis. A psychology of personal growth. In D. Bannister (Ed.), *Perspectives in personal construct theory.* New York: Academic Press, 1970. Pp. 197–221.

SAMUELS, H. The validity of personality-trait ratings based on projective techniques. *Psychological Monographs,* 1952, **66**, (5).

SANDLER, J. Masochism: An empirical analysis. *Psychological Bulletin,* 1964, **62**, 197–204.

SANFORD, N. The approach of the authoritarian personality. In J. L. McCary (Ed.), *Psychology of personality.* New York: Logos, 1956. Pp. 255–319.

SANFORD, N. Personality: Its place in psychology. In S. Koch (Ed.), *Psychology: A study of a science.* New York: McGraw-Hill, 1963, Pp. 488–592.

SARASON, I. G. *Personality: An objective approach.* New York: Wiley, 1966.

SARNOFF, I. Identification with the aggressor: Some personality correlates of anti-Semitism among Jews. *Journal of Personality*, 1951, **20**, 199–218.

SAWREY, W. L., and Weisz, J. D. An experimental method of producing gastric ulcers. *Journal of Comparative and Physiological Psychology*, 1956, **49**, 209–270.

SAWYER, J. Measurement and prediction: Clinical and statistical. *Psychological Bulletin*, 1966, **66**, 178–200.

SCHACHTER, S. The interaction of cognitive and physiological determinants of emotional state. In L. Berkowitz (Ed.), *Advances in experimental social psychology*. New York: Academic Press, 1964. Pp. 49–80.

SCHACHTER, S., and Singer, J. Cognitive, social, and physiological determinants of emotional state. *Psychological Review*, 1962, **69**, 379–399.

SCHAFER, R. *Psychoanalytic interpretation in Rorschach testing*. New York: Grune & Stratton, 1954.

SCHAFER, R. *A new language for psychoanalysis*. New Haven, Conn.: Yale, 1976.

SCHAFER, R. *Language and insight*. New Haven, Conn.: Yale, 1978.

SCHNEIDER, J. M. College students' belief in personal control. *Journal of Individual Psychology*, 1971, **27**, 188.

SCOTT, J. P. *Early experience and the organization of behavior*. Belmont, Calif.: Wadsworth, 1968.

SEARS, R. R. Experimental studies of projection. I. Attribution of traits. *Journal of Social Psychology*, 1936, **7**, 151–163.

SEARS, R. R. Relation of fantasy aggression to interpersonal aggression. *Child Development*, 1950, **21**, 5–6.

SEARS, R. R., Rau, Lucy, and Alpert, R. *Identification and child-rearing. Standford, Calif.: Stanford University Press, 1965.*

SECHREST, L. The psychology of personal constructs. In J. M. Wepman and R. W. Heine (Eds.), *Concepts of personality*. Chicago: Aldine, 1963. Pp. 206–233.

SECHREST, L. J. Personal constructs theory. In R. J. Corsini (Ed.) *Current personality theories*. Itasca, Ill.: Peacock, 1977. Pp. 203–241.

SECHREST, L. A passion for theory. *Contemporary Psychology*, 1979, **24**, 19–20.

SECHREST, L., and Jackson, D. N. Social intelligence

and accuracy of interpersonal predictions. *Journal of Personality*, 1961, **29**, 167–182.

SEEMAN, J. Perspectives in client-centered therapy. In B. B. Wolman (Ed.), *Handbook of Clinical Psychology*. New York: McGraw-Hill, 1965. Pp. 1215–1229.

SELIGMAN, M. E. P. *Helplessness*. San Francisco: Freeman, 1975.

SELLS, S. B. Structured measurement of personality and motivation: A review of contributions of Raymond B. Cattell. *Journal of Clinical Psychology*, 1959, **15**, 3–21.

SHEERER, Elizabeth T. An analysis of the relationship between acceptance of and respect for others in ten counseling cases. *Journal of Consulting Psychology*, 1949 **13**, 169–175.

SHERMAN, J. A. Imitation and language development. In H. W. Reese (Ed.), *Advances in child development and behavior*. New York: Academic Press, 1971. Pp. 239-272.

SHIELDS, J. Heredity and environment. In H. J. Eysenck & G. D. Wilson (Eds.), *A textbook of human psychology*. Baltimore: University Park Press, 1976.

SHIELDS, S. Functionalism, Darwinism, and the psychology of women: A study in social myth. *American Psychologist*, 1975, 30, 739–754.

SHONTZ, F. C. *Research methods in personality*. Englewood Cliffs, N.J.: Prentice-Hall, Inc., 1965.

SHOTWELL, Anna M., Hurley, J. R., and Cattell, R. B. Motivational structure of a hospitalized mental defective. *Journal of Personality*, 1961, **62**, 422–426.

SIGNELL, K. A. Cognitive complexity in person perception and nation perception: A developmental approach. *Journal of Personality*, 1966, **34**, 517–537.

SILVERMAN, L. H. A Q sort study of the validity of evaluations made from projective techniques. *Psychological Monographs*, 1959, **73**, No. (7, Whole No. 477).

SILVERMAN, L. H. Psychoanalytic theory: The reports of its death are greatly exaggerated. *American Psychologist*, 1976, **31**, 621–637.

Sixteen Personality Factor Inventory. Champaign, Ill. Institute for Personality and Ability Testing, 1962.

SKINNER, B. F. *Walden two*. New York: Macmillan, 1948.

SKINNER, B. F. Are theories of learning necessary? *Psychological Review*, 1950, **57**, 193–216.

SKINNER, B. F. *Science and human behavior*. New York: Macmillan, 1953.

SKINNER, B. F. A case history in the scientific method. *American Psychologist*, 1956, **11**, 221–233.

SKINNER, B. F. *Cumulative record*. New York: Appleton-Century-Crofts, 1959.

SKINNER, B. F. Behaviorism at fifty. *Science*, 1963, **140**, 951–958.

SKINNER, B. F. Autobiography. In E. G. Boring and G. Lindzey (Eds.), *A history of psychology in autobiography. New York: Appleton-Century-Crofts, 1967. Pp. 385–414.*

SKINNER, B. F. *Beyond freedom and dignity*. New York: Knopf, 1971.

SKINNER, B. F. I have been misunderstood. *The Center Magazine*, 1972, March–April, 63–65.

SKINNER, B. F. *About behaviorism*. New York: Knopf, 1974.

SKINNER, B. F., and Rogers, C. R. Some issues concerning the control of human behavior: A symposium. *Science*, 1965, **124**, 1057–1066.

SKINNER, N. S. F., and Howarth, E. Cross-media independence of questionnaire and objective test personality factors. *Multivariate Behavioral Research*, 1973, **8**, 23–40.

SKOLNICK, A. Motivational imagery and behavior over twenty years. *Journal of Consulting Psychology*, 1966, **30**, 463–478.

SMITH, M. B. The phenomenological approach in personality theory: Some critical remarks. *Journal of Abnormal and Social Psychology*, 1950, **45**, 516–522.

SNYDER, W. U. An investigation of the nature of nondirective psychotherapy. *Journal of General Psychology, 1945, 33*, 193–223.

SOLYOM, L., and Miller, S. A. Differential conditioning procedure as the initial phase of the behavior therapy of homosexuality. *Behavior Research Therapy*, 1965, **3**, 147–160.

SPENCE, K. W. The postulates and methods of behaviorism. *Psychological Review*, 1948, **55**, 67–78.

SPENCE, K. W. A theory of emotionally based drive (D) and its relation to performance in simple, learning situations. *American Psychologist*, 1958, **13**, 131–141.

STAMPFL, T. G. Implosive therapy: An emphasis on covert stimulation. In D. J. Levis (Ed.), *Learning approaches to therapeutic behavior change*. Chicago: Aldine, 1970. Pp. 182–204.

STEINER, J. F. *Treblinka*. New York: Simon & Schuster, 1966.

STEPHENSON, W. *The study of behavior*. Chicago: University of Chicago Press, 1953.

STEVENS, S. S. The operational definition of psychological concepts. *Psychological Review*, 1935, **42**, 517–527.

STOCK, D. An investigation into the interrelations between the self concept and feelings directed towards other persons and groups. *Journal of Consulting Psychology*, 1949, **13**, 176–180.

STONE, H. K., and Dellis, N. P. An exploratory investigation into the levels hypothesis. *Journal of Projective Techniques*, 1960, **24**, 333–340.

SUINN, R. M. Osborne, D., and Winfree, P. The self-concept and accuracy of recall of inconsistent self-related information. *Journal of Clinical Psychology*, 1962, **18**, 473–474.

SULLIVAN, H. S. *The interpersonal theory of psychiatry*. New York: Norton, 1953.

SZASZ, T. S. *The myth of mental illness*. New York: Harper, 1961.

TAVERSKY, A., and Kahneman, D. Judgment under uncertainty: Heuristics and biases. *Science*, 1974, **185**, 1124–1131.

TAYLOR, Janet A. Drive theory and manifest anxiety. *Psychological Bulletin*, 1956, **53**, 303–320.

TAYLOR, Janet A. Learning theory and personality. In J. M. Wepman and R. W. Heine (Eds.), *Concepts of personality*. Chicago: Aldine, 1963. Pp. 3–30. Technical recommendations for psychological tests and diagnostic techniques. *Psychological Bulletin Supplement*, 1954, **51**, Part, 2, 1–38.

THARP, R. G., and Wetzel, R. J. *Behavior modification in the natural environment*. New York: Academic, 1969.

THETFORD, W. N. An objective measurement of frustration tolerance in evaluating psychotherapy. In W. Wolff and J. A. Precker (Eds.), *Success in psychotherapy*. New York: Grune & Stratton, 1952. Chapter 2.

THORNDIKE, E. L. *The elements of psychology.* New York: A. G. Seiler, 1905.

THORNDIKE, R. L. The psychological value systems of psychologists. *American Psychologist,* 1954, **9**, 787–790.

TOMKINS, S. S. Commentary. The ideology of research strategies. In S. Messick and J. Ross (Eds.), *Measurement in Personality and Cognition.* New York: Wiley, 1962. Pp. 285–294.

TRIPOLDI, T., and Bieri, J. Cognitive complexity as a function of own and provided constructs. *Psychological Reports,* 1963, **13**, 26.

TRUAX, C. B. Reinforcement and nonreinforcement in Rogerian psychotherapy. *Journal of Abnormal Psychology,* 1966, **71**, 1–9.

TURNER, R. H., and Vanderlippe, R. H. Self-ideal consequence as an index of adjustment. *Journal of Abnormal and Social Psychology,* 1958, **57**, 202–206.

TYLER, L. E. *The psychology of human differences.* New York: Appleton-Century-Crofts, 1965.

TYLER, L. E. *Individuality.* San Francisco: Jossey-Bass, 1978.

ULLMANN, L. P., and Krasner, L. (Eds.), *Case studies in behavior modification.* New York: Holt, Rinehart and Winston, 1965.

ULLMANN, L. P., and Krasner, L. *A psychological approach to abnormal behavior.* Englewood Cliffs, N.J.: Prentice-Hall, 1975.

VALINS, S., and Ray, A. A. Effects of cognitive desensitization on avoidance behavior. *Journal of Personality and Social Psychology,* 1967, **7**, 345–350.

VANDENBERG, S. G. The hereditary abilities study: Hereditary components in a psychological test battery. *American Journal of Human Genetics,* 1962, **14**, 220–237.

VARGAS, M. J. Changes in self-awareness during client-centered therapy. In C. R. Rogers and R. F. Dymond (Eds.), *Psychotherapy and personality change.* Chicago: University of Chicago Press, 1951. Pp. 145–166.

VERNON, P. E. *Personality assessment.* New York: Wiley, 1963.

WADE, T. C., and Baker, T. B. Opinions and use of psychological tests. *American Psychologist,* 1977, **32**, 874–882.

WAHLER, R. G., and Pollio, H. R. Behavior and insight:

A case study in behavior therapy. *Journal of Experimental Research in Personality,* 1968, **3**, 45–56.

WALKER, A. M. Rablem, R. A., and Rogers, C. R. Development of a scale to measure process changes in psycho-therapy. *Journal of Clinical Psychology,* 1960, **16**, 79–85.

WALTERS, R. H. Some conditions facilitating the occurrence of imitative behavior. In E. C. Simmel, R. A. Hoppe, and G. A. Milton (Eds.), *Social facilitation and imitative behavior.* Boston: Allyn and Bacon, 1968. Pp. 7–30.

WALTERS, R. H. and Parke, R. D. Influence of the response consequences to a social model on resistance to deviation. *Journal of Experimental Child Psychology,* 1964, **1**, 269–280.

WATSON, J. B. *Behavior.* New York: Holt, Rinehart and Winston. 1914.

WATSON, J. B. *Psychology from the standpoint of a behaviorist.* Philadelphia: Lippincott, 1919.

WATSON, J. B. Autobiography. In C. Murchison (Ed.), *A history of psychology in autobiography.* Worcester, Mass.: Clark University Press, 1936. Pp. 271–282.

WATSON, J. B. *Behaviorism.* New York: People's Institute Publishing Co., 1925.

WATSON, J. B., and Rayner, Rosalie. Conditioned emotional reactions. *Journal of Experimental Psychology,* 1920, **3**, 1–14.

WATSON, J. D. *The double helix.* New York: Atheneum, 1968.

WEBB, W. B. The choice of the problem. *American Psychologist,* 1961, **16**, 223–227.

WEBER, S. J., and Cook, T. D. Subject effects in laboratory research: An examination of subject roles, demand characteristics, and valid inference. *Psychological Bulletin,* 1972, **77**, 273–295.

WEISS, J. M. Effects of coping response on stress. *Journal of Comparative and Physiological Psychology,* 1968, **65**, 251–260.

WEISS, J. M. Somatic effects of predictable and unpredictable shock. *Psychosomatic Medicine,* 1970, **32**, 397–409.

WEITZ, J. Criteria for criteria. *American Psychologist,* 1961, **16**, 228–231.

WESSMAN, A. E., and Ricks, D. F. *Mood and personality.* New York: Holt, Rinehart and Winston, 1966.

WHITE, B. J. The relation of self-concept and parental identification to women's vocational interests. *Journal of Counseling Psychology*, 1959, **6**, 202–206.

WHITE, R. W. Motivation reconsidered: The concept of competence. *Psychological Review*, 1959, **66**, 297–333.

WHITE, R. W. Competence and the psychosexual stages of development. In M. R. Jones (Ed.), *Nebraska Symposium on Motivation*. Lincoln: University of Nebraska Press, 1960.

WHITING, J. W. M., and Child, I. L. *Child training and personality: A cross-cultural study*. New Haven, Conn.: Yale University Press, 1953.

WIGGINS, J. S. *Personality and prediction: Principles of personality assessment*. New York: Addison-Wesley, 1973.

WILDE, G. J. S. Trait description and measurement by personality questionnaires. In R. B. Cattell and R. M. Dreger (Eds.), *Handbook of modern personality theory*. Washington, D.C.: Hemisphere, 1977. Pg. 69–103.

WILKINS, W. Desensitization: Social and cognitive factors underlying the effectiveness of Wolpe's procedure. *Psychological Bulletin*, 1971, **76**, 311–317.

WILLIAMS, J. *The psychology of women*. New York: Norton, 1976.

WILLIAMS, J. R. A test of the validity of the P-technique in the measurement of internal conflict. *Journal of Personality*, 1959, **27**, 418–437.

WILSON, G. Introversion/Extroversion. In H. London and J. E. Exner (Eds.), *Dimensions of personality*. New York: Wiley, 1978. Pp. 217–261.

WINETT, R. A., and Winkler, R. C. Current behavior modification in the classroom: Be still, be quiet, be docile. *Journal of Applied Behavior Analysis*, 1972, **5**, 499–504.

WING, C. W., Jr. Measurement of personality. In D. K. Whitla (Ed.), *Handbook of measurement and assessment in behavioral sciences*. Reading, Mass.: Addison-Wesley, 1968. Pp. 315–347.

WITTMAN, M. P. A scale for measuring prognosis in schizophrenic patients. *Elgin Papers*, 1941, **4**, 20–33.

WOLF, S. "Irrationality" in a psychoanalytic psychology of the self. In T. Mischel (Ed.), *The self: Psychological and philosophical issues*. Totowa, N.J.: Rowman & Littlefield, 1977. Pp. 203–223.

WOLPE, J. *Psychotherapy by reciprocal inhibition*. Standford, Calif.: Stanford University Press, 1958.

WOLPE, J. The systematic desensitization treatment of neuroses. *Journal of Nervous and Mental Disorders*, 1961, **132**, 189–203.

WOLPE, J. *The practice of behavior therapy*. New York: Pergamon, 1969.

WOLPE, J., and Lang, P. J. A fear survey schedule for use in behavior therapy. *Behavior research and therapy*, 1964, **2**, 27–30.

WOLPE, J. and Lazarus, A. A. *Behavior therapy techniques: A guide to the treatment of neuroses*. New York: Pergamon, 1966.

WOLPE, J. and Rachman, S. Psychoanalytic "evidence": A critique based on Freud's case of Little Hans. *Journal of Nervous and Mental Disease*, 1960, **130**, 135–148.

WOLPIN, M., and Raines, J. Visual imagery, expected roles and extinction as possible factors in reducing fear and avoidance behavior. *Behavior Research and Therapy*, 1966, **4**, 25–37.

WYLIE, Ruth C. *The self-concept*. Lincoln: University of Nebraska Press, 1961.

WYLIE, Ruth C. The present status of self theory. In E. F. Borgatta and W. W. Lambert (Eds.), *Handbook of personality theory and research*. Chicago: Rand McNally, 1968, Pp. 728–787.

WYLIE, R. C. *The self-concept*, rev. ed. Lincoln: University of Nebraska Press, 1974.

PHOTO CREDITS

INDEX

ABA research design, 495-497
ABC assessment, 445-448, 460
Abernethy, E. M., 164
Abnormal behavior, *see* Psychopathology
About Behaviorism, Skinner, 292
Abraham, K., 72
Abrahamson, L. Y., 506
Achenbach, T., 167
Acquiescence, 442-443
Acquisition, 364-367, 394-395
Action research, 515, 527-528
Actualization, 122, 157
Adams-Webber, J. R., 191, 218, 221
Adcock, C. J., 437
Adler, A., 32
    theories of, 84-86
Adolescence, ego identity in, 56
Adolescent Aggression, Bandura, 357
Adorno, T. W., 498
Age trends, in personality development, 258-259, 273
Aggression, 34-35, 373
    in personal construct theory, 208
    in social learning theory, 372-373
Aggressive instinct, 46
Aggressor, identification with, 54
Agnew, J., 218
Agras, W. S., 337
Akeret, R. V., 163-164
"Albert," case history of, 288
Alcoholism, and systematic desensitization, 326

Alexander, F., 78, 264
Allport, F., 234
Allport, G., 17, 232, 268, 272
    trait theory of, 234-237
Alpert, R., 99, 322
Anal personality, 57-59, 76
Anal stage of development, 52, 72-73
Anal triad, 58
Analytical psychology, school of, 86-89
Animal view of person, 15
Anomalies, 23
Anticathexis, 47
Anticipation of events, 194-196
Anti-Semitism, 498-499
    Freud's concern with, 29, 32-33
    among Jews, 54
Anxiety, 47-50, 95, 165-166
    hierarchies of, 327-328
    Horney's view of, 89-91
    Kelly's views of, 196
    and neurosis, 260-262
    psychoanalytic views of, 71-73
    Rogerian views of, 123, 165-166, 170
    social learning views of, 379
Approach-approach conflict, 324
Approach-avoidance conflict, 323
Archetypes, 87-88
Aronfreed, J., 340
Aronson, E., 125-126
Assessment, *see* Personality assessment
Assessment of Men, OSS Staff, 400
Atkins, A., 191
Attention processes, 367-368

Atthowe, J. M., 303
Attitudes, 253-257
Authoritarian personality, 498-499
Autistic children, behavior therapy for, 345-346
Avoidance learning, 296
Avoidance-avoidance conflict, 324
Awareness, states of, 18, 29, 536-537
Axelrod, B., 148-149
Ayllon, T., 302-303, 325
Azrin, H. H., 303

Baer, D. M., 297
Baker, T. B., 417-418
Baker, V., 346, 495
Baldwin, A. L., 130, 281
Bandura, A., 299, 300, 307, 325, 337, 345, 354, 355, 520, 532
    life of, 355-357
    social learning theory of, 360-396
Bannister, D., 207, 217, 218, 221
Barber, T. X., 524
Barlow, D. H., 339
Barr, H. L., 270
Barratt, B., 218
"Barrett, Ronald," case history of, 213-216
Bartsch, T. W., 262
Bateson, G. A., 13
"Beal, Mildred," case history of, 187-190
Beck, S. J., 417
Becker, W. C., 12, 266
Bed-wetting, 326

Beech, H. R., 346, 347
Behavior, 7, 533-536
    abnormal, see Psychopathology
    determinants of, 16-19
    goals of, 34
    influences on, 11, 537-538
    modification of, see Behavior change
    psychoanalytic theory of, 28-29
    self-consistency and, 125-128
    unity of, 17-18, 534-536
Behavior, Watson, 288
Behavior change, 14, 545-547
    Cattell's view of, 262-265
    construct theory of, 209-216
    learning theory of, 300-307
    phenomenological theory of, 143-155,
        167-168
    psychoanalytic theory of, 73-83, 103
    Rogerian theory of, 143-155
    social learning theory of, 380-386
    stimulus-response theory of, 325-334
Behavior therapy, 325, 337-340, 351
    evaluation of, 345-350
Behavioral approaches to personality,
        308-309, 332-333, 334-336, 350-351
    behavior change, 300-307, 325-334
    Dollard, J., theories of, 315-351
    evaluation of, 340-350
    growth and development, 296-297
    Hull, C. L., theories of, 314-315
    learning theories, 278-280, 308-309
    Miller, N. R., theories of, 315-351
    Pavlov, P., theories of, 283-286, 309
    person, view of, 280-281
    psychopathology in, 297-298, 322-324,
        350-351
    recent developments in, 334-340
    science, theory, and research
        methods, view of, 282-283
    Skinner, B. F., theories of, 289-308
    stimulus-response theories, 312-313,
        318-334, 350
    unconscious, views of, 298
    Watson, J. B., theories of, 286-289, 309
Behavioral Avoidance Test (BAT), 449,
    450
Behaviorism, Watson, 289
Benjamin, J. D., 416
Berberich, J. P., 326
Berger, S. M., 367
Bergin, A. E., 168
Bernstein, D. A., 449

Beyond Freedom and Dignity, Skinner,
    292, 335-336
Bias, in personality tests, 442, 443, 456
Bieri, J., 190-191, 210
Bijou, S., 326, 447
Bindra, D., 492, 499
Biofeedback research, 337
Birth order of siblings, 86
Bivariate methods of research, 245-247,
    280
Black Rage, Grier and Cobbs, 545
Blanchard, E. B., 337, 380
Blindness, hysterical, 302
Block Design Test, 403
Blum, G., 57
Bonarius, J. C. J., 193-194, 210, 220
The Book of the It, Groddeck, 39-40
Bootzin, R. R., 346
Boring, E. G., 548-549
Bouchard, T. J., 266
Brady, J. P., 302
Brady, J. V., 493-494
Brain, human, complexity of, 9
Brain injury, study of, 156-157
Breger, L., 343, 344
Breuer, J., 30
Briar, S., 191
Brierly, D. W., 218
Brown, N. O., 28
Brown, I. B., 506
Brucke, E., 29, 34
Bruner, J. S., 220-221
Bucher, B., 345, 346
Burt, C., 237, 243
Burton, R. V., 429
Butler, J. M., 10, 98, 121, 141-142, 144, 164

Campbell, D. T., 404-405
Cardinal traits, 236
Carlson, R., 16, 525
Cartwright, D. S., 124, 168
Case studies:
    "Albert," 288
    "Barrett, Ronald," 213-216
    "Eve," 427-428
    "Joey," 304-307
    "Little Hans," 79-83, 333-334
    "Mrs. Oak," 151-155, 162-163
Castration anxiety, 52-53
    "Little Hans" case study, 79-83
Catharsis, 30

Cathartic hypnosis, 73
Cathexis, 47
Cattell, R. B., 232, 242-243
    person, view of, 245
    personality theory of, 247-259
        clinical applications, 259-264
        evaluation of, 265-271
        science, theory, and research
            methods, views of, 245-247
    16 P. F., 250-252, 273, 435, 436-437,
        438-439, 443, 474-479
Cautela, R. J., 450
Center for Studies of the Person, 112
Central traits, 236
Change, see Behavior change
Character Education Inquiry, 444
Charcot, J., 30
Cheating, and self-esteem, 125-126
Child, I. L., 62
Childhood behavior, 61
    see also autistic children; parent-child
        relationships
Chodorkoff, B., 124
Cimenero, A. R., 449
Civilization and Its Discontents, Freud,
    35
Class, social, influences of, 11-13
Classical conditioning, 284-286, 309, 326
Cleaver, E., 148-149, 150
Cleckley, H., 427
"Clever Hans," 523
Client-centered theory, 113
Client-centered therapy, 143
    case study of, 151-155
    conditions for, 145-146
    evaluation of, 162-163
    history of, 143-145
    interview techniques, 423-425
    outcomes of, 149-151
    process of, 147-149
Client-Centered Therapy, Rogers, 143
Clinical analogue research, 517-521, 527
Clinical approach to behavioral
        assessment, 245-247, 268, 452-456,
        491-492
Clinical Treatment of the Problem Child,
    Rogers, 143
Coan, R. W., 259
Cognitive behavior, 341-342
Cognitive competencies, 371, 377, 380
Cognitive complexity-simplicity,
    190-191

Cognitive modification treatment, 517-520
Cognitive processes, 369-370, 394
Cognitive style, as personality characteristic, 191-193
Cognitive variables, 340
Cohen, J., 265
Cohen, Y. A., 61
Cole, J. K., 221
Collective unconscious, 86-87
Competence motivation, 10-11, 45, 122
Comprehensiveness of theories, 21-22
Computer view of person, 15
Conceptual thinking, 7
Concurrent validity of tests, 402-403
Conditioned anxiety reaction, 334
Conditioned emotional reaction, 288
Conditioned Reflexes, Pavlov, 290
Conditioning, classical, 284-286, 309, 326
Conflict, 256
    incongruence as, 165-166
Congruence, 122-128, 165-166, 170
    in client-centered therapy, 145-146
Conscience, 322
Conscious, concept of, 39, 103
Consciousness, states of, 18, 39-43
Consistency, see Self-consistency
Construct theory of personality, 176-177, 184-200, 226-228
    behavioral change, 209-216
    clinical applications, 204-216, 472-474
    evaluation of, 219-222
    growth and development, 197-198
    person, view of, 179-181
    process, 194-197
    psychopathology in, 204-209
    related points of view, 216-219
    structure, 184-194
    systems of constructs, 176-177, 185-186, 190-194, 199-200
Construct validity of tests, 403
Constructive alternatism, 181
Construing, 184
Content analysis of interviews, 420
Content validity of tests, 402
Contrast pole, 184
Control, 500-521
    locus of, 509-514
    process of, 281
Cook, T. D., 522
Cooke, G., 339

Coopersmith, S., 131-134, 163
Cordua, G., 346
Core constructs, 185
Correlational approach to personality research, 498-499
Counterconditioning, 325, 329-332
Counseling and Psychotherapy, Rogers, 143
Craighead, W. E., 338
Criterion method of test development, 437-440
Criterion-oriented validity of tests, 402
Crockett, W. H., 191-193, 218
Cronbach, L. J., 403, 429, 456, 458, 459, 490, 492-493, 499
Crowne, D. P., 164, 443
Crutchfield, R. S., 25
Cultural factors:
    in personality, 11, 13, 89-93
    in schizophrenia, 13
Culture, as learned behavior patterns, 7
Curtis, F. J., 131

Damarin, F. L., 259-266
Dana, R. H., 417
Dashiell, J. F., 491-492, 499
Data, sources of, 248-249
Davids, A., 164
Davison, G. C., 332, 349, 387, 490
Death, threat of, 196
Death instinct, 35, 46, 103
Defense processes, 48-50, 123
    Freudian, 71-73
    Rogerian, 141-142, 165-166, 170
    in social learning theory, 379, 396
Delay of gratification, in social learning theory, 374-377
Delhees, K. H., 247, 257
Demand characteristics, 522
Demian, Hesse, 140
Denial, as defense mechanism, 123-124, 170
Determinism, 180-181
Deutsch, F., 421-422
DeVellis, R. F. and B. M., 506
Development, 11-13, 14, 542-544
    psychoanalytic theory of, 50-60
    research on, 60-64
    see also Growth and development
Diggory, J. C., 164, 210
Discrimination, 285, 373-374
Discrimination learning, 325

Disguised-nondisguised tests, 404
Dishonest behavior, and self-esteem, 125-126
Displacement of instincts, 47
Distortion, as defense mechanism, 123-124, 141, 170
Dollard, J., 312, 313, 315-317
    stimulus-response theories of, 318-326
Drabman, R., 338
Dreams, 74
Drives, 46, 103, 318-319
Durkes, W., 50
Dymond, R. F., 142, 143
Dynamic lattice, 255-256, 269
Dysfunctional expectancies, 378, 379
Dysfunctional self-evaluations, 378-379

Eagle, M., 43
Early experience, and personality development, 60-65
Ebaugh, F. G., 416
Edwards, A. L., 443
Ego, concept of, 43-46, 71, 103
Ego identity, 56
Ego psychology, 45, 55-56
Empathetic understanding, in client-centered therapy, 145-146
Empirical keying, 437-440
Empirical-criterion method of test development, 435
Encounter groups, 160
Endler, N. S., 17
Energy, psychic, psychoanalytic theory of, 46-48
Energy system, man as, 34-36
Engel, E., 163
Environmental factors in personality, 11-13
Epstein, S., 534
Equilibrium, 10
Ergs, 254-255, 257
Erickson, E. H., 55-56
Erogenous zones, 51
Ethical issues in behavior therapy, 348-349
"Eve," case history of, 427-428
Expectancies, 369
Experimental approach to personality research, 491, 493-497
Extinction, 285, 325
Extroversion, 88, 240-242

Eysenck, H. J., 94, 232, 265, 271, 324, 333, 346, 347
  factor-analytic theory of, 237-242, 272-273
  hierarchy of traits, 233
Eysenck Personality Inventory, 241

Factor-analysis, 237-242, 247, 272-273
  evaluation of, 265-269
  technique of test development, 435-437
Family, influence on personality, 12-13
Fantasy, as defensive behavior, 141
Fear, in construct theory, 196-197
Fear Survey Schedule, 449-451, 482-483
Federn, P., 32
Feldman, M. P., 344, 347
Feminine Psychology, Horney, 91
Ferenczi, S., 32
Ferster, C. B., 299
Fiedler, F. E., 146
Fisher, S., 94
Fiske, D. W., 169
Fixation, 56-60, 70, 103
  psychopathology of, 71-73
Fixed-role therapy, 210-212
  Ronald Barrett case history, 213-216
Focus of convenience of theory, 182
Folkins, C., 339
Frank, L. K., 13, 407
Franks, C. M., 393
Fransella, F., 207, 217
Free association, 32, 74
Free will, 180-181
French, T. M., 78
Frenkel-Brunswick, E., 498
Freud, A., 45, 93
Freud, S., 28, 29-34, 70
  concepts of, 7, 65-66
  and Kelly, 222-223, 225-226
  person, view of, 34-35
  psychopathology, view of, 70-83
  and Rogers, 225-226
  science, theory, and research methods, views of, 36-38
  society, view of, 35-36
  see also Psychoanalytic theory
Fromm, E., 33, 83, 89
Frustration, 73
  in social learning theory, 372
Frustration and Aggression, Dollard and Miller, 317

Functional analysis of behavior, 279-280, 445
Functional autonomy, 234-236
Future, influence of, 18-19

Garfield, S. L., 168
Gendlin, E. T., 142
Generalization, 285
Generalized reinforcers, 194
Genetic factors in personality, 13
Genital stage of development, 54-55
Gewirtz, J. L., 296, 297, 391
Glass, D. C., 507-509, 521
Goal-oriented identification, 53
Goals, in social learning theory, 370
Goldfried, M. R., 332, 349, 387, 447, 450
Goldman-Eisler, F., 62-64
Goldstein, K., 155-157
Goodman, G., 169
Gordon, J. E., 270
Gottesman, I. I., 13
Gough, H. G., 452, 455
Greenspoon, J., 162, 420
Greenspoon effect, 420
Grinker, R. R., 388, 502-504
Groddeck, G., 39-40
Group therapy, 160
Growth and development, 10, 11-13, 542-544
  behavioral theory of, 296-297, 320-322
  Cattell's theory of, 257-259
  construct theory of, 197-198
  Rogerian theory of, 129-134, 166-167
  social learning theory of, 371-377
  stimulus-response theory of, 320-322
  see also Development
Grummon, D. L., 168
Grusec, J. E., 374, 381
Guided participation, 380-381, 396
Guilford, J. P., 265, 437
Gump, P. V., 144
Gynther, M. D., 442

Habit, 318
Haigh, G. V., 121, 141-142, 144, 149, 164
Halkides, G., 146
Hall, C. S., 21, 34, 118
Hall, G. S., 32
Harlow, H. F., 10, 60-61
Harris, B., 288
Harrison, R., 213
Hartshorne, H., 444

Haughton, E., 303
Havener, P. H., 167
Havens, L., 101
Hawkins, R. P., 447
Hayden, M. L., 346
Hebb, D. O., 20
Heine, R. W., 146
Helper, M. M., 130, 164, 340
Helplessness, 500-521
  learned, 504-506
Hendrick, I., 74, 75, 77
Herbert, E. W., 346
Heredity, and personality, 258
Herrnstein, R. J., 307, 342
Hersh, Jim, case study of, 464-487
Hesse, H., 140, 170
Higher mental processes, 321
Hinkle, D. N., 217
Hiroto, D. S., 505, 512-514
Holdstock, T. L., 113
Holmes, D. S., 48
Holt, R. R., 268, 412, 454
Holtzman, W. H., 267
Homeostasis, 10
Honikman, B., 217
Horn, J. L., 255, 256, 257
Horney, K., 9, 89-91, 101
Hostility, in personal construct theory, 207-208
Howarth, E., 265, 266
Hull, C., 237, 312, 314-315
  stimulus-response theories of, 318-326
  theories of, as seen by social-learning theorists, 363-364
Human potential movement, 155-159
Hundleby, J. D., 258, 266
Hunt, J. McV., 57, 60, 65
Huntley, C. W., 164
Hypnosis, 30, 40
  cathartic, 73
Hysterical personality, 59-60

Icheiser, G., 16
Id, concept of, 43-46, 71, 103
Ideal self, 117
  measurement of, 119-121
Identification, 363
  psychoanalytical concept of, 53-54
Illness, and socialization anxiety, 62
Imitation, 325, 326, 363
Imitative behavior, 321-322
Impermeability of constructs, 205

Implosive therapy, 337-338
Incongruence, 123, 165-166, 170
Individual Psychology, school of, 84-86
Infantile sexuality, 78-83
Inferiority, feelings of, 84-86
Inhibition, 35, 47
Inouye, D. K., 506
Instincts, 46-47, 103
  development of, 51-60
Instrumental learning, 319
Intellectualization, 49
Internal-External Scale (I-E Scale),
  509-514, 527
Interpersonal relationships, 89-93
Interpersonal Theory of Psychiatry,
  Sullivan, 91
The Interpretation of Dreams, Freud, 32
Interviews, 419-425
Introversion, 88, 239-242
Invitational mood of subjective
  thinking, 181-182
Isolation, as defense mechanism, 49
Izard, C. E., 167

Jackson, C., 346
Jackson, D. D., 13
Jackson, D. N., 198, 442
James, W., 39
Janis, I. L., 315, 502-504, 515
Jensen, A. R., 22
"Joey," case history of, 304-307
John, E. S., 168
Jones, E., 30, 32, 325, 326
Jourard, S. M., 130
Jung, C., 84
  theories of, 86-89

Kagan, J., 61, 64
Kahneman, D., 419, 455
Kallmann, F. J., 13
Kamin, L. J., 525
Kanfer, F. H., 342, 434, 445, 447
Karoly, P., 342
Karon, B. P., 418
Kastenbaum, R., 450
Katz, P., 166
Kazdin, A. E., 332, 336, 338, 339, 346, 349,
  516, 520
Kelly, G. A., 176-179, 359, 428
  behavioral change, view of, 209-216
  and Freud, 222-223, 225-226

growth and development, view of,
  197-198
person, view of, 179-181
personality theory of, 184-200, 226-228
psychopathology, view of, 204-205
  evaluation of, 222
and Rogers, 223-226
science, theory, and research
  methods, view of, 181-183
therapy, view of, 209
Klein, G. S., 43, 94, 270
Klein, M., 93
Kleinmuntz, B., 220, 420
Kline, P., 94
Klopfer, W. G., 400
Kluckhohn, C., 4, 11, 96
Knowledge, kinds of, 115
Koegel, R., 345
Kohut, H., 94
Krasner, L., 298-301, 303, 336, 340, 348,
  495
Krech, D., 25
Kuhn, T. S., 22-24, 25
Kupers, C. J., 374

L-data, 248-252, 273
Laboratory research, 504-509, 527
Laing, R. D., 101
Landfield, A. W., 217-219, 221
Lang, P. J., 328, 337, 338, 449
Langer, E. J., 515-516
Language, human ability for, 7, 321
Latency, 54
Law of Effect, Thorndike, 281, 283
Lawson, K. D., 339
Lazarus, A. A., 324, 327, 328, 339, 344, 347,
  490
Lazarus, R. S., 41, 123
Lazovik, A. D., 328, 449
Leaman, R. L., 191
Learned helplessness, 504-506, 512-514
Learning theory, 278-280, 340-344
  see also Behavioral approaches to
    personality
Lecky, P., 123
Leitenberg, H., 339
Lemondrop test, 241
Levels of consciousness, 39-43
Levinson, D. J., 498
Lewis, M., 93, 296
Liberman, R. P., 346, 495
Libido, 46, 103

Liebert, R. M., 374
Life instinct, 46, 103
Lilly, R. S., 164, 167
Lind, D. L., 302
Lindzey, G., 21, 60, 118, 407
Little, K. B., 416
"Little Hans," case history of, 78-83,
  333-334
Locke, E. A., 344
Locus of control, 509-514, 527
London, P., 333, 338, 343, 344, 348
Long, G., 345
Loosening, 205
Lovaas, O. I., 326, 345, 346
Luborsky, L. B., 263, 268-269
Lundin, R. W., 20, 278, 548
Luria, Z., 427
Lykken, D. T., 60, 268

McCauley, C., 506
McCleary, R. A., 41, 123
Maccoby, E. E. and N., 419
McDonald, F. J., 374
McDougall, W., 243
McEverly, C. P., 242
McGauch, J. L., 343, 344
McGinnies, E., 40
McGuire, W. J., 526
Machine view of person, 15
MacKinnon, D. W., 50
MacLeod, R. B., 161, 162, 169
Madison, P., 46
Magnusson, D., 17
Maher, B., 195
Mahoney, M. J., 337, 338
Manifest Anxiety Scale, 435
Markus, H., 127
Marlowe, D., 443
Maslow, A. H., 11, 157-159
Masochism, behaviorist view of, 300, 341
Matarazzo, J. D., 421
Matched-dependent behavior, 321
Mathematico-Deductive Theory of Rote
  Learning, Hull, 315
Maturation, 258, 262, 273, 371
Maudsley Personality Inventory, 240-241
May, M. A., 444
May, R., 501
Mayman, M., 418
Mayo, C. W., 191-193
Measures, 401
  see also Tests

Measurement, 247
Medinnus, G. R., 131
Mednick, S. A., 324
Meehl, P. E., 403, 452, 453-455
Meichenbaum, D., 336, 338, 386, 516-520
Men Under Stress, Grinker and Speigel, 502
Menlove, F., 374, 381
Mental illness, social class factors in, 12, 13
  see also Psychopathology
Messick, S., 442
Mettee, D. R., 125-126
Michael, J., 302, 325
Milgram, N. A., 164
Miller, D. R., 57
Miller, H., 191
Miller, N. E., 20, 312, 313, 315-317
  stimulus-response theories of, 318-326
Minnesota Multiphasic Personality Inventory (MMPI), 435-436, 437-442, 443
Mischel, W., 220, 268, 270, 354-355, 448, 534, 536
  life of, 357-360
  social learning theory of, 360-396
Modeling, 326, 363-368, 380-381, 396
  and delay of gratification, 375-377
Monkeys, research with, 60-61, 493-495, 507
Moral issues, in behavior therapy, 348-349
Moral judgments, 373-374
Morgan, C., 412
Morgan, W., 96
Morganstern, K. P., 337, 347
Morin, S. F., 524
Morotic reproduction processes, 368
Moses and Monotheism, Freud, 32-33
Moss, H. A., 61
Moss, P. D., 242
Motivation, 10-11, 122, 254, 368
  Cattell's theory of, 255-257
  Kelly's view of, 194
  Maslow's view of, 158-159
  Rogers' view of, 122
Mowrer, O. H. and W. A., 326
Multiple Abstract Variance Analysis (MAVA) Method, 257-258, 273
Multivariate method of research, 245-247, 268, 273
Murphy, W. F., 421-422

Murray, H. A., 4, 407, 412, 413, 415

Narcissistic identification, 53
Naturalistic observation, 501-504
Negative reinforcers, 295
Nervous system, human, 9
Nesselroade, J. R., 247, 257, 262
Neurosis, 260-262
  Horney's theory of, 89-91
  psychoanalytic theory of, 71-73
  Wolpe's view of, 326-327
Neurotic trends, 89-91
Neuroticism, 239
Noise, as stress, 507-508
Nondirective methods of therapy, 144

OT-data, 248-252, 273
"Oak, Mrs.," case history of, 151-155, 162-163
Objective knowledge, 115
Objective tests, 443-450
Objective-behavioral tests, 406
Object-loss identification, 53-54
Observational learning, 363-368, 394
Oedipus complex, 52-53, 72
  "Little Hans" case study, 79-83
O'Leary, K. D., 338, 445
Oliveau, D. C., 339
Olweus, D., 534
On Becoming a Person, Rogers, 109
On Encounter Groups, Rogers, 160
Operant conditioning, Skinner's theory of, 289-308, 309
  behavioral change, 300-306
  evaluation of, 307-308
  process, 293
  psychopathology, 297-299
  structure, 293-297
Operants, 293
Opler, M. K., 13
Opton, E. M., 339
Oral frustration, and smoking, 57
Oral personality, 62-63, 76
Oral socialization practices, study of, 61
Oral stage of development, 51-52, 57, 72-73
Organ weakness, Adler's study of, 84
Orne, M. T., 522-523, 524
Osborne, D., 125
Osgood, C., 426, 427
Overall, J. E., 267
Own-control research method, 495

P technique of case study, 263-264
Paradigm, in scientific development, 23
Parent-child relationships, 12-13
  and cognitive complexity, 198
  self-esteem and, 130-134
Parke, R. D., 377
Parsimony-simplicity of theories, 21-22
Past, influences of, 18-19
Pattern and Growth in Personality, Allport, 234
Patterson, G. R., 339, 495
Patterson, R., 346
Paul, G. L., 328-332
Pavlov, I. P., 283-286, 290, 291, 309, 315, 493
Pawlik, K., 258, 266
Penis envy, 53, 91, 101
Perceived inefficacy, 379
Perceptual defense, 40-41
Performance, 364-367, 394
Peripheral constructs, 185
Perloff, B. F., 326
Permeable constructs, 205
Person, philosophical views of, 15, 532-533
  behavioral view of, 280-281
  Cattell's view of, 245
  Freud's view of, 34-36
  Kelly's view of, 179-181
  Rogers' view of, 113-114
  social learning theory view of, 360-362, 390
Personal construct theory, see Construct theory of personality
Personality, 4-8
  environmental determinants of, 11-13
  genetic approach to, 60-62
  nature of, 6-7
  processes of, 10-11
  structural concepts of, 9
Personality: A Psychological Interpretation, Allport, 234
Personality and Assessment, Mischel, 16, 355
Personality and Psychotherapy, Dollard and Miller, 317
Personality assessment, 400, 456-462, 547-549
  bias in, 442, 443, 456
  case study of Jim Hersh, 464-487
  classification of tests, 404-429, 434-456
  evaluation of, 450-456

goals of, 401
  reliability, 401-402
  validity, 402-404
objective techniques, 443-450,
    458-459, 460
  behavioral assessment (ABC) test,
    445-447, 482-483
projective techniques, 405-418,
    429-430, 447-448, 458
  case study of, 465-470
  evaluation of, 416-418
  Rorschach Inkblot Test, 407-412,
    416-418, 458, 465-470, 483-484
  Thematic Apperception Test (TAT),
    412-416, 466-470
psychometric techniques, 434-443,
    460
  Cattell 16 P. F., 436-437
  evaluation of, 442-443
  Minnesota Multiphasic Personality
    Inventory (MMPI), 437-442
research in, 490-528
sign and sample approaches to,
    448-450
subjective techniques, 419-429, 430
  interviews, 419-425
  Q-sort, 425-426
  semantic differential, 426-428,
    470-472
Personality change, see Behavior
    change
Personality research, 490-528
Personality sphere, 249
Personality theory, 3-25, 179, 490,
    532-544
  and assessment data, 483-487
  behavioral approaches to, 308-309,
    332-333
  construct theory, 176-177, 184-200,
    226-228
  issues in, 14-21
  phenomenological theory, 108-109,
    135-136, 170-172
  psychoanalytic theory, 28, 102-104, 168
  research in, 490-528
  social learning theory, 354-355,
    386-388, 394-396
  trait theory, 232-234, 272-274
Personality Traits, Their Classification
    and Measurement, Allport and
    Allport, 234
Personality types, 56-60

Person-situation controversy, 16-17
Pervin, L. A., 15, 16, 167, 195, 210, 500, 524
Peterson, D. R., 266
Peterson, R. F., 297, 447
Pfungst, O., 523
Phallic character, 59-60, 76
Phallic stage of development, 52, 73
Phares, E. J., 510
Phenomenal field of individual, 115
Phenomenological theory of
    personality, 108-109, 135-136,
    170-172
  behavior change, 143-155, 167-168
  clinical applications, 140-155
  case study, 470-472
  evaluation of, 161-170, 171, 223-225
  growth and development, 129-134,
    166-167
  person, view of, 113-114
  process, 121-129
  psychopathology, 140-142, 167-168
  recent developments in, 159-161,
    171-172
  related points of view, 155-159
  self, view of, 117-121, 163-165, 170
  science, theory, and research
    methods, views of, 114-117
  structure, 117-121
Phillips, J. S., 434, 447
Philosophical views of person, see
    Person
Philosophy, Freud's view of, 36
Phobia, 333-334
  fear of snakes, 328, 380-381, 382-384,
    385
  of "Little Hans," 80-82, 333-334
Piaget, J., 218-219
Pildner, H., 164
Pinkston, E. M. and S., 346
Piotrowski, Z. A., 416, 418
Plans, in social learning theory, 370
Pleasure, as goal of behavior, 34
Pleasure principle, 35, 43-44, 97-98
Poch, S. M., 210
Pollio, H. R., 304-307
Positive regard, need for, 128-129, 166,
    170
  unconditional, in client-centered
    therapy, 145
Positive reinforcement, 325-326
Preconscious, psychoanalytical concept
    of, 39, 103

Predictive validity of tests, 402-403
Pregenital stages of development, 54,
    103
Present time, influences of, 18-19
Preverbal constructs, 185
Principles of Behavior, Hull, 315
Process, concepts of, 6, 10-11, 14, 541-542
  behavioral views of, 293, 319-320
  Kelly's view of, 194-197
  in psychoanalytic theory, 46-50, 103
  Rogers' view of, 121-129
  in social learning theory, 363-370
Progressive change, psychoanalysis as,
    73-78
Projection, as defense mechanism, 48,
    141
Projective tests, 405-418, 429-430,
    447-448
Proprium, concept of, 236
Psychoanalysis, 28, 38
  behavioral criticism of, 333-334
  as therapy, 70-83
  see also Psychoanalytical theory
Psychoanalytical interview, 421-423
Psychoanalytical theory of personality,
    28, 102-104, 168
  Adler, A., 84-86
  clinical applications of, 70-83
  evaluation of, 95-102, 222-223
  growth and development, 50-65
  research in, 60-65
  Horney, K., 89-91
  interview technique, 421-423
  Jung, C. G., 86-89
  person, view of, 34-36
  process, 46-50
  psychopathology, 70-73
  recent developments in, 93-95
  related points of view, 83-93
  structure, 38-46
  Sullivan, H. S., 91-93
Psychodynamic theory of personality,
    psychoanalysis as, 27, 28-29, 102
  and projective tests, 406-407, 430
Psychology, scientific, 491-499
Psychology From the Standpoint of a
    Behaviorist, Watson, 288
Psychometric tests, 406, 434-450
Psychopathology, 14, 544-547
  Cattell's approach to, 259-262
  in construct theory, 204-209
  Kelly's view of, 204-209

in learning theory, 297-298
in phenomenological theory, 140-142, 167-168
psychoanalytical theory of, 70-83
Rogers' view of, 140-155
Skinner's view of, 297-307
social learning views of, 378-380, 395-396
stimulus-response theory of, 322-334
Psychopathology of Everyday Life, Freud, 32
Psychosis, 72-73, 141
Psychosocial stages of development, 55-56
Psychotherapy, 209
  Kelly's view of, 209-216
  Rogers' view of, 140-155, 167-168
Psychotherapy and Personality Change, Rogers and Dymond, 142, 143
Psychotic personality factors, 260
Psychoticism, 239
Puberty, 54
Public policy, research and, 525
Punishment, 296, 341

Q-data, 248-250, 273
Q-sort, 119-121, 425-426

Rablen, R. A., 142
Rachman, S., 324, 333-334
Raimy, V. C., 119, 142
Raines, G. N., 420-421
Raines, J., 339
Range of convenience of theory, 182
Rank, O., 32
Rapaport, D., 418
Rational view of person, 15
Rationalization, 49-50, 141
Rational-theoretical tests, 435
Rau, L., 99, 322
Rayner, R., 288, 309
Reaction range, concept of, 13
Reaction-formation, 49
Reality principle, 44
Reciprocal determinism, 354
Reflected appraisal, 131
Regression, 56-57, 70, 72-73
Regressive change, 73
Reik, W., 452-453, 455
Reinforcement processes, 368
Reinforcement Survey Schedule, 450, 451, 482-483

Reinforcers, 294-295, 308
Reliability of test, 401-402, 456
  of interviews, 420-421
Religion, teachings of, 113
Remy, R. M., 130
REP (Role Construct Repertory) Test, 186-194, 217, 228, 472-474
  evaluation of, 220
Repression, 5, 50
Research, 490-528, 547-549
Research methods, 37
  behavioral view of, 282-283
  Cattell's view of, 245-247
  Freud's view of, 36-38
  Kelly's view of, 181-183
  Rogers' view of, 114-117
  social learning view of, 362
Research relevance of theories, 21-22
Response, 318
  patterns of, 6
  Skinner's view of, 293
  Pavlovian, 284-285
Retention processes, 367-368
Reynolds, G. S., 293
Rickels, K., 261
Rickers-Ovsiankina, M. A., 417
Riesman, D., 155
Ring, K., 526
Ritter, B. J., 380
Rodin, J., 515, 516
Rogers, C. R., 108-113
  behavior change, views of, 143-155, 167-168
  client-centered therapy of, 140-155, 516, 520
    interviews, 423-425
  and Freud, 225-226
  growth and development concepts of, 129-134, 166-167, 171
  and Kelly, 223-226
  person, view of, 113-114, 171
  personality, view of, 117-136
  phenomenological theories of, 108-109, 135-136, 170-172
    evaluation of, 161-170, 171-172
  science, theory, and research methods, views of, 114-117, 171, 458
  therapy, view of, 116-117, 140
Rohrer, J. H., 420-421
Role Construct Repertory (REP) Test, 186-194, 217, 220, 228, 428, 472-474

Rorschach, H., 407-408
Rorschach Inkblot Test, 406, 407-412, 416-418, 458, 465-470, 483-484
Rosenblum, L. A., 296
Rosenthal, R., 522-524
Rosenthal, T. L., 367, 371, 373, 385, 387
Rosenzweig, S., 37, 50
Ross, D. and S., 364
Rotter, J., 359, 388, 509-510
Rubinstein, E. A., 525
Russell, B., 290

Sajwaj, T. E., 346
Salmon, P., 218
Sample approach to behavior assessment, 448-450
Samuels, H., 458
Sandler, J., 300, 340
Sanford, R. N., 498
Sarnoff, I., 54
Saslow, G., 445
Sawrey, W. L., 493
Sawyer, J., 454
Schaeffer, B., 326
Schafer, R., 94, 409, 418
Schedules of reinforcements, 294
Scheier, I. H., 260, 262, 492, 499
Schizophrenia, 13
  behaviorist view of, 299
  and construct theory, 205-207
  stimulus-response theory of, 324
Schneider, J. M., 500
Schweid, E., 447
Science:
  behaviorist view of, 282-283
  Cattell's view of, 245-247
  Freud's view of, 36-38
  Kelly's view of, 181-183
  Rogers' view of, 114-117
  social learning view of, 362
The Scientific Analysis of Personality, Cattell, 243
Scientific development, stages of, 22-24
Scientist, person as, 179-180, 184, 194-195, 198-200, 208-209
Sears, R. R., 4, 8, 48, 99, 322
Sechrest, L., 177, 185, 198, 220, 221
Secondary dispositions, 236
Seeman, J., 143
Self, concept of, 17-18, 118, 378, 534-536
  and behavior, 125-128
  case study, 470-472

changes in, 148-151
Jung's theories of, 88
measurement of, 119-121, 425-428
Rogers' view of, 117-121, 170
  evaluation of, 163-164
social learning view of, 370, 395
Sullivan's concept of, 91
Self-actualization, 121-122, 135, 157, 159,
  165-166, 170
  and psychological development,
  129-130
Self-consistency, 122-128, 170
  see also Congruence
Self-control, 336-337
Self-efficacy, 381-384, 396
Self-esteem, 125, 131, 142
  and parent-child relationships,
  130-134
  study of, 163-164
Self-ideal self discrepancy, 166-168
Self-regulation, 368-370
Self-reinforcement, 336-337, 369-370
Self-report data, 428-429, 434-443
Seligman, M. E. P., 504-506
Sells, S. B., 266
Semantic differential, 426-428, 470-472
Sensitivity training, 212-213
Sentiments, 254-255, 257
Sex, duality of, 88
Sexual instinct, 46
Shannon, D. T., 329-332
Shaw, G. B., 44
Sherman, J. A., 297
Shields, J., 13, 241
Shields, S., 524
Shneidman, E. S., 416
Siblings, birth order of, 86
Siddhartha, Hesse, 170
Sign approach to behavior assessment,
  448-450
Signell, K. A., 197-198
Silverman, L. H., 94, 416
Similarity pole, 184
Simmons, J. Q., 345
Singer, J. E., 507-509
Singer, J. L., 13
Situational specificity, 279
Sixteen Personality Factor (16 P. F.)
  Inventory, 250-252, 273, 435,
  436-437, 438-439, 443, 474-479
Skinner, B. F., 16, 20, 116, 266, 278, 281,
  282, 289-293, 348

growth and development, view of,
  296-297
personality theory of, 293-297, 309, 318
  clinical applications of, 297-307
  evaluation of, 307-308
  utopian planning of, 335-336
Skinner box, 294
Smith, M. B., 161
Smoking, and frustration, 57
Snake phobia, 328, 380-381, 382-384, 385
Snyder, W. V., 147
Social class, influence of, 11-13
Social engineering, 335-336
Social Learning and Personality
  Development, Bandura and
  Walters, 357, 389
Social Learning and Imitation, Dollard
  and Miller, 317
Social learning theory, 354-355, 386-388,
  394-396
  behavior change, 380-386
  Bandura, A., theories of, 355-357
  evaluation of, 388-393
  growth and development, 371-377
  Mischel, W., theories of, 357-360
  person, views of, 360-362
  process, 363-370
  psychopathology, 378-380
  science, theory, and research
    methods, views of, 362-363
  structure, 370
Social Learning Theory, Bandura, 389
Social psychology of research, 522
Socialization anxiety, and illness, 62
Society, Freud's view of, 34-36
Source traits, 248, 252, 273
Spearman, C., 237, 242, 243
Specification equation, 256-257
Spence, K. W., 282
Spiegel, J. P., 388, 502-504
Stampfl, T. G., 337-338
Standards, 368-370, 394-395
State anxiety, 262
Statistical approach to behavior
  assessment, 452-456
Steiner, J. F., 49
Stephenson, W., 119
Stimulus-response (S-R) theory of
  personality, 312-334
Stone, H. K., 417
Stress, 500, 507-509, 520-521
Strong Vocational Interest Blank, 403, 435

Structural tests, 434-450
Structure, concepts of, 6, 9-10, 14,
  539-541
  behavioral, 293, 318-319
  psychoanalytic, 38-46
  Rogerian, 117-121
  in social learning theory, 370
Structured-nonstructured tests, 404
Studies in Hysteria, Freud and Breuer, 30
Subception, 123, 165-166, 170
Subjective knowledge, 115
Subjective tests, 405, 419-430
Sublimation, 50
Submerged constructs, 185, 197
Subordinate constructs, 185
Successive approximation, 295
Suicide, 207-208
Suinn, R. M., 125
Sullivan, H. S., 12, 89, 91-93
Superego, 43-46, 53, 54, 103
Superordinate constructs, 185
Superstitious behavior, 299
Surface traits, 248
Suspension, 197
Symbolization, 39-40
Symptom formation, 165
Symptoms, 71-73, 328
System, personality as, 6
Systematic desensitization, 326-332, 339,
  351, 380-381
Szasz, T. S., 101

Tachistoscope, 40
Target behaviors, 301, 309, 444
TAT (Thematic Apperception Test), 407,
  412-416, 466-470
Tatro, D. F., 260
Taulbee, E. S., 400
Taversky, A., 429
Taxonomy, 247
Taylor, J. A., 343, 435
Teasdale, J. D., 506
Teigen, J., 346, 495
Tension, 10-11, 34, 97-98
Tests, 401, 456-461
  classification of, 404-429, 434-456
  evaluation of, 483-487
  goals of, 401-404
  statistical, 450-456
  see also Personality assessment
Thematic Apperception Test (TAT), 407,
  412-416, 466-470

Theory, 19-25, 547-549
  behavioral view of, 282-283
  Cattell's view of, 245-247
  evaluation of, 21-22
  focus and range of convenience, 182
  Freud's view of, 36-38
  Kelly's view of, 181-183
  Rogers' view of, 114-117
  social learning views of, 362, 386-387
Therapeutic climate, 145-146, 150-151
The Therapeutic Relationship and its Impact, Rogers, 143
Therapy, 168
  client-centered, 143-151, 162-163
  fixed-role, 210-216
  see also Psychotherapy
Thigpen, C., 427
Thinking processes, 51
Thorndike, E. L., 281, 283, 309
Threat, in construct theory, 196-197
Three Essays on the Theory of Sexuality, Freud, 32
Tightening, 205
Token economy, 303-304, 336
Tomkins, S. S., 268
Trait approaches to personality, 232-234, 272-274
  Allport, theories of, 234-237, 272
  Cattell, theories of, 242-270, 273-274, 474-479
  evaluation of, 265-272
  Eysenck, theories of, 237-242, 272-273
  situationist criticism of, 270-272
  structural concepts from, 9

Transference, 75-78, 209
Tripoldi, T., 191
Truax, C. B., 171
Turner, R. H., 167
Tyler, L. E., 222, 266, 533
Type, structural concept of, 9, 233, 239

Ullman, L. P., 298, 299, 300, 336
Unconditional positive regard, in client-centered therapy, 145-146
Unconditioned response, 284-285
Unconscious, concept of, 7, 18, 38-43, 45, 103, 536-537
  experiment in, 41-43
  and learning theory, 298
Undoing, defense mechanism of, 49
Utopian planning, 335-336

Validity of tests, 402-404, 456, 457
Value judgment, personality as, 5
Vandenberg, S. G., 13
Vanderlippe, R. H., 167
Vargas, M. J., 168
Verbal constructs, 185
Vernon, P. E., 118, 167, 193, 220, 426
Vicarious conditioning, 367
Voluntary-objective tests, 405

Wade, T. C., 417-418
Wahler, R. G., 304-307
Walden Two, Skinner, 291, 335
Walker, A. M., 142
Walters, R. H., 325, 377, 389
Warburton, F. W., 269

Watson, J. B., 278, 281, 286-289, 309, 336
Weakland, J., 13
Weaning, age of, and personality, 62-64
Webb, W. B., 524
Weber, S. J., 522
Weiss, J. M., 507
Weisz, J. D., 493
White, R. W., 10, 45, 98, 122
Whiting, J. W. M., 62
Wilcoxon, L. A., 332, 339
Wilde, G. J. S., 266, 434, 442
Williams, J., 101
Williams, J. R., 260
Wilson, G. D., 94, 241, 349
Wilson, G. T., 393
Winfree, P., 125
Winston, H. D., 60
Wittman, M. P., 453
Wolf, S., 93
Wolfer, J. A., 515
Wolitzsky, D. L., 43, 270
Wolpe, J., 324, 326-332, 333, 334, 339, 347, 449
Wolpin, M., 339
Women, psychoanalytic views of, 91, 101
Wylie, R. C., 164, 167, 392

Young, L. D., 337

Zeitgeist, 15
  cognition and, 217
Zigler, E., 166, 167
Zimmerman, B. J., 371, 373